DESIGN STUDIES

Southampton
SOLENT
University

MOUNTBATTEN LIBRARY
Tel: 023 8031 9249

Please return this book no later than the date stamped.
Loans may usually be renewed - in person, by phone,
or via the web OPAC. Failure to renew or return on time
may result in an accumulation of penalty points.

ONE WEEK LOAN		

DESIGN

STUDIES

A Reader

EDITED BY HAZEL CLARK AND DAVID BRODY

Oxford • New York

English edition

First published in 2009 by

Berg

Editorial offices:
First Floor, Angel Court, 81 St Clements Street, Oxford OX4 1AW, UK
175 Fifth Avenue, New York, NY 10010, USA

Berg is the imprint of Oxford International Publishers Ltd.

Library of Congress Cataloging-in-Publication Data
Design studies : a reader / edited by Hazel Clark and David Brody. — English ed.
p. cm.
Includes bibliographical references and index.
ISBN 978-1-84788-236-3 (pbk.) — ISBN 978-1-84788-237-0 (cloth)
1. Design.   I. Clark, Hazel.   II. Brody, David Eric.
NK1510.D477   2009
745.4—dc22
2009008156

British Library Cataloguing-in-Publication Data

A catalogue record for this book is available from the British Library.

ISBN 978 1 84788 237 0 (Cloth)
978 1 84788 236 3 (Paper)

Typeset by Apex CoVantage, LLC, Madison, Wl, USA
Printed by the MPG Books Group in the UK

www.bergpublishers.com

To Our Families:
CSD, JCD & CC (HC)
James, Dad Bro, JB, Mom Bro (DB)

CONTENTS

LIST OF ILLUSTRATIONS

ACKNOWLEDGMENTS

Without the advice and good judgment of others, this *Reader* would never have been completed. In particular we thank Clive Dilnot and Miodrag Mitrasinovic for their insights and reflections on design studies. We also thank all the authors included here; both the newly commissioned work and the republished work in this book offer a diverse range of readings that we hope will guide our readers through the challenging terrain of design studies. Thanks are due to Hannah Alcasid and her colleagues in the New School Digital Library for scanning the texts and substantially lightening our load. Also to graduate students, including Michelle Everridge, Abbey Nova, and Christine Ritok, who hunted down obscure articles and facilitated the often Kafkaesque task of attaining permissions. Thanks also to the recitation leaders who facilitated the course, Introduction to Design Studies, and to the countless students who took the class. And, of course, thanks to Tristan Palmer, our editor at Berg, who guided this project in its earliest phases to completion, and whose rapid-fire e-mail responses were remarkably helpful and amiably comforting.

We are very grateful to those publishers, companies, and individuals who allowed us to print work free of charge or at a reduced rate. We also very much appreciate the contribution of Parsons The New School for Design toward the cost of producing the *Reader*. Individually, Hazel Clark would like to thank Clive and Jacob Dilnot for their unwavering support, and also Earl Tai for all his work while she was on sabbatical completing this project. David Brody would like to thank Laura Auricchio, Jonathan Brody, Michael Brody, Shelley Brody, James Castillo, John Davis, Larissa Goldston, Patricia Hills, Diana Linden, and Joshua Srebnick.

NOTES ON CONTRIBUTORS

Theodor Adorno (1903–1969) was a German philosopher and sociologist. Before his death, he was chair of the *Deutsche Gesellschaft für Soziologie.*

Hugh Aldersey-Williams is a British design journalist and author.

Arjun Appadurai is an anthropologist and currently John Dewey Professor in the Social Sciences at the New School in New York.

Judy Attfield (1937–2006) was a designer and design historian and Leverhulme Emeritus Fellow at Winchester School of Art, University of Southampton, England.

Peter Reyner Banham (1922–1988) was a renowned architectural historian and critic of design, born in Britain and a long-time resident in the United States.

Jean Baudrillard (1929–2007) was a renowned French cultural theorist, sociologist, and philosopher whose work is associated with postmodernism and poststructuralism.

Zygmunt Bauman is professor emeritus of sociology at the University of Leeds, England.

Dipti Bhagat is a design historian and cultural geographer and teaches design history and theory, with a focus on design and urban culture, at Sir John Cass Department of Art, Media and Design at London Metropolitan University.

Gui Bonsiepe is professor of at F H Koln, Germany and visiting professor at a number of universities including Carnegie Mellon; EUA, Chile; LBDI/FIESC, Brazil; Jan van Eyck Academy, The Netherlands.

Pierre Bourdieu (1930–2002) was a French sociologist who held the chair of sociology at the Collège de France.

Michael Braungart is a German chemist who worked with William McDonough to begin Braungart Design Chemistry in Charlottesville, Virginia.

David Brett is reader emeritus in design history at the University of Ulster.

David Brody is assistant professor of design studies in the School of Art and Design History and Theory at Parsons The New School for Design, New York. His research and teaching focus on design studies, material culture, and visual culture. He is currently completing his forthcoming book, *Visualizing Empire: Orientalism and American Imperialism in the Philippines*.

Richard Buchanan is Professor of Information Systems in the Weatherhead School of Management, Case Western Reserve University, Cleveland, Ohio.

Louis Bucciarelli is professor of engineering and technological studies at Massachusetts Institute of Technology.

Wava Carpenter is director of Culture + Content for Design Miami. Prior to joining Design Miami, Carpenter coordinated exhibitions for Cooper-Hewitt, National Design Museum. She holds a degree in the history of design and decorative arts, with a specialization in postwar design from Italy and the United States.

Michel de Certeau (1925–1986) was a French intellectual who worked in the fields of philosophy and other social sciences. He taught at a variety of universities throughout the world.

Hazel Clark is Dean of the School of Art and Design History and Theory at Parsons The New School for Design, New York. She is a design historian and theorist who has taught internationally and has a particular interest in design and culture, and fashion and textiles. Her most recent publications include co-editing *Old Clothes, New Looks: Second Hand Fashion (*Berg 2005) and *The Fabric of Cultures: Fashion, Identity and Globalization* (Routledge 2009).

Justin Clark is a Los Angeles-based freelance journalist and a graduate of the Columbia School of Journalism, He has written for *L.A. Weekly, Psychology Today, Architecture, BlackBook*, and other publications.

Margaret Crawford is a professor of urban planning and design at Harvard University's Graduate School of Design.

Arthur Danto is a renowned American art critic and Johnsonian Professor of Philosophy Emeritus at Columbia University, New York.

Clive Dilnot is currently professor of design studies at Parsons The New School for Design, New York. Previously he was professor of design studies and director of design initiatives at the School of the Art Institute in Chicago, and he taught in the Graduate School of Design and

Carpenter Center for the Fine Arts at Harvard University and in the United Kingdom, Asia, and Australia. His most recent publications are essays for *Chris Killip: Pirelli Work* (Steidl, 2006) and *Ethics? Design?* (Chicago, Archeworks, 2005).

Barbara Ehrenreich is an American feminist, socialist, and political activist. She is a widely read columnist and essayist. She is coauthor with Anette Fuentes of *Women in the Global Factory* (1983).

Adrian Forty is professor of architectural history at the Bartlett School of Architecture, the University of London.

Michel Foucault (1926–1984) was a French philosopher and historian whose work influenced other fields, such as sociology and literary criticism. He was a chair at the Collège de France.

Annette Fuentes is an American journalist who writes regularly on health and social policy. She is coauthor with Barbara Ehrenreich of *Women in the Global Factory* (1983).

Buckminster Fuller (1895–1983) was an American designer and thinker whose work revolutionized contemporary ideas about the potential of design.

Paul du Gay is professor of sociology and organization studies in the Faculty of Social Sciences at the U.K. Open University.

Alison Gill is a lecturer in visual communication design at the University of Western Sydney, and her Ph.D. in fashion theory and feminist philosophy of the body was received from the University of Sydney. Alison has written about visual and fashion culture for *Fashion Theory,* and *Form/work,* and her research interest in athletic shoes was explored in a chapter for *Shoes: A History from Sandals to Sneakers.*

Erving Goffman (1922–1982) was a Canadian sociologist. He was the Benjamin Franklin Professor of Anthropology and Sociology at the University of Pennsylvania.

Gerard Goggin is professor of digital communication and deputy director of the Journalism and Media Research Centre, University of New South Wales, Sydney, Australia. He has published widely on mobiles, Internet, and new media, and his books include *Digital Disability* (2003), *Cell Phone Culture* (2006), *Internationalizing Internet Studies* I (2008), and *Mobile Phone Technologies* (2009).

Donna Haraway teaches in the History of Consciousness Program at the University of California, Santa Cruz.

Daniel Harris is a New York–based author.

Wolfgang Fritz Haug is a German Marxist philosopher and former professor of philosophy at the Free University of Berlin.

Dick Hebdige is a British sociologist who teaches at the University of California, Santa Barbara.

John Hockenberry is an American journalist and Distinguished Fellow at the Massachusetts Institute of Technology.

D. J. Huppatz teaches design history at Swinburne University of Technology in the Design History and Critical Theory Department in Melbourne, Australia.

Heike Jenß, assistant professor of fashion studies at Parsons The New School for Design, New York, received her Ph.D. in cultural anthropology of textiles from Dortmund University in Germany, where she worked in the research project, "Uniform in Motion: The Process of Uniformity in Body and Dress." She has lectured and written about fashion, youth culture, consumption, and identity and is author of the book *Sixties Dress Only: Mode und Konsum in der Retro-Szene der Mods.*

John Chris Jones is a Welsh designer whose has worked extensively in the field of design methods.

Guy Julier is professor of design and head of research at Leeds Metropolitan University, England.

Naomi Klein is an award-winning writer and journalist whose work is syndicated widely.

Sarah Lichtman is assistant professor of design history in the School of Art and Design History and Theory at Parsons The New School for Design, New York.

Trish Lorenz is a British journalist who writes about design.

William McDonough is an architect and author who has been integral to the socially responsible design movement. He is also a partner in William McDonough + Partners.

Ezio Manzini is professor of industrial design at Politecnico di Milano, director of the Research Unit Design and Innovation for Sustainability, and coordinator of the Masters in Strategic Design and Doctorate in Industrial Design programs.

Victor Margolin is professor emeritus of design history at the University of Illinois, Chicago.

Karl Marx (1818–1883) was a German thinker whose political philosophies shaped the history of world political systems.

Daniel Miller is professor of anthropology at University College London.

Abraham Moles (1920–1992) was one of the first researchers to link aesthetic perception with information theory.

Donald A. Norman is a consultant and the Allen K. and Johnnie Cordell Breed Senior Professor in Design at Northwestern University in Evanston, Illinois.

Gavin O'Malley is a journalist who writes for a variety of publications.

Victor Papanek (1927–1999) was a designer and educator who strongly influenced the concepts of socially responsible and ecologically minded design.

Henry Petroski is professor of civil engineering at Duke University in Durham, North Carolina.

Sir Nikolaus Pevsner (1902–1983) was a renowned German-born British historian of art and architecture whose best-known work was the forty-six-volume guide, *The Buildings of England*.

Jules David Prown is Paul Mellon Professor Emeritus in the History of Art Department at Yale University in New Haven, Connecticut.

Bradley Quinn is a writer and curator specializing in fashion, design, and style, who lives in New York.

Vicente Rafael is professor of history at the University of Washington.

R. Roger Remington is the Massimo and Lella Vignelli Distinguished Professor of Design at Rochester Institute of Technology. He has authored: *Nine Pioneers in American Graphic Design; Lester Beall: Trailblazer of American Graphic Design; American Modernism—Graphic Design 1920–1960;* and *Design and Science—The Life and Work of Will Burtin.* He also developed the Graphic Design Archive, which preserves original source materials of thirty-three Modernist American design pioneers.

Katie Salen is a game designer and writer, and associate professor of design and technology at Parsons The New School for Design, New York.

Donald A. Schön (1930–1997) developed the theory and practice of reflective professional learning; he was Ford Professor of Urban Studies and Education at the Massachusetts Institute of Technology.

Herbert Simon (1906–2001) was a political scientist whose work influenced a number of fields. He taught at Carnegie Mellon University in Pittsburgh, Pennsylvania.

Susan Squires works on customer research ethnographies for a variety of corporations.

Kate Stohr is the cofounder, with Cameron Sinclair, of Architecture for Humanity.

John Stone is a journalist who often writes about design.

John Styles is research professor in history at the University of Hertfordshire, England.

Susan Szenasy is an educator, a design journalist and editor of *Metropolis* magazine, and an activist for sustainable design.

Earl Tai is an architect by training who also holds a Ph.D. in East Asian Languages and Culture. He is associate professor of design studies and former associate chair in the Department of Art and Design Studies at Parsons The New School for Design, New York. His scholarly specializations include cross-cultural design, particularly that of East Asia, and social ethics in design and art. He also serves as a design advisor for a number of not-for-profit organizations, including Friends of Tilonia, Hearts and Hands, and Community Rehabilitation leprosy projects.

Frederick Winslow Taylor (1856–1915) was an engineer who wrote extensively about labor.

Matthew Turner is a professor in the School of Creative Industries at Napier University, Edinburgh, Scotland.

Lucila Fernández Uriarte is a designer and professor at the Instituto Superior de Diseño Industrial (ISDI), Havana, Cuba.

Eric Van Schaak is professor emeritus of art and art history at Colgate University in Hamilton, New York.

Gregory Votolato is an architect, curator, teacher, and writer on design, technology, and culture. His publications include *American Design in the Twentieth Century* (Manchester University Press 1998), *Transport Design, A Travel History* (Reaktion 2007), and *Ship,* to be published in 2009, and his exhibitions, *Making Buildings,* a national touring exhibition for the British Crafts Council (2001).

Shirley Teresa Wajda currently teaches American material culture and United States history at Kent State University. She has published on a wide variety of topics, including nineteenth-century sterographs, children's cabinets of curiosities, commercial portrait photography, women's dress, Martha Stewart's stuff, and flea markets.

John Walker is a design and art historian and theorist and former faculty member at Middlesex University, London.

Stuart Walker is co-director of ImaginationLancaster at Lancaster University, U.K.

Catherine Walsh is a doctoral student in the Department of Art History at the University of Delaware. She specializes and teaches courses in American art and visual culture, and her current research revolves around the intersection of word and image in nineteenth-century American objects and literature.

Denise Whitehouse is a senior lecturer in design history at the Faculty of Design, Swinburne University of Technology, Australia. She has extensive experience in developing innovative design history programs within university art and design schools. Her research and publications focus on design history, criticism, and education, with a particular interest in shaping strategies for writing a critical history of design practice in Australia.

Bess Williamson is a Ph.D. candidate in the Program in the History of American Civilization at the University of Delaware. She is currently working on a dissertation on disability and design in mid- to late twentieth-century America.

Susan Yelavich is a fellow of the American Academy in Rome (FAAR) and an assistant professor in the School of Art and Design History and Theory at Parsons The New School for Design. She is the author of numerous articles and books, including *Contemporary World Interiors* (2007), *Pentagram/Profile* (2004); *Inside Design Now* (2003); *Design for Life* (1997); and *The Edge of the Millennium: An International Critique of Architecture, Urban Planning, Product and Communication Design* (1993).

Eric Zimmerman is a writer, academic, and game designer in New York.

GENERAL INTRODUCTION

Design is everywhere. Arguably, nothing today has a greater impact on human beings. The modern world is artificial, it is a world that we have made and designed and keep on remaking and redesigning. Professional designers have been important in this process from the early twentieth century on, but so are we all, as users, consumers, interrogators, and recipients of designed environments, objects, images, experiences, services, and messages. Design improves and gives direction to our lives, but rarely for everyone in the same instant. We define and control our surroundings through design, in ways that can make our lives easier or more complex. Design creates new possibilities in our physical world that are not based in nature, and design helps facilitate our needs. Design is about assistance, but it can also be a hindrance; it often sits in an ambiguous cultural position that can lead to both positive and negative outcomes, depending on time, place, and context. Design uses experiences from the past to create things for the present that look forward to the future. As the professionals working in design specialisms such as communication, industrial design, fashion, interior design, or architecture, as well as in intradisciplinary teams, designers hold an enormous responsibility. All this and more is the complicated substance of design studies.

Design Studies: A Reader is the first anthology to closely examine the diversity and complexities of design: as processes, as designed products (including signs and images), as systems, in use, as well as in effects on and relationship to human beings within a range of social and cultural contexts. The book takes its title and its concept from design studies, as an evolving academic discipline that looks at design holistically from idea to process, to finished products, to reception. This is *a* reader; it is not definitive, but rather it concentrates on design studies' interest in the more social and cultural dimensions of design, its consumption and production, identity, ethical issues, and globalization, in design as an instrument of social life and as an agent of change. In doing so the *Reader* documents what has been written on these subjects by design specialists and by those from other fields and disciplines, and it contributes to the further development of design studies.

WHAT IS DESIGN STUDIES?

Design studies is the academic discipline that addresses the complicated activity of design. The term appears to have originated in the title of the journal of the same name, founded in Britain in 1979, which today describes itself as "the only journal to approach the understanding of design from comparisons across all domains of application, including engineering and product design, architectural design and planning, computer artefacts and systems design" (http://www.elsevier.com). Design studies represents a pluralistic approach to design, which also developed in the research into design methods that was taking place in Britain in the 1960s (see Section 2 of the *Reader*). This encouraged reflection by designers on their own practices, and it also attempted to establish a community of researchers who embraced design via principles, thoughts, values, and practices, as well as things, and who brought this design thinking to bear on the world. The concept was further enhanced in the United States with the establishment of the academic journal *Design Issues* in 1984, edited by Victor Margolin, at the University of Illinois, Chicago.

Margolin originally set design studies as an approach that encompassed and exceeded the scope of design history, which had begun as an academic discipline in Britain in the 1970s (see Section 1). He has since developed that definition. *Design Issues* declares a concern with "History/Theory/Criticism," but it has also contributed to establishing a diverse, multidisciplinary, and multifaceted approach to understanding design. Margolin has conceptualized the scope of design studies as emphasizing: design practice, designed products, design discourse or the language that is used to discuss design, and design meta-discourse, which reflects upon critiques and analyses of design. Margolin's method has been particularly important to the way that we have approached design studies in this *Reader*. We share his belief that design is "a component of culture whose study concerns everyone" (Margolin 2002: 256) and that this approach is "strongest when organized by topics rather than by conventional academic disciplines" (Margolin 2002: 252).

While *Design Studies: A Reader* acknowledges these emphases, it also looks beyond them, and beyond design out into a wider world, practically and intellectually. The *Reader* therefore references on the one hand design in use, and on the other design's involvement with methodologies and areas of scholarship outside of itself, particularly in the social sciences, in the humanities, and in the field of cultural studies. In doing so the *Reader* provides a broad and multidisciplinary acknowledgement of design, relevant to a wide audience, as a social and cultural force that demands recognition.

The concept of the *Reader* developed from a course, "Introduction to Design Studies," which we, the co-editors, instigated and developed as part of a new curriculum for undergraduate design students at Parsons The New School for Design, in New York. As design theorists and historians, our courses presented a unique opportunity for students from the diverse range of design disciplines offered by Parsons to meet and study design as a common concern, beyond professional boundaries. Taking that opportunity meant recognizing that studying design in the way that we felt it must be studied involved accessing a wide and diverse range of literature, contemporary and historical, written by design specialists and from other fields. But our approach and that of the *Reader* is not just intended for design students; in fact, our teaching demands that those students also recognize their parallel existences as users and subjects of design.

Design studies, as a reflexive act (what Margolin has referred to as a meta-discourse) incites a type of thinking within the field that can radically alter the "business-as-usual" mentality that hinders progress. Thinking design is an imperative that leads to questioning "best practices," and this can also change how design is practiced. We assembled the *Reader* as a transdisciplinary endeavor that uses examples from design, theory, history, and practice as well as from other disciplines, to get those curious and interested in the artificial world to think about design holistically, rather than as a set of discrete practices.

READING THE *READER*

Rather than use lengthy essays, this book uses excerpts from longer pieces and includes shorter articles, as well as specially commissioned essays and other primary sources, to guide readers through the diversity of design-related subject matters and approaches. Four of these commissioned essays cover larger themes, including design history, ethics, mass-produced fashion, and social justice. In addition, a final section of specially commissioned essays analyzes ten seminal designs of the twentieth century, from Helvetica to the cell phone. The majority of these texts relate to design as material and visual culture—the "artificial things" that human beings conceive, produce, use, and interpret. Furthermore, the book's range of international readings is designed to work within a global context, especially in relation to those parts of the world where interest in design studies is most developed, that is, in the United Kingdom, the United States, continental Europe, Asia, and Australia.

To achieve this aim, we have divided this reader into seven sections. These separate sections should be thought about holistically, in that the themes, ideas, and concepts covered in each section are intimately interrelated to each other. For instance, a student of design cannot fully understand the realities of our current crisis in sustainability (Section 6.3) without also assessing topics such as Consumption (4.3), Labor (5.1), Industrialization (5.2), and Globalization (6.1). While it would be ideal if one read through the entire book, thinking about how and where these interconnections exist, *Design Studies: A Reader* can also be used discretely in sections or subsections and still convey important ideas in current and past thinking about design.

The seven main sections of this book cover enormous topics that raise heated conversations about design. Starting with the section on History is critical, in that history grounds the practice of design in context and explains the connection between our material world and the events that surround the thinking and making of specific things. The second section, Design Thinking, assesses various ways of analyzing design, as both a process and a complex activity. The Theorizing section then brings design into larger theoretical arenas, such as aesthetics and ethics, and claims that design needs to be understood as part of a larger dialogue about beauty, politics, and interpersonal and intercultural communication. The fourth section covers the critical link between Identity and Consumption. In a world where advertising claims that you are what you buy, these readings dissect this idea. The fifth section, on Labor, Industrialization, and New Technology, looks carefully at the history of design production and also points to new possible directions in our rapidly changing world. The penultimate section, Design and Global Issues, harkens back to the questions first raised in Section 3 and claims that designers and consumers have to be very aware of how their activities are disenfranchising the vast majority of the world population. Furthermore, this section questions how global use patterns are causing havoc in our world of supposed plenty. Finally, the last section includes ten separate essays on "Design Things." We commissioned these short essays to add texture to the reader, so that many of the abstract notions raised in the first six sections can be understood through actual things. Again, the hope is that multiple readings and various sections can work together to explain how, for instance, the bicycle, the Eames Lounge Chair, or the Bullet Train can be understood in relation to concerns about globalization, design history, or aesthetics.

While a number of anthologies closely examine aspects of design practice and its professions, no reader encapsulates the diversity and complexities of design—as a practice, profession, subject, and object, and as material and visual form—in a single volume. *Design Studies: A Reader* presents a range of perspectives that address the design process, the designed product (including signs and images), design and use, as well as its effect on and relationship to human beings within a range of social and cultural contexts. In doing so, the *Reader* not only documents what has been written on the subject, but it aims to contribute to the further development of this exciting field.

SECTION 1

HISTORY OF DESIGN

SECTION INTRODUCTION

Placing the historical context of design at the beginning of the *Reader* emphasizes our view of the importance of the history of design for design studies. We share the view that "the tripartite relationship between history, understanding, and practice is of central importance to design as a whole" (Dilnot 1989: 214). For greater clarity, we employ the distinction made by John Walker between *design history,* as a new academic discipline that emerged in Britain in the late 1970s, and *the history of design,* as the object of study of that discipline (Walker 1989: 1).

Design history has its origins as an academic discipline in Britain in the early 1970s. It was generated substantially in art and design schools by teachers who sought to inform design students about the history of their practices. The first British design history conference, held in 1975, was followed by a series of annual conferences and their ensuing publications, such as *Leisure in the Twentieth Century* (1977), and *Design History: Fad or Function?* (1978). Participants came from a diversity of backgrounds, including art and architectural history, social and economic history, and design practice. Many were involved in developing new courses and programs, such as the Open University's ground-breaking course and the ensuing book, *History of Architecture and Design 1890–1939.* In 1977 this interest was formalized with the founding of the Design History Society, and then in 1988 with the publication of its *Journal of Design History,* which has since established an international scope and readership. In the United States the journal, *Design Issues,* was launched in 1984, with a broader focus on the history, theory, and criticism of design.

At this stage, the histories of design available were of two types: those written before and adopted by the nascent discipline, such as Siegfried Giedion's *Mechanisation Takes Command* (1948), Herwin Schaeffer's *The Roots of Modern Design* (1970), and Nikolaus Pevsner's *Pioneers of Modern Design* (1991 [1949]), and those that were contemporary and determining to the establishment of the discipline and its methodologies. In the second category, John Heskett (1980) and Jeffrey L. Meikle (1979) are two scholars who produced detailed histories that also demonstrated the discipline's early interest in industrial design.

Over the years, the history of design has broadened its intellectual and its geographic scope, reflecting more intellectual diversity, encompassed by design history and the widening global impact of design (see Section 6). We can cite, as examples, Tony Fry's *Design History Australia* (1988), the *Scandinavian Journal of Design History,* launched in 1991, and in 2002, the first of an annual series of meetings of the Design History Workshop Japan. New scholarship has also been demonstrated via exhibitions. These have ranged from the detailed monographic approach, such as Flinchum on Henry Dreyfus (1997), to a focus on a particular region (Taragin 2002), or revisionist histories, such as Wilk's *Modernism* (2006).

While scholarship has moved far beyond the modernist canon, the state of design and its history still continues to be a subject for academic discourse. In 2008, for example, the editors of this *Reader* chaired a panel at the annual conference of the College Art Association on this topic. The fact that the debate does continue serves to enrich the discipline, as well as our greater understanding and study of design.

SECTION 1: HISTORY OF DESIGN

1.1: Design Histories

INTRODUCTION

Placing design objects and practices within the context of history helps discern where design has been, where it might be going, and how its past can be rethought. But the very breadth and depth of design, the questions over its definitions and origins, raise complex issues that cannot be ignored when researching, writing, and simply discussing the history of design. They emphasize how histories of design must be understood against the context from which they emerged, against their objectives and the biases of their authors. This subsection presents four distinct approaches to the history of design that also illustrate the development of design history as an academic discipline, considered in detail in the next subsection: Pevsner's modernist-based art historical approach, Forty's more sociological perspective, and then the postmodernist discourse (writing about the cultural geography of the subject of design history) of Turner, writing as a historian and cultural outsider, and Uriarte, as a designer and cultural insider.

Pevsner's extract is taken from a book that predated but was very influential on the establishment of design history as a discipline. *Pioneers of Modern Design from William Morris to Walter Gropius,* originally published in 1936 as *Pioneers of the Modern Movement from William Morris to Walter Gropius,* presents the thesis that a modern style emerged at the end of the nineteenth century, beginning with the work of William Morris and his circle, which also encompassed the development of steel building and Art Nouveau. At the time of the book's original publication, functionalism was the modern architectural style that was under development in Europe and the United States, and design was still emerging as a legitimate profession.

Pevsner identifies distinctive qualities of modernity through his choices of art, architecture, and functional objects, which are presented as aesthetically superior to mid-Victorian design, which the author saw as bourgeois and excessive, as epitomized in the British goods shown at the Great Exhibition of 1851. His emphasis on the primacy of certain pioneering artists and architects as aesthetic and moral saviors is represented in this extract by the work of Charles Annesley Voysey. The roots of his argument lie in art history and in German philosophy, where the quest to achieve the sublime is paralleled in *Pioneers* as the narrative of the modern movement.

Pevsner's canonical approach was subsequently criticized by scholars who viewed design more diversely in terms of its objects, its geographies, and its intellectual rationale (see Section 1.2). Adrian Forty takes particular issue with Pevsner's attribution of blame for a deterioration in design to the mechanical inventions of the Industrial Revolution, based largely on the arguments of mid-nineteenth-century British design reformers. But Pevsner's history must be understood (as must all histories) relative to the background and intentions of its author, and commended in its argument for the importance of design and its history in the modern world.

Forty was one of the first scholars to publish a history of design that focuses on machine-made objects and acknowledges their place as conveyors of meaning or "what design does, as opposed to who did it." Prior to this book he had contributed The Electric Home: A Case Study of the Domestic

Revolution of the Inter-War Years in Britain as a unit of the course History of Architecture and Design 1890–1939 (1975) for the U.K. Open University. Prepared by Tim Benton and others, the course and its supporting television and radio programs proved groundbreaking in its methodology and content. In The Electric Home and later in the book *Objects of Desire: Design and Society 1750–1980* (1986), Forty moves beyond design history premised on great designers, on style over content and meanings, and on the modernist form-follows-function aesthetic. In this extract, which concludes his book, he critiques the myth of the omnipotent designer and questions Pevsner's approach of representing design "purely as the creative act of individuals" as ultimately degrading to its complexities and its importance to everyday life. Forty also highlights for us the importance of reading historical sources critically, in context, and from multiple perspectives. This latter point is developed with particular reference to the geographical and the temporal scopes of the other two extracts in this subsection.

Matthew Turner begins his essay by addressing the issue of the geopolitical narrowness of the history of design as he saw it when he began his research on Hong Kong in the 1980s. The focus of design history on Western modernism, either as a principle, for Pevsner, or as a problem, for Forty, Turner considers limited geographically and politically. Turner raises important questions about design itself—where it can exist and has existed and who defines its existence. He observes that, in the late 1980s at least, "the history of design seems to be written by the economically powerful." If the history of design is embedded in the values of the First World, then "its retrospective application elsewhere is problematic." Turner therefore sees himself not simply as uncovering the history of design in early twentieth-century Hong Kong, but more ambitiously, in enlarging an understanding of world design, providing valuable material for disciplines beyond design history, and boosting the confidence of designers outside of the First World.

Turner's research emphasizes how the design historian needs a broad historical, social, cultural, and political understanding, especially when working beyond the established parameters of Western modernism. Design adaptation, for example, culturally acceptable in the Pearl River Delta and in Hong Kong, would be condemned as mere copying in the West (see also the extract by Daniel Huppatz in Section 2.3) But one cannot speak simply of modernity as a given outside of Europe and the United States, or beyond the 1960s, which was the decade before Cuba, the subject of the last essay, began its design development.

Lucila Fernández Uriarte's history of design in Cuba is distinctive on several levels. The two examples she discusses here illustrate a confluence of the impact of premodernity, modernity, and postmodernity (as one might see today in other regions of South America, in India, or in China). They address the specific historical and cultural conditions of Cuba, and the urban problems of its capital city, Havana. Uriarte is writing from a different perspective than the other historians in this subsection; she is charting a history that she herself has experienced, in her own lifetime as a designer and educator living and working in her country of origin.

The history of design continues to develop its parameters, relative to design practices, objects, and definitions, as well as to other intellectual disciplines. For design studies, the inclusion of design history remains a given, not an option.

1

PIONEERS OF MODERN DESIGN, EIGHTEEN-NINETY TO NINETEEN-FOURTEEN

Nikolaus Pevsner

We must first return to English architecture and design. At the end of the eighties, … Morris was the leader in design, Norman Shaw in architecture. The deliberate break with tradition, which characterized the style of Europe's greatest painters about 1890 and the style of the initiators of Art Nouveau, was not made and not desired in England. So it seemed appropriate to leave until now the discussion of the English development from 1890 onwards, though at least one English architect had ventured on a new style of an original and highly stimulating nature, before Art Nouveau had begun. This was C. F. Annesley Voysey (1857–1941).[1] It has already been said that his designs were a source of inspiration of Art Nouveau. Van de Velde told the author of the revolutionizing effect of Voysey's wallpapers on him and his friends.[2] His words were: 'It was as if Spring had come all of a sudden.' And indeed we have only to look at one of Voysey's wallpapers printed in the nineties and one of his somewhat later printed linens, to see the great difference between him and Morris. Not that he aimed at novelty; his modifications and progressiveness, it would seem, were almost unconscious. Doctrines and hard-and-fast rules were not his way. In the controversy between supporters of stylized and of naturalistic ornament, he did not take sides. For although, in an interview in 1893, he declared realism to be unsuitable for decoration, he was inclined to admit plants and beasts in patterns on condition that they be 'reduced to mere symbols'. This may seem in accord with Morris, but there is

a distinctly new note in Voysey's urgent desire to 'live and work in the present'.[3]

So he arrives at patterns which are happily near to nature, and at the same time full of decorative charm. The graceful shapes of birds flying, drifting, or resting, and of tree-tops, with or without leaves, are favourite motifs of Voysey's, and there is an unmistakable kindliness in his childlike stylized trees and affectionately portrayed birds and beasts. A comparison between these wallpapers or linens and Morris's *Honeysuckle* shows what a decisive step has been taken away from nineteenth-century Historicism into a new world of light and youth.

It is known that everywhere in English cultural life a longing for fresh air and gaiety expressed itself at the end of Queen Victoria's reign. The success of Liberty's about 1890 depended largely on their Eastern silks in delicate shades and their other Chinese imports. The history of the part played by China and Japan in European art since 1860 has not yet been written. It would be very interesting to show the influence of the East appearing here in a loose technique of painting, there in the greatest finesse of line and contours, there again in clear, soft, and pure colour, and in yet other works in flat pattern effects. Owing to the unique synthesis of ornamental and 'Impressionist' qualities in Eastern art, both the Impressionists and, at the opposite pole, the originators of Art Nouveau, could use what Japanese woodcuts and Chinese pottery had to teach them. The Impressionist went to Japan for a lightness that

Image 1 C. F. Voysey, 14 South Parade, Bedford Park, London, 1888–1891. Courtesy of The Bedford Park Society.

he took for *plein air,* for a sketchy handling of the brush, and a flatness of surfaces, which he wrongly interpreted as meaning the shadelessness of strong sunlight. His adversary, more justly, stressed the high degree of stylization in every line drawn and every surface decorated by an Eastern artist. That is why Japanese woodcuts can appear in the backgrounds of Manet's *Zola* and Degas's *Tissot* as well as van Gogh's *Père Tanguy* and Ensor's *Skeleton Studying Eastern Paintings.*[4] The case of Whistler is especially instructive; for it proves that in the same painter at the same time both aspects of the Eastern style might be reflected. The influence of Eastern colour, Eastern delicacy, and Eastern composition on his yet so clearly Impressionist portraits is evident and has no need of the Chinese costume in the *Princesse du Pays de la Porcelaine* to stress it. At the same time, however, Whistler could make this same picture the

chief accent of a room decorated in a style which, although not free from traces of Historicism obviously pointed forward to Art Nouveau.[5] Moreover Whistler pleaded for rooms with completely plain walls in light colours. In this he followed a lead given by his friend Edward Godwin whose house at Bristol has been mentioned in a previous chapter because of the plain walls and bare floors of its rooms and because of its Japanese prints. The date of these interiors, 1862, is remarkably early. Whistler's house in Tite Street, Chelsea, built for him by Godwin, had white and rich yellow walls, Japanese matting on the floors, plain curtains in straight folds, some pieces of Chinese porcelain, and a few simply framed pictures and etchings.[6] In trying to imagine such rooms, we feel ourselves at once in the early years of the twentieth century, no longer in the days of Morris and Ruskin. And yet, in theory (if that is not too heavy an expression for his casual *aperçus*) and in technique, Whistler was as complete an Impressionist as anybody, and therefore an object of passionate hatred to those who worked for a new outlook on life and art.[7] There is no need to go again into that unpleasant case, Whistler versus Ruskin. Morris was bound to follow Ruskin.[8] This was a matter of principle primarily, but also a matter of taste. The man who regarded Burne-Jones as the great living painter of the Late Victorian era could certainly not appreciate Whistler's superficial (truly superficial) pictorial impressions.

One would expect to find the same contrast between the disciples of the Arts and Crafts and the Impressionists as between Morris and Whistler. However, it is a fact which has already been mentioned in connection with the exhibitions of Les Vingt, that on the Continent the introduction of Impressionism, and of the new decorative style in both its forms, as Art and Crafts and as Art Nouveau, took place concurrently and were both due to the same persons. Meier-Graefe, who was one of the first to discover van de Velde, wrote books on Renoir and Degas, and also on van Gogh and Gauguin. And even today most people interested in art are unaware of the irreconcilable difference between Impressionism as a doctrine and the doctrine of Morris and all his followers. Yet, it is obvious that the antithesis, Impressionism versus Arts and Crafts, is but the artistic expression of a far more comprehensive cultural antithesis between two generations. On the one side there is a conception of art as a rapid rendering of momentary surface effects, on the other as an expression of what is final and essential; on the one side there is the philosophy of Art for Art's sake, on the other a renewed faith in a social message of art. The Impressionists stand for the exquisite luxuries of late-nineteenth-century Paris, the Arts and Crafts for 'roughing it' in the spirit of that Youth Movement which is so significant of the years around 1900 and after, and can be traced in Bergson as much as in the foundation of the first 'modern' public schools in England: Abbotsholme (1889) and Bedales (1892).

In design, Voysey is the outstanding but by no means the only representative of this new *joie de vivre*. Some of Crane's late wallpapers also depart from Morris's heaviness. Frank Brangwyn's designs for textiles are another example. As long as Continental architects believed in Art Nouveau, it was chiefly English designs for wallpapers, printed linens, chintzes, and so on which appealed to them. As soon as the new desire for *Sachlichkeit* spread, all the pioneer work done by the English architects and artists in the shaping (not the decoration) of objects became topical. It must have been a delightful surprise to those who—like Muthesius—came to England, weary not only of Victorian stuffiness but also of the licence of Art Nouveau, to see a toast rack or a cruet set designed by Voysey. The refreshing simplicity of his wallpapers is also the keynote of these small things of everyday use. Their charm lies solely in the cleanness and gracefulness of their shapes.

Of particular importance for the coming Modern Movement was the expression of this new spirit in furnishing. The entrance hall of Voysey's house, The Orchard, Chorleywood, Hertfordshire, of 1900 can serve as an example, with its lightness; the woodwork painted white, a pure intense blue for the tiles, unmitigated contrasts of uprights and horizontals, especially in the screen to the staircase (a motif which was for a time to become eminently popular), and furniture of bold, direct, if a little *outré* forms.

There is one more thing which must be said about Voysey and which places him further from Morris and close to us. He was a designer, not a craftsman. He could not in fact, so he told the author, work in any craft. Ernest Gimson (1864–1920),[9] the greatest of the English artist-craftsmen, was, as a matter of fact, in not too different a position, although not many people realize it. He had been trained, it is true, in craftsmanship, but his famous works of cabinetmaking, metal-work, and so on are only designed and not made by him. The chairs give an impression of his honesty, his feeling for the nature of wood, and his unrevolutionary spirit. Few of his works have this superb simplicity. As a rule, Gimson was more responsive to English tradition and did not despise the use of forms invented in the past.

On a really commercial basis good progressive furniture was at the same time made by Sir Ambrose Heal (1872–1959). The firm of Heal & Son had been producing Victorian furniture, until Ambrose Heal changed its course. A wardrobe which Heal's showed at the Paris Exhibition of 1900 has the same brightness which we found in Voysey's wallpapers. Plain surfaces of slightly fumed and waxed oak contrast with small panels decorated in pewter and ebony. There are no long curves; the patterns are composed of rectangles and gracefully-drawn little flowers. The close atmosphere of medievalism has vanished. Living amongst such objects, we breathe a fresher air.

Image 2 Dining chair designed by Harry Davoll or Fred Gardiner after Ernest Gimson and made by Gardiner in 1946. Seats were probably rushed by Neville Neal in Edward Gardiner's workshop. Copyright: Cheltenham Art Gallery & Museum (with photograph by Woodley and Quick).

Even more important historically than such exhibition pieces of Heal's was their production for the ordinary market. In 1898, the first catalogue of Heal's Plain Oak Furniture came out and started the revival of the simple wooden bedstead in England.[10] For more than twenty years these pleasant bedsteads were popular in the English furniture trade, until they were swept away by misguided supporters of modernistic forms.

Exactly the same contrast between 1890 and 1900 as in cabinetmaking is to be found in English printing. Morris's Kelmscott Press—founded in 1890—produced pages the effect of which depends largely on their exquisite medievalist decoration. Cobden-Sanderson's and Emery Walker's Doves Press—founded in 1900—secured for the plain unadorned type face its place in modern book production.

As far as English architecture is concerned, the historical position is not quite so simple as in applied art. It has been pointed out that, by 1890, Norman Shaw had attained a style which, based on Queen Anne, was so 'modern' in character and so perfectly suited to English needs and taste that it could hardly be improved on, as long as no open break with tradition was attempted. The earliest and most remarkable cases of independence—earlier in fact than that of Horta—are afforded by some of the early architectural works of Mackmurdo and Voysey. Mackmurdo's house, 8 Private Road, Enfield built about 1883 is of a surprisingly free carriage. The flat roof and the few horizontal windows of the upper floor are particularly noteworthy. Although much more orderly it forms in its independence of approach a parallel, the only European parallel, to Godwin's house of 1878 for Whistler. In 1882 Mackmurdo founded the Century Guild, the first of all those groups of artist-craftsmen-designers who followed the teaching of William Morris. Of 1883 was his amazing title page which started Art Nouveau on its way. In 1886 Mackmurdo put up the stand, for the products of his guild at an exhibition at Liverpool. The attenuated shafts with their excessive top cornices instead of capitals and the repetition of these odd forms on top of the fascia board are even more original, and started a fashion, when Voysey and then several others took them up. Of Mackmurdo's strong influence on Voysey there can be no doubt. He himself said to the author that when he was very young Mackmurdo had impressed him even more than Morris. Yet the first house which Voysey built, the one in The Parade at Norman Shaw's garden suburb, Bedford Park near London, is amazingly independent, considering the date, 1891. The arrangement of the windows is particularly striking. But whereas this kind of free grouping also prevails in the works of Norman Shaw and his school, the whiteness of the walls was an open protest against the surrounding red brick of Shaw's garden suburb. The tower-like tallness of the house also and the skipping rhythm of bare walls and horizontal window openings were innovations introduced deliberately and not without a youthful sense of mischief.

However, Voysey did not go on in that direction, or else he would have developed into an architect of Art Nouveau. Already in the tiny studio built in St Dunstan's Road, West Kensington, London, in the same year 1891, the general proportions are closer to English traditions, cottage traditions, than anything in the house in Bedford Park, although the detail is again remarkably novel, above all the massive chimney, the batter of the buttresses on the right and also the ironwork in front (obviously inspired by Mackmurdo's woodwork of 1886).

When Voysey began to get commissions for houses in the country, his appreciation of English traditions was decisively strengthened.[11] A man of intense feeling for nature, as his designs prove him to have been, he could not but think of his houses in conjunction with the surrounding countryside, and so shapes offered themselves which were more akin to the English manor house and cottage of the past than to those he had evolved in London. His country-house practice began in the early nineties and by 1900 had assumed very large dimensions. He never built a church, never a public building, and only once a small warehouse.

Perrycroft, Colwall, Malvern Hills, dates from 1893. It is typical of Voysey's ideas of what a country house should be like. In spite of such strikingly modern features as the consistently horizontal fenestration and the massive block shapes of the chimney-stacks, it is nowhere demonstratively anti-traditional, and it fits perfectly with its natural surroundings (a garden was planned and planted together with the house) and the architectural character of the country.

This is even more evident in another building, the house erected for Canon L. Grane at Shackleford in Surrey, in 1897. Today it is not easy to appreciate the candour and simplicity of its façade. For, in Britain at least, it has become too much of a standard example ineptly imitated by hundreds of speculative builders all along the arterial roads and all over the suburbs. However, from the historian's point of view, it remains no small feat to have created the pattern for the vast majority of buildings carried out over a period of thirty years and more. What was not copied from Voysey, needless to say, was what impresses us today as his most progressive motifs—the long- drawn-out window strips and the completely bare triangles of the gables, broken only in one place by a charmingly tiny and just a trifle precious window.

This introduction of an occasional effect of Art Nouveau piquancy helps a great deal to lighten the otherwise puritan honesty of many of Voysey's houses.

NOTES

Extracted from Nikolaus Pevsner, *Pioneers of Modern Design* (London and New York: Penguin Books, 1991), pp. 148–61.

1. There is as yet no book in existence on Voysey. The best paper is Brandon Jones, John, 'C.F.A. Voysey', *Architectural Association Journal*, lxxii, 1957, pp. 238–62. *See* also Pevsner, Nikolaus, 'Charles F. Annesley Voysey', *Elsevier's Maandschrift*, 1940, pp. 343–55. For earlier

publications of Voysey's work cf.: *Dekorative Kunst,* i, 1898, pp. 241ff.; Muthesius, H., *Das englische Haus,* Berlin, 1904–5, i, pp. 162 ff.

2. The clearest proof of this influence of Voysey's is Adolphe Crespin's wallpapers, designed at Brussels in the nineties. *Art et décoration,* ii, 1897, pp. 92ff.

3. *The Studio,* I, 1893, p. 234.

4. On the Japanese influence in the sixties see for instance Rewald, John, *The History of Impressionism,* New York (Museum of Modern Art), 1946, p. 176. On the influence of Japan on Art Nouveau *see* Lancaster, Clay, 'Oriental Contribution to Art Nouveau', *Art Bulletin,* xxxiv, 1952, and more recently Madsen, *Sources of Art Nouveau,* pp. 188, etc. A general treatment of the subject before 1900 is Gonse, L., 'L'art japonais et son influence sur le goût européen', *Revue des arts decoratifs,* xviii, 1898. A few key dates are 1854 for the first official treaty between the United States and Japan; 1854 for the first between Britain and Japan; 1859 for the first trade agreement between the United States and Japan; and 1859 for the first between Britain and Japan; 1856 for the chance discovery of Japanese woodcuts in a Paris shop by Braquemond, the etcher (who then introduced them to the Goncourts, Baudelaire, Manet, and Degas, and probably also Whistler); 1862 for the participation of Japan in the International Exhibition in London. Christopher Dresser's journey to Japan in 1876 has been referred to. Owen Jones … also … published *Examples of Chinese Ornament* in 1867.

5. The Peacock Room now at the Freer Gallery of Art in Washington was decorated by Whistler in 1876–7; the *Princesse* had been painted in 1863–4.

6. Pennell, E. R. and J., *The Life of J. McN. Whistler,* London, 1908, I, p. 219; and Way, T. R., and Dennis, G. R., *The Art of J. McN. Whistler,* London, 1903, p. 99. The exhibitions for which Whistler was responsible in 1883 and 1884 had white and lemon yellow and white and pink walls (Pennell, pp. 310 and 313).

7. [Another] interesting instance of this confusion between old—i.e., *l'art pour l'art* outlook—and new ideas [is] … Gatz, Felix M., ' Die Theorie des l'art pour l'art und Theophile Gautier', *Zeitschrift für Aesthetik und allgemeine Kunstwissenschaft, xxix,*1935, pp. 116–40.

8. He speaks of the 'impression on a very short-sighted person of divers ugly incidents seen through the medium of a London fog'. National Association for the Advancement of Art and its Application to Industry, *Transactions, Edinburgh Meeting, 1889,* London, 1890, p. 199.

9. *Ernest Gimson, His Life and Work,* Stratford-on-Avon, 1924.

10. Weaver, Sir Lawrence. 'Tradition and Modernity in Craftsmanship.' *Architectural Review,* lxiii, 1928, pp. 247–9.

11. Two examples of the sort of Tudor or seventeenth-century manor houses which must have impressed Voysey are: Westwood near Bradford-on-Avon, illustrated in Garner, T., and Stratton, A., *Domestic Architecture during the Tudor Period,* 2nd ed., London, 1929; and Perse Caundle in Dorset, illustrated in Oswald, A., *Country Houses of Dorset,* London, 1935.

2

DESIGN, DESIGNERS AND THE LITERATURE OF DESIGN

Adrian Forty

Because designers generally talk and write only about what they do themselves, design has come to be regarded as belonging entirely within their realm. This misunderstanding has reappeared in innumerable books and in the coverage of design in the press and on television. It has also, with more serious consequences, been taught in schools of design, where students are liable to acquire grandiose illusions about the nature of their skills, with the result that they become frustrated in their subsequent careers.

The second and more fundamental reason why so much has been made of what designers think and do has come out of an apparent paradox in their role. On the one hand, design is determined by ideas and material conditions over which designers have no control, yet, on the other hand, designs are the result of designers exercising their creative autonomy and originality. To put the paradox in the most extreme terms, how can designers be said to be in command of what they do, but at the same time merely be the agents of ideology, with no more power to determine the outcome of their work than the ant or worker bee? There is no answer to this question: it is a fact that both conditions invariably co-exist, however uncomfortably, in the work of design. The same apparent paradox occurs in all manifestations of culture: any painting, film, book or building contains ideas about the nature of the world, ideas which exist in other minds apart from that of the artist, author or designer, but which are mediated through his or her ability to conceive a form or means of representation. The paradox has been widely discussed, and there have been numerous attempts to give a theoretical explanation.[1]

For most designers, however, the solution to the problem lies not in theory, but in collusion with the myth of their own omnipotence and in wholly ignoring their role as agents of ideology. Although some designers do acknowledge that they are involved in the transmission of ideas over which they have no control and which they may not fully understand, it is more common to hear them describing their work as if they had overall power. Clearly, it is necessary for designers to believe, at least temporarily, in their own omnipotence in order for them to be able to create at all, but this does not mean, as they often assume, that everything they do is the result of their own conscious will and determination. The omnipotence is surely, like all such claims, a fantasy, but an attractive one: the myth of creative autonomy obliterates the problem of ideology as a determinant in design and releases designers from the uncomfortable prospect that they might be no more than actors in the theatre of history. That others, such as critics and historians, should have proved so attached to the myth is more surprising, and can only be explained by its accordance with the widespread assumption that, despite all evidence to the contrary, individuals are the masters of their own will and destiny.

One example of a successful design will suffice to illustrate how easily a designer's own view of a job can make him appear omnipotent. The design of the Lucky Strike cigarette packet has not, to the best of my knowledge, been written about by anyone except the man who designed it, Raymond Loewy: it therefore provides a subject fresh for exegesis.[2] In 1940, American Tobacco decided for reasons which are not known that the packet in which their Lucky Strike cigarettes were sold needed to be redesigned. They took the job to Loewy, a Frenchman who had emigrated to the United States in 1919 and had established a successful industrial design practice in New York. The changes Loewy made to the Lucky Strike packet were in fact very minor, so minor that one wonders why he has drawn so much attention to them: he changed the ground colour of the pack from green to white, altered the lettering of the word 'cigarettes', and made both sides of the pack the same, where before only one side had borne the red target symbol. The new design was evidently judged a success by the manufacturers, as it has continued unchanged to the present.

In his autobiography, *Never Leave Well Enough Alone*, Loewy has described the characteristics that he thought made the design a winner. The elimination of the green simplified the printing, as well as dealing with the problem of the unpleasant smell given off by the green ink. The white ground made the brand symbol more conspicuous, and placing it on both sides made it always visible. The design was also meant to change the way people thought about the cigarettes, as Loewy described: ' … owing to its impeccable whiteness, the Lucky pack looks, and is, clean. It automatically denotes freshness of content and immaculate manufacturing.'[3]

In the 1940s, of course, these signs did not serve the same purpose as they would now, since smoking was not then known to have any adverse effects upon health.

Loewy's account of the design and his reasons for its success made much of his own ingenuity and talent. Were we to accept this version and to take the single most important fact about the Lucky Strike packet as being that it was designed

by Raymond Loewy, we should be following the routine of conventional histories of design. Yet for all its apparent credibility, there are large flaws in this version. While one cannot deny that skill and creativity went into the design, it seems hard to believe that only Loewy could have come up with the idea of a white cigarette packet, and once we admit the possibility that other designers could have achieved similar results, the case for attributing the design's success entirely to Loewy's personal creativity falls away. If there were others who could have produced it, some of the reasons for the design's success must have lain elsewhere than in the individuality of the designer. Suppose for a moment that we did not know who designed the packet. In this condition of ignorance, which is how we normally experience designs, we would have no choice in trying to understand the causes of the design's success but to consider what ideas it signified.

Image 3 Lucky Strike packet as redesigned by Raymond Loewy, ca. 1942. Photo with permission of Laurence Loewy of Loewy Design.

The potency of the Lucky Strike design might, for instance, be understood in terms of the problem perceived by manufacturers in the United States of creating a single national market out of the heterogeneous assortment of different races and nationalities that have become the country's citizens. The massive influx of immigrants to the United States in the late nineteenth and early twentieth centuries had created a population which strenuously wanted to be identified as American, but in which individuals were daily reminded by their tongues, diets and customs of their origins as, say, Chinese, Irish or Italian. They could identify themselves as Americans only if they had ideas of what Americanness was, and these ideas, to be acceptable to them, had to be compatible with their own ethnic or national identities. Great efforts were therefore made to establish an American ideal with which all races and creeds could identify. American culture is full of affirmations of what it means to be American, a characteristic that seems odd to non-Americans, but has been very important to the development and cohesion of the nation: Canada, with its militant French separatist movement, is a warning of the consequences of the failure to establish a satisfactory national identity. The ideas by which the American was distinguished seem vague and so extraordinarily general as to be very hard to question or refute. Their very flabbiness, however, is one of their great qualities, for it enables them to be shared by all Americans without undermining the self-image of any sub-group of Italians, Jews or Poles. The following description of the characteristics said to distinguish Americans is taken from a book published in 1933:

'What according to the American standard is rated relatively high? Formal education certainly goes on that list … Protection of health—everything promoting physical health, bodily vigour and longevity—is also undoubtedly on the list of values rated relatively high. This motive without question justifies any expenditure of time and money. Physical comfort and bodily cleanliness too, it may be alleged, rank relatively high in the American standard of living. "Americanisation", it is quite frankly said at times, means inculcation of our passion for hot water, large and numerous towels, soaps, baths and other cleansing agents. The physical comfort motive shows itself in the widespread systems of central heating, electric fans, refrigeration and easy chairs.'[4]

Hygiene, cleanliness and comfort are general, unspecific qualities with which no reasonable person, whether Lithuanian Jew or Japanese, could possibly disagree. So suitable have they proved that they have been seized upon avidly by all who wish to show that they are indeed Americans, creating in the process all sorts of curious effects—Americans pay more for white-shelled eggs than for brown, whereas the converse is true in Britain.

If hygiene and purity were important constituents of the idea of Americanness, so too was the belief in material prosperity and the abundance of commodities, which thus needed to be not only freely available, but also identifiably American. An industry based upon markets consisting of specific minority groups could be expected neither to achieve mass sales nor to promote the idea of prosperity with a specifically American basis. The problem, then, was to discover the characteristics that would make products identifiable as American. In this task, design was to provide some answers, one of which would appear to have been represented by the Lucky Strike packet.

Drawing upon the existing association between cleanliness and Americanness gave the Lucky Strike packet an American image, which ensured it a national market. A member of any ethnic group could identify Lucky Strike as an American cigarette by virtue of the pack's conspicuous cleanliness, and perhaps, by purchasing a packet, instantly feel part of American culture. Indeed, the packet was so recognisably American that, within a very short space of time, Lucky Strike became famous throughout the world as a symbol of the American way of life.

Unless we are to invent some fiction about the design being 'timeless' (a device much favoured by design historians for evading the problem of design's relation to society), we can suggest two distinct factors as lying behind the Lucky Strike packet's success within a particular society at a particular point in history. The ideas of cleanliness and Americanness signified by the design belonged in the minds of all Americans and cannot in any way be said to have been an invention of the designer. The other factor in the design's success was the way in which an association between the ideas of whiteness, cleanliness and America was set up by means of a single image. This image was the creation of the designer, and Loewy and his office certainly deserve credit for their skill in devising a form that conveyed the association so effectively.

No design works unless it embodies ideas that are held in common by the people for whom the object is intended. To represent design purely as the creative acts of individuals, as Nikolaus Pevsner did in *Pioneers of Modern Design,* temporarily enhances the importance of designers, but ultimately only degrades design by severing it from its part in the workings of society. This book has set out to show the ways in which design turns ideas about the world and social relations into the form of physical objects. Only by exploring this process and by shifting our attention away from the person of the designer can we properly comprehend what design is, and appreciate how important it has been in representing to us the ideas and beliefs through which we assimilate and adjust to the material facts of everyday life.

NOTES

Extracted from A. Forty, 'Design, Designers and the Literature of Design', in *Objects of Desire: Design and Society 1750–1980* (London: Thames and Hudson, 1986), pp. 241–5. Reprinted by permission of Cameron Books.

1. For an introduction to the theoretical debates on the status of the artist in the production of culture, see Raymond Williams, *Marxism and Literature,* Oxford, 1977, and J. Wolff, *The Social Production of Art,* London, 1981.
2. Raymond Loewy, *Never Leave Well Enough Alone,* New York, 1951, chapter 12; and Raymond Loewy, *Industrial Design,* London and Boston, 1979, pp. 218–219.
3. Loewy, 1951, p. 148.
4. Kyrk, H, *Economic Problems of the Family,* New York, 1933, p. 382.

EARLY MODERN DESIGN IN HONG KONG

Matthew Turner

What distinguishes the history of design from the history of art or architecture is surely the narrowness of its geopolitical compass. The design literature is almost exclusively concerned with the First World, that is to say, with the industrial and commercial development of the Organization for Economic Cooperation and Development (OECD) region.

Whereas we may turn to historical studies of Chinese art or architecture, for example, and draw on a wealth of Chinese and foreign scholarship, a corresponding history of Chinese design is yet to be seen. There is no history of design in India or in a hundred other places that lie outside the triad of Western Europe, North America, and Japan. The effect is as though no significant design ever taken place in the rest of the world, except in the remote sense of the vernacular, or in oases of Western influence.[1]

The extent to which this imbalance in historical resources gives rise to a certain chauvinism, enjoyed by contemporary designers within the triad, and to the difficulties faced by designers elsewhere is a question that ought to concern practitioners of design history. For it may be asked whether the discipline has become a form of neoimperialism?

Most historians of design, particularly those writing from a Marxist viewpoint, would be affronted by such a question. Pretending that the discipline's horizons are expanding or that it will follow the history of science and reach the Sinic world before long is unacceptable. Clive Dilnot argues that the teleological character of design history, its mission to pave the *via regia* of Western modernism, has had its day;[2] Adrian Forty points out that factory production and standardization evolved contemporaneously, but independently, from mechanization,[3] John Heskett suggests somewhat radically that the study of design need not be predicated on modern sources of energy to the extent that third-century India may fall within the purview of the discipline,[4] and Simon Jervis claims that the greater number of significant designers lived and worked before the period conventionally studied by design historians.[5] Why, then, does there seem to be no evidence that the First World's monopoly on the history of design is about to be shaken.

The simplest explanations include that (1) nobody has yet looked for the history of design outside the modern, industrialized, capitalist nations, or (2) evidence is not readily available, and (3) by Western definitions, there can be no real history of design outside the First World. The first explanation is perhaps the most congenial to those who come to design history by way of art history. After all, is not the history of design a relatively new field, which has yet to establish itself even in many OECD nations, such as Yugoslavia? Perhaps the late Sir Nikolaus Pevsner should be regarded as a latter-day Vasari, and John Heskett, *et alia,* as figures such as Giordano Bruno ("There are only as many true rules as there are true artists"), or Zuccari ("Man forms within himself various designs … therefore his design is accidental")? Germany today, tomorrow the world?

However, only the third explanation seems plausible. Appeals to the novelty of the subject or to the dearth of subject matter are not well-founded. After all, more than half a century has passed since Pevsner's *Pioneers* was published in the West and design, as well as design education, was established in many non-Western countries. Given the twentieth-century internationalization of communications and the global expansion of industrial forms of production, the complete absence of any but a Western history of design for three-quarters of the world cannot be explained away by a lack of interest or evidence.

The proposition that, by Western definitions, there cannot be a history of *design,* properly speaking, outside the tradition of the First World has the merit of frankness and, moreover, offers greater explanatory power. In this form, the proposition does not deny that from ancient to modern times there was not a vast daily output of goods and images manufactured for domestic or export purposes, around the globe; it merely asserts that the planning and shaping of such goods and images should not be confused with modern, Western, industrial notions of design—for if everything is design, then design has no meaning.

Entering into a review of definitions of design may not be necessary because the laconic and generalized definitions that have been made do not in themselves preclude application to almost any form of visualization or productive activity. But who, then, advances such a proposition? Indeed, nobody has seriously proposed that the history of design is the exclusive inheritance of the First World, yet neither has anybody seriously contested the terms of the inheritance or suggested it to be a modern forgery. Rather, in line with the old saw that history is written by the victors, the history of design seems to be written by the economically powerful. Japan, for example, was not equipped with a history of design (or with a workable system of management) until her emergence as an economic superpower made such a history inevitable. Until the late 1960s, Japan was assumed to have copied her way onto the industrial

ladder; after that point, she was revealed to have possessed a long and complex history of innovation in design.[6]

The example of Japan suggests that the teleological current in design history runs deeper than merely the justification of whatever style currently happens to be in fashion or the provision of a hagiography of great names. The lineage it provides for modern industrial power may be on an altogether larger scale. Points of friction are instructive; for example, the interpretation of Russian design during the revolutionary period, the discussion of German design in the context of National Socialism or in the German Democratic Republic, and the accounts of design in developing countries. Talking about design in the context of Communism, Fascism, or poverty is never easy. Is this because the history of design is a discourse embedded in the ideological formations of the postwar, liberal, capitalist world?

For some time, now, Occam's razor has been hovering over this tenuous thread of reasoning and, having entered into Discourse's hall of mirrors, only an investigation on the scale of a Foucault or a Said[7] would be sufficient. Such an investigation must demonstrate that the history of design has developed into a useful buttress of values central to the First World and, to such an extent, that its retrospective application elsewhere is problematic. Of course, what these central values might be is a question open to much speculation. Supposing that the history of design embodies a number of key beliefs about First World development seems reasonable. These beliefs are in economic growth and technological development, in progress through free competition and consumer choice, in aspirations toward the comforts and sophistications of affluence, in the importance of individuality, creativity, and innovation fused with the benefits of standardization and mass production. If a demonstration that design is less a description of a process and more a representation of an ideology (conveniently depoliticized and positive, filling the vacuum left behind by science, which has lost so much of its innocence since the 1950s) could be made, a fruitless search for essences might be avoided. After all, an essence being distilled from practices as varied as engineering, design, and fashion design has never seemed likely.

Would such an investigation yield any positive result? Yes, for it would open a perspective on an immense, unexplored storehouse of knowledge about the developing world in the modern era. While enlarging the understanding of world design, valuable material for other disciplines would be provided and a much needed boost would be given to the growing confidence of designers working outside the First World.

The following discourse represents a fragmentary contribution to this ambitious program, focusing on early twentieth-century design in Hong Kong. Other methodologies and perspectives will need to be forged because Hong Kong is in many ways atypical of the developing world. Hong Kong is one of the newly industrialized countries (NICs) of Asia, which, although outside the triad, share many of its values. South Korea and Taiwan[8] had a long colonial history of manufacturing under Japanese colonialization, and Singapore and Hong Kong were industrialized during the period of British colonial rule.[9] In addition, all four "little dragons" are well-known for their unique postwar rates of growth and for the volume and variety of goods exported from their factories.

If the Asian NICs lack of indigenous histories of design seem surprising, remember that the "inheritance" of design history is administered by the First World. Delaying recognition of competing economic power centers as long as possible may be in the interest of the triad, whether by trade protectionism or intellectual protectionism. The intellectual property laws in Hong Kong, for example, protect foreign firms far more than local firms.[10] Uniquely, the trademarks and copyrights of all other countries are enforced within the Territory to attract foreign firms seeking a place to manufacture their goods. That such laws discourage local innovation (it is impossible for a company to check the registers in every country) has

not been considered a disadvantage by those who frame the law. The colonial view never considered it likely that Chinese design would make a significant contribution to exports. The corresponding instruments of trade protectionism toward the NICs need no elaboration.

These issues, however, concern postwar Hong Kong design. The concern here is rather to investigate earlier developments, that began some time before the British landed at Possession Point in 1841. China's foreign trade had been concentrated in its coastal cities for many centuries, particularly in the Pearl River delta. This region had been a center for foreign trade since the Han dynasty (202 BC–220 AD) and for export manufacturing since the Sung dynasty (960–1279 AD), when vast quantities of mass-produced ceramics were made in the provincial kilns of Guangdong. When Emperor Qianlong closed all trading ports with the exception of Guangzhou in 1757, the Pearl River delta became the focus of China's commerce and export industry.

THE DEVELOPMENT OF INDUSTRY IN CHINA'S PEARL RIVER DELTA[11]

The economic strategy of this region was characterized by first, a labor-intensive system of serial or mass production; second, a strong export orientation; and third, a process of adaptive design. As the successive waves of foreign merchants brought with them new products, the early industries of the Pearl River delta became the crucible for export designs that adapted the world's goods to Chinese materials and manufacture. From the tenth to the nineteenth century, Chinese export ceramics were designed in a vast range of adaptive styles, from rough Southeast Asian *kendi* to refined Japanese *imari* wares and Dutch coffee pots. Decorations ran from Arabic to Latin and English, interlaced with Chinese motifs and symbols. The epitome of mimicry was reached when fanciful Western *chinoiserie* designs were self-consciously copied by Chinese artists for European markets.

Design for manufacturing industries around the Pearl River delta, therefore, adopted a strategy unlike that developed by the textile manufacturers of Ahmedabad, where predominantly Indic designs were produced in varying quality to suit different markets. As industrialization gathered speed in Europe, the Chinese strategy of design adaptation, labor intensive production, and export orientation also ran counter to the strategies of manufacturers and traders in the West, preoccupied as they were with an integrated expansion of mechanization and empire.

From the perspective of a commercial and military power such as Britain at the turn of the nineteenth century, that all other systems of manufacturing should give way before the great partnership of machine production and expanded foreign markets must have seemed inevitable. Indeed, this situation became the fate of proto-industrialization outside the West. Traditional systems of trade and manufacture gave place to a colonial economy that depended on supplying raw materials to the West and importing machine made goods. The East-West flow in the world's circulation of goods was soon reversed.

But the trading and manufacturing centers of the Pearl River delta, together with Japan, were an exception to the rule. This exception is more surprising because Japan enjoyed a favorable situation in relation to the expansion of empires in the nineteenth century, whereas a good part of the Pearl River delta came under effective foreign control. Indeed, the survival of design adaptation, labor intensive production, and export orientation into modern times became, as with imperial *laissez-faire* capitalism, an economic anachronism. Yet this combination later led to industrial "hypergrowth" in the modern Asian economies of Hong Kong, Singapore, Taiwan, and South Korea.

Hong Kong was the direct descendant of a unique system of design and manufacturing that had established itself over the centuries along the commercial thoroughfares of the Pearl River delta. The evidence for this may be found in the remarkable continuities of design, during more than a century, in product types and styles, manufacturing and printing companies, and families of artist-designers, that can stretch back to the earliest years of Hong Kong.

If, a century later, Hong Kong artificial flowers were made of plastic and new products, such as radios and flashlights, had joined the list, the continuities rather than the new developments were more remarkable.

To those who assume Hong Kong's industrialization was a postwar phenomenon, its long history of manufacturing is equally surprising. In 1846, the second governor, Sir John Davis, noted: A large number of Chinese are employed in their respective shops in the exercise of industrial trades and manufactures, and there are scarcely any wants of the inhabitants which do not meet with a ready supply within the town.[12]

By 1846, one-third of all Chinese properties were registered as factories. With a Chinese population of 20,338 by 1848, some 700 industrial enterprises must have been founded within the first decade of Hong Kong's history. Records from 1853 suggest that more than 500 of these were ship chandlers, boat builders, and rope manufacturers, however, other arts and crafts also flourished. The 1865 census lists 44 silversmiths, 14 painters and photographers, 17 rattan furniture makers, 10 watch and clock makers, and 5 portrait artists.

During the late nineteenth century, local industry expanded and diversified to include feather-dressing, match factories, soap, cement, coal, briquette and rattan works, sugar refineries, and spinning mills. In 1906, Sir Matthew Nathan promoted the first exhibition of industrial arts to provide visual evidence of what could be made in Hong Kong. A forerunner of the annual industrial products exhibitions, organized by the Chinese Manufacturers' Association founded in 1934, Nathan's Arts and Crafts show was, in the memory of Horace Kadoorie: A revelation of the artistic temperament of Chinese craftsmen in our midst. Above all, it showed the way in which local artisans sought to express their feelings for beauty in the works of their hands.[13]

NOTES

Extracted from M. Turner, 'Early Modern Design in Hong Kong', in D. Doordan, ed., *Design History An Anthology: A Design Issues Reader* (Cambridge, Mass. and London: The MIT Press, 1995), pp. 200–5. Reprinted by permission of The MIT Press.

1. Objections may be made that aspects of design outside the OECD have been described, for example, by developmental economists or railway enthusiasts, but through conversations with designers across Asia, one learns that such accounts are not believed to comprise a history of design.
2. Clive Dilnot, "The State of Design History,' *Design Issues* Vol.1, No. 1 (Spring 1984): 4–23.
3. Adrian Forty, *Objects of Desire* (New York: Pantheon, 1986), chapter 1.
4. Hazel Conway, ed., *Design History—A Student Guide,* 1986/87 article by John Heskett.
5. Simon Jervis, *Penguin Dictionary of Design and Designers* (London: Penguin, 1984), Introductory Essay.
6. The transition point seems to be the *Exhibition of Modern Design in Japan* (Kyoto: National Museum of Modern Art, 1969); the catalog begins: "In the field of modern design, Japan's history is brief."
7. See Edward Said, *Orientalism* (New York: Pantheon, 1978).
8. See J.L. Lau, ed. *Models of Development: A Comparative Study of Economic Growth in South Korea and Taiwan* (San Francisco: ICS Press 1986).
9. The *Report on the Industrial Development of the Colonial Empire* (Colonial Office 1934) was intended to further "Mass production by highly mechanized industrial techniques, a Western device which the east has not found difficult to copy [leading to] progressive social development which will raise the standard of life and the demand for comfort, recreation, and even luxury on the part of Oriental populations" in Singapore and Hong Kong.
10. Michael Pendleton, "Discouraging Local Innovation and Design Expertise in Hong Kong's Colonial Intellectual Property Law," in Hong Kong University's Conference *Design and Development in South and Southeast Asia,* December, 1988.
11. The following account is a variation of my catalog essay published originally as "A History of Export Design in Hong Kong (1900–1960)" in *Made in Hong Kong: A History of Export Design 1900–1960* (Hong Kong: Hong Kong Museum of History with the Urban Council 1988).
12. In 1956, for example, the combined value of Hong Kong "Imperial Preference" export products to British Africa, Malaya, India, and Pakistan and the rest of the British Commonwealth amounted to more than HK$ 264,000,000 (excluding Great Britain) while exports to the United States totaled a mere HK$ 20,457,311.
13. Turner, "A History of Export Design," 9.

4

MODERNITY AND POSTMODERNITY FROM CUBA

Lucila Fernández Uriarte

This article addresses what the study of design history means to a historian with interests in theory and criticism. Regarding the Cuban design profession, there are only three decades of development, from the 1970s onwards. It is important, therefore, to find the points of focus and categories that allow us to investigate the history of material culture before industrialization. The first problem would be to distinguish the predecessors of industrial design.

There have been three decades in which design has been conditioned by social and political events and in which it has been severely limited by economic restraints. In the same way as in countries without an organic industrialization, design in Cuba grew from external influences. There is an urgent need, therefore, to begin to clarify what is specifically ours or the way in which those influences are re-interpreted. To give a view of the history of design that is not a cheap copy of 'universal' design, everyday life in Cuba was studied in the light of historical categories. What follows draws upon the anthropological views of two recognized Cuban historians who have worked on the history of material culture, one in the tobacco industry and the other in the sugar industry: Don Fernando Ortiz and Moreno Fraginal. I hope that they will forgive my interpretation of their work.

A TALE AND SOME INDISCREET ANECDOTES[1]

To make the content of this work more easily understandable, allow me to reminisce. Cuba is an island and, moreover, is situated in a privileged geographical position: 'Key to the unchartered new world of the West Indies'. With the settlement of Christianized Indians, it may be said that this has influenced its culture and history. Cubans have been open to all types of influence and at the same time have suffered violent periods of ostracism; the sea allows communication as much as isolation. For us, it is normal that the latest things that arrive by boat, plane or Internet live side by side with old, traditional things. This relationship has been the norm in our lives. The introduction of professional design in Cuba will be discussed with regard to the professions, institutions and groups in the 1970s and 1980s. In particular, the theoretical model within which it was implemented and the current situation will be discussed. I would like to suggest that the premises from which Cuban design originated were triply modern as they held three utopias: that of design itself, of politics and of history.

The first aimed at reaching a physical, rational and harmonic framework. The second aspired to eliminate the distance between the collective and individual elements in a society of social justice and the third had the intention of rising above the under-developed reality of the country.

In Cuba, as in other countries outside the European scene, one cannot talk about modernity but rather successive modernizations, which have been introduced by different events throughout our history. It could be said that the first modernization (if we accept that modernity started in the Renaissance) was the Discovery in 1492.

Subsequent changes might be identified with the rise of the great sugar industry through the nineteenth century; the wars of independence during that century; the interference of American capital in the twentieth century and the avalanche of its consumer products in the 1950s, or with the socialist revolution in 1960.

If part of modernity is historic action, which by nature is sudden and excessively dynamic, for us, this has been even more marked, leading to transformations without the necessary time to acclimatize and adjust to our reality. That is to say, without the necessary transfer of culture that allows a more intimate dialogue with immediate and appropriate issues. Modernizations are partial, because fusion over time is also characteristic of our countries. It means the parallel existence of different works, technology and cultural periods of historical evolution in the same historic phase. A clear example of this temporary imbalance was the co-existence in the last century in Cuba of the steam engine and the railway with the regime of slavery, which had already made an appearance in Spain.

One could ask, what does the appearance of design in Cuba in the 1970s have in particular, apart from the characteristic it shared with other peripheral countries, i.e. that it was imported? The triple utopia in which it found itself gave it its own characteristics but also, the moment at which it appeared within the dynamics of contemporary design history, contributed to its specificity.

It could be argued that in the 1960s the questioning of the modern movement started. However, what has happened up to now with the modern movement has been interpreted in different ways.

The industrial design which started in the nineteenth century had two problems from the beginning, indicating the emptiness which it needed to fill: one was the adaptation of objects for production and marketing. The other was the need to make the disastrous city atmosphere and architecture, a legacy of the industrial development, more coherent and human.

Schematically, it could be said that even today, these two challenges reflect the various interpretations of design. Both positivism and romanticism, two constants of contemporary culture, have also been intrinsically linked to the act of design. However, despite this start, over time, contemporary design did take into account the success of the adaptive line. Perhaps this was a result of the general influence of industrial society, which tended to eliminate critical options and include all in its pragmatics.

It was in the middle of this first crisis of the modern movement at the end of the 1960s that the image of design was exported to peripheral and non-industrialized countries. Perhaps it seemed that the ghost of romantic escapades of the last century and the idyllic lives outside Europe would surface again. When the ideal fades in Europe, hope places it beyond the seas. Therefore, for some of the main theorists of this second rationalist movement, critical action of design, which makes certain allowances for the environment and society that were already difficult to implement in Europe, found a new opportunity in the emergence of design in the 'Third World'.

With reference to one of the theories of neorationalism, Gui Bonsiepe commented in *Politica tecnologia, disetio industrial y modelos de desarrollo*:

> but if the industrial designer can carry out the aims of this projected model, which, to a certain extent has a general value, this profession of only 2 generations old, but already becoming senile, would be able to rejuvenate itself by accepting the only really important criterion on [sic]: that of affecting society, its value would not only be peripheral.[2]

At the same time, what would the periphery gain from the incorporation of design? Here the modern tale grows through the incorporation of another task through the incorporation of another task, because for the underdeveloped countries of the 'Third World', industrial design would become an indispensable factor in overcoming underdevelopment and dependence.

In this way the concepts of design rising from European modernity suffered an adaptive transfer of culture in order to play a part in the increased dynamics of social, economic and technological factors within the underdeveloped countries. An uneasy alliance was produced between the theoretical content of modern design and the 'Third World' theories and ideologies which, during the 1960s and 1970s, created hypotheses of social models to escape underdevelopment.

This new mission for design, unforeseen by William Morris, one of the most reputable defenders of its social content, nor by any of the fathers of the modern movement, is described thus by Bonsiepe:

> The dependent countries will fall into an endless whirlwind if they attempt to imitate the lifestyle and range of products of the industrialized countries without looking for an alternative … De-colonization in all its manifestations, economic, technological and cultural, should be the goal of project activity in the periphery (technological politics, industrial design and models of development).[3]

The extensive repercussions of this thesis in the first practical stage of industrial design in Latin America is recorded in the principles of ALADI (Latin American Association of Industrial Design), which in its constitutive act in 1980 defined industrial design as a necessary technological discipline whose most important objective is 'to support the rupture of economic, technological and cultural dependency to which underdeveloped countries find themselves tied and give an incentive to the design of Latin American technologies, objects and communication systems'.[4]

Similarly, in the specific case of Cuba, the comments of Ivan Espín[5] (promoter and founder of the design institutions in Cuba) could not be more incisive: 'The real problem that Cuba has, and it is a crucial problem, is that of escaping

underdevelopment and without industrial design, one can't make this move'.[6]

From this first argument about the contextual situation that gave rise to the origins of design in Cuba and other Latin American countries, it can be summarized that the meeting point of design and the periphery was conditioned by two historical factors of the 1960s and the start of the 1970s; the start of the crisis of the modern movement ideology and the ideologies of how to escape underdevelopment. In this hybrid of modernity and the periphery, both would find something worthwhile. For one, this meant reclaiming the social content of design; for the other, escape from underdevelopment. That is to say, entry into modernity. Paradoxical, wouldn't one say?

In the specific case of Cuba, which is of interest to us, there were also other conditions that influenced the initiation of design in this country.

Some concrete facts may help to provide a more precise framework for the Cuban experience. Since 1969, a Further Education college of Industrial and Computer Design, EDI, has existed in Cuba. In 1981 the National Office of Industrial Design, ONDI, was created, which had a remit to organize practical projects, promote design and carry out an evaluation of the products. In 1984 the Higher Institute of Industrial Design was created which, in its various faculties and departments offered different specialisms in both industrial and graphic design. From 1982 to 1984 the presidency of ALADI was held by Cuba.

In the theoretical basis of the institutions representative of Cuban design (ONDI and ISDI), the influence of the harder nucleus of the second phase of modernity that arrived in Cuba can be found through the personalities and theories of the school of Ulm. So while Europe opened to pluralism and to criticism of the modernist movement, in Cuba, design was watched over from a uniquely defensive perspective of modernity.

The absolute priority of usefulness, the strict rationality, the total rejection of conventionalism, whether it be 'good design' or 'styling', the priority of the relationship between design and science, technology and industry, and the orientation of the project towards a solution of social and environmental problems, were premises of these institutions. It could seem paradoxically contradictory or mistakenly fanciful to use a concept of design that had come out of the heat of the third scientific/technical European revolution in the 1960s in a country that was in the midst of escaping underdevelopment. However, from this understanding of design, Cuban industrial design has kept a strong basis of conceptualization and a rigour in its heritage characterized by rationality and scientific foundations. However, the imbalance between this concept and the specific social components of the country, among which were most noticeable the backwardness of industry, meant that aspirations were not achieved as expected.

To comprehend fully the origin of design in Cuba, the socialist character of Cuban society in which it arose should be added to all the previous considerations.

The history of design experienced another moment in which design and revolution were interrelated; the time of soviet Constructivism which, although it started well, had a tragic end known to all.

In Cuba, the socialism installed several decades ago after replacing the previous history was characterized by an open comprehension of modern, contemporary creativity, as much in the fine arts as in architecture and design. Cuban socialism found representation in its culture of modernity (perhaps owing to the adverse reaction to postmodernity) and, as a promoter of the creation of a physical framework ready for the development of a new lifestyle, supported design in all its forms.

During the 1970s and 1980s regional and urban plans were drawn up in the country for the first time and the industrialization of architecture was promoted in answer to the economic development and to satisfy the needs of the population.

Industrial design itself needed to take part in this transformation of the productive infrastructure, of transport and of the framework of life. Its perspectives could not agree more with the universality and abstraction, homogeneity and scale of modernity because the diversity of options and solutions to the problems of school furniture, school uniforms, kitchens or furniture for home or social housing, for example, became one problem with one solution. In this way, misuse of the Modern Movement's premises resulted in the repetition of its mistakes.

Despite the criticism that a certain distance permits, those of us who experienced design in the 1980s in Cuba remember its epic character with nostalgia and still have doubts and an ironic view of history: Was it the model that was wrong or was it industry that failed to respond? Or perhaps there was insufficient time to put it into practice, because 1989, when the first industrial designers of ISDI were graduating, coincided with the start of the economic depression and reduced productivity of the country.

After 1990 the 'special period'[7] as it is termed began; the profound economic crisis conditioned by the disappearance of the socialist European countries and by the intensification of the embargo. The country entered an economy of survival, as did the institutions and design. State institutions on which industrial design had depended in the previous period continued with their task of training designers and with promotion but now faced a difficult decision: how to make design survive if this was still not part of industry and had not received public recognition because it had not won public acclaim, nor had it made its quality felt in the environment or for consumers.

Different interpretations of the modern peripheral model seem to be at odds with these changes and among them are two of significance: the insertion of design in key industries to escape underdevelopment and the aspiration to use objects to create a new lifestyle.

In recent years (the 1990s) the theory has been lost but pluralism, particularly in the form of subjects that are experiencing a new wave, such as graphic design linked to corporate identity and marketing, and interior design, has gained ground.

For design in Cuba, the decade of the 1990s has meant the constant re-elaboration of answers to hitherto unasked questions related to marketing, management and the market, which have arisen from the new circumstances.

Various examples of design in the 1990s will now be discussed. They are not examples of tendencies, nor of exceptional works, but rather they are examples of how the experience of design takes place in our context and how pre-modernity, modernity and post-modernity go together. Categories are used such as fusion through time, transfer of culture, and archaism, commonly found in other areas of our culture, but now applied to design. The first two examples are related to essential aspirations of modernity that have ceased to exist: the relationship between design and industry and the creation of a new quality for everyday life.

FROM THE TRAINBUS TO THE 'CAMELS' OF HABANA

The following example is representative of how a project born of the heat of modern and peripheral ideas did not manage to survive the economic crisis (postmodern underdevelopment?)

The crisis of transportation en masse in Habana has been one of its fundamental urban

Image 4 The "Camel" on Havana Pier, Havana, Cuba. Photograph by Lucila Fernandez Uriarte.

problems. Its radiocentric, extensive structure and its continuous demographic growth which exceeds two million, led to excessively long, roundabout journeys. In 1990 this situation became worse, which led to the need for an urgent solution based on the industrial reality of the country and the available resources.

The proposed solution offered by the Department of Development of Equipment and Machinery of ONDI (together with SIME and the Habana Urban Development Group) consisted of the national construction of a gigantic omnibus (train or metro) capable of transporting around 300 people, which would circulate on express lanes along wide streets in the same way as a tram.

The proposed system was significantly more economical than that which was then in operation. It would be made with national technology and the theoretical model from which the project came was characterized by its roots in rationality and peripheral issues. Some comments on it show 'its usefulness means the satisfaction of a social need and in addition to measuring itself by how well it eliminates scarcity, it should be measured by the elimination of technological dependency'.[8]

Today the real versions of the initial project go through the streets of Habana; 'the camels', consequence of innumerable frustrations and changes. 'The camels' have prevented the collapse of the city but for the population that has to put up with it, the problem continues.

NOTES

Extracted from L. Fernández Uriarte, 'Modernity and Postmodernity from Cuba', *Journal of Design History*, 18/3 (2005), pp. 245–9.

This article has appeared previously, in the original Spanish, in *Historiar Desde la Periferia: Historia e Historias del Diseno/Design History Seen from Abroad: History and Histories of Design* edited by Anna Calvera and Miguel Mallol, Barcelona: Publications de la Universitat de Barcelona, 2001, ISBN: 84-475-2499-x).

1. The sub-title of the conference indicates the structure: the first part on modernity, is systematic and technical; the second, that on postmodernism, is divided into sections, plural refers to specific cases in an attempt to join form and content.
2. Gui Bonsiepe. Politics, technology, industrial design and development models.
3. Gui Bonsiepe. Politics, technology, industrial design and development models.
4. *Acta de constitución de la ALADI,* 1980.
5. Iván Espín was the promoter and founder of the design institutions in Cuba, ONDI and ISDI.
6. Ivan Espin, *Diseño y subdesarrollo,* La Habana, 1982.
7. Editor's note: with the fall of the Berlin Wall and the break up of the Soviet Union, under whose influence Cuba found itself during the Cold War, there was a great reduction in financial aid. In 1990 a period of shortages and serious economic crisis began, known as 'The special period'.
8. Adrian Fernández, *Prologo al proyes to del trembus,* La Habana, 1992.

SECTION 1: HISTORY OF DESIGN

1.2: Design History As a Discipline

INTRODUCTION

This subsection explores design history as a larger field, which was established over thirty years ago, but which still continues to be the subject of debate among academics. The writers quoted provide a historiographic and methodological perspective and also comment on design history's possible future iterations.

We begin with an extract in which Victor Margolin raises questions that are very pertinent to this *Reader,* the relationship between design history and design studies. Margolin reflects on design history's origins as a discrete academic discipline and also as a subject that has engaged researchers from fields beyond design history. He points out how the body of research that has accumulated since the late 1970s has indicated that there are almost limitless boundaries for the historical study of design activity, because of the increasing breadth and fluidity of what constitutes "design," intellectually and professionally. Margolin thus argues for design to be "conceived as broadly as possible" as a "process of invention" involved with "the conception and planning of the artificial world." This approach then enlarges not only what design is, but also how we think of its history.

Margolin proposes that design history should have two locations, one in relation to the discourse and concerns of its own practitioners—"design historians," and the other as part of a wider field of design discourse, in which it can address design and its future. In taking this approach, he gives historians a more active role relative to design practitioners and also reinforces the significance and diversity of historical research for design practice. Thus, design history is not seen discretely, but as a constituent of the more pluralistic field of design studies. Margolin defines design studies "as the field of inquiry that addresses questions of how we make and use products in our daily lives and how we have done so in the past." He sees a central role for historians in this broader view of design, one that they have not in general taken. Many scholars and teachers of the history of design would consider Margolin's location of design history within design studies as controversial. The different approaches can be recognized by comparing the approach of the journal *Design Issues,* which Margolin cofounded and co-edits, with that of the British *Journal of Design History*. In the next extract, British design theorist and academic John Walker considers such differences of approach as part of the task of "Defining the Object of Study."

Walker began his book by acknowledging design history's "problematic," that is, the definition of its theoretical and ideological frameworks within which the discipline gained its meaning and values. He does not go as far as Margolin in widening the scope of design history into design studies, but he nevertheless acknowledges that design history does not have one single homogeneous object of study. Of course the larger issue is, as he explains in this extract, that there is no consensus concerning the meaning and scope of the term/concept *design*. And as time advances, the possibility of concrete definition becomes more remote—this has been and remains both the blessing and the curse of design history. In unpacking the discipline's historiography, Walker reinforces Margolin's case for a wider perspective. One omission he notes is the absence of feminist approaches to design history at the time he was writing in the late 1980s. He addresses this specific issue by inviting a feminist design historian, Judy Attfield, to contribute a conclusion to his book, which is also extracted here.

Taking a feminist perspective is more than another methodology, but rather an overtly political stance from which to consider design and its history. Judy Attfield draws attention to the fact that in focusing its concerns on the machine, functionalism, and modernity, design history ultimately prioritizes a male point of view. Here and in her subsequent work, most notably her book, *Wild Things The Material Culture of Everyday Life,* Attfield draws attention to the fact that "women experience the designed world differently from men." Uncovering the nature and extent of women's role in the history of design is a complex task, and one that is not simply resolved by identifying the work of women designers. Women's interaction with design as users in the made world has provided some significant insights, for example the work of Matrix, the feminist architects' collective, which could, incidentally, be presented as a model of the integration of design history into design studies. Attfield presents a feminist critique of design and its history as a way of opening space for discussion, as it inevitably draws critical attention to certain cultural norms and givens such as "market forces or abstract aesthetics" (points explored in greater detail in Section 4.2, Gender and Design).

Finally, in this subsection, we commissioned a special essay from Australian scholar Denise Whitehouse, whom we invited to reflect on the current state of design history as a discipline. Whitehouse provides us with some of the discipline's own history and examines the need for disciplinary practice-based history. She also draws attention to recent scholarly approaches such as design as a mode of social and cultural production, explored in Section 6, Design and Global Issues. *Design and Culture* is also incidentally the focus and title of a new academic journal, edited by Elizabeth Guffey, and published by Berg in 2009.

Whitehouse draws attention to the geographies of design history, and its globalization, which demand the more regionally distributed approaches to the history of design, already mentioned. Where design history is written and by whom also affects what is written and how history, or more properly histories, are made. Whitehouse reminds us that "History is not a neutral practice; rather, individuals and institutions bring subjectivities, be they cultural, professional, ideological, or theoretical to the making and reading of history." Whitehouse makes substantial and informed references to the progress of scholarship after 1984 (Dilnot 1984), which confirms that design history has achieved the status of a recognized academic discipline. But as Whitehouse and the extracts in this subsection indicate, there is still considerable potential for the development of the role of design history for design studies.

5

DESIGN HISTORY AND DESIGN STUDIES

Victor Margolin

Design history as an academic subject received its first major impetus in the early 1970s in Great Britain. In 1960, the First Report of Britain's National Advisory Council on Art Education (NACAE), known as the Coldstream Report, stipulated that all students in art and design should learn the history of their own subjects. Ten years later, a joint committee of the NACAE and the National Council for Diplomas in Art and Design urged that art and design history courses embody sophisticated historical methods and relate their respective practices to social issues and concerns. The mandates in these reports, however, applied primarily to the polytechnics rather than to the university sector.[1]

Teachers of design history were drafted from other fields such as the history of art and then set to work developing curricula. The new courses established an initial narrative for the field, particularly as course topics were translated into textbooks and publications for a popular audience.

In the introduction to the proceedings of an early design history conference in Brighton, Penny Sparke wrote that

[a]s an academic discipline it [design history] is undoubtedly the child of the art schools, where the increasing number of design students need a historical perspective more relevant to their immediate needs than the one provided by traditional fine art history, and it is largely within their confines that it has blossomed and yielded fruit.[2]

Independent of the teaching activity in Britain, design history courses were also established in the United States, Scandinavia, and elsewhere.[3] Along with these courses, a loosely knit international community of design historians emerged, abetted by a number of institutional achievements—the founding of the Design History Society in Great Britain in 1977 and the Scandinavian Forum of Design History in 1983, the series of regular conferences and special events organized by these and other groups, several international design history conferences, and the establishment of scholarly journals that have given design historians a place to publish their research.[4]

The importance of design history has been intermittently recognized as well by design professionals. Sessions conducted by historians have been held at national and international design conferences and congresses such as those organized by the International Council of Graphic Design Associations (ICOGRADA) and by the Industrial Designers Society of America (IDSA). ICOGRADA formed a Design History Working Group that communicated by mail for several years in the mid-1980s and produced a design history bibliography.[5] Although the national and international design associations have not developed a sustained involvement with design history, this does not detract from the subject's powerful pedagogical effect on future designers. Through design history courses taught by design historians or studio design teachers, design students in many countries have come to understand the wider cultural context in which designers have worked in the past and in which they continue to work today.

To think of design history as a discipline based on firm assumptions of what design is and how we might study its past is to ignore the dynamic crossings of intellectual boundaries that are occurring elsewhere. For example, researchers outside design history have discovered design to be a rich topic of historical investigation, and some of the best of design history's incipient scholarly accomplishments have come from scholars in other fields such as art history, American studies, and history itself.

When design history first began to emerge in Great Britain, those involved felt it important to mark the subject "design" with boundaries that would shape the development of its historical accounts. In the late 1970s, John Blake, an administrator at the British Design Council, urged that design history become "a kind of coagulation of ideas" that could develop into "a recognizable body of knowledge which can be unequivocally labeled 'design history'—not as an appendage of the history of art, not as an appendage of the history of architecture, not as an appendage of the history of technology or of anything else for that matter though with obvious connections with all these things."[6]

Since that time a body of research has accumulated but, seen in retrospect, this material, which is diverse both in method and in subject matter, does not explain what the framework of investigation is for a design historian. We have, nonetheless, advanced far beyond the limited boundaries established by scholars who first began to write historical accounts of design activity.

[...]

What we have seen thus far is a progressive opening up of design history to include topics well beyond what Pevsner would have been willing to recognize as valid. As further material for inclusion we could cite design in Asia, Africa, Latin America, and other regions of the world outside the European and North American orbit.

But even having done that, we would still be faced with the nagging problem of whether and how we might establish boundaries for the field. We already have a fragmentation into histories of craft, graphic design, and industrial design. While these divisions serve expedient purposes for the education of students who are preparing for careers in one or another of the craft or design professions, they have no legitimate correspondence to fundamental categories of design activity and are simply stopgap measures to hold off the inevitable problem of trying to define "design" itself.

In the first chapter of his book *Disegno Industriale: Un Riesame* (Industrial Design: A Reexamination) entitled "Definition," Tomás Maldonado made an attempt to define industrial design, which is only one aspect of the larger topic: "By industrial design is meant, normally, the planning of objects fabricated industrially, that is, by machine, and in series."[7] But Maldonado notes that this definition is not quite satisfactory since it fails to distinguish between the activity of the industrial designer and what traditionally belonged to the engineer. It is difficult, he says, to demarcate where in the design of an industrial product the work of one ends and the other begins. Maldonado also finds problems with past attempts to produce a single history of modern design and concludes that "[s]trictly speaking, it is not a question of one history but of multiple histories."[8]

Maldonado is correct in pointing out the difficulty of demarcating distinctions between different kinds of design activity. The definition of what an industrial designer does has changed many times in the past and will continue to change in the future. As evidence of this phenomenon in engineering, Yves Deforge has discussed the nineteenth-century training of the engineer as follows:

During the transition period, which lasted in some cases until the beginning of the twentieth century, the training of engineers still included the knowledge of construction technology or industrial science, as well as *an initiation into the knowledge of styles* and to academic art design. This training let them conceive of interesting ensembles in which the sign function was manifested by forms and decorations inspired by classical styles or by the imitation of architectural effects.[9]

After many years of separation in the twentieth century between education for what Deforge calls the utility function, represented by the technical training of engineers, and the sign function, exemplified by the more aesthetic education of industrial designers, we now have a few designers who have revived the more comprehensive nineteenth-century practice by obtaining degrees in both engineering and industrial design.

The point I want to make here is that design does not signify a class of objects that can be pinned down like butterflies. Designing is an activity that is constantly changing. How, then, can we establish a body of knowledge about something that has no fixed identity? From a nineteenth-century point of view, this is a troubling question. The nineteenth-century mind thrived on classification. During this period, great museums were built to house collections of discrete objects such as flora and fauna, high art, decorative arts, and technology. Boundaries between the natural and the artificial were clearly drawn. Art was also differentiated from craft, and the two were further distinguished from technology. This is the legacy that clearly informed Pevsner's history and it continues to bedevil us today.

But currently in the universities, as in the museum world, powerful intellectual forces are breaking down the boundaries that once seemed to immutably separate fields of knowledge. Let us take art history as an example. Its subject matter has broadened to include such topics as billboards, museum displays, and souvenirs. Design history too has been incorporated within the art historian's purview without anyone batting an eye. And art history's methods have multiplied extensively as scholars have drawn upon critical theories in many other fields and disciplines such as anthropology, sociology, philosophy, and psychoanalysis. At this point, one could even argue that the term "art studies" more effectively accounts for the diverse range of practices that today constitute what is being researched and taught in departments of art history throughout the United States and elsewhere.

In a cogent essay entitled "Blurred Genres: The Reconfiguration of Social Thought," the anthropologist Clifford Geertz states that "the present jumbling of varieties of discourse has grown to the point where it is becoming difficult either to label authors (What is Foucault—historian, philosopher, political theorist? What Thomas Kuhn—historian, philosopher, sociologist of knowledge?) or to classify works (What is George Steiner's *After Babel*—linguistics, criticism, culture history? What William Gass's *On Being Blue*—treatise, causerie, apologetic?)."[10] Geertz continues:

> It is a phenomenon general enough and distinctive enough to suggest that what we are seeing is not just another redrawing of the cultural map—the moving of a few disputed borders, the marking of some more picturesque mountain lakes—but an alteration of the principles of mapping.[11]

Seen from Geertz's view of how intellectual discourse is changing, the expansion of design history's subject matter since the mid-1930s when Pevsner published *Pioneers* might be considered to be just another redrawing of the design map. Although this expansion has continued in recent years to include more new topics such as design in regions outside Europe and the United States and the investigation of issues related to consumption, it has not contributed to a radical rethinking of how we reflect on design itself.

When Geertz writes about "an alteration in the principles of mapping," he is referring to the contemporary suspicion of long-standing methods of interpretation in disciplines as diverse as ethnography, philosophy, and even economics.[12] Basic interpretive methods in what were once established disciplines are now being challenged, and in some instances, rejected. This is not simply a temporary phenomenon but a fundamental revolution in the kinds of reflection we want to engage in as human beings, since what we regard as knowledge is simply the codification of our collective experience in the world.[13]

Having begun with such a limited subject matter as Pevsner provided, it is understandable that significant energy would have been expended in broadening the range of topics that design historians might study. Although we have begun to incorporate new material from the less-developed regions of the world, we have also learned from a number of feminist historians that entire categories of objects, regardless of where they were designed or produced, are suspect because of their relation to patriarchal culture, which extends across all geographical regions.

Feminism has provided a powerful critique of design history, although feminist historians are divided among those who have maintained a static definition of "design" and history's relation to it and those who are interested in using history to explore what a new feminist design practice might be like.[14]

Despite these differences, however, feminists have had to break down the distinctions between history, theory, and criticism in order to establish a different vantage point from which to view design and design history.

But even when we look at design from new positions, we must still ask ourselves whether we are studying a specific class of things that are stabilized in categories such as crafts or industrially produced objects or whether the subject matter of design is really much broader. I think the latter is true. The history of design in the twentieth century shows us that designers have not been constrained by a set of principles and rules that proscribed the scope of their work. Rather, they have invented the subject matter of their profession as they have gone along.

Henry Dreyfuss and Norman Bel Geddes, for example, moved from designing products to creating model cities for the New York World's Fair in 1939, while Raymond Loewy designed a Rocketport of the future for the same fair and later went on to work for the National Aeronautics and Space Administration on the interior of the Skylab. In the postwar years, Charles and Ray Eames and many other designers invented entirely new projects that were not imagined by the earlier consultants. In Italy, several generations of designers, which includes Franco Albini, Ettore Sottsass Jr., Mario Bellini, and Andrea Branzi—all trained initially as architects—have continually moved back and forth between design, architecture, and urbanism. And we should not forget R. Buckminster Fuller, whose career as an engineer and designer defies all previous categories of practice.

Given this process of continual invention that expands our prior understanding of what designers do, it makes more sense to conceive of design as broadly as possible in order to lay the foundation for its study. If we consider design to be the conception and planning of the artificial world, we can recognize the artificial as a mutable category that is changing rapidly as human invention repeatedly challenges its relation to the natural. To grasp the significance of artificial intelligence, genetic engineering, and nanotechnology, we must progressively enlarge our understanding of what design is while we are simultaneously occupied with establishing its historical narratives.

The momentous changes that the world is currently undergoing are forcing us to reconsider how we approach design as a subject of study. I would argue that it is the broad activity of designing, with its multifarious results, that can open up for design historians a range of important new questions that have not been coherently posed before and simultaneously can enable designers to consider new possibilities for practice.

Using an enlarged conception of the artificial as the basis for our inquiries, we can thus undertake new investigations of what designing is and how it affects the way we organize possibilities for human action. These questions then force us to reconsider how we have previously constituted design's history. Since we cannot isolate a fixed class of products—whether material or immaterial—as the subject for design history and because we need to think instead of designing as an act of continuous invention, it is not realistic to believe that we can mark out a stable terrain that can be claimed by design historians. What I foresee instead is that design can serve as a powerful theme around which the most diverse kinds of inquiries, related to history as well as to the contemporary situation can be organized.

I therefore want to propose two locations for design history—one in relation to the discourse and particular concerns of its own practitioners and the other in relation to the wider field of design discourse, where it can contribute to the ongoing research about design and its future. Within this wider field, history can play a powerful role that is currently being neglected. Historians bear the knowledge of design's best practice from the past as well as the recognition of design policies and activities that need not be repeated.[15] They are also able to hold up standards based on experience and extrapolate from prior activities possibilities for the future. As the formation of a design research culture intensifies, it will be important to have historians involved in order to engage with the current issues of professional concern and to provide a "long view" that is otherwise lacking.

Until now, few design historians have sought such a role. While it may be argued that design history is a relatively new field and that the historian's energies are best turned to the development of his or her own research community, it can also be propounded that design historians are urgently needed to prevent design discourse from taking too strong a turn toward technique as the dominant topic of research. Historians have the capacity to help shape the consciousness of the design community and to contribute to the articulation of its ideals, principles, and research agendas.

The tension between reflection and technique, which I want to differentiate from the classic theory-practice dichotomy, is marginalized or subdued in many professions. In social work doctoral research, for example, at least as it is conducted in many American universities, there are courses in social work history, which are usually taught by social work academics, but students are strongly encouraged to do quantitative research projects for their dissertations. Such tensions exist in other fields like urban planning, where it is often those engaged with current policy issues who dominate the reflective side of planning education.

A stronger engagement by historians with the burgeoning culture of design research would not mean the end of the Design History Society or any other group of design historians that convenes to develop design history as a field. It would mean a greater openness on the part of design historians to confront and reflect on issues of current practice and to engage with design researchers who have different interests than their own.

This engagement should work in two directions. First, it can contribute to the wider discourse on design and help to shape design reflection as an activity grounded in historical experience as well as current technique; and second, it can open up the subject matter of design history to new topics that would otherwise be missed. Incorporating design history within a wider field of design studies invites a dialogue with other researchers besides historians. This does not detract from design history's own identity, but it counters the tendency to maintain it as a separate field of activity that has primary relevance to its own practitioners.

In "The Multiple Tasks of Design Studies," [...] I present a pluralistic vision of design studies that can encompass very different kinds of knowledge. For my purpose here, I will simply define design studies as the field of inquiry that addresses questions of how we make and use products in our daily lives and how we have done so in the past. These products comprise the domain of the artificial. Design studies addresses issues of product conception and planning, production, form, distribution, and use. It considers these topics in the present as well as in the past. Along with products, it also embraces the web of discourse in which production and use are embedded. Its subject matter includes visual and material culture, as well as the design of processes and systems.

Scholars in different spheres of research are already contributing to a wider discourse about design. In cultural anthropology, for example, Mary Douglas and Baron Isherwood, Grant McCracken, Daniel Miller, and others have written extensively about consumption, although they focus on it as a symbolic act while ignoring questions of how products are designed and made as well as how they are actually incorporated into the daily activities of users. In his important book, *Material Culture and Mass Consumption,* published in 1987, Miller was particularly critical of the kind of design history that is "intended to be a pseudo art history, in which the task is to locate great individuals such as Raymond Loewy or Norman Bel Geddes and portray them as the creators of modern mass culture."[16] Since *Material Culture and Mass Consumption* was published, Miller has participated in several conferences that have been sponsored or cosponsored by the Design History Society in Britain, and his book has been cited by some design historians as being an important work for the field. Miller has focused his attention on the consumer and asserted, along with other anthropologists, that consumption is not a passive act but a creative project through which people put products to use in ways that were not necessarily intended by those who designed and produced them. He has thus broadened the context within which to study products in contemporary culture.

However, I do not wish to privilege cultural anthropology as the disciplinary base for design studies. It is only one of a number of established disciplines and fields—the philosophy of technology, general systems theory, cultural studies, and cognitive psychology, among them—whose scholars are now beginning to recognize the significance of design in contemporary life. As I reflect on the form that design studies might take in a university setting, I do not envisage a new discipline that will close its boundaries to interventionists from elsewhere. I would follow the lead of Robert Kates who was instrumental in establishing a program on world hunger at Brown University. Instead of focusing on the issue of disciplinary boundaries, Professor Kates emphasized the definition of problems for research:

But we are not a discipline, nor should we be one, despite our proto-theory, scholarly materials, or university courses. We need to be inclusive, not exclusive; we will need new skills and insights as our current inquiries change.[17]

The challenge for those of us who study design at the beginning of the twenty-first century is to establish a central place for it in contemporary life. This requires bold new conceptions and the kind of openness Professor Kates advocates, rather than the more limited thinking that has characterized much of design's study thus far. Historians have a central role to play in this process, and the question of whether they will take up the challenge remains.

NOTES

Extracted from V. Margolin, "Design History and Design Studies," in *The Politics of the Artificial: Essays on Design and Design Studies* (Chicago: University of Chicago Press, 2002), pp. 218–21 and 224–30. Reprinted by permission of The University of Chicago Press.

1. For this account, I have drawn on a paper by Clive Ashwin, which was presented at a 1977 conference on design history at Brighton Polytechnic. See Ashwin, "Art and Design History: The Parting of the Ways?" *Design History: Fad or Function?* (London: Design Council, 1978): 98–102. See also Jonathan Woodham, "Recent Trends in Design Historical Research in Britain," in Anna Calvera and Miguel Mallol, eds., *Historiades de la periferia: Historia e historias del diseño. Actas de Ia 1°Reunión*

Científica Internacional de Historiadores y Estudios del Diseño, Barcelona 1999/Design History Seen from Abroad: History and Histories of Design. Proceedings of the 1st International Conference of Design History and Design Studies, Barcelona 1999, eds. Anna Calvera and Miguel Mallol (Barcelona: Universitat de Barcelona Publications, 2001), 85–97.

2. Penny Sparke, introduction to *Design History: Fad or Function? 5.*

3. See my essay "Design History in the United States, 1977–2000" in this volume [V. Margolin, *The Politics of the Artificial* (Chicago: University of Chicago Press, 2002)] .

4. An international gathering of design historians was organized by Anty Pansera, Fredrik Wildhagen, and myself in Milan in May 1987. This was followed by another, planned by Paul Greenhalgh, Fredrik Wildhagen, and myself at the Victoria and Albert Museum in London in December 1990. The most recent event, arranged by Anna Calvera and entitled "First International Conference of Design History and Design Studies" (though it was not the first), was held in Barcelona in April 1999 and a follow-up to this event was held in Havana, Cuba, in June 2000. The proceedings of the Milan conference were published as *Tradizione e Modernismo, 1918/1940: Atti del Convegno* (Tradition and Modernism: Design between the Wars, 1918–1940: Congress Minutes), ed. Anty Pansera (Milan: L'Arca Edizioni, 1988). The proceedings of the Barcelona conference, edited by Anna Calvera and Miguel Mallol, were published in 2001 (see note 1 above). The first academic design journal to publish design history articles may have been *Design Issues,* which was founded in 1984. The *Journal of Design History* began publication in Britain in 1988 and the annual *Scandinavian Journal of Design History*, based at the Danish Museum of Decorative Art in Copenhagen, started in 1991. Most recently, the Bard Graduate Center for Studies in the Decorative Arts, Design and Culture established a new scholarly journal, *Studies in the Decorative Arts,* which frequently crosses over into design history. The Catalan journal *Temes de Disseny* also publishes scholarly design history articles on occasion, as does the Brazilian journal *Arcos.*

5. ICOGRADA's initiatives in design history were due to the vision of its then president, Jorge Frascara. He established a working group and found resources to publish the bibliography. See Victor Margolin, *Design History Bibliography* (London: ICOGRADA, 1987).

6. John Blake, "The Context for Design History," in *Design History: Fad or Function? 56.*

7. Tomas Maldonado, *Design Industriale: Un Riesame,* rev. and enl. (Milan: Feltrinelli, 1991), 9. The first edition appeared in 1976, 16.

8. Ibid., 16.

9. Yves Deforge, "Avatars of Design: Design before Design," in Victor Margolin and Richard Buchanan, eds., *The Idea of Design: A Design Issues Reader* (Cambridge: MIT Press, 1995), 21–28.

10. Clifford Geertz, "Blurred Genres: The Reconfiguration of Social Thought," in Geertz, *Local Knowledge: Further Essays in Interpretive Anthropology* (New York: Basic Books, 1983), 20.

11. Ibid.

12. See, for example, John S. Nelson, Allan Megill, and Donald N. McCloskey, eds., *The Rhetoric of the Human Sciences: Language and Argument in Public Affairs* (Madison: University of Wisconsin Press, 1987); and Donald N. McCloskey, *If You're So Smart: The Narrative of Economic Expertise* (Chicago and London: University of Chicago Press, 1990).

13. A good example of a design study that cuts across different fields is the catalog *Household Choices,* which was edited by the Household Choices Project in Britain, Tim Putnam and Charles Newton, eds., *Household Choices* (n.p: Futures Publications, 1990). It includes essays by historians, anthropologists, urbanists, and specialists in housing and features

several photographic sequences as well. John Murdoch, in his introduction to the catalog, noted the influence of new methods in art history and literary criticism on the study of design:

The idea that the product, usually at the point of sale, might pass beyond the control of its manufacturer into a realm of variable understanding, interpretation and use, seemed less familiar than it had recently become to art historians, and certainly less familiar than it was to critics of written texts (5).

Household Choices has brought us a considerable distance from Pevsner's *Pioneers of the Modern Movement,* a book with which it can hardly be compared. It does not moralize about the quality of products nor does it privilege the artifacts of the modern movement as more worthy of our attention than others. Neither does it give primacy to the designer's intentions in defining the meaning of a product. It suggests a more complex identity for the product than as simply the outcome of a design process. Instead, it is located in a situation, and its meaning is created in part by its users.

14. Prominent in the feminist design history literature are Judy Attfield and Pat Kirkham, eds., *A View from the Interior: Feminism, Women, and Design* (London: Women's Press, 1989); Isabelle Anscombe, *A Woman's Touch: Women in Design from 1860 to the Present Day* (New York: Viking, 1984); Penny Sparke, *As Long as It's Pink: The Sexual Politics of Taste* (London: Pandora, 1995); and Pat Kirkham, ed., *Women Designers in the USA, 1900–2000:*

Diversity and Difference (New Haven and London: Yale University Press, 2000). The broader issue of how objects take on a gender identification is addressed in *The Gendered Object,* ed. Pat Kirkham (Manchester and New York: Manchester University Press, 1996). See also Cheryl Buckley, "'The Noblesse of the Banks': Craft Hierarchies, Gender Divisions, and the Roles of Women Paintresses and Designers in the British Pottery Industry, 1890–1939," *Journal of Design History* 2, no. 4 (1989): 257–274; and "Design, Femininity, and Modernism: Interpreting the Work of Susie Cooper," *Journal of Design History* 7, no. 4 (1994): 277–294; as well as Suzette Worden and Jill Seddon, "Women Designers in Britain in the 1920s and 1930s: Defining the Professional and Redefining Design," *Journal of Design History* 8, no. 3 (1995): 177–194.

15. A good example of the latter would be the critique of the British Ministry of Trade's attempt to shape public taste while producing "utility products" during World War II and the subsequent endeavor of the postwar Council of Industrial Design to further this intention. See the excellent set of essays on the subject of utility design in Judy Attfield, ed., *Utility Assessed: The Role of Ethics in the Practice of Design* (Manchester and New York: Manchester University Press, 1999).

16. Daniel Miller, *Material Culture and Mass Consumption* (Oxford: Basil Blackwell, 1987), 142.

17. Robert Kates, "The Great Questions of Science and Society Do Not Fit Neatly into Single Disciplines," *Chronicle of Higher Education* (May 17, 1989): 81.

6

DEFINING THE OBJECT OF STUDY

John Walker

Specifying the object of study, establishing the boundaries of the subject, are the first tasks of any new intellectual discipline. By so doing, it differentiates itself from other, rival disciplines. Although drawing a circle around a certain body of material may be essential in order to found a discipline, the very act gives rise to arguments about limits. Necessarily, it also disrupts the totality and continuity of reality and thereby prompts questions about the relations between inside and outside.

Design historians agree that their object of study is the history of design, but there is not yet a consensus concerning the meaning and scope of the term/concept 'design'. For example, does design include architecture? Is architecture part of the object of design history or art history or is architectural history an independent discipline in its own right? Similar uncertainties arise in respect of the crafts, the minor or decorative arts and the mass media. In relation to the latter, design is undoubtedly a *part* of film-making, television production, pop music and advertising but these are also the concern of film, media, cultural studies and sociology. Consequently, there is plenty of scope for territorial disputes.

What is certain is that the boundary line of any discipline is fuzzy rather than sharp and that it overlaps the circles of several other disciplines.

THE WORD/CONCEPT 'DESIGN'

'Design' is a word which occurs in many contexts: a design, graphic design, fashion design, interior design, engineering design, architectural design, industrial design, product design, corporate design, design methods. It is not immediately obvious that a common essence underlies all these different usages. Ludwig Wittgenstein's notion of family resemblance may be more appropriate as a linking concept than the idea of a single essence.[1]

Like all words and concepts, 'design' gains its specific meaning and value not only because of what it refers to but also differentially, that is, via its contrast with other, neighbouring terms such as 'art', 'craft', 'engineering' and 'mass media'. This is one reason why definitions of 'design' which purport to encapsulate an essential meaning tend to be so unsatisfactory. And, like most other words, 'design' causes ambiguities because it has more than one common meaning: it can refer to a process (the act or practice of designing); or to the result of that process (a design, sketch, plan or model); or to the products manufactured with the aid of a design (designed goods); or to the look or overall pattern of a product ('I like the design of that dress').

Another reason why definitions are inadequate and provisional is that language, like everything else, is subject to historical change. The word 'design' has altered its meaning through time: during the Renaissance *'disegno'* (which in practice meant drawing) was considered by art theorists such as Vasari to be the basis of all the visual arts; consequently these were often referred to as 'the arts of design'. At that time *disegno* described the inventive, conceptualizing phase which generally preceded the making of paintings, sculptures and so forth. All artists engaged in design as part of their creative activities, hence design was not yet considered the exclusive concern of a full-time professional. Designers as such only emerged later as a result of the growing specialization of functions which occurred in Europe and the United States as part of the industrial revolution of the eighteenth and nineteenth centuries. At least this is the generally accepted story. A different view is held by Simon Jervis whose ideas will be considered shortly. Thus, eventually, design came to mean a full-time activity undertaken by trained specialists employed or commissioned by manufacturers. The designer did not normally make the product he or she designed.

It is clear from the above that any comprehensive history of design ought to include a history of the evolution of the concept 'design' as well as a history of designers and designed goods. Such a history would need to explain the emergence of design as distinct from art and craft, and trace its subsequent development in relation to the changing status of the latter as a result of the transition from a feudal to a capitalist mode of production and the growth of industry, engineering, technology, mass production and mass media/communication. It would also need to clarify the meanings and usages of older expressions such as 'art manufactures', 'the industrial arts', 'the applied arts', 'commercial art', 'ornament' and 'the decorative arts'. An examination of the fluctuating fortunes of these terms would be valuable because changes of nomenclature are one sign of changes in material reality.

During the 1980s, when design was promoted as the solution to Britain's industrial decline, the words 'design' and 'designer' took on a new resonance. They became values in their own right. For example, people spoke of 'designer jeans' (and even 'designer drugs', 'designer socialism'). Since all jeans are designed, the adjective was redundant but its use demonstrated how 'the design' was being perceived as a desirable attribute rather than the product as a whole. One journalist described 'designer' as a marketing trigger word. Part of the same process was an emphasis on the names of particular designers—a Katherine Hamnett

T-shirt, a James Stirling museum, an Ettore Sottsass sofa. This habit derived from the fine arts where the signature of the artist was the guarantee of uniqueness, authenticity, individuality and creativity. In the end what counted was not the suitability and practicality of the designed object but merely the fact that it was by such and such a famous name. The designer's label on the product became more important than the product itself.

THE SCOPE OF THE SUBJECT

Novice design historians can be intimidated by the sheer number and variety of topics with which they are expected to be familiar. As an indication of the range and heterogeneity of the field, consider the subjects covered by the volumes displayed in London's Design Centre Bookshop: graphics, packaging, cinemas, streamlining, design for the disabled, the grammar of form and colour, signs and symbols, ergonomics, human factors engineering, anthropometry, town planning, textiles, ceramics, fashion, office lighting, interior design, modelmaking, transportation, arts and crafts, engineering, consumerism, copyright, safety standards, solar energy systems, patenting, shops and shopping, theories and methods of design, famous designers, art and design schools and academies, the design of nations and epochs, the styles of design, housing, landscape design, computers, computer-aided design, typography, histories of invention and industrial processes … the list is apparently endless.

Of course, some of these topics can be considered more central than others. It would be possible to arrange them in an order: central, closely related, marginal. The boundaries between design, art, craft, engineering and mass media are not sharply defined and some subjects, such as architecture, appear to overlap several realms. (Architecture can involve art, engineering, craft methods and industrial production.) As human knowledge develops both quantitatively and qualitatively, an increasing tendency towards fragmentation and specialization occurs. Whereas, initially, architectural history included design—because the discipline was based on great modern architects who also designed furniture and fittings—design history is now a separate field. Similarly, one finds that the subjects of art, craft, design, architecture, photography and film all have their separate museums and institutions. In part, these divisions represent real, material conditions: in the twentieth century the various arts have tended to go their separate ways. At the same time, such divisions have their disadvantages: mixed-media forms, for example, tend to be neglected because they cut across several categories and thus appear to belong to none of them. Pop music, for example, involves music, singing, clothes, make-up, hairstyling, musical instruments and sound systems, stage sets, lighting, record covers, posters, promotional goods, still photography, film, video and television.

[…]

Design historians can limit their object of study by concentrating upon examples of good or exceptional design. Hence the popularity of texts about the work of famous architect-designers or about so-called design classics or cult objects. This approach is derived from art history and architectural history. In the latter, for example, a qualitative distinction is often made between distinguished and undistinguished structures: a cathedral is an example of architecture, whereas a bicycle shed is a mere building. Since, in most cases, high quality structures are those designed by professionally-trained architects, the high/low distinction is equivalent to the professional/amateur distinction.

While some design historians ignore anonymous, vernacular design on the grounds of low quality or because there is too much of it, others, influenced by the anthropologist's concept of material culture as embracing all the artefacts of a society, seek to encompass all designed goods—good, bad and indifferent—whether by professional designers or not. The quantity problem, they contend, can be overcome by selecting representative examples. Good design histories are problematical, they argue, because of the contentious issue: whose taste or preference determines good

and bad? Are the tastes and value judgements of the historian or design world experts to prevail over those of other social groups? A negative answer does not mean, however, that the issue of the historian's value judgements and the question of quality can be dispensed with altogether. In this regard it would be helpful if design historians distinguished between their personal assessments and those of others and tried to explain any divergence of views. It would also be useful to examine changes in value judgements over time.

While design historians may agree that the central focus of their research is the designer, the design process and designed goods, other topics such as style, taste, the role of clients, management, marketing and consumers also need to be investigated. Furthermore, these topics cannot be studied in isolation because they are aspects of a dynamic system which itself is part of a larger social and historical process. It is for this reason that however sharply the boundaries of the subject are drawn, sooner or later the design historian has to address external factors.

[…]

Among contemporary design historians the dominant definition is the modern one, that is, design as a specialist activity associated with the industrial revolution, mass production manufacture, the modern movement in architecture, and the consumer society. There are, however, a few dissenting voices. One is Simon Jervis, a furniture expert, museum curator and author of *The Penguin Dictionary of Design and Designers* (1984). He is critical of the modern definition on the grounds that it excludes so much design dating from the period 1450 to 1800 and because it is anti-ornament like modernist design theory. Jervis' conception of design can be called, therefore, 'premodern' or 'anti-modern'. Jervis ingenuously admits that 'the question of the definition of design is begged'. Nevertheless, even if it is not explicit some concept of design must be implicit in the book by virtue of what it includes and excludes.

Jervis gives most attention to ceramics, furniture, glass, interior decoration, ornament and textiles. Graphics, consumer durables and typography are touched upon to a lesser extent while heavy industrial, theatre and dress design are 'almost wholly excluded'. Jervis sees design as closely linked to art and architecture hence he features biographies of many artists and architects. Premodern design, he argues, was the province of goldsmiths, engravers, sculptors, painters and architects. They produced engraved designs and cartoons for making such things as furniture, metalwork and tapestries. These designs were chiefly concerned with decoration and ornament. A clear distinction is made between designers and craftsmen. The former are judged to be superior in status and are regarded as generating luxury goods for the ruling strata, the wealthiest sector of society.

This dictionary proved controversial within the design history profession. An acrimonious exchange of letters occurred in the *Design History Society Newsletter* following a critical review.[2] Polytechnic historians felt that Jervis was unduly narrow in his definition of design and lamented the exclusion of fashion and engineering. They also considered that the emphasis in any dictionary of this kind should be on the modern design of the past 200 years and also that more women designers should have been featured. Jervis responded by claiming that the polytechnics' concept of design history had been 'created by committee'. No doubt to outsiders the dispute will seem a storm in a designer teacup. However, it did illuminate the fact that different institutions—museums, polytechnics—tend to generate different, antagonistic conceptions of design based upon their separate histories and social functions.

As the dispute between Jervis and his critics revealed, engineering is a bone of contention among design historians. While on the one hand the subject has more to do with science and technology than with design, craft and the decorative arts, on the other hand design *is* undertaken by engineers. In fact, in many cases they design the machines which make the products other designers design.

Because engineering design is highly technical in character and primarily concerned with function, it lacks the visibility and glamour of other kinds of design. Furthermore, the huge size of some of their structures precludes their display in shops or design exhibitions. Gui Bonsiepe once criticized a design show on precisely these grounds and regretted the domestic bias of its organizers: 'There was a total absence of producers of capital goods such as agricultural equipment and tools, manufacturing and building machinery. The narcissistic preoccupation with the perfection of the living room predominated.'[3]

Another dissenting voice is that of Victor Papanek (b. Austria 1925), a professional designer and ex-dean of the school of design at the California Institute of the Arts. His polemical book *Design for the Real World: Human Ecology and Social Change* (1972) is a sustained critique of modern industrial design and a plea for a different kind of design serving the needs of the poor, the sick, the handicapped and the peoples of Third World countries. Papanek's conception of design is also, to a certain extent, anti-modern but, unlike Jervis', his outlook is not traditionalist. His conception of design can be called 'libertarian', 'alternative' or 'ecological'.

His book begins with an all-embracing definition:

> All men are designers. All that we do, almost all the time, is design, for design is basic to all human activity. The planning and patterning of any act towards a desired, forseeable end constitues the design process ... Design is composing an epic poem, executing a mural, painting a masterpiece, writing a concerto. But design is also cleaning and reorganizing a desk drawer, pulling an impacted tooth, baking an apple pie, choosing sides for a back-lot baseball game, and educating a child ... Design is the conscious effort to impose meaningful order.[4]

The problems inherent in this definition are obvious and multiple.

Feminists will note the absence of women. Apparently, design includes art, poetry, music, dentistry, cooking, sport and education! It is also motivated by a utopian socialist perspective: the truism that design is a process all human beings engage in to some extent ignores the specialized, professional character of design in modern society though, in fact, Papanek later attacks the design profession for failing to meet the real needs of humanity. He also observes: 'The ultimate job of design is to transform man's environment and tools and, by extension, man himself.' This remark is valuable because it highlights the fact that design has a feedback effect upon human beings: it is not merely environmental change that is taking place but also self-transformation—for good or ill.

Design, for Papanek, is primarily a problem-solving activity. He provides a much more precisely defined notion of design via a diagram which he calls 'the function complex'. Around the central core of function are clustered six interlinked concepts—use, need, telesis, method, aesthetics, association.

It should be clear by now that the various definitions of design discussed above are inflected by the different ideological-political positions of those who devise them. Materialist historians of industrial design may argue: 'Our definition is the most objective, we simply try to describe the world as it is.' No doubt Papanek would respond by saying: 'It is not sufficient to accept the world as it is, our conception of design ought to encompass the world as it might be.'

THE CONCEPT 'DESIGN': OPEN OR CLOSED?

Who determines what the concept 'design' encompasses? Is design, like art, an 'open' concept in the sense that it can be extended, revised, changed? In answer to the first question: it is primarily the design world (that is, those professionally concerned with design—designers, critics, historians, museum curators, clients and associated institutions) who determine the contemporary meanings of the term 'design'. However, the fact that design has changed its meaning historically suggests that it is possible for individuals and groups to propose new definitions, new objects of study. Whether the design world and society as a whole accepts these new proposals is another matter.

Given the fact that design history is a new discipline, it is somewhat surprising that concepts of design have so quickly become conventional and orthodox. For example, new research on design usually focuses upon an extremely narrow range of topics: consumer goods, public transport, advertising, the home, etc. 'Safe' topics predominate. Why are design historians so unimaginative? Why are they so reluctant to consider military weapons, police equipment, scientific instruments, sexual aids, space vehicles, engineering machines, computer hardware and software, the role of the state in promoting design, the relation of design to pollution, profit and exploitation, as topics worthy of analysis? There appears to be a deeply-entrenched conservatism among design historians, an unwillingness to confront the relationship between design and politics, design and social injustice. Regrettably, a great deal of design in the twentieth century has been directed towards anti-social and anti-human ends: the design of concentration camps and gas chambers; the design of instruments of torture, surveillance and repression; the design of all kinds of dangerous products. What would we think of general histories which only described good people and happy events?

Even within the limits of present popular topics there is a need for a more sceptical, questioning and critical approach: are there not disadvantages to the ever-expanding production of goods? Is the continual redesign of 'old' products essential in all cases? Are the values promoted by design and advertising socially beneficial or socially detrimental? Is the design historian's function merely to celebrate and reinforce a particular kind of commercial culture?

It could be argued that design, in its most general sense, is a form of politics: humanity struggles to shape its environment and society in order to satisfy its needs. It follows that design historians could, legitimately, extend their object of study to include the design of political structures and ecological systems.

EXTERNAL FACTORS AND INTERDISCIPLINARY PERSPECTIVES

The design historian's task is complicated by the fact that besides issues internal to design, external factors also have to be considered. This is because design is affected by wars, revolutions, economic booms and slumps, technological innovations and so forth. At this point the problem of limiting the object of study becomes acute. To what extent, for example, should design historians study the economy of a society? They might decide to take a crash course in economics but they would quickly discover that there is not one economic theory which can be speedily grasped but a variety of competing theories about how the economy works. Attempting to apply the findings of another discipline is thus not a straightforward matter. Furthermore, it is surely impractical to expect design historians to master all the related fields of knowledge that impinge on design.

[…]

'Interdisciplinary' is a word increasingly associated with design. For instance, the activity of design is regarded by members of the Design Research Society as interdisciplinary in two respects: first, it occurs in various arts and industries (fashion, architecture, engineering, etc.); and second, it synthesizes information derived from a range of disciplines (ergonomics, sociology, psychology, etc.).

The word 'interdisciplinary' is also being applied to design history. Design historians envisage that they will use concepts, theories and methods drawn from other disciplines such as sociology, anthropology, linguistics, art history and economics. While it is perfectly proper that design historians should learn as much as possible from other disciplines, the importation of 'foreign' concepts is problematical because the objects of study and goals of such disciplines differ from one another.

(A synthesis of, say, Marxism, feminism, psychoanalysis and semiotics is extremely difficult to achieve; and what may result is a deformed hybrid.)[5] A critical, discriminating attitude towards all ideas no matter what their source is essential.

Furthermore, there is a problem of compatibility: ideas drawn from different disciplines may well contradict one another. Advocates of the multidisciplinary approach rashly assume that the greater the plurality of perspectives the better, but this ignores the problems of how fundamental ideological differences between various perspectives are to be reconciled.[6] Critics of pluralism argue that not all accounts of reality are equally valuable; some, they insist, are better, more truthful than others. (Marxists, for example, argue that historical materialist approaches to design are superior to idealist approaches.) A mere accumulation of different perspectives will tend to produce a relativistic confusion; again, discrimination is essential. In short, there is a danger that design history could suffer from scholarly eclecticism and become an incoherent ragbag.

Also, unless the object of study of design history is precisely defined the sheer magnitude of its possible subject matter will reduce the researcher to impotence. The young discipline could dissipate itself among a thousand topics and find itself disputing the roles and territories of a dozen existing academic disciplines.

Nonetheless, academic disciplines often share certain characteristics: for example, empirical methods of study and theories such as functionalism. In such areas of overlap the results obtained by different disciplines may well be commensurable. Even when two disciplines are far apart, new insights may be gained by applying the theories of one to the object of study of the other in an analogical fashion. For instance, some historians have found the biological theory of evolution useful in thinking about the temporal development of art and design.

Perhaps the most effective way in which design historians could benefit from a multidisciplinary approach would be to establish teams of scholars from different disciplines to work collaboratively on common themes and problems.

NOTES

Extracted from J. Walker, 'Defining the Object of Study', in J. Walker, ed., *Design History or the History of Design* (London: Pluto Press, 1989), pp. 22–36. Reprinted by permission of Pluto Press.

1. On the notion of family resemblance see L. Wittgenstein, Philosophical *Investigations* (Oxford: Blackwell, 1953) pars 66–7.
2. Hazel Conway (book review), *Design History Society Newsletter,* (23) November 1984 pp. 13–15. Plus letters: from Jervis, (24) 1985 pp. 6–7; D. Greysmith, (25) 1985 pp. 4–6.
3. G. Bonsiepe, quoted in, J. Bicknell and L. McQuiston (eds), *Design for Need* (Oxford: Pergamon Press, 1977) p. 16.
4. V. Papanek, *Design for the Real World: Human Ecology and Social Change* (London: Thames & Hudson, 1972) p. 17.
5. Possibly these remarks are too pessimistic. Sut Jhally's book *The Codes of Advertising* (London: Pinter, 1987) draws upon Marxism, psychoanalysis and anthropology; it also undertakes empirical research using the social science method of content analysis. These different elements are successfully combined to generate new insights into the nature of television advertising. One reason why this works is that the concept of fetishism—which Jhally foregrounds—is common to all three disciplines cited above.
6. Terry Eagleton remarks: 'Pluralists believe there is a little truth in everything.' He adds: 'This theoretical pluralism also has its political correlative: seeking to understand everybody's point of view quite often suggests that you yourself are disinterestedly up on high or in the middle, and trying to resolve conflicting viewpoints into a consensus implies a refusal of the truth that some conflicts can be resolved on one side alone.' *Literary Theory: an Introduction* (Oxford: Blackwell, 1983) p. 199.

7

FORM/FEMALE
FOLLOWS FUNCTION/MALE

Feminist Critiques of Design

Judy Attfield

It is symptomatic of our post-modern condition that it should be considered important to include a feminist critique of design here.[1] The current tendency to question dominant value systems and interpretations of history indicates a loss of faith in the single unitary view, which in the case of design history has always placed it in the male domain. The dominant conception prioritizes the machine (masculine) over the body (feminine). It assigns men to the determining, functional areas of design—science, technology, industrial production—and women to the private, domestic realm and to the 'soft', decorative fields of design. It places form in the feminine realm where its role is to reflect the imperatives of the 'real'. According to this kind of aesthetic theory then, form (female) follows function (male).[2]

Juliet Mitchell has argued that 'feminism is an ideological offspring of certain economic and social conditions.'[3] Her interpretation is a positive one which attributes to feminists the ability to imagine 'yesterday's future', i.e. a today in which machines replace gruelling labour, when there is more leisure and more sexual equality. But she also points out that the women's movement emanates from the dominant middle class. Thus, it essentially presents a Western point of view from within a consumer society which requires women as a cheaper part-time, non-unionized workforce, while depending on them as the main bulk of the consuming public. It is this condition which has indeed brought some women more power but has also kept others in positions of subservience.

Nicholas Coleridge, in *The Fashion Conspiracy* (1988) illustrates both these extremes in his description of the current condition of the international fashion design world where Tamil girls, under the age of 13, work in a Madras sweatshop to supply the American clothing trade, a country where some women can afford to spend $7,000 for a dress to attend a *charity* ball.

THE POLITICS OF EXPERIENCE

A fundamental starting point for feminist design historians is the fact that women experience the designed world differently from men. One of the most powerful and influential critiques of town planning, Jane Jacobs' *The Death and Life of Great American Cities* (1961), caused a transformation by introducing a critical element into the writing of architectural history which until then had glorified modernism without question.[4] It was precisely her female point of view which brought out new and valuable insights in the relationship between design ideals and lived experience.[5]

Design shapes the environment and makes assumptions about women's place in terms of buildings, public spaces and transport. It also provides the imagery women use to form their identity through fashion, advertising and the media generally. It assumes that particular areas of the design profession are 'women's work', thereby reflecting the predominant division of labour in society. Furthermore, it segregates the sexes through artifacts by endowing these with unnecessary gender definitions, while neglecting the special needs of women who want their own transport, places and spaces.[6] And, as already explained, it excludes women from the determining spheres of science, technology and industry.[7]

The role of design in forming our ideas about gender power relations often remains invisible, while at the same time it makes them concrete in the everyday world of material goods. 'White goods' such as washing machines and electric cookers may reduce the heavy manual labour women perform and those designed by women may satisfy their needs better than those designed by men, but such goods are still manufactured with women in mind—the implicit assumption is that it is they who will be doing the bulk of the washing and cooking, not men—hence the division of labour by gender remains unaffected by product innovation and improvement.

Design reflects our aspirations and arouses our expectations, but it is also a process and as such has a potential for transformation. Some professional feminist designers have attempted to reform gender relations through innovatory designs.[8] Feminist historians have been and are undertaking research to bring to light those designers' achievements as well as the achievements of women working in the field whose contributions remain unrecognized. It is also vital to consider the impact that women have had historically, and can continue to exert on design by means of individual and joint consumption.[9]

'WOMEN-DESIGNERS' VERSUS A FEMINIST CRITIQUE

Isabelle Anscombe's *A Woman's Touch* (1984) gives exclusive attention to women designers who have participated in 'the history of the major design movements since the 1860s'. It helps to set the record straight by giving more emphasis to those women who did manage to penetrate the professional arena—some of them, like Charlotte Perriand[10] and Eileen Gray,[11] already known in conventional design history—but who were often overshadowed by male designers with whom they associated through professional or personal ties. However, it soon becomes clear that this 'women-designers' approach does little except confirm the prejudice that women are inferior designers except in the so-called 'feminine' areas such as the decorative arts, textiles, interior design and fashion. Even where there was an opportunity to alter the emphasis by showing how some female designers were prevented from practising in the more exclusively male areas of design, as in the case of Eileen Gray, Anscombe fails to do so.[12]

There are other problems related to looking at women designers as the main focus. For instance, the restrictions of method in the conventional biography place them in a preset, hierarchical framework in which 'great', usually male, designers appear. Is this really because there have been no great women designers? Since Linda Nochlin's essay on women artists, written in the early 1970s, this has become a somewhat rhetorical question.[13] Design is even less of an autonomous activity than art and needs to be examined in close relationship with the social, cultural, economic and technological conditions which have nurtured its development as a practice. However, the historiography which has produced some of the seminal works of design history has established a tradition of pioneers of modern design and an avant garde aesthetic in which few women figure. There is an urgent need, therefore, to bring to light the work of women pioneers of design in order to provide role models for young women embarking upon design careers who, at present, face unwelcoming, male-dominated enclaves in architecture, engineering, product and industrial design, where all that *is* thought necessary to meet the needs of women is an equal opportunities policy.[14]

A considerable body of work has built up around an object-based study of the history of design, which avoids some of the more overtly sexist problems by not focusing on designers.[15] It also marks out for itself a methodology distinct from conventional art history in which the cult of the artist rubs off on the art work, thereby giving it a particular value distinct from the anonymously designed object. A women-designers' approach is based on the traditions of such an art history and cannot cope with anonymous design. This is not to say that object-based study is innocent and neutral in matters of gender. On the contrary, a hierarchy has built up around types of objects which gives importance to industrial design and the 'machine aesthetic'—i.e. the more obviously masculine—while considering areas such as fashion as trivial and synonymous with 'feminine'. But the limitations of a women-designers' approach not only diminishes women, it also devalues design history as a discipline by using a borrowed and inappropriate methodology.[16]

A feminist critique makes it possible to look at women designers in a new light and to assess their work in the context of the history of a profession which has consistently marginalized them. It also suggests a methodology for design history which is not based upon aesthetics or connoisseurship, but upon a concern for people.

USE-VALUE AND FEMINIST CRITIQUE

Some feminist design historians are not content to satisfy academic criteria. They want their research to be of value to practising designers. They conceive of design history as contributing to an understanding of different groups' needs as part of the design process. *Making Space* (1984) by Matrix (a feminist architects' collective) is one example of an interventionist text which seeks to bring theory and practice together and to relate knowledge of the past to the present and the future.

The problems of defining an object of study appropriate to design history have been fraught by precedents set by art history. Although feminist art history does present us with an excellent body of critique and methodology, it cannot be appropriated and applied directly to design unless we treat design as if it were art. There is some measure of agreement that it need *not* just be about the appreciation of something called 'good design', nor the attribution of authorship to particular designers of certain cult objects, lest the whole exercise deteriorate into one of connoisseurship. But what it *should* be is less clear. Not only is there confusion over *what* should be looked at, but *why*.

A feminist perspective can be quite specific in its focus on use-value. By providing historical explanations for women's lack of visibility at the production stage, it is possible to understand better why dominant masculine values are constantly reproduced in the material world. Thus a feminist critique of design history can become part of a more general movement of reform. It is at that particular intersection—between what we think and what we do—that the transitive meaning of design as a verb, as an action, can take place.

[…]

The purpose of a feminist critique of design and its history should be to discuss women's concerns so that women do not feel segregated or excluded in any way for reasons of gender. Though there are some radical feminists who choose permanent separatism as a form of refusal, this excludes many women as well as men. A gendered view, on the other hand, is a practical way of opening a space for discussion. It forms part of a wider move away from authoritarian, patriarchal values for both men and women. It also allows women to become involved as ungendered beings—as people who consider issues beyond those of gender: i.e. race, class, age, sexuality, religion, occupation and so on.

It should not be 'Woman' who is made the special case for treatment, but the culture which subordinates people by gender, class, race, etc., and does nothing to question the attitudes which position them as 'Other'. The concept of 'the Other' is one used to define the category of 'woman' in a negative relationship to the category of 'man'. (Man' enjoys the privilege of being the norm—'the measure of all things'—while 'woman' is that which deviates from it.) The acknowledgement of such a presence with particular needs and interests contests the privileged position of the dominant power. This includes the challenging of mainstream art which insists on purity and preserves itself from contamination of the ordinary, the everyday and the common. It will also allow traffic across the borders and the entry of the 'minor' arts, the crafts, ephemera, fashion and the popular. By transgressing the normal definition of art, it can redirect the search for an impossible, timeless 'classic' towards a more practical activity.

Design history presents a suitable case for treatment as it struggles to come to terms with its relationship to art and the all-pervasive postmodernism which threatens to shatter its confident, macho value system based on the prime importance of industrial production.

While post-modernism cannot replace the rules it shatters with anything nearly as comforting as the harmony and belief in technological progress offered by the myth of modernism, it does enable a decentred shift in the way in which we look at the world, and how we relate to it—not an unfamiliar experience to women who are accustomed to occupying the margins.[17] Feminist practice in design, history and critique offers a point at which a criterion can be constructed which doesn't refer everything back to market forces or abstract aesthetics.

NOTES

Extracted from J. Attfield, 'FORM/female FOLLOWS FUNCTION/male: Feminist Critiques of Design', in J. Walker, ed., *Design History or the History of Design* (London: Pluto Press, 1988), pp. 201–8. Reproduced by permission of Pluto Press.

1. J. Attfield, 'Invisible touch', *Times Higher Educational Supplement* 19 June 1987 p. 26.
2. 'Form follows function' is a catchphrase associated with the Modern Movement in architecture and attributed to the American architect Louis Sullivan. See 'The tall office building artistically considered', in T. and C. Benton and D. Sharp (eds), *Form and Function* (London: Crosby Lockwood Staples, 1975) p. 13.
3. J. Mitchell, 'Reflections on twenty years of feminism', in Mitchell and Oakley, *What is Feminism?*, p. 48.
4. The critique of modern town planning has become associated with a simplistic, reactionary post-modernism which is only to do with styling for the market, and a loss of faith in designing as a practice concerned with people's needs. Jacobs' critique is not about the so-called 'failure of modernism' but about an interventionist approach to designing in which the designer teams up with users and works with them to achieve an environment more in keeping with their needs. Whereas Robert Venturi's *Complexity and Contradiction in Architecture* (1966) which presented an aesthetic critique of modernism and a celebration of historical styles without considering social implications has been much more influential.
5. Marshall Berman acknowledges this in his book *All that is Solid Melts into Air* (London: Verso, 1985) pp. 312–29.
6. See A. Karf, 'On a road to nowhere', *Guardian* 8 March 1988.
7. See C. Cockburn, *Brothers: Male Dominance and Technological Change* (London: Pluto, 1983) and *Machinery of Dominance* (London: Pluto, 1985); T. Gronberg and J. Attfield (eds), *A Resource Book on Women Working in Design* (London: London Institute/Central School of Art, 1986).
8. See, for example, S. Torre, 'Space as Matrix', *Heresies* (11) 1981 pp. 51–2; D. Hayden, *The Grand Domestic Revolution* (London: MIT Press, 1982).
9. See, for example, S. Worden, 'A voice for whose choice?', in Design History Society, *Design History: Fad or Function?* (London: Design Council, 1978).
10. C. Benton, 'Charlotte Perriand: Un Art de Vivre', *Design History Society Newsletter* (25) May 1985 pp. 12–15.

11. Both have been associated with Le Corbusier and have suffered from having their designs attributed to him, or having work ignored if—as in the case of Perriand—it was not done in association with him.

12. See Peter Adam's biography, *Eileen Gray* (London: Thames & Hudson, 1987).

13. L. Nochlin's essay first appeared in V. Gornick and B. Moran (eds), *Women in Sexist Society. Studies in Power and Powerlessness* (New York: Basic Books, 1971) pp. 480–510. For an overview of feminism and art history see T. Gouma-Peterson and P. Mathews, 'The feminist critique of art history', *Art Bulletin* LXIX (3) Sept 1987 pp. 326–57.

14. Some design departments have responded to the needs of women by adopting a policy of positive discrimination in recruitment and in access courses, but this is still uncommon. For example, the 'Women into architecture and building' course (1985–) in the Department of Environmental Design, North London Polytechnic.

15. Represented by such texts as Hazel Conway (ed), *Design History: a Students' Handbook* (London: Allen & Unwin, 1987).

16. For example see A. Forty, 'Lucky Strikes and other myths', *Designer* November 1985 pp. 16–17.

17. I refer here to what Hal Foster calls 'a postmodernism of resistance' which is concerned with 'a critical deconstruction of tradition, not an instrumental pastiche of pop- or pseudo-historical forms, with a critique of origins, not a return to them. In short, it seeks to question rather than exploit cultural codes, to explore rather than conceal social and political affiliations'; from his introduction to *Postmodern Culture* (London: Pluto, 1985).

8

THE STATE OF DESIGN HISTORY AS A DISCIPLINE

Denise Whitehouse

Design history is a new field of knowledge that has developed in the international academy as a scholarly discipline during the last forty years. Its emergence within universities during the 1970s and 1980s was the product of an era of dynamic cultural and economic change that stimulated intellectual interest in design as a mode of cultural and economic production and created an increased demand for qualified designers to work in new and expanding specializations. As Dilnot (1984) asserts, the postwar expansion of capitalism and the explosion of popular culture and mass consumerism was pivotal to the institutionalization of design as a professional practice and academic discipline, and with this the intellectualization of the history of design. First-generation design historians tell of how the impetus to develop design history came from the impact of these changes on design education, which stimulated an acute need for a history that, in defining and explaining how design as we know it came into being, also identified its subject, players, and manifestations (Attfield 2007; Dilnot 1984; Margolin 2002a; Naylor 2000; Woodham 1995).

The postwar elevation of design (design here meaning a specialist practice, profession, and disciplinary field) to degree, postgraduate, and research status within universities created a demand for contextual studies that dealt not, as in the past, with art and architecture, but with design as a field of knowledge in its own right. The challenge, therefore, was to rescue the history of design from the margins of the modernist historiography's grand narratives of art, craft, and architecture, as exemplified by Nikolaus Pevsner's *Pioneers of Modern Design* (1960), and to create a new history, which Dilnot (1984a; 1984b) advocated in his vision statement, "The State of Design History," which would explore the boundaries of what design is and could be. He called for a new historical practice that initially took as its focus the task of defining and explaining design as a specialist activity within the wider context of its development as an economic, social, and cultural mode of production that was inextricably linked to the history of how the world was made modern.

The emergence of design history as an academic practice is usually dated to the formation of the Design History Society in Britain in 1977. The significance of this event was the existence of a critical mass of practitioners concerned with converting the study of the history of design into an independent disciplinary field. When the society's mouthpiece, the *Journal of Design History,* was first published in 1988, the field was beginning to take form with several texts, including Dilnot's "The State of Design History" essays (1984a; 1984b), Forty's *Objects of Desire* (1986), Fry's *Design History Australia* (1988), and Sparke's *Introduction to Design and Culture* (1986), all attempting to theorize its intellectual potential and its intent, methods, and challenges.

All these texts reflect the considerable impact that cultural studies (centered in Britain at the University of Birmingham's Centre for Contemporary Cultural Studies) was having on traditional academic fields such as history, literature, and art history within universities around the world (Frow 2005). For design historians the work of cultural theorists, including Bourdieu (1993), Baudrillard (1981), de Certeau (1984) and Williams (1965), in theorizing how meaning is constructed through the everyday engagement with visual and material culture, including mass consumer culture, was particularly useful in developing critical frameworks for writing about the history of design. By 1989 Walker was able to argue, in *Design History and the History of Design,* that the study of the history of design was being shaped into a disciplinary field with its own logic, set of concerns, and, importantly, methodology. The main value of design history is, according to Walker, "to deepen and strengthen the writing of histories of design" and play a critical role in shaping the discourse of design (Walker 1989: 19–20).

In reviewing the development of design history as a discipline, and the issues that have shaped and are shaping its practice, this essay is mindful that each era looks at the past through the lens of its own concerns, which for design history means seeking to understand how design as we are experiencing it today has come into being. This, as Dilnot (2003) argues, demands building an understanding of the processes of modernization and capitalist expansion that have driven the development of design as a global mode of economic and cultural production and consumption. Integral to this is using historical hindsight to question and understand the latest phase in the globalization of capitalism, which is witnessing the emergence of postcommunist and non-Western countries, such as China and India, as centers of low-cost production, the impact of which is felt by the design profession and design education. A question that underpins this essay, therefore, is: What role could and should design history take in building this understanding?

DEFINING THE OBJECT OF INQUIRY

Debate and controversy have been at the heart of design history since its beginnings, as competing stakeholders have debated the potential scope of its field of inquiry and the nature of its questions and definitions. As Woodham (1995) records, there have been the attacks from established disciplines such as social anthropology, questioning the credibility of such an endeavor. Within the discipline, feminist scholars have attacked the patriarchal ideologies of modernist historiography that marginalized women and their designing activities from the history of design (Attfield 1989: 199–225; Attfield and Kirkham 1989; Buckley 1989: 251–62). Another faction led by Margolin (2002a) and Buchanan (1998: 259–63) argues that, while excellent, the practice of design history lacks the consensus of disciplinary values and definitive boundaries necessary to be recognized as an established discipline. Yet another faction, questioning the pedagogical relevance of design history to design education, has promoted the development of design culture as an alternative field of study (Julier and Narotzky 1998; Julier 2006). Most recently, a new generation of multinational scholars are challenging design history's Anglo/Euro/American orientation and questioning whether the Western historiography that underpins its practice is appropriate for shaping local and regional histories of countries that have been historically outside or on the margins of Western capitalism's project of modernization (Calvera 2005; Uriarte 2005; Vyas 2006).

Pivotal to these academic debates is the challenge of how to shape a discipline and its methodology; the scope and boundaries of its knowledge, objects, and purpose; and the appropriateness of its questions and narratives to its audiences. There is also the challenge of how to shape a critical and rigorous form of history making that, as Dilnot (1984a; 1984b) and Walker (1989) posited, would be open to the possibility that there can be no one history of design. Rather, there are many different ways in which the history of the idea of design and the circumstances of its production, practice, and consumption can and should be told. Most important, there are the vexing questions, which troubled the formative years of design history and continues to bother it today, of whose interests should the practice of design history serve, and who should decide its purpose and focus of inquiry?

Should the primary intent of design history, as many within the design education and design research fields argue, be to raise the consciousness of design as a scholarly discipline and a professional practice (Buchanan 1998; Margolin 2002a)? If so, it would take the form of a practice-based history dedicated to the understanding of design's development as a specialist activity, with its roots in modern capitalism's project of industrialization and its economies of mass production and consumption. Historians accordingly would take up Margolin's (1995:14) proposal and focus their inquiry on the historical formulation of design as an industrial practice implicated in the translation of technologies and resources into modern products, and in the wider "practice of human invention and the conception of the artificial." Their task would be to build on the foundation studies of Heskett (1988), Meggs (1998), Meikle (1979), and Sparke (1983) in developing disciplinary and professional histories that investigate the development of design as an intellectual and professional practice from within the context of the histories of Anglo/European industry and modernism, as well as American capitalism's entrepreneurial systems of manufacturing and marketing.

A subtext would be to follow the lead of Freidman (1989), Fry (1988), Pulos (1983), and Remington (1989) in developing national and regional histories that trace the internationalization of design as integral to the growth of Western capitalism's industrial businesses. Design historians would also need to develop historical categories and narrative strategies for investigating the complex culture of the design artifact in all its different manifestations, from concept through to its abundant material presence and visual representation, within the spectacle of consumption and the fabric of everyday life. Within this schema, design history would function as a subdiscipline of the academic fields of design studies and design research and play a prescribed pedagogical role in advancing the status of design as a discipline, by providing it with a legitimizing discourse that, based in historical precedence, assists in establishing standards of professional quality and role models for young designers (Margolin 2002a; 2002b).

On the other hand, design history could, as its early protagonists advocated, be developed as an independent disciplinary practice, the focus of which is the historical coming to be of design in all the complexities and associated meanings of the word, be it verb or noun (Doordan 1995; Forty 1995; Fry 1988; Walker 1989; Woodham 1995). It could seek broader possibilities for understanding the value and meaning of design, by drawing inspiration from the wider fields of history and cultural studies, with their questioning of the role of material and visual culture in the construction of meaning. As a new field of academic inquiry, its intent could be, as Attfield (2007: 1–2) proposed, to produce a history of design that: "concerned with all aspects of the modern material world and … the multifarious ways it has threaded itself into our everyday lives … [would offer] … a way into the mysteries of how the artefactual world has been shaped and formed by the powerful determining forces of politics and economics, as well as the softer, but nevertheless equally influential, value-driven thrust of social dynamics."

A CONTEMPORARY HISTORY

In adopting this charter, design historians could position the history of design within the emergent field of contemporary historiography, the primary concern of which, Michel de Certeau (1988) argues, is not the grand narratives of empire building, great men, progress, and impressive deeds, but the practice of meaning. With the aim of challenging modernist historical practices, contemporary historians take up concerns formerly consigned to silence or situated outside the frame of traditional disciplines, including the impact of modernism's different material and visual languages on the unconscious relationships that inform the objects and practices that have shaped everyday life, concerns that might rightly include design. Practicing within this wider field of design, historians could rigorously question the value and significance of design as a fundamental human activity pertaining to the shaping of not only physical order but also the social and cultural order. They also could join with scholars from complementary fields, including material and visual culture, art and architectural history, sociology, cultural anthropology, psychology, the history of business, consumption, technology, retail, and postcolonialism, in building understanding of how individual and collective consciousness was constructed in the modern age of capitalist production and consumption, beginning with the Industrial Revolution and the birth of consumer society.

As a mode of contemporary history, design history has been able to formulate wide-ranging questions that, rather than narrowing the object of inquiry, test the possibilities for different varieties of histories of design, which would collectively build a scholarly depth of understanding. Some of these questions are posed in the *Journal of Design History*, about the history of design's implication in the production, distribution, and consumption of capitalism's world of goods, and its part in the everyday communication of ideological messages that pertain to issues ranging from political and economic power, to freedom and social justice, identity and ethnicity, and domesticity and gender (Berney 2001; Gerchuk 2000; Maynard 2000; Reed 1997). Other questions concern when and how the separation

of labor, together with the growth of industrial businesses (print, media, manufacturing, retailing, transport, leisure, urban development, trade, housing), created the need for a multiplicity of designing activities—graphic, typographical, industrial, product, and interior and fashion design, the purpose of which was the creation of cultures of consumption (Aynsley and Berry 2005; Hewitt 1995; Jobling and Crowley 1996; Lavin, 2001; Maffei 2000; Porter 1998).

This in turn stimulated questions about the gap between the ideal of the modernist designer as a creative social reformer who brings technical and aesthetic innovation to industry, and the reality of design's origins as a commercial practice serving the need of modern industry and commerce to shape consumer societies. Central to this, as Mazur Thomson (1997), Hewitt (1995), and Poynor (2002) show, is understanding the manner in which practitioners have collectively defined the role of the designer in response to demands of new industrial businesses, such as print, advertising, packaging, and product, shaping specialist work practices and career paths that they institutionalized through the development of unions, trade journals, education and training, and professional regulation. Also central is the questioning of the designer's role in the shaping of meaning: Is it the user who creates the meaning of the object (Attfield 2007), or does the designer as the "*sine qua non* of the modern commercial system" ensure "through the activities of production and consumption, that people's needs and desires ... are met by visual and material images and artifacts that enter the marketplace and help us define who we are"? (Sparke 2004: 2).

STRATEGIC NARRATIVES

But before this could be achieved, design historians had to retrieve the telling of the story of design from the ideological restrictions of modernist historiography, with its rhetoric of the avant-garde, high culture (art and architecture), and man's (white) creative contribution to the universal advance of civilization (Western). It needed to move, as Dilnot, Fry, and Walker argued, beyond Pesvnerian and art historical practices of canonization and connoisseurship, and the privileging of the innovative designer, aesthetic form, and zeitgeist, in order to develop a new historiography for design. A new methodology that is underpinned by contemporary theories of cultural production would, Fry (1989) theorized, allow for a greater understanding of the role of design in prefiguring and manufacturing the world in which we live.

While identifying a new set of objects, players, materials, technologies, theories, and practices to study, design historians had to develop narrative strategies for writing about design that moved beyond modernist concerns with formalism, innovation, and the functional object to the investigation of design as an economic and cultural practice. Social narratives such as those proposed by Forty (1986), Sparke (1986), and Lupton (1993) use a poststructuralist analysis of the encoded nature of mass consumer products and their promotional rhetoric, to reveal design's implication in the construction and mediation of social discourses, including those of family and home, work and leisure, the social body, gender, age, race, and class. And critical gender narratives have introduced women as producers and consumers to the history of design and in the process have opened the field to a new set of players and concerns, stimulating inquiry not only into gender and design (feminine and masculine), but also the marginal fields of interior, fashion, and retail design and their ephemeral modes of representation, such as in magazines, advertising, and the spectacle of shopping (Attfield and Kirkham 1989; Breward 1997; Colville 2004; Crowley 2006; McKellar and Sparke 2004; Sparke 2005).

As new historians of design, they also developed user narratives that examine the complex practices and self-understandings that people build of themselves as consumers as they negotiate the abundance of mass culture (Trentmann 2004). The concern arose that consumption, as opposed to production, was essential to rupturing modernism's ideal of good design and extending the understanding of the social dynamics of how ordinary people engage with the idea of design within the realities of their daily lives, be it within the home or beyond. This demanded widening the definition of design to include its practice by ordinary people, as they creatively engage in the selection and arrangement of goods and spaces and in do-it-yourself activities, within the processes of self-construction and identity formation (Atkinson 2006; Attfield 2007). It also involved opening the field to include the anonymous design of the high street manufacturers and traders, with their mélange of traditional and contemporary styles (Edwards 1994; 2001; Woodham 1997). The practices of styles, taste, and fashion also need recovery from the negativity of modernism's ideology of anti-consumerism, by rethinking their centrality to the urban spectacle of habitus, and with this the modern mode of identity and value formation (Breward 2004; Silverman 1989; Sparke 1995; Troy 1991). The unifying concern of these new narratives is to establish a more inclusive definition of design and culture that celebrates diversity and difference.

Underpinning these thematic narratives is the shared concern of contemporary historians with the pivotal role of capitalism's production and consumption in cultural formation, and the construction of modern identities and experiences for mass audiences (Brewer 2004). The identify formation, as Fry (1988) stresses, extends beyond social groups and individuals to the economics and politics of international trade and its conversion of regional and non-Western countries into primary industrial nations and markets for mass consumer goods and services. These narratives also are marked by design history's distinguishing focus on the materiality of the design object, and the processes informing its production and consumption, together with the mediating discourses that situate it within circulating systems of meaning (Lees-Maffei 2008; Meikle 1998).

Production, as Lees-Maffei (2008: 6–7) explains, not only involves the manufacture of physical objects, but also the production of the meaning of designed goods as "understood through mediating discourses of advertising, curatorial and retail strategies, advice discourses, education, consumer magazines, television, radio, film and internet media," and how "the goods themselves also mediate between production and consumption, maker and user, as advertisements for themselves and as carrier of messages about the people who own or use them." While Lees-Maffei's interest lies with the mediating role of the exhibition, Aynsley and Forde (2007) have interrogated the modern home magazine, analyzing its visual format and representational strategies, including drawings, plans, display rooms, typography, and photography, to reveal how design not only encodes the magazine object and the objects within it with performative possibilities, but also presents design itself as an experience to be consumed through the process of reading.

Finally, as the varied nature of the narratives indicates, there is the recognition that there can be no one totalizing, global paradise history of design (de Certeau 1988). Rather, there is belief in the importance of multiple histories, which foster complexities of understandings by focusing attention on specific themes and aspects of design practice, or specific geographical locations and moments, and which cumulatively shape depth and breadth of understanding.

THE STATE OF DESIGN HISTORY TODAY

Forty years on from when design historians began shaping these concerns into what is now an independent field of inquiry, there is still dispute as to whether a discipline of design history can be said to exist (Buchanan 1998; Margolin 2002a; 2002b; Meikle 1998). This stems from the inherently contested nature of history making. Like all histories, design history contributes to the shaping of public consciousness, as the stories it tells filter into the public imagination through various media: academic and popular publications, the press, museum and gallery exhibitions, television programs, and films. History is not a neutral practice; rather, individuals and institutions bring subjectivities, be they cultural, professional, ideological, or theoretical to the making and reading of history. Thus, while Margolin and Buchanan argue that design history lacks the definitive boundaries and identifying focus on professional practice necessary for it to be a recognized discipline, their rhetoric is to some extent political, being informed by the professional and ideological conflict between design academics and design historians over the purpose and intent of design history. There are also the unexplored historical and philosophical biases of design education toward certain modes of knowledge and learning, especially history, the roots of which are to be found in Enlightenment theories of creativity, which were institutionalized by Bauhaus and post–World War II art and design pedagogy (Golec 2004; Whitehouse 2002).

The reality is that design history is a well-established disciplinary field, which is increasingly being mapped through varied modes of exposition: academic journals, exhibitions, dictionaries, document and essay anthologies, catalogs, monographs, and TV and film documentaries, all grounded in scholarly research. While small, it draws strength from cooperation with historians from complimentary disciplines, such as the American Studies scholar Jeffrey Meikle, and from gallery and museum curators, who, like the London Victoria and Albert's Christopher Wilk (2006) and Australia's Powerhouse Museum's Ann Stephen (Stephen, McNamara, and Goad 2006; 2008), are making significant contributions to design history. It also draws strength from trans-disciplinary ventures (Aynsley and Grant 2006), in which design history concerns (cultures of consumption) are collectively analyzed by scholars from different disciplines (especially from material and consumer studies), who work to build a richly contextualized study with relevance to diverse audiences. This practice of historians (Betts 2004; Conekin, Mort, and Walters 1999), of working across different disciplines and various subject and thematic areas is a feature of contemporary historical practice that is troublesome for some, such as Margolin (2000a; 2000b), who views it as a threat to the establishment of design history's territorial boundaries.

In Britain, where the practice is strongest, the Design History Society and supportive government policies have provided a springboard for the formation of a disciplinary space with the supporting intellectual networks that cultural studies scholar John Frow (2005) argues are necessary to drive and generate a body of knowledge. These networks, as the *Journal of Design History* indicates, reach nationally and internationally across universities and the different disciplines therein, into archival, museum, and gallery systems, as well as design, publishing, and culture industries. As a result, a cohesive research culture has formed around a network involving London's Royal College of Art (RCA), the Victoria and Albert Museum (V&A), universities such as Kingston and Brighton, and a network of special interest study groups. Their unifying concern is the design of cultures of consumption, with the radiating center being the home (ideal and real), on which the energies of the design world, everyday consumerism, and identity formation are predominately focused.

The important point is that when one reviews the publications emanating from the V&A and RCA's Centre for the Study of the Domestic Interior (Aynsley and Berry 2005; Aynsley and Forde 2007; Aynsley and Grant 2006), and Manchester University Press's Studies in Design (Attfield 2007; Conekin 2003; Jobling and Crowley 1996; McKellar and Sparke 2004), it is evident that this research is marked by a cogent set of disciplinary questions and definitions that reflect the shared identification of materials for research, methods of interpretation, and interlinking narratives. This, together with the funding from the United Kingdom's preeminent Arts and Humanities Research Council, is evidence that design history is now recognized within the academy and beyond as a significant field of intellectual research.

While Britain has set the methodological framework and narratives for others to build on, there are signs of a strengthening of practice in the United States, where a younger generation of design historians with links in the design studies, decorative arts, galleries, and museum fields, are using the Design Studies Forum of the College Art Association to build networks with a particular interest in opening the field toward Asia (Margolin 2002b). While the U.S. field shares a concern with social narratives, including those of the consumer and the marginalized, it is distinctive in its focus on the regional, and on the history of design as a commercial practice, and in its professionalization within the wider development of U.S. manufacturing and marketing and the shaping of an American way of life.

The issue of how to shape professional and disciplinary histories is a source of friction between American academic historians and practitioners-cum-historians, as the critical debate around the Steven Heller–led Graphic Design Movement indicates (Golec 2004; Heller and Ballance 2001). In an effort to create scholarly, as opposed to celebratory, disciplinary histories, academic historians (Gorman 2001; 2003; Mazur Thomson 1997) argue the need to interrogate the "real" history of design, as in the shaping of its practices, processes, businesses, and discourses, and the dynamics informing the institutionalization of different design specializations, including graphic design and industrial design, into professional disciplines. By focusing on a particular moment in the development of design in a specific region, as did Mazur Thomson and the innovative Toledo Museum of Art's Alliance of Art and Industry (2002) exhibition, they are drawing attention to how specific sets of economic, technological, and human dynamics (gender, transportation, resources, labor, manufacturing and production technologies, entrepreneurship), inform the production of design centers and industries.

The push to demystify design is further evident in a growing concern among historians, galleries, and museums with the mainstream consultants and in-house designers such as Henry Dreyfuss (Flinchum 1997), Brooks Stevens (Adamson, 2003) and Russel Wright (Albrecht, Schonfeld, and Shapiro 2001). These exhibitions, and the monographs that accompany them, are building detailed and accurate understandings of the nature of design expertise and practice, including the collaborative nature of design work, the process of product development, advertising and market placement, the importance of self-promotion, and the mediating role of designers in shaping styles and market trends in response to the lifestyle aspirations of society. Importantly, they are developing methods for giving concrete form and intellectual understanding to the design process through the exploration of new evidential material in the form of plans, drawings, photography, publicity, and promotional materials, together with detailed product and project case studies.

A WORLD HISTORY OF DESIGN?

Thus far I have focused on two of the three driving concerns that I perceive are shaping design history as a disciplinary field: the need for a disciplinary practice-based history, and the dominant concern with design as a mode of social and cultural production. In concluding, I want to explore the third concern, the globalization of design history that is accompanying the international expansion of design education and practice and our entry into what Dilnot (2003) terms the fourth stage of capitalist expansion. While many countries produce local histories of design, the output is uneven and often driven by nationalist and trade agendas. Change is evident, however, in the formation of academic focus groups, such as the Japanese Design History Forum and the International Committee for Design History and Design Studies (ICDHDS), whose conferences are drawing together scholars from all regions: Western, non-Western, postcommunist, postcolonial, Asian, and Southern Hemisphere, to remap the scope and narrative concerns of design history. In their endeavor to develop histories to support the development of design education, research, and practice in their regions (long regarded as marginal or outside the history of modern design), these scholars are advocating a new geography of design that critically rethinks the impact of Western capitalism's dissemination of the idea and practice of design. The intent is to build this geography through the comparison and synthesis of the different histories of how specific countries, regions, and localities have responded to design as an agency of modernization.

Such a history, Calvera (2005) and her fellow global history protagonists (such as Woodham 2005) argue, would challenge the Euro/Anglo/American focus of design history and broaden its definitions of design beyond its concern with modern industrialization and consumer culture to address the value and historical systems of non-Western cultures and their distinctive modes of production and consumption, including craft-based industries. But before intellectual consideration can be given to the development of critical histories of different countries, regions, and localities within a global context, new systems of interpretation need to be developed that question the modernist ideological biases that underpin the conventional modes used for telling national and internationalist histories of design.

In calling for a new world history, Woodham (2005), Margolin (2005), and Calvera (2005) argue the need for a unifying narrative that rethinks design as a global and multicultural phenomenon. Calvera's aim is to create a theoretical narrative that brings intellectual logic to the multiple stories of how different countries—Australia (Jackson 2002), China (Wong 2001), Cuba (Uriarte 2005), Hong Kong (Turner 1995), India (Vyas 2006), South Africa (Eeden 2004), Spain (Calvera 2002)—have negotiated the process of Westernization and the idea of design according to their specific economic, geographical, political, and cultural circumstances.

For Margolin and Woodham, a way forward would be to widen the scope of the grand narratives of design history, as in the art and design dictionary and the international, disciplinary, and era surveys, to include a more comprehensive range of countries. These encyclopedic histories are much favored, because of their familiarity and their facility to map the totality of a field and give it definitive boundaries, while canonizing its significant definitions, centers of creative power, and key players, objects, and concerns. Ideal for textbooks and blockbuster exhibitions, their conventions were established by art historians in the post–World War II era of international modernism and were popularized within design history during the 1980s and 1990s. While many express concerns about the inherently Western and exclusive nature of these narratives and their practices of canonization, their appeal is strong, as the latest trend for totalizing texts, evidenced in Raizman (2003) and Eskilson (2007), indicates.

However, as de Certeau (1988) and Conekin, Mort, and Walters (1999) argue, the totalizing world narrative was born of an attempt to theorize the expansionist properties of the West's ideal of a modern world system and disseminate its systems of intellectual power, which, for those colonized, would demand multiple shifts in knowledge and material culture, including the reorganization of concepts of time, history, place, and space. Within histories of design, these imperialist ideologies have been signified through a European world consciousness, including chronological time, and a meta-narrative of the evolutionary "progress" of modern "civilization" as driven by man's "pioneering" spirit and quest for the new horizons. As Calvera notes, its geographical order, with its mapping of centers, regions, and peripheries, is also power-based, as its privileging of eurocentricity renders those distant from the "center" as silent or other, and their experience of modernism as nonexistence or, as the British-educated Fry (1989) once argued of Australia, a simulacrum of the real thing. This power play reaches further into design history's agreed definition of design as

the product of industrialization, technological innovation, and mass manufacture, which excludes countries that lack mass manufacturing and its technologies but that nevertheless shape sophisticated design cultures.

THE ISSUE OF SPECIFICITY: THE BUILDING BLOCKS OF A GLOBAL DESIGN HISTORY

Calvera proposes that the new geography of design history be built by working from the specific as opposed to the general. The focus should be on "particularities" and "specificities" that work to dismantle the power politics inherent in disseminated Western cultural practices and to identify the shared strategies of reception, resistance, and exchange that characterize postcolonial and non-Western cultures. Calvera's aim is to build new histories that strategically compare the stories of different countries, in order to identify the patterns of similarities and differences that characterize the world's experiences of modernization, and with this the development of multiple design cultures and multiple manifestations of modernisms.

The challenge for design history is the development of interpretative methods and narratives that can bring a critical focus to this process. Initially this demands posing new questions, most specifically about how the idea of modern design and the concepts of modernism, modernization, and modernity have been disseminated, understood, received, rejected, and negotiated in different places at different times, according to specific circumstances and needs. Questions such as the following need to be raised: When, how and for what purpose was modern design imported into, or rejected by, a country? Is this process always linked to the progress of industrialization and mass production, or can it be governed by other needs? Could the idea of modern design, as in the case of communist East Germany, provide inspiration for an industrial design aesthetic that is the antithesis of Western capitalism's ideal of good design (Rubin

2006)? Could it be rejected as a threat to national cultural identity, as in Catalonia (Calvera 2002)? Or could it be imported as a signifier of cultural change and prosperity as in 1950s Cuba (Uriarte 2005)? Or, as in Australia during the 1950s and 1960s, could it be used to signify a new nation's cultural maturity? And if this were the case, how then does Australia's experience of modern design align with that of other "new" and modern nations such as Brazil, India, Hong Kong, and Singapore?

There are also questions pertaining to the legacies of Western capitalist expansion, including how design historians in non-Western countries relate traditional historical values and practices with those imposed by modernist historiography when shaping their histories of design. How do they theorize the tension between the need to protect traditional modes of production and consumption that are central to cultural distinctiveness, and the economic and social need for the benefits of global capitalism? How do postcolonial design historians address the role of design in advancing the nationalist ideologies of white settlement and racism, and their impact on indigenous people (Connellan 2007; Whitehouse 2005)? Finally, how have and do the politics of world trade shape the economies of different countries, and how has this shaped the peculiarities of regional design cultures and industries and informed the internationalization of design as a profession and discipline?

The history of design history, as we have seen, is marked by an intense and productive debate about whose interests it should serve and what should be the objects of its inquiry. As a new mode of history, it is alive with the questioning and competing concerns of different interest groups, who are nevertheless united in their struggle to come to terms with the multiplicity of meanings and practices associated with the concept of design. By reviewing the past through the lens of contemporary concerns, design historians are building intellectual understanding of the significance of design within the history of how the world as we know it has come into being. As they are revealing, design can no longer be defined simply in terms of the designer, the object, technology, and manufacturing. Rather, it comprises a complex and changing dynamic that on the grand scale pertains to economic, social, and cultural production and consumption, and on the micro level to the collaborative practices of designers and ordinary people in the construction of everyday meaning. Central to this is an understanding of the role of design within the shaping of the human consciousness and materiality of everyday life: with how the world is continuously being made modern. As Dilnot (2003) argues, by critically rethinking the history of design, design history is casting light on the dilemmas and debates facing the design profession and education, as the global process of modernization enters its fourth stage, in the process changing the global order of production and consumption, and with this the nature of design as a significant global profession and cultural practice.

ANNOTATED GUIDE TO FURTHER READING

Anyone studying design history must read Clive Dilnot's seminal two-part essay, "The State of Design History" (1984a; 1984b). Part I maps the field of scholarship before 1984, and Part II considers the problems and possibilities of the emerging field. With its call for a broad consideration of design and its history, it still sets an agenda for scholarship. The essays were republished in the first of three anthologies of essays from *Design Issues* (Margolin 1989; Doordan 1995; Margolin and Buchanan 1995), each of which provides insight into early design history debates (for example Hannah and Putnam 1980). Both *Design Issues* and the *Journal of Design History* have remained the main scholarly mouthpieces for design history discourse.

The development of the discipline has been reflected in its adoption of new scholarly approaches, such as the feminist-based design histories of Cheryl Buckley (Section 4.2), Pat Kirkham, and Judy Attfield. Their interest in material culture has also brought new insights, particularly Attfield's *Wild Things: The Material Culture of Everyday Life* (2000), and Alison Clarke's *Tupperware: The Promise of Plastic in 1950s America* (1999). Insightful object-based interpretations have proved especially valuable to the history of design, with Dick Hebdige's essay, "Object as Image: The Italian Scooter Cycle" (1988), being exemplary in its interpretation of the changing meanings of a designed product. Raizman and Gorman's more recent *Objects, Audiences, and Literatures: Alternative Narratives in the History of Design* (2007) draws upon literary sources to examine how class, gender, and cultural context shaped the reception of design.

Object-based methodology has informed works such as Paul Betts's *The Authority of Everyday Objects: A Cultural History of West German Industrial Design* (2004), which is also a detailed nation-based study. Focused research into particular periods and geographies continues to create new historical insights, such as Nancy Troy's enlightening *Modernism and the Decorative Arts in France: Art Nouveau to Le Corbusier* (1991). Historical reappraisals are often publications that support exhibitions, as with Taragin's *The Alliance of Art and Industry: Toledo Design for a Modern America* (2002). The need to extend the geographic and cultural biases of design history beyond Britain, Europe, and the United States has continued to be discussed in scholarly essays (Woodham 2005). An example of a nation-based collection is Michael Bogel's very comprehensive *Designing Australia: Readings in the History of Design* (2002). A geographically comprehensive history of design has yet to be published; at the time of writing, Victor Margolin's long-awaited world history of design is expected to be the first of its type.

While we would encourage a broader and cross-disciplinary understanding of the history of design, subject-based histories still prove of value to those searching for the development of a particular design profession, such as Philip Meggs's *History of Graphic Design* (1992). Meggs's book raises additional questions of whether history might be written other than chronologically; Steven Heller and Georgette Balance's collection, *Graphic Design History* (2001), and Christopher Breward's *Fashion* (2003) indicates the potentialities of a more thematic approach.

Also, earlier approaches to what is now recognized as the history of design can still prove valuable methodologically and historically. Here Siegfried Giedion's *Mechanisation Takes Command: A Contribution to Anonymous History* (1948) comes particularly to mind. Finally, for those who want to sample a range of approaches to design history, Lees-Maffei and Houze's *The Design History Reader* will provide valuable insights (forthcoming from Berg at the time of writing).

SECTION 2

DESIGN THINKING

SECTION INTRODUCTION

The readings in this section explore three different approaches to thinking about design. The first subsection assesses theoretical and philosophical approaches. The second subsection focuses on how research helps discern design's process and power in the marketplace. Finally, the Communications subsection (2.3) reveals how branding forces the public to think about design in specific ways, which often deny the realities we associate with actual products. These three subsections question design's place in the world and investigate the idea of design as a medium through which complicated problems can be solved and novel ways of thinking about complex global concerns can be inspired.

Many design studies scholars explain that we tend to limit our capacity to think about design. As one optimistic theorist notes, we live on Earth without even understanding the marvels of the resources that are at our fingertips. Furthermore, we also underestimate the advantages of failure. Failure betters design thinking and improves upon current conditions. In a set of readings that reflects ideas found in other portions of the *Reader,* especially the Sustainability (6.3) and Politics (3.3) subsections, the first subsection sets the stage for the idea of thinking critically about design practice.

Research further develops our thinking about design. It is through research that we are able to attain knowledge about the inner workings that are integral to the design process and the reception of design in the marketplace. As the readings in the Design Research subsection contend, a careful analysis of design, from its creation to its consumption, leads to a better understanding of what design means in our contemporary world. Connected to the important work of the Design Research Society, the readings here posit design as a science that can be critiqued and investigated.

Theoretical analyses and research facilitate the power of design communications, which is most evident in the branding process. The brand is, for better or worse, the ultimate communicator in our capitalist society, where symbols and abstract thinking about a corporation become more important than what the company actually makes and sells. Branding, in short, initiates our consumer-based thinking about design. Thus, the readings in the Design Communications subsection (2.3) reveal the power of design's message in our brand-obsessed world. Indeed, cultural thinking about design is mediated by the dominance of branding.

These readings ask us to rethink design as a process, as a practice, and as a product that gives our lives meaning and sustains our economic and political systems. Design contains problems with shapeless borders that are at times impossible to define and at other times rather straightforward to understand in our consumer-oriented culture. Instead of asking that we clearly delineate design's boundaries, this section invites us to explore the complexities inherent to the task of thinking about design.

SECTION 2: DESIGN THINKING

2.1: Design Philosophies and Theories

INTRODUCTION

Design studies asks us to think about the meaning of design. On the surface, this seems like a simple idea, but when we try and understand the complexities of design in terms of its process, its use, and its applicability, the enormity of the topic can be overwhelming. The five authors in this subsection get us to assess design from a wide-angle perspective that does not focus too intently on one specific issue within design, but instead explores the big-picture questions about what makes design work, what makes design fail, and why we need to study and participate in the design process.

Buckminster Fuller contends in his 1982 book, *Critical Path*, that humanity can be saved by understanding how fortunate we are to have so many resources at hand. In a utopian call to action, Fuller claims that too many of our current designs are built to fritter away energy—cars, airplanes, and even spaceships waste too much energy that could be utilized to our benefit. Indeed, Fuller notes, "we now have four billion billionaires on board Spaceship Earth who are entirely unaware of their good fortune." The entire population of Earth focuses on the idea that technology can only be associated with weapons and machines "that compete with [us] for [our] jobs." Fuller, following a lifetime of work that attempted to create viable design solutions to help foster a better living experience, wants humankind to escape the "world's power structures" that have duped us into believing that doomsday is around the corner. In language that predates, but predicts, the readings on sustainability (Section 6.3), Fuller comments that design can rescue us from the pessimism that defines our way of life and stops us from looking for alternative energy and resources.

While Fuller looks at design thinking from a vantage point that is macro in scale and utopian in vision, John Chris Jones asks us to investigate a variety of new methods that designers can use in his seminal book *Design Methods*. Jones, who organized a 1962 conference at London's Imperial College on design methods, which many believe led to the Design Research Society (see the next subsection of the reader, 2.2), starts his book by asking: "What is designing?" He examines different and conflicting definitions of design and then does something remarkable for the 1970 publication date of this book: He notes that design has moral implications in which the choices designers make have increasingly large consequences. He uses the example of the supersonic jet, in which the noise of sonic booms "can drastically alter the circumstances of millions of people." Jones gets us to think about design as a more public and democratic activity, so that "the public effects of designing become the subjects of political debate."

Jones, like Fuller, wants the public to become more engaged in the ethics of the design process. If we think for a moment about the world of politics, in which our leaders claim to want our participation and our input, this same request for participation can be found in the forward-thinking language found in this subsection. And, in fact, this same notion is echoed by the readings in the subsection on ethics and the subsection on politics. By understanding the complex problems of design, humankind can improve the world through new design thinking that demands participation.

Louis Bucciarelli argues in his book, *Designing Engineers*, that part of the problem with design thinking is that there is a discrepancy between the "uncertainty and ambiguity" in the design process and the "ideal image" of the design process that designers believe exists. Using an anthropological method that is similar to the work of Susan Squires, discussed in Section 2.2, Bucciarelli claims that because designers think about their work in a specific way, this affects how design appears and functions in the world. An example is the telephone, which, he writes, means different things to different designers and different users. The system that is the telephone—from the receiver to the intricate web of interfaces that move sound across a distance to another receiver—is so complicated that very few people actually know how the phone works. According to Bucciarelli, the engineer who designs the phone uses an "object-world" type of thinking. In other words, a telephone designer will devise a phone in a particular way and this "patterns their thought and practice" when it comes to creating a telephone design that the rest of us must utilize. We need to assess the difference between what designers say happens during the design process and what actually occurs. In essence, this process affects the world of things that fill our lives with meaning and purpose.

Henry Petroski, in his book, *Success Through Failure: The Paradox of Design*, furthers our discussion of Bucciarelli's work by explaining that part of what designers look at when creating their worldview is failure. Thinking about failure, according to Petroski, leads to success. Using very straightforward examples in the world of technology and engineering, Petroski argues that earlier iterations of design lead to better models as a result of design's inability to "reach perfection."

The problems in design thinking that Petroski identifies are ultimately, according to Richard Buchanan in his essay, "Wicked Problems in Design Thinking," larger than we imagine. Buchanan identifies four areas of design: "symbolic and visual communications," "material objects," "activities and organized services," and "environments for living, working, playing, and learning." Because designers engage in these four contexts, which define our existence as human beings, we need to think about how design comes up with "definitions" and "solutions" to the different arenas that encompass design. The issue, however, is that these definitions and solutions are not so easily understood; they are, according to Buchanan, "wicked problems." A wicked problem is one that does not have a clear definition—it exists in an ambiguous state in which the potential resolution is so complicated that it has multiple meanings to multiple individuals. We could think of the issues around sustainable design, discussed in Section 6.3, as an example of a wicked problem, since its complexity does not allow for a simple solution. Buchanan's essay helps explain why thinking about design has complexities that do not permit a linear way of understanding how design works in our contemporary world.

The five authors here inspire us to think about design as a reflexive act, in which the design process can be pondered to help us understand the dramatic impact that design has on our lives. The design process can be analyzed in a way that provides us with more knowledge about why design exists, how design affects our lives, and where design will take us in the future. Thinking about design brings clarity to the design studies' mandate of helping us comprehend the complexities of our designed world.

9

SPECULATIVE PREHISTORY OF HUMANITY

Buckminster Fuller

Weighing only fifty-five pounds, with a wingspan of ninety-six feet, the human-powered *Gossamer Albatross* was able to fly across the English Channel because the structural materials of which it was built were many times tensilely stronger than an equal weight of the highest-strength

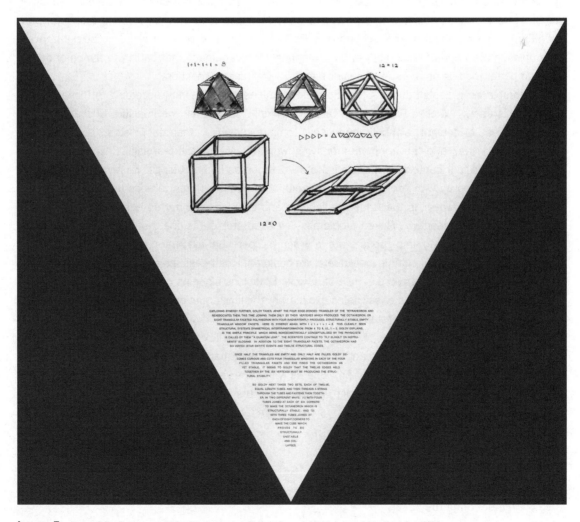

Image 5   Page 6 from *Tetrascroll* by Buckminster Fuller. Copyright Universal Limited Art Editions.

aircraft aluminum. The tensile strengths of the *Albatross's* structural materials were sixty times stronger per equivalent weight than the strongest structural materials available to Leonardo da Vinci for realizing the design of his proposed human-powered flying machine. The *Albatross's* high-strength carbon-fiber and Mylar materials were all developed only a short time ago—since World War II.

A one-quarter-ton communication satellite is now outperforming the previously used 175,000 tons of transatlantic copper cables, with this 700,000-fold reduction in system-equipment weight providing greater message-carrying capacity and transmission fidelity, as well as using vastly fewer kilowatts of operational energy.

Continuing to attempt to fit our late- twentieth-century astronautical man-on-Moon-visiting capability into a nineteenth-century horse-and-buggy street pattern, house-to-house-yoo-hooing life-style (and a land baron racket) is so inefficient that the overall design of humanity's present social, economic, and, political structuring and the physical technology it uses wastes ninety-five out of every 100 units of the energy it consumes. (Our automobiles' reciprocating engines are only 15-percent efficient, whereas turbines are 30 percent, jet engines 60 percent, and fuel cells used by astronauts 80 percent.) In the United States, throughout all twenty-four hours of every day of the year—year after year—we have an average of two million automobiles standing in front of red stoplights with their engines going, the energy for which amounts to that generated by the full efforts of 200 million horses being completely wasted as they jump up and down going nowhere.

Environment-controlling buildings gain or lose their energy as "heat or cool" only through their containing surfaces. Spheres contain the most volume with the least surface—i.e., have the least possible surface-to-volume ratio. Every time we double the diameter of a spherical structure, we increase its contained atmosphere eightfold and its enclosing surface only four-fold. When doubling the diameter of our sphere,

we are not changing the size of the contained molecules of atmosphere. Therefore, every time we double a spherical structure's diameter, we halve the amount of enclosing surface through which an interior molecule of atmosphere can gain or lose energy as "heat or cool." Flat slabs have a high surface-to-volume ratio, and so flat slab fins make good air-cooling motorcycle and light-airplane engines. Tubes have the highest surface-to-volume ratios. Triangular- or square-sectioned tubes have higher surface-to-volume ratios than have round-sectioned tubes. Tall slab buildings and vertical, square-sectioned, tubular-tower skyscrapers have the maximum possible energy (as heat or cool)- losing capability.

One two-mile-diameter dome enclosing all the mid-Manhattan buildings between Twenty-second and Sixty-second streets and between the Hudson and East rivers, having a surface that is only one eighty-fourth that of all the buildings now standing in that midtown area, would reduce the heating and cooling energy requirements of that area eighty-four-fold.

The human pedal-powered airplane and the communication satellite are only two out of hundreds of thousands of instances that can now be cited of the accomplishment of much greater performance with much less material. The inefficiency of automobiles' reciprocating engines—and their traffic-system-wasted fuel—and the energy inefficiency of today's buildings, are only two of hundreds of thousands of instances that can be cited of the design-avoidable energy wastage. But the technical raison d'être for either the energy-effectiveness gains or losses is all completely invisible to human eyes. Thus, the significance of their omni-integratable potentialities is uncomprehended by either the world's leaders or the led.

Neither the great political and financial power structures of the world, nor the specialization-blinded professionals, nor the population in general realize that sum-totally the omni-engineering-integratable, invisible revolution in the metallurgical, chemical, and electronic arts now makes it possible to do so much more with ever fewer pounds and volumes of material, ergs of energy, and seconds of time per given technological function that it is now highly feasible to take care of everybody on Earth at a "higher standard of living than any have ever known."

It no longer has to be you or me. Selfishness is unnecessary and henceforth unrationalizable as mandated by survival. War is obsolete.

It could never have been done before. Only ten years ago the more-with-less technology reached the point where it could be done. Since then the invisible technological-capability revolution has made it ever easier so to do. It is a matter of converting the high technology from weaponry to livingry. The essence of livingry is human-life advantaging and environment controlling. With the highest aeronautical and engineering facilities of the world redirected from weaponry to livingry production, all humanity would have the option of becoming enduringly successful.

All previous revolutions have been political— in them the have-not majority has attempted revengefully to pull down the economically advantaged minority. If realized, this historically greatest design revolution will joyously elevate all humanity to unprecedented heights.

The architectural profession—civil, naval, aeronautical, and astronautical—has always been the place where the most competent thinking is conducted regarding livingry, as opposed to weaponry. Now is the time for the comprehensive architectural profession to reorient itself from the six-months-per-one-residence work schedule to the millions-per-day, air-deliverable, sewer-and-water-mains-emancipated, energy-harvesting, dwelling-machine-production world with its unpurchasable, air-deliverable dwelling machines only rentable from a Hertz-Hilton-Bell-Tel service industry, able to accommodate at unprecedentedly high standards of living all humanity's remote-from-one-another living accommodations. Now is also the time for the architectural profession to reorient itself from the years-to-build, human-need-exploiting cities to the all-in-one-day-air-deliverable-or-removable, human-need-serving, singly-domed-over cities. We

have to satisfactorily rehouse the alternately convergent and divergent shuttling phases of four billion uprooting, around-the-world-integrating, sometimes transient, sometimes resident, sometimes in cities, sometimes in the country humans—before 2000 A.D.

Technologically we now have four billion billionaires on board Spaceship Earth who are entirely unaware of their good fortune. Unbeknownst to them their legacy is being held in probate by general ignorance, fear, selfishness, and a myriad of paralyzing professional, licensing, zoning, building laws and the like, as bureaucratically maintained by the incumbent power structures.

Dismaying as all this paralysis may be, it will lead eventually to such crisis that comprehensive dissemination of the foregoing truths ultimately will be accomplished through (1) the world-around-integrated electronic media broadcasting and (2) the computerized switchover from the inherently-inadequate-life-support accounting assumption of yesterday to the adequate-for-everyone-and-everything, time-energy accounting comprehensively employed by the multibillion-galaxied, eternally regenerative Universe itself. An exclusively-to-be-accomplished, world-around-integrated, computer-facilitated, cosmically compatible accounting switchover will make it popularly comprehensible that we do indeed have four billion billionaires on our planet, thereby publicizing that fact and thereby inducing the systematic release of their heritage to all Earthian humans. All this accounting switchover must also be accomplished before 2000 A.D.

Those who make money with money deliberately keep it scarce. Money is not wealth. Wealth is the accomplished technological ability to protect, nurture, support, and accommodate all growful needs of life. Money is only an expediency-adopted means of interexchanging disparately sized, non-equatable items of real wealth.

A shoemaker has ten milk-drinking children. He wants to acquire a milk cow to convert grass into milk to take care of his children. The shoemaker makes his shoes out of cowhide, but that is not the reason he wants the cow. If and when the cow gets too old for milk production, he can butcher it for its meat and obtain a goodly supply of cowhide for his shoemaking.

A cow breeder wants a pair of shoes. He and the shoemaker agree that it takes much more time and individual inputs to produce a milk cow than it does to make a pair of shoes. They agree that you can't cut the cow up and still milk it. So they employ metal, which, being scarce and physically useful, has high and known exchange value and which could be cut apart into whatever fractions are necessary to implement the disparate values of interexchanging. That's how we got money.

Computers do not have to see or feel anything. Computers do not deal in opinion judgments; they simply store, retrieve, and integrate all the information given them. The more relevant the information they are given and the more accurate that information, the better the answers that the computer can give as to the consequences of doing thus and so under a given set of circumstances. Only the computer can cope with the astronomical complexity of integrating the unpredicted potentials of the millions of invisible technology gains in physical capabilities already accomplished. Only world-considerate computer accounting will be able to produce the figures that will persuade all humanity to divert high-science technology from weaponry to livingry. Computer capability will clearly manifest that we indeed now have four billion real-wealth billionaires.

Computer capability will distribute only-computer-readable credit cards to all humanity, whose constant living, travel, and development use will continually integrate all the production starts and holds on world-wide coordinated supplying of the needs of a world-around dynamically dwelling humanity. Computers will relegate all gold to its exclusively functional uses as a supreme electromagnetic conduction-and-reflection medium—with its supremacy amongst metals also manifest as rated in weight and bulk per accomplished function. The computer will relegate all physical substances to their uniquely best functional uses.

All the foregoing considerations demonstrate clearly why the computer accounting switchover is not only possible but mandatory and must be accomplished before the fear and ignorance of the billions of humans involved in the power structure's bureaucracies panic and push the atomic-bomb release buttons. What makes us say "panic" of the major political, religious, and business bureaucracies? Bureaucracies will panic because all the great political, religious, and—most of all—big-business systems would find their activities devastated by the universal physical success of all humanity. All the strengths of all great politics and religion and most of business are derived from the promises they give of assuaging humanity's seemingly tragic dilemma of existing in an unalterable state of fundamental inadequacy of life support.

There are two more prime obstacles to all humanity's realization of its option to "make it." One is the fact that humanity does not understand the language of science. Therefore it does not know that all that science has ever found out is that the physical Universe consists entirely of the most exquisitely interreciprocating technology. Ninety-nine percent of humanity thinks technology is a "new" phenomenon. The world populace identifies technology with (1) weapons and (2) machines that compete with them for their jobs. Most people therefore think they are against technology, not knowing that the technology they don't understand is their only means of exercising their option to "make it" on this planet and in this life.

Fortunately the mathematical coordinate system that has been and as yet is employed by science is not the coordinate system employed by the physical Universe. Nature is always most economical. Science's coordinate system is not most economical and is therefore difficult. Nature never has to stop to calculate before behaving in the most economical manner. Scientists do. Also, fortunately, we have discovered nature's coordinate system, which is elegantly simple and popularly comprehensible. (See *Synergetics*, vols. 1 and 2—Macmillan, 1975, 1979.) Synergetics will make it possible for all humanity to comprehend that physical Universe is technology and that the technology does make possible all humanity's option to endure successfully.

The other prime obstacle to realization of the "great option" is the fact that the world's power structures have always "divided to conquer" and have always "kept divided to keep conquered." As a consequence the power structure has so divided humanity—not only into special function categories but into religious and language and color categories—that individual humans are now helplessly inarticulate in the face of the present crisis. They consider their political representation to be completely corrupted, therefore they feel almost utterly helpless.

Asking a computer "What shall I do?" is useless. You can get an informative answer, however, if you program your question into the computer as follows: "Under the following set of operative circumstances, each having a positive or negative number value in an only-one-value system, which of only two possible results will be obtained if I do so and so? And by how much?"

In 1953 my friend the late Walter Reuther, then president of the United Auto Workers, was about to meet with the board of directors of General Motors to form a new and timely post-World-War-II-oriented labor pact. At that time the first of the "new-scientists" prototyped computers ever to be industrially manufactured were being assembled, put in running order, and fine-tuned by Walter Reuther's skilled machinists. Walter had all his fine-tuning machinists put the following problem into their computers: "In view of the fact that most of General Motors' workers are also its customers, if I demand of General Motors that they grant an unheard-of wage advance plus unprecedented vacation, health, and all conceivable lifetime benefits for all of its workers, amounting sum-totally to so many dollars, which way will General Motors make the most money: by granting or refusing?" All the computers said, "General Motors will make the most profit by granting."

Thus fortified, Walter Reuther made his unprecedented demands on General Motors' directors, who were elected to their position of authority only by the stockholders and who were naturally concerned only with the welfare of those stockholders. Reuther said to the assembled General Motors board of directors: "You are going to grant these demands, not because you now favor labor (which, in fact, you consider to be your enemy), but because by so granting, General Motors will make vastly greater profits. If you will put the problem into your new computers, you will learn that I am right."

The directors said, "Hah-hah! You obviously have used the wrong computers or have misstated the problem to the computers." Soon, however, all their own computers told the directors that Walter was right. They granted his demands. Within three years General Motors was the first corporation in history to net a billion-dollar profit after paying all government taxes—with their profits increasing steadily thereafter for twenty years.

NOTE

Extracted from B. Fuller, *Critical Path* (New York: St. Martin's Press, 1981), pp. xxiii–xxix. Reprinted by permission of St. Martin's Press, LLC.

10

WHAT IS DESIGNING?

John Chris Jones

Literature on design methods began to appear in most industrialized countries in the nineteen fifties and sixties. Before that time it was sufficient to know that designing was what architects, engineers, industrial designers and others did in order to produce the drawings needed by their clients and by manufacturers. Now things are different. There are plenty of professional designers who doubt the procedures that they have been taught to use and plenty of new methods that have been invented to replace the traditional ones.

A common feature of both the criticisms of traditional methods and the proposals for new ones is the attempt to isolate the essence of designing and to write it down as a standard method, or recipe, that can be relied upon in all situations. Some recent definitions and descriptions of designing appear below.

Finding the right physical components of a physical structure (Alexander, 1963)

A goal-directed problem-solving activity (Archer, 1965)

Decision making, in the face of uncertainty, with high penalties for error (Asimow, 1962)

Simulating what we want to make (or do) before we make (or do) it as many times as may be necessary to feel confident in the final result (Booker, 1964)

The conditioning factor for those parts of the product which come into contact with people (Farr, 1966)

Engineering design is the use of scientific principles, technical information and imagination in the definition of a mechanical structure, machine or system to perform prespecified functions with the maximum economy and efficiency (Fielden, 1963)

Relating product with situation to give satisfaction (Gregory, 1966)

The performing of a very complicated act (Jones, 1966a)

The optimum solution to the sum of the true needs of a particular set of circumstances (Matchett, 1968)

The imaginative jump from present facts to future possibilities (Page, 1966)

A creative activity—it involves bringing into being something new and useful that has not existed previously (Reswick, 1965).

The first surprise about these quotations is that they differ so much: only about a tenth of the important words are mentioned more than once. There seem to be as many kinds of design process as there are writers about it. Another surprise is that nobody mentions drawing, the one common action of designers of all kinds. Certainly the above quotations give little support to the idea that designing is the same under all circumstances, and, as we will see later, the methods proposed by design theorists are just as diverse as are their descriptions of the design process.

Perhaps the variety which is so obviously present in the literature on designing is a useful clue. In getting away from drawing, and from the conventional ways of thinking about design, the theorists may together have produced the very thing that is needed to overcome the weakness of traditional designing, that 'thing' being variety itself, a greater variety than that which exists in the experience and expertise of any one designer, of any one design profession or, for that matter, of any one design theorist.

One thing that *is* common to all the above descriptions is that they refer, not to the outcome of designing, but to its ingredients. These, as we have seen, differ as much as do the ingredients in a recipe book, if not more so. If we seek a firmer basis for our thoughts we had better look outside the process itself and try to define designing by its results. A simple way of doing this is to look at the end of the chain of events that begins with the sponsor's wish and moves through the actions of designers, manufacturers, distributors and consumers to the ultimate effects of a newly designed thing upon the world at large. All one can say with certainty is that society, or the world, is not the same as it was before the new design appeared. The new design has, if successful, changed the situation in just the way that the sponsor hoped it would. If the design is unsuccessful (which in many cases is more likely) the final effect may be far from the sponsor's hopes and the designer's predictions but it is still a *change* of one kind or another. In either case we can conclude that the effect of designing is to *initiate change in man-made things*. This, for the moment at least, can be our simple but universal definition of the expanding process that formerly took place on a drawing board but now includes 'R and D', purchasing, design for production, product planning, marketing, system planning and other things besides. As soon as we think about this ultimate definition, we see that it applies not only to the work of engineers, architects and other design professionals but also to the activities of economic planners, legislators, managers, publicists, applied researchers, protestors, politicians and pressure groups who are in the business of getting products, markets, urban areas, public services, opinions, laws, and the like, to change in form and in content. What, in all this diversity, has happened to designers? Have they, under the modern pressures to become more scientific, to participate and to coalesce, lost the special quality that distinguished them from those who do 'uncreative' work? Surely the answer is 'yes'. 'Yes' because designing is outgrowing its reliance upon the mysteries of being able to draw and of being able to foresee future situations in visual form: and 'yes' because all the *non*-designing professions have now to plan their activities on an industrial basis making use of man-machine systems wherever possible.

THE DESIGNER'S OBJECTIVES

We have seen that the traditional objective of a designer was to produce drawings for the approval of his client and for the instruction of manufacturers. Our new definition of designing as the *initiation of change in manmade things* implies that there are other objectives that must be achieved before drawings can be completed, or even started. If the object that is drawn is to bring about prescribed changes in the world at large, the designers must be able to predict the ultimate effects of their proposed design as well as specifying the actions that are needed to bring these effects about. The objectives of designing become less concerned with the product itself and more concerned with the changes that manufacturers, distributors, users, and society as a whole, are expected to make in order to adapt to, and to benefit from, the new design. [...]

The process of bringing about change in manmade things is portrayed as a series of events which starts with the supply of materials and components to a producer and ends with the evolutionary effects upon society-at-large of the system of which the new product forms a part. Each of these events is a stage in the life history of the product and each is dependent upon the one before it. Neither the sponsors of the new design nor its designers play a direct part in product life history: their control ceases before the production process starts. [...]

[...] not all sponsors are financially affected at every stage in product life. More often than not at the present time, but possibly less often in the future, the sponsor does not lose or gain if the design has costs or benefits beyond, say, the point of purchase. Under these circumstances designers may well be aware of good or bad effects of alternative designs upon issues which are important to the people concerned but which are of no direct interest to their sponsor. In such cases the designers may be tempted to offer to the sponsor only those proposals that have 'good' effects. Designers who are tempted to do this are stepping outside their role and taking decisions on behalf of society as a whole. Those who are faced with this particular dilemma, and many are, should not be tempted to legislate by stealth but should instead persuade their sponsor to take the right decision himself. If he will not do so they can resign their positions and bring to the notice of the persons who will be affected by the new design the predictions which, as designers, they are able to make and on which the sponsor has decided not to act. An empirically minded designer might ignore the whole question of acting outside his sponsor's interests and decide to let the imperfections of the present position run their course.

This moral design dilemma is frequent today because the effects of design decisions are growing faster than are the organizations that sponsor design. Typical examples occur in, say, the designing of supersonic aircraft that can impose sonic bangs on large populations, or the planning of new cities that can drastically alter the circumstances of millions of people. The ultimate answer to the dilemma is not for designers to become as gods but for the design process to become more public so that everyone who is affected by design decisions can foresee what can be done and can influence the choices that are made. Such a change would mean that the public effects of designing become the subjects of political debate and also that some of the principles and methods that are the subject of this book become a part of general education.

WHY IS DESIGNING DIFFICULT?

[...] The fundamental problem is that designers are obliged to use current information to predict a future state that will not come about unless their predictions are correct. The final outcome of designing has to be assumed before the means of achieving it can be explored: the designers have to work backwards in time from an assumed effect upon the world to the beginning of a chain of events that will bring the effect about. If, as is likely, the act of tracing out the intermediate steps exposes unforeseen difficulties or suggests better objectives, the pattern of the original problem may change so drastically that the designers are thrown back to square one. It is as if, during a game of chess, one could choose to switch, or be obliged to switch, to a game of snakes and ladders. This instability of the *problem* is what makes designing so much more difficult and more fascinating than it may appear to someone who has not tried it.

The task of the design team is to ensure that each of the many different things of which the sponsor must be sure [...] has two characteristics:

(a) it is within the capacity of the suppliers, producers, distributors, etc., at each stage of product life
(b) it is compatible with that which precedes it and that which follows.

Strong dependencies between distant points in product life history make it difficult to design without much back-tracking and circularity. The role of imagination, the designer's trump card, is to enable him to avoid incompatibility between the one stage and another by changing his original aims to others that are more compatible but equally satisfactory in the long or short run. This sensitivity of aims to detailed decisions makes it difficult or impossible to solve design problems in a wholly logical way but does not prevent their solution within the adaptable apparatus of the human brain. The purpose of this book is to explore some first attempts at permitting many brains, rather than one, to grasp, and to explore, the complexities of designing.

IS DESIGNING AN ART, A SCIENCE OR A FORM OF MATHEMATICS?

The view put forward here is that designing should not be confused with art, with science, or with mathematics. It is a hybrid activity which depends, for its successful execution, upon a proper blending of all three and is most unlikely to succeed if it is exclusively identified with any one. The main point of difference is that of *timing*. Both artists and scientists operate on the physical world as it exists in the *present* (whether it is real or symbolic), while mathematicians operate on abstract relationships that are independent of historical *time*. Designers, on the other hand, are forever bound to treat as real that which exists only in an imagined *future* and have to specify ways in which the foreseen thing can be made to exist.

[…]

NOTE

Extracted from C. J. Jones, *Design Methods* (New York: Wiley, 1992), pp. 3–10. Reprinted with permission of John Wiley & Sons, Inc.

11

DESIGNING ENGINEERS

Louis Bucciarelli

DO YOU KNOW HOW YOUR TELEPHONE WORKS?

A few years ago, I attended a national conference on technological literacy, a topic that had recently attracted attention in the media as well as among scholars concerned with education at both secondary and postsecondary levels in the United States. One of the main speakers, a sociologist, presented data he had gathered in the form of responses to a questionnaire. After detailed statistical analysis, he had concluded that we are a nation of technological illiterates. As an example, he noted how few of us (less than 20 percent) know how our telephone works.

This statement brought me up short. I found my mind drifting and filling with anxiety. Did I know how my telephone works?

I squirmed in my seat, doodled some, then asked myself, What does it mean to know how a telephone works? Does it mean knowing how to dial a local or long-distance number? Certainly I knew that much, but this did not seem to be the issue here. Might it mean knowing how to install a phone, or perhaps knowing what to do when something goes wrong—no dial tone, noise on the line? But most of us do know that in such cases we need only call a service department. No, I suspected the question was to be understood at another level, as probing the respondent's knowledge of what we might call the "physics of the device."

I called to mind an image of a diaphragm, excited by the pressure variations of speaking, vibrating and driving a coil back and forth within a magnetic field, generating a variation in voltage across the terminals of the coil. I could even picture this signal traveling along the wire coming out of the phone into the wall and out onto the pole outside my house. But what then? How do all those different signals from different phones get sorted and routed to their proper destinations? I had no explanation for this.

If this was what the speaker meant, then, he was right: Most of us don't know how our telephone works, and I bet if he asked, most of us don't give a damn about knowing how it works as long as it does. Despair and guilt had yielded to cynicism.

Indeed, I wondered, does he know how his telephone works? Does he know about the heuristics used to achieve optimum routing for long-distance calls? Does he know about the intricacies of the algorithms used for echo and noise suppression? Does he know how a signal is transmitted to and retrieved from a satellite in orbit? Does he know how AT&T, MCI, and the local phone companies are able to use the same network simultaneously? Does he know how many operators are needed to keep the system working, or what those repair people actually do when they climb a telephone pole? Does he know about corporate financing, capital investment strategies, or the role of regulation in the functioning of this expansive and sophisticated communication system?[1]

Does anyone know how their telephone works?

How about the designer of the device? Surely, he or she must know. I followed this line of thought for a while, but again, I found my footing less sure than I had anticipated. Indeed, from my own observations, I can claim fairly confidently that there is no single individual alone who knows how all the ingredients that constitute a telephone system work together to keep each of our phones functioning. There is no one "maker." Instead, inside each firm, there are different interests, perspectives, and responsibilities—corporate planning, engineering, research, production, marketing, servicing, managing—and consequently different ways in which the telephone "works."

At this point I retreated from cynicism. The question now struck me as interesting, not as an instrument for testing technological literacy, but in its own right: What does it mean when someone claims to know how their telephone works? I conjectured that there could well be no unique criterion for judging responses; there could be as many legitimate, that is to say accurate, ways to describe how the telephone works as there are respondents.[2]

The narrow view of the workings of the telephone has the quality of a myth. But while the story about vibrating diaphragms and coils moving in a magnetic field may provide coherence amid complexity, may give us the confidence to respond in the affirmative to a sociologist on the track of technological literacy, and may encapsulate some particular facet of technical truth, taking it as the measure of a person's understanding of how today's sophisticated and dynamic system of communication works is naive.

This naivete is just one failing of the sociologist's research program; another is the presumption that you can test a person's "technological literacy" by literary means alone. Thus, if a respondent has just finished reading about the telephone in the *Encyclopedia of Science*, the sociologist would no doubt find him or her technologically literate. But this is neither sufficient nor necessary as a display of knowing how the telephone works. Indeed, it is little more than a test of reading retention.

No, the "knowing how it works" that has meaning and significance is knowing how to do

something with the telephone—how to act on it and react to it, how to engage and appropriate the technology according to one's needs and responsibilities. Thus the everyday user around the house from the age of seven to seventy, the person who repairs the lines, the new product engineer, and the corporate executive each appropriates the telephone to his or her own interests, and each knows how it works.

Refocusing in this way, dragging myself away from an instrumental story derived from a vision of the scientific origins of the device, led me to reformulate the question. Rather than "Do you know how your telephone works?" I would ask, "How does the telephone symbolize, alienate, serve, or have meaning for you?" With this question we might be able to test the breadth and depth of a person's technological understanding and competence. Note, too, how, with this reorientation, the object loses its grip and the social context of its workings assumes primacy.

It is the fixation on the physics of a device that promotes the object as an icon in the design process. For while different participants in design have different interests, different responsibilities, and different technical specialties, it is the object as they see and work with it that patterns their thought and practice, not just when they must engage the physics of the device but throughout the entire design process, permeating all exchange and discourse within the subculture of the firm. This way of thinking is so prevalent within contemporary design that I have given it a label—"object-world" thinking—and will now detour a bit to give a preview of what I mean by the term. I will start with a less complex and more ancient technology and explore what it might mean to know how it works from the perspective of an object world.

HOW A CHAIR WORKS—ONE PERSPECTIVE

Clearly we all know how to sit in a chair, so in this respect we know how it works: A chair is for sitting. That is how it functions. Unfortunately, this description is akin to saying that a telephone is for making telephone calls. Surely we can do better. (You never know when a sociologist is going to telephone to ask if you know how your chair works.) How about this?

A chair is a supported seat. A seat is a two-dimensional, finite, contoured surface, made of a rigid or flexible material, which provides immediate support to at least the buttocks of the human body. This support is sufficient to enable a person, when seated, to lift both feet off the ground without falling over. The surface is supported by a structure intervening with the ground.

A skeptic might interject here, "Does this mean that a hammock is a chair? Or a bed? Or a horse?" In response, we can start adding details. We might, for example, say that a chair is made of inanimate material. There goes the horse.[3] Or we can pass the buck back to a simpler precedent and build upon that:

A chair is a stool with a backrest, and a stool is a board elevated from the ground by supports.[4]

But this is still not good enough, for we still have to explain how a stool works. Why do most stools have three legs while a chair has four? We must strive to be even more scientific:

A chair is a four-legged stool with a back. Although three legs, or points of support, are sufficient to support the seat, the stability of seating is enhanced if we add a fourth point of support since, for said stability, a line connecting the center of gravity of an extended body (yours or mine) to the center of gravity of the earth (or whatever planetary body one happens to be seated upon) must intersect the plane through the feet of the legs of the stool or chair, at a point interior to the three- or four-sided plane figure having the feet as vertices. With four legs, one can assure stability with a square seat.[5]

This, then, is a chair and how it works. We can call this the principle of operation of the chair—what Robert Pirsig would call its underlying form.[6] This is the "physics of the device" knowledge that is often taken as the hallmark of technological literacy. It constitutes a sparse, efficient, generic, abstract identity of a chair, just as the identity of a circle is defined by the Platonic ideal of "all points equidistant from a fixed point."[7]

Given this principle, we can imagine an infinite variety of particular embodiments that would function as a chair. A chair can be finely carved or sparse yet stately. We can add arms and cushions to create a throne—or set the thing up on curved rails to make a rocker—a matter of controlled stability—if we want to get frivolous.

I don't claim that this generic description is the best possible in any sense. Nor is it unique. Indeed, there are other object worlds we should enter to define more fully how a chair works. We can talk about the forces borne by the legs, which distort and deform relative to the seat when a person sits down. We can even do a finite-element analysis on the computer and estimate the internal stresses in the legs, the seat, and the back. And we certainly ought to describe the craft knowledge of chair object worlds: how to join the legs and back to the seat, whether or not it is preferable to make the back an extension of the rear two legs. All of this is part of an object world perspective on how a chair works.

HISTORICAL ROOTS—OBJECT WORLDS

But this is neither a physics text nor a chair design manual. My intent instead is to illustrate a particular way of thinking about and framing an answer to the question "How does it work?" This way of thinking will prove essential to understanding the thought and practice of participants in contemporary engineering design.

This has not always been the case. The first chair makers did not need to enter the world of geometry, consider the conditions that ensure static equilibrium, or call upon mathematical theories describing stress and strain within beams, legs, and arms in order to do their work. Vernacular technique was all they needed. One might claim that the underlying form of the chair was embedded in the crafter's rules of thumb, sense of symmetry, feel for an awl in making a cut, or know-how about joining wood to wood, but that knowledge remained unarticulated, tacit, and sensual (as far as we know). It was not of a kind with contemporary scientific understanding—for example, a Ptolemaic astronomer's explanation of planetary orbits, which relied upon the abstract notion of uniform circular motion and the machinery of epicycles and deferents (the elements of underlying form of the motion of the planets) and was drawn out in texts for all to read who could. But then, until relatively recently, the heavens were of a different nature than the stuff of the sublunary region. Indeed this "underlying form" way of thinking about earthly, mundane things like chairs and telephones was very much a child of the Renaissance. With the shattering of the perfection of the heavens, with the connection of the terrestrial to the celestial (the earth is not below, on center; the sun has spots; the planets are not wandering stars and themselves have moons; our moon is mountainous and, like Newton's apple, is falling toward the earth), the decaying stuff of this world became a candidate for abstract philosophical thought and discourse. Some attribute to Galileo this new way of framing and responding to the question.

Image 6 shows Galileo's cantilever beam.[8] He wanted to know how it works in object-world terms. That is, he was seeking, and felt he had found, its underlying form. He made the following claim:

A solid prism or cylinder of glass, steel, wood, or other material capable of fracture, which suspended lengthwise will sustain a very heavy weight attached to it, will sometimes be broken across … by a very much smaller weight, according as its length exceeds its thickness.[9]

Already we note the generic nature of his vision of "glass, steel, wood, or other material capable of fracture" and the instrumental relationship, somewhat hidden to the modern eye, in the proposition "be broken across … by a very much smaller weight according as its length exceeds its thickness." His demonstration immediately follows:

Let us imagine the solid prism ABCD fixed into a wall at the part AB; and at the other end is understood to be the force of the weight E. (Assuming always that the wall is vertical and the prism or cylinder is fixed into the wall at right angles.) It is evident that if it must break, it will break at the place B, where the niche in the wall serves as support, BC being the arm of the lever on which the force is applied. The thickness BA of the solid is the other arm of this lever, wherein resides the resistance, … the moment of the force applied at C has, to the moment of the resistance which exists in the thickness of the prism (that is, in the attachment of the base BA with its contiguous part), the same ratio that the length CB has to one-half of BA. Hence the absolute resistance to fracture in the prism BD (being that which it makes against being pulled apart lengthwise) … has, to the resistance against breakage by means of the lever BC, the same ratio as that of the length BC to one-half of AB … . And let this be our first proposition.

The figure is striking—a fine etching in the Renaissance genre of nature observed. But it is also disconcerting. There is a lack of proportion in the weight hooked to the end of the beam relative to the beam itself. And the wall looks like the decaying remnant of some edifice that was perhaps once grand. How is it that the structure remains intact, supporting this massive weight, while the wall at the root of the beam seems fallen to such a sorry state? And the letters of the alphabet—what are they doing in this landscape?

The image is not to be read in this naturalistic way. No, it is a new kind of figure, a new image

Image 6   Telephone: *Model 302*. Designed by Henry Dreyfuss (American, 1904–1972). Manufactured by Western Electric Manufacturing Company for the Bell Telephone Company, ca. 1937. Metal, paper, rubber-sheathed cord. Cooper-Hewitt, National Design Museum, Smithsonian Institution; museum purchase with the Decorative Arts Association Acquisition Fund, 1994-73-2. Photo: Hiro Ihara.

to go with a new science. Galileo means to help the reader follow his argument—that the beam will fail at the end B if the weight at the end C becomes too large. But there is more to it than that. The reader must see in the figure an angular lever with its fulcrum at B, one arm extending out along the beam to the weight at the end C, the other, shorter arm, extending from B up to A. Then the reader must imagine an internal force, a "resistance" acting over the arm AB, directed to the left, and visualize how this resistance would balance the weight suspended at E through the action of the lever. From the principle of equilibrium of the lever one obtains that the ratio of the force that will break the beam when applied transversely at E to the force that will break the beam when applied longitudinally at AB—a

force Galileo calls "the prism's absolute resistance to fracture"—is the same as the ratio of one-half the distance AB to the distance BC.

This is how we are meant to read Galileo's proposition. He is explaining how a cantilever beam works by revealing its underlying form. His explanation is not a proof, though. The law of the lever was already well known. What is significant and innovative is the association of the workings of a load-bearing beam with the geometry and principle of the lever. The new science comes in positing a relation between the beam as physical artifact and vernacular technique and the beam as abstract lever and mathematical artifice.

As a *physical artifact*, the beam has a "thickness," a "length," a "mortise," and a "weight" at the end. These are significant, but the embellishments of these characteristics—the crumbling nature of the wall, the ivy, the grain in the wood, even the material from which the beam is made—are not.

As an *abstract lever*, there is a fulcrum at B, a force applied at C, and an (internal) resistance that "opposes the separation of the part BD lying outside the wall from that portion lying inside," and they bear the same ratio as half the length (lever arm) BA to the length (lever arm) BC. That is how the beam works.

Indeed, that is a cantilever beam. With Galileo, the questions "What is it?" and "How does it work?" collapse into one. When put, they solicit the same response. The attempt to answer either brings out the fact that a cantilever beam is a lever, just as a chair can be seen as a stable platform. In this, "we take for true being that which is only a method."[10]

WHO DEFINES THE WORKINGS?

Seeking underlying form is but one approach to defining how a telephone, a chair, or a cantilever beam works. It guides participants designing within object worlds but doesn't always make sense for those of us who don't engage technology in this intimate way. Indeed, it is not always relevant, or all there is to the workings of technique; and sometimes it sounds downright silly to speak of a chair in this way.

For example, as you stand before Napoleon's throne in the Louvre, you are probably not thinking about underlying form. Or if you encounter a Rietveld chair in the Centre Pompidou, with its bright red back, glossy black seat, and its spindly arms, legs, and interlacing struts all tipped with yellow, you might think about underlying form only if it crosses your mind to wonder whether or not it would collapse if you sat on it. Or if you spot a Le Corbusier lounge chair in the window of a fashionable shop along the Rue Rivoli, priced at 12,380 francs, its inner constitution is not likely to be the first thing that passes through your mind. You don't spend $2,000 on a four-legged stool with a back.

A Rietveld or Corbusier chair or Napoleon's throne "works" as something other than what you or I am seated on at the moment. They work as art, as fashion, as symbol of power and prestige. Their primary function is not to support bodies. Their one common characteristic is that they are uncommon. Each has its own special identity that renders irrelevant our generic and abstract description. Our object-world definition of chair is meaningful only if we are talking about an anonymous chair. The anonymity of this chair is of a piece with the generic and abstract response we give to the question of how it works. It is no coincidence that Galileo's vision takes root at the first glimmerings of an industrial revolution.[11]

Far removed from the Renaissance, most of us don't see technology in terms of underlying form. We live in a world where each object appears in its particularity, as an artifact made of hardware or as a system of rules and constraints. The underlying form remains hidden, sometimes intentionally; our perceptions of how a telephone, a chair, a photovoltaic module, or an x-ray inspection machine function can be correspondingly "superficial." Yet we do know how they work, as shown by our knowing how to pass them by, work through them, remake them, or use them, even if but briefly.

Not all relations are superficial. Often the connection is dictated. A worker in a machine shop who tends a semiautomatic tool, which requires the insertion, then removal of the workpiece in but a second or two, has little choice in how to relate to technique. Other relationships are direct and intense by choice. Bricolage and do-it-yourself are possible, as Pirsig has so beautifully demonstrated in *Zen and the Art of Motorcycle Maintenance*. For example, an owner's careful and constant ministrations might cause a motorcycle or automobile to reveal a personality; or an office worker might become enthused about "hacking," learning to navigate the computer system in a personal and deliberate way. Moreover, even an ephemeral connection can be quite intense, as when a family reacts to the siting of a recycling facility across the town field; they may never have seen one, but they still have enough of a sense of how one might work to want to know more before they go along with the idea.

The way in which one sees how technology works is very much a matter of the nature of the encounter—whether it is in passing, intense in bricolage or dictation, or lay-political. Our relations to and hence our perspectives on technology may vary, but in general, as user, traveler, player, viewer, or tender, we do not have the same connection to technology that its makers have. However we appropriate technique, most of us do not see technology in terms of its formal structure, underlying form, or *inner constitution*.[12]

Those who are concerned with technological literacy often seem to be claiming that this is a sad state of affairs. Others see a deeper problem in our relations with technology, one that won't necessarily be solved by a universal program of education. They claim that we have embraced a new brand of slavery as we accept subservience to technique over which we have little control, much less understanding. Or, to put this idea in terms of a less odious metaphor, technology now legislates and structures our lives, yet we seem not to have been given the opportunity to vote.[13]

How does your telephone work? How does your chair really function? These questions fade in significance next to those that ask about legislating and ruling lives. Even if we can answer the sociologist "correctly" and thus be counted among the technologically literate, we remain uncomfortable: What disturbs us is the thought that, whatever our level of technological literacy, we are powerless to affect the form and function of the machinery that surrounds us, aids and comforts us, alienates and confuses us, improves our productivity, makes too much noise, sometimes leaks, can be beautiful, can be ugly, is often indispensable … . There it is: the telephone rings, and we answer.

It is a small step from these thoughts to a grand vision of technology that is autonomous in its workings, running our lives and out of the control of not just us ordinary citizens but engineers,

managers, and corporate strategists who themselves don't fully understand what they are doing.

NOTES

Extracted from L. Bucciarelli, *Designing Engineers* (Cambridge, Mass.: MIT Press, 1994), pp. 2–12. © 1994 Massachusetts Institute of Technology, by permission of the MIT Press.

1. "Only 19 percent believe that they have a clear understanding of how their telephone works." From Jon D. Miller, Technological Literacy: Some Concepts and Measures," Public Opinion Laboratory, Northern Illinois University, 19 February 1986. Note the inferred wording of the question. In this form, it is as much a test of a consumer's confidence in his or her technical understanding as it is a test of the latter. The qualifier "clear" no doubt assures a low positive response. Evidently, we will never know what respondents do know about how their telephone works. But note that, with the question phrased in this way, it is not necessary for the sociologist to know the slightest thing about how a telephone works in order to complete his research. I assume that a graduate student did the dialing.

2. This is not to claim that "anything goes"— that is, that some respondents will not offer erroneous accounts in their attempts to please a sociologist. Nor should one conclude that the telephone can be put to use for any arbitrary purpose or that the telephone is value free or neutral. It is a long way from the claim that different persons have different relationships with one and the same technology, the claim made here, to the fantasy that depicts technique as the sterile embodiment of nature's laws, devoid of human intent and interests.

3. The exclusion of ludicrous but rational and logically possible readings of statements and claims from the serious business of design is a matter of context. The neophyte engineer's

suggestion will often be greeted with a laugh, and he or she learns, in this way, that "a horse is not a chair around here."

4. Christopher Dresser, *Principles of Decorative Design* (London; New York: Cassell, Peter & Galpin, 1873), quoted in E. Russell, P. Garner, and J. Read, *A Century of Chair Design* (Chicago: Academy Editions, 1980).

5. The knowledge that three points of support are all that are required to support a seat (and to define a plane) is reflected in ancient pottery vessels. Those pots and tankards showing four legs generally mimic some form of animal life. The problem with four legs is that you had better have a level surface to set your vessel down upon or to place your chair on if you don't want the contents sloshing about or yourself rocking in an uncontrolled way.

6. Robert Pirsig, *Zen and the Art of Motorcycle Maintenance* (New York: William Morrow, 1974).

7. Note how some sort of abstract sketch or figure would be extremely useful for describing the chair's principle of operation. Not a glossy picture of a Le Corbusier chaise lounge, but a simple, geometrical figure with a few lines for legs, the outline of the plane figure whose vertices are located at the four points where the feet hit level ground, a special symbol for center of gravity, and finally a line drawn from the center of gravity, through the plane at the base of the feet, directed toward the earth's center. For stability, the intersection of this line with the plane at the feet must lie within the interior of the plane figure.

8. For this image, see http://www.lindahall.org/events_exhib/exhibit/exhibits/civil/strength.shtml

9. Galilei Galileo, *Discorsi e dimastrazioni mateingtiche, intorno a due nuoue scienze* (Leida: Appresso gli Elsevivii, 1638). For a standard translation, see *Dialogues Concerning Two New Sciences*, trans. Henry Crew. Alfonso de Salvio (New York: Macmillan, 1914), p. 116 (fig. 17).

10. Husserl attributes to Galileo the conception of nature as, in reality, possessing a mathematical structure behind the appearances. The full Husserl quote is 'The *Ideenkleid* (the ideational veil) of mathematics and mathematical physics represents and (at the same time) disguises the empirical reality and leads us to take for True Being that which is only a method." Quoted in Robert Cohen and Marx Wartofsky, eds., *Boston Studies in the Philosophy of Science*, vol. 2 (New York: Humanities Press, 1965), p. 286. Or, as put by Aron Gurwitsch in his "Comments on Marcuse" in the same volume (p. 293), "The world is not in reality as it looks."

See also Michael Lynch, "The Externalized Retina: Selection and Mathematization in the Visual Documentation of Objects in the Life Sciences," in Michael Lynch and Steve Woolgar, eds., *Representation in Scientific Practice* (Cambridge, MA: MIT Press, 1990), pp. 153–186, especially pp. 169ff.

11. Even anonymity is not enough to ensure that we have an appropriate response to the question. Take an electric chair. Clearly, this is not particular in the "one-of-a-kind," museum-item sense (although no doubt some wax museum has one on display). How does an electric chair work? What is an electric chair? Our abstract way of answering would have to move beyond Galilean mechanics and refer to voltages and currents, resistive paths through the human body as well as the location of its center of gravity. But, again, we don't quite have it right.

12. Ian Hacking, *Representing and Intervening* (Cambridge: Cambridge University Press, 1983).

13. This line of criticism is forcefully presented in Langdon Winner, *The Whale and the Reactor* (Chicago: University of Chicago Press, 1986).

SUCCESS AND FAILURE IN DESIGN

Henry Petroski

Everything has two handles—by one of which it ought to be carried and by the other not.

—Epictetus[1]

Ur-implements were most likely those things found close at hand. Thus, the finger would have been the obvious choice to draw lines in the sand, and then to point out features of the plan. But the finger is blunt, and the hand to which it is attached obscuring. The humble twig or stick certainly became the natural extension of the finger, allowing the designer to stand away from a

Image 7   Frank Gehry's Disney Hall, Los Angeles. Photo by Eric Orner.

drawing and thus obscure it less. But even the act of picking up a stick can involve design. A good number of sticks lying about might be rejected as too short or too curvy, too flaccid or too brittle. They would not even have to be touched to be considered failures. A proper pointer might have had to be chosen from and broken off of a nearby bush or tree. Once chosen, it could have been held at either end—but the thicker generally feels better in the hand, leaving the more slender free to be more effective as a pointer. All these choices and decisions made in anticipation of the stick's use would have been ones of design.

An alternative, of course, was to shape a pointer out of a suitable piece of wood. In the nineteenth century, when the images projected by magic lanterns grew to great size, it took a larger and larger pointer to reach a detail that a lecturer wished to emphasize. This led to the making (and selling) of long, straight, and slender pointers out of appropriate pieces of timber. However, with considerable length came not inconsiderable mass, and a twelve-foot-long pointer could be rather unwieldy. Lecturers must have had a difficult time holding one at the very end, even for a short period of time, and the thicker end of the pointer might have had to be rested on the stage to be used without undue discomfort.[2]

The fabricated wooden pointer of more modest size was once standard equipment in the classroom. Though subtly tapered like a stick, it had the aesthetic and functional advantage of apt proportion. It was usually fitted with a rubber tip—to soften its tap and scratch on the blackboard—and a metal eye by which to hang it from a hook. The wooden pointer may be said to have been a "perfected" design in the twentieth century, but it had a propensity for being mislaid or being broken over a mischievous pupil and thus rendered less effective for its intended purpose. Even on college and university campuses, where corporal punishment is rare, wooden pointers had a habit of disappearing. Guest lecturers, wishing to stand away from the projected images they were describing, often were offered an ad-hoc pointer in the form of a disembodied automobile antenna, a yardstick or meterstick, a strip of slender wooden molding, or some other remnant from the lumberyard. These succeeded marginally as pointers but had severe aesthetic failings.

More fastidious lecturers began to carry their own mechanical pointers, usually in the form of a purposely designed telescoping wand fitted with a pocket clip.[3] Collapsed, these implements looked like just another pen or pencil in the engineer's pocket arsenal. Unfortunately, in larger auditoriums, the limited length of these and most pointers required lecturers to stretch in the spotlight of their slides to tap things at the top of the illuminated image. (Some speakers held the pointer in midair between projector and screen to cast a shadow on the object of interest.)

The laser pointer, which came into prominence in the 1990s, was at first typically thick in the hand (to accommodate its electronics and batteries) but had a good range. Before long, such pointers came in more slender pocket models and in shorter, key-chain styles. The laser pointer has clear advantages over the simple stick, but it also has its own shortcomings. Batteries are required and they run down, the shaky hand of a nervous lecturer is amplified in the jerky motions of the glowing red dot, and the eyes of the audience are at risk. Moreover, the red dot can be difficult to see against certain backgrounds, thus rendering the high-tech pointer inferior even to its low-tech predecessors. To correct this problem, more electronically complicated and thus more expensive green-beam laser pointers, which reportedly can be as much as thirty times as intense as the red, came to be introduced.

Technological advances generally tend toward but never reach perfection; there is always some way in which they can be improved. Lecturers found themselves encumbered with a slide changer in one hand, a laser pointer in the other, and thus no hand left to turn the pages of their notes. On more than one occasion, I have seen lecturers press the slide advance button when they wanted to activate the laser beam, and vice versa. Slide changer controls came to be added to laser pointers, whose casing had naturally to be enlarged—into devices that were shaped not unlike the familiar domestic remote control, which most hands feel quite comfortable holding and manipulating. The laser pointer was thus at the same time evolving toward both intensification and complexification. But not every combination worked for every user.

Success and failure are the two sides of the coin of design. This is nothing new. Like the stick pointer, virtually all of the earliest things used in prehistoric times can be assumed to have been found in nature: caves in which to seek shelter, rocks with which to hunt (and fight), fallen branches to reach fruit high on trees, sticks to poke into beehives and insect holes, shells to scoop up water from a lake, fallen logs and stepping-stones to cross a stream. Though such found things may have needed no essential crafting, their mere selection for a purpose made them designed. Everything we have used since has also been designed, in the sense that it has been acquired, adapted, altered, arranged, or assembled deliberately to accomplish a specific objective. Designed things are the means by which we achieve desired ends. If the ends have not always justified the means, they have at least inspired them. But how do things evolve from sticks and stones to bricks and mortar? From shells to spoons? From logs to bridges? From caves to castles?

Whenever we use some *thing* to do *some*thing we expect it to do, we test it. Such testing is not necessarily conscious, but it is always effective and consequential. Indeed, with the testing of each individual example of a thing we also test the general hypothesis on which our expectation is based, whether consciously or not. If the thing passes the test, we declare it a success—at least until the next test. Successful tests are unremarkable. If the thing does not pass a test, we say that it (and the hypothesis) has failed. Failures are remarkable. The failures always teach us more than the successes about the design of things. And thus the failures

often lead to redesigns—to new, improved things. Modern designers and manufacturers can do this on their own, or they can be encouraged to do it by consumers, who essentially are design critics who vote with their purchases.

I have a versatile piece of carry-on luggage that I have subjected to many tests. It is a roll-on that is sized to fit into the overhead bin of an airplane. The bag has a good many zippers, which give me access to a variety of outside pockets, one of which is expandable. When my carry-on was new, I often stuffed that pocket with books and folders, thinking that I would not have to carry a separate book bag. With the pocket so stuffed, the bag often failed to fit into the overhead. Such experiences taught me the limits to which I could expand the pocket, even though it itself had much more capacity. On the front of the bag there is a smaller pocket, which is not expandable but can be opened from either end. On one trip I put a book in that pocket and closed the top zipper but forgot to close the bottom one, which I had opened the night before to retrieve the same book. I only realized that my book had fallen out in the hotel lobby when a kind stranger ran after me with it. The bag functions as designed only when I use it as designed.

My roll-on has two conventional handles, one on the top and one on the side. I have found the top handle most convenient for carrying the bag up and down stairs, something I do often in taking commuter flights. The top handle is also good for carrying the bag down the aisle on larger planes. Early on, the way I lifted the bag into the overhead made the side handle inaccessible for retrieving it at the end of the flight. That had led to some torn fingernails. Now, I pay attention to how I stow the bag, making sure one of the handles is always facing out. Both handles are backed with Velcro, so that when they are not in use they hug the bag and do not get abused by the luggage of other passengers or by baggage handlers when I check my luggage.

Since it is a roll-on, my bag also has a collapsible handle by which I can pull it through airports and parking lots. When the bag is heavily packed, pulling it by this handle can get a bit uncomfortable. I have noticed that airline pilots and flight attendants, who almost invariably have this brand of luggage, tend to sling a second bag over the front rather than pile it on top, as I had tended to do. Now I follow the example of the professionals. The slinging method counterbalances somewhat the weight of the roll-on and thus lessens the downward force on the pulling hand, hence making it less likely for me to have to change hands frequently.

Once, when we were on a long trip, my wife bought a new roll-on bag. She did so in a store that carried a great variety, and so which one to choose among the many closely similar designs was not an easy decision. After narrowing down the choices to a few that had the right amount and arrangement of luggage space, she tested each of them by trying its handles and pulling the bag (empty) along the store's carpeted aisle. It was only after she had chosen and bought her bag and was rolling it back to the hotel that we realized that the wheel of her roll-on made a lot more noise than did mine, especially when pulled over a scored sidewalk. Furthermore, as I learned when I pulled her heavily loaded bag one day, its handle was shorter and thus closer to the ground than the handle on mine. This had not mattered so much when the bag was empty, but it did matter when the bag was full and heavy. The tests to which the bag had been subjected in the store did not represent the more trying conditions under which it would be used in an airport terminal. What had seemed to be a piece of luggage whose design differed from mine only in aesthetic ways proved to be functionally very different as well. Its performance was not up to what was expected, and we both have learned to be more critical shoppers the next time we buy a piece of luggage or anything else.

"Failure is an unacceptable difference between expected and observed performance," according to the comprehensive definition used by the Technical Council on Forensic Engineering of the American Society of Civil Engineers.[4] Good design is thus proactive failure analysis, something that both a designer and the chooser among designs ought to practice. Anticipating and identifying how a design can fail—or even just be perceived to fail—is the first step in making it a success. Still, whether we are designing or buying luggage, or building or occupying warehouses, we can overlook the details that make the difference between success and failure. Just as a roll-on need not fall apart completely to be a disappointment, so a building need not collapse catastrophically to be considered a failure. A warehouse with a door narrower than inventory it was built to store is a decided failure.

An "unacceptable difference between expected and observed performance" can result when a structure merely settles and cracks. In such a case, there can be considerable disagreement over how much should have been expected and how much should be considered unacceptable. Unfortunately, sometimes expectations are articulated only in retrospect—in a courtroom. Regardless, when a part of something engineered to be successful fails, the entire design has failed; and it is a signal for examination, for change, for redesign.

The new Walt Disney Concert Hall in Los Angeles is a striking piece of architectural and engineering design. Frank Gehry's imagination has given the hard stainless steel facade the appearance of soft and pliable flower petals. Shortly after completion of the building, however, an unexpected problem arose. The surface of one section—whose cladding had a bright finish instead of the brushed texture of the rest of the structure—reflected sunlight onto a condominium building across the street, blinding its tenants and raising the temperature in their living space by as much as 15 degrees Fahrenheit. Had the unacceptable result been anticipated, a nonreflecting finish might have been used. When I visited the concert hall, the offending surface was draped over with a netlike fabric to mitigate the unwanted effect while a permanent solution was being sought. That solution—or redesign—was, not surprisingly, to dull the bright finish, and it only remained to choose the process for doing so.[5] After almost a year of studying the problem, it was announced that the offending section would be sandblasted to "dull the finish so that it resembles the exterior of the rest of the building."[6]

Had the corner of the concert hall been oriented differently, the stainless steel cladding might not have reflected the sunlight into the condo or any other nearby building, and an issue would not have arisen. The Disney Hall facade might have been hailed as an unqualified success. Indeed, the critical acclaim for the structure might likely have reinforced Gehry's conviction that juxtaposing bright and brushed stainless steel produced the desired aesthetic effect. Without the corrective required by the reflection problem, future Gehry buildings might have been designed with increasingly daring variations on the use of such cladding—perhaps drawing further acclaim. As long as the facades did not concentrate excessive sunlight onto broiling neighbors, the bright cladding might have been used with increasing confidence, until what happened in Los Angeles happened to some subsequent project. That incontrovertible failure would have revealed a fault that had only been latent in all the earlier "successful" buildings.

The unintended consequence of reflected sunlight is only one of myriad ways in which an architectural design can fail. One winter, another new Gehry building—the Weatherhead School of Management at Case Western Reserve University—began to shed snow and ice off its sloping stainless steel roof, potentially endangering pedestrians. The smoothly curving surface provided no barrier to stop the accumulated frozen precipitation, once loosened, from arcing off the building like skiers racing over a mogul. "The benefits of a striking building outweigh a minor problem," one architect is reported to have said. He also said, "If you're going to have that building shining and beautiful and doing all the wonderful things it does, this is a small price to pay." Not everyone agreed. Among the fixes contemplated in Cleveland was the installation of heating cables to prevent the snow and ice from building up in the first place.[7]

Getting things just right can be tricky in any context. When a new commuter car—designated the M7—was being developed for the Long Island Rail Road, passenger complaints about earlier car designs were taken into consideration. After many years of service, the neoprene seats found on the earlier M1 and M3 model cars had "lost much of their bounce" and developed "sinkholes," which were blamed for backaches. So the seats on the M7 were "injected with silicone, given lumbar support and a headrest" to improve them ergonomically. Riders had complained also about the absence of an armrest for the window seat, and so in the redesign "one was molded into the wall of the car." Focus group members who otherwise liked the seats on another model car, the double-decker C3, reported of it that "they found the armrests just a tad short." So the armrests on the M7 were made four-tenths of an inch longer than those of the C3. Yet this seemingly insignificant but well-intended modification made by the designers "snagged their dream of design perfection on the railroad cars of the future." Within two years of the M7's introduction, "73 claims for torn clothing had been filed," blaming not only the extra length but also the "rubber eraser"-like material of the new armrests for catching trousers and not letting go when the unlucky commuter got up from his or her seat.[8]

Blaming an unfortunate occurrence on bad design may make for a convincing damage claim—or even a successful lawsuit—but the connection between intention and result, between cause and effect, is not always what it seems. Over three thousand intersections in New York City have signs instructing pedestrians, "To Cross Street/ Push Button/Wait for Walk Signal."[9] A good deal of time often elapses between pushing the button and getting the go-ahead, but conscientious citizens obediently wait. They presume, one presumes, that a delay is part of the system's design. It may be a "bad design," but the light does change—eventually.

New York intersections began to be fitted with these "semi-actuated signals" around 1964. They were the "brainstorm of the legendary traffic commissioner, Henry Barnes, the inventor of the 'Barnes Dance,' the traffic system that stops all vehicles in the intersection and allows pedestrians to cross in every direction at the same time." Walk buttons were installed mostly where a minor street intersected a major one, along which traffic would be stopped only if a pavement sensor detected a vehicle waiting to enter from the minor street or if someone pushed the button, causing the light to change ninety seconds hence. With increased traffic (by 1975, about 750,000 vehicles were entering Manhattan daily), the signals were being tripped frequently by minor-street traffic. The walk buttons hardly seemed necessary, and pushing them interfered with the coordination of newly installed computer-controlled traffic lights along many thoroughfares. Consequently, most of the devices were deactivated by the late 1980s, but the buttons themselves and the signs bearing the instructions for their use remained in place. Evidently there was never any official announcement about the status of the "mechanical placebos."[10]

Though most New York City traffic-crossing buttons are thus "off" when they appear to be "on," many familiar consumer electronics devices in fact remain "on" when we turn them "off." This passive design feature is necessary so that our stereos, televisions, and other home appliances can respond to the touch of a keypad or the signal from a remote control. According to one study, a sizable percentage of microwave ovens "consume more energy in standby (running their clocks and keeping their touch panels active) than in cooking" over the course of a year. This phenomenon has come to be termed "standby power waste" and amounts to as much as 10 percent of electricity used in U.S. homes.[11]

Similarly bizarre design quirks arise when computers are really "on." In 1998 IBM incorporated a very useful feature into its ThinkPad: The keyboard can be illuminated, which is obviously handy when typing in poor light, such as in the darkened cabin of an airplane. However, because there was no place to put an on-off switch or button or key dedicated to the lighted-keyboard feature, it is activated by pressing the unintuitive combination Fn+PgUp. Even though there is a lamp icon on the PgUp key, evidently few users knew its significance or that the keyboard could be lighted up, and so they continued to type in the dark. According to an IBM director of design, "Not everything can have a button. If we didn't limit them, we'd be looking at products with as many buttons as an accordion."[12] Judgment calls pervade design.

NOTES

Extracted from H. Petroski, *Success through Failure: The Paradox of Design* (Princeton, N.J.: *Princeton* University Press, 2006), pp. 44–57. Reprinted by permission of Princeton University Press.

1. *The Encheiridion*, trans. W. A. Oldfather (Loeb Classical Library), 43. Quoted from Bartlett's *Familiar Quotations*, 16th ed. (Boston: Little Brown, 1992), 108.

2. Long, slender pointers would naturally be prone to breaking, and few of them survive in lecture halls today. Professor David Billington, who employs two slide projectors when he lectures to his class in an auditorium at Princeton University, makes use of a long window pole as a pointer. Throughout much of the lecture that I attended in December 2004, he rested the end of the pole on the stage.

3. Some years ago, as a momento of a lecture that I gave to the Graduate Materials Engineering Program at the University of Dayton, I was presented with a collapsible pointer of a handsome design. Closed, it is the size and weight of a slender Cross pen, but with a smooth, matte black finish. Telescoped open, the pointer betrays the chrome of an automobile antenna, but with a black plastic tip, which shows up

well against the white background of the slides of equations, charts, and graphs typical of those then shown at a technical lecture.

4. Kenneth L. Carper, "Construction Pathology in the United States," *Structural Engineering International* 1 (1996), 57.

5. Jia-Rui Chong, "Whose Bright Idea Was This?" *Los Angeles Times*, February 21, 2004, B1.

6. Robin Pogrebin, "Gehry Would Blast Glare Off Los Angeles Showpiece," *New York Times*, December 2, 2004, B1, B9.

7. Damien Guevara, "Snow, Ice Slide Off New Building: CWRU Closes Sidewalk for Safety," *Cleveland Plain Dealer*, March 1, 2003, B1.

8. Michelle O'Donnell, "Rrrrrrrippp! Another Victim of Those Pesky Armrests," *New York Times*, May 28, 2004, B2. See also Terrence Neilan, "Grabbing Long Island, by the Pants Pocket," *New York Times*, July 7, 2005, B2.

9. Michael Luo, "For Exercise in New York Futility, Push Button," *New York Times*, February 27, 2004, A1, A23.

10. Ibid.

11. "Plugging The Leak," *IEEE Spectrum*, January 2001, 81.

12. Katie Hafner, "Looking for the Eurkea! Button," *New York Times*, June 24, 2004, G1, G7.

13

WICKED PROBLEMS IN DESIGN THINKING

Richard Buchanan

THE WICKED PROBLEMS THEORY OF DESIGN

Recent conferences on design are evidence of a coherent, if not always systematic, effort to reach a clearer understanding of design as an integrative discipline. However, the participants, who increasingly come from diverse professions and academic disciplines, are not drawn together because they share a common definition of design; a common methodology, a common philosophy, or even a common set of objects to which everyone agrees that the term "design" should be applied. They are drawn together because they share a mutual interest in a common theme: *the conception and planning of the artificial.* Different definitions of design and different specifications of the methodology of design are variations of this broad theme, each a concrete exploration of what is possible in the development of its meanings and implications. Communication is possible at such meetings because the results of research and discussion, despite wide differences in intellectual and practical perspectives, are always connected by this theme and, therefore, supplemental. This is only possible, of course, if individuals have the wit to discover what is useful in each other's work and can cast the material in terms of their own vision of design thinking.

Members of the scientific community, however, must be puzzled by the types of problems addressed by professional designers and by the patterns of reasoning they employ. While scientists share in the new liberal art of design thinking, they are also masters of specialized subject matters and their related methods, as found in physics, chemistry, biology, mathematics, the social sciences, or one of the many subfields into which these sciences have been divided.[1] This creates one of the central problems of communication between scientists and designers, because the problems addressed by designers seldom fall solely within the boundaries of any one of these subject matters.

The problem of communication between scientists and designers was evident in a special conference on design theory held in New York in 1974.[2] This conference was interesting for several reasons, the most significant directly related to the content of the meeting itself. Reviewed in one of the initial papers,[3] the "wicked problems" approach to design proved to be one of the central themes to which the participants often returned when seeking a connection between their remarkably diverse and seemingly incommensurate applications of design.[4] Also significant was the difficulty that most of the participants had in understanding each other. Although an observation of an outsider on the dynamics of the meeting, it is an excellent example of a "wicked problem" of design thinking.

The *wicked problems* approach was formulated by Horst Rittel in the 1960s, when design methodology was a subject of intense interest.[5] A mathematician, designer, and former teacher at the Hochschule fur Gestaltung (HfG) Ulm, Rittel sought an alternative to the linear, step-by-step model of the design process being explored by many designers and design theorists.[6] Although there are many variations of the linear model, its proponents hold that the design process is divided into two distinct phases: *problem definition* and *problem solution. Problem definition* is an *analytic sequence* in which the designer determines all of the elements of the problem and specifies all of the requirements that a successful design solution must have. *Problem solution is a synthetic* sequence in which the various requirements are combined and balanced against each other, yielding a final plan to be carried into production.

In the abstract, such a model may appear attractive because it suggests a methodological precision that is, in its key features, independent from the perspective of the individual designer. In fact, many scientists and business professionals, as well as some designers, continue to find the idea of a linear model attractive, believing that it represents the only hope for a "logical" understanding of the design process. However, some critics were quick to point out two obvious points of weakness: one, the actual sequence of design thinking and decision making is not a simple linear process; and two, the problems addressed by designers do not, in actual practice, yield to any linear analysis and synthesis yet proposed.[7]

Rittel argued that most of the problems addressed by designers are *wicked problems*.[8] As described in the first published report of Rittel's idea, *wicked problems* are a "class of social system problems which are ill-formulated, where the information is confusing, where there are many clients and decision makers with conflicting values, and where the ramifications in the whole system are thoroughly confusing."[9] This is an amusing description of what confronts designers in every new situation. But most important, it points toward a fundamental issue that lies behind practice: the relationship between *determinacy* and *indeterminacy* in design thinking. The linear model of design thinking is based on *determinate* problems which have definite conditions.

The designer's task is to identify those conditions precisely and then calculate a solution. In contrast, the *wicked-problems* approach suggests that there is a fundamental *indeterminacy* in all but the most trivial design problems—problems where, as Rittel suggests, the "wickedness" has already been taken out to yield determinate or analytic problems.

To understand what this means, it is important to recognize that *indeterminacy* is quite different from *undetermined. Indeterminacy* implies that there are no definitive conditions or limits to design problems. This is evident, for example, in the ten properties of *wicked problems* that Rittel initially identified in 1972.[10]

1. *Wicked problems* have no definitive formulation, but every formulation of a *wicked problem* corresponds to the formulation of a solution.
2. *Wicked problems* have no stopping rules.
3. Solutions to *wicked problems* cannot be true or false, only good or bad.
4. In solving *wicked problems* there is no exhaustive list of admissible operations.
5. For every *wicked problem* there is always more than one possible explanation, with explanations depending on the *Weltanschauung* of the designer.[11]
6. Every *wicked problem* is a symptom of another, "higher level," problem.[12]
7. No formulation and solution of a *wicked problem* has a definitive test.
8. Solving a *wicked problem* is a "one shot" operation, with no room for trial and error.[13]
9. Every *wicked problem* is unique.
10. The *wicked problem* solver has no right to be wrong—they are fully responsible for their actions.

This is a remarkable list, and it is tempting to go no further than elaborate the meaning of each property, providing concrete examples drawn from *every area* of design thinking. But to do so would leave a fundamental question unanswered. *Why are design problems indeterminate and, therefore, wicked?* Neither Rittel nor any of those studying *wicked problems* has attempted to answer this question, so the *wicked-problems* approach has remained only a description of the social reality of designing rather than the beginnings of a well-grounded theory of design.

However, the answer to the question lies in something rarely considered: the peculiar nature of the subject matter of design. Design problems are "indeterminate" and "wicked" because design has no special subject matter of its own apart from what a designer conceives it to be. The subject matter of design is potentially *universal* in scope, because design thinking may be applied to any area of human experience. But in the process of application, the designer must discover or invent a *particular* subject out of the problems and issues of specific circumstances. This sharply contrasts with the disciplines of science, which are concerned with understanding the principles, laws, rules, or structures that are necessarily embodied in existing subject matters. Such subject matters are undetermined or under-determined, requiring further investigation to make them more fully determinate. But they are not radically indeterminate in a way directly comparable to that of design.[14]

Designers conceive their subject matter in two ways on two levels: general and particular. On a *general level*, a designer forms an idea or a working hypothesis about the nature of products or the nature of the humanmade in the world. This is the designer's view of what is meant, for example, by the "artificial" in relation to the "natural." In this sense, the designer holds a broad view of the nature of design and the proper scope of its application. Indeed, most designers, to the degree that they have reflected on their discipline, will gladly, if not insistently, explain on a general level what the subject matter of design is. When developed and well presented, these explanations are philosophies or proto-philosophies of design that exist within a plurality of alternative views.[15]

They provide an essential framework for each designer to understand and explore the materials, methods, and principles of design thinking. But such philosophies do not and cannot constitute sciences of design in the sense of any natural, social, or humanistic science. The reason for this is simple: design is fundamentally concerned with the particular, *and there is no science of the particular*.

In actual practice, the designer begins with what should be called a *quasi-subject matter*, tenuously existing within the problems and issues of specific circumstances. Out of the specific possibilities of a concrete situation, the designer must conceive a design that will lead to *this* or *that* particular product. A *quasi-subject matter* is not an undetermined subject waiting to be made determinate. It is an indeterminate subject waiting to be made specific and concrete. For example, a client's brief does not present a definition of the subject matter of a particular design application. It presents a problem and a set of issues to be considered in resolving that problem. In situations where a brief specifies in great detail the particular features of the product to be planned, it often does so because an owner, corporate executive, or manager has attempted to perform the critical task of transforming problems and issues into a working hypothesis about the particular features of the product to be designed. In effect, someone has attempted to take the "wickedness" out. Even in this situation, however, the conception of particular features remains only a possibility that may be subject to change through discussion and argument.[16]

This is where placements take on special significance as tools of design thinking. They allow the designer to position and reposition the problems and issues at hand. Placements are the tools by which a designer intuitively or deliberately shapes a design situation, identifying the views of all participants, the issues which concern them, and the invention that will serve as a working hypothesis for exploration and development. In this sense, the placements selected by a designer are the same as what determinate subject matters are for the scientist. They are the *quasi-subject matter* of design thinking, from which the designer fashions a working hypothesis suited to special circumstances.

This helps to explain how design functions as an integrative discipline. By using placements to discover or invent a working hypothesis, the designer establishes a *principle of relevance* for knowledge from the arts and sciences, determining how such knowledge may be useful to design thinking in a particular circumstance without immediately reducing design to one or another of these disciplines. In effect, the working hypothesis that will lead to a particular product is the principle of relevance, guiding the efforts of designers to gather all available knowledge bearing on how a product is finally planned.

But does the designer's working hypothesis or principle of relevance suggest that the product itself is a determinate subject matter? The answer involves a critical but often blurred distinction between design thinking and the activity of production or making. Once a product is conceived, planned, and produced, it may indeed become an object for study by any of the arts and sciences—history, economics, psychology, sociology, or anthropology. It may even become an object for study by a new humanistic science of production that we could call the "science of the artificial," directed toward understanding the nature, form, and uses of humanmade products in all of their generic kinds.[17] But in all such studies, the activities of design thinking are easily forgotten or are reduced to the kind of product that is finally produced. The problem for designers is to conceive and plan what does not yet exist, and this occurs in the context of the indeterminacy of *wicked problems*, before the final result is known.

This is the creative or inventive activity that Herbert Simon has in mind when he speaks of design as a science of the artificial. What he means is "devising artifacts to attain goals" or, more broadly, "doctrine about the design process."[18] In this sense, Simon's science of the artificial is perhaps closer to what Dewey means by technology as a systematic discipline of experimental thinking. However, Simon has little to say about the difference between designing a product and making it. Consequently, the "search" procedures and decision-making protocols that he proposes for design are largely analytic, shaped by his philosophic view of the determinacies that follow from the natural laws that surround artifacts.[19]

For all of the insight Simon has in distinguishing the artificial as a domain of humanmade products different from objects created by natural processes, he does not capture the radical sense in which designers explore the essence of what the artificial may be in human experience.[20] This is a synthetic activity related to indeterminacy, not an activity of making what is undetermined in natural laws more determinate in artifacts. In short, Simon appears to have conflated two sciences of the artificial: an inventive science of design thinking which has no subject matter aside from what the designer conceives it to be, and a science of existing humanmade products whose nature Simon happens to believe is a manipulation of material and behavioral laws of nature.[21]

Design is a remarkably supple discipline, amenable to radically different interpretations in philosophy as well as in practice. But the flexibility of design often leads to popular misunderstanding and clouds efforts to understand its nature. The history of design is not merely a history of objects. It is a history of the changing views of subject matter held by designers and the concrete objects conceived, planned, and produced as expressions of those views. *One could go further and say that the history of design history is a record of the design historians' views regarding what they conceive to be the subject matter of design.*

We have been slow to recognize the peculiar indeterminacy of subject matter in design and its impact on the nature of design thinking. As a consequence, each of the sciences that have come into contact with design has tended to regard design as an "applied" version of its own knowledge, methods, and principles. They see in design an instance of their own subject matter and treat design as a *practical demonstration* of the scientific principles of that subject matter. Thus, we have the odd, recurring situation in which design is alternately regarded as "applied" natural science, "applied" social science, or "applied" fine art. No wonder designers and members of the scientific community often have difficulty communicating.

NOTES

Extracted from R. Buchanan, "Wicked Problems in Design Thinking," *Design Issues* 8, no. 2 (1992): 14–19. Reprinted by permission of the author and the University of Illinois at Chicago, School of Art and Design.

1. This list could also include the humanistic disciplines and the fine arts, because there is as much difficulty in communicating between some traditional humanists and designers as between designers and scientists. This is evident in the persistent view that design is simply a decorative art, adapting the principles of the fine arts to utilitarian ends, held by many humanists.

2. William It. Spillers, ed., *Basic Questions of Design Theory* (Amsterdam: North Holland Publishing Company, 1974). The conference, funded by the National Science Foundation, was held at Columbia University.

3. Vladimer Bazjanac, "Architectural Design Theory: Models of the Design Process," *Basic Questions of Design Theory*, 3–20.

4. Graph theory, developed by the mathematician Frank Harary, also served to connect the work of researchers in many areas. It was reported by the organizers that Harary, who attended this conference and delivered the paper "Graphs as Designs," suggested that the basic structure of design theory could be found in his work on structural models. Whether or not Harary made such a suggestion, it is possible to see in graph theory, and, notably, the theory of directed graphs, a mathematical expression of the doctrine of placements. Comparison may establish a surprising connection between the arts of words and the mathematical arts of things, with further significance for the view of design as a new liberal art. "Schemata" are the connecting link, for placements may be schematized as figures of thought, and schemata are forms of graphs, directed or otherwise. For more on graph theory see F. Harary, R. Norman, and D. Cartwright, *Structural Models: An Introduction to the Theory of Directed Graphs* (New York: Wiley, 1965).

5. A series of conferences on Design Methods held in the United Kingdom in 1962, 1965, and 1967, led to the formation of the Design Research Society in 1967, that today continues to publish the journal Design Studies. Parallel interest in the United States led to the establishment of the Design Methods Group in 1966, which published the DMG Newsletter (1966–71), renamed the *DMG-DRS Journal: Design Research and Methods*, and then renamed in 1976 and published to the present as *Design Methods and Theories*. For one attempt to describe and integrate a set of methods used in design thinking, see J. Christopher Jones, *Design Methods: Seeds of Human Futures* (1970; rpt New York: John Wiley & Sons, 1981). Many of the methods Jones presents are consciously transposed from other disciplines. However, they all can be interpreted as techniques for repositioning design problems, using placements to discover new possibilities.

6. Rittel, who died in 1990, completed his career by teaching at the University of California at Berkeley and the University of Stuttgart. For a brief biographical sketch, see Herbert Lindinger, *Ulm Design: The Morality of Objects* (Cambridge: M.I.T. Press, 1990), 274.

7. Bazjanac presents an interesting comparison of linear models and the wicked problems approach.

8. The phrase wicked problems was borrowed from philosopher Karl Popper. However, Rittel

developed the idea in a different direction. Rittel is another example of someone initially influenced by neo-positivist ideas who, when confronted with the actual processes of practical reasoning in concrete circumstances, sought to develop a new approach related to rhetoric.

9. The first published report of Rittel's concept of wicked problems was presented by C. West Churchman, "Wicked Problems," *Management Science* (December 1967), vol. 4, no. 14, B-141–42. His editorial is particularly interesting for its discussion of the moral problems of design and planning that can occur when individuals mistakenly believe that they have effectively taken the "wickedness" out of design problems.

10. See Horst W. J. Rittel and Melvin M. Webber, "Dilemmas in a General Theory of Planning," working paper presented at the Institute of Urban and Regional Development, University of California, Berkeley, November 1972. See also an interview with Rittel, "Son of Rittelthink," Design Methods Group 5th Anniversary Report (January 1972), 5–10; and Horst Rittel, "On the Planning Crisis: Systems Analysis of the First and Second Generations," *Bedriftsøkonomen*, no. 8: 390–96. Rind gradually added more properties to his initial list.

11. Weltanschauung identifies the intellectual perspective of the designer as an integral part of the design process.

12. This property suggests the systems aspect of Rittel's approach.

13. Rittel's example is drawn from architecture, where it is not feasible to rebuild a flawed building. Perhaps the general property should be described as "entrapment" in a line of design thinking. Designers as well as their clients or managers are often "entrapped" during the development phase of a new product and are unable, for good or bad reasons, to terminate a weak design. For a brief illustration of entrapment in the product development process of a small midwestern company, see Richard Buchanan, "Wicked Problems: Managing the Entrapment Trap," *Innovation* (Summer, 1991), 10:3.

14. There is one case in which even the subject matters of the sciences are indeterminate. The working hypotheses of scientists invariably reflect distinctive philosophic perspectives on and interpretations of what constitutes nature and natural processes. This is a factor in accounting for the surprising pluralism of philosophies among practicing scientists and suggests that even science is shaped by an application of design thinking, developed along the lines of Dewey's notion of "intentional operations." Even from this perspective, however, scientists are concerned with understanding the universal properties of what is, while designers are concerned with conceiving and planning a particular that does not yet exist. Indeterminacy for the scientist is on the level of second-intention, while the subject matter remains, at the level of first-intention, determinate in the manner described. For the designer, indeterminacy belongs to both first- and second-intention.

15. For a brief discussion of different conceptions of subject matter on this level held by three contemporary designers, Ezio Manzini, Gaetano Pesce, and Emilio Ambaz, see Richard Buchanan, "Metaphors, Narratives, and Fables in New Design Thinking," *Design Issues* VII-1 (Fall, 1990): 78–84. Without understanding a designer's view of subject matter on the general level, there is little intelligibility in the shifts that occur when a designer moves, for example, from designing domestic products to graphic design or architecture. Such shifts are usually described in terms of the designer's "personality" or "circumstances," rather than the continued development of a coherent intellectual perspective on the artificial.

16. Failure to include professional designers as early as possible in the product development

process is one of the sources of entrapment in corporate culture. Professional designers should be recognized for their ability to conceive products as well as plan them.

17. The earliest example of this science is Aristotle's *Poetics*. Although this work is directed toward the analysis of literary productions and tragedy in particular, Aristotle frequently discusses useful objects in terms of the principles of poetic analysis. "Poetics," from the *Greek* word for "making," is used by Aristotle to refer to productive science or the science of the artificial, which he distinguishes both from theoretic and practical sciences. Few investigators have recognized that poetic analysis can be extended to the study of making "useful" objects. When designer and architect Emilio Ambaz refers to the "poetics of the pragmatic," he means not only esthetic or elegant features of everyday objects, but also a method or discipline of analysis that may contribute to design thinking.

18. Simon, *The Sciences of the Artificial*, 52–53.

19. For Simon, the "artificial" is an "interface" created within a materialist reality: "I have shown that a science of artificial phenomena is always in imminent danger of dissolving and vanishing. The peculiar properties of the artifact lie on the thin interface between the natural laws within it and the natural laws without." Simon, *The Sciences of the Artificial*, 57. This is one expression of the positivist or empiricist philosophy that guides Simon's theory of design.

20. For Simon, the equivalent of a wicked problem is an "ill-structured problem." For Simon's views on how ill-structured problems may be addressed, see "The Structure of Ill-Structured Problems," *Models of Discovery* (Boston: D. Reidel, 1977), 305–25. This paper has interesting connections with the doctrine of placements because placements may be used to organize and store memories, and Simon is particularly concerned with the role of long-term memory in solving ill-structured problems. But Simon's methods arc still analytic, directed toward the discovery of solutions in some sense already known rather than the invention of solutions yet unknown.

21. Although Simon's title, *The Sciences of the Artificial*, is a perfectly adequate translation of what we have come to know in Western culture as Aristotle's Poetics, Simon seems unaware of the humanistic tradition of poetic and rhetorical analysis of the artificial that followed from Aristotle. This is not an antiquarian issue, because the study of literary production—the artificial formed in words—prefigures the issues that surround the study of the artificial in all other types of useful objects. Aristotle carefully distinguished the science of the artificial from the art of rhetoric. When Aristotle comes to discuss the thought that is presented in an artificial object such as a tragedy, he pointedly refers the reader to his treatise on the inventive art of rhetoric for the fullest elaboration of the issue. However, Simon deserves less criticism for overlooking this connection than humanists who have been amazingly neglectful, if not scornful, of the rise of design and technology in the twentieth century.

SECTION 2: DESIGN THINKING

2.2: Design Research

INTRODUCTION

During World War II, Great Britain, under the auspices of the Ministry of Information, began a design research project that could help with the war effort. This organization, led to the industry–based Design Research Unit (DRU), continued to influence the spread of design research after the war. As part of an outgrowth of the intellectual interests that grew under the DRU, scholars began to assert that design—even outside of the parameters of a military venue—warranted its own field of study (Kinross 1998). The British group that furthered this field of inquiry was the Design Research Society, which was founded in the 1960s and continues to play a significant role in design studies.

The readings in this subsection represent and extend the work of the Society by offering approaches that help us understand the relationship between research and design. The first reading, by Herbert Simon, suggests that there should be a new branch of science created to assess the importance of our man-made world. Donald Schön then examines the design process and how designers make choices. Finally, Susan Squires looks at design's connection to society by studying how products made by designers interact with consumers. The three readings in this subsection explore how research has changed our understanding of design.

Herbert Simon's *The Sciences of the Artificial* describes our contemporary world as a man-made place where design creates new possibilities that need to be researched and understood. Simon is one of the original thinkers behind the charge of the Design Research Society and the notion that there could be a scientific rigor applied to the study of design. He contends that we live as part of a "collective artifice" in which we receive information through "strings of artifacts called 'symbols.'" For centuries humans have been interested in natural sciences, as seen, for instance, in our study of biology or in our commitment to institutions like museums of natural history. However, Simon wants to know "whether there cannot also be 'artificial' science—knowledge about artificial objects and phenomena." For example, imagine a form of science that studied how our world of artificial design made us think, act, and create. How, as Donald Norman asks in the subsection of the *Reader* on technology (5.3), does computer software design, like Microsoft Word®, affect our lives as students and thinkers? Simon claims that for too long culture has ridiculed artifice and, as we continue to witness in popular culture, has a "deep distrust" in the products we make. In order to dispel many of the myths and misconceptions that we attach to artificiality, Simon asks us to develop a type of scientific study of the artificial realm that will help us explain design's place, function, and cultural consequences.

According to Simon, design products are artificial "meeting points" that "interface" between an inner and outer world. The inner world is the functional mechanism that makes the product work—the motor of the car, the gears of a bike—and the outer world is the environment in which the product performs its function. Simon sees this inner–outer dialog as key to his research agenda. Assessing the relationship between the "inner system" and "outer environment" can help us understand the nature of design. He uses the example of a clock on a ship. Today we take it for granted that a clock can tell time accurately, even when on a ship that is rising and falling with the swells of the ocean. However, initially, during the eighteenth century, the design of the ship's clock "had to be endowed with many delicate properties" to make certain that the ship's movement did not interfere with the clock's ability to function—like the car that has to be made with design details to insure that it will not crash when a road surface changes. The inner workings and outer environment of the clock had to be in sync to allow the natural world of the sea to be in harmony with the artificial mechanism of the clock.

While Simon investigates the larger field of artificiality, Donald Schön researches the way designers work in his article "Designing: Rules, Types and Worlds." This essay, which won an award from the Design Research Society when it came out in 1988, appeared in the journal *Design Studies,* which continues to be an important publication that "reports new research and scholarship in principles, procedures and techniques relevant to the practice, management and pedagogy of design" (http://www.elsevier. com/locate/destud). Schön explains how designers come up with types, or categories and reference points for specific situations. He gives the example of the New England green (the center of many towns in the American Northeast) as a "type" that helps us think about a specific location as a point of reference. Types lead to the creation of "rules," or sets of practices established through types. Schön gives the example of how for centuries symmetry in architecture was a rule, a given, based on the drawings of ancient Roman designers. Finally, these rules and types create "design worlds," which are the imaginative places filled with knowledge that are lived in by designers.

Schön's premise about the importance of research has found applications in the business world. As Susan Squires notes in her essay, "Doing the Work: Customer Research in the Product Development and Design Industry," design research has become actively engaged with different types of research platforms. In this excerpt from her longer article, she details her use of discovery research, and how this methodology enables her to look at consumers and their behaviors without preconceived notions. Definition research, in short, explores links between specific products and specific consumers. Squires takes us through her own work process, which is akin to an ethnographic study, in which she analyzes consumer behavior in everyday consumer settings. For instance, she explains the study she did for a breakfast cereal company, in which she went into homes and looked at how individuals thought about the foods they were eating and their nutritional habits. Squires's research led to some surprising conclusions about consumer behaviors, such as people not eating as healthily as they claim to be eating, which altered her client's approach to designing breakfast foods. Additionally, her analysis of consumer culture is connected to the material culture and consumption subsections that appear later in this book.

We can think about these readings as a three-tiered approach to design research. Simon investigates design as part of the grand order of things in our world, where artificiality forms the basis of our lives. Schön takes us closer to the working life of the designer, by giving us knowledge about how designers evaluate the problems within the artificial realm. Finally, Squires brings us to a more granular level of applicability, in which businesses can conduct research to come up with solutions that will ultimately make their products more viable in the marketplace. This subsection provides us with insight about how design research can lead to clearer ways of thinking about design practices and products.

14

UNDERSTANDING THE NATURAL AND ARTIFICIAL WORLDS

Herbert Simon

The world we live in today is much more a man-made,[1] or artificial, world than it is a natural world. Almost every element in our environment shows evidence of man's artifice. The temperature in which we spend most of our hours is kept artificially at 20 degrees Celsius; the humidity is added to or taken from the air we breathe; and the impurities we inhale are largely produced (and filtered) by man.

Moreover for most of us—the white-collared ones—the significant part of the environment consists mostly of strings of artifacts called "symbols" that we receive through eyes and ears in the form of written and spoken language and that we pour out into the environment—as I am now doing—by mouth or hand. The laws that govern these strings of symbols, the laws that govern the occasions on which we emit and receive them, the determinants of their content are all consequences of our collective artifice.

One may object that I exaggerate the artificiality of our world. Man must obey the law of gravity as surely as does a stone, and as a living organism man must depend for food, and in many other ways, on the world of biological phenomena. I shall plead guilty to overstatement, while protesting that the exaggeration is slight. To say that an astronaut, or even an airplane pilot, is obeying the law of gravity, hence is a perfectly natural phenomenon, is true, but its truth calls for some sophistication in what we mean by "obeying" a natural law. Aristotle did not think it natural for heavy things to rise or light-ones to fall (*Physics*, Book IV); but presumably we have a deeper understanding of "natural" than he did.

So too we must be careful about equating "biological" with "natural." A forest may be a phenomenon of nature; a farm certainly is not. The very species upon which man depends for his food—his corn and his cattle—are artifacts of his ingenuity. A plowed field is no more part of nature than an asphalted street—and no less.

These examples set the terms of our problem, for those things we call artifacts are not apart from nature. They have no dispensation to ignore or violate natural law. At the same time they are adapted to man's goals and purposes. They are what they are in order to satisfy man's desire to fly or to eat well. As man's aims change, so too do his artifacts—and vice versa.

If science is to encompass these objects and phenomena in which human purpose as well as natural law are embodied, it must have means for relating these two disparate components. The character of these means and their implications for certain areas of knowledge—economics, psychology, and design in particular—are the central concern of this book.

THE ARTIFICIAL

Natural science is knowledge about natural objects and phenomena. We ask whether there cannot also be "artificial" science—knowledge about artificial objects and phenomena. Unfortunately the term "artificial" has a pejorative air about it that we must dispel before we can proceed.

My dictionary defines "artificial" as, "Produced by art rather than by nature; not genuine or natural; affected; not pertaining to the essence of the matter." It proposes, as synonyms: affected, factitious, manufactured, pretended, sham, simulated, spurious, trumped up, unnatural. As antonyms, it lists: actual, genuine, honest, natural, real, truthful, unaffected. Our language seems to reflect man's deep distrust of his own products. I shall not try to assess the validity of that evaluation or explore its possible psychological roots. But you will have to understand me as using "artificial" in as neutral a sense as possible, as meaning man-made as opposed to natural.[2]

In some contexts we make a distinction between "artificial" and "synthetic." For example, a gem made of glass colored to resemble sapphire would be called artificial, while a man-made gem chemically indistinguishable from sapphire would be called synthetic. A similar distinction is often made between "artificial" and "synthetic" rubber. Thus some artificial things are imitations of things in nature, and the imitation may use either the same basic materials as those in the natural object or quite different materials.

As soon as we introduce "synthesis" as well as "artifice," we enter the realm of engineering. For "synthetic" is often used in the broader sense of "designed" or "composed." We speak of engineering as concerned with "synthesis," while science is concerned with "analysis." Synthetic or artificial objects—and more specifically prospective artificial objects having desired properties—are the central objective of engineering activity and skill. The engineer, and more generally the designer, is concerned with how things *ought* to be—how they ought to be in order to *attain goals,* and to *function.* Hence a science of the artificial will be closely akin to a science of engineering—but very different, as we shall see, from what goes currently by the name of "engineering science."

With goals and "oughts" we also introduce into the picture the dichotomy between normative and descriptive. Natural science has found a way to exclude the normative and to concern itself solely with how things are. Can or should we maintain this exclusion when we move from natural to artificial phenomena, from analysis to synthesis?[3]

We have now identified four indicia that distinguish the artificial from the natural; hence we can set the boundaries for sciences of the artificial:

1. Artificial things are synthesized (though not always or usually with full forethought) by man.
2. Artificial things may imitate appearances in natural things while lacking, in one or many respects, the reality of the latter.
3. Artificial things can be characterized in terms of functions, goals, adaptation.
4. Artificial things are often discussed, particularly when they are being designed, in terms of imperatives as well as descriptives.

THE ENVIRONMENT AS MOLD

Let us look a little more closely at the functional or purposeful aspect of artificial things. Fulfillment of purpose or adaptation to a goal involves a relation among three terms: the purpose or goal, the character of the artifact, and the environment in which the artifact performs. When we think of a clock, for example, in terms of purpose we may use the child's definition: "a clock is to tell time." When we focus our attention on the clock itself, we may describe it in terms of arrangements of gears and the application of the forces of springs or gravity operating on a weight or pendulum.

But we may also consider clocks in relation to the environment in which they are to be used. Sundials perform as clocks *in sunny climates—* they are more useful in Phoenix than in Boston and of no use at all during the Arctic winter. Devising a clock that would tell time on a rolling and pitching ship, with sufficient accuracy to determine longitude, was one of the great adventures of eighteenth-century science and technology. To perform in this difficult environment, the clock had to be endowed with many delicate properties, some of them largely or totally irrelevant to the performance of a landlubber's clock.

Natural science impinges on an artifact through two of the three terms of the relation that characterizes it: the structure of the artifact itself and the environment in which it performs. Whether a clock will in fact tell time depends on its internal construction and where it is placed. Whether a knife will cut depends on the material of its blade and the hardness of the substance to which it is applied.

THE ARTIFACT AS "INTERFACE"

We can view the matter quite symmetrically. An artifact can be thought of as a meeting point—an "interface" in today's terms—between an "inner" environment, the substance and organization of the artifact itself, and an "outer" environment, the surroundings in which it operates. If the inner environment is appropriate to the outer environment, or vice versa, the artifact will serve its intended purpose. Thus, if the clock is immune to buffeting, it will serve as a ship's chronometer. (And conversely, if it isn't, we may salvage it by mounting it on the mantel at home.)

Notice that this way of viewing artifacts applies equally well to many things that are not man-made—to all things in fact that can be regarded as adapted to some situation; and in particular it applies to the living systems that have evolved through the forces of organic evolution. A theory of the airplane draws on natural science for an explanation of its inner environment (the power plant, for example), its outer environment (the character of the atmosphere at different altitudes), and the relation between its inner and outer environments (the movement of an airfoil through a gas). But a theory of the bird can be divided up in exactly the same way.[4]

Given an airplane, or *given* a bird, we can analyze them by the methods of natural science without any particular attention to purpose or adaptation, without reference to the interface between what I have called the inner and outer environments. After all, their behavior is governed by natural law just as fully as the behavior of anything else (or at least we all believe this about the airplane, and most of us believe it about the bird).

FUNCTIONAL EXPLANATION

On the other hand, if the division between inner and outer environment is not necessary to the analysis of an airplane or a bird, it turns out at least to be highly convenient. There are several reasons for this, which will become evident from examples.

Many animals in the Arctic have white fur. We usually explain this by saying that white is the best color for the Arctic environment, for white creatures escape detection more easily than do others. This is not of course a natural science explanation; it is an explanation by reference to purpose or function. It simply says that these are the kinds of creatures that will "work," that is, survive, in this kind of environment. To turn the statement into an explanation, we must add to it a notion of natural selection, or some equivalent mechanism.

An important fact about this kind of explanation is that it demands an understanding mainly of the outer environment. Looking at our snowy surroundings, we can predict the predominant color of the creatures we are likely to encounter; we need know little about the biology of the creatures themselves, beyond the facts that they are often mutually hostile, use visual clues to guide their behavior, and are adaptive (through selection or some other mechanism).

Analogous to the role played by natural selection in evolutionary biology is the role played by rationality in the sciences of human behavior. If we know of a business organization only that it is a profit-maximizing system, we can often predict how its behavior will change if we change its environment—how it will alter its prices if a sales tax is levied on its products. We can sometimes make this prediction—and economists do make it repeatedly—without detailed assumptions about the adaptive mechanism, the decision-making apparatus that constitutes the inner environment of the business firm.

Thus the first advantage of dividing outer from inner environment in studying an adaptive or artificial system is that we can often predict behavior from knowledge of the system's goals and its outer environment, with only minimal assumptions about the inner environment. An instant corollary is that we often find quite different inner environments accomplishing identical or similar goals in identical or similar outer environments—airplanes and birds, dolphins and tunafish, weight-driven clocks and spring-driven clocks, electrical relays and transistors.

There is often a corresponding advantage in the division from the standpoint of the inner environment. In very many cases whether a particular system will achieve a particular goal or adaptation depends on only a few characteristics of the outer environment and not at all on the detail of that environment. Biologists are familiar with this property of adaptive systems under the label of homeostasis. It is an important property of most good designs, whether biological or artifactual. In one way or another the designer insulates the inner system from the environment, so that an invariant relation is maintained between inner system and goal, independent of variations over a wide range in most parameters that characterize the outer environment. The ship's chronometer reacts to the pitching of the ship only in the negative sense of maintaining an invariant relation of the hands on its dial to the real time, independently of the ship's motions.

Quasi independence from the outer environment may be maintained by various forms of passive insulation, by reactive negative feedback (the most frequently discussed form of insulation), by predictive adaptation, or by various combinations of these.

NOTES

Extracted from H. Simon, *The Sciences of the Artificial*, 3rd ed. (Cambridge, Mass.: MIT Press, 1996), pp. 2–8. © 1996 Massachusetts Institute of Technology, by permission of The MIT Press.

1. Throughout this book I will use "man" as an androgynous noun, encompassing both sexes, and "he," "his," and "him" as androgynous. I believe that we should not abandon these pronouns but include women and men equally in their scope.

2. I shall disclaim responsibility for this particular choice of terms. The phrase "artificial intelligence," which led me to it, was coined, I think, right on the Charles River, at MIT. Our own research group at Rand and Carnegie-Mellon University have preferred phrases like "complex information processing" and "simulation of cognitive processes." But then we run into new terminological difficulties, for the dictionary also says that "to simulate" means "to assume or have the mere appearance or form of, without the reality; imitate; counterfeit; pretend." At any rate, "artificial intelligence" seems to be here to stay, and it may prove easier to cleanse the phrase than to dispense with it. In time it will become sufficiently idiomatic that it will no longer be the target of cheap rhetoric.

3. This issue will also be discussed at length in my fifth chapter. In order not to keep readers in suspense, I may say that I hold to the pristine positivist position of the irreducibility of "ought" to "is," as in chapter 3 of my *Administrative Behavior* (New York: Macmillan, 1976). This position is entirely consistent with treating natural or artificial goal-seeking systems as phenomena, without commitment to their goals. *Ibid.*, appendix. See also the well-known paper by A. Rosenbluth, N. Wiener, and J. Bigelow, "Behavior, Purpose, and Teleology," *Philosophy of Science*, 10 (1943): 18–24.

4. A generalization of the argument made here for the separability of "outer" from "inner" environment shows that we should expect to find this separability, to a greater or lesser degree, in all large and complex systems, whether they are artificial or natural. In its generalized form it is an argument that all nature will be organized in "levels." My essay "The Architecture of Complexity," included in this volume as chapter 7 [in his volume, *The Sciences of the Artificial*], develops the more general argument in some detail.

15

DESIGNING

Rules, Types and Worlds

Donald A. Schön

TENSIONS IN A THEORY
OF DESIGNING

The study of architectural designing,[1] important in its own right, also contributes to the quest for a new and more satisfactory epistemology of practice, an alternative to a discredited but none the less resurgent model of technical rationality. As we explore what professional practitioners know and how they reason, especially in situations of uncertainty, uniqueness, and conflict, it becomes increasingly attractive to see these indeterminate zones of practice as *design-like* and to think of architectural designing as an exemplar of knowledge and reason in other professions.

A satisfactory theory of what architects know and how they reason, and more generally, a satisfactory theory of design-like practice, must take account of four fundamental tensions.

Tacit and Explicit Knowledge

Designers are usually unable to say what they know, to put their special skills and understandings into words. On the rare occasions when they try to do so, their descriptions tend to be partial and mistaken: myths rather than accurate accounts of practice. Yet their actual designing seems to reveal a great deal of intelligence. How, then, if we reserve 'knowledge' for what can be made explicit, are we to explain what designers 'know'? And if, on the contrary, we recognize designers'

tacit knowledge, what shall we say about the ways in which they *hold* it, or get access to it when they need it?

Uniqueness and Generality

If practised designers, especially the more skillful, tend to treat each design situation as a unique 'universe of one', how shall we explain design *reasoning*? Reasoning seems to require the use of general rules and, as Justice Cardozo pointed out long ago,[2] general rules never decide concrete cases. If we argue, on the other hand, that the premises of design reasoning consist in particular *judgments* (for example, that a space is 'cramped' or 'terrible'), how shall we describe the bases of the judgments? If we treat design judgments as acts of perception in which we recognize that something is matched or mismatched to its environment, as Christopher Alexander suggested,[3] then match or mismatch by reference to *what*?

Generativity and Cumulativeness

Designers appear to build up their knowledge in a cumulative fashion, developing knowledge in one design episode and carrying it over to the next. But how shall we conceive of this cumulative process? If designers frame situations and shape practice through general rules or principles carried over from past experience, how do they ever make anything new?

Pluralism and Commonality

Characteristically, designing is a social process. In every major building project, there are many different kinds of participants: architects, engineers, building contractors, representatives of clients and interest groups, regulators, developers, who must communicate with each other in order to bring a project to completion. These individuals in their different roles tend also to pursue different interests, see things in different ways, and even speak different languages. Yet they do sometimes come to agree on some thing to be built. How shall we account for the ways in which they do so?

A theory of designing worth its salt must somehow take account of these tensions. It must not ignore them. But they will present themselves differently depending on how we choose to represent designing and design knowledge. If we give priority to *rules,* for example, we will find it difficult to explain how practised designers come to see things in new ways as they respond to the perceived uniqueness of a design situation. If we give priority to particular intuitions, perceptions and judgments, it will be hard for us to explain how designers build up repertoires of broadly usable design knowledge. If we focus on the knowledge design participants hold in common, we tend to underplay the diversity, ambiguity and relative chaos inherent in much real-world designing. If we focus on idiosyncratic differences in designers' understandings, we pose, in a particularly intractable way, the problem of explaining how buildings do get designed and built.

Dilemmas associated with choosing fundamental elements and frameworks for design theory are as old as design theory itself. They come up in a new way, computational approaches to designing. From this however, as a result of the recent growth of interest in perspective, we must reckon not only with the traditional tensions of design theory but with the special characteristics and constraints of computers as vehicles for the representation and manipulation of knowledge.

A PERSPECTIVE ON DESIGNING AND DESIGN KNOWLEDGE

In this paper, I shall treat designing not primarily as a form of 'problem solving', 'information processing', or 'search', but as a kind of *making*. On this view, design knowledge and reasoning are expressed in designers' transactions with materials, artifacts made, conditions under which they are made, and manner of making. What architects make, as John Habraken has observed,[4] are *representations* of things to be built. Sketches, diagrams, drawings and models function as virtual worlds, representations of the real world of building on a site, within which architects can experiment at relatively low risk and cost.

It is useful to distinguish several levels of 'making', moving from a general view of designing to a more specifically architectural one.

In designing, first of all, things are made under conditions of *complexity*. Designers discover or construct many different variables. These interact in multiple ways, never wholly predictable ahead of time. As a result, a designer must fashion each move to satisfy a variety of requirements and can never make a move that has only the consequences intended for it.

Architects make things under conditions of *uncertainty*. This means not only that the consequences of design moves are never wholly predictable but that design situations are, in John Dewey's language, 'problematic'.[5] Although the programme or brief to be satisfied by a design may be highly specified, design situations are always partly indeterminate. In order to formulate a design problem to be solved, the designer must *frame* a problematic design situation: set its boundaries, select particular things and relations for attention, and impose on the situation a coherence that guides subsequent moves. Moreover, the work of framing is seldom done in one burst at the beginning of a design process. Designing triggers awareness of new criteria for design: problem solving triggers problem setting.

Finally, architectural designing is a *dialogue* with the phenomena of a particular site. An architect's 'making' has as much to do with appreciating a site as with imagining a building. As William Hillier has written, designing is 'a kind of dialectic between the designer's prestructuring of the world and the world as it is seen to be when examined in these terms'.[6]

Within this general framework, a designer's ways of knowing can be described, and the tensions inherent in design theory can be addressed, through the notions of *rules, types* and *worlds*.

We need a way of talking about the objects of designing—what we design *with*—that allow us both to take cognizance of multiple ways of seeing things, each a reality for those who hold it, and to make sense of strivings for commonality. Hence, I am led to the notion of *design worlds*. These are environments entered into and inhabited by designers when designing. They contain particular configurations of things, relations and qualities, and they act as *holding environments* for design knowledge. A designer's knowledge is not only in his ideas or actions, but in the things with which he deals. The objects of a design world are, in Seymour Papert's phrase, 'things to think with'.[7] As a designer brings understandings, strategies and images to a particular design situation, conducts a dialogue with that situation, and constructs in it a version of a more or less familiar design world, he instantiates a particular set of things to think with.

Designers *construct* their design worlds not only through the shaping of materials but through interlocking processes of perception, cognition and notation. As Nelson Goodman has pointed out,[8] we make the worlds in which we live through a kind of instant perceptual problem solving (Jeanne Bamberger's phrase) that takes the form of selective attention, grouping, boundary setting, and naming.

The idea of design worlds is inconsistent with an *objectivist* point of view, according to which things are what they are independent of our ways of seeing them. On this view, it is difficult to explain how different designers see things differently, have trouble talking with each other about them, and take radically different approaches to design. But design worlds are consistent with a *constructionist* perspective like Goodman's where miscommunication, novelty, and diversity of approach are exactly what we would expect. From a constructionist perspective, the seeming objectivity of a consensual design world is not a given but an achievement, a product of the work of communicative inquiry.

When we seek to describe the 'prestructurings' designers bring to the construction of their design worlds, the problem of representing design knowledge presents itself in another guise. How are we to account for the cumulative generality of design knowledge and for the designer's capacity to generate new understandings in response to the uniqueness of a particular design situation?

Considerations like these have led William Porter and me to adopt a variant of the familiar notion of 'type'. A type, in the sense we intend, is neither a general category, like 'church', nor does it consist only in a particular instance, like 'Richardson's Trinity Church'. In our sense, types should be seen as particulars that function in a general way, or as general categories that have the 'fullness' of particulars. Examples might be the 'New England Green', 'Oxbridge lawns', 'pavillion' and 'cave', mentioned in William Porter's essay in this issue (of *Design Studies*). Because of their fullness—the richness of imagery, ideas and commonplaces associated with them—types such as these can generate sequences of moves and guide designing. For this reason, I believe, Rudolph Arnheim suggests that 'the abstractions characteristic of productive thinking are types rather than containers',[9] and goes on to describe types as 'generative abstractions'.

Types can function as references. By invoking a type, a designer can *see* how a possible design move might be matched or mismatched to a situation, even when the designer cannot say with respect to what features there is a match or mismatch. In a designer's dialogue with a situation, types can function both to transform the situation and to be transformed by it. A design situation, seen as unique, both invites and resists the importation of a type. The transaction between familiar type and unique design situation is a metaphorical process, a form of *seeing*—and *doing-as,* in which a designer both transforms a design situation and enriches the repertoire of types available to him for further design.

A number of contemporary authors have introduced ideas that bear a family resemblance to our notion of types. The literary critic, William Wimsatt, introduced the term, 'concrete universal', to capture the peculiar combination of generality and concrete particularity characteristic of certain literary images.[10] In his account of scientific revolutions, Thomas Kuhn speaks of 'exemplars … concrete problem solutions, accepted [by a community of scientists] … as, in a quite usual sense, paradigmatic'. In Kuhn's view, a student learns a science—physics, for example—by learning to solve canonical problems like finding the acceleration of a ball rolling down an inclined plane, and then 'discovers a way to see his problem as like … the exemplary problems he has encountered before'.[11] The cognitive psychologists, Eleanor Rosch and Susan Carey-Block, have argued that we learn to recognize and reason about familiar things, not by amassing lists of features but by forming representations of 'prototypes' (the prototype of 'bird', for example: more like a robin than an ostrich) in relation to which we then recognize and reason about the things we perceive (see, for example, References[12] and[13]). Geoffrey Vickers has described the use of precedents in legal reasoning where, in debates about the correct formulations of rules of law, priority is given to the precedent from which the rule is derived.[14] In a context closer to the present one, Rudolph Arnheim has described the 'generative process [that] animates perception visibly, every time a perceived thing evokes its prototype.[15]

We believe that, in a sense closely related to the exemplars, precedents, images and concrete universals described by the authors cited above, the *rules* employed in design reasoning are derived from types. As rules of law are derived from judicial precedents, in Vickers's account, so design rules are derived from types, and may be subjected to test and criticism by reference to them. Moreover, a designer's ability to apply a rule correctly depends on familiarity with an underlying type, by reference to which the designer judges whether the rule 'fits the case' and fills the inevitable gap between the relatively abstract rule and the concrete context of its application.

Rule-descriptions are derivative constructs. By reflecting on existing types, we may construct and codify their constitutive rules. For example, the building types, codified by Vitruvius on the basis of his analysis of the design practice of his time, shaped designing and building in the West for hundreds of years. (An example of a Vitruvian type and an associated rule: 'In a house, the standard of symmetry—the part from which all other parts are to be calculated—is the atrium; it may have one of three different ratios of length to width: 5:3, 3:2, and the ratio of the diagonal of a square to its side'.)[16]

Over time, we may come to think of such rules as free-standing. But when a type shifts—when, for example, it comes to be seen as mismatched to its changing environment—then the codified rules collapse and the illusion of independence is exposed.

There is a two-way interaction between design types and design worlds. On the one hand, elements of a design world may be assembled to produce an artifact that comes to function—either in the practice of an individual designer or in a larger design culture—as a type; so it has been with Trinity Church. On the other hand, the direction of causality may be reversed. A vernacular building type—with its constituent things and relations, forms, materials, construction methods, ways of organizing space, and symbolic vocabularies—may 'loosen up' to provide the furniture of a design world. In a very similar vein, John Habraken has described 'thematic systems' like post-and-beam or pillar-and-arch construction, which are drawn from vernacular building types.[17] He has involved students in intensive 'conversations' with these thematic systems—kinds of design worlds, in our sense of the term—in order to help them become sensitive to the systems' constraints and potentials for generating new forms. Similarly, an individual designer may, in a project or series of projects, break apart objects and relations inherent in a type she has developed or adapted. She may live for a time in a design world made up of these objects and relations, exploring its limits and its potentials for generating new forms.

NOTES

Extracted from D. Schön, 'Designing: Rules, Types, and Worlds', *Design Studies* 9/3 (1988): 181–4. Used by permission of Elsevier.

1. This paper is drawn from my work over the past five years with William Porter and other members of the MIT's Design Theory and Method Group.
2. Cardozo, B. *The Nature of the Judicial Process* Yale University Press, New Haven, Conn. (1921).
3. Alexander, C. *Notes Toward a Synthesis of Form* Harvard University Press, Cambridge, Mass. (1968).
4. Habraken, J. *The Appearance of the Form* Atwater Press (1985).
5. Dewey, J. *Logic: The Theory of Inquiry* Holt, Rinehart and Winston, New York (1938).
6. Hillier, W. and Leaman, A. 'How is design possible? A sketch for a theory', *DMGIDRS Journal*, Vol. 8, No. 1.
7. Papert, S. *Mindstorms: Children, Computers and Powerful Ideas* Basic Books, New York (1980).
8. Goodman, N. *Ways of Worldmaking* Hackett, Indianapolis (1978).
9. Arnheim, R. *Visual Thinking* The University of California Press, Berkeley and Los Angeles, California (1969).
10. Wimsatt, W. K., Jr. 'The structure of the 'concrete universal' in literature' *Publications of the Modern Language Association of America*, Vol. LXII (1947) pp. 262–280.
11. Kuhn, T. 'Second thoughts on paradigms' In *The Essential Tension* The University of Chicago Press, Chicago, Illinois (1977).
12. Rosch, E. 'Principles of categorization' In *Cognition and Categorization* (Eds E. Rosch and B. Lloyd) Lawrence Erlbaum, Hillsdale, NJ (1978).
13. Carey, S. *Conceptual Change in Childhood* MIT Press, Cambridge, Mass. (1985).
14. Vickers, G. Information memorandum, Division for Study and Research in Education, MIT (1978).
15. Arnheim, R. *Visual Thinking* The University of California Press, Berkeley and Los Angeles, California (1969).
16. Vitruvius, M. P. *The Ten Books on Architecture* (trans. M.H. Morgan, 1914) Dover Publications, New York (1960) (Section I, ii, 4 and section VI, iii, 5) Quoted in Tom Heath *Lessons from Vitruvius*, mimeo Queensland Institute of Technology, Brisbane, Australia (1987).
17. Habraken, J. *The Appearance of the Form* Atwater Press (1985).

16

DISCOVERY RESEARCH

Susan Squires

DISCOVERY RESEARCH

The goal of discovery research is to uncover and understand the cultural system that frames human action to provide a direction for creating new products and services. Researchers collect and analyze a combination of verbal, observational, and contextual information to identify what people say and do in their natural environment. The consistencies and, more frequently, the inconsistencies help identify unarticulated or unrecognized needs, gaps, and adaptations called "work-arounds" and "disconnects." By reframing disconnects in terms of sociocultural systems, teams essentially change the assumptions that guide their own attempts to create products or services. Clients and consumers almost always perceive the new products and services as innovative or novel because existing products usually ignore many of the cultural attributes of a product or treat them in stereotypic ways.

[…]

The key to a successful discovery research project is the use of rapid ethnographic assessment methods. […] Since at least the mid-1970s, rural development projects requiring quick results have been called rapid appraisal, rapid assessment, and rapid rural appraisal (Chambers 1983; Hildebrand 1982; Rhoades 1982; Honadle 1979; Shaner, Philipp, and Schmehl 1982; Collinson 1981). More recently they have been used to describe new research directions in health (Beebe 1995; Bennett 1995; Higginbothom 1994;

Manderson and Aaby 1992; Manderson et al. 1996; Trotter and Schensul 1999) and product innovation (Squires 1999; Sunderland 1999).

The objective of rapid ethnographic assessment in discovery research is typically to construct a sociocultural model of the local living system that is both consistent with the way local people understand it and uses local (emic) categories to describe and categorize their reality (Galt 1985: 14). All rapid ethnographic approaches share three important characteristics "(1) a system perspective, (2) triangulated data collection, and (3) iterative data collection and analysis (Beebe 1995: 42)."

Rapid ethnography, as applied in product innovation, differs from other rapid ethnographic approaches in three important ways. First, whereas rapid rural appraisal requires the participation of sizable multidisciplinary teams, small teams usually do rapid ethnographic research for product development. Thus the teams have to be quick, almost self-supporting, and well coordinated. Second, the outcome of the work is most likely a product rather than complex state-subsidized programs and public policies. Third, the teams use video whenever possible to document interviews, behavioral activities, and the relationship among things so that individuals who could not be present might review and exchange information.

I use rapid ethnographic approaches that stress open-ended interviews, site tours (contextual observation), participant observation, literature reviews, cultural history, and semiotic (content) analysis. I occasionally use time series analysis, multidimensional scaling (cognitive mapping), focus groups, and telephone surveys. Let me give you an example of how discovery research can be used to generate cultural insights that lead to successful products.

My colleagues and I were asked to learn about family morning routines and breakfast time behavior. Our client, a large breakfast food company, was particularly interested in learning whether or not "participant observation," the hallmark of anthropological ethnographies, was useful in generating insights that might facilitate its own product development. We formed two teams. Each was composed of one social scientist and one designer. I teamed up with Sally.

We went to have breakfast with the Kellys, a family residing in a northern California suburb. They were one of several families we visited. We arrived at 6:30 A.M. with bags stuffed with video cameras, film, batteries, tape recorders, and paper and pens. I knocked on the door and waited. The door opened into a dark, empty hall, and a woman's voice echoed from the kitchen, "Come on in. We've been expecting you." And then she added, "Close the door, Jack." Sally and I looked down to see the silent upturned face of a smiling four year old. Jack pushed the door shut and ran ahead of us down the hall and into the kitchen. We followed.

The first minutes are always awkward, but soon Sally and I were sipping coffee at the kitchen table and engaging in small talk with Mom and Jack's older brother Kevin, age six. Jack had left us in favor of the family TV that was booming away in the living room.

Mom led the conversation. We let her talk. "Well, I'm not sure I have anything more to tell anyone. If you want, I'll tell you what I told the people at the focus group."

We had recruited Mrs. Kelly because she had participated in a traditional focus group sponsored by the client. As we normally do, we had already familiarized ourselves with the latest understanding of breakfast food consumption. The material included industry reports and market research. Market research is often a good source of information about what is currently the "right" or "acceptable" thinking on a topic. The focus group in which the Kelly mom participated provided us with information on what people say about breakfast and breakfast food. The focus group data indicated that the American breakfast of the 1990s was occurring very early in the morning. The data also revealed that American moms are very concerned about the quality of the breakfast food they buy. They want to give their kids a good start to the day, and a good breakfast, they told the market researchers, was key to providing that start. We were visiting the Kellys to learn whether their breakfast time activities matched what moms had told the market researchers in the focus group.

Jack's mother began our visit by telling us what she had told the market researchers at the focus group. "As I already said," Mom continued, "I only feed my kids whole grain, nutritious food. Gives 'em a good start to the day. I know Kevin does better on his tests when I make sure he's had a good breakfast."

Mom took out a package of whole grain waffles and put a couple in the toaster to back up what she had just told us. "Want some waffles?" she smiled. Sally and I shook our heads. I didn't feel like having a waffle at 6:45 A.M. It was tough enough to concentrate on the long list of questions we wanted to ask:

- What were the morning routines at the Kelly house?
- Who was there and who was not?
- What other foods might be available?
- What was it like to coax a four year old to eat at 6:30 in the morning?
- What else had to get done before the family left the house?
- Where did the family go after leaving the house?
- Did anyone pick up food after leaving the house?

Sally and I were looking for the answer to these and a multitude of other questions. We began by watching what Mom was doing as she spoke to us. As Mom talked, she moved rapidly around the kitchen, adding a banana from a bowl and yogurt from the fridge, packing lunch for the boys. The toaster popped up, and Mom put the waffles on plates and buttered them while she told us about her day.

"My husband left just before you got here. He never eats breakfast. I think he grabs something at a 7–11 later on. But I make sure the kids eat. Jack, get in here and eat your waffle," she interrupted to call the four year old. Jack paid absolutely no attention to her and continued to watch cartoons on TV.

Mom smiled at us and put a plate of waffles in front of Kevin. "Jack's in day care. I drop him off first. Then I take Kevin to school. He's in the first grade. I'm usually out of here by seven or seven-fifteen. It's so early for them, but what can I do? My husband has to be at work pretty early, so it's up to me to take the kids to school before I go to work."

While Mom was telling us about the nutritious lunch she had just made for her two sons, we made our first "discovery": a disconnection between Mom's verbal reports and the family's breakfast behavior. Kevin left the table. He returned with a bowl of red, white, and blue Trix cereal and milk. Meanwhile, Mom was showing us how she got her kids to eat fresh fruit by mixing it into their yogurt. She paid no attention to Kevin as he ate his cereal.

"Where did you get that?" I asked Kevin, pointing to the cereal. "From the cabinet, of course," he told me with a puzzled look. He knew I had seen him get the cereal.

"How is it?"

It makes the milk turn blue." Kevin stirred the cereal in his bowl to demonstrate. The milk turned blue.

"Pretty cool," I noted. "Did your mom buy this for you?"

Kevin looked at me. "Not her. My dad—he likes it, too."

Mom came over to the table and began taking things to the sink. "Oh, that." She pointed to the cereal. "His father buys that," she explained as she picked up Kevin's waffle and ate it, licking the syrup off her fingers. She headed to the dishwasher with Kevin's empty dish and Jack's uneaten waffle.

"Jack, are you ready to go?" she shouted at the living room as she shoved Jack's waffle down the garbage disposal. During the time we were with the Kelly family, we never saw Jack eat anything.

Jack appeared with a blanket wrapped around him. Mom handed him his lunch container and said, "Here, take this and get in the car. You too, Kevin." Mom picked up her car keys. "Well, that's about it," she told us.

Sally and I slowly began to pack up our equipment when the phone rang. Mom ran to the counter and picked it up.

"I'm late," she informed the caller. "Yeah, whole grain waffles, juice, milk. Hey, I've got to go. Talk to you this afternoon."

She hung up and turned to Sally and me. "My mother-in-law," she explained. "Calls almost every morning to see if the kids have had a good breakfast. She thinks I should stay home with the kids. Doesn't think I have time to feed them good food when we're always on the run. What does she know? In her day, she fed her kids (my husband being one of them) bacon and eggs in the morning—cholesterol. Just goes to show you. Hey, I'm watching out for my kids. I'm a good mom."

As Sally and I left the Kelly home, we talked about what we would need to do next. We recognized that spending breakfast at the Kelly home was only a first step in the discovery process. Back at our office we spent hours examining the videotapes and transcripts from this and other breakfast visits, looking for a pattern in what people had told us and what they did. If this were a typical research project, we knew we would probably identify more questions than insights during the first analysis phase. That would mean we would be out "in the field" again at 6:30 in the morning.

From the analysis of our visit to the Kelly home and other breakfast visits, we learned that morning food consumption is not just about the individual decisions that moms make. A network of family and friends is involved in defining what is acceptable and made available for breakfast.

The existence of this network of family and friends was not a surprise. Underlying the rapid ethnographic approach is the understanding that all people belong to one or more networks of interlocking social relationships in which all members share a common or core set of beliefs, values, and behaviors. Anthropologists and other trained ethnographers use various methods to uncover the core sets by

- gathering individual (emic) perspectives from members of these sociocultural groups;
- examining the collected information to identify patterns of shared beliefs, behaviors, values, and rules;
- constructing group "mental models" from identified patterns to understand the meaning at the core of the system;
- interpreting how the members of a sociocultural network use their mental models to construct and express appropriate shared behaviors, beliefs, and values, to provide a contextual frame of meanings for products and services;
- identifying disconnects in the mental model where shared beliefs don't match behavior or where beliefs are not shared or break down, causing points of stress. For example, among the Kelly family adults there was a shared understanding that breakfast is an important meal. What constituted a "good" breakfast, however, was in disagreement and was causing tension in the family.

Because we were interested in placing breakfast in the context of the Kelly family's lives, we continued to follow various Kelly members in the following days. We called Dad at work and conducted a telephone interview. He told us about Saturday morning breakfast with Kevin and about shopping with his kids, buying cereal like the "stuff [he] ate when [he] was a kid." We also arranged to observe at Jack's day care. We were interested in learning whether he ever got anything to eat during the day, and if so, when and what.

We made our second discovery the day we visited Jack's day care. The kids were playing outside. While some of the kids were participating in a teacher-led activity, we found Jack sitting on the grass near the edge of the playground area.

"Hey, Jack, remember us?" I asked, walking over to where he sat. "Sure, I have to go. Bye."

"Wait, Jack, what are you doing over here anyway?" Sally asked. She had noticed that Jack had his lunch container with him.

"Eating my lunch." Jack looked first at Sally, then me.

"Lunch at ten o'clock in the morning?"

"It's all right, you know—Miss Barbara said it's okay. I got hungry."

Now we knew that something was up. Jack may not have eaten in the early morning, but he could not wait until the school's proscribed lunchtime to eat. The fieldwork with the Kelly family and others confirmed much of the information collected in the focus group. Breakfast time for today's families is very different than the idealized breakfast of the 1950s. Other findings were more unexpected. We certainly didn't expect to see blue cereal or Jack eating his lunch before lunchtime.

We began to see the whole picture of food consumption in the morning once we constructed shared mental models and a contextual frame for observed behaviors. By doing so, we identified the disconnects between beliefs and behaviors that provided insight about what happened at breakfast, what didn't happen at breakfast, and what happened outside of the home. Although we recognize that we will never be able to actually get inside the heads of the Kelly family, we can infer quite a bit from what moms, dads, and kids told us, and from what we observed.

We began to look at what was common to all the families in the study. We constructed a set of understandings of the food consumption habits of families that put the focus group data in the context of an evolving American family.

Because both moms and dads are working, breakfast in today's American homes is under stress. There really is no time for breakfast. Yet, there is a belief among parents that breakfast is the most important meal of the day, especially for the kids. Kids, we are told, will do better in school and by extension better in life if they eat a good breakfast every morning. Parents are under a lot of pressure to provide their children with a good start to the day and to their future. Although it appears that moms, dads, and their relatives all share the belief that breakfast is the most important meal of the day, they differ about what constitutes a "good' breakfast. For Mom, a good breakfast is whole grain or preservative-free foods. Dads value foods similar to those they had as children. They enjoy sharing these "comfort" foods with their kids although they may not be the nutritional food moms value.

Grandparents are typically more worried about the changing role of moms in the family and more likely to doubt the ability of moms to juggle work and childcare. They are not convinced that today's mom can provide the breakfast their grandkids need to succeed in life. However, the foods of a generation ago that the "good mom" provided are not perceived as good by today's standards. As the mom in this story told us, she would never provide a breakfast of cholesterol-laden foods to her kids.

Finally, kids are not cooperating. They may not want to eat so early in the morning. Physiologically, they may not be ready to eat. If they do eat, they want something that has a value to them: blue milk. Getting kids to eat Mom's ideal breakfast is another point of stress.

The opportunities we found during this research were not just about trying to reconcile the differing beliefs about what constitutes a "good" breakfast for moms, dads, kids, and grandmothers. We also looked at the food consumption patterns of all the family members during the day, and it became clear that the "traditional" breakfast time at the beginning of the day might not be the best time to consume food. In fact, most of the family members in our study were not eating breakfast at home. Dad stopped at a convenience store. Mom picked up food where she worked. The kids were eating their lunch at school when they got hungry. Presented with this pattern of food consumption in the morning, it is easy to dismiss the eating at school and work as snacking. But it is not about snacking. It's breakfast; it's about a meal that has culturally proscribed beliefs about its appropriate time, activity, and location.

A deeper look at the food concerns of the family and the behavior using cultural and physical anthropological theory suggests a more pervasive nutritional problem in the American middle class. Selling people another snack food will not solve this problem, even if it is a healthful snack.

The combined information we gathered from the literature and our field studies suggest that Americans are facing a structural conflict. Time pressures are forcing American families to start their day earlier than ever before—so early that, for all intents and purposes, we are still "asleep." Recent studies of sleep cycles among children and teenagers suggest that they need more sleep time. The majority of us are ready to eat and begin our day between 8 and 10 in the morning. By looking for opportunities holistically, we found that the problem was not just about what to eat (breakfast food). It's about the inconsistency between when it is culturally appropriate to eat and when people are ready to eat.

We shared our insights with our client. It considered the evidence and created Go-curt. Despite limited distribution, Go-curt brought in $37 million in sales in its first year. Two years later, *Newsweek* featured Go-Gurt in a story. The magazine quoted one California mom who said that her child "thinks she's eating a Popsicle for breakfast, but it's better for her" (*Newsweek,* October 11, 1999). Go-Gurt succeeded because it resonates with the kid's need for fun and mobility and the mother's need to provide nutritious food.

[...]

NOTE

Extracted from S. Squires, "Doing the Work: Customer Research in the Product Development and Design Industry," in *Creating Breakthrough Ideas: The Collaboration of Anthropologists and Designers in the Product Development Industry,* ed. Bryan Byrne (Westport, Conn.: Bergin and Garvey, 2002), pp. 107–14. Reproduced with permission of Greenwood Publishing Group, Inc., Westport, CT.

SECTION 2: DESIGN THINKING

2.3: Design Communications

INTRODUCTION

Branding builds an organization's identity by communicating an impression through language, graphics, images, and sensory experiences. Governments, corporations, and individuals use branding to share meaning about their ideology, processes, and products with the larger public. Designers who work in branding often promote the identity of the brand over a tangible or material product to communicate ideas that change perceptions. Moreover, brands are rampant in our global culture. For example, think about the Nike swoosh and McDonald's arches. As Naomi Klein explains in the Politics subsection (3.3), corporations are now ignoring the realities of labor and production in order to extol the brand above everything else. This subsection includes three readings that explore design's communicative limits and cultural impact.

The first reading in the subsection discusses how the crises associated with war forced many governments to turn to the power of communication design during the twentieth century. Eric Van Schaak describes how the American government understood that the power of graphic design could be used to convince citizens about the importance of supporting the Allies during World War I. In his article, "The Division of Pictorial Publicity," Van Schaak writes about the Division's output of propaganda and how its designers worked closely with government officials to devise graphics that would inspire fear of the enemy. Ten specific designs, created to sell Liberty Bonds, "confronted the public with the horrors of a possible German invasion." By branding the war effort as a necessary struggle against the possibility of a barbaric invasion by German forces, the U.S. government raised close to seven billion dollars that helped pay for the war.

Like governments, corporations have long understood the power of communication design as a branding tool. Indeed, think about how brands are marketed during the Super Bowl, or the World Cup, where advertisements attempt to generate awareness without focusing on actual products or services. In the article, "Globalizing Corporate Identity in Hong Kong: Rebranding Two Banks," D. J. Huppatz writes about the changing corporate identities of the Hongkong and Shanghai Banking Corporation (HSBC) and the Bank of China. He reveals how design, both graphic and architectural, allowed the two banks to form a "new image that would not only distinguish each from their global competitors, but also distance each from their respective … histories." The act of rebranding allowed these institutions to have a fresh start that asked consumers to reimagine the global reach and economic power associated with these financial establishments.

The excerpt from the Huppatz article focuses on graphic design and the banks' shift toward using abstract corporate logos. The Hongkong and Shanghai Banking Corporation, for instance, had used a nineteenth-century seal that included a coat of arms (signifying the British Crown) and Chinese characters (signifying the nation associated with the bank). In 1983, designer Henry Steiner came up with an abstract form for the bank. "The logo consists of a minimal hexagram composed of red and white triangles derived from the company's old flag." Huppatz reveals how this abstract design erases Hong Kong's colonial past (the symbol of the British crown is gone) and distances the bank from its link to China (the Chinese characters have been cut). In place of this old logo is a new logo that gives a larger population of potential consumers the chance to associate with HSBC as a corporate brand. In the twenty-first century, it is easier for customers in cities such as New York to connect with HSBC through abstraction, rather than have to think about graphics that make the bank look too Chinese or too closely aligned with the British Empire.

Moving away from government propaganda and enormous financial institutions, the article on Martha Stewart allows us to evaluate branding on a more personal level. While abstraction might work for a bank that is trying to create a global brand, devising symbols about quality and comfort are Martha Stewart's aim for her corporation, Martha Stewart Living Omnimedia. Shirley Wajda contends that Stewart walks the fine line between two different types of American fantasies about individualism—utilitarian individualism and expressive individualism. According to Wajda's article, "Kmartha," Stewart collapses these categories into one brand in which a combination of the utilitarian side (the individual who is self-reliant) and the expressive side (the individual who is creative and feeling) become an unusual admixture that reveals "a deeper American concern about individualism and its place in society." Stewart, through a remarkable public relations machine and marketing genius, makes her own self—her brand—into this incredible amalgamation of American ingenuity and domestic sensitivity.

War propaganda, a bank's logo, and the design of domestic products are all forms of what Larry Ackerman, who works for the branding firm Siegel + Gale, describes as "societal brands." Ackerman, in a white paper (a position paper) titled "The Rise of the Societal Brand" (see the annotated guide at the end of the subsection for full citation), found on Sigel + Gale's Web site (http://www.siegelgale. com/dialogue/2007/02/07/the-rise-of-the-societal-brand/), notes that "we are witnessing the rise of a new phenomenon on the brand landscape: organizations whose sheer size, wide sphere of influence and fundamental impact on the national or world economy makes them, by definition, societal brands." These mega-brands "literally shape how society works, whether they intend to or not. They are agents of societal change." The articles in this subsection examine branding efforts that shape the way we think about the world as consumers and members of civic culture. The global influence of branding alters our perceptions of corporations and governments, fostering our own sense of identity in a world where "societal brands" define us as individuals and citizens.

17

THE DIVISION OF PICTORIAL PUBLICITY IN WORLD WAR I

Eric Van Schaak

When America entered World War I, Washington quickly realized that the successful prosecution of the war would require a sustained effort of a magnitude and an intensity hitherto unimagined. The need for men, supplies, and self-sacrifice on the home front was totally unprecedented. What is particularly interesting to an art historian is the government's decision to bring home this message through the visual arts.

On April 13, seven days after signing the joint Congressional resolution that declared war on the Imperial German Government, President Wilson issued Executive Order No. 2594 that created a Committee on Public Information (CPI) which was to act as an agency for releasing news of the government; issuing information to sustain morale in the United States, administering voluntary press censorship, and, later, developing propaganda abroad. Three of the ex officio directors of the Committee were members of President Wilson's cabinet: Newton D. Baker, Secretary of War, Josephus Daniels, Secretary of the Navy, and Robert Lansing, Secretary of State.[1] The fourth director and Chairman of the Committee was George Creel (1875–1953), a forty-one-year-old journalist, editor, magazine writer, and zealous advocate of reform causes. As the editor of the *Rocky Mountain News*, Creel had advocated Wilson's nomination for the presidency as early as 1911, and had corresponded with Wilson during his first administration.[2]

At first, there were several meetings of the full committee, but Creel soon took charge and the CPI was, essentially, George Creel and his staff. He had no illusions about the difficulty of his job, and he knew that, in spite of Congress's overwhelming support of the war resolution, the country was deeply divided over the war. Looking back on his work, he wrote:

During the three and a half years of our neutrality, the United States had been torn by a thousand diverse prejudices, with public opinion stunned and muddled by the pull and haul of Allied and German propaganda. The sentiment of the West still was isolationist; the Northwest buzzed with talk of a "rich man's war," waged to save Wall Street loans; men and women of Irish stock were "neutral," not caring who whipped England; and, in every state demagogues raved about "warmongers. … "[3]

The mission of the CPI, as he saw it, was to unify the country and to fight for "the verdict of mankind." To carry out this task, he created a large number of subcommittees, or "divisions," as he called them. By the time the CPI went out of existence, Creel had created twenty-one divisions devoted to domestic propaganda, including the News Division, the Film Division, the Advertising Division, and the Women's War Work Division. There also was a Foreign Section with sixteen divisions which dealt with the foreign press cable service, foreign mail service, and a Work with the Foreign Born Division that had nine national bureaus.[4]

One of the most successful of these divisions was the Division of Pictorial Publicity (DPP). Creel understood that posters could have an important role in influencing public opinion. He wrote:

Even in the rush of the first days ... I had the conviction that the poster must play a great role in the fight for public opinion. The printed word might not be read; people might choose not to attend meetings or to watch motion pictures, but the billboard was something that caught even the most indifferent eye. ... What we wanted—what we had to have—was posters that represented the best work of the best artists—posters into which the masters of the pen and brush had poured heart and soul as well as genius.[5]

Creel chose Charles Dana Gibson (1867–1944) to head the Division of Pictorial Publicity.[6] Gibson was the president of the Society of Illustrators, an organization of professional artists that had been founded in 1901 to promote the art of illustration and to hold exhibitions of its members' works. He was one of the best known and highest paid artists in America, and in the decade before the war, the elegant and attractive "Gibson Girl" had become a national institution.

[...]

The Division of Pictorial Publicity officially came into being in November, 1917, and by the beginning of January, 1918, Gibson was able to send Creel a summary of the Committee's work for December, 1917.[7] This was the earliest of the surviving reports of Gibson's committee. It was typed on letterhead which still had the logotype of the Society of Illustrators, but also identified the organization as the Division of Pictorial Publicity. The Division now had office space in Room 1203, 200 Fifth Avenue, in New York City. The report was entitled "Summary/Division of Pictorial Publicity for December 1917," and it had been prepared by Horace Devitt Welsh (1888–1942), the Assistant Secretary of the DPP. Welsh worked out of the CPI's Washington

office, and was the "contact man" who went to the government offices to determine what sort of publicity they needed. He then would pass this information on to Gibson, who would choose the artists. Welsh's report began:

I submit herewith summary of the work of the Art Department which was previously formed and has now branched out into a Division of Art for Pictorial Publicity.

Welsh then listed the officers. Gibson was the Chairman, and Frank De Sales Casey was the Vice Chairman and Secretary. The Board of Associate Chairmen consisted of Adams, Blashfield, and Gilbert, as well as the painter and etcher Joseph Pennell (1860–1926). There also was an Executive Board composed of fourteen artists: the painter William Jean Beauley (b. 1874), Frederick G. Cooper, Charles Buckles Falls, Louis Fancher, the sculptor Melvina Hoffman (1885–1966), the illustrator Wallace Morgan (1873–1948), the painter and illustrator Herbert Paus (1880–1946), the painter and illustrator William Allen Rogers (1854–1931), the illustrator and painter John E. Sheridan (1880–1948), the painter and print maker Harry Everett Townsend (1879–1941), the illustrator and writer Frank J. Sheridan, Jr., and Adolph Treidler (1886–1981). Casey and the illustrator Charles David Williams had been appointed to "secure for the government work of the highest merit along artistic lines."

The report outlined the way the Division intended to function. Government departments would contact the committee when they needed artwork, and the Division would provide it at no cost, since most of the artists, Casey pointed out, were volunteering their services. The Division would not be involved in printing the work, since this would be the responsibility of those who had commissioned the work. "The coordination of the various artistic resources," Casey wrote, "should do a great ways [sic] in enabling the United States to be in the front rank of artistic patriotic appeals for the duration of the War."

[...]

After the DPP's report of its activities during December, 1917, there are no more reports until July 23, 1918, when Casey and Gibson sent Creel a report of the Division's activities during the months of May and June. A report for March was sent to Creel, and he acknowledged its receipt in a letter dated April 5, but this has not been located. There also is a report dated August 5 for the month of July, a report dated August 22 for the week ending August 22, a report dated September 16 for the activities during the month of August, a report dated October 24 for the activities during September, and a final report dated November 18 for the work done during the month of October. These reports not only document the activities of the Division, they give us a good picture of the way the Division functioned.[8]

The reports are quite extensive, some of them as long as fifteen pages, and they list the governmental departments that had commissioned pictorial publicity and the artists who carried out the work. However, since the captions or slogans on the posters are seldom listed, it often is impossible to identify individual posters.

The amount of work produced by the DPP was astonishing. During May and June, the Liberty Loan Committee for the Fourth Liberty Loan Drive, which opened on September 28 and closed on October 19, 1918, requested some posters. More than fifty designs were submitted by forty-eight artists. All the designs were shipped to Liberty Loan Headquarters in Washington. After the Liberty Loan Committee had selected the designs for the drive, nine of which were chosen from among those submitted by the DPP, the Food Administration then chose five more. The remaining designs were sent back to New York. Eventually, ten of the DPP's designs were used.[9]

Most of the ten designs chosen by the Liberty Loan Committee confronted the public with the horrors of a possible German invasion. The lowering Hun in Fred Strothmann's *Beat Back the Hun* with his blood stained fingers and bayonet, still wears the *Pickelhaube* (spiked helmet), which Americans understood as a symbol of Prussian militarism, even though German forces had switched to the *Stahlhelm* (steel helmet) in 1916.[10] The bloody boots in John Norton's *Keep These Off the U.S.A.* were a grim warning of what Americans could expect from an invading Germany army.[11] But for dramatic effectiveness, none could match Joseph Pennell's striking portrayal of New York City under attack: *That Liberty Shall Not Perish from the Earth*. Pennell wrote that "My idea was New York City bombed, shot down, burning, blown-up by an enemy," and his original idea for the caption was "BUY LIBERTY BONDS OR YOU WILL SEE THIS".[12]

Ellsworth Young's *Remember Belgium*, of which more than a million copies were printed, played on American outrage at the atrocities committed by the German army in Belgium in 1914.[13] And the choice offered to Americans by the prolific magazine and book illustrator Henry Patrick Raleigh's *Hun or Home?* reminded Americans that only their dollars stood between them and an onslaught of merciless barbarians.[14]

While it may seem absurd to us today that Americans could actually believe that a German invasion force could land on American shores, there were millions of Americans who thought that a German invasion of the continental United States was not only possible, but quite likely and possibly even imminent. In 1915, Bernard Walker, an editor at *Scientific American*, had written *America Fallen*, a vivid account of a German invasion.[15] That same year, Hudson Maxim's *Defenseless America* appeared, in which the author claimed that an enemy power could land an invasion force of from 100,000 to 200,000 men on our shores in two weeks.[16] Robert R. McCormick, publisher of the influential *Chicago Tribune*, was so concerned about the threat of a German invasion that he urged the government to erect a series of fortifications in Albany, Boston, Pittsburgh, Atlanta, Vicksburg, and Houston, and in all the passes of the Sierra Nevadas and the Rockies. One member of Congress suggested that, since the Germans might attack the west and east coasts simultaneously, Americans living on the seaboards should retreat to safety behind the Allegheny and Rocky Mountains.[17]

The emphasis on the possibility of a German invasion in the publicity for the Fourth Liberty Loan was one of the reasons for its tremendous success. The Treasury estimated that more than twenty million people, more than half of the adult population of the United States, had purchased bonds. Nearly seven billion dollars was raised.

[...]

During its brief existence, the DPP had produced pictorial publicity for fifty-eight governmental departments and committees, submitted seven hundred designs for posters, one hundred and twenty-two for cards, three hundred and ten pieces of newspaper advertising, two hundred and eighty-seven cartoons, and nineteen designs for seals and buttons: a total of 1,438 designs created by 318 artists. Also, during the Third Liberty Loan Drive (April 6–May 4, 1918) Henry Reuterdahl and N. C. Wyeth had completed a 90-foot-high and 25-foot-long painting for the Sub-Treasury Building. To publicize the Fourth Liberty Loan (September 28–October 19, 1918) Reuterdahl had painted three paintings more than twenty feet long in Washington, DC.[18] And the total cost to the government for all this work was only $13,170.97.[19]

Reviewing the work of the Division of Pictorial Publicity in 1920, Creel wrote that he considered it one of the most remarkable parts of the Committee on Public Information.

At America's call, however, painters, sculptors, designers, illustrators, and cartoonists quickly and enthusiastically rallied to the colors, and no other class of profession excelled them in the devotion that took no account of sacrifice or drudgery ... [their posters] called to our own people from every hording like great clarions, and they went through the world, captioned in every language, carrying a message that thrilled and inspired.[20]

D. H. Lawrence once wrote that, for the generation that lived through the horrors of World War I, "all the great words were cancelled out,"[21] but the posters show no sign of this disillusionment; instead, they brought the "great words" to life for millions of Americans, inspiring them to make sacrifices for the war effort. They were the words men believed in and were willing to die for, and their power still resonates across the gulf that separates the beginning of the last century from its end.

NOTES

Extracted from E. Van Schaak, "The Division of Pictorial Publicity in World War I," *Design Issues* 22, no. 1 (2006): 32–33, 35–36, 39–43, and 45. © 2006 by the Massachusetts Institute of Technology.

1. Frank Hardee Allen, *Classification Scheme: Records of the Committee on Public Information, 1917–1919* (Washington, DC: Division of Classification, The National Archives, 1938), vii.

2. For Creel, see *The National Cyclopedia of American Biography* (New York: James T. White & Company, 1956), 41, 575–576, and Creel's autobiography, *Rebel at Large: Recollections of Fifty Crowded Years* (New York: G. P. Putnam's Sons, 1947).

3. Creel, 1947, 157.

4. The Committee's work was cut back after July 1, 1918. Its domestic activities ended after the armistice was signed on November 11, 1918, but its foreign operations continued until June 10, 1919. The fundamental studies of the Committee are James R. Mock and Cedric Larson, *Words that Won the War: The Story of the Committee on Public Information 1917–1919* (Princeton, NJ: Princeton University Press, 1939); and Stephen Vaughn, *Holding Fast the Inner Lines: Democracy, Nationalism, and the Committee on Public Information* (Chapel Hill, NC: The University of North Carolina Press, 1980). See also *Complete*

Report of the Chairman of the Committee on Public Information, 1917:1918:1919/Washington, DC: U.S. Government Printing Office); G. Creel, *How We Advertised America* (New York and London: Harper & Brothers Publishers, 1920); henceforth cited as Creel (1920); and *A Report Concerning Papers, Films, Records, Public Property, and Liabilities, etc. of the Committee on Public Information. Made by the Director of the United States Council of National Defense in response to Senate Resolution 323 of the 65th Congress, Second Session, adopted March 5, 1920* (Washington, DC: National Archives). See *Records of the Committee on Public Information, Record Group 63, CPI 1-02 Box 1, Entry 23,* and the hearings in the House of Representatives at which some CPI personnel were questioned. U.S. Congress, House Committee on Appropriations, *Hearings Before the Subcommittee of the House Committee on Appropriations in Charge of Sundry Civil Appropriations Bill for 1919, Part 3,* 65th Congress, 2nd Session, 1918.

5. Creel (1920), 133–134.

6. On Gibson, see Fairfax Downey, *Portrait of an Era as Drawn by C. D. Gibson (New* York: Charles Scribner's Sons, 1936); and Nick Meglin, "Charles Dana Gibson and the Age of Exclusivity," *American Artist* 39: 392 (March, 1975): 62.

7. The statement called for in Senate Resolution No. 323, adopted March 5, 1920 (see Footnote 4) gives the date of the organization of the DPP as November, 1917. For Welsh's report, see CPI 1-B1, Box 2.

8. CPI 1-131, Box 1, Entry 13.

9. *New York Times* (September 20, 1918): 4; and the DPP report for the months of May and June (CPI-B1, Box 1, Entry 13).

10. Fred Strothmann (1879–1958) was a pupil of Carl Hecker, and then studied in Paris and at the Berlin Royal Academy. He had wanted to be a portrait painter, but shifted to comic illustration. He was a regular contributor to the old *Life* Magazine, *Harper's Monthly, The Century, Hearst's International,* and *The Saturday Evening Post*; and also worked as a political cartoonist and a book illustrator. See Walter Reed, *The Illustrator in America 1860–2000* (New York: The Society of Illustrators, 2001), 124; *Who Was Who in American Art 1564–1975: 400 Years of Artists in America,* Peter Hasting Falk, ed. (Madison, Connecticut: Sound View Press, 1999), 3, 3207; and the *New York Times* (May 14, 1958): 33.

11. John Warner Norton (1876–1934) studied and later taught at the Chicago Art Institute, and was active as a muralist and as an easel painter. In 1926, at the Institute's annual exhibition, one of Norton's works won a bronze medal and a $300 prize and, in 1931, he won the Architectural League's Medal of Honor in painting for his paintings in the Tavern Club of Chicago. See *Who Was Who in American Art 1564–1975: 400 Years of Artists in America,* Peter Hasting Falk, ed., 2, 2440–2441; and the *New York Times* (January 8, 1934): 17.

12. Joseph Pennell (1860–1926) was one of the leading American illustrators of the late nineteenth and early twentieth centuries, and during World War I he created illustrations of the war production efforts in Britain, France, and the United States. He also was the author of a number of books including a biography of his friend, Whistler. See Reed, *The Illustrator in America 1860–2000,* 60; and *Who Was Who in American Art 1564–1975: 400 Years of Artists in America,* Peter Hasting Falk, ed., 3, 2567–2568. Pennell's poster is one of the best documented of the war. He wrote that "The idea came into my head on my way back from New York, where I had attended a meeting of the Committee on Public Information at which the loan was announced and posters asked for. See Joseph Pennell, *Joseph Pennell's Liberty Loan Poster: A Text Book for Artists and Amateurs, Governments and Teachers and Printers, with Notes, an Introduction and Essay*

on the Poster by the Artist (Philadelphia and London: J. P. Lippincott Company, 1918), 9 and 18.

13. Elsworth Young (1866–1953) was an illustrator and landscape painter who had come to Chicago in 1895 to work for *The Chicago Tribune*. Later, he did illustrations for *Popular Mechanics*. See *Memorial Fielding's Dictionary of American Painters, Sculptors & Engravers 2nd Newly-Revised, Enlarged, and Updated Edition,* Glen B. Opitz, ed. (Poughkeepsie, NY: Apollo Books, 1987), 1068; and the *New York Times* (September 27, 1952): 17.

14. Henry Patrick Raleigh (1880–1944) was one of America's most popular illustrators during the 1920s. He worked for the New York *World* and also did illustrations for *Harper's Bazaar, Saturday Evening Post, Colliers,* and Hearst. He also was active as an etcher, a lithographer, and a portrait painter. See *Who Was Who in American Art 1564–1975: 400 Years of Artists in America,* Peter Hasting Falk, ed.,

3, 2695; and Reed, *The Illustrator in America 1860–2000, 158–159.*

15. J. Bernard Walker, *America Fallen! The Sequel to the European War* (New York: Dodd, Mead and Company, 1915).

16. Hudson Maxim, *Defenseless America* (New York: Hearst's International Library Co., 1915), passim.

17. Edward Robb Ellis, *Echoes of Distant Thunder: Life in the United States 1914–1918* (New York: Coward, McCann & Geoghegan, Inc., 1975), 424–425.

18. Creel (1920), 137–138 and the list of artists in CPI 1-B1, Entry 13, Box 1.

19. For some time, Gibson paid the Division's operating expenses out of his own pocket. See James R. Mock and Cedric Larson, *Words that Won the War. The Story of the Committee on Public Information 1917–1919,* 102.

20. Creel (1920), 133.

21. Quoted in Barbara Tuchman, *The Guns of August* (New York: Macmillan Company, 1962), 440.

18

GLOBALIZING CORPORATE IDENTITY IN HONG KONG

D. J. Huppatz

By creating a uniform identity for the intangible processes and complex operations of a multinational corporation, designers play a crucial role in globalization. This article contrasts the rebranding of two multinational banks' corporate identity through a detailed semiological analysis of their graphic and architectural makeovers during the 1980s.[1] The increasingly global expansion of both the Hong Kong and Shanghai Banking Corporation and the Bank of China required a new image that would not only distinguish each from their global competitors, but also distance each from their respective colonial and communist histories. As key sites of identity, both the new corporate logos and the Hong Kong headquarters of each bank provide examples of the close link between two-dimensional and three-dimensional design disciplines in the service of global branding. The new identity programmes not only reveal these corporations' global aspirations but also their position in relation to the looming deadline of the British colony's 1997 return to China. A conduit for trade between China and the rest of the world, Hong Kong was the empty territory within which the two corporations metamorphosed, its local identity and culture suppressed by both designers and clients who instead utilized the language of international modernism, engaging geographically neutral references such as abstraction and high technology. Despite this apparent neutrality, however, both rebranding programmes are a product of their local context, and design, in its role of

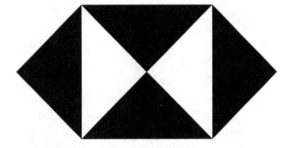

Image 8 HSBC Logo. Courtesy of Henry Steiner, Steiner & Co.

creating identity, emerges as one of Hong Kong's key assets during the 1980s.

THE GRAPHIC MAKEOVER

Founded in 1865, by a consortium of predominantly British traders, to fund the China trade, the Hong Kong and Shanghai Bank (HSBC) was both colonial and global at birth. With its headquarters in Hong Kong, a Shanghai branch for Northern China, a Yokohama branch for the Japan trade and a London branch, it grew within the networks of capitalism fostered by British colonialism in Asia. Although not established by the British government, by the 1880s it was banker for the Hong Kong colonial administration. As Asian trade expanded in the late nineteenth century, agents in various Asian cities became separate branches, so by the turn of the century there were branches in Singapore, Calcutta, Bombay, Colombo, Manila and Batavia, as well as in San

Francisco, New York, Lyons and Hamburg. The bank proved a particularly successful colonial enterprise, continuing to grow in the twentieth century, particularly after the Second World War, with extension into Indian and south-east Asian domestic markets. A more aggressive policy of expansion began in the 1970s, gaining foreign subsidiaries with their own identities and specializations, a trend which continued into the next decade. The takeover of the New York-based Marine Midlands Bank in 1980 further emphasized the HSBC's shift from an Asian-based to a dispersed multinational bank. However, as this brief paragraph from *The Times* (April 9, 1981) illustrates, the corporation still retained a distinctly colonial identity:

> The HK and Shanghai Banking Corporation is one of the great institutions of British commonwealth and colonial history. In its present manifestation it is one of the great banking empires of the modern commonwealth world. Based in Hong Kong, it is in most senses still a very British enterprise.[2]

At this time, the bank's visual image was also solidly colonial. Its nineteenth-century company crest, disseminated on banknotes and official correspondence, looked more like a royal seal than the logo of a modern financial corporation. The top part of the crest features the British Royal coat of arms—a lion and a unicorn holding a belt inscribed with the words 'Hon Y Soit Qui Mal Y Pense' ('Shame to him who evil thinks') which loop around a royal shield with a crown on top. The ribbon on which the lion and unicorn stand bears the motto 'Dieu et Mon Droit' ('God and My Right'). Below the ribbon is the only local reference, an image of a British clipper and a Chinese junk in a harbour, with some small figures on shore in the foreground, all framed by ornate foliage. The image of the two ships and the figures evidently engaged in trade is a local reference that situates the corporation's activities in a specifically Hong Kong colonial context as the premier financier for trade between Britain and China.

In 1983, Hong Kong designer Henry Steiner was commissioned to design a new corporate identity for the HSBC. The logo consists of a minimal hexagram composed of red and white triangles derived from the company's old flag. According to Steiner:

> The Hongkong and Shanghai Banking Corporation needed an updated name and identity for an international audience. The crest they were using was complicated and rather colonial. A bold, geometric symbol was designed using the shapes and colors from the company's old flag (a version of the Scottish Saint Andrew's flag) and is used together with a specially designed workmark.[3]

This design, closer to international modernist standards, would create a new identity for the increasingly global corporation while retaining some trace of the company's history. The HSBC website offers a similar reading:

> The Group's hexagon symbol was ... developed from the bank's house flag: a white rectangle divided diagonally to produce a red hourglass shape. A number of Hong Kong companies established in the 19th century were set up by Scottish businessmen and, like many other company flags of that era, the design was based on the Scottish flag, the cross of St Andrew.[4]

The shift from a distinctly colonial design to a more abstract symbol appears as seamless as the company's own shift from financier of the Britain—China trade to multinational financial giant. The shortened name, 'HSBC', also signalled a shift away from its Asian colonial roots to the neutrality of an abstract international corporate style. In rebranding this way, the bank followed what was an international standard by this time, as North American banks had already changed their complex heraldic marks to simple abstract logos, starting in the 1960s:

> In the United States, major banking institutions were advised by their design consultants to

discard eagles, lions, tigers and similar ferocious fauna in favour of simplified versions of currently fashionable and expensive works of art. Bridget Riley, Victor Vasarely, Max Escher and others became the inspiration for much of the US banking symbolism that emerged in the 1960s.[5]

In an Asian context, the new logo signalled the bank's alignment with Western international standards, distinguishing it from its local roots in Hong Kong and the China trade. Even the new wordmark suppressed its locality in an attempt to appeal to a broad international audience.

With the abstraction of international modernism, however, comes an ambiguity offering possibilities beyond the readings of the designer and client. In a 2000 edition of the British journal *Design Week*, a showcase of international identity design featured Steiner's HSBC logo. Designer John Powner nominated it as an outstanding logo but interpreted it very differently to both Steiner and the bank: 'Henry Steiner's clever symbol is a folded-out traditional Chinese purse, in the shape of an H—a wonderful reductive and appropriate idea'.[6] Thus, in this somewhat subversive reading,[7] the company's colonial flag metamorphoses into an abstracted Chinese purse, perhaps appropriate given the changing makeup of the bank. By the early 1980s, the traditionally British-born and Oxbridge-educated Board of Directors contained at least three Chinese businessmen. The new generation of Chinese entrepreneurs, represented by Yue-Kong Pao, Li Kashing and Hui Sai Fun, became permanent fixtures on the Board of the colony's premier financial institution from this time. While only three in a Board of twenty, they do represent the beginnings of a Chinese hold on the purse strings of an increasingly global corporation.

This ambiguity of the contemporary logo coincides with Fredric Jameson's reading of a logo as comprising a series of fragments whose ultimate meaning cannot be fixed, since its 'fundamental inner logic is the exclusion of the emergence of themes as such ... and which therefore systematically sets out to short-circuit traditional interpretive temptations ... '[8] Jameson's logo is:

a sign in its own right ... yet it is not yet clear what such new signs might be signs of, since no product seems identifiable, nor [sic] even the range of generic products strictly designated by the logo in its original sense, as the badge of a diversified multinational corporation.[9]

He argues that a logo does not operate alone, but as part of a constant stream or 'total flow' of visual material. It operates as a condensation of narratives, an abstract symbol standing in for a complex corporate enterprise comprising a diverse range of people and activities. As with Steiner's HSBC logo, the corporate logo is far from fixed in its meaning and its interpretative ambiguity highlights an excess of meaning beyond the designer's (or the client's) intentions.

One of the HSBC's major rivals in the China trade is the mainland-based Bank of China. Established in 1912 in Shanghai, the Bank of China (BOC) operated throughout the Maoist years as the specialized foreign trading bank of Communist China. With the opening of China to foreign trade in the late 1970s, the BOC needed a new identity to present to the world. In addition to growing to meet the expanding China trade, the bank also became more than just a foreign trading bank, moving into commercial banking and, later, insurance and other financial services. As Hong Kong had traditionally functioned as a mediator between China and the rest of the world, it was the natural place for the redesign of the bank's identity. This mediating practice was embodied in the nineteenth century figure of the comprador, a Chinese merchant whose knowledge of both Chinese Western commercial practices and culture made him an invaluable figure in the colony's economy. As a similar kind of middleman, Hong Kong designer Kan Tai-Keung was commissioned by the Bank of China in 1981 to redesign the bank's graphic image in a way that would bring it in to line with current global standards as well as signal its Chinese origins.

Kan's corporate logo of a simple red circle with a square in the middle specifically refers to an old Chinese coin while still adhering to international modernism's abstract style.[10] Lines above and below the square suggest the Chinese character zhong (middle), a shortened version of the characters for China, zhong guo. His 1989 Annual Report for the Bank of China took the Chinese coin idea a step further, using a real coin tied vertically with red string onto the cover. More than just a surface appropriation of traditional Chinese culture applied to a contemporary financial network, Kan's initial logo marked the Chinese state-controlled bank's entrance into global finance. Rather than yellow stars on a red background or hammers and sickles, the traditional Chinese coin and reference to the character zhong appeared to a global market to be safer than any design with a hint of Communism. This is not surprising since the CCP has been trying to downplay its Maoist past, and this now historical era was closely associated with the political symbolism of the national flag and the hammer and sickle.

Kan reworked the Bank of China's corporate image in 1992 to include a calligraphic rendering of Zhongguo Yinhang (Bank of China) with the English words in type below. Again emphasizing Chinese tradition, the calligraphy is not in simplified characters (the official script of the People's Republic), but traditional characters, the script most commonly used in Hong Kong and Taiwan. In his use of traditional calligraphy for Chinese characters, featured with English type, Kan emphasized the bank's cultural origins, but without specific reference to mainland China.

In choosing a Hong Kong designer for the mainland's most important financial logo, the Chinese government appears to have made a political decision to entrust its image-making to a designer of international renown but one with no obvious ties to the party state. This suggests a degree of cross-border fluidity in 1981 not normally associated with Hong Kong-China relations until

much later. However, Geremie Barmé argues that Hong Kong-Taiwan (Kong-Tai) consumer culture already had a marked influence on the mainland at that time: 'In the 1980s, the Kong-Tai style, with its evocation of hip, modernized Shanghai decadence, worldly petit-bourgeois patina, and consumer sheen, profoundly influenced the face of mainland culture'.[11]

In an essay entitled 'CCP Inc.', Barmé even links the development of party identity to the influence of the Kong-Tai commercial environment, with Hong Kong designers providing an appropriately international corporate image for state institutions. In this way, a Hong Kong designer such as Kan functions in a comprador role, aestheticizing the Chinese bank in an appropriate language for the global marketplace. The China evoked in Kan's logo is not the Communist China of the 1970s or early 1980s, but one constructed from an existing Western code of representation in which calligraphy and Chinese coins already have an iconic status.

Infinitely reproducible and instantly recognizable, both the HSBC and the BOC logos lose specific geographical connections. Both feign neutrality and displace the complexity of colonial British as well as Chinese history with the safety of abstraction. Wally Olins argues that multinational banking institutions tend to favour modernist identity programmes and that: 'although their products and services may be different from those of their competitors, they aren't necessarily that different; and it might be the case that the apparent differences between themselves and others in the market reside principally in the way they use their identities'.[12]

Thus despite their abstraction, both the logos are encoded with compressed historical narratives, however generalized—Kan's Chinese coin suggests the legacy of Chinese commerce while Steiner's link to a Scottish flag suggests a colonial history. Rather than a potentially threatening Communist China, Kan's logo alludes to a timeless traditional China, while Steiner's abstract logo alludes vaguely to a colonial commercial legacy while its minimal abstraction aligns it to Western corporate models. Importantly, both corporations employed Hong Kong designers for their redesign, not only marking the city as an important financial centre but also as a culturally fluid design centre in which new identities can be created. Ackbar Abbas describes the city during the 1980s and 1990s as a neutral cultural space, receptive to a wide variety of design styles and influences, an 'open city' whose 'extreme receptivity is unusual and could be related as much to its "floating" identity as to its growing affluence and accelerated development'.[13] He further argues that this is symptomatic of an identity in flux, as cultural memory is erased by the city's constant programme of building and rebuilding. However, Abbas also points out that the apparent neutrality of Hong Kong culture actually serves the interests of global capitalism, as seen in the examples of the two banks' rebranding programmes.

NOTES

Extracted from D. J. Huppatz, 'Globalizing Corporate Identity in Hong Kong', *Journal of Design History* 18/4 (2005): 357–61. Reprinted by permission of the author and Oxford University Press.

1. The approach taken here is informed by the semiology developed by Charles Sanders Peirce and Ferdinand de Saussure, and more particularly in relation to design, the work of Roland Barthes. See C. S. Peirce, *Collected Papers,* 8 volumes, Harvard University Press, 1931–58. F. de Sassure, *Course in General Linguistics,* trans. Roy Harris, Open Court Press, 1986, and R. Barthes, *Mythologies,* Paladin, 1972.

2. *The Times,* quoted in F. H. H. King, *The Hongkong Bank In the Period of Development and Nationalism, 1941–1984: From Regional Bank to Multinational Group, Volume IV of the History of the Hongkong and Shanghai Banking Corporation,* Cambridge University Press, 1991, p. 555.

3. From Steiner's portfolio on the Hong Kong Designer's Association webpage, see: http://www.hkda.com.hk.

4. HSBC website: http://www.hsbc.com.

5. W. Olins, *Corporate Identity: Making Business Strategy Visible Through Design,* Thames and Hudson, 1989, p. 59.

6. J. Powner, 'International Corporate Identity insert', *Design Week* (UK), Vol. 15, No. 33, August 2000, between pp. 24–25.

7. Such subversive readings rest in what Per Mollerup refers to as 'aberrantly decoded meanings', derived from readers who 'may add some unintended meaning by aberrant decoding apart from, or instead of, the encoded meanings.' P. Mollerup, *Marks of Excellence: The Function and Variety of Trademarks,* Phaidon Press, 1997, p. 89.

8. F. Jameson, *Postmodernism, or, the Cultural Logic of Late Capitalism,* Duke University Press, 1991, pp. 91–2.

9. Ibid., p. 86.

10. For this image, see http://www.boc.cn/en/static/index.html

11. G. R. Barmé, *In The Red: On Contemporary Chinese Culture.* Columbia University Press, 1999, ja. 241.

12. W. Olins, *Corporate Identity: Making Business Strategy Visible Through Design,* Thames & Hudson, 1989, p. 88.

13. A. Abbas, *Hong Kong: Culture and the Politics of Disappearance,* University of Minnesota Press, 1997, p. 80.

19

KMARTHA

Shirley Teresa Wajda

With the 1999 offering of Class A common stock to the public, Martha Stewart has made the street—that is, Wall Street—her home. On October 18, 1999, Martha Stewart herself served to the denizens of Wall Street a homemade breakfast of scrambled egg-stuffed, scallop-shaped brioche, chocolate croissants, and fresh squeezed orange juice. The coffee and bagel street vendors in downtown New York stood little chance of a good thing—that is, good business—that morning.

Martha Stewart Living Omnimedia (MSLO) fared much better. By day's end, the company's stock had soared from the initial public offering (IPO) of 7.2 million shares at $18.00 per share to $35.56 per share.[1] That's a lot of brioche. Indeed, it's a lot of food for thought. The phenomenon that is Martha Stewart—whether the person, the brand, the many companies, or the lifestyle Stewart advocates and sells—stuns by its success, measured in the material evidence of sales and in the advice displayed in material form in many American homes. Others scorn Stewart's enterprises as materialistic, "new Gilded Age" excess, the result of an overbearing (female) CEO driven by (take your choice) greed, perfectionism, or a problematic personal life. (What next, detractors ask, invading Poland with spatulas and fondue forks?)

That Stewart *herself* elicits both avid praise and acrid derision is telling, and what I wish to explore tentatively in this essay is why those responses occur, and so loudly. Despite the "Martha-bashing," Martha Stewart Living Omnimedia is wildly successful; any discussion of "Martha-meaning"

must thus account for consumerism's relationship to Americans' notions of the self at the heart of this phenomenon. Indeed, when we speak of Martha Stewart we are really speaking of a contested ideal, a "Kmartha," if you will. Kmartha comprises the celebrity, the corporation, the confounding image of American tradition and progress, all brought, literally, home. Martha Stewart offers brioche to Wall Street speculators but brings home the bacon, and this boundary "transgression" of public and private is the one that seems to provoke so much anxiety. Just as quickly, however, Kmartha offers a salve in material goods and comforting advice, nostalgic re-creations of family cohesion and community well-being, all the while advocating both disciplined system and self sufficiency.

In this respect Martha Stewart taps into a deeper American concern about individualism and its place in society. In a special issue of *The New York Times Magazine* entitled "The Me Millennium" (17 October 1999), sociologist and public policy expert Andrew J. Cherlin explored the contradictory definitions of individualism found in the newspaper's survey conducted for that special issue. The American public is extremely selfish. "The selfishness is not shameless," Cherlin writes,

in fact, the public seems somewhat conflicted. People bemoan the self-centeredness they see around them. They regret that family ties are weakening. They complain that they can't trust most people. But at the same time, they express starkly individualistic views. When presented with a list of basic values, they strongly identify with personal responsibility, self-sufficiency and self-expression. And not many see the contradiction—that if everyone puts highest priority on one's own interests, then family and community ties may weaken further.[2]

Such a contradiction, Cherlin observes, is the product of Americans' ongoing struggle between an older "utilitarian individualism"—that of Franklinesque achievement and Emersonian self-reliance—and a newer "expressive individualism"— one in which "emotional gratification, self-help, getting in touch with feelings, expressing personal needs" define the self. What is so seductive about expressive individualism is that it is so seemingly democratic: middle-class affluence has allowed more Americans more "time and money to cultivate their own emotional gardens." Nevertheless, in their responses to the survey Americans across the spectrums of class, sex, age, race, ethnicity, and political identity exhibited collectively a split personality between these dueling individualisms and commitment, projecting, for Cherlin, a widespread anxiety about their own pursuit of the American dream.[3]

Both individualisms are available commercially to Americans. The phenomenal success of Oprah Winfrey (with whom Martha Stewart is often compared) depends greatly on expressive individualism. Oprah's Book Club, for example, offers participants (in the main, women) "good reads" with which to explore their feelings. Winfrey's recently launched magazine *O* tenders the same advice of "self-actualization." And Winfrey's daily television show has altered its format in the last several years to exclude sensational topics of social and individual depravity and to emphasize emotional well being and spiritual growth.

If Oprah Winfrey cultivates women's emotional gardens by discussing book plots, Martha Stewart sows, mulches, composts, and weeds a quite different form of plot. As *New York Times* columnist

Molly O'Neill points out, Martha Stewart's enterprises "are professionalizing the traditional sphere of 'women's work' into an even bigger, and more demanding arena: 'couples' work'." Indeed, this was Stewart's original intent: to fill in "the hole women left after entering the work force en masse." Stewart offers working Americans of both sexes an example of utilitarian individualism: she raises her own food, tends her own chickens, and recycles, all the while remembering to tend meticulously to traditional rituals that bring together family, friends, and community.[4]

Yet Martha Stewart also stewards a phenomenal business enterprise. In 1991, the eponymous home and decorating magazine *Martha Stewart Living* was introduced through Time, Inc., to 250,000 subscribers. The magazine, reacquired by Stewart in February 1997, now boasts a circulation of 2.1 million, and was expanded in January 2001 from ten to twelve issues a year. Quarterly special issues (entitled *Weddings and Baby*) now include holiday issues (Halloween and Christmas). Stewart's weekend television show, launched in September 1993, attracts 2.6 million viewers, while her daily show, "Living with Martha Stewart" (launched in September 1997), expanded from thirty to sixty minutes in January 1999, and, according to Stewart's website, reaches 88 percent of households in the United States. The program now airs in Brazil and Japan, and Stewart's other programs air on cable networks HGTV and the Food Network ("From Martha's Kitchen"). Holiday specials are now primetime events. From 1991 to 1997 Stewart appeared weekly on NBC's "Today," and now she visits CBS's "The Early Show." Martha by Mail debuted in Fall 1995, as did *askMartha,* her *New York Times* syndicated column carried by 235 newspapers across the nation. Ninety-second *askMartha* radio broadcasts are currently carried by 285 stations. The corporation's website, introduced on 8 September 1997, attracts 300,000 hits per week. Since 1982, Martha Stewart has written or coauthored with her magazine's editors over thirty books. (Her first work, *Entertaining,* appeared in 1982 and has undergone thirty printings.) In the last four years, Martha Stewart has signed deals with Kmart, Sherwin-Williams, Jo-Ann Fabrics, and Zellers (a Canadian concern), to put her name on lines of home furnishings—kitchen tools, bed and bath items, interior paints, outdoor furniture and garden tools.[5]

Despite this outsized success—or because of it—Martha Stewart herself is parodied on popular television shows such as "Saturday Night Live" (SNL) or "Late Night With David Letterman." Martha Stewart's own private life has weathered biting, even mean-spirited scrutiny, in part to the rage of the age for "investigative expose" masquerading as fully considered biography. In an era in which the former First Lady (and now United States Senator) is known popularly (and in some quarters derogatorily) as "Hillary" (one may imagine the raised eyebrows of Mrs. Roosevelt if addressed as "Hey, Eleanor!"), the popular assumptions of behavior and ambition "proper" to one's gender come fully into public view. Performance artist Karen Finley noted in a 1996 interview that the public's reaction to Hillary Rodham Clinton and Martha Stewart indicates much about the conflicted roles women play. First winning and then losing an advance and contract for her book, *Living It Up: Humorous Adventures in Hyperdomesticity,* because the publisher (Crown) also published Martha Stewart's works, Finley noted that her book (eventually produced by Doubleday in 1996) "criticizes how women spend their days and the fact that the only place a woman can exercise creative dominion or power or decision-making is in the safe haven of domestic territory." Finley sees such territoriality at work in public life as well.

We've seen similar things happen to more famous public figures, like Hillary with the baking cookies line, a simple sentence, but the whole world caved in and she's never gotten over it. …

… .I think Martha Stewart is our first lady. That's why everybody is so into her. The way she's blonde, the way she looks and handles herself

… .She's smart, she went to Barnard, she has credentials. What they'd really like for Hillary Clinton is to disguise that. Martha Stewart has all the education, but she decided to stay home and bake cookies. That's why the country's all behind her.[6]

On the other hand, Stewart's ambition is at times conflated with her company, characterized by *Salon* critic Mary Elizabeth Williams as "Martha's tastefully decorated evil empire" which grows "ever more ominous by the day." Martha Stewart Living Omnimedia, however ominous its corporate name, is not perceived by business analysts as a threat to free enterprise; no trustbusting action is about take place, even as MSLO's success is causing venerable domestic magazines such as *McCall's* and *Redbook* and *Better Homes and Gardens* to suffer major losses, or helping to cause chain department stores such as Sears and Caldor's to lay off workers by the thousands. Noting that MSLO's revenues doubled in the third quarter of 2000 but few financial presses took notice, *Salon* writer Sara Hazlewood surmised that such blindness was the result of MSLO's devotion to "domestic interests." "If Martha Stewart sold routers instead of linens, would the financial press take notice?" Hazlewood asked. By extension, would the American consumer recognize the enormity of Stewart's power if she sold, say, computers?[7]

Consider the media's treatment of Martha Stewart to that of Microsoft CEO Bill Gates—an oft-made comparison of two "New Gilded Age" titans. Gates is often feminized (as in "Saturday Night Live's" whiny, teenish nerd seeking world domination) for not taking recent federal antitrust suits "like a man." Confronted with damning testimony of his personal knowledge of his corporation's monopolistic activities, Gates as a witness acted petulantly, not defiantly; in deposition he was emotional, not commanding. Subdued not by government force but by the folly of his own deeds and words, Gates appears as a nonthreatening Oz-ian wizard behind the curtain. Perhaps given this characterization, Mary Elizabeth Williams predicted Stewart triumphant in a hypothetical head-to-head (perhaps a "Celebrity Death Match"?) with Gates:

> There have even been rumors of a proposed Martha Stewart computer—designed especially for the kitchen, bien sur. Although Martha could probably slice Bill Gates like a handful of fresh strawberries, mix him with steel-cut Irish oatmeal and eat him for breakfast, her publicist, alas, denies the story.[8]

Stewart's "omnivorous" behavior is parodied also in a popular "Top Ten" (and now lengthened to a "Top Fifteen") list lighting its way across the Internet. The title of the list reveals the cultural apprehension of strong-willed, successful women: "The Top Ten [Fifteen] Clues That Martha Stewart is Stalking You." Several of these "clues" are harmless if recast on a list entitled "Signs that Martha Stewart Has Been Visiting Your Home"—for example, "The telltale lemon slice in the dog's water bowl." Nevertheless, other "clues" compare Stewart's persona to that of the Glenn Close character, a successful publisher, stalking an ex-lover and his family in the much debated 1987 film *Fatal Attraction*: "You find your pet bunny on the stove in an exquisite tarragon, rose petal and saffron demiglace, with pecan-crusted hearts of palm and a delicate mint-fennel sauce." In short, in the celebrity of Stewart and Gates we see popular curiosity about personality and power, but more important we discern a cultural anxiety and confusion about gender and power and changes in the way Americans live: Gates, no Edison as the whiny wizard of Silicon Valley; Stewart, no helpful hintful Heloise but rather the dominatrix of domesticity.

What Cherlin and others seem to have ignored is the implication of gender in the historical generation(s) of the definition of individualism. Franklin and Emerson are evoked as progenitors and exemplars here, and this sort of ideological inheritance is inherently masculine. The "separate spheres" ideology so pervasive in American culture carries with it a stigma for those men and women who cross over. "It … seems clear that the fabric of public life has frayed," writes Chemin, and the reasons he offers for that unraveling are revealing. "One notable change is the loss of job security, which uproots workers and undermines community."

Another is the infusion of many more women into the work force, meaning more two-earner families and more employed single parents. "Between work and taking care of my children, who are 3 and 5, I don't have much time for community involvement," says Delisa Hunter, a 23-year-old from Norfolk, Va.

Public life, community, and *civic engagement* are interchangeable terms in Chemin's essay, and this muddies the historical evolution of individualism and its meanings for certain groups and not for others. Of course, the author could not, in the course of a Sunday newspaper magazine feature, offer readers the breadth of any or all respondents' backgrounds and views. But the example he offers here confuses more than it clarifies: a woman who balances family as a "traditional" mom and "modern" worker, and who hasn't much time for the sort of "community involvement" that elsewhere in the essay is defined as voluntary associations for men, associations that often served as ancillary sites for professional growth and business transactions. Chemin's mention of the decline of the League of Women Voters (along with the Masons, it must be mentioned) is in itself indicative of the way many define civic or public engagement and women's entrance into that public life.

It's not that I'm faulting Chemin for inaccuracy or ideological bias: comprehending individualism as a changing historical construct is an exceedingly complex task, and how Americans define public and private is equally if not more complicated a conundrum to solve. Still, it's difficult to read that job insecurity is undermining community and that, in a parallel manner, the phenomenon that more women are working (that is, outside the home for pay) also serves to loosen the bonds of community. No matter that job insecurity likely necessitates that both parents work, and that men are increasingly the single parent raising children (according to the 2000 United States Census); it's women in the workplace (and "single parents" who are still primarily women) who are part of the problem.

It's also women who are thought to be the (stereo)typical consumers in American society. *Consumption, consumerism,* and *consumer culture* are at times interchangeable and at other times discrete, dependent on the critic's politics or scholarly discipline. Scholars such as Ann Douglas, Christopher Lasch, and William Leach view the "culture of consumption" as therapeutic, inauthentic, nonproductive, feminine, antithetical and, indeed, harmful to American civic culture—the same criticisms levied against expressive individualism. Others, such as Mary Douglas, Daniel Miller, and Janice A. Radway, see in consumption the means by which selves are fashioned, identities defined, confirmed, or, importantly, transformed. Kmartha stirs up Americans' anxieties about consumption and its meanings because, paradoxically, those anxieties are brought home. At one and the same time a homemaker and CEO, Martha Stewart crosses traditional gender boundaries in an area often ignored by critiques of consumer culture. "Keep within compass," an eighteenth-century print charged women; this Oprah Winfrey does, and is adored, if at times ridiculed for weepy sentimentalism. Kmartha, despite the emphasis on the domestic, does not keep within compass: Martha Stewart exemplifies the (masculine) utilitarian individualism at the heart of the "do-it-yourself" movement, through her business acumen, self-reliance, and undeniable achievement.[9]

All that said, however, Martha Stewart also re-enacts the selflessness embedded in women's domestic roles. Fans, for example, tune in to "Martha Stewart Living" not to see what she is wearing, but what she is doing. As one GardenWeb forum respondent wrote: "What I like about her is her casual style, the jeans-and-tennies look."[10] Unlike other female celebrities (including First Ladies) who tend to their respective "look" as work, Stewart tends to the work itself. Another GardenWeb forum participant observed:

> I usually crawl out of bed, pull on yesterdays [sic] jeans and maybe a clean T-shirt if making dinner last night got messy, slip into my garden clogs, brush my teeth, put my hair back into the bun that it slipped out of in the night (foregoing the brush of course), and then my girls and I go out into the yard and weed, trim, chop or do anything that might need us. ... I guess that's why I love Martha. ... [s]he's not out to impress by her outward physical appearance. ... She lets her ability speak louder than her appearance.[11]

Mirrored in Stewart's lack of attention to her physical self-presentation is the attitude conveyed by this fan when she observes that the various plantings in her yard "might need us."

Kmartha promotes a lifestyle in which the individual is not only laborer but also CEO of his or her own household—with all the attendant anxieties about gender and power. Kmartha relies equally upon Americans' expressive consumption to make a living: Martha Stewart Living Omnimedia, that is, in which the divide between private and public is confounded. Though Martha Stewart Living Omnimedia generates over $200 million a year in sales in the United States, the company's stock certificate was designed in-house. How appropriate for the doyenne of the "do-it-yourself" generation.[12]

NOTES

Extracted from S. Wajda, "Kmartha," *American Studies* 42, no. 2 (2001): 71–77. Reprinted by permission from *American Studies*.

1. On the initial price offering of Martha Stewart Living Omnimedia (hereafter MSLO), see "Martha Stewart Tidies up Wall St.," *New York Times,* 19 October 1999. "The Markets: Market Place; Big Board Fumbles Martha Stewart Deal," New York Times, 21 October 1999, CI. For a spoof on the coincidental pairing of MSLO and the World Wrestling Federation, see Tom Kuntz, "Culture Clash; Martha vs. the W.W.F.—the Final Confit," *New York Times,* 24 October 1999, 4:7.

2. Andrew J. Cherlin, "I'm OK, You're Selfish," *The New York Times Magazine,* 17 October 1999, at <http://www.nytimes.com/library/millennium/m5/poll-cherlin.html>. *The New York Times* survey was conducted between 17–19 July 1999, and included 1,178 Americans interviewed by telephone.

   Cherlin is basing his formulation on the insights of sociologist Robert M. Bellah and his colleagues in *Habits of the Heart: Individualism and Commitment in American Life* (Berkeley, 1985). Bellah and his team surveyed white, middle-class Americans between 1979 and 1984. I thank Norman Yetman for pointing out the connection.

3. Ibid.

4. Molly O'Neill, "But What Would Martha Say?" *The New York Times Magazine,* 16 May 1999, at <http://www.nytimes.com/library/magazine/millennium/m2/recipes.html>.

5. Information supplied by a variety of sources: see, for example, "Martha Stewart Living Omnimedia Acquires Martha Stewart Living From Time Inc.," *PR Newswire,* 4 February 1997; Simon Worrell, "Million Dollar Apple Pie; Profile: Martha Stewart; She's Turned Herself Into a Saint, Home-making Into an Industry," *The Independent* (London), 12 October 1997, 3.

   On the repurchase of Martha Stewart Living (hereafter MSL) from Time Inc. see "The Media Business: Martha Stewart to Buy Her Company," *New York Times,* 5 February 1997, D5; Angela G. King, "Right Time for Martha to Control Her Empire," *Daily News* (New York), 5 February 1997, 26; Mary Elizabeth Williams, "Perfect World," *Salon,* 14 March 1997 at <http://www.salon.com/march 97/media/media970314.html>.

   On website see George Manner, "Martha Has a New Home on the Web," *Daily News* (New York), 5 September 1997, 83, and <www.marthastewart.com>.

   On partnership with Kmart Corporation see press releases archived at Kmart Corporation's website <www.kmartcorp.com>.

   On partnerships with Jo-Ann Fabrics see Mary Vanac, "Hudson, Ohio-Based Fabrics Retailer Signs Up Martha Stewart," *Akron Beacon Journal,* 28 July 1999; Nancy Romanenko, "Material Girl; Martha Stewart Unfolds Fabric Collection," *Asbury Park Press* (Neptune, NJ), 19 August 1999, D1.

   On MSLO's relationship with Zellers, see Donna LaFramboise, "'Tell them Martha sent you': Lifestyle-Guru Stewart In Marketing Pact With Zellers," *The Gazette* (Montreal), 30 May 1998, F3; Francois Shalom, "Curtain Fell So Fast: Bonavista Fabrics Is Suing Zellers and Martha Stewart. ..." *The Gazette* (Montreal), 7 September 1999, El.

   On introduction of garden furniture, see Marianne Rohrlich, "Personal Shopper: Perches for the Armchair Gardener," *New York Times,* 25 March 1999, F10; Nancy Meyer, "Martha Stewart Garden Furniture Rolls Out," *Brandmarketing* 6:4 (April 1999): 6; Tim Moran, "Kmart Corp.'s Billion-Dollar 'Brand-Aid' Is Martha Stewart," HFN, May 24, 1999: 1.

6. Christopher Busa, "Talking with Karen Finley," Provincetown Arts, 12 (1996), at <http://www.capecodaccess.com/Gallery/Arts/talkingKaren.html>.

7. Mary Elizabeth Williams, "Perfect World," at <http://www.salon.com/march97/media/media970314.html>; Sara Hazlewood, "Martha Stewart Kicks Ass," at <http://www.salon.com/business/feature/2000/11/07/Martha/index.html>.

On competition, see "Sluggish National Chains Continue to Lose Ground," *HFN,* 9 August 1999, 6.

8. Williams's observation seemingly takes a page from John Kasson's *Rudeness & Civility: Manners in Nineteenth-Century Urban America* (New York, 1990), in which Kasson observes that at the turn of the twentieth century, metaphors of eating were applied to Robber Barons and trustbusters alike. See "Table Manners and the Control of Appetites," 182–214, esp. 195–200.

9. The literature on consumption and consumer culture is plentiful: I've mentioned here only a few authors whose work is known to American studies scholars. "Culture of consumption," of course, comes from the title of Richard Wightman Fox and Jackson Lears, eds., *The Culture of Consumption: Critical Essays in American History,* 1880–1980 (New York, 1983); Ann Douglas, *The Feminization of American Culture* (New York, 1977); Christopher Lasch, *The Culture of Narcissism* (London, 1979); William Leach, *Land of Desire: Merchants, Power, and the Rise of a New American Culture* (New York, 1993). Those studies exploring what Arjun Appadurai calls the "social life of things" (*The Social Life of Things* [Cambridge, 1986]) through attention to material culture (or specific genres) see at least a paradox in empowerment and exploitation within capitalism: Mary Douglas with Baron Isherwood, *The World of Goods* (New York, 1979); Daniel Miller, *Material Culture and Mass Consumption* (Oxford, Eng., 1987); Janice A. Radway, "Reading is Not Eating: Mass-Produced Literature and the Theoretical, Methodological, and Political Consequences of a Metaphor," *Book Research Quarterly* 2 (Fall 1996): 7–29; idem, "On the Gender of the Middlebrow Consumer and the Threat of the Culturally Fraudulent Female," *South Atlantic Quarterly* 93:4 (1994): 871–93; and idem, *Reading the Romance: Women, Patriarchy, and Popular Literature* (Chapel Hill, 1991).

For a useful statement of the overlapping fields of material culture and consumer culture, consult Celia Lury, *Consumer Culture* (New Brunswick, 1996). "Keep Within Compass," English, laid paper, 1785–1805. Winterthur Museum 54.93.1, Winterthur, D.E.

10. "Jen—SoCal-9/19," "RE: Resentful of Martha Stewart," 21 March 2000, "Resentful of Martha Stewart? forum, GardenWeb, at <http://forums.gardenweb.com/forums/load/favorite/ msg1214041713693.html>.

11. "Amy," "RE: Resentful of Martha Stewart?", 2 April 2000, "Resentful of Martha Stewart?" forum, Garden Web, at <http://forums.gardenweb.com/forums/load/favorite/msgl 214041713693 .html>.

12. Diana B. Henriques, "Martha Stewart, the Company, Is Poised To Go Public. But Is It a Good Thing?", *New York Times,* 12 October 1999, C 1.

ANNOTATED GUIDE TO FURTHER READING

The literature about design thinking and philosophy has been expanding since the 1960s. For new directions on design in relation to cognition see Charles Eastman et. al.'s edited volume, *Design Knowing and Learning* (2001), which contains essays that attempt to crack the complex code of design practice as it unfolds in the designer's mind. Bryan Lawson's *How Designers Think* (1980) looks at how the various methods designers use, such as drawing and computer-assisted technologies, alter our conceptualization of design. And, for more on design's ability to reflect back on specific practices, the first section of Victor Margolin and Richard Buchanan's edited book, *The Idea of Design* (1995), is essential.

Approaching design as a viable research endeavor can be traced back to the conference on Design Methods held at Imperial College in London in 1962. Many of the papers from this conference can be found in J. C. Jones and D. G. Thornley's edited volume, *Conference on Design Methods* (1963). In the early 1960s, other scholars, such as Thomas Kuhn, in his *The Structure of Scientific Revolutions* (1962), were starting to look at the field of science as an arena in which the practice of research shifts paradigms of understanding. Kuhn's ideas impacted the design methods movement, which continues to thrive under the organization called the Design Research Society. Another example of an important volume of essays that grapple with this area of design studies is the book edited by Nigel Cross, *Developments in Design Methodology* (1984). Additionally, a contemporary example of a design firm that uses specific methodologies in their assessment of projects is IDEO, and a discussion of their practice can be found in Thomas Kelly's *The Ten Faces of Innovation* (2005).

Design is, of course, a tool for communication, and there is within the business and academic communities a growing interest in exploring the limits of design's power to disseminate messages. Steven Heller has edited the indispensable *Graphic Design Reader* (2002), in which interviews and writing by designers who were integral to the history of communication design can be found. Also, Jorge Frascara's *Communication Design* (2004) offers a comprehensive overview, including issues ranging from aesthetics to an overall assessment of the field. It is the subject of branding that has become one of the major foci of those interested in design communications. Outside of Naomi Klein's insightful critique included in our reader, Alice Tybout and Tim Calkin's edited work, *Kellogg on Branding* (2005), provides numerous essays and case studies used by students at Northwestern University's business school. Several firms not only practice branding for clients, but also offer position papers that discuss the importance of branding in our culture. For an extensive archive of these papers by one of the leading brand management companies, see Siegel + Gale's "dialogue" link on their Web site, which can be found at http://www.siegelgale.com/dialogue/.

SECTION 3

THEORIZING DESIGN AND VISUALITY

SECTION INTRODUCTION

Aesthetics, ethics, politics, and the close study of material culture are integral to design studies. Aesthetics explains why we have certain notions of beauty. Ethics describes how our actions affect others. Politics provides us with the tools and knowledge to alter our lived experiences. Moreover, it is in the analysis of material things that we can gain a theoretical understanding through artifacts, which often tell us more about history and contemporary society than traditional forms of documentation.

The authors in the first subsection explain how capitalism, hierarchies, and our perceptions of design, both real and imagined, affect our understanding of aesthetics, or sensory experiences. These readings explore ideas about beauty's conflicted history in relation to art and design. Several of these theorists assert that traditional boundaries between utility (everyday design) and high art (painting and sculpture) are contested and closely aligned with cultural context. Taking the notion of aesthetics into the realm of popular culture, others claim that we often think about design in ways that fib about status and aesthetic context. Indeed, as consumers we have preconceived ideals about aesthetics that we project onto objects incorrectly. We tend to have faith in certain aesthetic conceptions that frequently differ from a design's actual appearance and history.

The categories that often pervade aesthetic judgments have ethical consequences; thus, the second subsection includes essays that investigate the relationship between design and ethics. More critics are beginning to claim that ethical design begins in the classrooms of art and design schools, while others challenge professional designers to rethink the focus of their practice. This subsection assesses design's obsession with profit and fosters the expectation—like several of the readings in the Sustainability subsection (Section 6.3)—that the design community should begin to reflexively understand how it impacts the world.

Politics drives our understanding of ethics, as civic culture defines value systems. The readings in the Politics subsection describe how design can help us pursue democracy and give power to those who have been disenfranchised for too long. Furthermore, these readings critique capitalism and how it defines our experiences by forming privilege and class stratification. Relying heavily on a Marxist perspective, several of these authors inquire about our fetishization of objects, which denies the reality of labor, thus casting a long shadow about the plight of workers that other passages in the *Reader,* especially in the sections that delve into history, communications, and labor, explore.

Design is ultimately a world of products and ideas that provides us with cultural knowledge, individual identities, and socioeconomic meaning. In the material culture subsection, we read how the shape of things, and the built environment, can create power dynamics (another ethical conundrum), while these authors also describe how analyses of material culture can offer insights into history and contemporary society. In a group of readings that should be associated with the subsection on consumption (4.3), these excerpts on material culture and social interaction help us discern why we purchase specific goods and why our world reinforces notions of authority, paradigms of control, categories of beauty, and ethical standards.

The theoretical ideas considered in this section offer perspectives that familiarize us with different approaches to design. These texts proffer insights about design that touch on a range of topics from beauty to capitalism, concerns that should be pursued in design studies. The study of aesthetics, ethics, politics, and the material realm require careful consideration, since these are the very concepts that delimit design.

SECTION 3: THEORIZING DESIGN AND VISUALITY

3.1: Aesthetics

INTRODUCTION

Ideas about aesthetics and design have become increasingly contested, as many theorists assert that traditional boundaries between utility and high art are no longer applicable. Furthermore, many now argue that the ideal of aesthetics needs to embrace multivalent voices. One of the problems in constructing "an aesthetics of design" is that design and aesthetics refer to different traditions of understanding creative activity. Unlike the fine arts, which often employ universal and nonutilitarian aesthetic criteria, design automatically implies a utilitarian role, which is socially, economically, culturally, and historically determined. Design has been intimately linked to capitalism since the Industrial Revolution, which served to define the contemporary usage of the term. At the same time, design is linked to art, although the boundaries between the two are fluid, relative to the extent to which a design might serve a want or need, and/or be a subject of the imagination.

The three extracts in this subsection do not resolve this issue; rather, they are chosen as examples of different contemporary approaches to design and aesthetics. Their authors come from diverse but related intellectual traditions. Each is a respected critic of contemporary culture who draws our attention to ways of conceptualizing an aesthetic of design and reinforces the historical specificity and subjectivity of the activity. They recognize the necessity of combining functional and aesthetic judgments for design. In doing so they underscore the limitations of the modernist aesthetic of "form follows function" that governed so much of what was considered good design for most of the twentieth century. Aesthetic considerations of design reference larger questions of the relationship between human beings and objects that have remained integral to philosophical debates.

We begin with "Aesthetics and the Work of Art," in which Arthur Danto tackles the issue of the object as artwork, conventionally a prime candidate for aesthetic appreciation and debate. Danto distinguishes between appreciation and aesthetic appreciation with his reference to "ordinary" everyday objects, what might be termed anonymous designs. He argues that the thumbtack or the white envelope can be the subjects of functional, but not aesthetic, appreciation, not, that is, unless they "become" artworks. The comparison reinforces how aesthetic appreciation is dependent on knowledge, formed by cultural distinction and historical moment, rather than by any inherent properties of a given object. It also challenges the modern view of universal beauty, based on the philosophy of Immanuel Kant. Danto argues that while everything that human beings design and make has some potential aesthetic value, certain fields, art in particular, have their own special aesthetics and languages of appreciation, which are made and shared by their cognoscenti. Design also has its experts and critics, but how much harder is their task of aesthetic discrimination than that of the art critic, when their subject is so public, so ordinary, so changing, and so essential to the lives of human beings?

In the second reading, Jean Baudrillard cites the significance of the Bauhaus as the point of departure for the modernist aesthetic in design. After the Bauhaus, Baudrillard argues, design is encountered increasingly as a sign and as a commodity. These factors also affect how it is judged aesthetically—crudely speaking, by how it looks and is represented and by how much it costs (note how Danto refers us to *cheap* white envelopes and *plastic* forks). The outcome, Baudrillard explains, is that the modern sense of aesthetics has "no longer anything to do with categories of beauty and ugliness." Aesthetic judgment is unable to reference the style or content of an object, only how it functions as a commodity and as a sign. He continues to accuse design of reducing objects to their utilitarian and aesthetic properties, which it then isolates and opposes. Even if we do not share Baudrillard's argument, he nevertheless reinforces the complexities of attempting to establish an aesthetic understanding of design, something our final essay on the Airstream also demonstrates.

In this essay written in the 1970s, Reyner Banham raises questions about modernist aesthetic judgments of design. Architectural historian, critic, and writer, Banham has written incisively about, not the first machine age of the 1920s, but "the second machine age," a time of pop art, urban and industrial design, automobile styling, gadgets, gizmos, and ultimately the impact of America. A mobile home with a shiny polished exterior, the Airstream is considered an icon of the American streamlined aesthetic of the 1930s. The Airstream is beloved by modernist architects from "ex-Bauhausier" Marcel Breuer to Le Corbusier and their followers as a classic of universal beauty, which translates across time and space, and it is part of the design collection of the Museum of Modern Art in New York. Yet Banham cautions against a design aesthetic in which beauty is skin deep. The shell of the Airstream underwent forty-five years of detailed refinement and did not achieve its idealized streamlined form

Image 9   Constantin and Laurene Boym, *Christ Chair*, 2006. Photographed by Constantin and Laurene Boym at Moss Gallery, New York.

until the 1970s, when it benefited from revived interest in and nostalgia for "the streamlined decade." Also, its external appearance belies its interior, which, with its deep carpets and wood grain, resembles "a piece of regular American suburbia."

The Airstream, in fact, represents an aesthetic idealization of 1930s American modernism. Banham cautions against the elitism of European modernism in favor of an aesthetic that also can embrace, objectively, contemporary design and culture. His essay also brings to mind Roland Barthes's account of the new Citroen D.S.19, in *Mythologies* (1957), in which cars are likened to Gothic cathedrals and the "Deesse" is depicted as an object from another universe, "a new Nautilus" in the public imagination.

As the theoretical lines blur between the material object and its image, so do the more pragmatic ones between art and design. Recently "DesignArt" or "defunctionalism" have been coined to describe design that may or may not be functional but will certainly have an emotional appeal (Hage 2008). Its products can incorporate hand, machine, and technological methods, link conceptual approaches from other arts and other disciplines, and distort or erase the assumed function of objects. As design takes new trajectories of this sort, the task of considering aesthetic criteria by which to judge it becomes all the more complex.

20

AESTHETICS AND THE WORK OF ART

Arthur C. Danto

There is another consequence of perhaps even greater moment to us. If knowledge that something is an artwork makes a difference in the mode of aesthetic response to an object—if there are differential aesthetic responses to indiscernible objects when one is an artwork and the other a natural thing—then there would be a threat of circularity in any definition of art in which some reference to aesthetic response was intended to play a defining role. For it would not be just aesthetic response that belonged to works of art in contrast with the kind that belongs to natural things or blasé artifacts like Brillo boxes (when not works of art)—and we should have to be able to distinguish works of art from natural things or mere artifacts in order to define the appropriate kind of response. Hence we could not use that kind of response to define the concept of the artwork.

Anyway, aesthetic considerations have always been viewed as having a natural place in discussions of art, and this is as good a place as any to come to terms with this easy association. The question is whether aesthetic considerations belong to the definition of art. If they do not, then they simply will be among the things which go with the concept without pertaining to its logic, and not really more important philosophically than countless other things, such as preciousness or collectability, which have also been part of the practice if not of the concept of art.

An aesthetic condition has been deemed necessary in the definition of art formulated by George Dickie in his influential discussion of the institutional theory of art. A work of art is a "candidate for appreciation," a status conferred upon an artifact by "the artworld," in Dickie's use of the term—an institutionally enfranchised group of persons who serve, so to speak, as trustees for the generalized *musée imaginaire,* the occupants of which are the artworks of the world. "If something cannot be appreciated," Dickie writes, "it cannot be a work of art." Dickie denies that he means specifically *aesthetic* appreciation, but he has been taken to mean that by a prominent critic, Ted Cohen, whose argument, if sound, has some meaning for us. It is that there are certain objects which cannot be appreciated, hence cannot be works of art by Dickie's own contrapositive formula. Hence the citizenry of the artworld is bounded by the constraints of appreciability and cannot by fiat declare just anything a work of art. So there are at least negative conditions on what a work of art can be, and this is evidently not as wholly an institutional matter as Dickie pretends. Presumably, unappreciable objects would be those which would not support the claim that every object can be viewed practically *or* aesthetically. These objects cannot be psychically distanced, and so the objection pertains to more than Dickie's theory and has in consequence a conspicuous philosophical importance.

There nevertheless are two difficulties with this position as defended by Cohen. Among the objects alleged immune to aesthetic appreciation, Cohen cites "ordinary thumbtacks, cheap white envelopes, the plastic forks given at some drive-in restaurants" and, most particularly, "urinals." Now I do not know whether the claim is that these cannot be appreciated or simply cannot be appreciated favorably. Terms like "cheap," "ordinary," and "plastic" are expressions of distaste, and it is not clear that even by Dickie's criterion every object elevated to the stature of an artwork by the artworld must *ipso facto* be favorably appreciated. As a matter of textual fact, Dickie does say something like this: "I am saying that every work of art must have some minimal *potential* value of worthiness." But in fact aesthetic qualities compass, it seems to me, negative considerations as arising only with persons and actions which had considerations; we are repelled, disgusted, even sickened by certain works of art. To restrict to the favorable cases the application of the epithet "work of art" would be parallel to regarding moral considerations as arising only with persons and actions which had some "minimal potential value or worthiness." And while there may indeed be good in everything, moral theory had better accommodate the swine, the wicked, the morally lazy, the bad, the evil, the revolting and the mediocre. So "appreciation," if aesthetic at least, can be negative, and the very use of the adjectives he does use tells us a lot about the way in which Cohen appreciates throwaway forks, vulgar envelopes, and ordinary thumbtacks (in contrast with pushpins?). I should be astonished if negative aesthetic appreciation entailed that the objects which elicited it could not be works of art.

These questions can obviously not be settled without some discussion of aesthetic appreciation—or of appreciation *tout court*—but there is another and more damaging difficulty that would remain even if these questions were resolved in such a way as to leave Cohen's objection unshaken. Even were we to grant that an ordinary thumbtack could not be aesthetically appreciated (positively or negatively), it would not follow that a thumbtack could not be a work of art. Of course a thumbtack that is a work of art would have to differ in some way from a thumbtack otherwise

like it in every external respect that is not a work of art. This we have seen from the beginning (remember the canopener). But in that case it is far from plain how things would stand with appreciation. Even granting that the thumbtack itself was beneath appreciation, it would not follow that an artwork materially like a mere thumbtack could not be appreciated; and that to which we might respond appreciatively would be the properties of the artwork without necessarily being the properties of the thumbtack. To be sure, the connection between the two may be very intricate to work out—as intricate perhaps as the connection between a person and his body. We may see this somewhat more clearly perhaps by pondering the notorious example of Duchamp's *Fountain* and Dickie's own analysis of it.

Dickie is adamant in insisting that there is no such thing as "a special kind of aesthetic consciousness, attention, or perception." And he goes on to say, "The only sense in which there is a difference between the appreciation of art and the appreciation of nonart is that the appreciations have different *objects.*" Presumably he does not mean by "different objects" the difference between artworks and mere things, for then his definition would go circular: he would be defining appreciation of art in terms of its objects, whereas candidacy for appreciation was supposed to have gone into the explanation of why something is an artwork. So I gather he is trying to say that what we appreciate in artworks is just what we would appreciate in nonartworks, when in fact they happen materially to be the same, as *Fountain* is from countless urinals distributed for the convenience of gentlemen wherever they congregate. "Why," Dickie says, "Cannot the ordinary qualities of *Fountain*—its gleaming white surface, the depth revealed when it reflects images of surrounding objects, its pleasing oval shape—be appreciated? It has qualities similar to those works by Brancusi and Moore which many do not balk at saying they appreciate." These *are* qualities of the urinal in question, as they are qualities of any urinal made of white porcelain, which do resemble certain qualities of *Bird in Flight*. But the question is whether the artwork *Fountain* is indeed identical with that urinal, and hence those gleaming surfaces and deep reflections are indeed qualities of the artwork. Cohen has supposed that Duchamp's work is not the urinal at all but the gesture of exhibiting it; and the gesture, if that indeed is the work, has no gleaming surfaces to speak of, and differs from what Moore and Brancusi did roughly as gestures differ from bits of brass and bronze. But certainly the work itself has properties that urinals themselves lack: it is daring, impudent, irreverent, witty, and clever. What would have provoked Duchamp to madness or murder, I should think, would be the sight of aesthetes mooning over the gleaming surfaces of the porcelain object he had manhandled into exhibition space: "How like Kilamanjaro! How like the white radiance of Eternity! How Arctically sublime!" (Bitter laughter at the *Club des artistes*.) No: the properties of the object deposited in the artworld it shares with most items of industrial *porcelainerie,* while the properties *Fountain* possesses as an artwork it shares with the *Julian Tomb* of Michelangelo and the *Great Perseus* of Cellini. If what made *Fountain* an artwork were only the qualities it shared with urinals, the question would arise as to what makes it an artwork and not those—the offense to egalitarianism being of a piece with what moved J's political indignation [. ....] Is it just an oversight of the artworld? Should there be a mass transfiguration, like a mass conversion to Buddishm of all the untouchables in Calcutta? What Dickie has overlooked is an ambiguity in the term "makes" as it occurs in the question: what makes something a work of art? He has emphasized how something gets to be a work of art, which may be institutional, and neglected in favor of aesthetic considerations the question of what qualities constitute an artwork once something is one.

My own view is that a work of art has a great many qualities, indeed a great many qualities of a different sort altogether, than the qualities belonging to objects materially indiscernible from

them but not themselves artworks. And some of these qualities may very well be aesthetic ones, or qualities one can experience aesthetically or find "worthy and valuable." But then in order to respond aesthetically to these, one must first know that the object is an artwork, and hence the distinction between what is art and what is not is presumed available before the difference in response to that difference in identity is possible. After all, we have been struck from the beginning by Aristotle's insight that the pleasure one derives from works of mimesis presupposes knowledge that they are imitations, for one will not derive that pleasure from the originals, however indiscernible originals and imitations may be. And Diderot has brilliantly argued that we may be moved to tears by representations of things which by themselves will move us not at all, or move us differently. We may cry at a representation of a mother's despair at the death of a child, but he would be hardhearted who just wept at the correspondant [sic] reality; the thing is to comfort and console. What I wish to say, then, is that there are two orders of aesthetic response, depending upon whether the response is to an artwork or to a mere real thing that cannot be told apart from it. Hence we cannot appeal to aesthetic considerations in order to get our definition of art, inasmuch as we need the definition of art in order to identify the sorts of aesthetic responses appropriate to works of art in contrast with mere real things. True, something may not be a work of art without, as Dickie says, the minimal potential for aesthetic value. But I wonder if there is anything at all of which that is not true? He himself allows, against Cohen, that "thumbtacks, envelopes, and plastic forks have qualities that can be appreciated if one makes the effort to focus on them." So what cannot? Yet there is, I shall argue, a special aesthetics for works of art and indeed a special language of appreciation, and inasmuch as both seem to be involved with the concept of art, it will not be amiss to address ourselves to some features of aesthetic and thence of artistic experience, even if it will not especially help us in finding the definition we seek.

NOTE

Extracted from A. C. Danto, "Aesthetics and the Work of Art," in his *The Transfiguration* *of the Commonplace* (Cambridge: Harvard University Press, 1981) pp. 91–95. Reprinted by permission of the publisher from *The Transfiguration of the Commonplace: A Philosophy of Art* by Arthur C. Danto, pp. 91–95, Cambridge, Mass.: Harvard University Press, Copyright 1981 by Arthur C. Danto.

21

DESIGN AND ENVIRONMENT OR HOW POLITICAL ECONOMY ESCALATES INTO CYBERBLITZ

Jean Baudrillard

Not all cultures produce objects: the concept is peculiar to ours, born of the industrial revolution. Yet even industrial society knows only the *product,* not the *object.* The object only begins truly to exist at the time of its formal liberation as a sign function, and this liberation only results from the mutation of this properly industrial society into what could be called our techno-culture,[1] from the passage out of a *metallurgic* into a *semiurgic* society. That is to say, the object only appears when the problem of its finality of meaning, of its status as message and as sign (of its mode of signification, of communication and of sign exchange) begins to be posed beyond its status as product and as commodity (beyond the mode of production, of circulation and of economic exchange). This mutation is roughed out during the 19th century, but the Bauhaus solidifies it theoretically. So it is from the Bauhaus' inception that we can logically date the "revolution of the object."

It is not a question of simple extension and differentiation, however extraordinary, of the field of products on account of industrial development. It is a question of a mutation of status. Before the Bauhaus there were, properly speaking, no objects; subsequently, and according to an irreversible logic, everything potentially participates in the category of objects and will be produced as such. That is why any empirical classification (Abraham Moles, etc.) is ludicrous. To wonder whether or not a house or a piece of clothing is an object, to wonder where the object begins, where it leaves off in order to become a building, etc.—all this descriptive typology is fruitless. For the object is not a thing, nor even a category; it is a status of meaning and a form. Before the logical advent of this object form, nothing is an object, not even the everyday utensils—thereafter, everything is, the building as well as the coffee spoon or the entire city. It is the Bauhaus that institutes this universal semantization of the environment in which everything becomes the object of a calculus of function and of signification. Total functionality, total semiurgy. It is a "revolution" in relation to the traditional mode, in which objects (for lack of a better word) are bound together and not liberated, have no status of their own and do not form a system among themselves on the basis of a rational finality (functionality).

This functionality inaugurated by the Bauhaus defines itself as a double movement of analysis and rational synthesis of forms (not only industrial, but environmental and social in general). It is a synthesis of form and function, of "beauty and utility," of art and technology. Beyond "style" and its caricatured version in "styling," the commercial kitsch of the 19th century and the modern style, the Bauhaus projects the basis of a rational conception of environmental totality for the first time. Beyond the genres (architecture, painting, furnishings, etc.), beyond "art" and its academic sanction, it extends the aesthetic to the entire everyday world; at the same time it is all of technique in the service of everyday life. The possibility of a "universal semiotic of technological experience"[2] is in effect born of the abolition of the segregation between the beautiful and the useful. Or again from another angle: the Bauhaus tries to reconcile the social and technical infrastructure installed by the industrial revolution with the superstructure of forms and meanings. In wishing to fulfill technology *(la technique)* in the finality of meaning (the aesthetic), the Bauhaus presents itself as a second revolution, the crowning perfection of the industrial revolution, resolving all the contradictions that the latter had left behind it.

The Bauhaus is neither revolutionary nor utopian. Just as the industrial revolution marked the birth of a field of political economy, of a systematic and rational theory of material production, so the Bauhaus marks the *theoretical extension of this field of political economy* and the practical extension of the system of exchange value to the whole domain of signs, forms and objects. At the level of the mode of signification and in the name of *design,* it is a mutation analogous to that which has taken place since the 16th century on the level of the mode of material production and under the aegis of political economy. The Bauhaus marks the point of departure of a veritable *political economy of the sign.*

The same general schema emerges: on the one hand, nature and human labor are disengaged from their archaic constraints, liberated as productive forces and as objects of a *rational calculus of production.* On the other, the whole environment becomes a signifier, objectified as an element of signification. Functionalized and liberated from all traditional implications (religious, magical, symbolic), it becomes the object of a rational calculus of signification.

THE OPERATION OF THE SIGN

Behind the transparency of the object in relation to its function, behind that universal moral law imposed upon it in the name of design, behind that functional equation, that new "economy" of the object that immediately adopts aesthetic value, behind the general scheme of synthesis (art-technique, form-function), a whole labor of

dissociation and abstract restructuration in fact takes place:

1. The dissociation of every complex subject-object relation into simple, analytic, rational elements that can be recombined in functional ensembles and which then take on status as the environment. For it is only on that basis that man is separated from something he calls the environment, and confronted with the task of controlling it. Ever since the 18th century the concept of nature has emerged as a *productive force to be mastered.* That of the environment only shifts it and intensifies it to mean a *mastery of signs.*

2. A generalized division of labor at the level of objects. Analytic fragmentation into 14 or 97 functions, an identical technical response reuniting several functions of the same object, or the same function in several objects, etc.—in short, the whole analytic grid that permits disassembling and reassembling an ensemble.

3. Even more fundamental is the semiological (dis)articulation of the object, from which the latter takes on the force of a sign. And when we say that it becomes a sign, it is according to the strictest definition; it is articulated into a "signifier" and a "signified," it becomes the signifier of a rational, objectifiable "signified" that is its function. This differs sharply from the traditional symbolic relation, where things have meaning, but a meaning that does not come to them from an objective "signified" to which they refer as "signifier." Such, in contrast, is the modern status of the sign-object, which in this respect obeys the linguistic schema: "functionalized" means also "structuralized," that is to say, split into two terms. Design emerges simultaneously as the project of their ideal articulation and the aesthetic of resolution of their equation. For aesthetic is nothing other

than that which, as if by excess, seals this *operational semiology*.

In fact, aesthetics in the modern sense of the term no longer has anything to do with the categories of beauty and ugliness. Critics, the public and designers all mix up the two terms beauty and aesthetic value indiscriminately, but they are logically incompatible (the confusion is strategic: in a system dominated by fashion, that is, by sign exchange value, it allows the conservation of the aura of a pre-industrial value, that of style).

A thousand contradictory definitions of beauty and of style are possible. One thing is certain: they are never a calculus of signs. They come to an end with the system of functional aesthetics, as the earlier modes of economic exchange (barter, gift exchange) perished with the rise of capitalism, and with the institution of a rational calculus of production and exchange. The category of the aesthetic succeeds that of beauty (liquidating it) as the semiological order succeeds the symbolic order. Contemporary aesthetics, once the theory of the forms of beauty, has become the theory of a generalized compatibility of signs, of their internal coherence (signifier-signified) and of their syntax. Aesthetic value connotes the internal functionality of an ensemble, it qualifies the (eventually mobile) equilibrium of a system of signs. It simply translates the fact that its elements *communicate* amongst themselves according to the economy of a model, with maximal integration and minimal loss of information (a harmonized interior in the tonality of blue, or "playing" upon the blues and greens; the crystalloid structures of the residential ensemble; the "naturalness" of "green spaces"). The aesthetic is thus no longer a value of style or of content; it no longer refers to anything but to communication and sign exchange. It is an idealized semiology, or a semiological idealism.[3]

In the symbolic order of style frolics a forever unresolved ambivalence—but the semio-aesthetic order is one of operational resolution, of an interplay of referrals, of equivalence and of controlled dissonances. An "aesthetic" ensemble is

a mechanism without lapses, without fault, in which nothing compromises the interconnection of the elements and the transparency of the process: that famous absolute *legibility* of signs and messages—the common ideal of all manipulators of codes, whether they be cyberneticians or designers. This aesthetic order is a cold order. Functional perfection exercises a cold seduction, the functional satisfaction of a demonstration and an algebra. It has nothing to do with pleasure, with beauty (or horror), whose nature is conversely to rescue us from the demands of rationality and to plunge us once more into an absolute childhood (not into an ideal transparency, but into the illegible ambivalence of desire).

This operation of the sign, this analytic dissociation into the functional duo signifier-signified, always caught in an ideological scheme of synthesis, is found even in the key concepts of design. It is at the bottom of all the current systems of signification (media, political, etc.), just as the operational bifurcation use value-exchange value is at the foundation of the commodity form and of the whole of political economy.[4] All possible valences of an object, all its ambivalence, which cannot be reduced to any model, are reduced by design to two rational components, two general models—utility and the aesthetic—which design isolates and artificially opposes to one another. It is useless to emphasize the hot-housing (*le forçage*) of meaning, the arbitrariness of circumscribing it by these two restrained finalities. In fact, they form only a single one: they are two dissociated forms of the same rationality, sealed by the same system of values. But this artificial separation then permits evoking their reunification as an ideal scheme. Utility is separated from the aesthetic, they are *named* separately (for neither has any reality other than *being named separately*), then they are ideally reunited and all contradictions are resolved by this magical operation. Now, the two equally arbitrary agencies exist only to mislead. The real problem, the real contradictions are at the level of form, of sign exchange value; but it is precisely these that are obscured by the operation.

Such is the ideological function of design: with the concept of the "functional aesthetic," it proposes a model of reconciliation, of formal surpassing of specialization (division of labor at the level of objects) by a universally enveloping value. Thus it imposes a social scheme of integration by the elimination of real structures. The functional aesthetic that conjugates two abstractions is thus itself no more than a superabstraction that consecrates the system of sign exchange value by delineating the utopia behind which the latter dissimulates. The operation of the sign, the separation of signs, is something as fundamental, as profoundly *political,* as the division of labor. Bauhaus theory, like semiology, ratifies this operation and the resultant division of labor of meaning, in the same way that political economy sanctifies economic separation as such, and the material division of labor that flows from it.

The term design must be given all its etymological scope. It can be unfolded in three senses: sketch *(dessin),* plan *(dessein),* and design *(design).* In all three cases one finds a scheme of rational abstraction: graphic for the sketch, reflexive and psychological for the plan (conscious projection of an objective) and more generally, for design: passage to sign status, sign-operation, reduction and rationalization into sign elements, transfer to the sign function.

From the beginning, this process of signification is systematic: the sign never exists apart from a code and a language. Thus, the semiotic revolution (as in its time the industrial revolution) concerns virtually all possible practices. Arts and crafts, forms and techniques both plastic and graphic (keeping to domains that have obvious affinity with design, but once again the term goes far beyond the plastic and architectural), which until then were singular and distinct, are synchronized, and homogenized according to the same model. Objects, forms, and materials that until then spoke their own group dialect, which only emerged from a dialectical practice or an original style, now begin to be thought of and written out in the same tongue, the rational esperanto of design.[5] Once functionally liberated,

they begin to make signs, in both sense [sic] of the phrase (and without a pun): that is, they simultaneously *become* signs and communicate among themselves. Their unity is no longer that of a style or practice, it is that of a system. In other words, as soon as the object is caught up in the structural rationality of the sign (cloven into a signifier and signified), it is simultaneously hooked into a functional syntax (like the morpheme in a syntagm), and assigned to the same general code (like the morpheme in a language). The whole rationality of the linguistic system regains possession of it. On the other hand, if we speak mainly of "structural" linguistics and of the "functionalism" of design, it must be seen that:

1. If the structural vision (signifier-signified, language-speech) is imposed in linguistics it results from, and is contemporaneous with, a purely functionalist vision of language (strictly finalized as a method of communication). The two are the same thing.

2. With "design," objects are also born simultaneously to functionality and to sign status. In the same instant, this restrained and rational finality assigns them to structural rationality. Function and structure involve the same "revolution." This means that functional "liberation" amounts to nothing more than being assigned to a code and a system. Once again, the homology is immediately visible in the liberation of labor (or of leisure, or of the body, etc.), which is never more than their assignment to the system of exchange value.

Let us summarize the essential characteristics of the homology (of the same logical process, even if they are separated chronologically) between the emergence of a political economy of the sign and that of political economy (of material production):

1. Political economy: Under the cover of utility (needs, use value, etc., the anthropological reference of all economic rationality), it institutes a coherent logical system, a calculus of productivity in which all production is resolved into simple elements, in which all products are equivalent in their abstraction. This is the logic of the commodity and the system of exchange value.

2. The political economy of the sign: Under the cover of functionality (objective finality, homologous to utility), it institutes a certain mode of signification in which all the surrounding signs act as simple elements in a logical calculus and refer to each other within the framework of the system of sign exchange value.

In the two cases, use value (utility) and functionality, the one given as final reference of political economy, the other of design, serve in fact only as the concrete alibi for the same process of abstraction. Under the pretext of producing maximal utility, the process of political economy generalizes the system of exchange value. Under the pretext of maximizing the functionality of objects (their legibility as meaning and message, that is in the end their use value as sign), design and the Bauhaus generalize the system of sign exchange value.

Just as a product's utility, unattainable when no coherent theory of needs is capable of establishing it, is revealed to be simply its utility for the system of exchange value—so an object's functionality, illegible as a concrete value, no longer qualifies anything other than the coherence of this sign-object with all the others, its commutability and thus its functional adaptation to the system of sign exchange value. Thus the functionality of an object (of a line, of a form) in an oblique architecture is not to be useful or equilibrated, but to be oblique (or vertical by contrast). It is the coherence of the system that defines the aesthetic-functional value of the elements, and

this value is an exchange value insofar as it always refers to a model as general equivalent (same abstraction as for economic exchange value).

It is no accident if this homology is even reflected on the ethical level. Like the capitalist revolution that instituted "the spirit of enterprise" and the basis of political economy as early as the 16th century, the Bauhaus' revolution is *puritan.* Functionalism is ascetic. This fact is revealed in the sobreity [sic] and geometric lines of its models, its phobia of décor and artifice, in short, in the economy of its discourse. But this is only what one might call the writing effect (which moreover has once again become a rhetoric like any other) of the fundamental doctrine: that of rationality in which the functional liberation of the object has the effect of establishing an ethic of objects just as the emancipation of labor as a productive force has the consequence of establishing a work ethic. Three centuries apart[6] an identical morality (and an identical psychology) corresponds to an identical logic. And the terms in which Weber *(The Protestant Ethic and the Spirit of Capitalism)* analyzes the rational economic calculus as worldly asceticism are, *mutatis mutandis,* entirely valid for the rational calculus of signs.

NOTES

Extracted from J. Baudrillard, "Design and Environment or How Political Economy Escalates into Cyberblitz," in *For a Critique of the Political Economy of the Sign,* trans. with an Introduction by Charles Levin (St Louis, Mo.: Telos Press Ltd., 1981), pp. 185–92. Reproduced with permission of Telos Press Ltd.

1. Echoing Galbraith's "techno-structure." Neo-capitalist, neo-industrialist, postindustrial: many terms can designate this passage from an industrial political economy to *a trans*-political economy (or *meta*-political economy).

2. Jeremy J. Schapiro, "One Dimensionality: The Universal Semiotic of Technological Experi-

ence," in Paul Breines, ed., *Critical Interruptions* (New York: Herder & Herder, 1970).

3. As early as 1902 Bernadetto Croce was writing an "Aesthetic as Science of Expression and *General Linguistic.*"

4. But this fundamental operation of form is what is never mentioned, in either case.

5. In his own way, using Marcusian terms, Schapiro (*op. cit.*) gives a similar analysis, but with more stress on machinery and technology: "The evolution of modern design is an essential component of the process of one-dimensionality (and indeed serves as an index of the latter's temporal development), since it derives from the machine process the forms for creating a total (totalitarian) environment in which technological experience defines and closes the experiential and aesthetic universe" (p. 161). Totalizing abstraction, undimensional homogeneity, certainly, but the machine or technology are neither the causes of this process nor its original models. Technological mutation and semio-linguistic mutation (passage to the abstraction of the code) are the two concurrent aspects of the same passage to structural-functional rationality.

6. Rather, these are logical guideposts to mark what in fact was a continuous historical process. However, the moment of formal theorization (which the Bauhaus is for the political economy of the sign) always marks a crucial point in the historical process itself.

22

TAKING IT WITH YOU

Reyner Banham

"It's not that caravans are bad housing … but that most housing isn't as good as caravans," or so said Alison Smithson (architect, novelist, spouse of architect and Edinbrugian *philosophe* of a prime Brodieish vintage). The remark was given the automated brush-off then, much as it would be today. "Everybody knows … " that caravans are portable slums and that caravan-sites are "ghettoes of poverty." Indeed it remains a fact that even the best-built caravan, if mounted on a brick foundation, not wheels, could be condemned by the district surveyor as a legally "dangerous structure" (so could a London bus!), but it is also still a fact that if you are buying basic habitability, a caravan gives you more for your money than anything on foundations the district surveyor could approve.

Footloose intellectual freebooters like Buckminster Fuller may have no difficulty with this concept of mobile homes as high-value housing … but most of the rest of us, and especially architects, are not at home with the idea, particularly when we contemplate the seemingly permanent environmental mess that usually surrounds them. The learned Smithson herself has been pretty acid about most of the mobile homes that actually cross her field of vision. So what was she on about? Just being flip and ala-mode in the modish sixties, or is there some shining Platonic ideal of a mobile home that once blessed her eyes?

You bet your re-cycled Mary Quant wellies there is! It shines forth upon the roads of America, but gleams quite frequently upon the highways of Europe, Africa and Asia as well. Three or four generations of modern architects have worshipped it, after their fashion and usually from afar, though ex-Bauhausler Marcel Breuer built one into his own house in the forties.

It's called the Airstream; it's been around since the early thirties, when it was dreamed up by one Wally Byam, and its smoothly streamlined polished-metal form is accounted one of the classics of modern American design. Like all classics (or Platonic ideals) it is supposed to be "for ever," changeless. Like that other Platonic ideal on wheels, the V W Beetle, it has in fact undergone continual detailed changes while being praised by bat-eyed liberals for its avoidance of "annual face-lifts à la Detroit."

The outline (if not the details) of the dream has changed little since it was first invented—not by Byam but by pioneer aviator Glenn Curtis. Like many another elegant snob in the late twenties, Curtis was appalled by the motley roadside hostelries he had to stay in while motorin' to Miami, and decided to take his own stateroom with him, in a streamlined capsule articulated to the back of his touring car. The Byam version was a regular towed trailer, not an artic, but was essentially the same proposition: a clean, efficient, highly-serviced, totally independent living-unit "wherever and whenever you choose to go or stay."

Air travel (as much as yachting) and aircraft technology were the inspiration of these

Image 10   Airstream, Design Within Reach, 2008. Photograph by Jim Bastardo. Reproduced by permission.

streamlined sleepers, which were near enough contemporary with the first transcontinental sleeper airliner, the Douglas DST, later to become that workhorse of the air, the Dakota or DC3.

What's odd about the Byam-waggon, however, is that it has only lately come to actually *look* like its distinguished contemporaries such as the DC3 or Bucky Fuller's (equally aircraft-inspired) Dymaxion cars. Unlike the Volkswagen, which has gone on looking like the same made-in-Germany tin jelly-mould from its beginnings to its recent end, the Airstream has contrived to finish up looking like a Classic of Early-Thirties American Functional Styling, but only after 45 years of detail refinement.

From its beginning until the middle sixties, the Airstream's metal panels did not join in smooth three-dimensional curves, but were faceted, like the planking of a boat, almost, and its windows were not round cornered and flush with its sides,

but had bent metal guttering over the top. Even after the plank effect had been smoothed away, the windows still had awkward corners, and it is only in the seventies that the Airstream has really been stylistically fit to stand alongside, say, the gantry-cranes of the TVA dams as proud witness to the spirit of the New Deal!

Not surprisingly, therefore, it bathes in the glow of nostalgia playing around "The streamlined decade," and its design-styles—the current Broadway smash, *On the Twentieth Century,* celebrates that great thirties train in sorry lyrics and tepid tunes, but the sets are a *knockout;* it's the first musical about industrial design! The Airstream fits that scene obviously, but what about ten years ago, or 20, or even 30 years ago when Breuer discovered it?

The fascination, for architects and designers, lay in its nearness to a full realisation of Le Corbusier's dream (the whole profession's dream, therefore) of *une machine a habiter fabriquee en serie; a* house engineered like an aircraft and manufactured like a car, Bucky Fuller's "Standard of Living Package." It was thus that the tragically late and lamented Ray Wilson celebrated the Airstream at Cambridge in the sixties; a snug weatherproof shell stuffed with capital-intensive technology, delivered to your address and replaced when it obsolesced. In spite of the vastly greater prestige of Apollo, Salyut, Soyuz and Skylab, and fighting off the earthbound challenges from the self-propelled Clark *Cortez* camper in the sixties, and General Motors Motorhome in the seventies, the Airstream has visibly remained the *beau ideal* of capsule-fanciers like Archigram, who frequently collaged it directly into their Plug-in, clip-on cities—where you could "live in the same house at several different addresses or several different houses at the same address."

The appeal of the Airstream, however, was always more visual than intellectual. It may be a very neat concept, but even in its facetted primitive forms it was an immensely appealing image. And it still is. Its polished aluminum exterior skin has the craftsmanly elegance of a Douglas aircraft; its miscellaneous doors and flaps and plug-points and ventilators have that aptness and tidy detailing which is supposed to derive from unaffected engineering practice, but which actually requires enormous self-effacing sophistication on the part of the designer. Overall, it sustains those neoclassical traditions that were built into the soul of western engineering around the time of James Watt, memorialised in aphorisms like: "Style is a word that has no plural."

That's the outside; what about the interior? Go on, guess! Wrong, wrong, all of you! Except for the cynic in the corner who has been reading Martin Pawley's *Private Future*. At least one of the fascinations of the capsule-dream was always the supposed private fantasies that could be contained within those sealed shells. Imagine convoys of gleaming streamliners zipping along

the interstates, passing boring farms and tedious state capitals and dull townships while those within conduct Japanese tea ceremonies, perform exquisite tortures with obscure Transylvanian leather objects or declaim Pindaric odes while dusky maidens anoint their heads with rare unguents. Imagine away ... the facts of the case are that the interiors of Airstreams are of a studied, deep-carpeted, wood-grained, value-free neutrality hard to match outside a Holiday Inn, and leave (physically) no room for fantasy.

This concentrated ordinariness has always been part of the deal, I suspect. Wally Byam's creed (oh, yes—it's a movement, practically a religion, being an Airstreamer) speaks of "bringing the world to your doorstep" but what he must have meant was "taking your doorstep to the world." Whether the view through the aircraft-style windows is Miami, Monument Valley or Mount Ararat, you are snug and secure in a piece of regular American suburbia.

In some ways this is an even more sensational situation than if an Airstream should prove to contain a cinema-organ or a seraglio, and it is a cultural fact that Americans have been warily shaping up to of late. A recent cartoon showed a man unloading tables, chairs, a standard-lamp and a television from a trailer home in the middle of some wild forest glade, what time his wife says: "I thought we came here to get away from it all, but you've brought it all with you!" Within the Airstream's perfect technological shell lies the promise that, after all, you *can* take it with you.

NOTE

Extracted from R. Banham, "Taking It with You," in *A Critic Writes* (Berkeley: University of California Press, 1996), pp. 223–26. Originally appeared in *New Society* 45, no. 826 (3 August 1978): 252–53. Reprinted by permission of the University of California Press via Copyright Clearance Center.

SECTION 3: THEORIZING DESIGN AND VISUALITY

3.2: Ethics

INTRODUCTION

Ethics deals with how our actions affect others, with an emphasis on right action. The raison d'être of design is in its relationships to human beings—design holds the possibility of structuring life in certain ways. Ideally design should result in the greater good for individuals or social groups, but unfortunately it does not always do so. These readings consider ethics in an increasingly artificial modern world, in design education, and as fundamental to the activity of designing. Two of the extracts are written by university professors, Zygmunt Bauman, a sociologist, and Clive Dilnot, a design theorist, and two by design journalists Rick Poyner and Susan Szensay. In their own way each is committed to the fundamental importance of education to achieve a greater confluence between design and ethics.

Bauman considers design relative to waste, and in particular the "wasted lives" of people who have become outcast and redundant in global modernization. He emphasizes how design is interwoven with and crucial to the constant change of modernity. Later in the extract he even states that "Modernity is a condition of compulsive and addictive designing." Designing itself is seen as "a self-perpetuating process," which is also "intrinsically wasteful." We can take a number of ethical perspectives on Bauman's thesis, from the very simple waste of the designed products that are thrown away before the end of their useful lives, to Marxist considerations of the "wasted" and alienated lives of those involved in producing, and in consuming, the artificial, that is the designed, world. Whichever we choose, the consideration of design and waste, which underpins contemporary concerns about sustainability (discussed in Section 6.3), offers many dimensions for theoretical and pragmatic approaches to design and ethics.

Such considerations tax design educators, especially those wishing to provide an ethical design education, which is the title of the second extract, by Susan Szenasy, who recounts her experience teaching undergraduate design students at Parsons The New School for Design, in New York City. She defines herself as the "sixties idealist" confronted with worldly and cynical students from a later generation. The issue of ethical design is by no means new; it is a by-product of modernity, as Bauman emphasizes. In the classroom, Szenasy evokes historical predecessors: William Morris, Henry Dreyfus, Walter Gropius and the Bauhaus, Ray and Charles Eames, as well as contemporary examples. Sustainability is a problematic issue for her students, by definition. Szenasy redefines "good design," not on the basis of modernist aesthetics, but as "responsible design," in which appearance is only one criterion. But how difficult is it for designers and other design professionals to work responsibly and to take an ethical position on what they do?

Advertising is an enormous global industry, not known for high ethical standards. The American Institute of Graphic Arts (AIGA) design manifesto, "First Things First," confirms that advertising has become an employment mainstay for many graphic designers, but what they are asked to do is often trivial and does not conform to any ethical standards. The long-standing and active AIGA produced the original manifesto in 1964. Forty years on the world has changed, but the concerns remain.

The millennium provided a point of reflection and led to the reissue of the manifesto, signed by designers and educators in Britain, Europe, and the United States.

In his introduction, Rick Poyner shares the view of designers as powerful cultural intermediaries, as expressed also by Paul du Gay and his colleagues in their study of the Sony Walkman (extracted in Section 5.1). What designers do is not value free; it has wide social and political ramifications. Simply put, design does not only have to be for economic profit, it can be for social good, and arguably this should be its primary purpose. But so much design activity is tied into capitalist economics, and many designers, and design students, are not attracted to the profession because of its potential as an ethical practice.

In the final essay, commissioned especially for this *Reader,* Clive Dilnot poses some hard questions for design professionals and nonprofessionals alike, beginning with the fundamental question of why we might need an ethics of design. Dilnot references a substantial range of scholarly perspectives to make his case as to how design might become an ethical practice. His words are not for the faint-hearted, nor do they apply only to Susan Szenasy's atypical design students, or to members of design professional bodies such as the AIGA. They apply to all design professionals everywhere, and to us all. For by inhabiting and using the artificial world, we share the responsibility for the ethics of its design.

23

IN THE BEGINNING WAS DESIGN OR THE WASTE OF ORDER-BUILDING

Zygmunt Bauman

Left to its own devices, unlit by the spotlights of the story and before the first fitting session with the designers, the world is neither orderly nor chaotic, neither clean nor dirty. It is human design that conjures up disorder *together with* the vision of order, dirt together with the project of purity. The thought trims the image of the world first, so that the world itself can be trimmed right after. Once the image has been trimmed, the trimming of the world (the desire to trim it, the effort to trim it—though not necessarily the feat of the trimming accomplished) are a foregone conclusion. The world is manageable and demands to be managed, in as far as it has been remade to the measure of human comprehension. Francis Bacon's injunction 'Nature, to be commanded, must be obeyed' was not an intimation of humility and even less a counsel of meekness. It was an act of defiance.

Nature has been obeyed—willy-nilly, knowingly or not—since the beginning of time. Being not of human making and so stretching beyond human reach and eluding human power was, after all, the very meaning of the idea of 'Nature'. Bacon's heresy lay in the idea that nature so understood need not and should not be let alone, as owing to regrettable neglect and unforgivable lack of resolve it had heretofore been, but can be *commanded*—providing we learn its laws that need to be obeyed. Three centuries later Karl Marx would reprimand philosophers for failing to follow Bacon's precept to the end: travelling along the track leading from obedience to command,

philosophers stopped halfway and left the train at the station Explanation. But, Marx would say, with all the honeycomb's perfection even the most wretched and bungling architect is superior to a bee, and that is thanks to the image of the finished product that he holds in his head before the work of construction starts.

Designs, of course, are called for because something *new* is about to be created; something extant, present already out there, in the world as it is, is to be changed. And just as the proof of the pudding is in the eating, knowledge proves itself by changing the world.

There are, though, two radically different ways of creating the new. Lewis Mumford used the allegory of farming versus mining to capture the difference between them. Agriculture, says Mumford, 'returns deliberately what man subtracts from the earth'. The process of mining, on the contrary 'is destructive ... and what is once taken out of the quarry or the pithead cannot be replaced'. Mining, therefore, 'presents the very image of human discontinuity, here today and gone tomorrow, now feverish with gain, now depleted and vacant'.[1] We may say that a fashion most commonly deployed among the modern ways to create (or should we rather say to creatively destroy?) has been shaped after the pattern and in the likeness of mining.

Farming stands for continuity: one grain is replaced by more grain, one sheep gives birth to more sheep. *Plus ça change—plus c'est la même chose.* The growth as reassertion and reaffirmation of being … A growth without losses … Nothing is lost on the way. Death is followed by rebirth. No wonder that societies of farmers took eternal continuity of beings for granted; what they witnessed and what they practised was an uninterrupted chain of endings indistinguishable from the incessant repetition of beginning—nay a perpetual resurrection. They did not live towards death as Martin Heidegger, pondering the ways and means of techne at the time of its ultimate triumph, suggested, but towards perpetual rebirth, whether in the form of an infinite reincarnation or of fleshy mortal bodies reborn as spirits, as immaterial but immortal souls.

Mining on the other hand is an epitome of rupture and discontinuity. The new cannot be born unless something is discarded, thrown away or destroyed. The new is created in the course of meticulous and merciless dissociation between the target product and everything else that stands in the way of its arrival. Whether precious or base, pure metals can be obtained only by removing slag and cinders from the ore. And one can get down to the ore only by removing and disposing of layer after layer of the soil that bars access to the ledge—having first cut down or burnt out the forest that barred access to the soil. Mining denies that death carries in its womb a new birth. Instead, mining proceeds on the assumption that the birth of the new requires the death of the old. And if so, then each new creation is bound to share sooner or later in the lot of that which has been left behind to rot and decompose to pave the way for a yet newer creation. Each point through which mining proceeds is a point of no return. Mining is a one-way movement, irreversible and irrevocable. The chronicle of mining is a graveyard of used up, repudiated and abandoned lodes and shafts. Mining is inconceivable without *waste*.

Asked how he obtained the beautiful harmony of his sculptures, Michelangelo reputedly answered: 'Simple. You just take a slab of marble and cut out all the superfluous bits.' In the heyday of the Renaissance, Michelangelo proclaimed the precept that was to guide modern creation. *Separation and destruction of waste was to be the trade secret of modern creation:* through cutting out and throwing away the superfluous, the needless and the useless, the beautiful, the harmonious, the pleasing and the gratifying was to be divined.

The vision of a perfect form hidden inside the formless slab of raw stone precedes its birth-act. Waste is the wrapping that conceals that form. To lay the form bare, to make it emerge and be, to admire its perfection in all its unalloyed harmony and beauty, the form must first be unwrapped. For something to be created, something else must be consigned to waste. The wrapping—the waste of the creative act—must be torn apart, shredded and disposed of lest it clutter the floor and cramp the sculptor's moves. There can be no artistic workshop without a rubbish heap.

This however makes waste into an indispensable ingredient of the creative process. More: it endows waste with an awesome, truly magic power, equivalent to that of the alchemists' philosopher's stone—the power of a wondrous transmutation of base, paltry and menial stuff into a noble, beautiful and precious object. It also makes waste an embodiment of ambivalence. Waste is simultaneously divine and satanic. It is the midwife of all creation—and its most formidable obstacle. Waste is sublime: a unique blend of attraction and repulsion arousing an equally unique mixture of awe and fear.

But remember Mary Douglas: no objects *are* 'waste' by their intrinsic qualities, and no objects can *become* waste through their inner logic. It is by being assigned to waste by human designs that material objects, whether human or inhuman, acquire all the mysterious, awe-inspiring, fearsome and repulsive qualities listed above. In his remarkable study of the ritual significance and magical proprieties commonly ascribed to human hair, Edmund Leach notes that in many cultures

head hair, while it is a part of the body, is treated with loving care, oiled and combed and dressed in the most elaborate fashion, but as soon as it is cut off it becomes 'dirt', and is explicitly and consciously associated with the … polluting substances, faeces, urine, semen and sweat … The 'dirt' is clearly magical stuff; it endows the barber and the washerman with dangerous aggressive power, but it is not the power of a particular individual …

it is the power of the 'magic hair' itself, or more correctly of the remarkable act of transmutation performed through its detachment from the human body. All the operations performed on the hair—cutting, shaving or styling—amount to a conjuring up of a new person out of the old, since in many cultures head hair is remodelled as an integral part of a rite of passage from one socially allocated identity to another. And so the act of separation 'not only creates two categories of persons; it also creates a third entity, the thing that is ritually separated …' In other words, 'it is the ritual situation which makes the hair "powerful", not the hair which makes the ritual powerful.'[2]

The cut-off hair shares some of its imputed magical attributes (black magic, to be precise) with urine, sweat and other similarly 'polluting' substances that are shunned and abhorred because of the ambiguity of their status—trespassing on the barricade that should not be crossed lest the world lose its transparency and actions their clarity—because of the questioning and compromising of the sacrosanct boundary between the embodied self and the rest of the world. But the cut-off hair also shares in the potent and sinister attributes of all waste. Like all waste, it is instrumental in the miraculous act of extracting the new out of the old, the better out of the worse, the superior out of the inferior. That coveted and welcome transmutation is not complete, and certainly not secure, as long as the 'waste' is still around instead of having been swept away and deposited in a leak-proof, distant location. The act of creation reaches its culmination, completion and true fulfilment in the act of the separation and disposal of waste.

The modern mind was born together with the idea that *the world can be changed*. Modernity is about rejecting the world as it has been thus far and the resolution to change it. The modern way of being consists in compulsive, obsessive change: in the refutation of what 'merely is' in the name of what could, and by the same token ought, to be put in its place. The modern world is a world containing a desire, and a determination, to defy its *mêmete* (as Paul Ricoeur would say)—its sameness. A desire to make *itself* different from what the self is, to remake itself, and to go on remaking it. The modern condition is to be on the move. The choice is to modernize or perish. Modern history has therefore been a history of designing and a museum/graveyard of designs tried, used up, rejected and abandoned in the ongoing war of conquest and/or attrition waged against nature.

When it came to designing, the modern mind had no equals. Designs were one article of which modern societies, and their members, never ran short. The history of the modern era has been a long string of contemplated, attempted, pursued, seen through, failed or abandoned designs. Designs were many and different, but each one painted a future reality different from the one the designers knew. And since 'the future' does not exist as long as it remains 'in the future', and since in dealing with the non-existent one cannot 'get one's facts straight', there was no telling in advance, let alone with certainty, what the world emerging at the other end of the efforts of construction would be. Would it indeed be, as anticipated, a benign, user-friendly and pleasurable world, and would the assets budgeted and laid aside for the purpose and the approved work schedules prove adequate for transferring that world from the drawing board into the future present?

A high probability of negative answers to both questions was always and always will remain an undetachable attribute of designing. 'The idea of an unalloyed good seems to be drawn from an illusion,' warns Tzvetan Todorov.[3] Greater good can only be had at a price: alongside its benefits, it is bound to bring consequences as undesirable as they are unpredictable, though the latter are usually played down or ignored at the designing stage on the pretext of the nobility of the overall intentions. Designs are fraught with risks; as modern times went by, an ever larger part of the designing zeal and design-drawing efforts was prompted by the urge to detoxicate, neutralize or remove out of sight the 'collateral damage' done by past designing. Designing becomes its own paramount cause; designing is, ultimately, a self-perpetuating process. It is also an intrinsically wasteful endeavour. If no design can be fully and truly 'on target' and cannot but affect, in an unpredictable and often unprepossessing fashion, aspects of reality overlooked or deliberately left out of account—then only excessive designing, a *surplus of designs,* may salvage the designing process as a whole, compensating for the unavoidable fallibility of each of its parts and stages.

A foolproof, risk-proof design is very nearly a contradiction in terms.

To be seen as 'realistic', as capable of implementation, design needs to simplify the world's complexity. It must set apart the 'relevant' from the 'irrelevant', strain the manageable fragments of reality out of such parts as are resistant to manipulation, and focus on the objectives which are rendered 'reasonable' and 'within our power' by currently available means and skills, supplemented by means and skills it is hoped will be acquired soon.

Between them, all the conditions listed, in order to be met, require that a lot of things be cast aside—out of view, out of thought and out of action. They also require that whatever has been left out is turned—turns immediately—into the *waste* of the designing process. The underlying strategy and the inevitable effect of designing is the division of the material outcomes of the action into 'what counts' and 'what does not count', into the 'useful product' and 'waste'. Because the drawing of designs is (for the reasons spelled out before) bound not only to be continuous but also to continuously expand in volume, designing cannot but portend a perpetual accumulation of waste and an unstoppable growth of unresolved or perhaps unresolvable waste disposal problems.

NOTES

Extracted from Z. Bauman, 'In the Beginning Was Design or The Waste of Order-Building', in *Wasted Lives: Modernity and Its Outcasts* (New York: Blackwell, 2004), pp. 19–25. Reprinted with the permission of Blackwell Publishers.

1. Lewis Mumford, *The City in History: Its Origins, its Transformations, and its Prospects* (New York, 1961), pp. 450–1.
2. See Edmund R. Leach, 'Magical hair', in *Myth and Cosmos: Readings in Mythology and Symbolism,* ed. John Middleton (Natural History Press, 1967), pp. 77–108.
3. Tzvetan Todorov, *Devoirs et delices. Une vie de passeur* (interviews with Catherine Portevin) (Seuil, 2002), p. 304.

24

ETHICAL DESIGN EDUCATION

Confessions of a Sixties Idealist

Susan S. Szenasy

"Sustainability is not my issue," protests one senior, a student in Parsons's product design department. She's presenting her term paper on a designer and maker of lamps. Two others in the class, also product majors, are appalled by this statement; so am I. We've just spent a semester returning, again and again, to discussions of our degrading natural environment and the need for everyone to figure out how to use this knowledge to design more sensitively.

We're a group of twenty-eight fledgling professionals, pursuing courses of study in architecture; interior, product, and graphic design; fashion; and photography; I'm number twenty-nine, their teacher and a design magazine editor. Having observed every kind of designer at work for several decades, I know that the creative professions make a huge difference in the ways we live. I see designers as active participants in the decisions businesses make about the land they occupy and the resources they use, the technologies they rely on, and the ideas they communicate.

Every Tuesday afternoon we gather in a windowless room in a hulking New School building on Fifth Avenue (New York)—the kind of soulless, mechanically aired space we've all grown to tolerate—and discuss the Ethics of Design. I have been teaching this senior seminar, part of Parsons's liberal arts offering, since 1997, when the school first asked me to develop it. The course is all about responsibility: to the planet, to the regions we live in, to the community, to the profession, to the client, and to the self. I interpret ethics to mean

that we have a moral duty, an obligation to our fellow humans and to other living creatures. And that obligation calls on us to be prudent stewards of the natural environment that supports and sustains our lives. Sustaining the environment, in turn, is our highest priority as thinking, verbal, tool-using creatures blessed with free will; yes, we have a choice. In my view, it's ethical to choose fresh water, clean air, nutritious food—the bounties our home planet provides for us—and safeguard these for future generations.

We begin each September by watching *Mind-Walk,* a 1991 film that argues for abandoning the Cartesian, mechanistic, linear thinking that lit up the road to industrialization and made the modern world possible. Now, if we are to survive, we need to switch to an ecological-systems thinking which considers interconnectedness and relationships. This is the crux of the 110-minute conversation between a politician, a poet, and a physicist—a brilliant script based on the thinking of physicist Fritjof Capra. There's no sex, no drugs, no rock and roll, nothing but talk about life, all kinds of life, and glorious views of Mont-Saint-Michel, a tiny island built up during the Middle Ages in France's Gulf of St. Malo, photographed to the music of Philip Glass.

As they watch the video monitor, the students see a gigantic metal mechanism in an ancient tower and hear the physicist say that the microchip has taken the place of the clockwork. This is a dramatic visual and verbal reminder of how invisible technology is replacing much of the bulkily visible. What's called for, says the scientist, is a drastic change in the way we see the world: no longer as a machine with replaceable parts, but as a system of relationships modeled on nature's own systems.

And so we build on this thought throughout our four months together, probing how designers can become active participants in the great system of living organisms that dwell on our fragile, blue-green planet. We try, as the physicist urges us to, to figure out how we might live and work inside a "web of relationships" and connect to the "web of life."

The first to resist ecological thinking this semester are the fashion students. They're skeptical, even cynical. Their lament: The big companies are in control. There's nothing any one designer can do. We're all slaves of seasonal trends and fickle consumers; we're creatures of a throw-away culture. Why should we care about being sensitive to the environment when nobody wants us to be? The world is a polluted, mean, ugly place ruled by greed and ego. To be part of the fashion industry, to make a living in it, we need to figure out how to make money, how to become stars.

I, the sixties idealist who wholeheartedly believes we can turn that ugly world into something more beautiful, try to keep my cool, though I hear my voice turn shrill. I bring up examples from Paul Hawken's 1993 book, *The Ecology of Commerce.* (I've stopped assigning it this year. Experience tells me that only a few students would actually read any part of it, so why waste all that paper?) I call their attention to large, multinational businesses like Ikea that are making changes in the way they procure and use materials and distribute their furniture, all to reflect their own, and presumably their customers', growing interest in the environment. I mention post-consumer materials now on the market, like the luxurious fleece we wear as parkas and use as blankets, made from recycled soda bottles. Yes, but look at us, we're slaves to mindless acquisition. You're dreaming a naive dream, Susan, argue the students.

We press on and read William Morris on the "morality of materials," on the importance of craft and the human touch in an industrialized world, on the social responsibility of designers. We learn about his interest in and advocacy of such varied but related areas of aesthetic expression as historic restoration, furniture and furnishings, wallpapers and textiles, polemical writings, and book publishing. Through this eccentric nineteenth-century genius we are introduced to the designer as an advocate, a revolutionary who looks back to medieval times to reclaim human creativity. His life and work teach us that a strong and brave designer can take on the powerful socioeconomic forces, like Morris took on the Industrial Revolution, and have influence far beyond his own times.

We read Walter Gropius on his struggles to establish the Bauhaus, a breakthrough art school in a provincial town in war-ravaged Germany. We learn about the dire economic conditions that plagued the early years of his school and how Gropius overcame these limitations by sheer will and conviction while collaborating with likeminded people. Though his ideas helped bring our world into modern times, we also learn that initially the Bauhaus was shaped by Morris's thinking: a deep understanding of craft materials and methods. We discuss how a great hardship, like the post-World War I collapse of social and economic values, can propel creative thinking and awaken social responsibility among formgivers. We talk about the need for material invention in such times. And we realize that design, as Gropius saw it (as Morris did before him), has a significant contribution to make in the reshaping of institutions as well as our lives. The word "responsibility" runs through our discussions.

We watch A *Story of Healing,* a short film that follows American surgeons and nurses in Vietnam doing reconstructive facial surgery on children. Working under primitive conditions, these highly skilled professionals bring all their technical knowledge and love of humanity to the task. It's a heartbreaking and an exhilarating thirty-three minutes that leads to two hours of spirited conversation on professional behavior: It's important, at times, to step out of our comfort zone. For the medical team, that meant leaving behind the fancy, well-run, high-tech hospitals they worked in every day. What does it mean for designers? We wonder.

The nurses and surgeons set up shop in a small, provincial hospital, some spending their vacations working there. They talk, between the many procedures they perform, about finding satisfaction in the work. No one mentions money or wealth or prestige. Their faces beam as they come to realize, one after another, "this is why I went into medicine in the first place." They all talk about the joys and surprises of helping those in need, being part of a dynamic team, testing their skills and imaginations at every turn, and learning that even though people's circumstances and cultures are different, they value the same things. They teach us that acting on our obligation to our human family can result in rewards far beyond our expectations.

Then, sometime around midterm, a fashion student mentions that an instructor gleefully showed off a forbidden cache of monkey fur in class. The room blows up. The kids are outraged. The architects, interior designers, and the product and graphic designers face the fashion designers, arguing the immorality and illegality of hunting monkeys for their fur. The thought of killing primates purely for their coats so some fashionista can parade around in them offends all of us, including the fashion designers.

One architecture student starts talking about hearts of palm. Apparently, she says, whole groves of a kind of palm tree are cut down and wasted so that some gourmand can buy a precious little snack in a can. Monkey fur and hearts of palm. Everyone agrees, eventually, that we can do without these ill-gotten luxuries. What else can we do without, I ask.

But the bigger question now, for everyone in the room, is how to think about the materials we use and what designers must teach themselves about these materials. One industrial design student explains that we have to look at the full life-cycle costs of materials, from resource harvesting to processing to manufacturing to distribution to use and recycling or, better yet, working to engineer materials for nontoxic degradation. It took monkey fur and hearts of palm to grasp the complex system lurking behind every material choice designers make, from the paper we print on, to the clothing we wear, to the furniture we sit on, to the buildings we live and work in, to the appliances we use.

Last year, our second class of the fall season happened to have been scheduled for 9/11, and so, of course, did not happen. The semester was foreshortened by the attacks on the World Trade Center. For a while the New School buildings served as staging areas for some emergency services. Several students came closer to the carnage than anyone should. Our academic world became more real as we talked about America's arrogant and profligate energy use, which was dramatically embedded in the twin towers, now turned to one big toxic pile of dust. The rubble was burning not far from where we sat. Those who will give forms to our physical environment—my twenty-eight hopes for the future of a new design ethic—had a hard time ignoring this fact of their lives. The collapse shows, among other things, that our current American lifestyle is unsustainable.

But what can we do? Ask the students. Henry Dreyfuss provides a helping hand from beyond the grave. He got involved. We discuss Dreyfuss's dogged concerns about how people use things, what we need to lead useful and happy lives, how we see the world around us, how our unique body measurements and movements determine our relationship to tools and rooms and other things. He reminds us that there is considerate, sympathetic thought behind every great object.

Dreyfuss learned to type before he designed a typewriter, he drove a tractor before he designed one, he hung around department stores before he would design a shop. It's inspiring to talk about this "man in the brown suit," as the conservatively suited, Depression-era industrial designer came to be known. He connected with humanity. That's what a responsible designer does. This gift for making connections becomes the glue that holds us together after our world is torn apart on that sunny September day.

Also providing inspiration are Charles and Ray Eames. We read about their irrepressible, all-American, mid-century-vintage enthusiasm for both the designed and natural environment. What would they do with the information we now have about the life cycles of materials, we wonder. They would use it to great effect, we surmise. This was, after all, the couple who explored interconnectivity in a most memorable way. In their now classic film, *Powers of Ten,* the Eameses showed the many scales that make up our knowledge and experience of the world, zooming from the molecular to the cosmic and points in between. How about re-examining these scales of existence to help us think about our resources and ourselves, I ask, and prod the students to imagine how they would see the world with the Eameses adventurous, educated, and playful eyes.

Standing on the shoulders of these design giants, who have laid the foundations for responsible behavior, we get ready to explore the ethics of today's designers. To that end, each student has chosen a practitioner they'll interview, preferably in person. This exchange becomes the subject of their presentations and final papers. Incidentally, the fashion designers end up choosing small shop owners, independent shoemakers, up-and-coming dress makers—more in line with William Morris's thinking than Ralph Lauren's—creative and principled people struggling to find their own way.

What of the student who professed to be untouched by sustainability? Though her presentation shows a shocking insensitivity to the subject, her paper does not. As I read it, I'm gratified to learn that the lamp maker she interviewed uses recycled materials and searches out nontoxic processes. Perhaps her disclaimer was a moment of youthful rebellion or an honest confusion about the meaning of a difficult word; sustainability, after all, is hard to wrap your brain around. Perhaps when we understand that good design is responsible design, we will no longer need to rely on clumsy, descriptive words. We'll just call it design—a noble and necessary human activity.

NOTE

Extracted from S. S. Szenasy, "Ethical Design Education Confessions of a Sixties Idealist," in Steven Heller and Veronique Vienne, ed., *Citizen Designer: Perspectives of Design Responsibility* (New York: Allworth Press, 2003), pp. 20–24. Reprinted by permission of the author.

25

FIRST THINGS FIRST 2000

A Design Manifesto Published Jointly by 33 Signatories in *Adbusters*, the *AIGA journal, Blueprint, Emigre, Eye, Form, Items* fall 1999/spring 2000

AIGA

We, the undersigned, are graphic designers, art directors and visual communicators who have been raised in a world in which the techniques and apparatus of advertising have persistently been presented to us as the most lucrative, effective and desirable use of our talents. Many design teachers and mentors promote this belief; the market rewards it; a tide of books and publications reinforces it.

Encouraged in this direction, designers then apply their skill and imagination to sell dog biscuits, designer coffee, diamonds, detergents, hair gel, cigarettes, credit cards, sneakers, butt toners, light beer and heavy-duty recreational vehicles. Commercial work has always paid the bills, but many graphic designers have now let it become, in large measure, *what graphic designers do*. This, in turn, is how the world perceives design. The profession's time and energy is used up manufacturing demand for things that are inessential at best.

Many of us have grown increasingly uncomfortable with this view of design. Designers who devote their efforts primarily to advertising, marketing and brand development are supporting, and implicitly endorsing, a mental environment so saturated with commercial messages that it is changing the very way citizen-consumers speak, think, feel, respond and interact. To some extent we are all helping draft a reductive and immeasurably harmful code of public discourse.

There are pursuits more worthy of our problem-solving skills. Unprecedented environmental, social and cultural crises demand our attention. Many cultural interventions, social marketing campaigns, books, magazines, exhibitions, educational tools, television programs, films, charitable causes and other information design projects urgently require our expertise and help.

We propose a reversal of priorities in favor of more useful, lasting and democratic forms of communication—a mindshift away from product marketing and toward the exploration and production of a new kind of meaning. The scope of debate is shrinking; it must expand. Consumerism is running uncontested; it must be challenged by other perspectives expressed, in part, through the visual languages and resources of design.

In 1964, 22 visual communicators signed the original call for our skills to be put to worthwhile use. With the explosive growth of global commercial culture, their message has only grown more urgent. Today, we renew their manifesto in expectation that no more decades will pass before it is taken to heart.

signed:

Jonathan Barnbrook
Nick Bell
Andrew Blauvelt
Hans Bockting
Irma Boom
Sheila Levrant de Bretteville
Max Bruinsma
Siân Cook
Linda van Deursen
Chris Dixon
William Drenttel
Gert Dumbar
Simon Esterson
Vince Frost
Ken Garland
Milton Glaser
Jessica Helfand
Steven Heller
Andrew Howard

Tibor Kalman
Jeffery Keedy
Zuzana Licko
Ellen Lupton
Katherine McCoy
Armand Mevis
J. Abbott Miller
Rick Poynor
Lucienne Roberts
Erik Spiekermann
Jan van Toorn
Teal Triggs
Rudy VanderLans
Bob Wilkinson

and many more
original Manifesto, 1964

NOTE

"First Things First 2000" Extracted from "First Things First 2000: A Design Manifesto," *AIGA Journal,* 2000, http://www.xs4all.nl/~maxb/ftf2000.htm. Reprinted by permission of the American Institute of Graphic Arts (AIGA).

DESIGN IS ABOUT DEMOCRACY

Rick Poyner

When Ken Garland published his First Things First manifesto in London thirty-five years ago, he threw down a challenge to graphic designers and other visual communicators that refuses to go away. As the century ends, this brief message, dashed off in the heat of the moment, and signed by twenty-one of his colleagues, is more urgent than ever; the situation it lamented incalculably more extreme.

It is no exaggeration to say that designers are engaged in nothing less than the manufacture of contemporary reality. Today, we live and breathe design. Few of the experiences we value at home, at leisure, in the city or the mall are free of its alchemical touch. We have absorbed design so deeply into ourselves that we no longer recognise the myriad ways in which it prompts, cajoles, disturbs, and excites us. It's completely natural. It's just the way things are.

We imagine that we engage directly with the "content" of the magazine, the TV commercial, the pasta sauce, or perfume, but the content is always mediated by design and it's design that helps direct how we perceive it and how it makes us feel. The brand-meisters and marketing gurus understand this only too well. The product may be little different in real terms from its rivals. What seduces us is its "image." This image reaches us first as a visual entity—shape, colour, picture, type. But if it's to work its effect on us it must become an idea: NIKE! This is the tremendous power of design.

The original First Things First was written at a time when the British economy was booming.

People of all classes were better off than ever before and jobs were easily had. Consumer goods such as TVs, washing machines, fridges, record players and cars, which North Americans were the first to take for granted, were transforming everyday life in the wealthier European nations—and changing consumer expectations for ever. Graphic design, too, had emerged from the austerity of the post-war years, when four-colour printing was a rarity and designers could only dream of American clients' lavish production budgets and visual panache. Young designers were vigorous and optimistic. They organised meetings, debates and exhibitions promoting the value of design. Professional associations were started and many leading figures, still active today, began their careers.

Ken Garland studied design at the Central School of Arts and Crafts in London in the early 1950s, and for six years was art editor of Design magazine, official mouthpiece of the Council of Industrial Design. In 1962, he set up his own company, Ken Garland & Associates, and the same year began a fruitful association (a "do-it-for-love consultancy," as he once put it) with the Campaign for Nuclear Disarmament. He was a committed campaigner against the bomb, and his "Aldermaston to London Easter 62" poster, with its huge, marching CND symbol, is a classic piece of protest graphics from the period. Always outspoken, in person and in print, he was an active member of the socialist Labour Party.

Garland penned his historic statement on 29 November 1963, during a crowded meeting of the Society of Industrial Artists at London's

Institute of Contemporary Arts. At the end he asked the chairman whether he could read it out. "As I warmed to the task I found I wasn't so much reading it as declaiming it," he recalled later; "it had become, we all realised simultaneously, that totally unfashionable device, a Manifesto." There was prolonged applause and many people volunteered their signatures there and then.

Four hundred copies of First Things First were published in January 1964. Some of the other signatories were well-established figures. Edward Wright, in his early forties, and the oldest, taught experimental typography at the Central School; Anthony Froshaug was also a Central typographer of great influence. Others were teachers, students, or just starting out as designers. Several were photographers.

The manifesto received immediate backing from an unexpected quarter. One of the signatories passed it to Caroline Wedgwood Benn, wife of the Labour Member of Parliament, Anthony Wedgwood Benn (now Tony Benn). On 24 January, Benn reprinted the manifesto in its entirety in his weekly Guardian newspaper column. "The responsibility for the waste of talent which they have denounced is one we must all share," he wrote. "The evidence for it is all around us in the ugliness with which we have to live. It could so easily be replaced if only we consciously decided as a community to engage some of the skill which now goes into the frills of an affluent society."

That evening, as a result of the Guardian article, Garland was invited on to a BBC TV news program to read out a section of First Things First and discuss the manifesto. It was subsequently reprinted in Design, the SIA Journal (which built an issue round it), the Royal College of Art magazine, Ark, and the yearbook Modern Publicity 1964/65, where it was also translated into French and German. This publicity meant that many people, not just in Britain but abroad, heard about and read First Things First. Garland has letters in his files from designers, design teachers and other interested parties as far afield as Australia, the United States and the Netherlands requesting copies, affirming support for the manifesto's message, or inviting him to come and speak about it.

That First Things First struck a nerve is clear. It arrived at a moment when design was taking off as a confident, professionalised activity. The rapid growth of the affluent consumer society meant there were many opportunities for talented visual communicators in advertising, promotion and packaging. The advertising business itself had experienced a so-called "creative revolution" in New York, and several influential American exponents of the new ideas-based graphic design were working for London agencies in the early 1960s. A sense of glamour and excitement surrounded this well-paid line of work. From the late 1950s onwards, a few sceptical designers began to ask publicly what this non-stop tide of froth had to do with the wider needs and problems of society. To some, it seemed that the awards with which their colleagues liked to flatter themselves attracted and celebrated only the shallowest and most ephemeral forms of design. For Garland and the other concerned signatories of First Things First, design was in danger of forgetting its responsibility to struggle for a better life for all.

The critical distinction drawn by the manifesto was between design as communication (giving people necessary information) and design as persuasion (trying to get them to buy things). In the signatories' view, a disproportionate amount of designers' talents and effort was being expended on advertising trivial items, from fizzy water to slimming diets, while more "useful and lasting" tasks took second place: street signs, books and periodicals, catalogues, instruction manuals, educational aids, and so on. The British designer Jock Kinneir (not a signatory) agreed: "Designers oriented in this direction are concerned less with persuasion and more with information, less with income brackets and more with physiology, less with taste and more with efficiency, less with fashion and more with amenity. They are concerned in helping people to find their way, to understand what is required of them, to grasp new processes and to use instruments and machines more easily."

Some dismissed the manifesto as naive, but the signatories were absolutely correct in their assessment of the way that design was developing. In the years that followed, similar misgivings were sometimes voiced by other designers, but most preferred to keep their heads down and concentrate on questions of form and craft. Lubricated by design, the juggernaut rolled on. In the gentler, much less invasive commercial climate of the early 1960s, it was still possible to imagine that if a few more designers would only move across to the other side of the vehicle balance would be restored. In its wording, the manifesto did not acknowledge the extent to which this might, in reality, be a political issue, and Garland himself made a point of explaining that the underlying political and economic system was not being called into question. "We do not advocate the abolition of high pressure consumer advertising," he wrote, "this is not feasible."

But the decision to concentrate one's efforts as a designer on corporate projects, or advertising, or any other kind of design, is a political choice. "Design is not a neutral value-free process," argues the American design educator Katherine McCoy, who contends that corporate work of even the most innocuous content is never devoid of political bias. Today, the imbalance identified by First Things First is greater than ever. The vast majority of design projects—and certainly the most lavishly funded and widely disseminated—address corporate needs, a massive over-emphasis on the commercial sector of society, which consumes most of graphic designers' time, skills and creativity. As McCoy points out, this is a decisive vote for economic considerations over other potential concerns, including society's social, educational, cultural, spiritual, and political needs. In other words, it's a political statement in support of the status quo.

Design's love affair with form to the exclusion of almost everything else lies at the heart of the problem. In the 1990s, advertisers were quick to coopt the supposedly "radical" graphic and typographic footwork of some of design's most celebrated and ludicrously self-regarding stars, and these designers, seeing an opportunity to reach national and global audiences, were only too happy to take advertising's dollar. Design styles lab-tested in youth magazines and obscure music videos became the stuff of sneaker, soft drink and bank ads. Advertising and design are closer today than at any point since the 1960s. For many young designers emerging from design schools in the 1990s, they now appear to be one and the same. Obsessed with how cool an ad looks, rather than with what it is really saying, or the meaning of the context in which it says it, these designers seriously seem to believe that formal innovations alone are somehow able to effect progressive change in the nature and content of the message communicated. Exactly how, no one ever manages to explain.

Meanwhile, in the sensation-hungry design press, in the judging of design competitions, in policy statements from design organisations, in the words of design's senior figures and spokespeople (on the few occasions they have a chance to address the public) and even in large sections of design education, we learn about very little these days other than the commercial uses of design. It's rare to hear any strong point of view expressed, by most of these sources, beyond the unremarkable news that design really can help to make your business more competitive. When the possibility is tentatively raised that design might have broader purposes, potential and meanings, designers who have grown up in a commercial climate often find this hard to believe. "We have trained a profession," says McCoy, "that feels political or social concerns are either extraneous to our work or inappropriate."

The new signatories' enthusiastic support for Adbusters' updated First Things First reasserts its continuing validity, and provides a much needed opportunity to debate these issues before it is too late. What's at stake in contemporary design, the artist and critic Johanna Drucker suggests, isn't so much the look or form of design practice as the life and consciousness of the designer (and everybody else, for that matter). She argues that the process of unlocking and exposing the underlying ideological basis of commercial culture boils down to a simple question that we need to ask, and keep on asking: "In whose interest and to what ends? Who gains by this construction of reality, by this representation of this condition as 'natural'?"

This is the concern of the designer or visual communicator in at least two senses. First, like all of us, as a member of society, as a citizen (a word it would be good to revive), as a punch-drunk viewer on the receiving end of the barrage of commercial images. Second, as someone whose sphere of expertise is that of representation, of two-dimensional appearances, and the construction of reality's shifting visual surface, interface and expression. If thinking individuals have a responsibility to withstand the proliferating technologies of persuasion, then the designer, as a skilled professional manipulator of those technologies, carries a double responsibility. Even now,

at this late hour, in a culture of rampant commodification, with all its blindspots, distortions, pressures, obsessions, and craziness, it's possible for visual communicators to discover alternative ways of operating in design.

At root, it's about democracy. The escalating commercial take-over of everyday life makes democratic resistance more vital than ever.

FTF2000:
foreword by Chris Dixon, Adbusters
original Manifesto, 1964
reaction by Jouke Kleerebezem
discussion Info Design Cafe mailing list
miscellaneous reactions

NOTE

Extracted from Rick Poyner, "Design Is about Democracy," 2000, http://www.xs4all. nl/~maxb/ftfpoyn.htm. Reprinted by permission of the American Institute of Graphic Arts (AIGA).

26

ETHICS IN DESIGN

10 Questions

Clive Dilnot

1. WHY MIGHT WE NEED AN ETHICS OF DESIGN?

Here is one reason. It comes from designer and educator Victor Papanek, from *Design for the Real World,* first published in 1974 but still unparalleled in its attack on the economic and social irresponsibility of design.

> There are professions more harmful than industrial design, but only a very few of them. Never before in history have grown men sat down and seriously designed electric hairbrushes, rhinestone covered file boxes, and mink carpeting for bathrooms, and then drawn up elaborate plans to make and sell these gadgets to millions of people. Before … if a person liked killing people, he had to become a general, purchase a coal-mine, or else study nuclear physics. Today, industrial design has put murder on a mass-production basis. By designing criminally unsafe automobiles that kill or maim nearly one million people around the world each year, by creating whole new species of permanent garbage to clutter up the landscape, and by choosing materials and processes that pollute the air we breathe, designers have become a dangerous breed. … As long as design concerns itself with confecting trivial 'toys for adults', killing machines with gleaming tailfins, and 'sexed up' shrouds for toasters, telephones, and computers, it … is about time that design *as we have come to know it,* should cease to exist.

> (Papanek 1974: 9,10).

Here is another. It comes from the Dutch communications and graphic designer Jan van Toorn.

> Capitalist culture organizes people as buyers of commodities and services [and] … transform[s] information and knowledge into commodities. … The corporate conglomerates of the culture industry have created a global public sphere which does not offer any scope for discussion of the social and cultural consequences of the 'free flow of information' organized by them. The fusion of trade, politics and communication has brought about the sophisticated one-dimensional character of our symbolic environment, which is at least as menacing as the pollution of the natural environment.

> This is partly due to the lack of a critical attitude to the social-cultural conditions of professional mediation. … Cooperation with institutions and adaptation to their structures has resulted in ideological accommodation, expressed in a lack of insight into the social role of the profession. … Under the pressure of neoliberalism and the power relationships of the free market … not only is the designer's individual freedom, 'ostensibly still existing within a space of its own … infiltrated by the client's way of thinking,' but design ends up discovering that at best it serves today as little more than a 'theatrical substitute for [missing] essential forms of social communication'—whilst at worst, 'drawing on its roles in the organization of production and in helping to stimulate consumption', it is

both hand-in-glove the 'extensive disciplining of the general public' in the terms of the market— a disciplining 'whose most far-reaching consequence is undoubtedly a political neutralization that is at odds with the functioning of an open and democratic society'

(van Toorn 1994: 151; 1997: 154).

Here is yet a third, this time by the architectural historian and critic Kenneth Frampton, reflecting on the contemporary urban condition.

A recent publication by the artists Laurent Malone and Dennis Adams recorded in photographic form the random topographic panorama that unfurled as they took a walk in a straight line from a storefront in Manhattan to the initial threshold of Kennedy airport. A more unaesthetic and strangely repetitive urban fabric would be hard to imagine. It is a dystopia from which we are usually shielded by the kaleidoscopic blur of the taxi window. Looked at through [a] pedestrian optic this is an in-your-face urban fabric. It is oddly paranoid, rather ruthless, instrumental, and resentful landscape compounded of endless chain-link fences, graffiti, razor wire, rusted ironwork, fast food [outlets], signs of all kinds, housing projects that are barely distinguishable from penal institutions, the occasional fading ad or former cinema … and as one gets further out … closely packed parsimonious suburban homes with their white plastic siding. And everywhere, of course … the signs of hardscrabble economic survival about to get harder. … One cannot help asking oneself if these are truly the shades of the American dream for which we are ostensibly liberating the Middle East. Is there some fatal, inescapable paralysis that prevails, separating the increasingly smart, technological extravagance of our armaments from the widespread dumbness and meanness of our environment?

(Frampton 2003: 3)

2. WHAT DO THESE THREE QUOTATIONS HAVE IN COMMON? WHAT DO THEY SUGGEST IN RELATION TO THE ETHICS OF DESIGN?

Each of these three quotations—which touch respectively on the design of products, on the roles of image culture and the graphic designer, and on the forces that shape contemporary urban environments—have some things in common. Each

- attacks, in different ways, the venality, triviality, and paralysis of the imagination that market brings to design
- bemoans the loss of a public sphere outside of the market
- condemns the way that market forces tend to eclipse or obliterate the human

  — by turning the human being into nothing other than a consumer and the designer as the irresponsible servant of those who wish to promote ever more unbridled consumption (Papanek)
  — by inducing into a world that is daily being *made* more unsustainable an additional "dumbness and meanness" into the built and made environments within which we try to exist (this is Frampton's point when he looks at the degraded humanscapes of Brooklyn and Queens in New York)
  — by reducing the conditions of our political and public life (at extreme, as van Toorn insists, helping to destroy the conditions that make democratic society possible)

In relation to design, each

- refuses the "false truth" of design as a practice that is only of occasion for the market
- opposes the denial of the other and of persons and their interests implicit in so much

contemporary making, whether that of the world as a whole or within the specialist practices of design

- sees current modes of designing or making the world as a betrayal of design's potential
- feels that design has become blind to its own possibility and therefore has lost the sense of its critical and affirmative capabilities

Overall, all three, implicitly or explicitly

- consider design's role as serving the wider (longer-term) interests of subjects rather than the narrow (and necessarily short-term) interest of private profit
- want to create an ethics and a politics of design sufficiently powerful to contest *both* the overall reduction of the human by the market and design's self-eclipsing as a critical agency
- understand design as an agency capable of helping us shape, in humane and sustainable directions, our relations with the artificial and natural worlds

3. IS WHAT IS NEEDED THEREFORE AN ETHICS?

The first answer is "Yes." We need to recover what the veteran designer Gui Bonsiepe has called the "virtues" of design (Bonsiepe, 1997). But, the answer must be conditioned with caution, for this cannot be ethics as we used to think of it, as a "weak practice," something external to design; a moral overlay that is "applied" to professional practice but which does not enter the act of designing. Neither is the ethics we need simply something that is called up to salve a conscience.

The ethics that Papanek, van Torn and Frampton are all implicitly calling for is

- not a "bandage"
- not an ethical statement of intent that has no force for practice (as the International Council

of Societies for Industrial Design and other design organizations are fond of creating)

- not an excuse for inaction
- not a covert plea for maintaining the status quo, particularly the status quo of unequal, venal, and destructive economic forces. (On the problem of weak ethics see Badiou 2001 passim)

On the contrary, the ethics we need

- is against the capitulation of human interests to those of the market
- is emphatically opposed to the destructiveness of what is and to the catastrophe-inducing economic rapacity that global capitalism is now inducing
- sees itself as interruption of the processes of economic "errancy" (Badiou, 2005, 145) and "de-futuring" (Fry 1999) and therefore as a way of helping contend with the consequences of negative globalization
- refuses resignation in the face of the given and refuses to acquiesce to the current domination of modes of reactive, negative, and destructive actions (Badiou 2001: 30)

Affirmatively, whether couched as responsibility (Papanek), as the ability of the designer to address the public as citizens and not consumers (van Toorn), or as the infusing of "humane intelligence" into the made environment (Frampton) *this* ethics would

- counter the nihilism of our cultural and social inability to designate the dimensions of a human good beyond that of the market—and instead insist that the many and varied dimensions of the good can be articulated substantively and made evident
- have the confidence to reassert—over against the market—the absolute primacy of the interests of human beings in a humane future

- posit the possibility of truly human—humane, sustainable—ways of making and remaking the world

4. BUT WHAT, SPECIFICALLY, CAN DESIGN—CONSIDERED AS ETHICS—ADDRESS?

If we bracket the narrow professional concerns of design and rather begin to look structurally at design in this expanded field of relations—which is what positing the possibility of sustainable ways of making and remaking the world involves—we can understand that essentially design relates to four moments: those of persons, relations, situations, and contexts. The ethics of design concerns how we address these.

The First Is Persons

Design begins and ends with its relation to persons: the ethical core of design lies in the relation of reciprocity established in any act of human making. A perception about the frailty, resilience, and dependence upon things of persons is projected into an artifact that can reciprocally answer these needs (as the pain of standing is relieved by constructing a chair). Design—in no matter what form—is nothing more (or less) than the self-conscious elaboration and exploration of this fundamental relationship. The problem with this exploration is that, turned into a quasi-autonomous activity (or worse, into a profession), design forgets its ontological roots. The work of design ethics is to bring back design to these origins—and to think about the consequences of so doing. (On the relation of persons and making see Scarry, 1985, chapter 5; Dilnot 2005, especially 87–104).

The Second Is Relations

Relations means here the infinitely multiple, complex, and variegated relations of human beings to the things they make—*including, of course, themselves and, today, the world as a whole* (for today

that too is a made thing). Design is, of course, in its essence, *about* relations. What design *designs* are the relations between things and persons and things and nature. Nonethical design reduces these to commodity relations (reduces all that a thing can be for us to the imaginary of the act of its purchase) or to a utilitarian operative relations (the kind that Adorno criticized when he lamented that

> technology is making gestures precise and brutal and with them men. It expels from movements all hesitation, deliberation, civility. … Not least to blame for the withering of experience is the fact that things, under the law of pure functionality, assume a form that limits contact with them to mere operation, and tolerates no surplus … which … is not consumed in the moment of action.
>
> (Adorno 1974: 40).

By contrast, ethically informed design (in the sense meant here) *contests* both reductions. It reverses the "loveless disregard for things that eventually turns against persons" (Adorno 1974: 39) and insists that if indeed evil is the reduction of things—including the reduction in the complexity and density of relations that a thing or a person is permitted to enjoy—then the good is the enhancement of relations. Ethics, we might say, works to *proliferate* relations.

The Third Is Situations

In the best and simplest definition of design we have (that by Herbert Simon in *The Sciences of the Artificial*), design is the process of planning and devising how we transform "existing into preferred" situations (Simon 1996: 111). Specifically, design addresses the infinite potential in situations. *Infinite* means here two things. It means, first, that the potential network of relations that a situation actually or potentially sustains always exceeds the state in which we encounter any situation (were this not the case no transformation could ever happen). Situations then are inherently open, inherently full of possibility. Second, *infinite* means the ability *of all situations* to be transformed, for the better, in our interests. Design is the process, then, of seizing and realizing the potential of situations (a) to be transformed; (b) to be so on behalf of or in the interests of or for the project of, *persons.* (On the ethics of situations see for example Badiou 2005 and Bauman and Keith 2001: 13).

To put this another way, the difference between ethical design and design that eschews ethics is that the former insists that what matters in situations is not their market value, not the capacity to be exploited and reduced for profit, but the human implications of the situation: its capacity to hold promise for how we can better—*which today means more sustainably*—live our lives.

The fourth address is to the *context(s)* we inhabit. We will consider this in the next section.

5. IS THE ARTIFICIAL THE REAL SUBJECT MATTER OF DESIGN?

In truth, the contexts that design potentially addresses are multiple. Persons, relations, and situations are all contexts. It is easy to add to this the physical contexts of the environments within which we exist. But is the deepest context of design the artificial?

The Artificial

Design is bound to artifice. It exists only because we make things and because in making things we sunder them from us—and therefore require design to ameliorate this sundering. On the other hand, and particularly today, the artificial is the context for our lives. Industrialization induced the major break from modes of existence in which it was still possible to posit nature (and gods) as the horizons of our existence. Today, at least as far as our finite lives are concerned, these horizons have vanished. The years 1945 (Hiroshima) and then again 2005 (global warming) mark the points at which human society entered a watershed in which the artificial became the horizon and medium of

our existence. Since then we have experienced a break not only with the past but with the continuity of the future. The destructive potentials first of unleashed technology (the A-bomb and then the H-bomb) and then of unlimited and rapacious economic growth (global warming) has instituted a break with the future such that today the future is no longer assured to us. This changes the work our culture has to do. Our work today is to create the conditions for a (humane) future to come about and to prefigure the possibility of a humane and mature attitude toward the artificial (and hence toward nature). But to do this we must know what the artificial can be, and this we do not know. Design is a way—in many arenas the only way—of exploring the artificial in terms of exploring what are its possibilities *for us.* (See Dilnot 2005: 15–35; 41–53.)

The Ethics of Discovery

As is made clear below, this is not without ethical or social importance. Milan Kundera makes the point that the ethics of the novel lives on the discovery of hitherto unforeseen possibilities for human existence (Kundera 1988). The same point applies to design: design is the discovery of what the artificial can be for us. Since the artificial is also today the frame of our possibilities as human beings, to discover what the artificial can be *for us* is to discover what our possibility can be, and hence (here its third dimension), it is also a discovery of what possibility can be. This too is ethically significant since for us, possibility has been reduced, very largely, either to the economic extrapolation of what is (more) or to what, technologically, can be made into a product. It is germane to the crises we face that we no longer think about possibility in general, nor do we by any means fully understand what artifice and the artificial can mean for us (meaning here: mean for us—for our lives—other than as the production of things for consumption and profit). By contrast, design is a deliberation about the possible conducted not only in thought (though its speculative, conceptual dimension should not be ignored), but through emblematic constructions in the form of propositions—prototypes—that have the typographical form "this!?"—meaning that they are at once assertions and questions, both real and prefigurative (real and fictive) in the same moment.

What designed products emblematically explore are the possibilities of how we can live (well, badly) with the artificial, which is our product. Design is a teaching (which means also a learning) concerning how we can contend with what we have made.

6. WHAT IS THE RELATION BETWEEN THE ETHICS OF DESIGN AND ACTING ETHICALLY IN THE WORLD IN GENERAL?

We can answer this question three ways:

1. Traditionally, ethics concerns the assessment of well-being (in Greek, the search for the "good" way of being). Today, we understand that the search for well-being takes us *through* making. But this means that ethics today has to be not (only) a series of prescriptions for how we might behave but also—or even primarily—a mode of transitively and substantively acting in the world. Ethics in general is therefore a process of *exploring* the ways that we can live well with making. This is not different from the work of design.

2. One problem we now face in the world is that as the horizon and medium of the world becomes, increasingly, artificial—as, in effect, we displace nature and re-create our world over as artificial—so we have to think and understand what it means to live, well, in an artificial world. This, as we know, we are failing (dramatically) to do. Not only do we need a mode of acting in relation to the artificial that can allow us to develop more sensitive and attuned relations between persons and things and between the

artificial and the natural as a whole, but we need to *learn* what it might be to act well in a world defined by the artificial. Design can be conceived of as par excellence an activity of learning how we can be (well) with the artificial.

3. Although conventionally we separate designing from acting in the world in general, this is a product of a historical division of labor induced by the Industrial Revolution, whose relevance may now be passing. That this might be so—and that therefore the difference between design action and acting in the world might be so much less than we have thought is suggested by work of the late English philosopher Gillian Rose. In her last book, *Mourning Becomes the Law* (Rose 1996), it is possible to discern the plan for a mode of acting that is simultaneously ethical in the work it can achieve and wholly congruent with design. In Rose's formulation, what she called "activity-beyond-activity" has as its characteristics that it privileges

- learning: for learning "mediates the social and the political: it works precisely by making mistakes, by taking the risk of action, and then by reflecting on its unintended consequences, and then taking the risk, yet again, of further action" (Rose 1996: 38)
- risk, or action without guarantee: "for politics does not happen when you act on behalf of your own damaged good but when you act, without guarantee, for the good of all—this is to take the risk of the universal interest" (Rose 1996: 62)
- creative action as negotiation: for acknowledgment of the "creative involvement of action in the configurations of power and law" and of "the risk of action, arising out of negotiation with the law" (Rose 1996: 12, 36, 77) is a precondition to being able

to act in relation to these configurations, as against merely evading the ambiguities and anxieties that they give rise to

- positing: which refers, in Rose's language, to the "temporarily constitutive positings" (Rose 1996: 12–13) of actors, which "form and reform both selves"; this "constant risk of positing and failing and positing again I shall call "activity beyond activity"' (Dilnot 2005: 78)

Note that these characteristics of action are not only highly congruent with design; *they are a way of describing design.*

7. HOW DO THE SINGULAR ETHICS OF DESIGN CONNECT TO CRUCIAL QUESTIONS IN CONTEMPORARY ETHICS AS A WHOLE?

Learning; risk, or action without guarantee; creative action as negotiation with power and law, and an understanding of action as iterative positing are all, and particularly in their combination, potentially modes of acting in the world in a design-congruent way that have resonance beyond the usual limits of what we think of as (nontransitive) ethical action. For example, against the failure of the (traditional) ethical imagination in relation to the "fast expanding realm of our ethical responsibilities" (Bauman 2006: 99) and in the absence of (other) modes of acting in the world that can put "what-is" and its de-futuring consequences at a distance (that can measure it and, in gauging it and its consequences for lives, reassert the primacy of the latter over the "errancy" of the former), then transitive and substantive imagination of design conjoined with Rose's "activity-beyond-activity" has something powerful to offer in terms of ethics as a whole.

In particular, an ethics that could conjoin (as an ethics informed by design could) imagination, transitive action, the perception of the possibility inhering in situations, and the capacitive to be prefigurative (to give only a random list of what

would be within the ethics of design as sketched earlier) would have at least a chance of addressing, for example,

- the fear and trepidation, not to say stasis, that we feel vis-à-vis the future—since to break the grip of the latter we need prefigurative possibility as a core attribute
- the unsustainability of what is—since it is only as a praxis that combines ethical and behavioral injunctions with material inscriptions and enactments that sustainment can even begin to be realized as a project
- the radical incompatibility between the destructive potential of unleashed technological and economic forces and the weakness of ethical injunctions or social abilities to productively direct or orient technological and economic potential—since it is only when the latter is internalized in praxis is there the possibility of dealing with this threat

If this is the case, then it becomes possible to see design as one element in a militant material practice, executed on behalf of subjects and on behalf of the project of the sustainable and the humane.

8. HOW IS THE ETHICAL AXIOM MANIFEST IN DESIGN?

We will neglect here the interesting question of the ethics latent in the processes of design and the capabilities that it patterns and subtends. Answering these questions would confirm further a conclusion that should be already apparent—that ethics is internal to design, properly understood.

But if ethics is internal to design, there is also an ethics of drawing out and making manifest this potential. The modes of so doing are infinite, for no prescription can be given in advance as to what might constitute an ethical drawing out of these possibilities. Nonetheless, three strategies in particular stand out—the exercise of radical compassion, the address to dignity, and the reconception of the "achievement of the ordinary."

Radical Compassion

At the core of design is an ontological and anthropological act—making as the making of self—which is also a meditation on and a realization of being. The obliteration of this origin is what marks most nonethical design and is the cause of the attacks that Papanek, van Toorn, and Frampton were each impelled to make. Conversely, all ethics begins with compassion. It is inconceivable to imagine an ethics (as against a morality) that does not begin from a solidarity toward living beings, which is founded upon something other than their formal rights as subjects, and which is grounded in substantive apperception of the suffering and possibility of others.

This is by no means only (only!) a moral injunction. We should equally see it as a historical project—for it is, after all, the loss of global compassion, or more precisely, the inability to make compassion matter and therefore keep it in play as more than a weak, transitory, and essentially personal matter (we could say: the inability to make compassion political)—that marks the last century and that already threatens this one. In this context, compassion and solidarity are political as well as ethical moments, and this should not be forgotten, particularly by those for whom compassion seems a somewhat less than sufficiently engaging political concept.

The element of compassion translates, in the first instance in design, in the language of one of the best accounts we have so far concerning this—the final chapter of Elaine Scarry's *The Body in Pain* (Scarry 1985)—to a perception concerning the pain of others and the ability of the designer to relieve that pain, not merely through expressions of sympathy but though the translation of that understanding into a self-standing artifact that is operative in relation to that pain. The ethical moment of this designing–action is captured most economically in the formulation Scarry

offers when she notes that although the resulting artifact cannot itself "be sentiently aware of pain, it is ... [in] itself the objectification of that awareness; itself incapable of the act of perceiving, its design, its structure, is the structure of a perception" (Scarry 1985: 289). What Scarry's observation immediately conveys is the sense that what the designer offers, ethically, is two-fold: that is, a quantum of (empathic and imaginative) perception concerning a situation, together with (and this is where professional expertise comes in) the capacity to translate that perception into an objective or standing form that is capable, simultaneously, of understanding, recognizing, meeting, and extending needs. All three are significant. None of the three are merely technical; none can be dispensed with, and in none can the question of ethics as we are posing it here be bracketed.

The Reconception of the "Achievement of the Ordinary"

If "radical compassion" equates, roughly, to the address to the subject, the reconception of the "achievement of the ordinary" equates to the manner in which we bring back under thought—under the aegis of a human project—the relations, situations, and contexts that constitute everyday life. This can easily be seen from a traditional point of view (conservative or radical it scarcely matters) as a descent into banality. Nietzsche might make us think differently about this, as might also a poet like Wallace Stevens. For Stevens, the task of the poet is the saying of the plainest things, to get "straight to the transfixing object" (Stevens 1955: 471). In turn, for Nietzsche, it is the plainest things that deliver us from the forgetting of being—or in Vattimo's paraphrase: "when the origin has revealed its insignificance ... then we become open to the meaning and riches of proximity. ... [In those moments,] the nearest reality, that which is around us and inside of us, little by little starts to display color and beauty and enigma and wealth of meaning—things which earlier men never dreamed of" (Vattimo 1988: 177, 169).

Perhaps this suggests that what Stevens elsewhere calls the "vulgate" of experience, or what Nietzsche calls the realm of the "nearest things" are the spaces in which design operates at once at its most subversive, and at its most ethical. The trope of modesty folded with those of the "plainest things" and the "nearest things" gives a double ethic: to deal at once, *as tenderly as possible,* with the proximity of things and life (my example would be the adult Shaker rocking cradle found in the infirmary in Hancock Shaker Village, used to ease with gentleness the last hours of aged Shakers) and, on the other side, to understand design as the activity in which one pursues a practice that can help deliver us, in Simon Critchley's words, from the "actual ... to the *eventual everyday*" (Critchley 1997: 118).

The first of these moments fulfills the requirement of responsivity identified by both Bahktin and Levinas (if differently) as the core of our ethical "answerability" to the world and to the other. To be *practically disposed* toward responsivity may in fact be the most fundamental mark of the ethical. But what is interesting about design is that the responsivity called for here is *double:* The subject is *also a situated possibility.* The situation is the everyday. Design lives in the impurity and even banality of the everyday: Its ethical work in this respect is the enhancement of the density of discriminated affirmative relations that a situation or an object is capable of delivering on behalf of the subject, seen, of course, not as a consumer, but as a project (the project of "becoming (finally) human").

The Address to Dignity

Finally, no adequate ethics is possible that does not address and today defend—to the point of extremity—the dignity of the subject. We are realizing today that only the defense of dignity saves the subject as a political subject and therefore preserves the possibility of our having some defense against the possibility that we may be dismissed even from the fragile position of the consumer and thus find ourselves literally in the wasteland of the superfluous—those declared outside the realm of the social. (On the day that I write this in May 2008, there are reports of attacks on refugees in South Africa; meanwhile, in Italy, the new government begins moves to expel the Romany population—whom, shades of 1933, it is treating as the scapegoats for the state of the Italian economy). In this respect there can be no compromise: the axiom or the criteria of dignity toward the subject or subjects to whom work is addressed is the beginning of the act.

If for design, the defense of dignity begins with the degree of recognition accorded the subject to whom work is addressed, design has a particular role, as is widely recognized, in terms of the public sphere. Gui Bonsiepe, in the paper referred to earlier, makes the case most elegantly:

> As the third design virtue in the future, I would like to see maintained the concern for the public domain, and this all the more so when registering the almost delirious onslaught on everything public that seems to be a generalized credo of the predominant economic paradigm. One does well to recall that the socially devastating effects of unrestricted private interests have to be counter-balanced by public interests in any society that claims to be called democratic and that deserves that label.
>
> (Bonsiepe 1997: 107)

This is a wonderful statement, which economically nails the case—the ethical, but also, in the broad sense, the political case—for the public domain.

It seems to me essential, politically speaking, but also on behalf of ourselves as subjects, that the public domain be revalued, and in more than honorific ways. This is not just a matter, though in my view this is not insignificant, of helping to create the "public sphere" (much maligned though that concept has been in the last decades). It is also an issue of creating the kinds of spaces and domains, mental as much as physical (though the latter seem to me in large part the necessary initiators of the former) in which subjects can again find themselves as "citizens"—and this term seems necessary to revive in the sense that the term "subject" has today almost entirely lost all connotations of citizenship.

So denuded, in fact, is this latter concept that it becomes almost possible to forget that there is a complex realm of subjective life that is not delimited by work, the immediate demands of family, or consumption. This forgetting is not merely in the mind. In the last half-century it has begun to be reflected in the "habitus" we inhabit, literally as well as ideologically. When Bonsiepe talks about "the almost delirious onslaught on everything public that seems to be a generalized credo of the predominant economic paradigm," one aspect he is surely referring to is the erosion of the urban to a condition in which, particularly in the United States, but also in Europe (as well as globally across nearly all pockets of the "developed" economy), the urban is reduced to nothing but a finely calibrated machine or system for consumption. Today, generalized distributed and privatized settlement is linked not to the city as the locus of the public realm beyond the life of the family, but only to sites of consumption. In effect, the latter has consumed the former. The significant results of this process are not only such developments as the effective loss of the small town (with its, however small, sense of urban complexity and density introduced into rural areas; the necessary counterpoint to what was historically relative rural isolation), but, much more seriously, the wider flattening and closure of spaces and realms of experience, such that nothing else is now able to obtain except a spiraling interaction between family/home, consumption, and entertainment. In these spaces and environments, what is lost is everything that does not pertain to consumption in the moment.

9. WHAT EXAMPLES OF ETHICAL APPROACHES TO DESIGN MIGHT BE OFFERED?

Space does not permit elucidating examples. But in any case, they could be legion. For even in its

most repressed moments, the negation of the ethical is rarely wholly complete—which is why, with much complacency, the design professions assure themselves that they are indeed, at heart, ethical. Given that we do not have the space to discuss individual cases, it might be better to list the virtues (in the old-fashioned sense) on which a radical ethics (one that takes the measure of a life and a practice) can be grounded. One of these is renunciation, in the sense of the ability to renounce what is false, for example, the architect Luis Barragan, in Mexico, in 1940, renouncing speculative modern architecture on the grounds that the activity corroded the conditions necessary for dwelling. The ability to take that critique and, rather than capitulate to what is, or retreat to cynicism or into the profession, to turn that critique into critical affirmation, is what makes ethical courage. Similarly, I think of the courage to originate: to place a paradigm at a distance and to draw on previously unthought configurative possibilities—and, in the case of Henry Beck and the London Underground Diagram, to create one of the exemplary *gifts* of twentieth-century design (the gift itself being one of the figures of the ethical). One wishes therefore to foreground *courage,* but also the ability that Richard Ellman, James Joyce's great biographer, discerned in *Ulysses,* namely the capacity—*without illusion*—to be able to disengage what is affirmable in life and to affirm that (Ellman 1972: 185).

10. WHAT, IN THE END, IS RESPONSIBILITY?

Since the essay opened with Papenek's attack on the irresponsibility of designers, it is right and proper to finish on the question of responsibility. To do so I will conclude with the paragraph with which I ended my extended Archeworks lecture on ethics (Dilnot 2005: 147–48):

The demand for the ethical is, at best, a demand for a way of being responsible. But even more emphatically, the demand for the ethical is a search for *lessons* in how to be responsible.

This sense is captured, if incompletely, by Peter Sloterdijk in the conclusion to his essay on Nietzsche. He says this:

> One's misery consists not so much of one's sufferings as in the inability to be responsible for them—one's inability to *want* to be responsible for them. The will to accept one's own responsibility—which is, as it were, the psychonautical variant of *amor fati*—indicates neither narcissistic hubris nor fatalistic masochism, but rather the courage and the composure to accept one's life in all its reality and potentiality. He who wants to be responsible for himself stops searching for guilty parties: he ceases to live theoretically and to constitute himself on missing origins and supposed causes. Through the drama, he himself becomes the hero of knowledge.
>
> (Sloterdijk 1989: 90)

For all its peculiarity, there is something in Sloterdijk's formulation that catches precisely what is required here. His formulation speaks to the precariousness of the enterprise of thinking and acting responsibly—the same precariousness-with-courage that was evident between-the-lines of Gillian Rose's "activity beyond activity," and that is present, to some degree, in each act of designing that takes the ethical axiom seriously and thinks and acts out its consequences. The ethical in this sense is a risk-taking activity, and the best conclusion to this essay is therefore to repeat the formulation that we gave earlier on this, namely, that the ethical "does not happen when you act on behalf of your own damaged good, but when," as Gillian Rose put it, "you act, without guarantees, for the good of all—this is to take the risk of the universal interest" (Rose 1996: 62).

SECTION 3: THEORIZING DESIGN AND VISUALITY

3.3: Politics

INTRODUCTION

Many scholars and designers have identified the relationship between design practices and politics, exploring everything from the propagandistic power of graphics to the democratic possibilities of the Internet. This subsection continues this dialog by including six readings that challenge us to look at design as a response to social and economic situations produced by politics. Rather than only seeing design as a reaction to politics, several of these excerpts also hint at design's power to create change within the political sphere. These readings can be divided into three groups: Karl Marx, Pierre Bourdeiu, and Naomi Klein each assess our capitalist condition and explain how design reinforces our political economy. Dick Hebdige and John Stones reveal that design can appear to subvert the political order, and they raise questions about the efficacy of design. Finally, Gui Bonsiepe discusses how design can be used to create a governing structure based on humanistic principles and democracy.

Karl Marx helps us understand the politicized dimension of design within the framework of his critique of capitalist culture, in which owners (the bourgeoisie) exploit workers (the proletariat). The excerpt included here, titled by Marx "The Fetishism of Commodities and the Secret Thereof," appears in his *Capital: A Critique of Political Economy*. In this passage, Marx discusses the strange power with which society imbues material commodities as markers of class and social stratification, which further separate the worker (laborers who produce the commodity) from consumers (purchasers who are often the owners of the means of production). Marx explains these commodities as fetishized objects. He notes that we "have absolutely no connection with their physical properties and with the material relations arising therefrom." Marx explores how culture "changes the forms of the material furnished by nature" into something mysterious, the fetishized (designed) commodity "endowed" with special powers and abstracted value. Marx's discussion about the material culture produced in an industrialized economy has led many scholars in design studies to focus on consumption and socio-economic class.

Pierre Bourdieu took Marx's ideas about the political power of capital further, to explain how society creates taste by endowing things and ideas with cultural importance. Like Marx, Bourdieu understood the idea of social stratification. Bourdieu observes that taste is "the practical affirmation of inevitable difference." He further explains, "In matters of taste, more than anywhere else, all determination is negation; all tastes are perhaps first and foremost distastes, disgust provoked by horror or visceral intolerance ('sick making') of the tastes of others." Therefore, when it comes to objects we associate with design, such as "cosmetics, clothing or home decoration," these "are opportunities to experience or assert one's position in social space, as a rank to be upheld or a distance to be kept." The things we bring with us through life, those material goods that fill our existence with meaning, are important markers of "distinction" that help us assert our place within a larger political economy.

Naomi Klein brings the Marxist critique of politics and design into a contemporary context. Klein writes that corporations are now only invested in the brand and its power to signify "deep inner meanings." She explains that production has been degraded in our world, where nothing is as important as the brand. In an excerpt from her book, *No Logo,* we learn how workers and factories are being "treated like detritus—the stuff left behind." Things are made cheaply with no commitment to quality. Indeed, as discussed by D. J. Huppatz in the Design Communications subsection (2.3), image is everything in our current world, where corporations establish the importance of style to create the distinctions and values that further capitalist interests.

Within capitalism there are subcultures that can, according to Dick Hebdige, resist the political systems that Marx and Bourdieu describe as rigid. Hebdige, in his book, *Subculture, the Meaning of Style,* points to specific subcultures, such as "mods and rockers, the skinheads and the punks—who are alternately dismissed, denounced and canonized; treated at different times as threats to public order and as harmless buffoons." These groups challenge the political order by consuming and creating designed objects that will help develop what Hebdige describes as a style that defines and mediates codes of meaning within a particular subculture. Hebdige raises the possibility of subverting the political system through style found in subcultures, yet he understands that this attempt at questioning the norm merely provides a small degree of independence from the dominant culture.

In a short piece from *Design Week,* John Stone looks at the difficulty of subverting the norm in his article, "Incendiary Devices." He asks whether the contemporary designer's attempts to create political commentary is effective, or nothing more than "headline-grabbing opportunism." He brings up the loaded example of Philippe Starck's gun lamp, designed in the form of a golden-colored Kalashnikov rifle. Many understood the lamp as subversive, a type of material manifestation of a commentary on war, but others in the design world simply claimed that Starck's use of weaponry to create form was an absurd joke that tried to be politically engaging but instead only managed to be frivolous, an illustration of "fashion and novelty."

Gui Bonsiepe agrees with Klein and Stones' contention that design has become "a media event," in which the intended message and hyperbole of the brand is now more important than the appearance and effectiveness of the actual design. Bonsiepe is encouraged, however, that there is a way to incite new design processes that will be tied to what he describes as a humanistic endeavor. "Design humanism is the exercise of design activities in order to interpret the needs of social groups, and to develop viable emancipative proposals in the form of material and semiotic artifacts." Bonsiepe asks us to think about ways in which design can shift "the enormous imbalance between the centers of power and the people submitted to these powers, because the imbalance is deeply undemocratic insofar as it negates participation." We may live in a world where brands, class, and socioeconomic disparities are a way of life, but Bonsiepe sees other possibilities that will potentially help shift the political power structure in new directions. He believes that this can be accomplished through new types of democratic design initiatives.

These essays offer the reader a way to connect design practice and products with the political sphere. While each author writes from a different perspective, their ideas can be categorized as a critique of capitalism, a discussion about the potentiality of subversive design, or a visionary quest for ending disenfranchisement through new types of design praxis. These six authors will incite discussions about the political quandaries that face the future of politics and the future of design.

27

THE FETISHISM OF COMMODITIES AND THE SECRET THEREOF

Karl Marx

A commodity appears, at first sight, a very trivial thing, and easily understood. Its analysis shows that it is, in reality, a very queer thing, abounding in metaphysical subtleties and theological niceties. So far as it is a value in use, there is nothing mysterious about it, whether we consider it from the point of view that by its properties it is capable of satisfying human wants, or from the point that those properties are the product of human labour. It is as clear as noon-day, that man, by his industry, changes the forms of the materials furnished by nature, in such a way as to make them useful to him. The form of wood, for instance, is altered, by making a table out of it. Yet, for all that the table continues to be that common, every-day thing, wood. But, so soon as it steps forth as a commodity, it is changed into something transcendent. It not only stands with

Image 11   Goyard. Palace trunk, 70cm, in black (with a personalization). (Courtesy of Goyard)

its feet on the ground, but, in relation to all other commodities, it stands on its head, and evolves out of its wooden brain grotesque ideas, far more wonderful than "table-turning" ever was.

The mystical character of commodities does not originate, therefore, in their use-value. Just as little does it proceed from the nature of the determining factors of value. For, in the first place, however varied the useful kinds of labour, or productive activities, may be, it is a physiological fact, that they are functions of the human organism, and that each such function, whatever may be its nature or form, is essentially the expenditure of human brain, nerves, muscles, &c. Secondly, with regard to that which forms the ground-work for the quantitative determination of value, namely, the duration of that expenditure, or the quantity of labour, it is quite clear that there is a palpable difference between its quantity and quality. In all states of society, the labour-time that it costs to produce the means of subsistence must necessarily be an object of interest to mankind, though not of equal interest in different stages of development. And lastly, from the moment that men in any way work for one another, their labour assumes a social form.

Whence, then, arises the enigmatical character of the product of labour, so soon as it assumes the form of commodities? Clearly from this form itself. The equality of all sorts of human labour is expressed objectively by their products all being equally values; the measure of the expenditure of labour-power by the duration of that expenditure, takes the form of the quantity of value of the products of labour; and finally, the mutual relations of the producers, within which the social character of their labour affirms itself, take the form of a social relation between the products.

A commodity is therefore a mysterious thing, simply because in it the social character of men's labour appears to them as an objective character stamped upon the product of that labour; because the relation of the producers to the sum total of their own labour is presented to them as a social relation, existing not between themselves, but

between the products of their labour. This is the reason why the products of labour become commodities, social things whose qualities are at the same time perceptible and imperceptible by the senses. In the same way the light from an object is perceived by us not as the subjective excitation of our optic nerve, but as the objective form of something outside the eye itself. But, in the act of seeing, there is at all events, an actual passage of light from one thing to another, from the external object to the eye. There is a physical relation between physical things. But it is different with commodities. There, the existence of the things *qua* commodities, and the value relation between the products of labour which stamps them as commodities, have absolutely no connection with their physical properties and with the material relations arising therefrom. There is a definite social relation between men, that assumes, in their eyes, the fantastic form of a relation between things. In order, therefore, to find an analogy, we must have recourse to the mist-enveloped regions of the religious world. In that world the productions of the human brain appear as independent beings endowed with life, and entering into relation both with one another and the human race. So it is in the world of commodities with the products of men's hands. This I call the Fetishism which attaches itself to the products of labour, so soon as they are produced as commodities, and which is therefore inseparable from the production of commodities.

This Fetishism of commodities has its origin, as the foregoing analysis has already shown, in the peculiar social character of the labour that produces them.

As a general rule, articles of utility become commodities, only because they are products of the labour of private individuals or groups of individuals who carry on their work independently of each other. The sum total of the labour of these private individuals forms the aggregate labour of society. Since the producers do not come into social contact with each other until they exchange their products, the specific social character of each producer's labour does not show itself except in the act of exchange. In other words, the labour of the individual asserts itself as a part of the labour of society, only by means of the relations which the act of exchange established directly between the products, and indirectly, through them, between the producers. To the latter, therefore, the relations connecting the labour of one individual with that of the rest appear, not as direct social relations between individuals at work, but as what they really are, material relations between persons and social relations between things. It is only by being exchanged that the products of labour acquire, as values, one uniform social status, distinct from their varied forms of existence as objects of utility. This division of a product into a useful thing and a value becomes practically important, only when exchange has acquired such an extension that useful articles are produced for the purpose of being exchanged, and their character as values has therefore to be taken into account, beforehand, during production. From this moment the labour of the individual producer acquires socially a two-fold character. On the one hand, it must, as a definite useful kind of labour, satisfy a definite social want, and thus hold its place as part and parcel of the collective labour of all, as a branch of a social division of labour that has sprung up spontaneously. On the other hand, it can satisfy the manifold wants of the individual producer himself, only in so far as the mutual exchangeability of all kinds of useful private labour is an established social fact, and therefore the private useful labour of each producer ranks on an equality with that of all others. The equalization of the most different kinds of labour can be the result only of an abstraction from their inequalities, or of reducing them to their common denominator, viz., expenditure of human labour power or human labour in the abstract. The two-fold social character of the labour of the individual appears to him, when reflected in his brain, only under those forms which are impressed upon that labour in everyday practice by the exchange of products. In this way, the character that his own labour

possesses of being socially useful takes the form of the condition, that the product must be not only useful, but useful for others, and the social character that his particular labour has of being the equal of all other particular kinds of labour, takes the form that all the physically different articles that are the products of labour, have one common quality, viz, that of having value.

Hence, when we bring the products of our labour into relation with each other as values, it is not because we see in these articles the material receptacles of homogeneous human labour. Quite the contrary; whenever, by an exchange, we equate as values our different products, by that very act, we also equate, as human labour, the different kinds of labour expended upon them. We are not aware of this, nevertheless we do it. Value, therefore, does not stalk about with a label describing what it is. It is value, rather, that converts every product into a social hieroglyphic. Later on, we try to decipher the hieroglyphic, to get behind the secret of our own social products; for to stamp an object of utility as a value, is just as much a social product as language. The recent scientific discovery, that the products of labour, so far as they are values, are but material expressions of the human labour spent in their production, marks, indeed, an epoch in the history of the development of the human race, but, by no means, dissipates the mist through which the social character of labour appears to us to be an objective character of the products themselves. The fact, that in the particular form of production with which we are dealing, viz., the production of commodities, the specific social character of private labour carried on independently, consists in the equality of every kind of that labour, by virtue of its being human labour, which character, therefore, assumes in the product the form of value—this fact appears to the producers, notwithstanding the discovery above referred to, to be just as real and final, as the fact, that, after the discovery by science of the component gases of air, the atmosphere itself remained unaltered.

What, first of all, practically concerns producers when they make an exchange, is the question, how much of some other product they get for their own? in what proportions the products are exchangeable? When these proportions have, by custom, attained a certain stability, they appear to result from the nature of the products, so that, for instance, one ton of iron and two ounces of gold appear as naturally to be of equal value as a pound of gold and a pound of iron in spite of their different physical and chemical qualities appear to be of equal weight. The character of having value, when once impressed upon products, obtains fixity only by reason of their acting and re-acting upon each other as quantities of value. These quantities vary continually, independently of the will, foresight and action of the producers. To them, their own social action takes the form of the action of objects, which rule the producers instead of being ruled by them. It requires a fully developed production of commodities before, from accumulated experience alone, the scientific conviction springs up, that all the different kinds of private labour, which are carried on independently of each other, and yet as spontaneously developed branches of the social division of labour, are continually being reduced to the quantitive proportions in which society requires them. And why? Because, in the midst of all the accidental and ever fluctuating exchange-relations between the products, the labour-time socially necessary for their production forcibly asserts itself like an over-riding law of nature. The law of gravity thus asserts itself when a house falls about our ears. The determination of the magnitude of value by labour-time is therefore a secret, hidden under the apparent fluctuations in the relative values of commodities. Its discovery, while removing all appearance of mere accidentality from the determination of the magnitude of the values of products, yet in no way alters the mode in which that determination takes place.

Man's reflections on the forms of social life, and consequently, also, his scientific analysis of those forms, take a course directly opposite to that of their actual historical development. He begins, post festum, with the results of the process of development ready to hand before him. The characters that stamp products as commodities, and whose establishment is a necessary preliminary to the circulation of commodities, have already acquired the stability of natural, self-understood forms of social life, before man seeks to decipher, not their historical character, for in his eyes they are immutable, but their meaning. Consequently it was the analysis of the prices of commodities that alone led to the determination of the magnitude of value, and it was the common expression of all commodities in money that alone led to the establishment of their characters as values. It is, however, just this ultimate money form of the world of commodities that actually conceals, instead of disclosing, the social character of private labour, and the social relations between the individual producers. When I state that coats or boots stand in a relation to linen, because it is the universal incarnation of abstract human labour, the absurdity of the statement is self-evident. Nevertheless, when the producers of coats and boots compare those articles with linen, or, what is the same thing with gold or silver, as the universal equivalent, they express the relation between their own private labour and the collective labour of society in the same absurd form.

The categories of bourgeois economy consist of such like forms. They are forms of thought expressing with social validity the conditions and relations of a definite, historically determined mode of production, viz., the production of commodities. The whole mystery of commodities, all the magic and necromancy that surrounds the products of labour as long as they take the form of commodities, vanishes therefore, so soon as we come to other forms of production.

NOTE

Extracted from K. Marx, *Capital: A Critique of Political Economy*, trans. S. Moore and E. Aueling (New York: The Modern Library, 1906), pp. 81–87.

28

THE AESTHETIC SENSE AS THE SENSE OF DISTINCTION

Pierre Bourdieu

Thus, the aesthetic disposition is one dimension of a distant, self-assured relation to the world and to others which presupposes objective assurance and distance. It is one manifestation of the system of dispositions produced by the social conditionings associated with a particular class of conditions of existence when they take the paradoxical form of the greatest freedom conceivable, at a given moment, with respect to the constraints of economic necessity. But it is also a distinctive expression of a privileged position in social space whose distinctive value is objectively established in its relationship to expressions generated from different conditions. Like every sort of taste, it unites and separates. Being the product of the conditionings associated with a particular class of conditions of existence, it unites all those who are the product of similar conditions while distinguishing them from all others. And it distinguishes in an essential way, since taste is the basis of all that one has—people and things—and all that one is for others, whereby one classifies oneself and is classified by others.

Tastes (i.e., manifested preferences) are the practical affirmation of an inevitable difference. It is no accident that, when they have to be justified, they are asserted purely negatively, by the refusal of other tastes.[1] In matters of taste, more than anywhere else, all determination is negation;[2] and tastes, are perhaps first and foremost distastes, disgust provoked by horror or visceral intolerance ('sick-making') of the tastes of others. 'De gustibus non est disputandum': not because 'tous les gouts sont dans la nature', but because

each taste feels itself to be natural—and so it almost is, being a habitus—which amounts to rejecting others as unnatural and therefore vicious. Aesthetic intolerance can be terribly violent. Aversion to different life-styles is perhaps one of the strongest barriers between the classes; class endogamy is evidence of this. The most intolerable thing for those who regard themselves as the possessors of legitimate culture is the sacrilegious reuniting of tastes which taste dictates shall be separated. This means that the games of artists and aesthetes and their struggles for the monopoly of artistic legitimacy are less innocent than they seem. At stake in every struggle over art there is also the imposition of an art of living, that is, the transmutation of an arbitrary way of living into the legitimate way of life which casts every other way of living into arbitrariness.[3] The artist's life-style is always a challenge thrown at the bourgeois life-style, which it seeks to condemn as unreal and even absurd, by a sort of practical demonstration of the emptiness of the values and powers it pursues. The neutralizing relation to the world which defines the aesthetic disposition potentially implies a subversion of the spirit of seriousness required by bourgeois investments. Like the visibly ethical judgments of those who lack the means to make art the basis of their art of living, to see the world and other people through literary reminiscences and pictorial references, the 'pure' and purely aesthetic judgments of the artist and the aesthete spring from the dispositions of an ethos;[4] but because of the legitimacy which they command so long as their relationship to the dispositions and interests of a group defined by strong cultural capital and weak economic capital remains unrecognized, they provide a sort of absolute reference point in the necessarily endless play of mutually self-relativizing tastes. By a paradoxical reversal, they thereby help to legitimate the bourgeois claim to 'natural distinction' as difference made absolute.

Objectively and subjectively aesthetic stances adopted in matters like cosmetics, clothing or home decoration are opportunities to experience or assert one's position in social space, as a rank to be upheld or a distance to be kept. It goes without saying that the social classes are not equally inclined and prepared to enter this game of refusal and counter-refusal; and that the strategies aimed at transforming the basic dispositions of a life-style into a system of aesthetic principles, objective differences into elective distinctions, passive options (constituted externally by the logic of the distinctive relationships) into conscious, elective choices are in fact reserved for members of the dominant class, indeed the very top bourgeoisie, and for artists, who as the inventors and professionals of the 'stylization of life' are alone able to make their art of living one of the fine arts. By contrast, the entry of the petite bourgeoisie into the game of distinction is marked, inter alia, by the anxiety of exposing oneself to classification by offering to the taste of others such infallible indices of personal taste as clothes or furniture, even a simple pair of armchairs, as in one of Nathalie Sarraute's novels. As for the working classes, perhaps their sole function in the system of aesthetic positions is to serve as a foil; a negative reference point, in relation to which all aesthetics define themselves, by successive negations.[5] Ignoring or ignorant of manner and style, the 'aesthetic' (in itself) of the working classes and culturally most deprived fractions of the middle classes defines as 'nice', 'pretty', 'lovely' (rather than 'beautiful') things that are already defined as such in the 'aesthetic' of calendars and postcards: a sunset, a little girl playing with a cat, a folk dance, an old master, a first communion, a children's procession. The striving towards distinction comes in with petit-bourgeois aestheticism, which delights in all the cheap substitutes for chic objects and practices—driftwood and painted pebbles, cane and raffia, 'art' handicrafts and art photography.

NOTES

Extracted from P. Bourdieu, *Distinction: A Social Critique of the Judgment of Taste,* trans. R. Nice (Cambridge: Harvard University Press, 1984), pp. 56–58. Reproduced by permission of Taylor & Francis Books UK and Harvard University Press.

1. Two examples, chosen from among hundreds, but paradigmatic, of explicit use of the scheme 'something other than': *'La Fiancée du pirate* is one of those very rare French films that are *really* satirical, *really* funny, because it does not resort to the carefully defused, prudently inoffensive comedy one finds in *la Grande Vadrouille* and *le Petit Baigneur ...* . In short, it is *something other than* the dreary hackwork of boulevard farce' (J. L. Bory, *Le Nouvel Observateur,* 8 December 1969; italics mine). 'Through distance, or at least, through difference, to endeavour to present a text on pictorial modernity *other than* the hackneyed banalities of a *certain style of art criticism. Between* verbose aphasia, the textual transcription of pictures, exclamations of recognition, *and* the works of specialized aesthetics, perhaps *marking* some of the ways in which conceptual, theoretical work gets to grips with contemporary plastic production' (G. Gassiot-Talabot et al., *Figurations* 1960–1973 [Paris, Union generale des editions, 1973], p. 7; italics mine).

2. This essential negativity, which is part of the very logic of the constitution of taste and its change, explains why, as Gombrich points out, 'the terminology of art history was so largely built on words denoting some principle of exclusion. Most movements in art erect some new taboo, some new negative principle,

such as the banishing from painting by the impressionists of all "anecdotal" elements. The positive slogans and shibboleths which we read in artists' or critics' manifestos past or present are usually much less well defined' (E. H. Gombrich, *Norm and Form: Studies in the Art of the Renaissance* [London, New York, Phaidon Press, 1966], p. 89).

3. This is seen clearly in the case of the theatre, which touches more directly and more overtly on the implicit or explicit principles of the art of living. Especially in the case of comedy, it presupposes common values or interests or, more precisely, a complicity and connivance based on immediate assent to the same self-evident propositions, those of the *doxa,* the totality of opinions accepted at the level of pre-reflexive belief. (This explains why the institutions supplying the products, and the products themselves, are more sharply differentiated in the theatre than in any other art.)

4. For an analysis of 'art for art's sake' as the expression of the artistic life-style, see P. Bourdieu, 'L'invention de la vie d'artiste,' *Actes,* 2 (1975), 67–93.

5. This is true despite the apparent exception in which some artists return to certain popular preferences, which had a totally different meaning in a cultural configuration dominated by choices which for them would be quite improbable or even impossible. These returns to the 'popular' style, which often pass for a return to the 'people', are determined not by any genuine relationship to the working classes, who are generally spurned—even in idealization, which is a form of refusal—but by the internal relations of the field of artistic production or the field of the dominant class. (This point has a general validity, and one would need to examine what the writings of intellectuals on the working classes owe to the specific interests of intellectuals in struggles in which what is at stake, if not the people, is the legitimacy conferred, in certain conditions, by appearing as the spokesman for popular interests.)

29

NO LOGO

Naomi Klein

Our strategic plan in North America is to focus intensely on brand management, marketing and product design as a means to meet the casual clothing wants and needs of consumers. Shifting a significant portion of our manufacturing from the U.S. and Canadian markets to contractors throughout the world will give the company greater flexibility to allocate resources and capital to its brands. These steps are crucial if we are to remain competitive.

—John Ermatinger, president of Levi Strauss Americas division, explains the company's decision to shut down twenty-two plants and lay off 13,000 North American workers between November 1997 and February 1999

Many brand-name multinationals, as we have seen, are in the process of transcending the need to identify with their earthbound products. They dream instead about their brands' deep inner meanings the way they capture the spirit of individuality, athleticism, wilderness or community. In this context of strut over stuff, marketing departments charged with the managing of brand identities have begun to see their work as something that occurs not in conjunction with factory production but in direct competition with it. "Products are made in the factory," says Walter Landor, president of the Landor branding agency, "but brands are made in the mind."[1] Peter Schweitzer, president of the advertising giant J. Walter Thompson, reiterates the same

thought: "The difference between products and brands is fundamental. A product is something that is made in a factory; a brand is something that is bought by a customer."[2] Savvy ad agencies have all moved away from the idea that they are flogging a product made by someone else, and have come to think of themselves instead as brand factories, hammering out what is of true value: the idea, the lifestyle, the attitude. Brand builders are the new primary producers in our so-called knowledge economy.

This novel idea has done more than bring us cutting-edge ad campaigns, ecclesiastic superstores and utopian corporate campuses. It is changing the very face of global employment. After establishing the "soul" of their corporations, the superbrand companies have gone on to rid themselves of their cumbersome bodies, and there is nothing that seems more cumbersome, more loathsomely corporeal, than the factories that produce their products. The reason for this shift is simple: building a superbrand is an extraordinarily costly project, needing constant managing, tending and replenishing. Most of all, superbrands need lots of space on which to stamp their logos. For a business to be cost-effective, however, there is a finite amount of money it can spend on all of its expenses—materials, manufacturing, overhead *and* branding—before retail prices on its products shoot up too high. After the multimillion-dollar sponsorships have been signed, and the cool hunters and marketing mavens have received their checks, there may not be all that much money left over. So it becomes, as always, a matter of priorities; but those priorities are changing. As Hector Liang, former chairman of United Biscuits, has explained: "Machines wear out. Cars rust. People die. But what lives on are the brands."[3]

According to this logic, corporations should not expend their finite resources on factories that will demand physical upkeep, on machines that will corrode or on employees who will certainly age and die. Instead, they should concentrate those resources in the virtual brick and mortar used to build their brands; that is, on sponsorships, packaging, expansion and advertising. They should also spend them on synergies: on buying up distribution and retail channels to get their brands to the people.

This slow but decisive shift in corporate priorities has left yesterday's non-virtual producers—the factory workers and craftspeople—in a precarious position. The lavish spending in the 1990s on marketing, mergers and brand extensions has been matched by a never-before-seen resistance to investing in production facilities and labor. Companies that were traditionally satisfied with a 100 percent markup between the cost of factory production and the retail price have been scouring the globe for factories that can make their products so inexpensively that the markup is closer to 400 percent.[4] And as a 1997 UN report notes, even in countries where wages were already low, labor costs are getting a shrinking slice of corporate budgets. "In four developing countries out of five, the share of wages in manufacturing value-added today is considerably below what it was in the 1970s and early 1980s."[5] The timing of these trends reflects not only branding's status as the perceived economic cure-all, but also a corresponding devaluation of the production process and of producers in general. Branding, in other words, has been hogging all the "value-added."

When the actual manufacturing process is so devalued, it stands to reason that the people doing the work of production are likely to be treated like detritus—the stuff left behind. The idea has a certain symmetry: ever since mass production

created the need for branding in the first place, its role has slowly been expanding in importance until, more than a century and a half after the Industrial Revolution, it occurred to these companies that maybe branding could replace production entirely. As tennis pro Andre Agassi said in a 1992 Canon camera commercial, "Image is everything."

Agassi may have been pitching for Canon at the time but he is first and foremost a member of Team Nike, the company that pioneered the business philosophy of no-limits spending on branding, coupled with a near-total divestment of the contract workers that make its shoes in tucked-away factories. As Phil Knight has said, "There is no value in making things any more. The value is added by careful research, by innovation and by marketing."[6] For Phil Knight, production is not the building block of his branded empire, but is instead a tedious, marginal chore.

Which is why many companies now bypass production completely. Instead of making the products themselves, in their own factories, they "source" them, much as corporations in the natural-resource industries source uranium, copper or logs. They close existing factories, shifting to contracted-out, mostly offshore, manufacturing. And as the old jobs fly offshore, something else is flying away with them: the old-fashioned idea that a manufacturer is responsible for its own workforce. Disney spokesman Ken Green gave an indication of the depth of this shift when he became publicly frustrated that his company was being taken to task for the desperate conditions in a Haitian factory that produces Disney clothes. "We don't employ anyone in Haiti," he said, referring to the fact that the factory is owned by a contractor. "With the newsprint you use, do you have any idea of the labour conditions involved to produce it?" Green demanded of Cathy Majtenyi of the *Catholic Register.*[7]

From El Paso to Beijing, San Francisco to Jakarta, Munich to Tijuana, the global brands are sloughing the responsibility of production onto their contractors; they just tell them to make the damn thing, and make it cheap, so there's lots of money left over for branding. Make it *really* cheap.

EXPORTING THE NIKE MODEL

Nike, which began as an import/export scheme of made-in-Japan running shoes and does not own any of its factories, has become a prototype for the product-free brand. Inspired by the swoosh's staggering success, many more traditionally run companies ("vertically integrated," as the phrase goes) are busy imitating Nike's model, not only copying the company's marketing approach, as we saw in "No Space," but also its on-the-cheap outsourced production structure. In the mid-nineties, for instance, the Vans running-shoe company pulled up stakes in the old-fashioned realm of manufacturing and converted to the Nike way. In a prospectus for an initial public stock offering, the company lays out how it "recently repositioned itself from a domestic manufacturer to a market-driven company" by sponsoring hundreds of athletes as well as high-profile extreme sporting events such as the Vans Warped Tour. The company's "expenditure of significant funds to create consumer demand" was financed by closing an existing factory in California and contracting production in South Korea to "third party manufacturers."[8]

Adidas followed a similar trajectory, turning over its operation in 1993 to Robert Louis-Dreyfus, formerly a chief executive at advertising giant Saatchi & Saatchi. Announcing that he wanted to capture the heart of the "global teenager," Louis-Dreyfus promptly shut down the company-owned factories in Germany, and moved to contracting-out in Asia.[9] Freed from the chains of production, the company had newfound time and money to create a Nike style brand image. "We closed down everything," Adidas spokesperson Peter Csanadi says proudly. "We only kept one small factory which is our global technology centre and makes about 1 percent of total output."[10]

Though they don't draw the headlines they once did, more factory closures are announced in North America and Europe each week—45,000

U.S. apparel workers lost their jobs in 1997 alone.[11] That sector's job-flight patterns have been equally dramatic around the globe. Though plant closures themselves have barely slowed down since the darkest days of the late-eighties/early-nineties recession, there has been a marked shift in the reason given for these "reorganizations." Mass layoffs were previously presented as an unfortunate necessity, tied to disappointing company performance. Today they are simply savvy shifts in corporate strategy, a "strategic redirection," to use the Vans term. More and more, these layoffs are announced in conjunction with pledges to increase revenue through advertising spending, with executives vowing to refocus on the needs of their brands, as opposed to the needs of their workers.

Consider the case of Sara Lee Corp., an old-style conglomerate that encompasses not only its frozen-food namesake but also such "unintegrated" brands as Hanes underwear, Wonderbra, Coach leather goods, Champion sports apparel, Kiwi shoe polish and Ball Park Franks. Despite the fact that Sara Lee enjoyed solid growth, healthy profits, good stock return and no debt, by the mid-nineties Wall Street had become disenchanted with the company and was undervaluing its stock. Its profits had risen 10 percent in the 1996–97 fiscal year, hitting $1 billion, but Wall Street, as we have seen, is guided by spiritual goals as well as economic ones.[12] And Sara Lee, driven by the corporeal stuff of real-world products, as opposed to the sleek ideas of brand identity, was simply out of economic fashion. "Lumpy-object purveyors," as Tom Peters might say.[13]

To correct the situation, in September 1997 the company announced a $1.6 billion restructuring plan to get out of the "stuff" business by purging its manufacturing base. Thirteen of its factories, beginning with yarn and textile plants, would be sold to contractors who would become Sara Lee's suppliers. The company would be able to dip into the money saved to double its ad spending. "It's passe for us to be as vertically integrated as we were," explained Sara Lee CEO John H. Bryan.[14]

Wall Street and the business press loved the new marketing-driven Sara Lee, rewarding the company with a 15 percent jump in stock price and flattering profiles of its bold and imaginative CEO. "Bryan's shift away from manufacturing to focus on brand marketing recognizes that the future belongs to companies—like Coca-Cola Co—that own little but sell much," enthused one article in *Business Week*.[15] Even more telling was the analogy chosen by Crain's *Chicago Business*: "Sara Lee's goal is to become more like Oregon-based Nike Inc., which out-sources its manufacturing and focuses primarily on product development and brand management."[16]

In November 1997, Levi Strauss announced a similarly motivated shake-up. Company revenue had dropped between 1996 and 1997, from $7.1 billion to $6.8 billion. But a 4 percent dip hardly seems to explain the company's decision to shut eleven plants. The closures resulted in 6,395 workers being laid off, one-third of its already downsized North American workforce. In this process, the company shut down three of its four factories in El Paso, Texas, a city where Levi's was the single largest private employer. Still unsatisfied with the results, the following year Levi's announced another round of closures in Europe and North America. Eleven more of its North American factories would be shut down and the total toll of laid-off workers rose to 16,310 in only two years.[17]

John Ermatinger, president of Levi's Americas division, had a familiar explanation. "Our strategic plan in North America is to focus intensely on brand management, marketing and product design as a means to meet the casual clothing wants and needs of consumers," he said.[18] Levi's chairman, Robert Haas, who on the same day received an award from the UN for making life better for his employees, told *The Wall Street Journal* that the closures reflected not just "overcapacity" but also "our own desire to refocus marketing, to inject more quality and distinctiveness into the brand."[19] In 1997, this quality and distinctiveness came in the form of a particularly funky international ad campaign rumored to have cost $90 million, Levi's most expensive campaign ever, and more

than the company spent advertising the brand in all of 1996.

"THIS IS NOT A JOB-FLIGHT STORY"

In explaining the plant closures as a decision to turn Levi's into "a marketing company," Robert Haas was careful to tell the press that the jobs that were eliminated were not "leaving," they were just sort of evaporating. "This is not a job-flight story," he said after the first round of layoffs. The statement is technically true. Seeing Levi's as a job-flight story would miss the more fundamental—and more damaging—shift that the closures represent. As far as the company is concerned, those 16,310 jobs are off the payrolls for good, replaced, according to Ermatinger, by "contractors throughout the world." Those contractors will perform the same tasks as the old Levi's-owned factories—but the workers inside will never be employed by Levi Strauss.

For some companies a plant closure is still a straightforward decision to move the same facility to a cheaper locale. But for others—particularly those with strong brand identities like Levi Strauss and Hanes—layoffs are only the most visible manifestation of a much more fundamental shift: one that is less about where to produce than how. Unlike factories that hop from one place to another, these factories will never rematerialize. Mid-flight, they morph into something else entirely: "orders" to be placed with a contractor, who may well turn over those orders to as many as ten subcontractors, who—particularly in the garment sector—may in turn pass a portion of the subcontracts on to a network of home workers who will complete the jobs in basements and living rooms. Sure enough, only five months after the first round of plant closures was announced, Levi's made another public statement: it would resume manufacturing in China. The company had pulled out of China in 1993, citing concerns about human-rights violations. Now it has returned, not to build its own factories, but to place orders with three contractors that the company vows to closely monitor for violations of labor law.[20]

This shift in attitude toward production is so profound that where a previous era of consumer goods corporations displayed their logos on the facades of their factories, many of today's brand-based multinationals now maintain that the location of their production operations is a "trade secret," to be guarded at all costs. When asked by human-rights groups in April 1999 to disclose the names and addresses of its contract factories, Peggy Carter, a vice president at Champion clothing, replied: "We have no interest in our competition learning where we are located and taking advantage of what has taken us years to build."[21]

Increasingly, brand-name multinationals—Levi's, Nike, Champion, Wal-Mart, Reebok, the Gap, IBM and General Motors—insist that they are just like any one of us: bargain hunters in search of the best deal in the global mall. They are very picky customers, with specific instructions about made-to-order design, materials, delivery dates and, most important, the need for rock-bottom prices. But what they are *not* interested in is the burdensome logistics of how those prices fall so low; building factories, buying machinery and budgeting for labor have all been lobbed squarely into somebody else's court.

And the real job-flight story is that a growing number of the most high-profile and profitable corporations in the world are fleeing the jobs business altogether.

NOTES

Extracted from N. Klein, *No Logo* (New York: St. Martin's Press, 2002), pp. 195–202. Reproduced with permission of St. Martin's Press, Harper Collins UK, Random House, and the author.

1. Landor Web site.
2. "People Buy Products Not Brands," by Peter Schweitzer (J. Walter Thompson White Papers series, undated).
3. "Big Brand Firms Know the Name Is Everything," *Irish Times,* 27 February 1998.
4. Bob Ortega, *In Sam We Trust* (New York: Times Books, 1999), 342.
5. "Trade and Development Report, 1997." United Nations Conference on Trade and Economic Development.
6. Donald Katz, *Just Do It* (Holbrook, MA: Adams Media, 1994), 204.
7. Cathy Majtenyi, "Were Disney Dogs Treated Better Than Workers?" *Catholic Register,* 23–30 December 1996, 9.
8. "Extreme Spreadsheet Dude," *Baffler* no. 9, 79, and *Wall Street Journal,* 16 April 1998.
9. John Gilardi, "Adidas Share Offer Set to Win Gold Medal," Reuters, 26 October 1995.
10. *Globe and Mail,* 26 September 1997.
11. Charles Kernaghan, "Behind the Label: 'Made in China,'" prepared for the National Labor Committee, March 1998.
12. *Los Angeles Times,* 16 September 1997, D5. Furthermore, Sara Lee's investors had been getting a solid return on their investment but the stock "had gained 25 per cent over the prior 12 months, lagging the 35 per cent increase of the benchmark Standard & Poor's 500-stock index."
13. Peters, *The Circle of Innovation* (New York: Vintage Books, 1999), 16.
14. David Leonhardt, "Sara Lee: Playing with the Recipe." *Business Week,* 27 April 1998, 114.
15. Ibid.
16. Jennifer Waters, "After Euphoria, Can Sara Lee Be Like Nike?" *Crain's Chicago Business,* 22 September 1997, 3.
17. Nina Munk, "How Levi's Trashed a Great American Brand," *Fortune,* 12 April 1999, 83.
18. "Levi Strauss & Co. to Close 11 of Its North American Plants," Business Wire, 22 February 1999, B1.
19. *Wall Street Journal,* 4 November 1997, B1.
20. Joanna Ramey, "Levi's Will Resume Production in China After 5-Year Absence," *Women's Wear Daily,* 9 April 1998, I.
21. "Anti-Sweatshop Activists Score in Campaign Targeting Athletic Retailers," *Boston Globe,* 18 April 1999.

30

SUBCULTURE AND STYLE

Dick Hebdige

I managed to get about twenty photographs, and with bits of chewed bread I pasted them on the back of the cardboard sheet of regulations that hangs on the wall. Some are pinned up with bits of brass wire which the foreman brings me and on which I have to string coloured glass beads. Using the same beads with which the prisoners next door make funeral wreaths, I have made star-shaped frames for the most purely criminal. In the evening, as you open your window to the street, I turn the back of the regulation sheet towards me. Smiles and sneers, alike inexorable, enter me by all the holes I offer … . They watch over my little routines.

—Genet, 1966

In the opening pages of *The Thief's Journal*, Jean Genet describes how a tube of vaseline, found in his possession, is confiscated by the Spanish police during a raid. This 'dirty, wretched object', proclaiming his homosexuality to the world, becomes for Genet a kind of guarantee–'the sign of a secret grace which was soon to save me from contempt'. The discovery of the vaseline is greeted with laughter in the record-office of the station, and the police 'smelling of garlic, sweat and oil, but … strong in their moral assurance' subject Genet to a tirade of hostile innuendo. The author joins in the laughter too ('though painfully') but later, in his cell, 'the image of the tube of vaseline never left me'.

I was sure that this puny and most humble object would hold its own against them; by its mere presence it would be able to exasperate all the police in the world; it would draw down upon itself contempt, hatred, white and dumb rages. (Genet, 1967)

I have chosen to begin with these extracts from Genet because he more than most has explored in both his life and his art the subversive implications of style. I shall be returning again and again to Genet's major themes: the status and meaning of revolt, the idea of style as a form of Refusal, the elevation of crime into art (even though, in our case, the 'crimes' are only broken codes). Like Genet, we are interested in subculture—in the expressive forms and rituals of those subordinate groups—the teddy boys and mods and rockers, the skinheads and the punks—who are alternately dismissed, denounced and canonized; treated at different times as threats to public order and as harmless buffoons. Like Genet also, we are intrigued by the most mundane objects—a safety pin, a pointed shoe, a motor cycle—which, none the less, like the tube of vaseline, take on a symbolic dimension, becoming a form of stigmata, tokens of a self-imposed exile. Finally, like Genet, we must seek to recreate the dialectic between action and reaction which renders these objects meaningful. For, just as the conflict between Genet's 'unnatural' sexuality and the policemen's 'legitimate' outrage can be encapsulated in a single object, so the tensions between dominant and subordinate groups can be found reflected in the surfaces of subculture—in the styles made up of mundane objects which have a double meaning. On the one hand, they warn the 'straight' world in advance of a sinister presence—the presence of difference—and draw down upon themselves vague suspicions, uneasy laughter, 'white and dumb rages'. On the other hand, for those who erect them into icons, who use them as words or as curses, these objects become signs of forbidden identity, sources of value. Recalling his humiliation at the hands of the police, Genet finds consolation in the tube of vaseline. It becomes a symbol of his 'triumph'—'I would indeed rather have shed blood than repudiate that silly object' (Genet, 1967).

The meaning of subculture is, then, always in dispute, and style is the area in which the opposing definitions clash with most dramatic force. Much of the available space in this book will therefore be taken up with a description of the process whereby objects are made to mean and mean again as 'style' in subculture. As in Genet's novels, this process begins with a crime against the natural order, though in this case the deviation may seem slight indeed—the cultivation of a quiff, the acquisition of a scooter or a record or a certain type of suit. But it ends in the construction of a style, in a gesture of defiance or contempt, in a smile or a sneer. It signals a Refusal. I would like to think that this Refusal is worth making, that these gestures have a meaning, that the smiles and the sneers have some subversive value, even if, in the final analysis, they are, like Genet's gangster pin-ups, just the darker side of sets of regulations, just so much graffiti on a prison wall.

Even so, graffiti can make fascinating reading. They draw attention to themselves. They are an expression both of impotence and a kind of power—the power to disfigure (Norman Mailer calls graffiti—'Your presence on their Presence … hanging your alias on their scene' (Mailer, 1974)). In this book I shall attempt to decipher the graffiti, to tease out the meanings embedded in the various post-war youth styles. But before we can proceed to individual subcultures, we must first define the basic terms. The word 'subculture' is loaded down with mystery. It suggests secrecy, masonic oaths, an Underworld. It also invokes the larger and no less difficult concept 'culture'. So it is with the idea of culture that we should begin.

[…]

HEGEMONY: THE MOVING EQUILIBRIUM

'Society cannot share a common communication system so long as it is split into warring classes' (Brecht, A Short Organum for the Theatre).

The term hegemony refers to a situation in which a provisional alliance of certain social groups can exert 'total social authority' over other subordinate groups, not simply by coercion or by the direct imposition of ruling ideas, but by 'winning and shaping consent so that the power of the dominant classes appears both legitimate and natural' (Hall, 1977). Hegemony can only be maintained so long as the dominant classes 'succeed in framing all competing definitions within their range' (Hall, 1977), so that subordinate groups are, if not controlled, then at least contained within an ideological space which does not seem at all 'ideological': which appears instead to be permanent and 'natural', to lie outside history, to be beyond particular interests (see *Social Trends*, no. 6, 1975).

This is how, according to Barthes, 'mythology' performs its vital function of naturalization and normalization and it is in his book *Mythologies* that Barthes demonstrates most forcefully the full extension of these normalized forms and meanings. However, Gramsci adds the important proviso that hegemonic power, precisely *because* it requires the consent of the dominated majority, can never be permanently exercised by the same alliance of 'class fractions'. As has been pointed out, 'Hegemony … is not universal and "given" to the continuing rule of a particular class. It has to be won, reproduced, sustained. Hegemony is, *as* Gramsci said, a "moving equilibrium" containing relations of forces favourable or unfavourable to this or that tendency' (Hall *et al.*, 1976).

In the same way, forms cannot be permanently normalized. They can always be deconstructed, demystified, by a 'mythologist' like Barthes. Moreover commodities can be symbolically 're-possessed' in everyday life, and endowed with implicitly oppositional meanings, by the very groups who originally produced them. The symbiosis in which ideology and social order, production and reproduction, are linked is then neither fixed nor guaranteed. It can be prised open. The consensus can be fractured, challenged, overruled, and resistance to the groups in dominance cannot always be lightly dismissed or automatically incorporated. Although, as Lefebvre has written, we live in a society where '… objects in practice become signs and signs objects and a second nature takes the place of the first—the initial layer of perceptible reality' (Lefebvre, 1971), there are, as he goes on to affirm, always 'objections and contradictions which hinder the closing of the circuit' between sign and object, production and reproduction.

We can now return to the meaning of youth subcultures, for the emergence of such groups has signalled in a spectacular fashion the breakdown of consensus in the post-war period. In the following chapters we shall see that it is precisely objections and contradictions of the kind which Lefebvre has described that find expression in subculture. However, the challenge to hegemony which subcultures represent is not issued directly by them. Rather it is expressed obliquely, in style. The objections are lodged, the contradictions displayed (and, as we shall see, 'magically resolved') at the profoundly superficial level of appearances: that is, at the level of signs. For the sign-community, the community of myth-consumers, is not a uniform body. As Volosinov has written, it is cut through by class:

> Class does not coincide with the sign community, i.e. with the totality of users of the same set of signs of ideological communication. Thus various different classes will use one and the same language. As a result, differently oriented accents intersect in every ideological sign. Sign becomes the arena of the class struggle. (Volosinov, 1973)

The struggle between different discourses, different definitions and meanings within ideology is therefore always, at the same time, a struggle within signification: a struggle for possession of the sign which extends to even the most mundane areas of everyday life. To turn once more to the examples used in the Introduction, to the safety pins and tubes of vaseline, we can see that such commodities are indeed open to a double inflection: to 'illegitimate' as well as 'legitimate' uses. These 'humble objects' can be magically appropriated; 'stolen' by subordinate groups and made to carry 'secret' meanings: meanings which express, in code, a form of resistance to the order which guarantees their continued subordination.

Style in subculture is, then, pregnant with significance. Its transformations go 'against nature', interrupting the process of 'normalization'. As such, they are gestures, movements towards a speech which offends the 'silent majority', which challenges the principle of unity and cohesion, which contradicts the myth of consensus. Our task becomes, like Barthes', to discern the hidden messages inscribed in code on the glossy surfaces of style, to trace them out as 'maps of meaning' which obscurely re-present the very contradictions they are designed to resolve or conceal.

NOTE

Extracted from D. Hebdige, *Subculture: The Meaning of Style* (London: Routledge, 1987), pp. 1–4 and 15–18. Reproduced by permission of Taylor & Francis Books UK.

31

INCENDIARY DEVICES

John Stones

Designers who try to make dramatic political comments with their creations should tread carefully, says John Stones. When you exploit the victims and paraphernalia of war or poverty you negotiate a minefield that could blow up in your face ...

Amid the air kissing and swirl of beautiful people at this year's Milan fair; there were a couple of new objects that clamoured for attention in a particular way.

One was a lamp with a gold plated Kalashnikov as its stand, designed by Philippe Starck for Italian lighting company Flos. The other, the Baghdad Table, uses aerial views of the heavily bombed and stricken Iraqi capital to form a metal surface grid. It was designed by Israeli designer Ezri Tarazi for Italian manufacturer Edra.

The provocative nature of these products was enhanced by the lack of context in which they were presented. The Baghdad Table was merely accompanied by aerial photos and the designer's name, a citizen of Israel, anything but an impartial player in the Middle East. Edra says the tables are 'assemblages of diversity' and they 'represent the ritual dimension of hospitality'. It even suggests they are Biblical, in spite of Baghdad's Islamic culture.

Starck's gun lamps use gold-plated handguns and assault rifles as stands. It is even believed that Starck wished to donate royalties to Lieutenant General Mikhail Kalashnikov, designer of one of the most unintended product design classics. Of course, the rifle has played a part in the death of thousands.

Image 12   Philippe Starck, Gun Lamp. Courtesy of Philippe Starck.

Are these cynical or even offensive attempts to grab headlines? Is this yet another shift in design towards fashion and spin? Or are they attempts, ill-conceived or otherwise to make design relevant, to reinterpret the function of 'fashion' furniture?

Lighting designer Arnold Chan of Isometrix is dismissive of the Starck lamp, saying, 'It's advertising for Flos. It's hype, the company is not going to be selling them by the crate.'

Professor Sir Christopher Frayling, rector of the Royal College of Art, is more trenchant. He says, 'A Kalashnikov on the coffee table–gold or not–is not my thing. I know someone whose close friend was shot by one. You can carry Postmodernist jokes too far. This doesn't mean design can't make political statements with a little 'p'. But the Starck object carries bad associations. It also encourages cynicism about important life and death issues'.

Product designer Mark Delaney also finds the products offensive. He describes the Kalashnikov lamp as, 'Starck at his attention-grabbing worst. Neither particularly beautiful nor artistically insightful, these lamps seem to exist only to create a few more column inches for the French designer'. The Baghdad table comes in for similar criticism: 'It takes up where the Campana brothers' Favela chair left off, continuing the company's obsession with odd philosophy and shallow political comment,' says Delaney.

Alongside the Baghdad table Edra presented another 'sculpture table', also dedicated to a city—the Brasilia table by Fornando and Humberto Campana, with an impractical if visually arresting surface made up of fractured mirror 'reflecting' their thoughts on the Brazilian city that is so often seen as an object lesson for the failure of Modernism.

Delaney says, 'These products are symptomatic of design's continuing obsession with fashion and novelty. If they had appeared in the satellite exhibition, presented by a young unknown designer neither would have warranted a second glance.'

But the work also has its defenders, Mike Curtis, managing director of Start Creative, suggests 'the controversial nature of Starck's latest work reinforces how the design industry can provoke and stimulate the consciousness'. He adds, 'Designers

are well placed to challenge conventions, especially at a time in the economic cycle when clients tend to be more conservative and much work is commercially focused and, by definition, safer'.

And Flos cites Cristina Morozzi: 'Neither self-made toy weapons nor table lamps are the cause of wars. Think about the pure gold plating on these fake weapons, which is just as powerful a symbol of the greed, not love, that appears to drive life with ever more devastating effects'. She places the work in context with Caralan designer Marti Guixe's new book on Toy Guns, which shows how a coat hanger can be shaped to look like a gun.

Both the gun lamps and the 'sculpture tables' are going into production. Younger designers are also adopting the use of furniture design as a vehicle for controversial statements. John Angelo Benson, a young British designer showing at the Salone Satellite, presented 'the most expensive chair in the world—to die for', a wooden recreation of Andy Warhol's infamously aestheticised chair of death, with leather straps now adorned with diamonds too. It presents itself as pillorying the media need for controversy and unambiguously criticises design, while not entirely escaping the clutches of that game itself.

If the intention or function of furniture was to get people talking, these pieces are no doubt successful. While some are already writing out no doubt sizeable cheques, others are left foaming at the mouth.

Sophisticated or well-intentioned attempts to make design relevant to wider debates and events in our culture or crass, insensitive, headline-grabbing opportunism? You decide.

NOTE

Extracted from J. Stones, 'Incendiary Devices', *Design Week* 20/17 (2005): 16–17. Reprinted by permission of Design Week, www.designweek.co.uk

32

DESIGN AND DEMOCRACY

Gui Bonsiepe

I shall present a few thoughts about the relationship between democracy and design, and about the relationship between critical humanism and operational humanism. This issue leads to the question of the role of technology and industrialization as a procedure for democratizing the consumption of goods and services, and finally to the ambivalent role of esthetics as the domain of freedom and manipulation.

The main theme of my lecture is the relationship between design—in the sense of projecting—and autonomy. My reflections are open-ended, and do not pretend to give quick and immediate answers. The university still offers a place to pursue these questions that normally will not be addressed in professional practice, with its pressures and contingencies.

Looking at the present design discourse, one notes a surprising—and I would say alarming—absence of questioning design activities. Concepts such as branding, competitiveness, globalization, comparative advantages, lifestyle design, differentiation, strategic design, fun design, emotion design, experience design, and smart design prevail in design magazines and the all too few books about design. Sometimes, one gets the impression that a designer aspiring to two minutes of fame feels obliged to invent a new label for setting herself or himself apart from the rest of what professional service offers. I leave aside "coffee table" books on design that abound in pictures and exempt the reader from intellectual efforts. The issue of

design and democracy doesn't enjoy popularity—apart from a few laudable exceptions.

If we look at the social history of the meaning of the term "design," we note on the one side a popularization that is a horizontal extension, and on the other side a contraction that is a vertical reduction. The architectural critic Witold Rybczynski recently commented on this phenomenon: "Not so long ago, the term 'designer' described someone such as Eliot Noyes, who was responsible for the IBM Selectric typewriter in the 1960s, or Henry Dreyfuss, whose clients included Lockheed Aircraft and the Bell Telephone Company ... or Dieter Rams, who created a range of austere-looking, but very practical, products for the German company Braun. Today, 'designer' is more likely to bring to mind Ralph Lauren or Giorgio Armani, that is, a fashion designer. While fashion designers usually start as couturiers, they—or at least their names—often are associated with a wide variety of consumer products including cosmetics, perfume, luggage, home furnishings, and even house paint. As a result, 'design' is popularly identified with packaging: the housing of a computer monitor, the barrel of a pen, and a frame for eyeglasses."[1]

More and more, design has moved away from the idea of "intelligent problem solving" (James Dyson) and drawn nearer to the ephemeral, fashionable and quickly obsolete, to formal aesthetic play, to the "boutiquization" of the universe of products for everyday life. For this reason, design today often is identified with expensive, exquisite, not particularly practical, funny, and formally pushed, colorful objects. The hypertrophy of fashion aspects is accompanied and increased by the media with their voracious appetite for novelties. Design thus has become a media event—and we have a considerable number of publications that serve as resonance boxes for this process. Even design centers are exposed to the complicity of the media, running the risk of failing to reach their original objective: to make a difference between design as intelligent problem solving and styling. After all, it is a question of a renaissance of the tradition of the Good Design Movement, but with different foci and interests. The advocates of Good Design pursued socio-pedagogical objectives, while the life style centers of today pursue exclusively commercial and marketing aims to provide orientation for consumption patterns of a new—or not that new—social segment of global character, that can be labeled with the phrase: "We made it."

The world of everyday products and messages, of material and semiotic artifacts, has met—with rare exceptions—in cultural discourse (and this includes the academic discourse) in a climate of benign indifference that has its roots in classical culture in the medieval age, when the first universities in the West were founded. This academic tradition did not take note of the domain of design (in the sense of project) in any of its disciplines. However, in the process of industrialization, one could no longer close one's eyes to technology and technical artifacts that more and more made their presence felt in everyday life. But the leading ideal continued to be cognitive character in the form of the creation of new knowledge. Design never established itself as a leading, parallel ideal. This fact explains the difficulties of integrating design education in institutions of higher learning, with their own traditions and criteria of excellence. This is evident in doctoral programs in design that favor the production of discursive results, and don't give projects the same value or recognition as the production of texts. The sciences approach reality from the perspective of cognition, of what can be known, while the design disciplines approach reality from the perspective of "projectability," of what can be designed. These are different perspectives, and it is hoped that, in the future, they will transmute into complementary perspectives. So far, design has tried to build bridges to the domain of the sciences, but not vice versa. We can speculate that, in the future, design may become a basic discipline for all scientific areas. But this Copernican turn in the university system might take generations, if not centuries. Only the creation of radically new universities can shorten this process. But the decision freedom of government institutions is limited due to the weight of academic traditions, and the bureaucratization emphasis on formal procedures of approbation (title fetishism). Therefore, the new university probably will be created outside of established structures.

Relating design activities to the sciences should not be misinterpreted as a claim of a scientific design, or as an attempt to transform design into a science. It would be foolish to "design" an ashtray using scientific knowledge. But it would not be foolish—and even mandatory—to tap scientific knowledge when designing a milk package with a minimal ecological footprint. It is no longer feasible to limit the notion of design to design disciplines such as architecture, industrial design, or communication design because scientists also are designing. When a group of agricultural scientists develops a new candy from the carob bean that contains important vitamins for school children, we have a clear example of a design activity.[2]

I now want to focus on the central issue of my lecture: the relationship between democracy and design. Indeed, during recent years, the notion of democracy has been exposed to a process of wear and tear, so it is advisable to use it with care. When looking at the international scene, we cannot avoid stating that, in the name of democracy, imperialistic invasions, bombardments, genocides, ethnical cleaning operations, torture, and the breaking of international laws have been—and are—committed, almost with impunity, at least for the moment. The cost of this lack of humanity is not known. Future generations probably will have to carry the burden. With democracy, these operations have nothing in common.

Neoliberals believe that democracy is synonymous with the predominance of the market as an exclusive and almost sanctified institution for governing all relations within and between societies. So we face such questions as: How can we recover the true meaning of democracy? How can democracy regain credibility? How can one counteract the arrogant and condescending attitude of the centers of power that consider democracy as nothing more than a tranquilizer for public opinion, in order to continue undisturbed "business as usual"?

I am using a simple interpretation of the term "democracy" in the sense of participation, so that dominated citizens transform themselves into subjects opening a space for self-determination, and that means ensuring room for a project of one's own accord. Formulated differently: democracy involves more than the formal right to vote. Similarly, freedom goes farther than the right to chose between a hundred varieties of cellular telephones; or a flight to Orlando to visit the Epcot Center, or to Paris to look at paintings in the Louvre.

I favor a substantial, and thus less formal, concept of democracy as the reduction of heteronomy (i.e., domination by external forces). It is no secret that this interpretation fits into the tradition of the Enlightenment that has been criticized so intensively by, among others, Jean-Francois Lyotard when he announced the end of the grand narratives. I do not agree with this approach or other postmodern variants. Without a utopian element, another world is not possible, and would remain the expression of a pious ethereal wish without concrete consequences. Without a utopian ingredient, residual though it may be,

heteronomy cannot be reduced. For this reason, the renunciation of the project of enlightenment seems to me the expression of a quietist, if not conservative, attitude—an attitude of surrender that no designer should be tempted to cherish.

In order to illustrate the necessity to reduce heteronomy, I am using a contribution from a linguist—a specialist in comparative literature—Edward Said, who died last year. He characterizes, in an exemplary manner, the essence of humanism; of a humanistic attitude. As a philologist, he limits the humanist attitude to the domain of language and history: "Humanism is the exertion of one's faculties in language in order to understand, reinterpret, and grapple with the products of language in history, other languages, and other histories."[3] But we can extend this interpretation to other areas, too. Certainly, the intentions of the author will not be bent when transferring his characterization of humanism—with corresponding adjustments—to design. Design humanism is the exercise of design activities in order to interpret the needs of social groups, and to develop viable emancipative proposals in the form of material and semiotic artifacts. Why emancipative? Because humanism implies the reduction of domination. In the field of design, it also means to focus on the excluded, the discriminated, and economically less-favored groups (as they are called in economist jargon), which amounts to the majority of the population of this planet. I want to make it clear that I don't propagate a universalistic attitude according to the pattern of design for the world. Also, I don't believe that this claim should be interpreted as the expression of a naive idealism, supposedly out of touch with reality. On the contrary, each profession should face this uncomfortable question, not only the profession of designers. It would be an error to take this claim as the expression of a normative request of how a designer—exposed to the pressure of the market and the antinomies between reality and what could be reality—should act today. The intention is more modest, that is to foster a critical consciousness when facing the enormous imbalance between the centers of power and the people submitted to these powers, because the imbalance is deeply undemocratic insofar as it negates participation. It treats human beings as mere instances in the process of objectivization *(Verdinglichung)* and commodification.

Here we come to the role of the market and the role of design in the market. In a recently published book, the economist Kenneth Galbraith analyses the function of the concept of the market that, according to him, is nothing more than a smokescreen for not talking openly about capitalism—a term that doesn't enjoy a high rating on the popularity scale in all social classes and in all countries. Galbraith puts design in the context of techniques of corporations for gaining and consolidating power:

> Product innovation and modification is a major economic function, and no significant manufacturer introduces a new product without cultivating the consumer demand for it. Or forgoes efforts to influence and sustain the demand for an existing product. Here enters the world of advertising and salesmanship, of television, of consumer manipulation. Thus an impairment of consumer and market sovereignty. In the real world, the producing firm and the industry go far to set the prices and establish the demand, employing to this end monopoly, oligopoly, product design and differentiation, advertising, [and] other sales and trade promotion.[4]

Galbraith criticizes the use of the term "market" as an anonymous and impersonal institution, and instead insists on talking about corporate power. Against this use of design—after all, a tool for domination—stands the intent not to remain fixed exclusively on the aspects of power and of the anonymous market. In this contradiction, design practice is unfolding and resisting a harmonizing discourse that is camouflaging the contradictions. One can deny the contradictions, but one cannot bypass them.

The issue of manipulation has a long tradition in design discourse, especially in advertising. I remember a popular book that, at the time, provoked a wide resonance, *The Hidden Persuaders* by Vance Packard (1957). But one should be on guard against a critique with declamatory character that merely denounces. More differentiation is required. Manipulation and design share one point of contact: appearance. We design, among others and certainly not only, appearances. For this reason, I once characterized the designer as a strategist of appearances, phenomena that we perceive through our senses—above all visual senses, but also tactile and auditory senses. Appearances lead us to the issue of aesthetics—an ambivalent concept. On the one side, aesthetics represent the domain of freedom, of play—and some authors claim that we are only free when we play. On the other side, aesthetics opens the access to manipulation, that is the increase of outer, directed behavior. When designing products and semiotic artifacts, we want to seduce, that is foster, a positive—or according to context, negative—predisposition towards a product and sign combination. Depending on intentions, design leans more to one pole or the other, more to autonomy or more to heteronomy.

At this point, I want to insert a few reflections on technology. The term "technology" generally is understood as the universe of artifacts and procedures for producing merchandise with which companies fill the stage of everyday practice. Technology implies hardware and software—and software implies the notion of design as a facet of technology that cannot be dispensed with. Here in Latin America, we face the problem of technology policy and industrialization policy. Research on these issues reveals interesting details about progress and setbacks. But these seem to me to favor a reductionistic interpretation of technology. Only in exceptional cases do texts mention the question of what is done with technology. The question for the design of products remains unanswered. This presents a weak point, without wanting to underestimate the efforts by historians. But one cannot defend them against the reproach of being blind to the dimension of design, the dimension of projects, or at least of facing this dimension with indifference. The motives for industrialization include the wish to diversify exports, and not to remain an exporting economy of commodities without added value. But behind this plausible argument is hidden another generally not explicitly formulated motif. I am referring to the idea that, apart from the growth of the GNP, industrialization is the only possibility for democratizing consumption to provide for a broad sector of the population access to the world of products and services in the different areas of everyday life: health, housing, education, sports, transport, and work, to mention only a few.

However, to mention today the role of government in promoting industrialization can appear almost as an offense to good manners. The role of public intervention has been demonized with one exception, paying the debt of a bankrupt, privatized service. In that case, public resources are welcome, thus reinforcing the idea that politics is the appropriation of public goods for private purposes. But when the history of industrialization and technology of this subcontinent is written, one shall see with clarity that the role of government has been decisive, even though the detractors of the public sector with their bellicose voices have belittled its function and contributions. If we look at the recent history of Argentina—a country that, until a few years ago, followed in subservient manner the impositions of the International Monetary Fund, and that, in a moment of delirium, enthusiastically praised its "carnal relationships" with the leading military and economic power—then we see that this country didn't fare very well with this policy of relentless privatization and reduction of government presence. This process plunged a great part of the population into a state of poverty unknown until then, and led to an income concentration with the corresponding bipolarization of society into two groups: the excluded and the included.

Privatization, in this context, is synonymous with de-democratization, because the victims of this process have never been asked whether they approved the credits and sales of public property that led the country into bankruptcy. Relentless privatization and the reduction of the role of government—the unconditional opening of the economy for imports—initiated the de-industrialization of Argentina, thus destroying the foundations for productive work, including work for industrial designers.

The industrialization policies in various countries in which I have participated, above all Chile, Argentina, and Brazil, concentrated exclusively on hardware, leaving the communication and information industries untouched. Today, the constellation has changed radically. An updated industrialization policy would have to include the information sector of the economy, for which graphic design and information design can provide essential contributions. New problems show up there that confront designers with 'cognitive demands that generally are not taken into consideration in design education programs. The expanding process of digitalization fostered a design current which today claims that the important design questions essentially are of symbolic character. As the second argument for the semantization of products—and thus the semantization of the designer's work—miniaturization is mentioned, made possible by printed circuits and cheap chips. These do not allow us to see how the products are working because functions become invisible. Therefore, the designer's task consists of making these invisible functions visible. Though it would be blind to deny the communication and symbolic aspects of products, their role should not be overvalued as some authors do. Between the alternative to put a nail into a wall with a hammer or the symbolic value of a hammer, the choice is clear. The material base of products with their visual, tactile, and auditory conformation provides a firm base for the designer's work.

With concern, one can observe the growth of a generation of designers that obsessively focuses on the symbolic aspects of products and their equivalents in the market—branding and self-branding—and that doesn't know anymore how to classify joints. The search for a balance between the instrumental/operational aspects of technical objects and their semantic aspects constitutes the core of the designer's work, without privileging one or the other domain. As the historian Raimonda Riccini writes:

> The polarity between the instrumental and symbolic dimension, between internal structure and external structure is a typical property of artifacts, insofar as they are tools and simultaneously carriers of values and meanings. Designers face the task to mediate between these two polarities, by designing the form of products as result of an interaction with the sociotechnical process.[5]

It is revealing that Riccini does not speak of the form of products and their interaction with functions, that is the affordances, but that she alludes to sociotechnical development. In this way, she avoids the outdated debate about form and function. The once secure foundations for arriving at the configuration of products have been dissolved today—if ever they existed. It would be naive to presuppose the existence of a canon of deterministic rules. He who defends such a canon, commits the error of essentializing Platonic forms. At the same time, it would be equally naive to claim that a limitless fickleness of forms would arise from the demiurgic actions of a handful of creatively inspired designers. We face a paradox here. To design means to deal with paradoxes and contradictions. In a society plagued by contradictions, design also is affected. It might be convenient to remember the dictum of Walter Benjamin that there is no document of civilization that is not, at the same time, a document of barbarism.

NOTES

Extracted from G. Bonsiepe, "Design and Democracy,:" *Design Issues* 22, no. 2 (2006): 27–34. Reprinted by permission of the author.

1. Witold Rybczynski, "How Things Work," *New York Review of Books* 10 (June 9, 2005): 49–51.
2. www.clarin.com/diario/2005/05/09/sociedad/s-03101.htm (Crean un nuevo alimento para escolares en base a algarroba.) (May 9, 2005).
3. Edward W. Said, *Humanism and Democratic Criticism* (New York: Columbia University Press, 2003), 28.
4. John Kenneth Galbraith, *The Economics of Innocent Fraud* (Boston: Houghton Mifflin Company, 2004), 7.
5. Raimonda Riccini, *Design e teorie degli oggetti. it verri 27* (February 2005): 48–57.

SECTION 3: THEORIZING DESIGN AND VISUALITY

3.4: Material Culture and Social Interactions

INTRODUCTION

Culture is constituted by our social exchanges with each other and our interactions with things. Since its inception, anthropology has assessed culture—its people (cultural anthropology) and its material manifestations (archaeology)—to try to better understand human complexity and diversity. As one of culture's most important artifacts, design, a form of material culture, can tell us about the history of its makers and the cultural condition of the society associated with the artifact. Looking closely at society through a critical lens, knowledge about different material worlds and cultural milieus can be furthered. Four of these readings (Prown, Miller, Foucault, and de Certeau) assess culture through an examination of our material culture, and the other reading in this subsection (Goffman) assesses our ever-changing cultural circumstances by studying our interpersonal interactions.

In his seminal essay on a methodological approach to understanding material culture, Jules Prown writes that "material culture is the study through artifacts of the beliefs—values, ideas, attitudes, and assumptions—of a particular community or society at a given time." He runs through a long list of potential categories of material culture, ranging from landscape to bodily adornment and then takes us through a step-by-step method of how to conduct a sound study of material culture. Prown argues that by going from description to deduction to speculation, we can better understand the world of things and gain historical insight into objects that we want to interpret. Ultimately, he dispels the primacy of written documents and celebrates the potential of artifacts.

Daniel Miller goes beyond methodology to make pronouncements about what material culture can tell us about the history of objects and ideas about possession. Specifically, he notes that objects can describe our relationship to our self and our society. For instance, some societies fetishize objects, and "the clothing, ornaments and tools belonging to an individual may be considered so integral to him or her that to touch or do harm to these inanimate objects is considered" akin to "taking the same action against the person." Miller also gives us insight into the importance of exchange, value, and ownership of material culture. It is, Miller reveals, the importance of private property that illuminates our modern-day relationship with objects. In language that is closely tied to the work of design anthropologist Susan Squires in the research subsection (2.2), Miller explains that through ownership we create our most extreme connection with the material realm.

Extending the study of the material sphere to a larger system, Michel Foucault, in his seminal book, *Discipline and Punish,* discusses the panopticon. This type of prison architecture, designed by Jeremy Bentham in late eighteenth-century England, created a structure of inferred and actual surveillance. Rather than physically punish the body of a criminal, individuals were now sent to prison and disciplined through the regulatory confines of a type of architecture that facilitated observation. To Foucault, whose thinking about issues from madness to sexuality changed the nature of academic inquiry, the panopticon is a material manifestation of a larger historical transformation where, through systems of surveillance, bodies could be watched and trained to perform in ways that were approved by cultural norms.

Using Foucault's ideas about the materiality of panoptic space, Michel de Certeau traces the experiences intertwined with *The Practice of Everyday Life.* In his chapter on "Walking in the City," he poetically describes the view of the city from the bird's-eye perspective on top of the World Trade Center in New York City, which was, at the moment that he wrote this book, the tallest building in the world. The view from the 110th floor was dizzying, but it was also unifying. It allowed for the entire system of the city to be encapsulated as a grid of knowledge that city planners and city governments regulated with the all-knowing mechanism of maps. However, the experience of the street level is different from the unifying perspective on high, and here is where de Certeau claims that the material culture of the urban environment can be transgressed. On the street we can escape "the imaginary totalizations produced by the eye, the everyday has a certain strangeness that does not surface, or whose surface is only its upper limit, outlining itself against the visible." Walking "transgresses" and allows for other possibilities within the real and imagined context of the designed city.

Foucault and de Certeau take on systems of power that regulate normativity and are not always overt; they are hidden behind an Oz-like veil of secrecy that should remind us of several of the issues raised in the subsection on ethics (3.2). However, sociologist Erving Goffman, in his seminal book *The Presentation of Self in Everyday Life,* claims that individuals are agents who make particular decisions about how they want to be perceived by others in social situations. From the vantage point of an omniscient sociologist, Goffman writes about encounters through the lens of what sociologists refer to as the study of symbolic interactions. However, he understood that each interaction that we have is unique. Goffman, in this reading, contends that "when an individual appears before others he will have many motives for trying to control the impression they receive of the situation." His book explores what we do when we interact and how these encounters lead to different performances of the self.

Unlike Prown, Miller, Foucault, and de Certeau, Goffman does not write directly about material culture. However, his insights into our everyday circumstances—our most banal interactions, utterances, and performances—should be understood as integral to how we consider design as a form of material culture. In language that is reminiscent of the Filipino texters in Rafael's essay from the Technology subsection (5.3), Goffman elucidates how it is design that facilitates our interactions and it is design that mediates our comprehension of, and commitment to, civic and social structures.

The study of design, as a material manifestation of culture, can help us understand our history and current condition. These readings offer ways in which we can frame our analyses of design. Through a close reading of objects, a discussion of property, a theory of spatial discipline, an investigation of urban spaces, and an explication of everyday encounters, these readings offer possible modes of inquiry into both our contemporary world and its multifaceted history.

33

MIND IN MATTER

Jules David Prown

Although art museums, historical societies, museums of history and technology, historic houses, open-air museums, and museums of ethnography, science, and even natural history, have long collected, studied, and exhibited the material of what has come to be called material culture, no comprehensive academic philosophy or discipline for the investigation of *material culture* has as yet been developed. Recently, however, there has been increased scholarly interest in the subject, as witnessed by the establishment of this periodical, *Winterthur Portfolio,* devoted specifically to material culture; graduate programs in material culture at University of Delaware, University of Notre Dame, and Boston University; an experimental Center for American Art and Material Culture at Yale University; and a substantial amount of innovative scholarship, especially in such emerging academic areas as folk life and cultural geography (a selective material culture bibliography is appended below). These developments and activities have been spontaneous and largely uncoordinated responses to a perceived scholarly need and opportunity. This essay attempts to define material culture and considers the nature of the discipline. It makes no claim to be either the first or the last word on material culture, but it does seek to illuminate the subject and to provide a basis for further discussion. It also proposes a particular methodology based on the proposition that artifacts are primary data for the study of material culture, and, therefore, they can be used actively as evidence rather than passively as illustrations.[1]

WHAT IS MATERIAL CULTURE?

Material culture is the study through artifacts of the beliefs—values, ideas, attitudes, and assumptions—of a particular community or society at a given time. The term *material culture* is also frequently used to refer to artifacts themselves, to the body of material available for such study. I shall restrict the term to mean the study and refer to the evidence simply as *material* or *artifacts*.

Material culture is singular as a mode of cultural investigation in its use of objects as primary data, but in its scholarly purposes it can be considered a branch of cultural history or cultural anthropology. It is a means rather than an end, a discipline rather than a field. In this, material culture differs from art history, for example, which is both a discipline (a mode of investigation) in its study of history through art and a field (a subject of investigation) in its study of the history of art itself. Material culture is comparable to art history as a discipline in its study of culture through artifacts. As such, it provides a scholarly approach to artifacts that can be utilized by investigators in a variety of fields. But the material of material culture is too diverse to constitute a single field. In practice it consists of subfields investigated by specialists—cultural geographers or historians of art, architecture, decorative arts, science, and technology.

Material culture as a study is based upon the obvious fact that the existence of a man-made object is concrete evidence of the presence of a human intelligence operating at the time of fabrication. The underlying premise is that objects made or modified by man reflect, consciously or unconsciously, directly or indirectly, the beliefs of individuals who made, commissioned, purchased, or used them, and by extension the beliefs of the larger society to which they belonged. The term *material culture* thus refers quite directly and efficiently, if not elegantly, both to the subject matter of the study, *material,* and to its purpose, the understanding of *culture.*

Despite its concision and aptness, the term *material culture* seems unsatisfactory, indeed, self-contradictory. *Material* is a word we associate with base and pragmatic things; *culture* is a word we associate with lofty, intellectual, abstract things. Our unease with this apparent disjunction is not superficial; it derives from a fundamental human perception of the universe as divided between earth and sky. That empirically observed opposition of lower and higher provides a powerful and pervasive metaphor for the distinctions we make between such elemental polarities as material and spiritual, concrete and abstract, finite and infinite, real and ideal. In its theological formulation this metaphor invariably locates heaven upward, above the earth, accessible not to the body but only to the mind or spirit (with mortification of the flesh [material] one way to achieve spiritual ends), and places hell in the bowels of the earth, down deep in the midst of matter. Material things are heir to all sorts of ills—they break, get dirty, smell, wear out; abstract ideas remain pristine, free from such worldly debilities.

The Western conception of history is that it has been characterized by man's increasing understanding and mastery of the physical environment, by the progressive triumph of mind over matter. The evidence of human history seems to confirm our sense that abstract, intellectual, spiritual elements are superior to material and physical things. This has led inevitably to a hierarchical ordering that informs our apprehension and judgment of human activities and experiences.[2] This unconscious ordering makes us uncomfortable with the terminological coupling of base material and lofty culture. Nevertheless, the term material culture, if not ideal, has the advantage of being concise, accurate, and in general use.

MATERIAL

The word *material* in material culture refers to a broad, but not unrestricted, range of objects. It embraces the class of objects known as artifacts—objects made by man or modified by man. It excludes natural objects. Thus, the study of material culture might include a hammer, a plow, a microscope, a house, a painting, a city. It would exclude trees, rocks, fossils, skeletons. Two general observations should be made here. First, natural objects are occasionally encountered in a pattern that indicates human activity—a stone wall or a row of trees in an otherwise random forest, a concentration of chicken bones in a pit or a pile of oyster shells, topiary or a clipped poodle, a tattooed body or a prepared meal. In the broadest sense these natural materials are artifacts—objects modified by man—and are of cultural interest. Second, works of art constitute a large and special category within artifacts because their inevitable aesthetic and occasional ethical or spiritual (iconic) dimensions make them direct and often overt or intentional expressions of cultural belief. The self-consciously expressive character of this material, however, raises problems as well as opportunities; in some ways artifacts that express culture unconsciously are more useful as objective cultural indexes.[3] For the moment, however, let it simply be borne in mind that all tangible works of art are part of material culture, but not all the material of material culture is art.

The range of objects that fall within the compass of material culture is so broad as to make some system of classification desirable. Sorting by physical materials does not work because of the multiplicity of substances used, even at times in a single artifact. The same is true of methods of fabrication. The most promising mode of classification is by function. The following list is arranged in a sequence of categories that progresses from the more decorative (or aesthetic) to the more utilitarian.

MIND IN MATTER

1. Art (paintings, drawings, prints, sculpture, photography)
2. Diversions (books, toys, games, meals, theatrical performances)
3. Adornment (jewelry, clothing, hairstyles, cosmetics, tattooing, other alterations of the body)
4. Modifications of the landscape (architecture, town planning, agriculture, mining)
5. Applied arts (furniture, furnishings, receptacles)
6. Devices (machines, vehicles, scientific instruments, musical instruments, implements)

These categories are broad; they undoubtedly require modification and refining; the list is intended simply to define the terrain and suggest the outlines of a system. Many objects straddle categories, but taxonomic shortcomings do not cause analytical problems. Classification for purposes of manageability and discussion does not affect the actual process of material culture analysis described below which applies to all artifacts. Although the range of categories suggests the potential applicability of a variety of specialized techniques and methodologies, no systematic attempt is made in this general essay to correlate categories of objects with particular analytical methods or with the production of particular kinds of cultural data. However, further consideration is given to these categories in the final section.

WHY MATERIAL CULTURE?

Why should one bother to investigate material objects in the quest for culture, for a society's

systems of belief? Surely people in all societies express and have expressed their beliefs more explicitly and openly in their words and deeds than in the things they have made. Are there aspects of mind to be discovered in objects that differ from, complement, supplement, or contradict what can be learned from more traditional literary and behavioral sources?

Inherent and Attached Value

The most obvious cultural belief associated with material objects has to do with *value.* There are different kinds of value. One, intrinsic in the fabric of an object itself, is established by the rarity of the materials used. Such value will inhere in the object for as long as the material continues to be valuable. With gold or silver or precious stones, this kind of value is quite persistent. More transient or variable are those values that have been attached by the people who originally made or used the object, by us today, or by people at any intervening moment. A value that accrues from utility will inhere as long as an object continues to be useful and can return when an obsolete object again becomes useful (wood stoves in an oil shortage). In addition to material and utilitarian values, certain objects have aesthetic value (art), some possess spiritual value (icons, cult objects), and some express attitudes toward other human beings (a fortress, a love seat) or toward the world (using materials in their natural condition as opposed to reshaping them).

Obviously, then, objects do embody and reflect cultural beliefs. But, although such embodiments of value differ in form from verbal and behavioral modes of cultural expression, they do not necessarily differ in character or content. In the following regards, however, objects do constitute distinctive cultural expressions.

Surviving Historical Events

Objects created in the past are the only historical occurrences that continue to exist in the present.

They provide an opportunity by which "we encounter the past at first hand; we have direct sensory experience of surviving historical events."[4] Artifacts may not be important historical events, but they are, to the extent that they can be experienced and interpreted as evidence, significant.

More Representative

Henry Glassie has observed that only a small percentage of the world's population is and has been literate, and that the people who write literature or keep diaries are atypical. Objects are used by a much broader cross section of the population and are therefore potentially a more wide-ranging, more representative source of information than words.[5] They offer the possibility of a way to understand the mind of the great majority of non-literate people, past and present, who remain otherwise inaccessible except through impersonal records and the distorting view of a contemporary literary elite. This promise perhaps explains why many of the leading early proponents, indeed pioneers, of material culture have come from the field of folklore and folk life and have studied vernacular objects. Such study has required a considerable amount of scholarly innovation. Vernacular objects pose interpretive difficulties because our scholarly traditions and experience, especially in regard to art, architecture, and the decorative arts, have focused on high style objects.

[...]

Veracity

Certain fundamental beliefs in any society are so generally accepted that they never need to be articulated (see *Cultural Perspective* below). These basic cultural assumptions, the detection of which is essential for cultural understanding, are consequently not perceivable in what a society expresses. They can, however, be detected in the way in which a society expresses itself, in the configuration or form of things, in *style*.[6] Stylistic evidence can be found in all modes of cultural expression, whether verbal, behavioral, or material. But a society puts a considerable amount of cultural spin on what it consciously says and does. Cultural expression is less self-conscious, and therefore potentially more truthful, in what a society produces, especially such mundane, utilitarian objects as domestic buildings, furniture, or pots.

Cultural Perspective

Perhaps the most difficult problem to recognize and surmount in cultural studies is that of cultural stance or cultural perspective. The evidence we study is the product of a particular cultural environment. We, the interpreters, are products of a different cultural environment. We are pervaded by the beliefs of our own social groups—nation, locality, class, religion, politics, occupation, gender, age, race, ethnicity—beliefs in the form of assumptions that we make unconsciously. These are biases that we take for granted; we accept them as mindlessly as we accept the tug of gravity. Is it possible to step outside of one's own cultural givens and interpret evidence objectively in terms of the beliefs of the individuals and the society that produced that evidence? If not, if we are irredeemably biased by our own unconscious beliefs, if we are hopelessly culture bound, then the entire enterprise of cultural interpretation should be avoided since our interpretations will inevitably be distorted. It is possible to argue, as Arnold Hauser does in response to the contention of Karl Marx that we see all things from the perspective of our social interest and our view is therefore inevitably distorted, that once we become aware of the problem we can struggle against subjectivity, against individual and class interests, and can move toward greater objectivity.[7] Awareness of the problem of one's own cultural bias is a large step in the direction of neutralizing the problem, but material culture offers a scholarly approach that is more specific and trustworthy than simple awareness. The study of systems of belief through an analysis of artifacts offers opportunities to circumvent the investigator's own cultural perspective. By undertaking cultural interpretation through artifacts, we can engage the other culture in the first instance not with our minds, the seat of our cultural biases, but with our senses. "This affective mode of apprehension through the senses that allows us to put ourselves, figuratively speaking, inside the skins of individuals who commissioned, made, used, or enjoyed these objects, to see with their eyes and touch with their hands, to identify with them empathetically, is clearly a different way of engaging the past than abstractly through the written word. Instead of our minds making intellectual contact with minds of the past, our senses make affective contact with senses of the past."[8]

The methodology of material culture, with its affective approach that aspires to the objectivity of scientific method, affords a procedure for overcoming the distortions of our particular cultural stance, and, of almost equal importance, it makes visible the otherwise invisible, unconscious biases of our own cultural perspective. Awareness of what one normally takes for granted occurs only in the forced confrontation with another norm. For example, we become particularly aware of gravity as gravity when it is not there, as in our observation of astronauts working in a spacecraft. When we identify with another culture through the affective, sensory apprehension of its artifacts, we have an opportunity to accept the other culture as the norm and become aware of the differentness, the special qualities, of our own culture. The culture being studied provides a platform, a new cultural stance, for a perspective on our culture. This can be of interest for its own sake, but specifically and practically in terms of the study of material culture, increasing awareness of the biases of one's own cultural perspective helps achieve objectivity in subsequent investigations.

The fact is that cultural perspective is only a problem or liability to the extent that one is unaware or unable to adjust for it. Indeed, it is our quarry, the cultural patterns of belief, of mind, that we seek.

Final Note

A disclaimer should be entered regarding the completeness of what can be learned from material culture. In certain instances—prehistoric or preliterate societies, for example—artifacts constitute the only surviving evidence, so there is little choice but to use them as best one can to determine cultural values as well as historical facts. But it would be a delusion to assume we acquire complete access to the belief systems of a culture through its material survival. Cultural expression is not limited to things. But the techniques of material culture should be part of the tool kit of the well-equipped cultural scholar. The obverse of this disclaimer is the argument advanced here: although the study of artifacts is only one route to the understanding of culture, it is a special, important, and qualitatively different route. An investigation that ignores material culture will be impoverished.

[...]

METHODOLOGY

How does one extract information about culture, about mind, from mute objects? We have been taught to retrieve information in abstract form, words and numbers, but most of us are functionally illiterate when it comes to interpreting information encoded in objects. Several academic disciplines, notably art history and archaeology, routinely work with artifacts as evidence and over the years have built up a considerable amount of theoretical and methodological expertise. Work done in these fields is often directed inward, toward the accumulation and explication of information required by the discipline itself. In the history of art this takes the form of resolving questions of stylistic and iconographic influence, of dating and authorship, of quality and authenticity. In archaeology it is the basic task of assembling, sorting, dating, and quantifying the assembled data. But art history and archaeology also have fundamental concerns with the cultures that produced the objects, and the methodologies of these two fields, to the extent that they provide means for the interpretation of culture, are essential to material culture. At present they are the two disciplines most directly relevant to the actual work of investigating material culture. But, as they are usually defined, they are not adequate to the total task. The exploration of patterns of belief and behavior, in an intellectual borderland where the interests of humanities and social sciences merge, requires an openness to other methodologies, including those of cultural and social history, cultural and social anthropology, psychohistory, sociology, cultural geography, folklore and folk life, and linguistics. But the approach to material culture set forth below dictates that these broader concerns and methodologies *not* be brought into play until the evidence of the artifact itself has been plumbed as objectively as possible. Therefore the first steps are most closely related to the basic descriptive techniques of art history and archaeology, and in this there is more overlap with the natural than with the social sciences. The initial descriptive steps in the approach to objects resembles fieldwork in a science such as geology, and description can also involve the use of scientific equipment.

The method of object analysis proposed below progresses through three stages. To keep the distorting biases of the investigator's cultural perspective in check, these stages must be undertaken in sequence and kept as discrete as possible. The analysis proceeds from *description,* recording the internal evidence of the object itself; to *deduction,* interpreting the interaction between the object and the perceiver; to *speculation,* framing hypotheses and questions which lead out from the object to external evidence for testing and resolution.[9]

Description

Description is restricted to what can be observed in the object itself, that is, to internal evidence.

In practice, it is desirable to begin with the largest, most comprehensive observations and progress systematically to more particular details. The terminology should be as accurate as possible; technical terms are fine as long as they can be understood. The analyst must, however, continually guard against the intrusion of either subjective assumptions or conclusions derived from other experience.

This is a synchronic exercise; the physical object is read at a particular moment in time. The object is almost certainly not identical to what it was when it was fabricated; time, weather, usage will all have taken their toll. At this stage no consideration is given to condition or to other diachronic technological, iconographic, or stylistic influences.

Substantial analysis. Description begins with substantial analysis, an account of the physical dimensions, material, and articulation of the object. To determine physical dimensions, the object is measured and perhaps weighed. The degree of precision depends on the interests of the investigator. If he will be considering a series of objects, a certain amount of precision is desirable, given the possible subsequent significance of and need for quantification. However, it is not desirable to carry decimals to the point of losing an immediate sense of dimension in a welter of numbers; real significance may lie in general measure, as with Glassie's discovery of the modal importance of spans and cubits in the vernacular architecture of Virginia.[10] Next comes a description of the materials—what they are, how extensively they are used, and the pattern of their distribution throughout the object. Finally, the ways in which the materials are put together in the fabrication of the object, the articulation, should be noted. For example, with fabrics one would look at the weave; with metals, the welding, soldering, riveting; with wood, the dovetails, dowels, miter joints, mortise-and-tenon joints, glue.

Substantial analysis is a descriptive physical inventory of the object. It is achieved with the assistance of whatever technical apparatus is appropriate and available. Simple tape measures and scales, ultraviolet lamps and infrared photographs, or complex electron microscopes and X-ray defraction machines are all basically enhancements of one's ability to perceive and take the measure of the physical properties and dimensions of the object.[11]

Content. The next step in description is analysis of content. The investigator is concerned simply with subject matter. This is usually a factor only with works of art or other decorated objects. The procedure is iconography in its simplest sense, a reading of overt representations. In the case of a painting, this may simply be what is represented, as if the work were a window on the world (or on some kind of world). Content may include decorative designs or motifs, inscriptions, coats of arms, or diagrams, engraved or embossed on metal, carved or painted on wood or stone, woven in textiles, molded or etched in glass.

Formal analysis. Finally, and very important, is analysis of the object's form or configuration, its visual character. It is useful to begin by describing the two-dimensional organization—lines and areas—either on the surface of a flat object or in elevations or sections through a solid object.[12] Next comes the three-dimensional organization of forms in space, whether actual in a three-dimensional object or represented in a pictorial object. Subsequently, other formal elements such as color, light, and texture should be analyzed with, as in the case of the initial description of materials, an account of their nature, extent, and pattern of distribution (rhythm) in each case. Determination of the degree of detail must be left to the discretion of the investigator; too much can be almost as bad as too little, the forest can be lost for the trees.

Deduction

The second stage of analysis moves from the object itself to the relationship between the object and the perceiver. It involves the empathetic linking of the material (actual) or represented world of the object with the perceiver's world of existence and experience. To put it another way, the analyst contemplates what it would be like to use or interact with the object, or, in the case of a representational object, to be transported empathetically into the depicted world. If conditions permit, he handles, lifts, uses, walks through, or experiments physically with the object. The paramount criterion for deductions drawn from this interaction is that they must meet the test of reasonableness and common sense; that is, most people, on the basis of their knowledge of the physical world and the evidence of their own life experience, should find the deductions to be unstrained interpretations of the evidence elicited by the description. If these deductions are not readily acceptable as reasonable, they must be considered hypothetical and deferred to the next stage.

Although the analyst in the deductive stage moves away from a concern solely with the internal evidence of the object and injects himself into the investigation, the process remains synchronic. Just as the object is only what it is at the moment of investigation, and as such may be more or less different than what it was when it was made, so too the analyst is what he is at the moment of investigation. Ten years hence he might respond differently to the object because of different interests and a different mix of life experiences near the surface of conscious awareness. The particular encounter between an object with its history and an individual with his history shapes the deductions. Neither is what they were nor what they may become. Yet the event does not occur within a vacuum. The object is at least in some ways what it was or bears some recognizable relationship to what it was; the same, although less germane, is true of the investigator. The object may not testify with complete accuracy about its culture, but it can divulge something. It is the analyst's task to find out what it can tell and, perhaps, deduce what it can no longer tell.

Sensory engagement. The first step in deduction is sensory experience of the object. If possible, one touches it to feel its texture and lifts it to know its heft. Where appropriate, consideration should be given to the physical adjustments a user would have to make to its size, weight, configuration, and texture. The experience of architecture or a townscape would involve sensory perceptions while moving through it. If the object is not accessible, then these things must be done imaginatively and empathetically. In the case of a picture, the engagement is necessarily empathetic; the analyst projects himself into the represented world (or, in Alois Riegl's sense, considers that the pictorial space continues into the viewer's world of existence) and records what he would see, hear, smell, taste, and feel.[13]

Intellectual engagement. The second step is intellectual apprehension of the object. With a tool or implement this is a consideration of what it does and how it does it, and in such cases may need to precede or accompany the sensory engagement. The degree of understanding at this stage (prior to the admission of external evidence) depends on the complexity of the object and the analyst's prior knowledge and experience. It is unnecessary to ignore what one knows and feign innocence for the appearance of objectivity, but it is desirable to test one's external knowledge to see if it can be deduced from the object itself and, if it cannot, to set that knowledge aside until the next stage.

In the case of a pictorial object, there are a number of questions that may be addressed to and answered by the object itself, especially if it is representational. What is the time of day? What is the season of the year? What is the effect on what is depicted of natural forces such as heat and cold or the pull of gravity? In the relation between the depicted world and our world, where are we positioned, what might we be doing, and what role, if any, might we play? How would we enter pictorial space? What transpired prior to the depicted moment? What may happen next?

Emotional response. Finally, there is the matter of the viewer's emotional response to the object. Reactions vary in kind, intensity, and specificity, but it is not uncommon to discover that what one

considered a subjective response is in fact widely shared. A particular object may trigger joy, fright, awe, perturbation, revulsion, indifference, curiosity, or other responses that can be quite subtly distinguished. These subjective reactions, difficult but by no means impossible to articulate, tend to be significant to the extent that they are generally shared. They point the way to specific insights when the analyst identifies the elements noted in the descriptive stage that have precipitated them.

I have stressed the importance of attempting to maintain rigorous discreteness and sequence in the stages of object analysis. In fact, this is difficult if not impossible to achieve. Deductions almost invariably creep into the initial description. These slips, usually unnoted by the investigator, are undesirable since they undercut objectivity. But in practice, while striving to achieve objectivity and to maintain the scientific method as an ideal, the investigator should not be so rigorous and doctrinaire in the application of methodological rigor as to inhibit the process. Vigilance, not martial law, is the appropriate attitude. Often an individual's subjective assumptions are not recognized as such until considerably later. In fact, it is instructive in regard to understanding one's own cultural biases, one's own cultural perspective, to mark those assumptions that remain undetected the longest in the descriptive stage. These are often the most deeply rooted cultural assumptions.

Speculation

Having progressed from the object itself in description to the interaction between object and perceiver in deduction, the analysis now moves completely to the mind of the perceiver, to speculation. There are few rules or proscriptions at this stage. What is desired is as much creative imagining as possible, the free association of ideas and perceptions tempered only, and then not too quickly, by the analyst's common sense and judgment as to what is even vaguely plausible.

Theories and hypotheses. The first step in speculation is to review the information developed in the descriptive and deductive stages and to formulate hypotheses. This is the time of summing up what has been learned from the internal evidence of the object itself, turning those data over in one's mind, developing theories that might explain the various effects observed and felt. Speculation takes place in the mind of the investigator, and his cultural stance now becomes a major factor. However, since the objective and deductive evidence is already in hand, this cultural bias has little distorting effect. Indeed, it is an asset rather than a liability; it fuels the creative work that now must take place. Because of cultural perspective, it is impossible to respond to and interpret the object in exactly the same way as did the fabricating society, or any other society that may have been exposed to and reacted to the object during its history and perigrinations. Where there is a common response, it provides an affective insight into the cultural values of another society. Where there is divergence, the distinctive cultural perspective of our society can illuminate unseen and even unconscious aspects of the other culture. There was gravity before Newton; there was economic determinism before Marx; there was sex before Freud. We are free to use the insights afforded by our cultural and historical perspective, as long as we do not make the mistake of assigning intentionality or even awareness to the fabricating culture. Our cultural distance from the culture of the object precludes affective experience of those beliefs that are at variance with our own belief systems, but the process now begun can lead to the recovery of some of those beliefs. That is a goal of the exercise.

Program of research. The second step in the speculative stage is developing a program for validation, that is, a plan for scholarly investigation of questions posed by the material evidence. This shifts the inquiry from analysis of internal evidence to the search for and investigation of external evidence. Now the methodologies and techniques of various disciplines can be brought into play according to the nature of the questions raised and the skills and inclinations of the scholar.

The object is not abandoned after the preliminary analysis—description, deduction, speculation—is complete and the investigation has moved to external evidence. There should be continual shunting back and forth between the outside evidence and the artifact as research suggests to the investigator the need for more descriptive information or indicates other hypotheses that need to be tested affectively.

[…]

NOTES

Extracted from J. Prown, "Mind in Matter: An Introduction to Material Culture Theory and Method," *Winterthur Portfolio* 17, no. 1 (1982): 1–4 and 7–10. Reprinted by permission of The University of Chicago Press on behalf of The Henry Francis du Pont Winterthur Museum.

1. There are material culture studies that do not require object analysis, in part because they address questions posed by the very existence of artifacts that lead directly to the consideration of external evidence. This is particularly true of socio-economic studies that deal with artifacts abstractly, often statistically, to address issues of class, patronage, patterns of usage, levels of technology, availability of materials, means of distribution, and so on.

2. For example, poetry, because more abstract, is considered loftier than prose, chess than wrestling, or the practice of law than collecting garbage. In the world of scholarship the more abstract subjects—mathematics, philosophy, literature—are more highly regarded than concrete and practical subjects such as engineering. Such ordering takes place even within the material realm of artifacts where all things are not equal. Higher value has been attached to works of art than to utilitarian craft objects since the Renaissance when a distinction was made between the arts, which require intellectual activity and creative imagination in their making, and the crafts, which require greater

physical exertion and mechanical ingenuity. Even in a specific art such as painting, there has long been an ordering of genres, ranging from history painting, which springs from the painter's imagination, at the top of the scale, to still-life painting, the replication of worldly objects, at the bottom. In architecture, the mental activity of design has been considered an appropriate pursuit for gentlemen (for example, Thomas Jefferson), while the actual physical labor of building has been carried out by laborers of the lower classes. In sculpture in the nineteenth century, the realization of the form indwelling in the marble was the work of the artist; hacking out replications was the work of stonemasons.

3. See the section on veracity below.
4. Jules David Prown, "Style as Evidence," *Winterthur Portfolio* 15, no. 3 (Autumn 1980): 208. Peter Gay has observed that "the most undramatic work of art presents precisely the same causal puzzles as the eruption of a war, the making of a treaty, or the rise of a class" (*Art and Act: On Causes in History—Manet, Gropius, Mondrian* [New York: Harper & Row, 1976], p. 3).
5. Henry Glassie, "Meaningful Things and Appropriate Myths: The Artifact's Place in American Studies," in *Prospects: An Annual of American Cultural Studies,* ed. Jack Salzman, vol. 3 (New York: Burt Franklin, 1977), pp. 29–30.
6. For an extended discussion of this issue, see Prown, "Style as Evidence," esp. pp. 197–200.
7. Arnold Hauser, "Sociology in Art," in *Marxism and Art: Writings in Aesthetics and Criticism,* ed. Berel Lang and Forrest William (New York: David McKay Co., 1972), p. 272.
8. Prown, "Style as Evidence," p. 208.
9. The issue of sequence undoubtedly needs further study. I am aware that the insistence upon strict adherence to a particular series of steps seems rigid and arbitrary, an uncalled-for fettering of the investigator. Yet, I have come to

appreciate the virtues of sequence empirically on the basis of considerable classroom experience with artifact analysis. It simply works better. The closer the sequence suggested below is followed, especially in regard to the major stages, and the greater the care taken with each analytical step before proceeding, the more penetrating, complex, and satisfying the final interpretation. Obviously, the procedure is time-consuming, and there is a natural impatience to move along. My experience has been, however, that this should be resisted until the analysis is exhausted and the obvious next question requires advancing to the next step.

10. Henry Glassie, *Folk Housing in Middle Virginia: A Structural Analysis of Historic Artifacts* (Knoxville: University of Tennessee Press, 1975).
11. The procedures outlined here for collecting internal evidence have other significant applications. Physical analysis, including the use of scientific apparatus, can provide crucial information in regard to authenticity. Other procedures noted below, notably formal analysis, can also be exceedingly useful in determining authenticity. These applications of the methodology can take place at any time, but it is preferable for the issue of authenticity to be resolved before the analysis proceeds beyond *description.* If a material culture investigator is to arrive at cultural conclusions on the basis of material evidence, the specimen being studied *must* be an authentic product of the culture in question. The investigator must determine what aspects of the objects, if any, are not authentic products of the presumed culture. A fake may be a useful artifact in relation to the culture that produced the fake, but it is deceptive in relation to the feigned culture.
12. The procedures of formal analysis summarized briefly here will be familiar to any art historian. They are not, however, arcane, and investigators need not be specially trained.

Formal analysis is a matter of articulating and recording what one sees, preferably in a systematic sequence as suggested here.

13. See Sheldon Nodelman, "Structural Analysis in Art and Anthropology," in *Structuralism,* ed. Jacques Ehrmann (Garden City, N.Y.: Anchor Books/Doubleday, 1970), p. 87. This splendid article sets forth succinctly the basis for contemporary structural analysis in the early art historical work of the German school of *Strukturforschung,* especially as initiated by Riegl and developed by Guido von Kaschnitz-Weinberg, and the *anthropologie structurale* of Claude Lévi-Strauss.

34

THE ARTEFACT AS MANUFACTURED OBJECT

Daniel Miller

The factor which distinguishes the artefact from the natural object is that it is the product of human labour. Although structuralism, in its extension of the Kantian position, has constantly asserted the cultural nature of those natural phenomena which impinge upon us only through being assimilated by our own categorizing processes, these may still be differentiated from artefacts, within which such a system of categorization is an inherent attribute. In formulating the category 'artefact', some notion of intention is also usually attributed to their creation; for example, a gas cloud may emerge as an unpredicted by-product of a technological process, though this product of human labour is only marginally an artefact.

Since manufacture always has to be practised upon materials, its first implication is that it may show signs of the constraints these materials bring to the technological process (Gombrich 1979: 63–94). Some materials, such as stone or wood, are largely subtractive, in that there is a natural substance from which parts are taken away, through chipping, sawing and other means, to create the finished artefact; while others, such as cast metal or clay, are additive, in that a quantity is utilized in a plastic state which can take the shape of a template or mould. Any such artefact may seek either to proclaim or to hide the material used and the constraints the material has imposed upon the technological process: a mask may be thought to incorporate the spiritual properties of the wood from which it is taken; a group of people may refuse to purchase an item known

to be of seal skin; a plastic may seek to copy a more traditional material; the gold from which an object is made may have far greater significance than the actual form into which it has been hammered.

In a society with a relatively unpronounced division of labour, it may be difficult to distinguish manufacture as a separate arena of social relations which are specifically signified by its products. As in the case of the construction of canoes for the Kula (Munn 1977), technology may be thoroughly embedded in cosmology, and even social theorists who would eschew a technological determinism, but wish to characterize societies through more mediated concepts such as 'modes of production', have often had to subordinate the organization of production to a host of other elements of social organization such as kinship and ritual (e.g. Godelier 1972; Hindless and Hirst 1975; Kahn and Llobera eds 1981).

An insight into the relationship which may be found between technology and cultural form in such societies is offered by the argument formulated by Franz Boas (1955) concerning the origins of primitive art (see also Gombrich 1979). Boas identified two major sources for this art: the drive towards representation and the tendency to create pattern. The latter, he suggested, stems from the basic motor-habits involved in simple technological processes which revolve around regular and repetitive movements, such as those of the hand in sewing, basketry, or weaving. These sequences may give rise to a kind of play, in which they are exaggerated, inverted or otherwise re-ordered in such a manner that a regular pattern or rhythm emerges in the finished product. The interplay between these sequences and the tendency either to see representational figures in pattern, or alternatively to repeat representational figures in such a way that they reduce to pattern, was held by Boas to be the foundation of art and design, providing the basic dimensions which united the diverse media of craft production, music, dance and poetry.

Using material from the Kwakiutl peoples of the north-west coast of America, Boas showed how the major stylistic features of their material culture, such as an extensive use of bilateral symmetry and the disintegration of animal representations into pattern, could be understood as emerging from the interplay of technology and constraint. For example, the problem of representing three-dimensional figures in two dimensions lent itself to the splitting of animal forms so that they faced out in both directions, joined by a centre line around the mouth and spine. In turn, these tended to become complex and ambiguous images such that, as anthropomorphized animals, they could represent the transformation of human and animal forms (Vastokas 1978), or through the focus upon the mouth could illustrate the principle of voracity according to which human killing and eating of animals ensured the cyclic reproduction of all life in the world (Walens 1981). Here, then, manufacture as technology involving materials with certain properties becomes an integral part of the emergence of culture incorporating the visual embodiment of the nature and legitimacy of a certain social order, which in turn forms part of an encompassing ontology (Goldman 1975: chapter nine).

With a more developed division of labour, and particularly with industrial production, the separation of the sphere of manufacture, as found, for example, in Marx's privileging of this particular domain, has tended to become more pronounced. An object may then become a conspicuous example of non-industrial production, such as the homespun *Khadi* cloth of India popularized by Gandhi as a symbol of Indian independence, and still a potent emblem for Indian political parties (Bayly 1986). The nineteenth-century arts and crafts movement developed by William Morris and others was also successful in advertising the hand-crafted status of their products. This kind of 'natural' product gains its meaning entirely from its opposition to industrialization, and is thus always indirectly produced by industrialization. The contradictory nature of this relationship is illustrated by the experiences of a community of potters in Japan, who, through the equivalent of the arts and crafts movement, were held as exemplifying a natural, anonymous and traditional form of production. When publicized as such through a visit by the British potter Bernard Leach and Japanese enthusiasts, however, the potters were forced to adopt new forms of marketing and production in order to meet the demand for these symbols of their purity, whilst at the same time preserving for the benefit of the tourists, the appearance of producing works of art untainted by industrialization (Moeran 1984). As is evident from the writing of Hegel, Marx and many later writers, technology itself, as the deliberate imposition of rational will upon the world, may become the foundation for the dominant ideologies of the industrialized world (e.g. Castoriadis 1984: 299–59).

These cases suggest that when manufacture as the signified of the object becomes reified as having a separate and particular connotation, it is not the actual process of manufacture which is of importance, but the ability of the object to stand for a particular form of production and its attendant social relations. The object has always had the ability to proclaim one technological origin while actually deriving from another. The *skeumorph*, in which, for example, a stone blade copies the style of a metal object, is a classic find in archaeological excavations of early bronze age sites. With the development of machinery, the mass produced object intended to disguise its origins and look like the product of hand labour has become well established. In many cases, this symbolism is part of a more general ability to proclaim or deny a distance from nature.

Although the artefact may stand for a particular form of production, it cannot be assumed that it will do so, or that the divisions which appear as significant from one perspective upon modern society will necessarily emerge as the major dimensions of differentiation in the object world. It might be thought, for example, that the major distinction between socialist and capitalist development, terms which are founded in contrasting philosophies of the proper relations of production, would be a prime subject for the symbolic capacity of the modern artefact. In practice, when making a purchase, it is very rare for us to note whether an object is made by a cooperative or a private factory, or in East or West Germany, and extraordinarily this division appears hardly, if at all, within the major symbolic dimensions of the contemporary world of commodities. We do not think in terms of capitalist shoes and socialist shoes. From this example, we can draw a conclusion of crucial importance for the analysis of material culture: divisions which may appear important in language and ideology may be absent from object differentiation, while distinctions within the domain of artefacts may constitute important divisions which would elsewhere be ignored or denied.

ARTEFACTS AND FUNCTION

In no domain is it as difficult as it is in the matter of function and utility to distinguish the actual place of artefacts in human practices from the particular legitimations and assumptions we have about them. In many societies, the classification and labeling of objects appears to indicate a close relationship between artefact and particular function, and the labels 'kitchen chair' or 'frying-pan' in Britain may be matched, for example, by an equivalent close relationship between pots and their labels in Nepal (Birmingham 1975). Function appears to play a key role in infant

recognition and naming of objects (Miller and Johnson-Laird 1976: 229–35), and, in adulthood, continues to play an important, though highly flexible, role in the description of objects in daily life (Miller 1978). What is problematic about this is the common assumption that it is caused by, and in turn indicates, some relationship of efficiency between the object and its use, such that this is the prime reason for its particular form, being either the natural outcome of adaptation, or the product of deliberate design processes for industrial goods.

Although functional purpose must impose a certain constraint on the shape and form of an object, that constraint is generally a very loose one for everyday forms (though obviously not for machine parts). A moment's reflection upon the several hundred different shapes of glass bottle in an off licence, all of which serve essentially the same purpose of containing liquids, or upon the variety of clothing in the high street, or china in the store, indicates this high degree of variability. Even though the individual shopper will often find some functional justification for his or her particular choice, as being especially practical, other reasons, some of which will be analysed in later chapters, may be adduced, relating to social rather than functional considerations which may more convincingly account for the majority of purchases.

While for some this may be evident enough in the society of mass consumption, it has equally commonly been assumed that this degree of variability is an aberrant result of the wastage of modern capitalism, and that the 'pristine' subjects of social anthropology live in a far closer relationship with the given needs of their environment (e.g. Forde 1934). The vast arrays of artefacts to be found in ethnographic museums which serve as simple vessels or clothing are, however, eloquent evidence for the distance between form and function in non-industrial as well as industrial societies. In parts of Melanesia such as the Solomon Islands, for example, relatively homogeneous tropical forest may be the setting for an extreme variety of cultural forms, such as spears or armbands, as one moves across an island archipelago. Detailed observation of the hand-made containers used in a South Asian village reveals a wide variety of forms designed to serve identical purposes, and a very loose relationship between form and fitness for function (Miller 1985: 51–74).

Just as with manufacture, the artefact may be used to express not actual efficiency but an ideal of function. In modern practices, this ideal has been conceived of as a principle of utility, to be embodied in the creation of the artefactual world. With modernism, the strongest assertion of the value of utility is found in the assumption that aesthetics may be subordinated to function. The proper modernist artefact is always held to be aesthetically pleasing precisely to the degree to which it exemplifies the adage that form follows function (Benton and Benton 1975). However, the actual reproduction of modernist form over the last century and a half has revealed exactly the opposite tendency, since objects formed entirely on the basis of utility have proved singularly unattractive (which accounts for their general absence from commercial marketing). This has not in any way curtailed enthusiasm for the principle that good design is based upon utility among its acolytes in London's Design Centre or the Boilerhouse Project of the Victoria and Albert Museum, London, where beauty through ergonomics may still be an avowed aim.

Once again, this division does not accord with political affiliation; Baudrillard attacks Marx and Marxist assertions of natural utility with as much vehemence as contemporary critics attack modernist architecture as an elitist imposition of ideology upon the general public. This embodiment of utility and technological rationality in the object as modernist form may be a powerful example of the much more general tendency towards the legitimizing role being played by technological rationality in the modern world (e.g. Habermas 1970; Sahlins 1976a). In movements such as 'hi-tech', objects most clearly come to exhibit a principle of utility quite detached from

any consideration of actual purpose, as the style is applied (as was streamlining in its day) indiscriminately to steam irons or armchairs. With hi-tech style, as with much of modernism, it is evident that the theoretical articulation of these principles is far less developed than their material expression. Indeed, hi-tech could be better understood as a set of principles distilled from a collection of material forms than as objects intended to embody prior principles.

The object form which has always been seen as most clearly exemplifying the utility principle is the tool. Tools, after all, extend the very possibility of humanity as productive agent, and thus make for obvious analogies with biological function. When understood as our 'extra-somatic means of adaption [sic]' they have become almost definitional of culture (White 1959). This notion of the instrumental object as an extension of being should not, however, be reduced to a relationship of efficiency, since an agriculturalist may wax more lyrical about a musical instrument than a plough, and the microcomputer's popularity may be greater among those who in common parlance 'waste time' in obsessive programming or games, than among those who use it as a practical means to some other end. It is the object's relationship to the social group which is crucial, rather than its ability to perform a transformation of nature under the sign of utility.

The artefact's capacity to separate itself from the immediacy of a relationship embodied in the concept of utility is most evident in the manner in which it is used for precisely the opposite function, that is, to separate the individual from productive activity. Although one means of detachment from the world is a spiritual asceticism based upon a lack of material possessions, more common has been the desire to accumulate luxuries and objects which themselves signify the lack of any need to engage directly in productive labour. The object's ornate and fragile form is an emblem of the leisure class which is constituted precisely by this distance (Veblen 1970). Civilization is most commonly defined not as greater efficiency in crop-growing and manufacture, but precisely as the preservation of distance from these activities.

ARTEFACTS, THE SELF AND SOCIETY

One of the limitations of anthropological investigations of the social meaning of artefacts is the tendency to Romanticize non-industrial societies as prior to objectification in the Marxist sense of rupture. The classic statement on this question with respect to the person was by Mauss (1979), who argued that the contemporary concept of the self is a relatively recent creation, strongly tied to the rise of various legalistic notions of the person in relation to property in ancient Rome and emerging in its modern form after certain developments in eighteenth-century German philosophy. Recent objectivist approaches in the social sciences and philosophy have attempted to equate all reference to the self with a particular and historical bourgeois self inextricably related to capitalism. Anthropologists, in turn, have attempted to argue that, for example, the transition from brideservice, in which labour is performed by the prospective groom, to bridewealth, where objects are given in exchange for the bride, marks a significant difference in the development of a phenomenon whereby objects may stand for human labour, with the implication that this is the first stage towards the conditions of property and alienation as we know them today (Strathern 1985). This theme, which relates the development of individualism and alienability specifically to *homo economicus,* has been a longstanding concern in philosophical and political anthropology (e.g. Dumont 1977).

Although we may find a particularly explicit conceptualization of the autonomous self in certain contemporary societies, this may be only an aspect of the more general separation and autonomy of concepts evident in modernist theory. While some capitalist societies may practise an extreme individualism, it is surely only a Romantic tendency to dichotomize which denies the possibility

of this characteristic to all other societies. The specific objectification of a moral and juridical individual through the use of objects may be found in a wide range of societies, including those where kinship rather than the economy appears to be the dominant organizational principle.

The phenomenon of certain mundane objects becoming so firmly associated with an individual that they are understood as literal extensions of that individual's being was discussed in some detail by Levy-Bruhl (1966: 100–27). In many societies, the clothing, ornaments and tools belonging to an individual may be considered so integral to him or her that to touch or do harm to these inanimate objects is considered indistinguishable from taking the same action against the person. Such property is identical to the person and may stand for that person in his or her absence. It may well be burnt together with the corpse as an equal form of the physical detritus of death. The 'self' objectified in the object will be differentially constructed according to the cosmological context. Tambiah (1984) has recently described an example of the transformation from one form of embodiment to another in Thailand, where buddhist amulets objectifying the charisma of forest saints are exploited by certain individuals as a means of gaining material advantage in their business dealings in the city.

As was noted in chapter 4 with respect to recent work on the *hau,* by embodying ancestral links objects may be the basis of an individual's present social identity such that loss of the object would itself constitute a danger to the legitimacy and viability of the personage and the group he or she leads (Wiener 1985). At the other extreme, societies may allow claims upon that which we consider inalienable. For example, in areas of the South Pacific it is not uncommon for parents to have to relinquish a new baby to admiring kin who have claimed it (Sahlins 1976b; Silk 1980). It is more useful to argue the variable nature of the relationship between the individual and society than to assume a linear evolution towards the autonomous self. Even between societies which may be subsumed under the label of late capitalism, such as the USA and Japan, there may be considerable differences in this regard (Abercrombie et al. 1986)

Anthropological discussion of this relationship between self, object and society is dominated by the more general analysis of exchange. Until recently, emphasis was most commonly placed on the object as gift in the tradition of Mauss, but some consideration is now also being given to what is too often taken merely as the gift's antithesis, that is the commodity. Appadurai (1986) provides a survey of some of the relevant literature, pointing out that in some respects commodities are not necessarily as divorced from wider cultural considerations as is often supposed. Almost all societies have elements of an exchange of objects in which persons are directly implicated, market exchange in which they are not implicated, and separate spheres of exchange which constrain the equivalences between things (e.g. Douglas 1967; Miller 1986).

Mauss's underlying concern was with individualism as an aspect of the fragmentation and disembedded nature of capitalist society. The problem is not, however, unique to capitalism. The fundamental opposition which may erupt between economy and society was noted by Simmel, who observed that the merchant is identified with the relative autonomy and abstraction of flexible exchange and is therefore often, as 'stranger', held in an ambiguous and partially anomalous relation to the host society (e.g. Simmel 1950: 402–8). Indeed, Parry has recently argued that it is only under the conditions of a relatively free market that there is evidence for the entirely disinterested gift, in which calculation should be entirely absent, this being a product of the same emergent duality (Parry 1986).

Any consideration of the relationship between commodities and persons is overshadowed by the concept of property which, as Sartre (1969: 575–600), Simmel (1978: 306), and others have noted, cannot be separated from the basic relationship between being and having. In turn,

discussion on this topic often focuses less upon the effect of property relations today than on the links established between property as an institution and Locke's concepts of individuality and natural rights, and, in turn, Marx's critique of private property. Unfortunately, the particular division most often invoked in contemporary political rhetoric concerning private and public property is misleading with regard to this issue, since the concept of private property suggests a close relationship between person and thing, whilst in practice private property is an institution which works to produce precisely the opposite effect. Private property as a notion conflates the direct relationship between the individual and those objects with which he or she is associated in self-construction with those over which he or she has legal rights. As an institution, private property is the foundation of abstract relationships between anonymous people and postulated objects, an extreme example of which is the relationship between shareholder and investment. In terms of the legalistic concept of private property, an individual is able to own an object with which he or she may have no personal relationship, thus preventing others from realizing their potential for achieving such a relationship. The claim to legitimacy of particular possession is based entirely upon the institutionalization of rights.

With respect to the object as objectification it might be better to use a term such as personal property, which assumes a genuinely self-productive relationship between persons and objects. The classic case of private property would than become not home ownership but the ownership of somebody else's home. The confusion of private and personal property as the subject of criticism has led most people, who for good reason wish to defend property with which they are intimately associated also to defend institutions which may result in their alienation from such property. People wishing to own their council house may thereby be led to believe mistakenly, that the present institutionalization of private property is in their interests.

Using a concept such as objectification, in which the cultural nature of the subject-object relationship is brought to the fore, the lines of this particular debate might be redrawn with important political consequences. Personal property is best linked with communal rather than private property, such as state or kin-held property, since it is a statement of relative inalienability, such that the social subject, individual or collective, associated with the object retains control over the conditions under which it may be alienated.

NOTE

Extracted from D. Miller, *Material Culture and Mass Consumption* (London: Blackwell, 1987), pp. 112–21. Reprinted by permission of John Wiley & Sons, Inc.

35

PANOPTICISM

Michel Foucault

Bentham's *Panopticon* is the architectural figure of this composition. We know the principle on which it was based: at the periphery, an annular building; at the centre, a tower; this tower is pierced with wide windows that open onto the inner side of the ring; the peripheric building is divided into cells, each of which extends the whole width of the building; they have two windows, one on the inside, corresponding to the windows of the tower; the other, on the outside, allows the light to cross the cell from one end to the other. All that is needed, then, is to place a supervisor in a central tower and to shut up in each cell a madman, a patient, a condemned man, a worker or a schoolboy. By the effect of backlighting, one can observe from the tower, standing out precisely against the light, the small captive shadows in the cells of the periphery. They are like so many cages, so many small theatres, in which each actor is alone, perfectly individualized and constantly visible. The panoptic mechanism arranges spatial unities that make it possible to see constantly and to recognize immediately. In short, it reverses the principle of the dungeon; or rather of its three functions—to enclose, to deprive of light and to hide—it preserves only the first and eliminates the other two. Full lighting and the eye of a supervisor capture better than darkness, which ultimately protected. Visibility is a trap.

To begin with, this made it possible—as a negative effect—to avoid those compact, swarming, howling masses that were to be found in places of confinement, those painted by Goya or described by Howard. Each individual, in his place, is securely confined to a cell from which he is seen from the front by the supervisor; but the side walls prevent him from coming into contact with his companions. He is seen, but he does not see; he is the object of information, never a subject in communication. The arrangement of his room, opposite the central tower, imposes on him an axial visibility; but the divisions of the ring, those separated cells, imply a lateral invisibility. And this invisibility is a guarantee of order. If the inmates are convicts, there is no danger of a plot, an attempt at collective escape, the planning of new crimes for the future, bad reciprocal influences; if they are patients, there is no danger of contagion; if they are madmen there is no risk of their committing violence upon one another; if they are schoolchildren, there is no copying, no noise, no chatter, no waste of time; if they are workers, there are no disorders, no theft, no coalitions, none of those distractions that slow down the rate of work, make it less perfect or cause accidents. The crowd, a compact mass, a locus of multiple exchanges, individualities merging together, a collective effect, is abolished and replaced by a collection of separated individualities. From the point of view of the guardian, it is replaced by a multiplicity that can be numbered and supervised; from the point of view of the inmates, by a sequestered and observed solitude (Bentham, 60–64).

Hence the major effect of the Panopticon: to induce in the inmate a state of conscious and permanent visibility that assures the automatic functioning of power. So to arrange things that the surveillance is permanent in its effects, even if it is discontinuous in its action; that the perfection of power should tend to render its actual exercise unnecessary; that this architectural apparatus should be a machine for creating and sustaining a power relation independent of the person who exercises it; in short, that the inmates should be caught up in a power situation of which they are themselves the bearers. To achieve this, it is at once too much and too little that the prisoner should be constantly observed by an inspector: too little, for what matters is that he knows himself to be observed; too much, because he has no need in fact of being so. In view of this, Bentham laid down the principle that power should be visible and unverifiable. Visible: the inmate will constantly have before his eyes the tall outline of the central tower from which he is spied upon. Unverifiable: the inmate must never know whether he is being looked at at any one moment; but he must be sure that he may always be so. In order to make the presence or absence of the inspector unverifiable, so that the prisoners, in their cells, cannot even see a shadow, Bentham envisaged not only venetian blinds on the windows of the central observation hall, but, on the inside, partitions that intersected the hall at right angles and, in order to pass from one quarter to the other, not doors but zig-zag openings; for the slightest noise, a gleam of light, a brightness in a half-opened door would betray the presence of the guardian.[1] The Panopticon is a machine

Image 13   Security cameras. Photograph by Tyler McCully.

for dissociating the see/being seen dyad: in the peripheric ring, one is totally seen, without ever seeing; in the central tower, one sees everything without ever being seen.[2]

It is an important mechanism, for it automatizes and disindividualizes power. Power has its principle not so much in a person as in a certain concerted distribution of bodies, surfaces, lights, gazes; in an arrangement whose internal mechanisms produce the relation in which individuals are caught up. The ceremonies, the rituals, the marks by which the sovereign's surplus power was manifested are useless. There is a machinery that assures dissymmetry, disequilibrium, difference. Consequently, it does not matter who exercises power. Any individual, taken almost at random, can operate the machine: in the absence of the director, his family, his friends, his visitors, even his servants (Bentham, 45). Similarly, it does not matter what motive animates him: the curiosity of the indiscreet, the malice of a child, the thirst for knowledge of a philosopher who wishes to visit this museum of human nature, or the perversity of those who take pleasure in spying and punishing. The more numerous those anonymous and temporary observers are, the greater the risk for the inmate of being surprised and the greater his anxious awareness of being observed. The Panopticon is a marvelous machine which, whatever use one may wish to put it to, produces homogeneous effects of power.

A real subjection is born mechanically from a fictitious relation. So it is not necessary to use force to constrain the convict to good behaviour, the madman to calm, the worker to work, the schoolboy to application, the patient to the observation of the regulations. Bentham was surprised that panoptic institutions could be so light: there were no more bars, no more chains, no more heavy locks; all that was needed was that the separations should be clear and the openings well arranged. The heaviness of the old 'houses of security', with their fortress-like architecture, could be replaced by the simple, economic geometry of a 'house of certainty'. The efficiency of power, its

constraining force have, in a sense, passed over to the other side—to the side of its surface of application. He who is subjected to a field of visibility, and who knows it, assumes responsibility for the constraints of power; he makes them play spontaneously upon himself; he inscribes in himself the power relation in which he simultaneously plays both roles; he becomes the principle of his own subjection. By this very fact, the external power may throw off its physical weight; it tends to the non-corporal; and, the more it approaches this limit, the more constant, profound and permanent are its effects: it is a perpetual victory that avoids any physical confrontation and which is always decided in advance.

Bentham does not say whether he was inspired, in his project, by Le Vaux's menagerie at Versailles: the first menagerie in which the different elements are not, as they traditionally were, distributed in a park (Loisel, 504–7). At the centre was an octagonal pavilion which, on the first floor, consisted of only a single room, the king's salon; on every side large windows looked out onto seven cages (the eighth side was reserved for the entrance), containing different species of animals. By Bentham's time, this menagerie had disappeared. But one finds in the programme of the Panopticon a similar concern with individualizing observation, with characterization and classification, with the analytical arrangement of space. The Panopticon is a royal menagerie; the animal is replaced by man, individual distribution by specific grouping and the king by the machinery of a furtive power. With this exception, the Panopticon also does the work of a naturalist. It makes it possible to draw up differences: among patients, to observe the symptoms of each individual, without the proximity of beds, the circulation of miasmas, the effects of contagion confusing the clinical tables; among schoolchildren, it makes it possible to observe performances (without there being any imitation or copying), to map aptitudes, to assess characters, to draw up rigorous classifications and, in relation to normal development, to distinguish 'laziness and stubbornness' from

MICHEL FOUCAULT, Panopticism | 241

'incurable imbecility'; among workers, it makes it possible to note the aptitudes of each worker, compare the time he takes to perform a task, and if they are paid by the day, to calculate their wages (Bentham, 60–64).

So much for the question of observation. But the Panopticon was also a laboratory; it could be used as a machine to carry out experiments, to alter behaviour, to train or correct individuals. To experiment with medicines and monitor their effects. To try out different punishments on prisoners, according to their crimes and character, and to seek the most effective ones. To teach different techniques simultaneously to the workers, to decide which is the best. To try out pedagogical experiments—and in particular to take up once again the well-debated problem of secluded education, by using orphans. One would see what would happen when, in their sixteenth or eighteenth year, they were presented with other boys or girls; one could verify whether, as Helvetius thought, anyone could learn anything; one would follow 'the genealogy of every observable idea'; one could bring up different children according to different systems of thought, making certain children believe that two and two do not make four or that the moon is a cheese, then put them together when they are twenty or twenty-five years old; one would then have discussions that would be worth a great deal more than the sermons or lectures on which so much money is spent; one would have at least an opportunity of making discoveries in the domain of metaphysics. The Panopticon is a privileged place for experiments on men, and for analysing with complete certainty the transformations that may be obtained from them. The Panopticon may even provide an apparatus for supervising its own mechanisms. In this central tower, the director may spy on all the employees that he has under his orders: nurses, doctors, foremen, teachers, warders; he will be able to judge them continuously, alter their behaviour, impose upon them the methods he thinks best; and it will even be possible to observe the director himself. An inspector arriving unexpectedly at the centre of the Panopticon will be able to judge at a glance, without anything being concealed from him, how the entire establishment is functioning. And, in any case, enclosed as he is in the middle of this architectural mechanism, is not the director's own fate entirely bound up with it? The incompetent physician who has allowed contagion to spread, the incompetent prison governor or workshop manager will be the first victims of an epidemic or a revolt. '"By every tie I could devise", said the master of the Panopticon, "my own fate had been bound up by me with theirs"' (Bentham, 177). The Panopticon functions as a kind of laboratory of power. Thanks to its mechanisms of observation, it gains in efficiency and in the ability to penetrate into men's behaviour; knowledge follows the advances of power, discovering new objects of knowledge over all the surfaces on which power is exercised.

The plague-stricken town, the panoptic establishment—the differences are important. They mark, at a distance of a century and a half, the transformations of the disciplinary programme. In the first case, there is an exceptional situation: against an extraordinary evil, power is mobilized; it makes itself everywhere present and visible; it invents new mechanisms; it separates, it immobilizes, it partitions; it constructs for a time what is both a counter-city and the perfect society; it imposes an ideal functioning, but one that is reduced, in the final analysis, like the evil that it combats, to a simple dualism of life and death: that which moves brings death, and one kills that which moves. The Panopticon, on the other hand, must be understood as a generalizable model of functioning; a way of defining power relations in terms of the everyday life of men. No doubt Bentham presents it as a particular institution, closed in upon itself. Utopias, perfectly closed in upon themselves, are common enough. As opposed to the ruined prisons, littered with mechanisms of torture, to be seen in Piranese's engravings, the Panopticon presents a cruel, ingenious cage. The fact that it should have given rise, even in our own time, to so many variations, projected or realized,

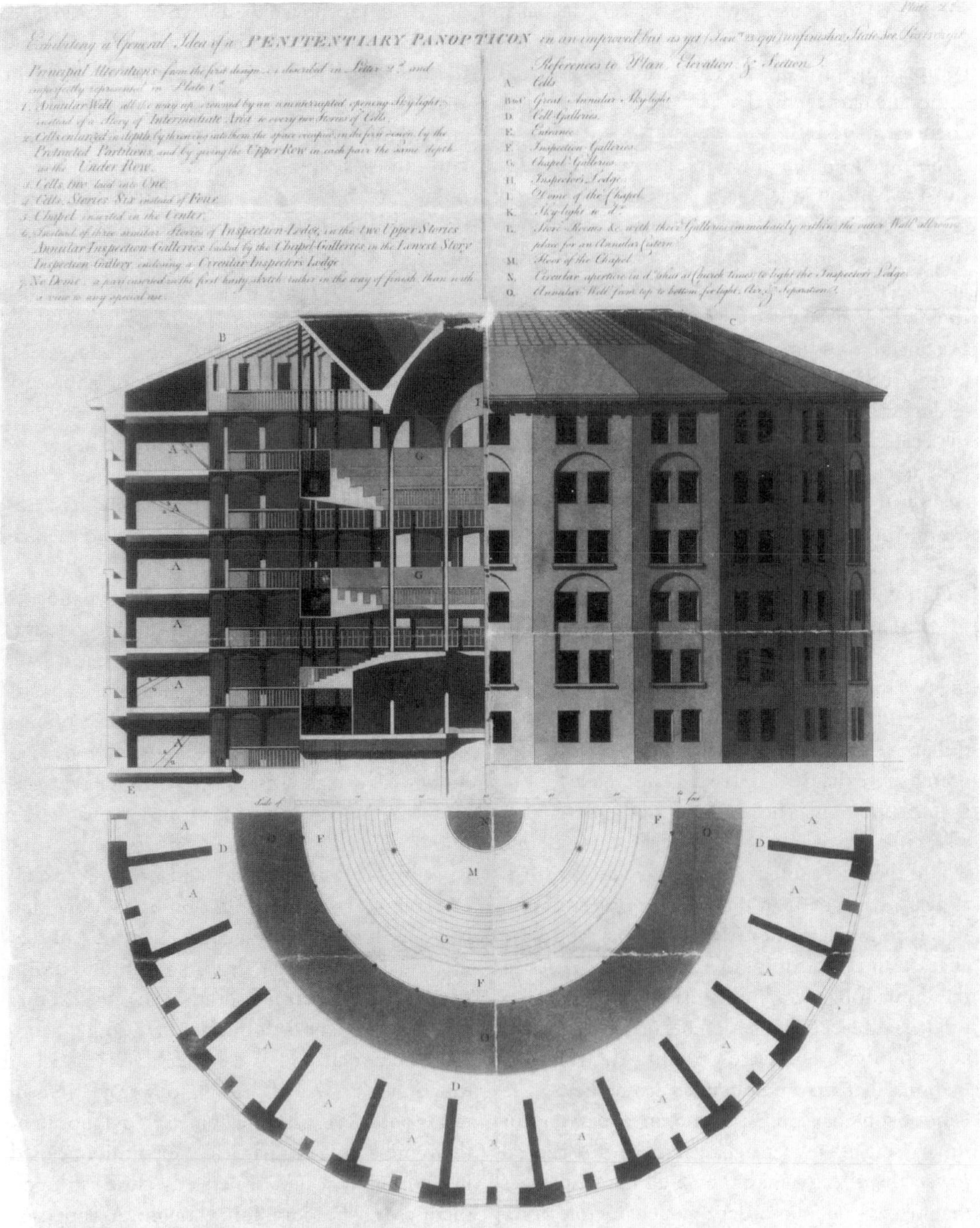

Image 14   Jeremy Bentham, Panopticon. Courtesy of University College, London.

is evidence of the imaginary intensity that it has possessed for almost two hundred years. But the Panopticon must not be understood as a dream building: it is the diagram of a mechanism of power reduced to its ideal form; its functioning, abstracted from any obstacle, resistance or friction, must be represented as a pure architectural and optical system: it is in fact a figure of political technology that may and must be detached from any specific use.

It is polyvalent in its applications; it serves to reform prisoners, but also to treat patients, to instruct schoolchildren, to confine the insane, to supervise workers, to put beggars and idlers to work. It is a type of location of bodies in space, of distribution of individuals in relation to one another, of hierarchical organization, of disposition of centres and channels of power, of definition of the instruments and modes of intervention of power, which can be implemented in hospitals, workshops, schools, prisons. Whenever one is dealing with a multiplicity of individuals on whom a task or a particular form of behaviour must be imposed, the panoptic schema may be used. It is—necessary modifications apart—applicable 'to all establishments whatsoever, in which, within a space not too large to be covered or commanded by buildings, a number of persons are meant to be kept under inspection' (Bentham, 40; although Bentham takes the penitentiary house as his prime example, it is because it has many different functions to fulfill—safe custody, confinement, solitude, forced labour and instruction).

In each of its applications, it makes it possible to perfect the exercise of power. It does this in several ways: because it can reduce the number of those who exercise it, while increasing the number of those on whom it is exercised. Because it is possible to intervene at any moment and because the constant pressure acts even before the offences, mistakes or crimes have been committed. Because, in these conditions, its strength is that it never intervenes, it is exercised spontaneously and without noise, it constitutes a mechanism whose effects follow from one another. Because, without any physical instrument other than architecture and geometry, it acts directly on individuals; it gives 'power of mind over mind'. The panoptic schema makes any apparatus of power more intense: it assures its economy (in material, in personnel, in time); it assures its efficacity by its preventative character, its continuous functioning and its automatic mechanisms. It is a way of obtaining from power 'in hitherto unexampled quantity', 'a great and new instrument of government ...; its great excellence consists in the great strength it is capable of giving to any institution it may be thought proper to apply it to' (Bentham, 66).

It's a case of 'it's easy once you've thought of it' in the political sphere. It can in fact be integrated into any function (education, medical treatment, production, punishment); it can increase the effect of this function, by being linked closely with it; it can constitute a mixed mechanism in which relations of power (and of knowledge) may be precisely adjusted, in the smallest detail, to the processes that are to be supervised; it can establish a direct proportion between 'surplus power' and 'surplus production'. In short, it arranges things in such a way that the exercise of power is not added on from the outside, like a rigid, heavy constraint, to the functions it invests, but is so subtly present in them as to increase their efficiency by itself increasing its own points of contact. The panoptic mechanism is not simply a hinge, a point of exchange between a mechanism of power and a function; it is a way of making power relations function in a function, and of making a function function through these power relations. Bentham's Preface to Panopticon opens with a list of the benefits to be obtained from his 'inspection-house': *Morals reformed—health preserved—industry invigorated—instruction diffused—public burthens lightened—Economy seated, as it were, upon a rock—the gordian knot of the Poor-Laws not cut, but untied—all by a simple idea in architecture!'* (Bentham, 39).

Furthermore, the arrangement of this machine is such that its enclosed nature does not preclude a permanent presence from the outside: we have seen that anyone may come and exercise in the central tower the functions of surveillance, and that, this being the case, he can gain a clear idea of the way in which the surveillance is practised. In fact, any panoptic institution, even if it is as rigorously closed as a penitentiary, may without difficulty be subjected to such irregular and constant inspections: and not only by the appointed inspectors, but also by the public; any member of society will have the right to come and see with his own eyes how the schools, hospitals, factories, prisons function. There is no risk, therefore, that the increase of power created by the panoptic machine may degenerate into tyranny; the disciplinary mechanism will be democratically controlled, since it will be constantly accessible 'to the great tribunal committee of the world'.[3] This Panopticon, subtly arranged so that an observer may observe, at a glance, so many different individuals, also enables everyone to come and observe any of the observers. The seeing machine was once a sort of dark room into which individuals spied; it has become a transparent building in which the exercise of power may be supervised by society as a whole.

The panoptic schema, without disappearing as such or losing any of its properties, was destined to spread throughout the social body; its vocation was to become a generalized function. The plague-stricken town provided an exceptional disciplinary model: perfect, but absolutely violent; to the disease that brought death, power opposed its perpetual threat of death; life inside it was reduced to its simplest expression; it was, against the power of death, the meticulous exercise of the right of the sword. The Panopticon, on the other hand, has a role of amplification; although it arranges power, although it is intended to make it more economic and more effective, it does so not for power itself, nor for the immediate salvation of a threatened society: its aim is to strengthen the social forces—to increase production, to develop the economy, spread education, raise the level of public morality; to increase and multiply.

How is power to be strengthened in such a way that, far from impeding progress, far from weighing upon it with its rules and regulations, it actually facilitates such progress? What intensificator of power will be able at the same time to be a multiplicator of production? How will power, by increasing its forces, be able to increase those of society instead of confiscating them or impeding them? The Panopticon's solution to this problem is that the productive increase of power can be assured only if, on the one hand, it can be exercised continuously in the very foundations of society, in the subtlest possible way, and if, on the other hand, it functions outside these sudden, violent, discontinuous forms that are bound up with the exercise of sovereignty. The body of the king, with its strange material and physical presence, with the force that he himself deploys or transmits to some few others, is at the opposite extreme of this new physics of power represented by panopticism; the domain of panopticism is, on the contrary, that whole lower region, that region of irregular bodies, with their details, their multiple movements, their heterogeneous forces, their spatial relations; what are required are mechanisms that analyse distributions, gaps, series, combinations, and which use instruments that render visible, record, differentiate and compare: a physics of a relational and multiple power, which has its maximum intensity not in the person of the king, but in the bodies that can be individualized by these relations. At the theoretical level, Bentham defines another way of analysing the social body and the power relations that traverse it; in terms of practice, he defines a procedure of subordination of bodies and forces that must increase the utility of power while practising the economy of the prince. Panopticism is the general principle of a new 'political anatomy' whose object and end are not the relations of sovereignty but the relations of discipline.

The celebrated, transparent, circular cage, with its high tower, powerful and knowing, may have been for Bentham a project of a perfect disciplinary institution; but he also set out to show how one may 'unlock' the disciplines and get them to function in a multiple, polyvalent way throughout the whole social body. These disciplines, which the classical age had elaborated in specific, relatively enclosed places—barracks, schools, workshops—and whose total implementation had been imagined only at the limited and temporary scale of a plague-stricken town, Bentham dreamt of transforming into a network of mechanisms that would be everywhere and always alert, running through society without interruption in space or in time. The panoptic arrangement provides the formula for this generalization. It programmes, at the level of an elementary and easily transferable mechanism, the basic functioning of a society penetrated through and through with disciplinary mechanisms.

NOTES

Extracted from M. Foucault, *Discipline and Punish: The Birth of the Prison,* trans. Alan Sheridan (New York: Vintage Books, 1977), pp. 200–209. Originally published in French as *Surveiller et Punir.* Copyright © 1975 by Editions Gallimard. Reprinted by permission of Georges Borchardt, Inc., for Editions Gallimard. Additionally reproduced by permission of Penguin Books Ltd.

1. In the Postscript to the Panopticon, 1791, Bentham adds dark inspection galleries painted in black around the inspector's lodge, each making it possible to observe two storeys of cells.
2. In his first version of the Panopticon, Bentham had also imagined an acoustic surveillance, operated by means of pipes leading from the cells to the central tower. In the Postscript he abandoned the idea, perhaps because he could not introduce into it the principle of dissymmetry and prevent the prisoners from hearing the inspector as well as the inspector hearing them. Julius tried to develop a system of dissymmetrical listening (Julius, 18).
3. Imagining this continuous flow of visitors entering the central tower by an underground passage and then observing the circular landscape of the Panopticon, was Bentham aware of the Panoramas that Barker was constructing at exactly the same period (the first seems to have dated from 1787) and in which the visitors, occupying the central place, saw unfolding around them a landscape, a city or a battle. The visitors occupied exactly the place of the sovereign gaze.

36

WALKING IN THE CITY

Michel de Certeau

Seeing Manhattan from the 110th floor of the World Trade Center. Beneath the haze stirred up by the winds, the urban island, a sea in the middle of the sea, lifts up the skyscrapers over Wall Street, sinks down at Greenwich, then rises again to the crests of Midtown, quietly passes over Central Park and finally undulates off into the distance beyond Harlem. A wave of verticals. Its agitation is momentarily arrested by vision. The gigantic mass is immobilized before the eyes. It is transformed into a texturology in which extremes coincide—extremes of ambition and degradation, brutal oppositions of races and styles, contrasts between yesterday's buildings, already transformed into trash cans, and today's urban irruptions that block out its space. Unlike Rome, New York has never learned the art of growing old by playing on all its pasts. Its present invents itself, from hour to hour, in the act of throwing away its previous accomplishments and challenging the future. A city composed of paroxysmal places in monumental reliefs. The spectator can read in it a universe that is constantly exploding. In it are inscribed the architectural figures of the *coincidatio oppositorum* formerly drawn in miniatures and mystical textures. On this stage of concrete, steel and glass, cut out between two oceans (the Atlantic and the American) by a frigid body of water, The tallest letters in the world compose a gigantic rhetoric of excess in both expenditure and production.[1]

To what erotics of knowledge does the ecstasy of reading such a picture, cosmos belong? Having taken a voluptuous pleasure in it, I wonder what is the source of this pleasure of "seeing the whole," of looking down on, totalizing the most immoderate of human texts.

To be lifted to the summit of the World Trade Center is to be lifted out of the city's grasp. One's body is no longer clasped by the streets that turn and return it according to an anonymous law; nor is it possessed, whether as player or played, by the rumble of so many differences and by the nervousness of New York traffic. When one goes up there, he leaves behind the mass that carries off and mixes up in itself any identity of authors or spectators. An Icarus flying above these waters, he can ignore the devices of Daedalus in mobile and endless labyrinths far below. His elevation transfigures him into a voyeur. It puts him at a distance. It transforms the bewitching world by which one was "possessed" into a text that lies before one's eyes. It allows one to read it, to be a solar Eye, looking down like a god. The exaltation of a scopic and diagnostic drive: the fiction of knowledge is related to this lust to be a viewpoint and nothing more.

Must one finally fall back into the dark space where crowds move back and forth, crowds that, though visible from on high, are themselves unable to see down below? An Icarian fall. On the 110th floor, a poster, sphinx-like, addresses an enigmatic message to the pedestrian who is for an instant transformed into a visionary: *It's hard to be down when you're up.*

The desire to see the city preceded the means of satisfying it. Medieval or Renaissance painters

Image 15 Street scene in New York City on September 11, 2001. Photograph by Ryuichi Sakamoto.

represented the city as seen in a perspective that no eye had yet enjoyed.[2] This fiction already made the medieval spectator into a celestial eye. It created gods. Have things changed since technical procedures have organized an "all-seeing power"?[3] The totalizing eye imagined by the painters of earlier times lives on in our achievements. The same scopic drive haunts users of architectural productions by materializing today the utopia that yesterday was only painted. The 1370 foot high tower that serves as a prow for Manhattan continues to construct the fiction that creates readers, makes the complexity of the city readable, and immobilizes its opaque mobility in a transparent text.

Is the immense texturology spread out before one's eyes anything human more than a representation, an optical artifact? It is the analogue of facsimile produced, through a projection that is a way of keeping aloof, by the space planner urbanist, city planner or cartographer. The panorama-city is a "theoretical" (that is, visual) simulacrum, in short a picture, whose condition of possibility is an oblivion and a misunderstanding of practices. The voyeur-god created by this fiction, who, like Schreber's God, knows only cadavers,[4] must disentangle himself from the murky intertwining daily behaviors and make himself alien to them.

The ordinary practitioners of the city live "down below," below the thresholds at which visibility begins. They walk—an elementary form of this experience of the city; they are walkers, *Wandersmänner,* whose bodies follow the thicks and thins of an urban "text" they write without being able to read it. These practitioners make use of spaces that cannot be seen; their knowledge of them is as blind as that of lovers in each other's arms. The paths that correspond in this intertwining, unrecognized poems in which each body is an element signed by many others, elude legibility. It is as though the practices organizing a bustling city were characterized by their blindness.[5] The networks of these moving, intersecting writings compose a manifold story that has neither author nor spectator, shaped out of fragments of trajectories and alterations of spaces: in relation to representations, it remains daily and indefinitely other.

Escaping the imaginary totalizations produced by the eye, the everyday has a certain strangeness that does not surface, or whose surface is only its upper limit, outlining itself against the visible. Within this ensemble, I shall try to locate the practices that are foreign to the "geometrical" or "geographical" space of visual, panoptic, or theoretical constructions. These practices of space refer to a specific form of *operations* ("ways of operating"), to "another spatiality"[6] (an "anthropological," poetic and mythic experience of space), and to an *opaque* and *blind* mobility characteristic of the bustling city. A *migrational,* or metaphorical, city thus slips into the clear text of the planned and readable city.

FROM THE CONCEPT OF THE CITY TO URBAN PRACTICES

The World Trade Center is only the most monumental figure of Western urban development. The atopia-utopia of optical knowledge has long had the ambition of surmounting and articulating the contradictions arising from urban agglomeration. It is a question of managing a growth of human agglomeration or accumulation. "The city is a huge monastery," said Erasmus. Perspective vision and prospective vision constitute the twofold projection of an opaque past and an uncertain future onto a surface that can be dealt with. They inaugurate (in the sixteenth century?) the transformation of the urban *fact* into the *concept* of a city. Long before the concept itself gives rise to a particular figure of history, it assumes that this fact can be dealt with as a unity determined by an urbanistic *ratio*. Linking the city to the concept never makes them identical, but it plays on their progressive symbiosis: to plan a city is both to *think the very plurality* of the real and to make that way of thinking the plural *effective;* it is to know how to articulate it and be able to do it.

An Operational Concept?

The "city" founded by utopian and urbanistic discourse[7] is defined by the possibility of a threefold operation:

1. The production of its *own* space (*un espace propre*): rational organization must thus repress all the physical, mental and political pollutions that would compromise it;

2. the substitution of a nowhen, or of a synchronic system, for the indeterminable and stubborn resistances offered by traditions; univocal scientific strategies, made possible by the flattening out of all the data in a plane projection, must replace the tactics of users who take advantage of "opportunities"

and who, through these trap-events, these lapses in visibility, reproduce the opacities of history everywhere;

3. finally, the creation of a *universal* and anonymous *subject* which is the city itself: it gradually becomes possible to attribute to it, as to its political model, Hobbes' State, all the functions and predicates that were previously scattered and assigned to many different real subjects—groups, associations, or individuals. "The city," like a proper name, thus provides a way of conceiving and constructing space on the basis of a finite number of stable, isolatable, and interconnected properties.

Administration is combined with a process of elimination in this place organized by "speculative" and classificatory operations.[8] On the one hand, there is a differentiation and redistribution of the parts and functions of the city, as a result of inversions, displacements, accumulations, etc.; on the other there is a rejection of everything that is not capable of being dealt with in this way and so constitutes the "waste products" of a functionalist administration (abnormality, deviance, illness, death, etc.). To be sure, progress allows an increasing number of these waste products to be reintroduced into administrative circuits and transforms even deficiencies (in health, security, etc.) into ways of making the networks of order denser. But in reality, it repeatedly produces effects contrary to those at which it aims: the profit system generates a loss which, in the multiple forms of wretchedness and poverty outside the system and of waste inside it, constantly turns production into "expenditure." Moreover, the rationalization of the city leads to its mythification in strategic discourses, which are calculations based on the hypothesis or the necessity of its destruction in order to arrive at a final decision.[9] Finally, the functionalist organization, by privileging progress (i.e., time), causes the condition of its own possibility—space itself—to be forgotten; space thus becomes the blind spot in a scientific and political technology. This is the way in which the Concept-city functions; a place of transformations and appropriations, the object of various kinds of interference but also a subject that is constantly enriched by new attributes, it is simultaneously the machinery and the hero of modernity.

Today, whatever the avatars of this concept may have been, we have to acknowledge that if in discourse the city serves as a totalizing and almost mythical landmark for socioeconomic and political strategies, urban life increasingly permits the re-emergence of the element that the urbanistic project excluded. The language of power is in itself "urbanizing," but the city is left prey to contradictory movements that counterbalance and combine themselves outside the reach of panoptic power. The city becomes the dominant theme in political legends, but it is no longer a field of programmed and regulated operations. Beneath the discourses that ideologize the city, the ruses and combinations of powers that have no readable identity proliferate; without points where one can take hold of them, without rational transparency, they are impossible to administer.

The Return of Practices

The Concept-city is decaying. Does that mean that the illness afflicting both the rationality that founded it and its professionals afflicts the urban populations as well? Perhaps cities are deteriorating along with the procedures that organized them. But we must be careful here. The ministers of knowledge have always assumed that the whole universe was threatened by the very changes that affected their ideologies and their positions. They transmute the misfortune of their theories into theories of misfortune. When they transform their bewilderment into "catastrophes," when they seek to enclose the people in the "panic" of their discourses, are they once more necessarily right?

Rather than remaining within the field of a discourse that upholds its privilege by inverting its content (speaking of catastrophe and no longer of progress), one can try another path: one can analyze the microbe-like, singular and plural practices which an urbanistic system was supposed to administer or suppress, but which have outlived its decay; one can follow the swarming activity of these procedures that, far from being regulated or eliminated by panoptic administration, have reinforced themselves in a proliferating illegitimacy, developed and insinuated themselves into the networks of surveillance, and combined in accord with unreadable but stable tactics to the point of constituting everyday regulations and surreptitious creativities that are merely concealed by the frantic mechanisms and discourses of the observational organization.

This pathway could be inscribed as a consequence, but also as reciprocal, of Foucault's analysis of the structures of power. He moved it in the direction of mechanisms and technical procedures, "minor instrumentalities" capable, merely by their organization of "details," of transforming a human multiplicity into a "disciplinary" society and of managing, differentiating, classifying, and hierarchizing all deviances concerning apprenticeship, health, justice, the army, or work.[10] "These often miniscule ruses of discipline," these "minor but flawless" mechanisms, draw their efficacy from a relationship between procedures and the space that they redistribute in order to make an "operator" out of it. But what *spatial practices* correspond, in the area where discipline is manipulated, to these apparatuses that produce a disciplinary space? In the present conjuncture, which is marked by a contradiction between the collective mode of administration and an individual mode of reappropriation, this question is no less important, if one admits that spatial practices in fact secretly structure the determining conditions of social life. I would like to follow out a few of these multiform, resistance, tricky and stubborn procedures that elude discipline without being outside the field in which it is exercised, and which should lead us to a theory of everyday practices, of lived space, of the disquieting familiarity of the city.

THE CHORUS OF IDLE FOOTSTEPS

"The goddess can be recognized by her step"

—Virgil, *Aeneid,* I, 405

Their story begins on ground level, with footsteps. They are myriad, but do not compose a series. They cannot be counted because each unit has a qualitative character: a style of tactile apprehension and kinesthetic appropriation. Their swarming mass is an innumerable collection of singularities. Their intertwined paths give their shape to spaces. They weave places together. In that respect, pedestrian movements form one of these "real systems whose existence in fact makes up the city."[11] They are not localized; it is rather they that spatialize. They are no more inserted within a container than those Chinese characters speakers sketch out on their hands with their fingertips.

It is true that the operations of walking on can be traced on city maps in such a way as to transcribe their paths (here well-trodden, there very faint) and their trajectories (going this way and not that). But these thick or thin curves only refer, like words, to the absence of what has passed by. Surveys of routes miss what was: the act itself of passing by. The operation of walking, wandering, or "window shopping," that is, the activity of passers-by, is transformed into points that draw a totalizing and reversible line on the map. They allow us to grasp only a relic set in the nowhen of a surface of projection. Itself visible, it has the effect of making invisible the operation that made it possible. These fixations constitute procedures for forgetting. The trace left behind is substituted for the practice. It exhibits the (voracious) property that the geographical system has of being able to transform action into legibility, but in doing so it causes a way of being in the world to be forgotten.

Pedestrian Speech Acts

A comparison with the speech act will allow us to go further[12] and not limit ourselves to the critique of graphic representations alone, looking from the shores of legibility toward an inaccessible beyond. The act of walking is to the urban system what the speech act is to language or to the statements uttered.[13] At the most elementary level, it has a triple "enunciative" function: it is a process of *appropriation* of the topographical system on the part of the pedestrian (just as the speaker appropriates and takes on the language); it is a spatial acting-out of the place (just as the speech act is an acoustic acting-out of language); and it implies *relations* among differentiated positions, that is, among pragmatic "contracts" in the form of movements (just as verbal enunciation is an "allocution," "posits another opposite" the speaker and puts contracts between interlocutors into action).[14] It thus seems possible to give a preliminary definition of walking as a space of enunciation.

We could moreover extend this problematic to the relations between the act of writing and the written text, and even transpose it to the relationships between the "hand" (the touch and the tale of the paintbrush [*le et la geste du pinceau*]) and the finished painting (forms, colors, etc.). At first isolated in the area of verbal communication, the speech act turns out to find only one of its applications there, and its linguistic modality is merely the first determination of a much more general distinction between the *forms used* in a system and the *ways of using* this system (i.e., *rules*), that is, between two "different worlds," since "the same things" are considered from two opposite formal viewpoints.

Considered from this angle, the pedestrian speech act has three characteristics which distinguish it at the outset from the spatial system: the present, the discrete, the "phatic."

First, if it is true that a spatial order organizes an ensemble of possibilities (e.g., by a place in which one can move) and interdictions (e.g., by a wall that prevents one from going further), then the walker actualizes some of these possibilities. In that way, he makes them exist as well as emerge. But he also moves them about and he invents others, since the crossing, drifting away, or improvisation of walking privilege, transform or abandon spatial elements. Thus Charlie Chaplin multiplies the possibilities of his cane: he does other things with the same thing and he goes beyond the limits that the determinants of the object set on its utilization. In the same way, the walker transforms each spatial signifier into something else. And if on the one hand he actualizes only a few of the possibilities fixed by the constructed order (he goes only here and not there), on the other he increases the number of possibilities (for example, by creating shortcuts and detours) and prohibitions (for example, he forbids himself to take paths generally considered accessible or even obligatory). He thus makes a selection. "The user of a city picks out certain fragments of the statement in order to actualize them in secret."[15]

He thus creates a discreteness, whether by making choices among the signifiers of the spatial "language" or by displacing them through the use he makes of them. He condemns certain places to inertia or disappearance and composes with others spatial "turns of phrase" that are "rare," "accidental" or illegitimate. But that already leads into a rhetoric of walking.

In the framework of enunciation, the walker constitutes, in relation to his position, both a near and a far, a *here* and a *there*. To the fact that the adverbs *here* and *there* are the indicators of the locutionary seat in verbal communication[16]—a coincidence that reinforces the parallelism between linguistic and pedestrian enunciation—we must add that this location (*here*—*there*) (necessarily implied by walking and indicative of a present appropriation of space by an "I") also has the function of introducing an other in relation to this "I" and of thus establishing a conjunctive and disjunctive articulation of places. I would stress particularly the "phatic" aspect, by which I mean the function, isolated by Malinowski and Jakobson, of terms that initiate, maintain, or interrupt contact, such as "hello," "well, well," etc.[17] Walking, which alternately follows a path and has followers, creates a mobile organicity in

the environment, a sequence of phatic *topoi*. And if it is true that the phatic function, which is an effort to ensure communication, is already characteristic of the language of talking birds, just as it constitutes the "first verbal function acquired by children," it is not surprising that it also gambols, goes on all fours, dances, and walks about, with a light or heavy step, like a series of "hellos" in an echoing labyrinth, anterior or parallel to informative speech.

The modalities of pedestrian enunciation which a plane representation on a map brings out could be analyzed. They include the kinds of relationship this enunciation entertains with particular paths (or "statements") by according them a truth value ("alethic" modalities of the necessary, the impossible, the possible, or the contingent), an epistemological value ("epistemic" modalities of the certain, the excluded, the plausible, or the questionable) or finally an ethical or legal value ("deontic" modalities of the obligatory, the forbidden, the permitted, or the optional).[18] Walking affirms, suspects, tries out, transgresses, respects, etc., the trajectories it "speaks." All the modalities sing a part in this chorus, changing from step to step, stepping in through proportions, sequences, and intensities which vary according to the time, the path taken and the walker. These enunciatory operations are of an unlimited diversity. They therefore cannot be reduced to their graphic trail.

NOTES

Extracted from M. de Certeau, *The Practice of Everyday Life*, trans. S. Rendail (Berkeley: University of California Press, 1984), pp. 91–99. Reproduced with permission of University of California Press via Copyright Clearance Center.

1. See Alain Médam's admirable "New York City," *Les Temps modernes,* August-September 1976, 15–33; and the same author's *New York Terminal* (Paris: Galilée, 1977).

2. See H. Lavedan, *Les Réprésentations des vales dans l'art du Moyen Age* (Paris: Van Oest,

1942); R. Wittkower, *Architectural Principles in the Age of Humanism* (New York: Norton, 1962); L. Marin, *Utopiques: Jeux d'espaces* (Paris: Minuit, 1973); etc.

3. M. Foucault, "L'Oeil du pouvoir," in J. Bentham, *Le Panoptique* (Paris: Belfond, 1977), 16.

4. D. P. Schreber, *Mémoires d'un névropathe* (Paris: Seuil, 1975), 41, 60, etc.

5. Descartes, in his Regulae, had already made the blind man the guarantor of the knowledge of things and places against the illusions and deceptions of vision.

6. M. Merleau-Ponty, *Phénoménologie de la perception* (Paris: Gallimard Tel, 1976), 332–333.

7. See F. Choay, "Figures d'un discours inconnu," *Critique,* April 1973, 293–317.

8. Urbanistic techniques, which classify things spatially, can be related to the tradition of the "art of memory": see Frances A. Yates, *The Art of Memory* (London: Routledge and Kegan Paul, 1966). The ability to produce a spatial organization of knowledge (with "places" assigned to each type of "figure" or "function") develops its procedures on the basis of this "art." It determines utopias and can be recognized even in Bentham's *Panopticon.* Such a form remains stable in spite of the diversity of its contents (past, future, present) and its projects (conserving or creating) relative to changes in the status of knowledge.

9. See André Glucksmann, "Le Totalitarisme en effet," *Traverses,* No. 9, 1977, 34–40.

10. M. Foucault, *Surveiller et punir* (Paris: Gallimard, 1975); *Discipline and Punish,* trans. A. Sheridan (New York: Pantheon, 1977).

11. Ch. Alexander, "La Cité semi-treillis, mais non arbre," *Architecture. Mouvement, Continuite,* 1967.

12. See R. Barthes's remarks in *Architecture d'aujourd'hui,* No. 153, December 1970–January 1971, 11–13: "We speak our city … merely by inhabiting it, walking through it, looking at it." Cf. C. Soucy, *L'Image du centre dans quatre romans contemporains* (Paris: CSU, 1971), 6–15.

13. See the numerous studies devoted to the subject since J. Searle's "What is a Speech Act?" in *Philosophy in America,* ed. Max Black (London: Allen & Unwin; Ithaca, N.Y.: Cornell University Press, 1965), 221–239.

14. E. Benveniste, *Problèmes de linguistique générale* (Paris: Gallimard, 1974), II, 79–88, etc.

15. R. Barthes, quoted in C. Soucy, *L'Image du centre,* 10.

16. "Here and now delimit the spatial and temporal instance coextensive and contemporary with the present instance of discourse containing I": E. Benveniste, *Problèmes de linguistique générale* (Paris: Gallimard, 1966), I, p. 253.

17. R. Jakobson, *Essais de linguistique générale* (Paris: Seuil Points, 1970), p. 217.

18. On modalities, see H. Parret, *La Pragmatique des modalités* (Urbino: Centro di Semiotica, 1975); A. R. White, *Modal Thinking* (Ithaca, N.Y.: Cornell University Press, 1975).

37

THE PRESENTATION OF SELF IN EVERYDAY LIFE

Erving Goffman

Given the fact that the individual effectively projects a definition of the situation when he enters the presence of others, we can assume that events may occur within the interaction which contradict, discredit, or otherwise throw doubt upon this projection. When these disruptive events occur, the interaction itself may come to a confused and embarrassed halt. Some of the assumptions upon which the responses of the participants had been predicated become untenable, and the participants find themselves lodged in an interaction for which the situation has been wrongly defined and is now no longer defined. At such moments the individual whose presentation has been discredited may feel ashamed while the others present may feel hostile, and all the participants may come to feel ill at ease, nonplussed, out of countenance, embarrassed, experiencing the kind of moony that is generated when the minute social system of face-to-face interaction breaks down.

In stressing the fact that the initial definition of the situation projected by an individual tends to provide a plan for the co-operative activity that follows—in stressing this action point of view—we must not overlook the crucial fact that any projected definition of the situation also has a distinctive moral character. It is this moral character of projections that will chiefly concern us in this report. Society is organized on the principle that any individual who possesses certain social characteristics has a moral right to expect that others will value and treat him in an appropriate way. Connected with this principle is a second, namely that an individual who implicitly or explicitly signifies that he has certain social characteristics ought in fact to be what he claims he is. In consequence, when an individual projects a definition of the situation and thereby makes an implicit or explicit claim to be a person of a particular kind, he automatically exerts a moral demand upon the others, obliging them to value and treat him in the manner that persons of his kind have a right to expect. He also implicitly forgoes all claims to be things he does not appear to be[1] and hence forgoes the treatment that would be appropriate for such individuals. The others find, then, that the individual has informed them as to what is and as to what they ought to see as the "is."

One cannot judge the importance of definitional disruptions by the frequency with which they occur, for apparently they would occur more frequently were not constant precautions taken. We find that preventive practices are constantly employed to avoid these embarrassments and that corrective practices are constantly employed to compensate for discrediting occurrences that have not been successfully avoided. When the individual employs these strategies and tactics to protect his own projections, we may refer to them as "defensive practices"; when a participant employs them to save the definition of the situation projected by another, we speak of "protective practices" or "tact." Together, defensive and protective practices comprise the techniques employed to safeguard the impression fostered by an individual during his presence before others. It should be added that while we may be ready to see that no fostered impression would survive if defensive practices were not employed, we are less ready perhaps to see that few impressions could survive if those who received the impression did not exert tact in their reception of it.

In addition to the fact that precautions are taken to prevent disruption of projected definitions, we may also note that an intense interest in these disruptions comes to play a significant role in the social life of the group. Practical jokes and social games are played in which embarrassments which are to be taken unseriously are purposely engineered.[2] Fantasies are created in which devastating exposures occur. Anecdotes from the past—real, embroidered, or fictitious—are told and retold, detailing disruptions which occurred, almost occurred, or occurred and were admirably resolved. There seems to be no grouping which does not have a ready supply of these games, reveries, and cautionary tales, to be used as a source of humor, a catharsis for anxieties, and a sanction for inducing individuals to be modest in their claims and reasonable in their projected expectations. The individual may tell himself through dreams of getting into impossible positions. Families tell of the time a guest got his dates mixed and arrived when neither the house nor anyone in it was ready for him. Journalists tell of times when an all-too-meaningful misprint occurred, and the paper's assumption of objectivity or decorum was humorously discredited. Public servants tell of times a client ridiculously misunderstood form instructions, giving answers which implied an unanticipated and bizarre definition of the situation.[3] Seamen, whose home away from home is rigorously he-man, tell stories of coming back home and inadvertently asking mother to "pass the fucking butter."[4] Diplomats tell of the time a near-sighted queen asked a republican ambassador about the health of his king.[5]

To summarize, then, I assume that when an individual appears before others he will have many motives for trying to control the impression they receive of the situation. This report is concerned with some of the common techniques that persons employ to sustain such impressions and with some of the common contingencies associated with the employment of these techniques. The specific content of any activity presented by the individual participant, or the role it plays in the interdependent activities of an on-going social system, will not be at issue; I shall be concerned only with the participant's dramaturgical problems of presenting the activity before others. The issues dealt with by stagecraft and stage management are sometimes trivial but they are quite general; they seem to occur everywhere in social life, providing a clear-cut dimension for formal sociological analysis.

It will be convenient to end this introduction with some definitions that are implied in what has gone before and required for what is to follow. For the purpose of this report, interaction (that is, face-to-face interaction) may be roughly defined as the reciprocal influence of individuals upon one another's actions when in one another's immediate physical presence. An interaction may be defined as all the interaction which occurs throughout any one occasion when a given set of individuals are in one another's continuous presence; the term "an encounter" would do as well. A "performance" may be defined as all the activity of a given participant on a given occasion which serves to influence in any way any of the other participants. Taking a particular participant and his performance as a basic point of reference, we may refer to those who contribute the other performances as the audience, observers, or co-participants. The pre-established pattern of action which is unfolded during a performance and which may be presented or played through on other occasions may be called a "part" or "routine."[6] These situational terms can easily be related to conventional structural ones. When an individual or performer plays the same part to the same audience on different occasions, a social relationship is likely to arise. Defining social role as the enactment of rights and duties attached to a given status, we can say that a social role will involve one or more parts and that each of these different parts may be presented by the performer on a series of occasions to the same kinds of audience or to an audience of the same persons.

NOTES

Extracted from E. Goffman, *The Presentation of Self in Everyday Life* (New York: Doubleday, 1959), pp. 12–16. Reprinted by permission of Doubleday, a division of Random House and Reproduced by permission of Penguin Book Ltd.

1. This role of the witness in limiting what it is the individual can be has been stressed by Existentialists, who see it as a basic threat to individual freedom. See Jean-Paul Sartre, *Being and Nothingness,* trans. by Hazel E. Barnes (New York: Philosophical Library, 1956), p. 365 ff.

2. Goffman, [E., "Communication Conduct in an Island Community" (Ph.D. dissertation, University of Chicago, 1953),] pp. 319–27.

3. Peter Blau, "Dynamics of Bureaucracy" (Ph.D. dissertation, Department of Sociology, Columbia University, forthcoming, University of Chicago Press), pp. 127–29.

4. Walter M. Beattie, Jr., "The Merchant Seaman" (unpublished M.A. Report, Department of Sociology, University of Chicago, 1950), p. 35.

5. Sir Frederick Ponsonby, *Recollections of Three Reigns* (New York: Dutton, 1952), p. 46.

6. For comments on the importance of distinguishing between a routine of interaction and any particular instance when this routine is played through, see John von Neumann and Oskar Morgenstern, *The Theory of Games and Economic Behaviour* (2nd ed.; Princeton: Princeton University Press, 1947), p. 49.

ANNOTATED GUIDE TO FURTHER READING

In terms of aesthetics, there is an enormous history of thinkers who have related visual form to our sense-based experiences. A very thorough collection of seminal essays on aesthetics from our modern period can be found in Clive Cazeaux's *The Continental Aesthetics Reader* (2000), which contains important writings by authors such as Immanuel Kant, Martin Heidegger, and Julia Kristeva. For more on design-specific readings that utilize aesthetic theory, Jerry Palmer and Mo Dodson have edited a collection titled *Design and Aesthetics* (1996).

For a wide range of readings on the history, practice, and philosophy of ethics, see Peter Singer's volume, *Practical Ethics* (1993). The study of ethics in relation to design practice has been gaining interest in the past decade, and a series of important books have emerged that assess the sometimes difficult marriage between the art of making things and the imperative for adhering to cultural values. Judy Attfield's edited volume, *Utility Reassessed* (1999), approaches design and ethics from a historical perspective. Steven Heller and Véronique Vienne's *Citizen Designer* (2003), on the other hand, provides insight about what "design responsibility" means in our contemporary world. Additionally, Barry Wasserman et. al. have written a helpful book titled *Ethics and the Practice of Architecture* (2000), about the relationship between ethics and architectural practice. Two recent books that look into ethics and sustainable design are Tony Fry's *Design Futuring: Sustainability, Ethics and New Practice* (2008), and Ezio Manzini and Carlo Vezzoli's *Design for Environmental Sustainability* (2008).

A good place to begin an exploration of political theory is Michael Morgan's edited book, *Classics of Political and Moral Theory* (1992). Morgan includes the writings of political thinkers from Sophocles to Weber, giving the reader an excellent variety of sources. Contemporary critics, such as Langdon Winner in his essay, "Do Artifacts Have Politics" (1986), have written about the political nature of manmade things. Two books that explore political conundrums that attend specific areas of design are Maud Lavin's *Clean New World* (2002), which focuses on graphic design, and Robin Manzell and Roger Silverstone's edited volume, *Communication by Design* (1998), which stresses the political nature of information systems and new technology in the realm of communications.

There is a growing body of sources that focus on design-related issues in terms of material culture studies. Ian Woodward's *Understanding Material Culture* (2007) provides an overview of the field. Susan Küchler and Daniel Miller's edited volume, *Clothing as Material Culture* (2005), includes essays that focus on clothing from an international perspective. Furthermore, two important earlier works that utilize a material culture approach are Dell Upton's *Holy Things and Profane* (1986), and Henry Glassie's *Folk Housing in Middle Virginia* (1975). Both of these model studies give students a method for investigating the built environment.

SECTION 4

IDENTITY AND CONSUMPTION

SECTION INTRODUCTION

Today, most people encounter design through consumption, either by purchasing designed commodities, by consuming design through the signs used in advertising and other forms of mediation, or simply as users. The "consumer society" emerged in Western capitalist systems, in which, as goods were produced in excess of needs, they came to represent the status and power of those able to afford them through conspicuous consumption (Veblen [1899] 2007). Industrialized and urban societies continue to use consumption and consumerism to create and display their social selves and to judge their peers through culturally defined, symbolic meanings of commodities. The question of identity is most likely to be answered in terms of patterns of consumption, or consumer lifestyle. Design is the interface in this process—a vital frontier of the display of identity through the processes of consumption. Personal style is designed through choices of commodities. Particular areas of design attention are what is worn on the body, and what is purchased for the home, both of which are strongly influenced by fashion in the consumer market. Identity tensions and ambivalences are highlighted in processes of consumption, in which commodities can be seen to "design" the person, as part of a collective or brand image, begging the very question of consumer individuality.

Definitions that once were considered fixed, such as gender identity, are now subjects for discussion, as stereotypes are simultaneously challenged by individuals and reinforced in the media. American artist Barbara Kruger's 1987 graphic image, *Untitled (I Shop Therefore I Am),* famously captured the stereotyping of women and the perceived role of consumption in the creation of identity. More recently, masculinity has also become a sign in popular culture, in the way that femininity has been historically.

Now, virtual worlds are designed as extensions of personal identity and as channels of consumption. The Internet enables anyone, anywhere, with access to a computer, to consume images and trade real and imagined products and contexts, in virtual "worlds" such as Second Life. The popularity of sites such as MySpace is based on the design and consumption of fluid identities. The fact that "identity theft" has come into common parlance to refer to stealing key documents of identification points both to the institutionalization and also the mutability of how identities are defined.

Design has facilitated the massive changes in the relationships between identity and consumption, which are largely symbolic. Design not only generates products as commodities, but also the systems of representation that make them desirable. Aesthetics, taste, and design are drivers in consumption, just as they are in the construction of identity. Consumers seek to distinguish themselves from one another, but they can only do so within the prevailing canons of taste of their preferred peer groups. In contemporary capitalist societies, individuals do not choose their identities; they choose where to shop, but in doing so they in turn affect the role and impact of design in this complex feedback process.

SECTION 4: IDENTITY AND CONSUMPTION

4.1: Virtual Identity and Design

INTRODUCTION

As Abraham Moles explains in "Design and Immateriality" (a reading from Section 5), we live in a world that is increasingly less connected to material reality. The real has become distanced from our everyday lives. In its place we experience a virtual scape, a place of digital connections facilitated by machines, computers, and software. The design of these virtual scapes raises queries about who we are and how we project ourselves in these new contexts. This is especially important in relation to the Internet—the most profound conduit of the virtual—where knowledge and consumerism unfold with a type of ease that has transformed design's relationship to culture. The readings in this subsection introduce questions about how design facilitates our interactions with a world that skews the realities of the physical self. These readings are also, of course, closely tied to the Rafael and Norman readings in Section 5, since the entire idea of virtuality is predicated on the advent of new technology and our ability to cope with the cultural shifts caused by technology.

One of the most feared forms of the virtual is the cyborg, that science fiction amalgamation of human and machine. Frightening images in Hollywood blockbusters, such as *The Terminator* series, reveal the problematic of morphing man into machine. Our terror of this new being is, however, according to theorist Donna Haraway, wrongheaded. To Haraway, the cyborg manifests utopian potential. In her "A Cyborg Manifesto," she details how by mixing physical corporeality with virtual possibility, the cyborg can traverse the human realm beyond the stereotypes and misogynist regimes that have historically made gender and sex dangerous categories. Haraway revels in the cyborg as "a creature in a post-gender world," where narratives about patriarchy and sexism can be overcome. While illuminating about the potential virtues of this new life form, Haraway never mentions the designers of circuits and brave new bodies that will continue to create cyborgs. She believes that we all have become cyborgs, but clearly the intervention of design has helped promote this transformation. It is the designer's challenge to make "our time, a mythic time[,]" into a possibility.

Haraway's utopic desire has been attempted in the world of virtual design, but these experiments are, thus far, commercial and military ventures; or, as seen in the example of video games, a combination of the two. In their groundbreaking work on game theory, titled *Rules of Play,* Katie Salen and Eric Zimmerman include a helpful discussion of cybernetic systems. Salen and Zimmerman explain in detail how video games, probably the most profitable medium of the virtual, use cybernetics to create an engaging gaming experience. They start by mentioning Haraway's title but then quickly reveal that although "appropriated by science fiction and technoculture," "cybernetics precedes the advent of the digital computer." Cybernetics is a way of calibrating a system so that the system responds to various stimuli through adjustments. They use the example of a thermostat that triggers an air conditioner. When a room goes above a specific temperature, the air goes on, thus cooling the room and bringing the temperature in the room back into the range that the user has set. This is a negative feedback system, since "the new data produces a result in opposition to the previous result (the temperature is rising, it will now be lowered)." There are also positive feedback systems, which react in the opposite way. Salen and Zimmerman explain, "Instead of bringing the system to a steady state, a positive cybernetic circuit encourages the system to exhibit more and more extreme behavior."

These positive and negative feedback systems are the basis for the virtual worlds of video-game designs that have sparked enormous consumer demand since games, such as Asteroids and Space Invaders, filled arcades in the late 1970s. These initial forays into game design utilized either positive or negative feedback systems to make games more enjoyable. For instance, moving from one level of difficulty to the next, with more obstacles and potential pitfalls in place, represents a classic example of a negative feedback system, in which the cybernetic system attempts to challenge the user with thornier situations—for example, more bullets—as the game progresses. Today digital games utilize a new programming technique called Dynamic Difficulty Adjustment (DDA). This type of game makes even more modifications to a player's experience than the positive and negative feedback scenarios, adding complexity to the gaming experience.

These games create venues in which, thinking back to Haraway's manifesto, we become part of a virtual realm as our minds become in tune with game designs. These games foster entertainment by making us feel as though we are in another world, surrounded by the virtual realm displayed on a screen. However, the Internet, a digital scape whose popularity has transformed our lived experience over the past two decades, has advanced not only new forms of entertainment, but also virtual realms that were previously considered mere fantasy. Indeed, one wonders what Haraway would have said about the Internet if she had written her manifesto ten years later than its 1991 publication date.

One space that could provide Haraway with the utopian vision she proposes is Second Life (http://www.secondlife.com), where players socialize, build, sell, and consume goods, all within an online world. As Justin Tyler Clark notes in his article from *I.D.,* "Second Life is one of the first virtual spaces in which users, rather than art teams, supply the content." While individual avatars can, in fact, enact alternative ways of living signaled by Haraway, the reality of Second Life is that the space has started to become successful as a marketing tool, in which stores, such as American Apparel, and brands, such as Coke, now advertise. As Gavin O'Malley reports in his article from *Advertising Age,* with American Apparel, for instance, "virtual shoppers who buy virtual clothes get 15% off the same items in real life." Interestingly, however, "real life" now often means purchasing items from online retailers.

Unlike the games that Salen and Zimmerman describe, we, as end-users, have more power within the context of Second Life. This has led many to praise the virtues of Second Life and similar sites, such as Whyville.net, where we make decisions, we build things, and we create, rather than becoming the digital trigger to cybernetic feedback systems. What will the future bring as our existence becomes more integrated with the virtual? Will commercial activity, as discussed in Section 4 of the *Reader,* influence all of our interactions in this brave new world, or will there be alternative possibilities as our experiences become more integrated with the virtual? These readings will foster a debate about the role of design within the context of our new virtual reality.

38

A CYBORG MANIFESTO

Donna Haraway

By the late twentieth century, our time, a mythic time, we are all chimeras, theorized and fabricated hybrids of machine and organism; in short, we are cyborgs. The cyborg is our ontology; it gives us our politics. The cyborg is a condensed image of both imagination and material reality, the two joined centres structuring any possibility of historical transformation. In the traditions of 'Western' science and politics—the tradition of racist, male-dominant capitalism; the tradition of progress; the tradition of the appropriation of nature as resource for the productions of culture; the tradition of reproduction of the self from the reflections of the other—the relation between organism and machine has been a border war. The stakes in the border war have been the territories of production, reproduction, and imagination. This chapter is an argument for *pleasure in* the confusion of boundaries and for *responsibility* in their construction. It is also an effort to contribute to socialist-feminist culture and theory in a postmodernist, non-naturalist mode and in the utopian tradition of imagining a world without gender, which is perhaps a world without genesis, but maybe also a world without end. The cyborg incarnation is outside salvation history. Nor does it mark time on an oedipal calendar, attempting to heal the terrible cleavages of gender in an oral symbiotic utopia or postoedipal apocalypse. As Zoe Sofoulis argues in her unpublished manuscript on Jacques Lacan, Melanie Klein, and nuclear culture, *Lacklein,*

the most terrible and perhaps the most promising monsters in cyborg worlds are embodied in non-oedipal narratives with a different logic of repression, which we need to understand for our survival.

The cyborg is a creature in a post-gender world; it has no truck with bisexuality, pre-oedipal symbiosis, unalienated labour, or other seductions to organic wholeness through a final appropriation of all the powers of the parts into a higher unity. In a sense, the cyborg has no origin story in the Western sense—a 'final' irony since the cyborg is also the awful apocalyptic *telos* of the 'West's' escalating dominations of abstract individuation, an ultimate self untied at last from all dependency, a man in space. An origin story in the 'Western', humanist sense depends on the myth of original unity, fullness, bliss and terror, represented by the phallic mother from whom all humans must separate, the task of individual development and of history, the twin potent myths inscribed most powerfully for us in psychoanalysis and Marxism. Hilary Klein has argued that both Marxism and psychoanalysis, in their concepts of labour and of individuation and gender formation, depend on the plot of original unity out of which difference must be produced and enlisted in a drama of escalating domination of woman/nature. The cyborg skips the step of original unity, of identification with nature in the Western sense. This is its illegitimate promise that might lead to subversion of its teleology as star wars.

Image 16 Cyborg performer isa gordon.

The cyborg is resolutely committed to partiality, irony, intimacy, and perversity. It is oppositional, utopian, and completely without innocence. No longer structured by the polarity of public and private, the cyborg defines a technological polis based partly on a revolution of social relations in the *oikos,* the household. Nature and culture are reworked; the one can no longer be the resource for appropriation or incorporation by the other. The relationships for forming wholes from parts, including those of polarity and hierarchical domination, are at issue in the cyborg world. Unlike the hopes of Frankenstein's monster, the cyborg does not expect its father to save it through a restoration of the garden; that is, through the fabrication of a heterosexual mate, through its completion in a finished whole, a city and cosmos. The cyborg does not dream of community on the model of the organic family, this time without the oedipal project. The cyborg would not recognize the Garden of Eden; it is not made of mud and cannot dream of returning to dust. Perhaps that is why I want to see if cyborgs can subvert the apocalypse of returning to nuclear dust in the manic compulsion to name the Enemy. Cyborgs are not reverent; they do not re-member the cosmos. They are wary of holism, but needy for connection—they seem to have a natural feel for united front politics, but without the vanguard party. The main trouble with cyborgs, of course, is that they are the illegitimate offspring of militarism and patriarchal capitalism, not to mention state socialism. But illegitimate offspring are often exceedingly unfaithful to their origins. Their fathers, after all, are inessential.

I will return to the science fiction of cyborgs at the end of this chapter, but now I want to signal three crucial boundary breakdowns that make the following political-fictional (political-scientific) analysis possible. By the late twentieth century in United States scientific culture, the boundary between human and animal is thoroughly breached. The last beachheads of uniqueness have been polluted if not turned into amusement parks—language, tool use, social behaviour, mental events, nothing really convincingly settles the separation of human and animal. And many people no longer feel the need for such a separation; indeed, many branches of feminist culture affirm the pleasure of connection of human and other living creatures. Movements for animal rights are not irrational denials of human uniqueness; they are a clear-sighted recognition of connection across the discredited breach of nature and culture. Biology and evolutionary theory over the last two centuries have simultaneously produced modern organisms as objects of knowledge and reduced the line between humans and animals to a faint trace re-etched in ideological struggle or professional disputes between life and social science. Within this framework, teaching modern Christian creationism should be fought as a form of child abuse.

Biological-determinist ideology is only one position opened up in scientific culture for arguing the meanings of human animality. There is much room for radical political people to contest the meanings of the breached boundary.[1] The cyborg appears in myth precisely where the boundary between human and animal is transgressed. Far from signalling a walling off of people from other living beings, cyborgs signal disturbingly and pleasurably tight coupling. Bestiality has a new status in this cycle of marriage exchange.

The second leaky distinction is between animal-human (organism) and machine. Pre-cybernetic machines could be haunted; there was always the spectre of the ghost in the machine. This dualism structured the dialogue between materialism and idealism that was settled by a dialectical progeny, called spirit or history, according to taste. But basically machines were not self-moving, self-designing, autonomous. They could not achieve man's dream, only mock it. They were not man, an author to himself, but only a caricature of that masculinist reproductive dream. To think they were otherwise was paranoid. Now we are not so sure. Late twentieth-century machines have made thoroughly ambiguous the difference between natural and artificial, mind and body, self-developing and externally designed, and many other distinctions that used to apply to organisms and machines. Our machines are disturbingly lively, and we ourselves frighteningly inert.

Technological determination is only one ideological space opened up by the reconceptions of machine and organism as coded texts through which we engage in the play of writing and reading the world.[2] 'Textualization' of everything in poststructuralist, postmodernist theory has been damned by Marxists and socialist feminists for its utopian disregard for the lived relations of domination that ground the 'play' of arbitrary reading.[3] It is certainly true that postmodernist strategies, like my cyborg myth, subvert myriad organic wholes (for example, the poem, the primitive culture, the biological organism). In short, the certainty of what counts as nature—a source of insight and promise of innocence—is undermined, probably fatally. The transcendent authorization of interpretation is lost, and with it the ontology grounding 'Western' epistemology. But the alternative is not cynicism or faithlessness, that is, some version of abstract existence, like the accounts of technological determinism destroying 'man' by the 'machine' or 'meaningful political action' by the 'text'. Who cyborgs will be is a radical question; the answers are a matter of survival. Both chimpanzees and artefacts have politics, so why shouldn't we (de Waal, 1982; Winner, 1980)?

The third distinction is a subset of the second: the boundary between physical and non-physical is very imprecise for us. Pop physics books on the consequences of quantum theory and the indeterminacy principle are a kind of popular scientific equivalent to Harlequin romances[4] as a marker of radical change in American white heterosexuality: they get it wrong, but they are on the right subject. Modern machines are quintessentially microelectronic devices: they are everywhere and they are invisible. Modern machinery is an irreverent upstart god, mocking the Father's ubiquity and spirituality. The silicon chip is a surface for writing; it is etched in molecular scales disturbed only by atomic noise, the ultimate interference for nuclear scores. Writing, power, and technology are old partners in Western stories of the origin of civilization, but miniaturization has changed our experience of mechanism. Miniaturization has turned out to be about power; small is not so much beautiful as pre-eminently dangerous, as in cruise missiles. Contrast the TV sets of the 1950s or the news cameras of the 1970s with the TV wrist bands or hand-sized video cameras now advertised. Our best machines are made of sunshine; they are all light and clean because they are nothing but signals, electromagnetic waves, a section of a spectrum, and these machines are eminently portable, mobile—a matter of immense human pain in Detroit and Singapore. People are nowhere near so fluid, being both material and opaque. Cyborgs are ether, quintessence.

The ubiquity and invisibility of cyborgs is precisely why these sunshine-belt machines are so deadly. They are as hard to see politically as materially. They are about consciousness—or its simulation.[5] They are floating signifiers moving in pickup trucks across Europe, blocked more effectively by the witch-weavings of the displaced and so unnatural Greenham women, who read the cyborg webs of power so very well, than by the militant labour of older masculinist politics, whose natural constituency needs defence jobs. Ultimately the 'hardest' science is about the realm of greatest boundary confusion, the realm of pure number, pure spirit, C^3I, cryptography, and the preservation of potent secrets. The new machines are so clean and light. Their engineers are sun-worshippers mediating a new scientific revolution associated with the night dream of post-industrial society. The diseases evoked by these clean machines are 'no more' than the minuscule coding changes of an antigen in the immune system, 'no more' than the experience of stress. The nimble fingers of 'Oriental' women, the old fascination of little Anglo-Saxon Victorian girls with doll's houses, women's enforced attention to the small take on quite new dimensions in this world. There might be a cyborg Alice taking account of these new dimensions. Ironically, it might be the unnatural cyborg women making chips in Asia and spiral dancing in Santa Rita jail[6] whose constructed unities will guide effective oppositional strategies.

So my cyborg myth is about transgressed boundaries, potent fusions, and dangerous possibilities which progressive people might explore as one part of needed political work. One of my premises is that most American socialists and feminists see deepened dualisms of mind and body, animal and machine, idealism and materialism in the social practices, symbolic formulations, and physical artefacts associated with 'high technology' and scientific culture. From *One-Dimensional Man* (Marcuse, 1964) to *The Death of Nature* (Merchant, 1980), the analytic resources developed by progressives have insisted on the necessary domination of technics and recalled us to an imagined organic body to integrate our resistance. Another of my premises is that the need for unity of people trying to resist world-wide intensification of domination has never been more acute. But a slightly perverse shift of perspective might better enable us to contest for meanings, as well as for other forms of power and pleasure in technologically mediated societies.

From one perspective, a cyborg world is about the final imposition of a grid of control on the planet, about the final abstraction embodied in a Star Wars apocalypse waged in the name of defence, about the final appropriation of women's bodies in a masculinist orgy of war (Sofia, 1984). From another perspective, a cyborg world might be about lived social and bodily realities in which people are not afraid of their joint kinship with animals and machines, not afraid of permanently partial identities and contradictory standpoints. The political struggle is to see from both perspectives at once because each reveals both dominations and possibilities unimaginable from the other vantage point. Single vision produces worse illusions than double vision or many-headed monsters. Cyborg unities are monstrous and illegitimate; in our present political

circumstances, we could hardly hope for more potent myths for resistance and recoupling. I like to imagine LAG, the Livermore Action Group, as a kind of cyborg society, dedicated to realistically converting the laboratories that most fiercely embody and spew out the tools of technological apocalypse, and committed to building a political form that actually manages to hold together witches, engineers, elders, perverts, Christians, mothers, and Leninists long enough to disarm the state. Fission Impossible is the name of the affinity group in my town. (Affinity: related not by blood but by choice, the appeal of one chemical nuclear group for another, avidity.)[7]

[...]

NOTES

Extracted from D. Haraway, *Simians Cyborgs, and Women: The Reinvention of Nature* (London: Routledge, 1991), pp. 150–5. Reprinted with permission of the author and the Cathy Miller Foreign Rights Agency.

1. Useful references to left and/or feminist radical science movements and theory and to biological/biotechnical issues include: Bleier (1984, 1986), Harding (1986), Fausto-Sterling (1985), Gould (1981), Hubbard *et al.* (1982), Keller (1985), Lewontin *et al.* (1984), *Radical Science Journal* (became *Science as Culture* in 1987), 26 Freegrove Road, London N7 9RQ; *Science for the People*, 897 Main St, Cambridge, MA 02139.

2. Starting points for left and/or feminist approaches to technology and politics include: Cowan (1983), Rothschild (1983), Traweek (1988), Young and Levidow (1981, 1985), Weizenbaum (1976), Winner (1977, 1986), Zimmerman (1983), Athanasiou (1987), Cohn (1987a, 1987b), Winograd and Flores (1986), Edwards (1985). *Global Electronics Newsletter*, 867 West Dana St, #204, Mountain View, CA 94041; *Processed World*, 55 Sutter St, San Francisco, CA 94104; ISIS,

Women's International Information and Communication Service, PO Box 50 (Cornavin), 12II Geneva 2, Switzerland, and Via Santa Maria Dell'Anima 30, 00186 Rome, Italy. Fundamental approaches to modern social studies of science that do not continue the liberal mystification that it all started with Thomas Kuhn, include: Knorr-Cetina (1981), Knorr-Cetina and Mulkay (1983), Latour and Woolgar (1979), Young (1979). The 1984 Directory of the Network for the Ethnographic Study of Science, Technology, and Organizations lists a wide range of people and projects crucial to better radical analysis; available from NESSTO, PO Box 11442, Stanford, CA 94305.

3. A provocative, comprehensive argument about the politics and theories of 'postmodernism' is made by Fredric Jameson (1984), who argues that postmodernism is not an option, a style among others, but a cultural dominant requiring radical reinvention of left politics from within; there is no longer any place from without that gives meaning to the comforting fiction of critical distance. Jameson also makes clear why one cannot be for or against postmodernism, an essentially moralist move. My position is that feminists (and others) need continuous cultural reinvention, postmodernist critique, and historical materialism; only a cyborg would have a chance. The old dominations of white capitalist patriarchy seem nostalgically innocent now: they normalized heterogeneity, into man and woman, white and black, for example. 'Advanced capitalism' and postmodernism release heterogeneity without a norm, and we are flattened, without subjectivity, which requires depth, even unfriendly and drowning depths. It is time to write *The Death of the Clinic*. The clinic's methods required bodies and works; we have texts and surfaces. Our dominations don't work by medicalization and normalization any more; they work by networking, communications redesign, stress management.

Normalization gives way to automation, utter redundancy. Michel Foucault's *Birth of the Clinic* (1963), *History of Sexuality* (1976), and *Discipline and Punish* (1975) name a form of power at its moment of implosion. The discourse of biopolitics gives way to technobabble, the language of the spliced substantive; no noun is left whole by the multinationals. These are their names, listed from one issue of *Science:* Tech-Knowledge, Genentech, Allergen, Hybritech, Compupro, Genen-cor, Syntex, Allelix, Agrigenetics Corp., Syntro, Codon, Repligen, MicroAngelo from Scion Corp., Percom Data, Inter Systems, Cyborg Corp., Statcom Corp., Intertec. If we are imprisoned by language, then escape from that prison-house requires language poets, a kind of cultural restriction enzyme to cut the code; cyborg heteroglossia is one form of radical cultural politics. For cyborg poetry, see Perloff (1984); Fraser (1984). For feminist modernist/postmodernist 'cyborg' writing, see HOW(ever), 871 Corbett Ave, San Francisco, CA 94131.

4. The U.S. equivalent of Mills and Boon.

5. Baudrillard (1983). Jameson (1984, p. 66) points out that Plato's definition of the simulacrum is the copy for which there is no original, i.e., the world of advanced capitalism, of pure exchange. See *Discourse* 9 (Spring/Summer 1987) for a special issue on technology (cybernetics, ecology, and the postmodern imagination).

6. A practice at once both spiritual and political that linked guards and arrested anti-nuclear demonstrators in the Alameda County jail in California in the early 1980s.

7. For ethnographic accounts and political evaluations, see Epstein (1991), Sturgeon (1986). Without explicit irony, adopting the spaceship earth/whole earth logo of the planet photographed from space, set off by the slogan 'Love Your Mother', the May 1987 Mothers and Others Day action at the nuclear weapons testing facility in Nevada none the less took

account of the tragic contradictions of views of the earth. Demonstrators applied for official permits to be on the land from officers of the Western Shoshone tribe, whose territory was invaded by the US government when it built the nuclear weapons test ground in the 1950s. Arrested for trespassing, the demonstrators argued that the police and weapons facility personnel, without authorization from the proper officials, were the trespassers. One affinity group at the women's action called themselves the Surrogate Others; and in solidarity with the creatures forced to tunnel in the same ground with the bomb, they enacted a cyborgian emergence from the constructed body of a large, non-heterosexual desert worm.

39

INTRODUCING CYBERNETIC SYSTEMS

Katie Salen and Eric Zimmerman

Cyberspace. Cyberpunk. A *Cyborg Manifesto.* The term *cybernetic* has been appropriated by science fiction and technoculture to mean anything associated with computer technology. In point of fact, the field of cybernetics precedes the advent of digital computers. Mathematician Norbert Weiner coined the term "cybernetics" in his 1948 book *Cybernetics or Control and Communication in the Animal and the Machine.* The word is derived from the Greek word for *steersman* or *navigator,* and appropriately enough, cybernetics studies the regulation and control of systems.

Cybernetics grew out of systems theory and information theory, and like these fields, cybernetics studies a range of subjects, from mechanical and electrical systems to social and biological systems. In looking at the basic principles of cybernetics, we are touching on a field filled with great debates and a rich history, a field that greatly influenced contemporary ideas about computer technology and society.

This chapter can only offer a brief introduction to cybernetics, focusing on the ways dynamic systems change over time and the formal structures that allow these changes to occur. What are the rule structures that monitor change within a game system? How does a game system adjust to change over time? What constitutes feedback within a game? How can positive and negative feedback loops be used in the design of meaningful play? Within this schema on *Games as Cybernetic Systems,* we bring cyber-

netics to bear on these important game design questions.

ELEMENTS OF A CYBERNETIC SYSTEM

Cybernetics deals with the ways a system gauges its effect and makes necessary adjustments. The simplest cybernetic device consists of a sensor, a comparator, and an activator. The sensor provides feedback to the comparator, which determines whether the machine is deviating from its established norm. The comparator then provides guidance to the activator, which produces an output that affects the environment in some way. This fundamental process of output-feedback-adjustment is the basis of cybernetics.

—Stephen Littlejohn,
Theories of Human Communication

As communications theorist Stephen Littlejohn makes clear, cybernetics studies particular kinds of systems. The cybernetic conception of a system is based on the interaction of inputs and outputs with the internal mechanism of a system. Inputs are how the system monitors the environment—they allow the environment to influence the system. Outputs are the ways that the system takes action—they are how the system influences the environment. Through the back-and-forth exchange between the environment and the system, the system changes over time.

A cybernetic system contains three elements: a *sensor*, a *comparator*, and an *activator*. The sensor senses something about the environment or the internal state of a system. The comparator decides whether or not a change to the system needs to be made as a result of the sensor's reading, and the activator activates that change. Together, these three elements regulate how a system operates and changes over time.

A common example of a cybernetic system is a thermostat. Imagine a hot summer day and a room with an air conditioner that is attached to a thermostat. The thermostat contains the system's *sensor*, a thermometer. The thermostat also contains a *comparator* it can use to compare the temperature of the room to a user-set temperature. If the thermostat measures the air temperature above the set amount, it activates the air conditioner, the *activator* of the system, which cools down the room.

As the air begins to cool, the system continues to monitor the room temperature. When the room is sufficiently cooled so that the thermostat's sensor doesn't register the temperature as being above the set limit, the thermostat no longer sends a signal to activate the air conditioner, and so shuts off the cold air. However, the hot summer sun will begin to heat up the room again. When the temperature rises above the thermostat's limit, the air conditioner will again be activated. This cyclic behavior of the system is the "process of output-feedback-adjustment" Littlejohn describes. The fact that the cybernetic system is running as a circuit, constantly monitoring itself to see whether or not conditions have been met, is the reason why cybernetic systems are sometimes called *feedback systems*, or *feedback loops*.

In every feedback loop, information about the result of a transformation or an action is sent back to the input of the system in the form of input data. With the thermostat, the input data is information about air temperature. If this data causes the system to continue moving in the same direction (the temperature continues to rise), then it is *positive* feedback. This means that the effect is *cumulative*. If, on the other hand, the new data produces a result in opposition to the previous result (the temperature is rising, it will now be lowered), the feedback is *negative*. The effects of negative feedback *stabilize* the system.

Positive feedback loops create an exponential growth or decline; negative feedback loops maintain an equilibrium. As cyberneticist J. de Rosnay explains,

> Positive feedback leads to divergent behavior: indefinite expansion or explosion (a running away toward infinity) or total blocking of activities (a running away toward zero). Each plus involves another plus; there is a snowball effect. The examples are numerous: chain reaction, population explosion, industrial expansion, capital invested at compound interest, inflation, proliferation of cancer cells. However, when minus leads to another minus, events come to a standstill. Typical examples are bankruptcy and economic depression.
>
> Negative feedback leads to adaptive, or goal-seeking behavior: sustaining the same level, temperature, concentration, speed, direction. In a negative loop every variation toward a plus triggers a correction toward the minus, and vice versa. There is tight control; the system oscillates around an ideal equilibrium that it never attains. A thermostat or a water tank equipped with a float are simple examples of regulation by negative feedbacks.[1]

The thermostat example represents a negative feedback system. The system is negative because it seeks to sustain the same temperature. Instead of letting the room get hotter and hotter from the sun, the system acts to return the room to its normative state.

A positive feedback system works in the opposite fashion. Instead of bringing the system to a steady state, a positive cybernetic circuit encourages the system to exhibit more and more extreme behavior. For example, if the thermostat were reversed so that it only activated the air conditioner when the room was *below* a certain temperature, we would have a positive feedback system. If the room temperature ever went below the comparator's threshold, it would continue to run, making the room colder and colder, so that the temperature would steadily get lower and lower. Brrr!

We could also construct negative and positive feedback loops with a heater. In a negative feedback loop, the heater would turn on when the temperature was *below a* certain level, raising the temperature until it reached its original state, at which point the heater would shut off. In a positive feedback loop, the heater would turn on when the temperature rose *above a* certain level, continuing to heat the room indefinitely. Hot hot hot!

Now imagine what would happen if we combined two simple cybernetic systems using an air conditioner and a heater. This dual system would have a sensor to detect the temperature, a double-comparator to compare the room temperature to a pre-established setting, and heating and cooling activators. Using a dual system allows us to control the room temperature in more subtle ways. If both sub-systems were negative feedback systems, the room temperature would be very stable, as both would seek to sustain a middle room temperature. The cooler or heater would turn on when the room became too hot or too cold, and the temperature would always be brought back to its normative position. The system would never let the temperature vary too greatly. This is, in fact, how central heating and cooling works in many homes.

Alternately, both the heating and cooling circuits could be made into positive feedback sub-systems. Whenever the temperature became too hot or too cold, one of the activators would turn on and keep pushing the temperature in that direction. If the temperature setting for the heater were above the temperature setting for the air conditioner, once the room temperature strayed from the middle range, it would never reach the center again. On the other hand, imagine that the heater's activation temperature was below the air conditioner's activation temperature. If the room started out in a middle temperature range somewhere between the two activation temperatures, when the two systems were turned on, both activators would begin battling with each other in a tug-of-war to either raise or lower the temperature.

The important thing to notice in all of the heating and cooling examples is that cybernetic systems affect phenomena like temperature in very specific ways. When more than one cybernetic system is operating together, things get complex quite quickly.

FEEDBACK SYSTEMS IN GAMES

How do feedback systems operate in games? As a cybernetic system, the rules of a game define the sensors, comparators, and activators of the game's feedback loops. Within a game, there are many sub-systems that regulate the flow of play, dynamically changing and transforming game elements. Do you want your game to move toward a balanced, steady state? Or do you want it to spin wildly toward one extreme or another? Designing feedback loops within your game can help you shape these tendencies. Feedback loops can be tricky to grasp, but they offer a crucial way of understanding how formal game systems function.

Game designer Marc LeBlanc has done a great deal of thinking about the relationship between game design and feedback systems, and this schema is indebted to LeBlanc's important work on the subject. In 1999, LeBlanc gave a presentation at the Game Developer's Conference, titled "Feedback Systems and the Dramatic Structure of Competition."[2] In this lecture, LeBlanc proposed a way of thinking about games as feedback systems […] In this model, the *game state* represents the current condition of the game at any given moment. In a Chess game, for example, the game state is represented by the arrangement of the pieces on the board, the captured pieces, and which player is about to move next. In a console fighting game such as Virtua Fighter 4, the game state includes which two combatants were chosen, the health and other fixed and variable stats of the two fighters, their relative spatial positions, and the arena in which they are fighting. The game state is a *formal* way of understanding the current status of the game, and does not take into account the skills, emotions, and experience of the players. Of course, these player-based factors will definitely affect the game state. If you are a masterful Virtua Fighter 4 player and your opponent is not, this will be evident in the play of the game. However, the game state itself refers only to the formal, internal condition of the game.

The other elements of LeBlanc's model correspond directly to the components of a cybernetic system as we have discussed them. The *scoring function* is the system's *sensor* that measures some aspect of the game state. The *controller* is the *comparator,* which looks at the sensor's reading and makes the decision whether or not to take action. The *game mechanical bias* is the *activator,* a game event or set of events that can be turned on or off depending on the decision of the comparator.

When looking at games as cybernetic systems, it is important to note that we are not necessarily considering the entire game as a single feedback system. Instead, our emphasis is on the ways that cybernetic systems are embedded in games. Embedded cybernetic systems affect a single aspect of a larger game, such as determining which player goes first next round or the relative speed of players in a race. We know from our study of systems that all parts of a game are interrelated in some way. A cybernetic system within a game that directly affects just one component of a game will indirectly affect the game as a whole.

[...]

DYNAMIC DIFFICULTY ADJUSTMENT

Increasingly, digital game designers are incorporating more sophisticated feedback techniques into their game designs. The game developer Naughty Dog Entertainment is known in the game industry for what it calls "Dynamic Difficulty Adjustment," a technique it has used in the Crash Bandicoot series of games, as well as the more recent Jak and Daxter.

Dynamic Difficult Adjustment, or DDA, uses feedback loops to adjust the difficulty of play. For example, in the original Crash Bandicoot game, the player is generally maneuvering the character Crash through a series of jumping and dodging obstacles, trying to overcome damaging hazards and reach objectives to finish the level. When a player dies, the game restarts at the beginning of the level or at the most recent "save point" reached in the level.

The danger in designing this kind of game is that players possess widely varying skill levels. An experienced gamer might breeze through a level, whereas a beginner might become frustrated after dying several times without making any progress.

The DDA operations in Crash Bandicoot evaluate the number of times that a player is dying at a particular location in a level, and make the game easier as a result. A player having trouble might suddenly find that there are more helpful objects nearby, or fewer enemies to avoid. This kind of attention to the balancing of player experience is evident in the play of Crash Bandicoot games, and it helps explain the fact that a wide audience of both hardcore and less experienced players enjoys them.

Using DDA and other feedback mechanisms in games raises some fascinating game design issues. If we consider the millennia-old tradition of pre-computer play, games are traditionally about a player or players competing within a formal system that does not adjust itself automatically to player performance. As you play a game such as Baseball or Othello, your fluency with the system and your ability to manipulate it grows. The game itself and the other players provide the challenge for you. As your play deepens, you find new forms of play, new ways of expressing yourself within the system of the game.

DDA points to a different kind of game, a game that constantly anticipates the abilities of the player, reads the player's behavior, and makes adjustments accordingly. Playing a game becomes less like learning an expressive language and more like being the sole audience member for a participatory, improvisational performance, where the performers adjust their actions according to how you interact with them. Are you then playing the game, or is it playing you? Is a game "cheating" if it constantly adjusts its own rules? Could such a scheme be designed into a multiplayer experience and still feel "fair" for everyone involved? These questions have no definitive answers, as there are always many solutions for any given game design problem. Dynamic Difficulty Adjustment could be considered a heavy-handed design tool that takes agency away from the player, or it could be considered an elegant way of invisibly shaping game play so that every player has an optimal experience. Regardless of your opinion on the matter, DDA is an important tool, and as digital games rely more and more on their ability to automate complex processes, this kind of design strategy will become more common.

[…]

NOTES

Extracted from K. Salen and E. Zimmerman, *Rules of Play: Game Design Fundamentals* (Cambridge: MIT Press, 2003), pp. 214–18 and 222–23, text only. © 2003 Massachusetts Institute of Technology, by permission of MIT Press.

Editor's note: Please note that this excerpt has been slightly altered since there are no images or references to images in this extract. This has been done with the permission of the publisher.

1. <pespmc1.vub.ac.be>.
2. Marc LeBlanc, presentation at Game Developer's Conference, 1999.

40

GET A LIFE

Justin Clark

Glancing around the headquarters of Linden Labs, you'd never suspect that the basketball court–size room contains thousands of art deco skyscrapers, fashion malls, and dance clubs.

None of them are real, of course. The San Francisco software company is the creator of *Second Life,* an online virtual simulation populated by 17,000 real world users from 75 countries. Don't call it a game. There is no "object" to speak of in *Second Life*—no killing, no possibility of death. Instead, the simulated universe serves many users as a design laboratory, networking, and marketing tool.

Other than socializing, the principal activity in *Second Life* is raising virtual currency through creating and selling a range of virtual products, including clothes to outfit fellow users' alter egos, concept cars to navigate *Second Life*'s roads, and

Image 17 From *Second Life*. *Second Life* is a trademark of Linden Research, Inc. COPYRIGHT © 2001–2008 LINDEN RESEARCH, INC. ALL RIGHTS RESERVED.

fantasy real estate. Through a system of civic development incentives known as Dwell, one can also earn income by designing popular public spaces that attract other users to one's land. Just as websites earn advertising revenue based on their traffic, land owners who entice fellow users to "teleport" to their developments earn virtual currency. These range from malls, casinos, and nightclubs, to Iraq War memorials, and reconstructions of nineteenth-century London and the World Trade Center. The virtual currency, Linden Bucks, can then be redeemed for real money through online currency exchange websites such as Gaming Open Market, or reinvested in the *Second Life* economy. Most commissions are under $100, but the world's creators argue that this may be a blessing: freedom from market pressures breeds vision.

"This is an environment where it's a hundred times easier to make something than in real life," says Philip Rosedale, Linden Lab's CEO. Rosedale says he foresaw the potential of collaborative design environments back in the 1980's, after building networking software for architecture firms. "There's no cost to goods. There's no concept of transport, you don't have to cut metal to make a shape."

Indeed, *Second Life* is one of the first virtual spaces to allow users to supply the content instead of an art team. It also gives users the intellectual property rights to their creations. While relatively few users earn more than a few thousand dollars a year, real life architects and designers are finding other rewards for their work.

John Zapf, a Toronto architect with the Architects' Alliance, first used *Second Life* to design a modular Home Depot store design in a class at the University of Texas, one of a handful of colleges using *Second Life* in their design curriculum. Zapf, who won a traveling fellowship and an Excellence in Design award from his university for the project, says that *Second Life* offers a collaborative and immersive experience unavailable in CAD programs. "It's a way of truly testing buildings before they become a sixty year blight on the landscape," Zapf says.

One possibility: a limitless number of users can stand on a piece of *Second Life* land property and collectively manipulate virtual building shapes, known as primitives. While a number of collaborative online design tools already exist, *Second Life* and competing simulations, such as San Jose-based *There,* offer the added benefit of immersing designs into virtual economies. One can put up a virtual mall overnight and see how it affects foot traffic in the area. Moreover, *Second Life* allows designers without real-world connections to meet and collaborate.

One user, Tim Shepard, says *Second Life* embodies the vision of architect Christopher Alexander, who foresaw pattern repetition algorithms as an efficient means of creating a universal design language. But other users complain that the opportunity to create good design and urban planning is wasted on less inspired purposes. A lack of building codes or incentives has contributed to pre-fabricated, cookie cutter architecture, and virtual sprawl. (Inexplicably, many users insist on creating bathrooms in their virtual homes, for instance.)

A New York programmer who goes by the user name Prokofy Neva (*Second Life* lets users freely choose their first names, but forces them to pick such high-brow surnames as Koolhaas and Fassbinder from a pool) encourages users to exploit the possibilities of virtual space, such as buildings that defy gravity. Neva recently invested $1,500 in a plot of land where he has regularly held competitions to promote architectural excellence. Past winners have ranged from Norman-style houses to modernist skyscrapers.

At this stage, the limits of real-time 3D rendering encourage architects to use geometrically minimalist styles such as Art Deco and Bauhaus, though with effort, some users have managed to create the parabolic arches and organic curves of Art Nouveau. In spite of the software limitations, designers like Zapf consider their *Second Life* work compelling enough to add to their design portfolios.

User Scott McMillin, a real life designer for Target and Sears who has made $500 a month on virtual clothing sales, recently recruited a fellow *Second Life* user for his design company. The company is using *Second Life* to market a real world multimedia system, Oculas, by embedding ads for the product within the virtual world. The advantage is that the ads are 3-D versions of the real product, and appear just as real as anything else in *Second Life*.

"We feel that virtual worlds will provide the perfect arena for extending brand awareness in innovative ways," explains McMillin. He isn't alone. Corporations such as McDonald's, Levi's, and Nike, have begun seeding similar virtual worlds with advertisements. But for designers seeking an innovative laboratory, no sales pitch may be necessary.

NOTE

Extracted from J. Clark, "Get a Life," *I.D.* 52, no. 4 (2005), pp. 35–36. Reprinted by permission of the author.

41

VIRTUAL WORLDS: THE LATEST FASHION

American Apparel, Coke Pioneer
New Marketing Frontier

Gavin O'Malley

Before American Apparel launches its first denim line this fall, the offerings are getting a virtual debut and being bought and worn by virtual people. Just as other marketers—from Coca-Cola to Wells Fargo—are creating their own virtual niches, the hip clothing company is letting members of the online game Second Life try the line on for size.

"Since we opened in May, we've sold over 2,000 items to people outfitting their avatars," said Raz Schionning, director of web services for American Apparel, which opened an elaborate retail store last month in Second Life with the help of ad agency Ad Option and web developer Aimee Weber. Virtual shoppers who buy virtual clothes get 15% off the same items in real life.

Second Life, created by San Francisco-based Linden Lab, is one of several virtual online worlds where trendsetters are flocking to exchange ideas, egos and virtual property using IM-equipped "avatars," or highly-customized 3D representations of themselves. With nearly 200,000 "residents," and its open-ended structure, Second Life has become something of a testing ground for marketers to explore this new genre known as "massively multiplayer" games.

Second Life currency, known as Linden, can actually be exchanged for U.S. dollars, but American Apparel didn't set up virtual shop to turn a profit. And, of course, the company has to pay Second Life in real dollars. Linden Lab charges $1,250 for an island like the one on which American Apparel's virtual store is located, plus another $195 a month.

Another Second Life locale, dubbed Baseball Island, will host live ESPN coverage of this year's Major League Baseball home-run derby on several virtual stadium Jumbotrons—while the event is simulated on the virtual field. The event, engineered by Electric Sheep—a company that builds games and environments in Second Life—is being sponsored by Budweiser.

Image 18 American Apparel Advertisement. Image Courtesy of American Apparel.

"What's special here is us participating in a new phase of the social-networking evolution," said Mr. Schionning.

And Mr. Schionning's sentiment is shared by a growing number of media agencies and marketers. "There's an opportunity here for marketers to communicate the real meaning of their brands," said Chad Stoller, executive director of emerging platforms at agency Organic. "Think if Snickers puts its candy bars in Second Life, and they gave players real energy."

MORE INTEREST

"I'm getting an inquiry about Second Life basically every day," said Tim Harris, senior VP and co-founder of Play, a division of Publicis' Denuo Group. "Hosting virtual events seems like a logical first step, but we're looking into far more creative ways to make brands relevant in this space."

The key is adding value to the virtual experience, said Greg Smith, exec VP-media insights, planning and analysis at Carat Fusion. "Games like Second Life could literally be a real marketplace for a lot of our clients," he said. "We're still thinking about the best way to add value, not just brand messaging."

But while Mr. Smith and others in the industry contemplate the possibility of effective virtual marketing, some brands are already enjoying success in the space. Coca-Cola's mycoke.com already offers a virtual setting in which visitors can play games, listen to music and chat. Wells Fargo's Stagecoach Island is an independent world where one can find all the comforts of virtual life, and even learn something about personal finance.

Simpler versions of the massively multiplayer phenomenon have found a following with tween audiences as well. One of the more popular is Whyville.net, which has accumulated nearly

Image 19   American Apparel Factory. Image Courtesy of American Apparel.

1.7 million members since it was hatched in 1999 by Numedeon. In April, Toyota signed up for a 14-week experiment with Whyville to promote its Scion brand of cars. Members can visit Club Scion and trick out a car. If they have enough virtual currency, they can even buy one and drive it around Whyville with their friends.

"When you're going after young trendsetters, you have to stay on the cutting edge," said Adrian Si, interactive-marketing manager for Scion. "We did MySpace about two years ago, but … I think it's a little too mainstream now."

And, he added, "studies show that kids start thinking seriously about what type of car they'd like to drive as early as eight or nine."

Other advertisers in the Whyville space include Adobe, NASA and the Getty Museum. Cost-per-thousand rates range from $6 to $30, while one-time sponsorship setup fees range from $25,000 to $250,000. Numedeon plans to launch five more virtual worlds, each targeting different demographics[. …]

In May, technology startup Doppelganger launched a 3D virtual lounge where fans of Interscope Records' Pussycat Dolls can hang out and dance with members of the bands.

Doppelganger CEO Andrew Littlefield has ambitions that go far beyond the Pussycat Dolls lounge, however. What he and his team of engineers have created is a virtual 3D world—imagine a trendier version of L.A. and Tokyo combined—where young people can hang.

Beyond Doppelganger's initial partnership with Interscope, Mr. Littlefield said deals with clothing labels and other brands are in the works. "This is the next generation of interaction between people and brands online," Mr. Littlefield told Advertising Age at launch.

But it goes without saying that marketers' entrance into unfamiliar virtual worlds will be tricky. One early misstep is the now-dead Cadbury-Adams deal to sponsor a "World of Warcraft" tournament.

Aware that the wildly popular virtual environment might not be an ideal world for direct product placement, the company had planned on teaming this summer with GameSpot-CNET Networks' online gaming review to sponsor a four-month gaming tournament in order to introduce its Stride gum brand.

These tournaments have been gaining momentum, with the final games averaging more than 100,000 on-demand streams and more than 10,000 spectators watching and participating in the live broadcasts, via GameSpot "TournamentTV." But the partnership fell through at the last minute, and, while no official reason was given, people close to the deal say the popular massively multiplayer role-playing game wasn't ready for such overt brand sponsorship.

NOTE

Extracted from G. O'Malley, "Virtual Worlds: The Latest Fashion," *Advertising Age* (July 10, 2006), 3. Reprinted with permission from the July 10, 2006 issue of Advertising Age, Copyright, Crain Communications Inc. 2006.

SECTION 4: IDENTITY AND CONSUMPTION

4.2: Gender and Design

INTRODUCTION

Gender affects design practice, products, and discourse through stereotype. The readings in this subsection explore how designed objects have become gender-identified, and how some design professions are seen as male spheres, while others are deemed only appropriate for women. While the term *gender* has both female and male forms, femininity and masculinity, the authors excerpted here refer specifically to the condition of women, in discourse, in production, and finally as designers.

A feminist design historian and professor at the University of Northumbria in the United Kingdom, Cheryl Buckley provides a context with a reworked version of her seminal essay, "Made in Patriarchy: Towards a Feminist Analysis of Women in Design," published originally in 1986. That essay aimed to analyze patriarchy as the context in which women interact with design, which also impacts the methods used by historians to record that interaction. In doing so, she challenges modernist design history's concern with experimentation, innovation, and mass-produced objects as serving to erase or distort women's roles as producers and consumers. Her reworking takes account of the effect on design history of postmodern theory, and the particular development of scholarly interest in masculinity within the study of gender and sexuality, an interest, she argues, that has deflected attention away from feminist concerns. She quotes the opinion of another feminist design historian, Pat Kirkham, "Postmodernism has helped broaden appreciation of the multivalency of objects, but it has made more respectable the study of objects out of context." Buckley calls for reclaiming feminist theory in order to explore the relationship of women and design within a social and historical context.

Buckley's call resonates with the second reading, "Life on the Global Assembly Line," first published in 1984 and reprinted in 2002 in the feminist magazine *Ms.* Unlike Buckley's essay, this is not a reworking of an earlier argument, but a restatement of an article concerning the disadvantaged role of women in the "new international division of labor," which still remains valid. Many women are employed to manufacture what might be called "design-intensive" products, particularly fashionable clothing and electronics. Women workers are a high percentage of the global labor force, yet their contributions are anonymous, unacknowledged and, when revealed, a source of embarrassment and discomfort to the consumers they serve.

In production, as in design, women's roles are often justified by myths, such as references to the small hands and manual dexterity of the Oriental female. Small hands imply small brains, as racism is layered on patriarchal and misogynous justifications of women's lowly and poorly paid positions in factories. Saralee Hamilton, a staff organizer at the American Friends Service Committee, an organization dedicated to social justice, including immigrant's rights, lays blame on multinational corporations for having "deliberately targeted women for exploitation." This point is developed further in Lorraine Gray's Emmy award–winning documentary, *The Global Assembly Line,* which portrays the lives of working women, and men, in the "free trade zones" of developing countries and North America, seen against the closure of U.S. factories as corporations for lower-paid workforces. It is also contextualized by the extract from Marx's *Capital* reproduced in Section 3.3, Politics, and with the readings in Section 6.2, Equality and Social Justice.

The question of difference between women and men designers is the subject of Hazel Clark's essay, from *Dish,* a book that followed an exhibition of the work of contemporary women designers, *Transformation: New International Design,* an exhibition held at Parsons The New School for Design, New York, June 18–October 3, 2003. Both the book and the exhibition examined design for the home, although perplexingly, neither emphasized that all the featured work was designed by women. Clark also identifies the domestic context as a center of female experience, as mothers, in child care, and also we learn, as designers. The domestic focus is not biologically given, but defined by social and cultural practices that facilitate greater understanding of design's role as "an interface between people and their activities, experiences, needs, and desires." Gender is often overlooked in that equation, or treated superficially. This is particularly the case in consumption (the subject of the next subsection), in which design is often promoted using crude gender stereotypes.

Casey and Martens (2007) have considered in detail *Gender and Consumption* in their edited anthology, and Sparke (1995) has discussed the sexual politics of taste in *As Long As It's Pink,* while Kirkham (1996) has focused on *The Gendered Object.* Each reinforces the way that gender definitions are constructed historically, socially, and culturally, but by the same token they are subject to change. Clothes are a good example, linked as they are so intimately with human identities, both public and private, and with consumption. The suit, for example, a sartorial convention for Westernized males and masculine culture since the nineteenth century, was appropriated by women to symbolize their challenge to male power, while simultaneously and unintentionally reinforcing that power. The issue here of course is not the object itself, which has no inherent gender, but how and in what context it is used.

So, we can conclude that gender does matter for design, not least because it focuses attention on how design operates as product, in production, professionally, relative to the history and understanding of human beings, and increasingly since the nineteenth century. Whether we share Cheryl Buckley's concern for the need for more feminist theory to challenge and problematize patriarchal norms or not, consideration of gender undoubtedly offers the potential for a greater and more nuanced understanding of design in all its many dimensions. Relative to consumption, for example, is the subject of the Section 4.3, where one of the readings, "Do-It-Yourself Security," by Sarah Lichtman, investigates the role of gender stereotypes in the postnuclear world, with the construction of the home fallout shelter in Cold War America. Consideration of gender and design implicates the identity of the consumer or user, thus widening the subject of study and its surrounding discourse.

42

MADE IN PATRIARCHY

Theories of Women and Design—A Reworking

Cheryl Buckley

This essay reconsiders some of the arguments raised in my earlier article "Made in Patriarchy: Towards a Feminist Analysis of Women and Design," which was first published in *Design Issues* in 1986.[1] That article, prepared over ten years ago, had two main aims. The first was to analyze the patriarchal context within which women interact with design as practitioners, theorists, consumers, historians, and as objects of representation. The second was to examine the methods used by historians to record that interaction.[2]

These methods, which involve the selection, classification, and prioritization of types of design, categories of designers, distinct styles and movements, and different modes of production, are inherently biased against women and, in effect, serve to exclude them from history. To compound this omission, the few women who make it into the literature of design are accounted for within the framework of patriarchy: they are either defined by their gender as designers or users of feminine products, or they are subsumed under the name of their husband, lover, father, or brother. Feminist theory, I argued, offered the theoretical tools to challenge the ways in which women's interaction with design was recorded. In particular, feminist theory enabled us to delineate the operation of patriarchy; it provided a method for conceptualizing gender and femininity, the sexual division of labor, and the hierarchal positioning of certain aspects of design over others.

The impetus for the article came from the growing interest within design history, practice, and theory in the relationship of women to design and was the culmination of related research, teaching, conferences, and publishing. At the time, it seemed as though the expansion of the field would bring about substantial changes to the various disciplines associated with design.[3]

In retrospect, this was overoptimistic. Arguably, although feminist interventions in design and design history still contribute to the debate, women's agenda has yet to be integrated into the mainstream. Questions about women's role in design remain tangential to the discipline and are tackled with reluctance. In design history, for example, women's position is still sidestepped, and in architectural and design practice women's needs as consumers/users often remain unaddressed. My aim, then, is to look at how the debate regarding women's relationship to design has developed since the mid-1980s in Britain within the context of design history and theory, and to offer some thoughts as to how we might progress beyond the millennium.

My intention is not to argue that women remain hapless victims, incapable of challenging the vagaries of patriarchy. There is much to celebrate in terms of women's achievements over the last decade. The conference "Re-Visioning Design and Technology: Feminist Perspectives" for which this essay was first produced is evidence of the continuing debate.[4] And yet it seems to me that we are at a critical point. In some respects the debate is faltering and we are losing our original focus. We risk disempowerment and marginalization particularly at the hands of postmodern theorists who pay scant attention to women. As Meaghan Morris has argued, "In a number of recent discussions of postmodernism, a sense of intrigue develops around a presumed absence—or withholding—of women's speech in relation to what has certainly become one of the boom discourses of the 1980s."[5] This sense of absence is especially worrying within a theoretical framework which ostensibly challenges established values. Perhaps, as Susan Faludi has argued in *Backlash,* an "anti-feminist backlash has been set off not by women's achievement of full equality but by the increased possibility that they might win it."[6]

As an academic discipline, design history has been eclectic in its intellectual influences since its inception, and inevitably it has incorporated aspects of postmodern theory. The way that this has shaped accounts of women's role in design can be demonstrated by the recent publication of two books. The Women's Press has reissued Attfield and Kirkham's A *View from the Interior: Women and Design,* first published in 1989 but in preparation from the mid-1980s.[7] This book made a major contribution to the development of a feminist design history by demonstrating the enormous scope of research on women's role in design at the end of the 1980s in Britain. Except for one essay, it concerned itself entirely with women and their relationships at different historical points to design. Coinciding with this reissue was the publication of a new book, edited by Pat Kirkham, entitled *The Gendered Object.* This studies "the ways in which objects, particularly objects of everyday life, are made socially acceptable and 'appropriate' for either men and women."[8]

Between the publication of these two books is a marked change, clearly evident from the titles, in the way that women's relationships to design has [sic] been described by design and cultural historians. In the first book, the focus was women and the theoretical underpinning was clearly feminist, whereas in the second, although there is still a concern with analyzing gender, there is as much emphasis on masculinity as on femininity.

One of the theoretical contexts from which this interest in gender has emerged in addition to feminism is postmodernism, and what is distinctive about this latter context is its emphasis on masculinity: "Much postmodern theory seems to be about a shifting in the position of masculinity, an uncertainty about manhood, a loss of faith in patriarchal authority."[9] Questioning masculinity is clearly important for feminism, and indeed feminists have been at the vanguard of this.[10] However, as Jane Flax has argued, "Postmodernist discourses, or even commentaries about them, notably lack any serious discussion of feminist theories, even when these theories overlap with, supplement, or support postmodernist writers' ideas."[11]

What interests me here is the question of whether postmodern theory enables the feminist design historian to write histories of women's relationship to design or, as I suspect, works against such work. In questioning postmodernism in this way, I am open to the charge of naïveté, but clarity rather than obscurity is my primary goal in utilizing any theory, whether postmodernist or feminist. In the first part of this essay, I will briefly discuss some of the key literature from design history over the last ten years (mainly from the United Kingdom, but also from the United States), and in the second part I want to explore the interplay between this literature and cultural and feminist theory, particularly as it relates to women and design.

Undoubtedly the feminist agenda in design has continued and developed. At an academic level, literature, research, conferences, and teaching programs have all proliferated in the last ten years. From a practical standpoint, user-sensitive designs have gained more legitimacy as architects and designers realize that the user of products and buildings is not a universalized "type" man but is instead socially and culturally constituted by sex, race, class, age, sexual orientation, and national identity. We have seen a number of important conferences which have provided a forum for developing new ideas, sharing information and research, and establishing common objectives.[12]

These emerged within the context of intense interest in design in the latter part of 1980s, and they focused on design to provide solutions to some of the problems facing women.

The literature relating to women and design expanded substantially in the late 1980s and early 1990s. Within this there are different categories and approaches. Some books and compilations of essays focused exclusively on women and design.[13] In addition, there have been major exhibition catalogs dealing with women designers and architects based on empirical research, which show women's involvement in design mainly as producers, although others look at the effect of design on women consumers.[14] Alongside these, there have been theoretical pieces which have examined the relationships between design and women and between design and feminism, including, in the United States, Martha Scotford's piece on graphic design in *Visible Language* and, in Britain, Judy Attfield's excellent feminist analysis of design in *Design History and the History of Design*.[15] The positioning of Attfield's piece as a supplementary section at the end of the book was very revealing, sending a clear signal about the relationship of feminism to design history as an optional extra—at least in the eyes of some.

Indeed we have to look no further than to the 1995 Spring issue of *Design Issues* for confirmation of this type of backsliding. In this special issue devoted to the question of how to define design history, a bevy of male scholars fought it out.[16] Their central purpose was to determine the nature and boundaries of design history and its relationship to design studies. Significantly, feminist critiques of design history were heavily drawn on by each side in their arguments, but none of the protagonists bothered to ask what had been happening to feminist design history in the last decade.[17] As I read their deliberations, I was struck by two main points. First, their interest in feminism was merely functional in the sense that it enabled them to come to a definition of design history. Genuine interest would have required a more substantial contribution than that

demonstrated by a few citations in the footnotes. Second, it was highly frustrating to see how feminist critiques of design history had been ransacked to sustain a particular viewpoint about the nature of the discipline. Feminist arguments, when they were referred to, were incorporated as but one of many "approaches," all potentially valid and equally important.

In addition to those books and journals which have directly addressed women's role in design, there have been numerous books which include aspects of women's relationship to design alongside other subjects, particularly film. This development has been stimulated by organizations such as the British Film Institute and individual researchers who have crossed the subject divide.[18] Fashion often figures prominently in these texts, and although it is an activity still neglected by mainstream design historians, it has been scrutinized by academics from outside the field, frequently with the aim of examining representations of femininity.[19] The neglect of fashion by design historians provides further evidence, in my view, of the intrinsic misogyny of much design history. Fashion is still collapsed into the realm of "the feminine" by all but the most gender-conscious of design historians.

Within the recent literature of fashion history and design history, however, are writings that evidence a growing trend to address gender instead of women. Together with these are books which deal with sexuality and gender within the context of postmodernism.[20] The focus for these is the body, usually the female body, and the processes of representation and consumption associated with this. Indeed, a shift of interest toward consumption rather than production has been a characteristic of design history generally, and this has been important to our understanding of women's role in design. Increasingly, however, the dominant tendency in research and publishing is gender, not women. Gender studies replaces women's studies in academic programs; masculinity is investigated as much as, if not more than, femininity; and the young women academics just starting out are as likely to be writing their Ph.D.'s about masculinity as they are about femininity. The question, then, is why should this be? Has the woman question been answered at long last? Or are we indeed witnessing a backlash in our subject, and if so where did it come from and why?

Arguably, some of my questions can be answered by examining the relationship between recent cultural theory, particularly postmodern, and feminism. A key question for me is where feminism as a tool for cultural as well as political analysis fits into the theoretical rethinking prompted by postmodernism. In fact, it is possible to argue that postmodern theory, although ostensibly challenging the value systems of moribund academic disciplines, has remained largely ignorant of and uninterested in feminism. In two specific ways, it seems to me, postmodernism has delivered a preemptive strike against women disguised as liberation. First, it has replaced one set of patriarchal discourses with another set which is equally patriarchal, as Meaghan Morris has argued: "It would be hard to deny that in spite of its heavy (if lightly acknowledged) borrowings from feminist theory, … postmodernism … has pulled off the peculiar feat of re-constituting an overwhelming male pantheon of proper names to function as ritual objects of academic … commentary."[21] Postmodernism is dominated by yet more "great" men—for example, Baudrillard, Barthes, Lacan, Lyotard—who have introduced a "new kind of gender tourism, whereby male theorists are able to take package trips into the world of femininity."[22]

Second, the postmodern approach to key concepts such as "feminine," "gender," and "subjectivity" poses problems for feminists. One of feminism's main achievements has been to counter essentialist definitions of gender difference and to undermine the notion that gender is rigidly fixed. In this, feminists have turned to psychoanalysis and to some of the same theorists who have proved so influential to postmodernism, although with a different end in view. The feminist study of gender seeks to highlight the situation of women and the analysis of male domination or patriarchy; it aims to problematize issues of identity, power, and knowledge, leading feminists to recover and explore aspects of social, cultural, and political lives which have been suppressed, remain unarticulated, or have been denied within male-dominated accounts. In contrast, when postmodern theory addresses the issue of gender it seems to do so with the intention of understanding masculinity, and any interest in femininity is there to provide a counterpoint to masculinity. As Suzanne Moore put it, "In deciphering the language of the 'other' and then claiming it for themselves, these theoretical drag queens don the trappings of femininity for a night on the town without so much as a glance back at the poor woman whose clothes they have stolen."[23]

The attack on the subject within contemporary cultural theory poses problems for those who are interested in histories of things and people normally marginalized by mainstream writers. One feminist strategy for writing histories of design has been to articulate women's presence as historical subjects rather than as objects. But in their critique of subjectivity, postmodern theorists consign women yet again to the margins of history. As Flax writes, "Post-modernists intend to persuade us that *we* should be suspicious of any notion of self or subjectivity. Any such notion may be bound up with and support dangerous and oppressive 'humanist' myths. However, I am deeply suspicious of the motives of those who would counsel such a position at the same time as women have begun to *re-member their selves* and to *claim an agentic subjectivity* available always before only to a few privileged white men" (my emphasis).[24]

How to frame the subject and subjectivity, and how to respond theoretically to the attack on these from postmodern theorists, are questions at the core of feminist approaches to history and design history. Feminist writers and historians including Sally Alexander, Carolyn Steadman, Rosi Braidotti, Doreen Massey, bell hooks, and Meaghan Morris have consistently tried to think differently about how women's histories can be written, and there are common threads in their work.[25] In particular there is the idea of speaking differently in order to articulate women's voices. For hooks this involves choosing to speak from the margins as a place of resistance, whereas Braidotti uses the terms "figuration" and "nomadic" to articulate the notion of the "situated" nature of subjectivity.[26] In a similar vein, Alexander sees memory as a way of glimpsing individual subjectivities: "Life histories, as they tell us something of what has been forgotten in cultural memory, always describe, or rehearse a history full of affective subjectivity. As with a poem, they may suggest the metonymic signs of femininity particular to a generation."[27] A sense of place increasingly informs feminist studies of women's lives and experiences. Using Adrienne Rich's term "the politics of location" to theorize the specificity of female subjectivities, Rosi Braidotti argues: "The politics of location means that the thinking, the theoretical process, is not abstract, universalized, objective, and detached, but rather that it is situated in the contingency of one's experience, and as such it is a necessarily partial exercise. In other words, one's intellectual vision is not a disembodied mental activity; rather, it is closely connected to one's place of enunciation, that is, where one is actually speaking from."[28] She goes on to equate the abstract generalities of certain theories (read postmodern) with the "classical patriarchal subject," asserting, "What is at stake is not the specific as opposed to the universal, but rather two radically different ways of conceiving the possibility of legitimating theoretical remarks. For feminist theory the only consistent way of making general theoretical points is to be aware that one is actually located somewhere specific."[29] Throughout, Braidotti and others such as Meaghan Morris and Doreen Massey remind us that within the context of postmodernism women are not merely abstracted, they are nowhere, and although the category "gender" is ostensibly at the core of postmodern discourse, women and femininity have been neatly sidestepped. However, they also propose a variety of theoretical strategies for

rethinking and re-articulating women's histories which are relevant for those interested in a feminist intervention in the history of design.

Influenced by cultural studies, film studies, anthropology, and architectural history, design history has been particularly susceptible to postmodernism over the last few years. From the postmodern viewpoint, design is an ideal subject for scrutiny. According to Judy Attfield and Pat Kirkham, "Design is posited here as material artefact, commodity, aesthetic object, aide-memoire, souvenir, lifestyle, political symbol; signifier supreme."[30] All aspects of design are fruitful sources for postmodern investigations, but fashion has a particular appeal for those very qualities that led to its devaluation by modernist design historians: "The fashion-object appears as the most chaotic, fragmented, and elusive of commodities, yet it circulates a pervasive and enveloping logic … . It constitutes an exemplary site for examining the cultural dislocation and contradictions of the transition from modernity to the late capitalist, new wave, postmodern era."[31] However, from a different, feminist viewpoint, fashion embodies numerous ideas about what it is to be woman, to be feminine, and to be gendered differently than men. Fashion images and advertisements in magazines and on TV are formulated historically, and they relate to specific "located" feminine identities, not generalized ones. As Pat Kirkham observes, " 'Postmodernism' has helped broaden appreciation of the multi-valency of objects, but it has made more respectable the study of objects out of context."[32] It is the analysis of design within its context and history which aids our understanding of its significance in women's lives. History enables us to interpret and understand, and perhaps to conceive of change.

In my view, postmodernism has deflected us from these concerns. Whereas the needs of women were our central objective ten years ago, we now deliberate over gender—indeed, theorizing about women and not gender has been intellectually insupportable over the last few years as the old polarities of femininity and masculinity have apparently dissolved. To some extent the problem facing us as feminist design historians is how to rearticulate the categories "feminine," "gender," "woman," and "subjectivity" in order to move beyond postmodern discourse. Taking our cue from feminist historians, geographers, cultural historians, and theorists, we need to remove these terms from the abstract and relocate them in the specificity of history. We must integrate these feminist categories into our discussions of design history, practice, and theory in order to demonstrate that women's experiences of design are still only partially accounted for. If, as a consequence, we are theoretically at odds with our peers, we should recall Jane Flax when she said, "Postmodernists have not offered adequate concepts of or spaces for the practice of justice. What memories or history will our daughters have if we do not find ways to speak of and practice it?"[33]

NOTES

Extracted from C. Buckley, "Made in Patriarchy: Theories of Women and Design—A Reworking," in *Design and Feminism Re-Visioning Spaces, Places, and Everyday Things,* ed. Joan Rothschild (New Brunswick, N.J. and London: Rutgers University Press, 1999), pp. 109–18. Rothschild Copyright © 1999 by Rutgers, The State University. Reprinted by permission of Rutgers University Press.

1. Cheryl Buckley, "Made in Patriarchy: Towards a Feminist Analysis of Women and Design," *Design Issues* 3:2 (Fall 1986): 1–31, and in Victor Margolin, ed., *Design Discourse: History, Theory, Criticism* (Chicago: University of Chicago Press, 1989), pp. 251–62.
2. Ibid., p. 251.
3. In Britain this began with a conference at the Institute of Contemporary Arts in London in 1983 entitled "Women and Design." This was followed by a number of key conferences throughout the 1980s and early 1990s culminating in "Cracks in the Pavements:

Gender/Fashion/Architecture" at the Design Museum in London in 1991. On a personal level it coincided with the period in which I wrote my Ph.D. thesis, which dealt with women designers in the British pottery industry, 1914–1940. This brought me face-to-face with numerous problems of historiography and theory in relation to a feminist design history.
4. "Re-Visioning Design and Technology: Feminist Perspectives," Graduate School and University Center of the City University of New York, November 16–18, 1995.
5. Meaghan Morris, *The Pirate's Fiancée: Feminism, Reading, Postmodernism* (London: Verso, 1988), p. 11.
6. Susan Faludi, *Backlash* (New York: Crown, 1991; London: Chatto & Windus, 1991), p. 11.
7. Judy Attfield and Pat Kirkham, A *View from the Interior: Women and Design* (London: Women's Press, 1989).
8. Pat Kirkham, *The Gendered Object* (Manchester: Manchester University Press, 1996), preface.
9. Suzanne Moore, "Getting a Bit of the Other: The Pimps of Postmodernism," in Rowena Chapman and Jonathan Rutherford, eds., *Male Order: Unwrapping Masculinity* (London: Lawrence & Wishart, 1988), p. 179.
10. See, for example, Lynne Segal, *Slow Motion. Changing Masculinities, Changing Men* (London: Virago, 1990).
11. Jane Flax, *Thinking Fragments: Psychoanalysis, Feminism, and Postmodernism in the Contemporary West* (Berkeley and Los Angeles: University of California Press, 1990), p. 211.
12. As an example, I recently attended a conference at the University of Trier in Germany entitled "Marginalisierung und Geschelechter-konstruction in den Angenwandten Kunsten," October 3–6, 1996. This was the second of three conferences organized by German, Austrian, and Swiss art historians which set out to explore aspects of women's art and design history.
13. See, for example, Rozsika Parker, *The Subversive Stitch* (London: Women's Press, 1984); Cheryl

Buckley, *Potters and Paintresses: Women Designers in the Pottery Industry, 1870–1955* (London: Women's Press, 1990); Jude Burkhauser, *Glasgow Girls: Women in Art and Design, 1880–1920* (Edinburgh: Canongate Press, 1990).

14. See, for example, Lynne Walker, *Drawing on Diversity: Women, Architecture, and Practice* (London: Royal Institute of British Architects, 1997); Elizabeth Cumming, *Phoebe Anna Traquair* (Edinburgh: National Galleries of Scotland, 1993); Jill Seddon and Suzette Worden, *Women Designing: Redefining Design in Britain between the Wars* (Brighton: University of Brighton, 1994); Philippa Glanville and Jennifer Faulds Goldsborough, *Women Silversmiths, 1685–1845* (Washington: National Museum of Women in the Arts, 1990).

15. Martha Scotford, "Messy History vs. Neat History: Toward an Expanded View of Women in Graphic Design," *Visible Language* 28: 4 (1994); John Walker, *Design History and the History of Design* (London: Pluto, 1989).

16. *Design Issues* 11: 1 (Spring 1995).

17. See, for example, the essays by Victor Margolin, Adrian Forty, and Jonathan Woodham.

18. See, for example, Beatriz Colomina, ed., *Sexuality and Space* (Princeton: Princeton Architectural Press, 1992); Jane Gaines and Charlotte Herzog, *Fabrications: Costume and the Female Body* (London and New York: Routledge, 1990).

19. See, for example, Elizabeth Wilson, *Adorned in Dreams: Fashion and Modernity* (London: Virago, 1985); Juliet Ash and Elizabeth Wilson, *Chic Thrills: A Fashion Reader* (London: Pandora, 1992); Caroline Evans and Minna Thornton, *Women and Fashion* (London: Quartet, 1989); Susan Porter Benson, *Counter Cultures: Saleswomen, Managers, and Customers in American Department Stores, 1890–1940* (Urbana: University of Illinois Press, 1988).

20. See, for example, Arthur Kroker and Marilouise Kroker, *Body Invaders: Sexuality and the Postmodern Condition* (London: New World Perspectives, 1988); Rosa Ainley, ed., *New Frontiers of Space, Bodies, and Gender* (London: Routledge, 1998); Elizabeth Grosz and Elspeth Probyn, eds., *Sexy Bodies: The Strange Carnalities of Feminism* (London: Routledge, 1995).

21. Morris, *Pirate's Fiancée,* p. 12.

22. Moore, "Getting a Bit of the Other," p. 167.

23. Ibid., p. 185.

24. Flax, *Thinking Fragments,* p. 220.

25. Sally Alexander, *Becoming a Woman and Other Essays in Nineteenth- and Twentieth-Century Feminist History* (London: Virago, 1994); Carolyn Steadman, "Landscape for a Good Woman," in Liz Heron, ed., *Truth, Dare, or Promise: Girls Growing Up in the Fifties* (London: Virago, 1985); Rosi Braidotti, *Nomadic Subjects. Embodiment and Sexual Difference in Contemporary Feminist Theory* (New York: Columbia University Press, 1994); Doreen Massey, *Space, Place, and Gender* (London: Polity, 1994); bell hooks, *Yearning: Race, Gender and Cultural Politics* (London: Turnaround, 1991); Morris, *Pirate's Fiancée.*

26. Braidotti, *Nomadic Subjects.*

27. Alexander, *Becoming a Woman,* p. 234.

28. Braidotti, *Nomadic Subjects,* p. 237.

29. Ibid., p. 238.

30. Attfield and Kirkham, Introduction, in Kirkham, *Gendered Object,* p. 3.

31. Gail Faurschou, "Fashion and the cultural logic of postmodernity," in Kroker and Kroker, *Body Invaders,* p. 79.

32. Kirkham, *Gendered Object,* preface.

33. Flax, *Thinking Fragments,* p. 221.

43

LIFE ON THE GLOBAL ASSEMBLY LINE

Barbara Ehrenreich and Annette Fuentes

Every morning, between four and seven, thousands of women head out for the day shift. In Ciudad Juárez, they crowd into ruteras (run-down vans) for the trip from the slum neighborhoods to the industrial parks on the outskirts of the city. In Penang they squeeze, 60 or more at a time, into buses for the trip to the low, modern factory buildings of the Bayan Lepas free trade zone. In Taiwan, they walk from the dormitories—where the night shift is already asleep in the still-warm beds—through the checkpoints in the high fence surrounding the factory zone.

This is the world's new industrial proletariat: young, female, Third World. Viewed from the "first world," they are still faceless, genderless "cheap labor," signaling their existence only through a label or tiny imprint—"made in Hong Kong," or Taiwan, Korea, the Dominican Republic, Mexico, the Philippines. But they may be one of the most strategic blocs of womanpower in the world. Conservatively, there are 2 million Third World female industrial workers employed now, millions more looking for work, and their numbers are rising every year.

It doesn't take more than second-grade arithmetic to understand what's happening. In the U.S., an assembly-line worker is likely to earn, depending on her length of employment, between $3.10 and $5 an hour. In many Third World countries, a woman doing the same work will earn $3 to $5 a day.

And so, almost everything that can be packed up is being moved out to the Third World:

garment manufacture, textiles, toys, footwear, pharmaceuticals, wigs, appliance parts, tape decks, computer components, plastic goods. In some industries, like garment and textile, American jobs are lost in the process, and the biggest losers are women, often black and Hispanic. But what's going on is much more than a matter of runaway shops. Economists are talking about a "new international division of labor," in which the process of production is broken down and the fragments are dispersed to different parts of the world, while control over the overall process and technology remains safely at company headquarters in "first world" countries.

The American electronics industry provides a classic example: circuits are printed on silicon wafers and tested in California; then the wafers are shipped to Asia for the labor-intensive process by which they are cut into tiny chips and bonded to circuit boards; final assembly into products such as calculators or military equipment usually takes place in the United States. Garment manufacture too is often broken into geographically separated steps, with the most repetitive, labor-intensive jobs going to the poor countries of the southern hemisphere.

So much any economist could tell you. What is less often noted is the gender breakdown of the emerging international division of labor. Eighty to 90 percent of the low-skilled assembly jobs that go to the Third World are performed by women in a remarkable switch from earlier patterns of foreign-dominated industrialization.

Until now, "development" under the aegis of foreign corporations has usually meant more jobs for men and—compared to traditional agricultural society—a diminished economic status for women. But multinational corporations and Third World governments alike consider assembly-line work—whether the product is Barbie dolls or missile parts—to be "women's" work.

It's an article of faith with management that only women can do, or will do, the monotonous, painstaking work that American business is exporting to the Third World. The personnel manager of a light assembly plant in Taiwan told anthropologist Linda Gail Arrigo, "Young male workers are too restless and impatient to do monotonous work with no career value. If displeased, they sabotage the machines and even threaten the foreman. But girls? At most, they cry a little."

A top-level management consultant who specializes in advising American companies on where to relocate gave us this global generalization: "The [factory] girls genuinely enjoy themselves. They're away from their families. They have spending money. Of course it's a regulated experience too—with dormitories to live in—so it's a healthful experience."

What is the real experience of the women in the emerging Third World industrial work force? Rachael Grossman, a researcher with the Southeast Asia Resource Center, found women employees of U.S. multinational firms in Malaysia and the Philippines living four to eight in a room in boardinghouses, or squeezing into tiny extensions built onto squatter huts near the factory. Where companies do provide dormitories, they are not of the "healthful," collegiate variety. The American Friends Service Committee reports that dormitory space is "likely to be crowded—while one shift works, another sleeps, as many as twenty to a room."

Living conditions are only part of the story. The work that multinational corporations export to the Third World is not only the most tedious, but often the most hazardous part of the production process. The countries they go to are, for the most part, those that will guarantee no interference from health and safety inspectors, trade unions, or even free-lance reformers.

Consider the electronics industry, which is generally thought to be the safest and cleanest of the exported industries. The factory buildings are low and modern, like those one might find in a suburban American industrial park. Inside, rows of young women, neatly dressed in the company uniform or T-shirt, work quietly at their stations. There is air conditioning (not for the women's comfort, but to protect the delicate semiconductor parts they work with), and high-volume piped-in Bee Gees hits (not so much for entertainment, as to prevent talking).

For many Third World women, electronics is a prestige occupation, at least compared to other kinds of factory work. They are unlikely to know that in the United States the National Institute on Occupational Safety and Health (NIOSH) has placed electronics on its select list of "high health-risk industries using the greatest number of toxic substances." If electronics assembly work is risky here, it is doubly so in countries where there is no equivalent of NIOSH to even issue warnings. In many plants toxic chemicals and solvents sit in open containers, filling the work area with fumes that can literally knock you out. "We have been told of cases where ten to twelve women passed out at once," an AFSC field worker in northern Mexico told us, "and the newspapers report this as 'mass hysteria.'"

[...]

In the competition for multinational investment, local governments advertise their women shamelessly. An investment brochure issued by the Malaysian government informs multinational executives that: "the manual dexterity of the Oriental female is famous the world over. Her hands are small, and she works fast with extreme care. ... Who, therefore, could be better qualified by nature and inheritance, to contribute to the efficiency of a bench-assembly production line than the Oriental girl?"

[...]

But the most powerful promoter of exploitative conditions for Third World women workers is the United States government itself. For example, the notoriously repressive Korean textile industry was developed with the help of $400 million in aid from the U.S. State Department. Malaysia became a low-wage haven for the electronics industry thanks to technical assistance financed by AID [Agency for International Development] and to U.S. money (funneled through the Asian Development Bank) to set up free trade zones.

But the most obvious form of United States involvement, according to Lenny Siegel, the director of the Pacific Studies Center, is through "our consistent record of military aid to Third World governments that are capitalist, politically repressive, and are not striving for economic independence."

[...]

So far, feminism, first-world style, has barely begun to acknowledge the Third World's new industrial womanpower. Jeb Mays and Kathleen Connell, cofounders of the San Francisco-based Women's Network on Global Corporations, are two women who would like to change that: "There's still this idea of the Third World woman as 'the other'—someone exotic and totally unlike us," Mays and Connell told us. "But now we're talking about women who wear the same styles in clothes, listen to the same music, and may even work for the same corporation. That's an irony the multinationals have created. In a way, they're drawing us together as women."

Saralee Hamilton, an AFSC staff organizer, says: "The multinational corporations have deliberately targeted women for exploitation. If feminism is going to mean anything to women all over the world, it's going to have to find new ways to resist corporate power internationally." She envisions a global network of grass-roots women capable of sharing experiences, transmitting information, and—eventually—providing direct support for each other's struggles. It's a long way off; few women anywhere have the money for intercontinental plane flights or even long-distance calls, but at least we are beginning to see the way. "We all have the same hard life," wrote Korean garment worker Min Chong Suk. "We are bound together with one string."

NOTE

Extracted from B. Ehrenreich and A. Fuentes, "Life on the Global Assembly Line," *MS Magazine* (Spring 2002). http://www.msmagazine.com/spring2002/ehrenreichandfuentes.asp (accessed January 15, 2008). Reprinted by permission of *MS* magazine, © 1981.

44

THE DIFFERENCE OF FEMALE DESIGN

Hazel Clark

Giving recognition, duly deserved, to the output of women designers begs an important question: do women design differently? And, if so, how? By what processes? Through what impulses? Do women practice design as a subtly different activity from the men who dominate the profession? These are difficult questions, not the least for women designers, especially if they do not necessarily want to be thought of as women designers, but rather as designers who happen to be women. But the publication of *Dish* by its very nature draws attention to the questions.

It remains a fact that even in the twenty-first century, with some exceptions, design is still a largely male-dominated profession (even though the majority of design students in the United States are female). Women tend to be more active in certain areas of design practice than in others, notably design for the home (including furnishings and textiles), and design related to the body (including clothing, accessories, and jewelry). But at the same time women designers remain cautious about promoting their gender. Why is this? Perhaps it is because when the female (the biological given) is expressed as the feminine (the culturally acquired characteristics associated with womanhood), it carries an implicit association with triviality and passivity.

Design emerged as a profession in the early twentieth century at the same time that modernism was developing. Modernism was predicated on polarized binary oppositions where the masculine was always superior to the feminine: rationality over intuition, culture over nature, function over decoration, progress over tradition, public over private, production over consumption, and design over taste equated male over female. In the late twentieth century new ways of thinking and acting, which we now often describe as postmodern, enabled a distancing from these binary equations—an embracing of gender and cultural diversity—and paved the way for the proper acknowledgment and valuing of difference. But this was not difference in the sense of "other," as the alien or the inferior (almost the only ways in which difference could previously be thought). It was difference in its true sense, where what is other is recognized and accepted affirmatively on its own terms.

Today we should have reached the point of being able to respect the talent of women designers and what they offer to design—but have we? Much has changed and continues to change. But the question of how much female difference is actually incorporated into what is, inevitably if unconsciously, a male design canon still remains. Will design produced by women continue to be treated less seriously than that produced by men? Is it to be marginalized as somehow not quite design? The difficulty of negotiating this impasse raises a dilemma for women designers in declaring their gender and identity. But in searching for answers we must be wary of reinforcing the old binary stereotypes. If the work in *Dish* strikes us as different it cannot simply be because of some essentialist notion of "female" or of the "feminine." We must rather look at the work for what it offers and consider both what the designers choose to address and how they do so.

First, there are a series of factors in considering what is addressed. The most central is an attention to context and use and the way that the object is seen as an interface between people and their wants and needs. This includes designs that address exclusively female experience. The most literal example is Ana Mir's tampon—a witty acknowledgement of how an anonymous yet indispensable object can warrant redesign. Mir's Hair Distinguisher bathroom tiles and Nicolette Brunklaus' Blonde printed textile similarly recognize the female body as women experience it—as visceral and transitory—rather than as objectified in much contemporary design and advertising. The experiential is often missing from design, which tends to instead rely on the visual for its impact. *Dish* develops our understanding of what design might be about when initiated by women's experience.

The experience of some of *Dish*'s designers is that of motherhood, and a number of the designs are for children: Sophie Demenge's Oeuf products for babies, Jennifer Carpenter's Truck furniture, and Laurene Leon Boym's animal rugs, designed originally for her son. Not just miniaturized adult designs, these objects originate from the actual experience of having children. Becoming mothers has contributed to expanding some women's concerns as designers.[1] Family has made a difference to these women as it has for their creative predecessors. Famously, the patchwork quilt that Sonia Delaunay made for her son's crib marked her highly successful move from painting to designing textiles.

Design for the home provides the core focus for *Dish,* but if women designers do have a stronger relationship to the home than their male counterparts, it is one that is defined more by social and cultural practice than by biology. The designs demonstrate an empathy with context and use. The rugs, textiles, furniture, and objects in *Dish* are largely one-of-a-kind, functional but not functionalist. Many provide sensory pleasure and humor and invite participation. Louise Campbell's SeeSaw and Dejana Kabiljo's SCRIBOman table are forms that demand use. Lily Latifi's felt and foam stools and felt mats call for reconfiguration by the user. Much of the work draws upon

an understanding of our wants and needs from our homes—the practical, but also the comforting, the relaxing, the sensual, and the playful. Of course some of the designs—Patricia Urquiola's furniture, for example—do not appear to allude to "women's work" at all but still retain a high level of sensitivity toward the user.

The designs draw our attention to the everyday. Experiences that might otherwise be ignored or considered mundane—the simple act of eating, for example—are highlighted and reevaluated. Catherine Lande's Munyal porcelain plates are utilitarian and explore tactile as well as visual qualities; she calls them "the invisible tools of everyday life," and as such they help celebrate the fundamental human activity of eating.

Recognizing that home is a place of consumption highlights design's social responsibility; in the process of using we need also to be aware of what is used-up and what is left over. Inna Alesina's Good Egg footstool, made from post-consumer paper egg crates, is part of a product line she has designed and manufactured from recycled materials. Monica Nicoletti's Place Holder cardboard moving boxes are embellished with images that can both reflect their contents and allow them to serve as temporary furniture—thus challenging conventions of what is to be consumed and what is permanent.

Many of *Dish*'s designers not only design for the home but also work at home, often collaboratively with male domestic partners or with other women. A preoccupation with human relationships characterizes their working methods as much as what they design. A number of the designers are committed to education; in teaching and promoting design they give support to students and younger designers. The how of what they choose to do is as much a consideration as the what—this is evident in their processes, techniques, and materials.

Some of the designs herein reference the traditionally feminine areas of design in innovative ways. Textiles, for instance, are not only superficially designed in color and pattern; their material traits are also explored. Lauren Moriarty takes

Image 20 Nicolette Brunklaus, Blonde, Curtains with digital printed image on velvet or silk. Brunklaus Amsterdam Interior Products, 2002.

thread and weaving as the point of departure for her three-dimensional products and cut neoprene fabrics. The decorative is explored, but not merely as an application, as an implied outcome of feminine leisure activity. In Elizabeth's Chandelier designed by Lyn Godley, for example, the decorative is fully integrated with the product.

This lamp is characteristic of the work in *Dish,* many of which are prototypes or one-offs that suggest the hand-made. This is often a deceit, with products such as Moriarty's textiles deriving from highly sophisticated technological processes. But the designs are not rhetorically technological—technology does not become a barrier between the thing and the user as it does with so many contemporary designs.

This collection begins to redress the binary opposition of modernism, not only for women designers but also for design itself. By restating the ways that design acts as an interface between people and their activities, experiences, needs, and desires, *Dish* brings a different voice to design—different but no less equal.

NOTES

Extracted from H. Clark, "The Difference of Female Design," in *Dish: International Design for the Home,* ed. Julie Stahl (New York: Princeton University Press, 2005), pp. 158–61. Reprinted by permission of Princeton Architectural Press.

1. Jane Margolies, "Getting Tough About Kids' Stuff: Four Designing Mothers Sound Off on Baby Products," *I.D.*, March/April 2004, 42–9.

SECTION 4: IDENTITY AND CONSUMPTION

4.3: Consumption

INTRODUCTION

Design is inextricably linked to consumption and to consumerism. What we buy, and what we chose not to buy tells others about our socioeconomic status and aspirations. Increasingly, consumption depends on design. As more commodities are promoted by images and advertising, and shopping is conducted virtually, the idea of a design-centric society has infiltrated popular culture. Taking examples from the domestic sphere, and from the experience of shopping, this subsection considers the relationship between design, identity, and consumption. The texts chosen resonate with themes already addressed: technology, taste, gender, and the larger issue of how the consumption of designed products, images, services, and messages makes, or unmakes, the individual.

The first extract is from *The World of Goods,* a book jointly authored by anthropologist Mary Douglas and economist Baron Isherwood. Originally published thirty years ago, the message is still relevant: For an understanding of design, social and economic factors are determinants in why people want and need objects, and in what they choose. The text concentrates on the adoption of technology as luxury in British homes and questions why the television had become more ubiquitous than the telephone in the 1970s. The answer to the question rests on "the way that the distribution of status interlocks with the technology of consumption." The task of determining "needs" has increased in complexity from fundamental Marxist discourse (Section 3.3), spurred by the pace of change and the absorption of technological objects, which remain luxuries for shorter and shorter periods of time before they become socially absorbed as necessities. Douglas and Isherwood reiterate how human relationships to designed objects are part of a process of communication—with the objects themselves and with one another, symbolically, and also literally in the case of technology.

These relationships are developed further, from a different perspective, in the next extract, in which Daniel Harris examines "quaintness" as a judgment of taste that references consumer products by means of an aesthetic of clutter. But quaintness should not simply be dismissed as mere nostalgia. In common with "cuteness," "coolness," and the other adjectives Harris uses to explore the aesthetics of consumerism, it is a product of its times, presented here as the antithesis of modernist functionalism and rationality. This extract might be read also in combination with the texts in Section 3.1, Aesthetics, especially "Design and Environment," by Jean Baudrillard. The difference is that Harris is analyzing taste from the realm of consumerism, how meanings are attributed to designed objects by consumers and how those meanings change (as also discussed in Section 3.4, Material Culture and Social Interactions). Many of Harris's examples reference the home—that place which (along with the body) is the main economic focus of contemporary consumption, as well as the base root of our identity.

The next text also references the home, though differently, through a case study. "Do-It-Yourself-Security," by design historian Sarah Lichtman, further focuses our thoughts on the variables that underlie consumer choices, socially, politically, and historically, and their interpretations. The home

Image 21 Barbara Kruger, *Untitled (I Shop Therefore I Am)*, 111" by 113" (282 cm by 287 cm), photographic silkscreen/ vinyl, 1987. COPYRIGHT: BARBARA KRUGER, COURTESY: MARY BOONE GALLERY, NEW YORK.

fallout shelter in the United States during the Cold War period is presented as "an ideologically charged national do-it-yourself project," which is examined as an idea as much as an artifact. While the shelter was intended to reassure against nuclear attack, that reassurance was only symbolic; the shelters were a source of anxiety—always potentially having to face the reality of being tested and failing the ultimate challenge. They represented quasi-safety while also reinforcing gender stereotypes and evoking comfortingly nostalgic images of the past, supported and promoted by government agencies. In this instance the thing being consumed was of much less real worth than what it meant in the construction of national and individual identities in postwar America.

The different ways that identities are constructed, not only by what is purchased, but also in the very process of consumption, is the subject of the final two texts. The first is by Wolfgang Fritz Haug, translated from the original German, from *The Critique of Commodity Aesthetics,* an influential book that traces the aesthetic dimensions of contemporary commodity production, most particularly advertising and design. In this extract Haug focuses attention on "the sales act" and more particularly on the development of "shopping entertainment." The display of commodities, themed stores, and shopping malls are but some examples of the theatricality that now impacts retail environments. Haug considers the manipulation of the consumer in this environment, the success of which is heavily dependent on design. The experience of consumption is as important as what is being purchased and is factored into the price of the merchandise. The aestheticization of commodities is dissolved into enjoyable experiences, which are transitory and independent from what is being purchased—this process leaves the market unsatiated and always seeking more. Where one shops and what brand label one wears can be as important for identity and status as the actual commodity itself.

This issue of branding identity is especially true for clothing, and in particular fashionable clothing, which is the subject of the final essay. Here Heike Jenß considers the way that the sportswear brand Puma has successfully introduced mass customization to its shoes. In common with W. F. Haug, she considers the role of sensual experience as part of the consumer experience. This essay distinguishes the transformation of the consumer into a codesigner, who selects and handles the material components of the actual shoes. Theoretically, this form of consumption acknowledges exhaustion with mass fashion and its failure to fulfill modernity's desire for individualization. These new "prosumers" become not only more invested in the clothes they helped to create, but also in the brand, which facilitated and also validates their choices. The "contemporary fashioning of uniqueness" is not in fact a desire to be individual and different, but a desire to achieve social status, acceptance, and a sense of belonging within a given community or culture that is distinguished by its adherence to the given brand. Individuality is redefined as "mass-desire," fulfilled through more and more specialized forms of commodities and their consumption.

THE TECHNOLOGY OF CONSUMPTION

Mary Douglas and Baron Isherwood

COMPOSITE COMMODITIES

Man is a social being. We can never explain demand by looking only at the physical properties of goods. Man needs goods for communicating with others and for making sense of what is going on around him. The two needs are but one, for communication can only be formed in a structured system of meanings. His overriding objective as a consumer, put at its most general, is a concern for information about the changing cultural scene. That sounds innocent enough, but it cannot stop at a concern merely to get information; there has to be a concern to control it. If he is not in any position of control, other people can tamper with the switchboard, he will miss his cues, and meaning will be swamped by noise. So his objective as a rational consumer also involves an effort to be near the center of transmission and an effort to seal off the boundaries of the system. Being near the center requires a strategy of organizing the exchange of marking services so as not to be excluded from shared civilities, from neither drinks, nor board, nor the possible matrimonial bed.

So here we are, with an interpretation of consumer behavior that lines us all up together, us with our machine-made merchandise and the tribesmen with their home-bred flocks and herds and hand-hafted hoes and hand-woven baskets. But it promises nothing of value unless it can improve the economist's computations. He is a professional with a job to do.

The more anxiously we urged on economists this idea of why people really want goods, the more we came to realize that economists are very busy people. Their own professional bias is neither politically inspired nor haphazard, but grounded instead in a powerful technology of measurement and calculation. It will serve no purpose to skate on the surface of their work. If there is to be any useful insight from anthropology for the theory of consumption, the eager anthropologist has to plunge into the trap-bestrewed forest, the most recondite area of demand theory, and try to see if any of the problems which interest economists there is likely to yield to a new approach.

In the end, after threshing around hopefully, the theoretical fields that seemed most susceptible were those in which economists try to interpret major consumption trends, and in which they seek ways of combining goods into large composite classes that respond in the same way to changes in income and prices. Food is the clearest example of a composite commodity. It includes all kinds of drinks, appetizers, staples, and garnishing, yet something meaningful can be said about the average cost of or demand for food. To assume that there are in real life other big partitions between goods fits well the intuition that people do first allocate their expenditures broadly between categories and then, at later stages of decision and choice, make subdivisions within these categories. For instance, having chosen a house in a certain neighborhood, of a certain size, I have committed myself to heating and flooring of some kind, but later comes the choice of possible types of heating and of carpets or tiles. But the distance of the house from my place of work and its selection implies a set of interdependent decisions about transport. It would be extremely convenient and helpful to economists to know more about the basis on which those practical groupings are habitually made by individual consumers. However, the ramifications are so closely meshed and interdependent that it is hard to find an overall principle of grouping goods that will actually simplify their estimates. What makes it particularly difficult is the weakness of economists' assumptions about why people want goods. So it is here, by introducing the social dimension of needs, that anthropology may be able to help. If goods fall into large separable groupings such that "marginal rates of substitution for certain pairs of commodities are functionally independent of the quantities of certain other commodities,"[1] then it must be because certain consumption activities can be clumped together and separated out from others. We take consumption activities to be always social activities. It would seem then that the clue to finding real partitioning among goods must be to trace some underlying partitioning in society.

By far the most common of the attempts at grouping goods is the Engel curve, which separates necessities from luxuries according to income elasticity.[2] Necessities are defined as those goods which are bought in the same quantities regardless of changes in prices or incomes. So needful are they to the consumer's way of life that when his income falls, he still buys much the same amount. Food is the class of goods on which the poor spend a larger part of their income than the rich. This proportion holds good so widely over the world (with some adaptations in the mode of calculation) that it is known as Engel's law. Food as a composite commodity is also the prime necessity. Luxuries, by contrast, are a completely heterogeneous class defined as those goods on which the individual will quickly cut down, in response to a drop in income. The distinction is culturally neutral and purely technical. That it happens to slot neatly into the veterinary prejudice (that food is what the poor most want) has

perhaps been seen as an added advantage of the analysis. Also implied is the idea that expenditure on luxuries is slightly immoral. This is ever-tempting but misleading, as we shall see. Part of our task will be to restore the neutrality of luxuries in the eyes and hearts of economists.

NEW COMMODITIES

An interesting and central problem is how to spot a new necessity in advance of the signal from price movements and ownership levels. Goods arrive in the shops today: some of them will become tomorrow's necessities. What is the direction and power that selects among the modern luxuries and procures that shift in status, so that from being first unknown, then known but dispensable, some goods become indispensable?

"Twenty years ago I had no car, no television, no refrigerator, no washing machine and no garden, how in heaven's name could I have been happy then?"[3]

In their turn each of these things came in as new commodities—all except the garden; in turn (including the garden), demand for them has spread right through the population, or almost. The curve that started to show a slow demand quickened and steepened, and then gradually flattened off, so that over time it shows the S-shaped form which generally characterizes new commodities. The flat head of the S shows saturation, the point where few new markets are being opened up. The main sales are for replacements and improved versions. At this point the market is defined as saturated. It may be saturated at any level of possible ownership, whether it is 90 percent or 30 percent of households, when demand turns downward. The economist can assume that all who want the thing have now got it. That saturation can set in long before even the 70 percent of households are equipped poses no special problem. Tastes and habits are not within the technical competence of economists; they are content to leave them to anthropologists. But surely we must be interested in asking why demand for some goods slackens off somewhere very short of complete acceptance, while for others it rushes on until 80 percent of households count it as basic equipment. The question is what makes yesterday's luxuries turn into today's necessities—not forgetting that some of yesterday's luxuries have dropped out completely. For instance, consider the solid silver cigarette cases of forty to fifty years ago, which, no longer carried, have not yet joined the display of Georgian snuffboxes in the curiosity cabinet, but lie instead stacked in attics, awaiting a decision as to their value—antiques or just their weight in silver.

Regarding the long term, the economist seems to have no answer. For the short term, the answer is in terms of prices and incomes, within the theory of demand. But the theory expects that a buoyant demand will make it worthwhile for suppliers to search for ways of lowering their costs of production: prices will eventually come down to an acceptable level, or credit facilities will help to bridge the consumer's financing problem.

To consider saturation from an anthropological perspective, we will keep in view the history of two innovations that have entered our homes in the past century: one is a universally agreed necessity, the television set; while the other, the telephone, is a necessity in upper-class homes. In England, for example, this innovation has not penetrated to all the potential users. In 1948 the percentage of householders owning television sets was 0.3 percent. By 1958 it was 52 percent, while the telephone, introduced in 1877, by the same date was installed in only 16.5 percent of households. Dividing the distribution according to social class, the television is very evenly spread, contrasting with the telephone, which clusters thickly at the top.

Two years later the proportion of all households owning television sets had gone up to 65 percent. By contrast, telephone penetration had actually reached no further than 21.4 percent by 1965. By 1973 there had been some catching up. The penetration rates for television were about 90 percent in all social classes, and for the telephone they were about 45 percent overall, with

Table 45.1 Distribution of television and telephone services, 1958

Class	Television Sets Ownership* (%)	Telephone Installation** (%)
Upper (A, B)	57.3	67.8
Middle (C1)	53.4	25.3
Lower (C2, D, E)	51.1	5.0

* "The Demand for Domestic Appliances," *National Institute of Economists Review*, p. 21, 1960, data from p. 27, Table 2, The Social Pattern of Ownership.

** Courtesy of the Post Office, Central Headquarters, Statistics, and Business Research Department, "Forecasting of Residential Telephone Penetration by Use of the Techniques of Social Sectors, Revised estimates."

88 percent in class A, B; 67 percent in C1; 44 percent in C2; and 20 percent in D, E.

Since TV and telephone are both relatively new means of communication, it will be instructive to compare their paths. Economists' usual practice is to treat television as one more household durable. The *National Institute of Economic and Social Research Review,* from which the figures are drawn, compared television sets with refrigerators, washing machines, and vacuum cleaners. Graham Pyatt improved on this by selecting two sets of durables, one, a kitchen consisting of cooker, vacuum cleaner, washing machine, and refrigerator, and the other apparently an entertainment set, radio, record player, radiograph, and television,[4] but he ignored the telephone. Lancaster tried grouping all goods—including men's clothing, automobiles, vegetables—on the basis of their intrinsic properties,[5] but he does not mention telephones. The whole problem of choosing a relevant grouping for the sake of comparisons of consumer behavior is like a corpse-strewn battlefield, and usually too technical for an outsider to comment upon.[6] We hope, however, to show that an anthropological understanding of the consumer's objectives will afford new ways of grouping. Unfortunately, there has been no close comparative study of the rates of advance of television and the telephone in the United Kingdom. Nevertheless, as one has had a meteoric spread, while the other has advanced slowly, it is interesting to use the comparison as a testing ground of the current theories of economists.

SPREAD-OF-INFECTION MODEL

The spread of television is a good illustration of the infectious disease model, or the epidemiological model of the spread of the innovation. Each household as it acquires a set becomes itself, as it were, immune, but its presence is likely to infect other households with the bug. People usually buy what they see their friends using and enjoying. Social contacts are not random. The likelihood of a TV owner influencing anyone he never meets is low. Each member of the population who becomes an owner reduces the number of susceptible nonowners in a circle of friends. So the rate of spread is affected by any discontinuities, regional and social, in personal relationships. Bain found that the rate of spread of TV was influenced by the size of families: the smaller families could afford the opportunity sooner than the larger ones, a smaller family being, in this argument, equivalent to a higher per capita income for the household.[7] Apart from this, the rate of spread of TV between different classes depended on the numbers in each social class: the more numerous, the slower the rise in proportion of ownership. It took twice as long to reach 50 percent in class D as in class A, one and a half times as long as in class B, and one and a quarter times as long as in class C. He showed that the main process that slows up the spread of ownership is the equivalent of immunity against disease. In the end, everyone has had it once and the population is then immune. For future sales, unless the population expands, the interest focuses on replacement of existing TV sets, or, by means of improvements, convincing owners that their set is obsolete, or that they now need two kinds, or perhaps one of the same kind for each member of the family. The epidemiological model fits perfectly the case of television spread. But it says nothing to help us understand the nonspread of telephones in the same period.

Purely economic reasons (in terms of the high initial cost of installing a telephone) do not take us far. If the price of subscribing to a telephone was too high, a steady demand would have eventually brought it down. By 1959 all four appliances studied in the *NIESR Review* (1960) were being sold at relative prices far below what they had been in the consumer prices index of 1959. Evidently, the principle of immunity itself needs to be examined. Indeed, the comparison of a new commodity with a diagnosable nameable disease is misleading, because each commodity is linked to others whose relations as complements and substitutes should be scanned altogether. We must move away from considering each commodity separately towards considering a particular level of technology that sustains a community at a given place and time.

Several economists have recognized that in the long term, prices, being responses to demand, can hardly be used as explanations of demand. Only the most short-term and superficial effects can be explained by price changes, even by incomes. Trying to analyze changes in the demand for tea, beer, spirits, and tobacco in the 1870–1958 period (omitting the war years), Prest concluded that price and income explained 1 percent of the variance of consumption of tea and tobacco, 9 percent of spirits, and 17.5 percent of beer.[8] Commenting upon this exercise, Farrell agrees that the strictly economic variables were quite unimportant in determining demand. In the long run social variables, which he put together as time trends and discontinuities, swamped price and income effects.[9] This reads like another invitation to the less exact social sciences to come into the discussion. Ironmonger takes up the theme even more emphatically.[10] He divides commodities between those remaining steady, those starting on the upward demand trend, and those having dropped out of fashion in the period between 1920 and 1938. They can be called the established, the inmoding, and outmoded. The outmoded commodities in this important exercise turned out to be dried fruits and legumes, once luxuries, flour and cocoa, once necessities, but gradually going downward in importance. Something was happening to the shopping lists during those 19 years which does not yield its secret to the straight inspection of prices and incomes. Like Prest and Farrell, Ironmonger is ready to concede some non-economic factors, and, following Bain, he elaborates the infection model of spread of innovations to trace them. But this model focuses the rate of change in the upward swing of demand and leaves a clutter of mysteries at the slowing down phase, where tastes are invoked to explain why everyone who has not got the thing does not want to have it.

What were those tastes? Twenty years earlier than 1938 was another culture with another technology base. As far as marking services were concerned, we need to be able to show how changes in the technological base (defined by consumption activities), due to increasing industrialization, affect the scale of activities open to people and the means by which they are pursued. For example, the outmoded commodities, dried fruits, legumes, cocoa, and flour, meant the joys of sharing rich hot puddings, some with outrageous names—spotted Dick, baby's leg, jam rolypoly, as well as prune mold, chocolate shape, rich soggy suet puddings, pease pudding, and so on. All those things themselves were only items in an exchange of marking services. We need to get closer to the conditions for getting and giving marking services to be able to analyze changing tastes in economic terms.

ORDER OF ACQUISITION

Industrialization has complicated life for the consumer. Regarding material goods there are, indeed, more of many things. But to keep up with the exchange of marking services necessary to happiness and necessary to a coherent, intelligible culture, he has to run harder to keep in the same place. Industrial growth means nothing more or less than extending the scale of operations. This is how per capita product is increased. The division of labor, as Adam Smith saw, inexorably drives producers to find economies of scale, and this drives them to finer and finer differentiations of their product and to search for wider markets. Large-scale plants

need a dense population to supply labor, hence the shift of rural populations into cities. Life in a city entails higher costs of sanitation, water supply, and so on, and new costs in transporting, distributing, packaging, and preserving food. New trades and professions arise, themselves calling for new kinds of goods. Responding to the change in the structure of society, the household transfers its production processes to the market, and buys more and more of its goods there with the money it has earned. No wonder canned foods have taken the place of home-bottling, and no wonder home deep-freezers are competing with canned foods. The household, like the manufacturer, seeks economies of scale in time and energy in its productive processes.

Some idea of efficient consumption could be worked out if the technology would only stay fixed. One would take into account the social demands for expenditure at various stages in the life cycle and allow for size of households and age of members. One would be able to say roughly that a youth requires the wherewithal to find a wife, that a married couple needs a home of some sort, that needs will expand with the birth of children and contract with old age and retirement. This is very much what the anthropologist does to describe the economy of a tribe at a given time. Among the pastoral Turkana the average head of household needed to deploy his family as herdsmen and dairymaids over 100 to 150 head of small livestock (sheep and goats), 25 to 30 head of cattle, and a few camels and donkeys. These quantities would cover the daily subsistence of humans, the replacement of flocks and herds, and also the contingencies of debt, loans to friends, bad years, and so on. A few rich men held up to 100 cattle, and over 300 small stock. A very few paupers eked out existence on wild fruits and occasional labor for wealthier people.[11] The average Lele man in the Congo would have to reckon on spending 300 to 400 raffia cloths, plus camwood bars, axes, and hoes, for admission fees, fines, and gifts before he had established his first wife's family.[12] If, for some reason (such as the early death of his own father), he were not able to raise the right amounts for goods at the crucial time, he would be forced to pawn one of his sisters and suffer a severe diminution of his civil rights.

The task of assessing needs in real terms is much more complicated if the basic technology is changing rapidly, as in the modern industrial world. However, the changes are always in roughly the same direction, toward more industrialization, more specialization in the division of labor. Consequently, it ought to be possible to work out the shifting technological basis of consumption at least in respect of essentials, and to use the levels of ownership of major pieces of equipment as a measure of standard of living.

Paroush has set out to do just this. Indeed, he finds that the order of acquisition of certain key items is roughly the same in all industrial countries.[13] His technique for establishing the common order of acquisition is highly empirical. Surveying the distribution of goods between households, he selects those which 90 percent of all consumers will purchase in the same order. He rigorously limits his work to those goods and excludes all others. His method is explicitly designed to take account of the shifts in needs which arise from demographic changes. There are some consumer durables whose usefulness rises with the size of family, such as the washing machine. A bachelor need not own an oven till he marries, so the order radio-before-oven is likely to hold good, by reason of the social definition of bachelor. But Paroush rules out idiosyncratic needs because no universal order of preference is likely to show for them. For example, he cites the need of an able-bodied individual for crutches, and the need of the unmusical for a piano: a piano "is really essential for a pianist, but luxury piece of furniture for a music-hater."[14]

Paroush rightly sets great store by the possible applications of his method. The stage of acquisition of a given household, once the general pattern of acquisition is established, can serve as an ordinal index of the standard of living, and changes in the standard of living can be traced by noting percentages of ownership of certain goods.

The household's commodity composition being the result of past income, and influenced by expectation of future income, should provide a good index of normal income. Obviously, the method could lend itself to many interesting analyses. Dividing the population of Israel into income levels, and examining the distribution of families by income within each level, he finds "a conspicuous correlation between income and ownership from the poorest through the richest level. For every level of outlay, the percentage of families with less than the given outlay declines as the level becomes richer." But the conclusion he draws is premature. "As a by-product we get a natural definition of the relative essentiality of various goods." Since the levels of ownership are measured within defined income levels, his method, as it stands, can only say how much an individual household deviates from the commodity composition deemed essential in its income group. Unless he boldly plumps for an arbitrary level of ownership which every household in this day and age should reach to be competent in current technological performance, he cannot talk about essentiality except for a given class of incomes.

There are two snags about his assumptions. First, the concept of efficiency is tied to the normal performance of each income group. This puts him in good company, as it is the same snag that besets utility theory in general. Second, his method necessarily selects the goods which lend themselves to grouping in a strict scale and structure. Any goods on which tastes disagree systematically will escape through the meshes of his net. This means that he can never use it to capture the existence of two or more distinct technologies of consumption in the same economy. These shortcomings could be repaired. Some combination of this method with Graham Pyatt's technique for assessing the probability of owning a particular set of goods could be devised to ferret out the different patterns. In the survey that Pyatt analyzed, "highly significant differences were found between the estimated probability patterns for different social classes."[15] This being so, the task of giving a technological basis to the idea of essentiality or necessity must not be shirked, though it may have to take a different turn.

Paroush's comment on music-haters is misleading and inconsistent. It implies a practical, technological basis for the order of acquisition, which is belied by his discovery that radio, record player, and transistor are more essential for bachelors than are ovens. Even if he insists that the radio and transistor are wanted for tuning in to useful information, surely the record player at least suggests a priority for the wish for music. For how is the bachelor ever going to get married unless he has some social accomplishments? Graham Pyatt speaks more realistically to the anthropological ear when he remarks that the trend to diffusion of durables, which may be described as a change of tastes, would be more fully understood as learning: "the implications of genuine technological development are the same as those of a learning process."[16] Some people are born musical and others can try to learn music, but the learning may well be held to be very necessary. In Gilray's cruel caricature, "Farmer Giles and his wife put their daughter through her paces for a prospective husband,"[17] evidently the girl had to play the piano or be condemned to a lowly marriage and poorer home. After the Rotterdam bombings in 1940 and 1941, middle and upper class families used household inventories for claiming compensation from the government. At that time, refrigerators, washing machines, and water heaters were comparatively recent innovations, and ownership of these appliances was rare and restricted to the highest income groups. But for all the rest, the ownership frequency and saturation levels showed upon the Rotterdam inventories as in Table 45.2:[18] Evidently learning the piano was a necessary accomplishment for Dutch boys and girls of a certain social class.

Paroush writes as if efficiency were a matter of keeping up with the advanced technology of speed and physical comfort. He refers to up-market goods such as air conditioners, and he fully realizes that his technique ought to explain

Table 45.2 The Rotterdam inventories

	Saturation level (%)
Vacuum cleaner	100
Sewing machine	90
Piano	85

something about the up-market concept. But unless he can take marking services and the culturally standardized norms of social interaction into account, he is limited arbitrarily to those few goods which can be scaled by 90 percent agreement in their ordering.

PERSONAL AVAILABILITY

Too much open-mindedness and gentility about the possible reasons for choosing goods, and too much delicacy and embarrassment at the idea that human beings might need to keep level with each other so as to be able to enjoy perfect reciprocity—this is the main reproach against economists who have done the most thinking about consumption. Kelvin Lancaster, for example, produces a finely tuned engine for analyzing consumer choice, and he knows that in the last resort it can apply even to the choice of lighting and food at dinner tables.[19] But his total open mindedness and lack of preconception about the objectives of shared consumption are his undoing. He starts by deploring the fact that traditional demand theory has ignored the properties of the goods themselves:

> With no theory of how the properties of goods affect preferences at the beginning, traditional analysis can provide no predictions as to how demand would be affected by specified change in one or more properties of a good, or how a "new" good would fit into the preference pattern over existing goods. Any change in any property of any good implies that we have a new preference pattern for every individual: we must throw away any information derived from observing behavior in the previous situation and begin again from scratch.[20]

Lancaster directs attention to the agreed physical properties of goods and their uses, whether social or psychological or nutritional. He argues that individuals are more interested in the characteristics of goods than in the goods themselves. When they choose, they are showing direct preferences for particular collections of characteristics and the preference for the actual goods that carry them is derived or indirect. His project for providing a fully integrated theory of consumer demand starts with an attempt to separate those properties of demand which are universal and depend on agreed characteristics that supply universal wants, and those which depend only on the idiosyncratic preferences of individuals. His exercise is made unduly cumbersome by the inability to conceive systematically of the consumer as a social being. Consequently, when he thinks of universal needs he is driven back to universal physical needs. His examples are drawn from automobile performance, speed, comfort, noise, or from calories and proteins as the needed properties in food which underlie the demand for food. The materialist approach to human needs works well enough for the limited purposes to which his theory has been applied. But a more consistently sociological approach would give it added power and the promise of a really strong theory of the technology of consumption. As it is, Lancaster is no more able than anyone else to explain which properties of today's luxuries will make some of them, but not others, become tomorrow's necessities.

To get a theoretical grip on the relationship between technology and consumption, it is no good starting with an unbiased mind as to what physical properties of goods are relevant, nor will the enlightenment come by devising an analytical tool that can deal with all possible appreciations of all possible physical properties in all possible consumer activities. Some simplifying assumptions are needed. As far as anthropology is concerned, there is only one type of physical property of consumption goods that need be considered: the capacity of goods to increase personal availability.

The demand for marking services implies a demand for personal availability. Sending a telegram to be read out at a friend's wedding is not the same quality of service as traveling a thousand miles to be there. Sending flowers by telegraph to a friend in the hospital is not the same quality of personal service as arriving in person at the usual visiting hours. But however willing, one cannot attend two friends' consumption rituals in person at close intervals of time in two distant places unless travel can be speeded up. Nor can a household increase the number of friends attending its own consumption rituals without increasing the power for dealing with large quantities. More space is needed, more relief from time-consuming household processes. Other things being equal, our theory supposes that a rise in real income will tend to be accompanied by an increase in the frequency of large-scale private social events. The rise in real income will be signaled by a demand for equipment and services which release individuals from a chain of high-frequency tasks in household production. An anthropological definition allows of two kinds of luxuries—one, the mere rank signifiers, such as the best china for the family christening; the other, the newest technological aids, the innovating capital equipment, which relieve the pressure on available time, space, and energy. They remain luxuries until they have become part of the normal technological base from which all consumption activities proceed. Though we cannot tell which new scale-facilitating equipment will slot into the existing cost structure and gradually transform it, we can be fairly sure that rising, real income is expressed as a demand for household scale facilitators.

Surely, one would expect the telephone to have been one of these as soon as it appeared on the market. One would have expected it to quickly become part of the technology base, as it did in the United States and as electric lighting has now done in the United Kingdom. But it did not. What does the epidemiological model say about the slow spread of the telephone in England? That there must have been some principle of immunity to the infection, other than the immunity which comes from acquisition, is an empty answer. We have to seek that *cordon sanitaire* in the status system and in the way that the distribution of status interlocks with the technology of consumption.

NOTES

Extracted from M. Douglas and B. Isherwood, "The Technology of Consumption," in *The World of Goods* (London and New York: Routledge, 1996 [1979]), pp. 67–76 and 78–81. Reprinted with permission of Taylor and Francis Books U.K.

1. Muth, Richard F. "Household Production and Consumer Demand Functions." *Econometrica* 24(3): 699–708, 1966.
2. Houthakker, H. S. "The Influence of Prices and Incomes on Household Expenditures." *Bulletin of International Institute of Statistics* 37, 1960.
3. Van Praag, B. S. *Individual Welfare and Consumer Behavior. A Theory of Rationality,* pp. 129, 211–213. New York: Elsevier-North Holland Publishing Co., 1968.
4. Pyatt, F. Graham. *Priority Patterns and the Demand for Household Durable Goods.* Cambridge: Cambridge University Press, 1966.
5. Lancaster, Kelvin. *Consumer Demand: A New Approach.* New York: Columbia University Press, 1971.
6. Strotz, "The Empirical Implication of a Utility Tree." *Econometrica* 25: 269–280, 1957; "The Utility Tree—A Correction and Further Appraisal." *Econometrica* 27: 482–488, 1959; Gorman, W. M. "Separable Utility and Aggregation." *Econometrica* 27: 469–481.
7. Bain, A. D. *The Growth of Television Ownership in the United Kingdom Since the War: A Lognormal Model,* pp. 68ff. Cambridge: Cambridge University Press, 1964.
8. Prest, A. R. "Some Experiments in Demand Analysis." *Review of Economics and Statistics* 13: 33–49, 1949.
9. Farrell, M. J. "Irreversible Demand Function." *Econometrica* 20: 171–186, 1952.
10. Ironmonger, D. S. *New Commodities and Consumer Behaviour,* pp. 73–78, 100, 121–126. Cambridge: Cambridge University Press, 1972.
11. Gulliver, P. H. *The Family Herds, a Study of Two Pastoral Tribes in East Africa: The Jie and the Turkana,* pp. 38–39. London: Routledge & Kegan Paul, 1955.
12. Douglas, Mary. *The Lele of the Kasai.* Oxford: Oxford University Press (for International African Institute), 1963.
13. Paroush, J. "The Order of Acquisition of Consumer Durables." *Econometrica* 33: 225–235, 1965.
14. Paroush, J. "Efficient Purchasing and Order Relations in Consumption" *Kyklos* 26:91, 1963.
15. Pyatt. *Priority Patterns,* p. 88.
16. Ibid., p. 77.
17. Chamberlin, E. R. *The Awakening Giant: Britain in the Industrial Revolution.* London: Batsford, 1976.
18. Cramer, J. S. "Ownership Elasticities of Consumer Durables." *Review of Economic Studies,* pp. 87–96, 1958.
19. Lancaster, Kelvin, J. "A New Approach to Consumer Theory." *Journal of Political Economy* 174: 132–157, 1966.
20. Lancaster, Kelvin, J. *Consumer Demand: A New Approach,* pp. 4–5. New York: Columbia University Press, 1971.

46

QUAINTNESS

Daniel Harris

In a consumerist society, collecting serves a very specific psychological function. While roaming around the countryside, hunting for bargains, the gourmand of garbage gives a clever spin to the act of shopping. He recharacterizes his materialism as an activity of a higher magnitude, not a selfish act of purchasing a product but a custodial one of salvaging the past, the conscientious work of a dedicated folk archeologist who excavates forgotten windfalls that might otherwise have ended up, with potentially disastrous consequences, in careless hands. Collecting is part of a dialogue that the consumer is having with his own conscience, a way of venting remorse for his acquisitiveness by reconfiguring his spending sprees as the freelance scholarship of a disinterested pseudo-scientist who performs a selfless civic duty of curating and conserving the material culture of the past.

Quaintness is also an aesthetic of clutter because it presents different periods simultaneously. Its chaotic style, reminiscent of many chain restaurants, which cram their dining rooms with old pickle barrels, buggy wheels, and antique German salt pigs, is the outcome of its historical fallaciousness, its scrambled sense of chronology, which mixes together disparate epochs and cultures, collapsing the time line like an accordion. Homeowners rarely have the knowledge, patience, or even interest to recreate a single style of interior decoration, but instead cobble together a generic past, a moody, atmospheric gestalt of what might be called "pastness," a perfectly imaginary representation of the good old days that pays cursory homage to the artifacts of any number of archaic civilizations. Quaintness rides roughshod over authenticity. It avoids verisimilitude and presents a hodgepodge of oldnesses, with ten-gallon cowboy hats displayed on the same shelf with colonial milk pitchers, Deco cake mixers with nineteenth-century pewter mugs, lava lamps with "classic wooden replicas of yesteryear's mantel clocks."

Quaintness is an aesthetic not only of clutter but also of imperfections, of scratches, chips, and cracks. It loathes the regularity of modern products so completely that it goes out of its way to create artificial irregularities in brand new things, thus faking the necessary dilapidation of quaintness, as when decorators "distress" exposed beams with motor oil and drill bits to counterfeit smudges of soot and the ravages of woodworm. Women's magazines frequently offer advice on improvising a "convincing and comforting air of antiquity," of the "authentically rustic," by "worrying" flea market finds "with sandpaper to simulate years of affectionate use," laundering Pendleton blankets fifty times in cold water to create "a little false aging," "mellowing" towels in a weak solution of cold tea, and staining concrete floors with shoe polish to create "authentic-looking discolorations that suggest the passage of time." Just as cuteness sadistically disfigures representations of children to make them pitiable, so quaintness actively disfigures possessions to eradicate the stigma of their newness, their disturbingly characterless perfection, which smacks of the alienating anonymity of assembly lines. These consumerist hate crimes express the discontent of a culture trapped in an eternal present, one in which everything is brand new, squeaky-clean, packaged in Styrofoam peanuts and shrink-wrapped. No sooner do our possessions begin to deteriorate, becoming scuffed and dented, dulled by grime and corroded by rust, than they are summarily discarded for ever-more-advanced models of the same appliances, ever-more-gleaming and untarnished ice crushers and trash compactors. In a consumerist society, signs of obsolescence become a social liability, an indication that one is financially unable to replace the aging product: to ditch the broken-down jalopy, to get rid of the patched blue jeans and the threadbare overcoat, whose shabbiness becomes a conspicuous badge of economic hardship, of the demeaning poverty of the disadvantaged, who must dress themselves and furnish their houses with the dusty white elephants and tattered hand-me-downs of more affluent classes. To ensure that consumers constantly replace their possessions, manufacturers have stigmatized the worn and out-of-date and in the process have produced a world that, out of psychological necessity, purges the environment of objects that betray use, creating a timeless landscape from which all signs of history, of wear and tear, have been eerily eradicated.

The scarification rituals of quaintness offer a way of registering a complaint against the tyranny of the new, an environment that has obtained factitious immortality through the constant replacement of our possessions. And yet the controlled nonconformity of quaintness never really seeks to substitute wood-burning stoves for Westinghouse range tops or old corrugated washboards for new Maytags. Instead, it seeks to preserve the consumerist status quo by restoring to our lives an artificial sense of the passage of time, a token presence of history, which we manufacture by torturing new possessions with heat guns or by acquiring forgeries of anachronistic appliances. Elmira Stove Works, for example, offers self-cleaning black metal ovens and "antique-styled" dishwashers that counteract the laboratory featurelessness of the modern kitchen's white Frigidaires and chrome-and-steel toasters with clunky reproductions of cast-iron warhorses with claw feet and pop-up drawers that conceal the control knobs: "It's like taking a step back in time with Cook's Delight. Stoves that look like 19th century heirlooms but are decidedly new in features and conveniences beyond their historic and inviting facades." Even as we claim to detest the present and portray ourselves as the saboteurs and malcontents of consumerism, committing strategic atrocities against store-bought goods, our rebellion against the tyranny of the new is patently ineffectual.

Descriptions of quaint objects use the words "character" and "charm" to distinguish them from mass-produced products bereft of "aura," as in statements that assert that "a great deal of the charm of antique furniture lies in the loving care that previous owners have expended on it," that handmade things retain "strong dashes of the owner's character," and that "a few nicks and scratches to the paint add character and a touch of whimsy" to one's furnishings. Such comments suggest that quaintness is highly anthropomorphic. It is animistic in its belief that old things absorb the emotions and personalities of the people who use them, that they have photographic memories, total recall, so that creaky Adirondack chairs and soggy four-poster beds become ghost-ridden mausoleums haunted by family spirits. From generations of contact with people, old Hoosier cabinets and massive eighteenth-century sideboards transcend their inanimacy to become eyewitnesses of our lives, historians that emanate an almost occult energy, as if they had stored up the vital forces of their former proprietors. Behind the superstitious belief that quaint furnishings retain the quirks and habits of the human beings who rub up against them, tenaciously hoarding their passions until they are engorged with "character," is the equally superstitious belief that modern materials such as plastic, Formica, and stainless steel, with their smooth impermeable surfaces and "aggressively shiny finishes," repel human emotions and therefore never acquire the "friendliness" and "warmth" of quaint "porous" things. Quaintness sets up a dialogue between non-consumerized and consumerized objects, between anti-commodities and commodities, between soulful woods and soullessly inanimate plastics whose pristine surfaces are hermetically sealed against the world, unlike the scratched surfaces of wormy oaks and knotty pines whose chips and cracks function as the orifices of quaintness, the perforations that permit the absorption of their owners' spirit. The primitive belief that our possessions have souls has never disappeared from our culture, and in fact has been reawakened in the twentieth century by consumerism and the tyranny of the new, which have given rise to a new folk religion whose purpose is to restore to our possessions their inner lives.

NOTE

Extracted from D. Harris, *Cute, Quaint Hungry and Romantic: The Aesthetics of Consumerism* (New York: Basic Books/Perseus Books Group, 2001), pp. 33–39. Reprinted by permission of Basic Books Perseus Books Group.

47

DO-IT-YOURSELF SECURITY

Sarah Lichtman

At the height of the cold war, from the 1950s to the early 1960s, the United States government embarked on a series of civil defence initiatives centred on the home fallout shelter. Combining sophisticated technology with domesticity, the home fallout shelter encouraged Americans to define 'home' in terms of safety, nationalism, consumption and the nuclear family. Both government propaganda and popular magazines advocated programmes for protecting the nation against nuclear attack, and civil defence became a component of the post-war phenomenon of do-it-yourself.

This case study examines the home fallout shelter as an ideologically charged national do-it-yourself project that permeated America's post-war consciousness more than its physical landscape; few Americans actually built shelters. Nevertheless, the government requested citizens, through a series of publications reinforced by the mass media, to furnish their own security, and fallout shelters presented homeowners with a do-it-yourself activity that combined home improvement with family safety. The fallout shelter is an instance of a largely imagined design phenomenon that can only be understood within the contexts of the broader political and social realities of cold war politics, and therefore, will be examined not only as an artefact, but also as an idea. The desire to protect the imperilled home, long a bulwark of American frontierism and self-defence, now translated to staving off the physical and psychological devastation of nuclear attack.

As part of the home, in basements or buried in backyards, the fallout shelter was a highly gendered realm, with men and women assigned separate roles. For centuries, women had been creating do-it-yourself projects, from home dressmaking to interior decoration, but during the post-war years, do-it-yourself became increasingly focused on tasks such as construction and carpentry, which were categorized as tasks for men. While do-it-yourself projects provided a curative and creative outlet from the workaday world for both sexes, they allowed men to demonstrate competence and strength—major markers of masculinity throughout the twentieth century.[1]

In safeguarding the nuclear family from nuclear attack, men assumed the role of capable protectors and providers. They did so at a time when masculinity was in considerable flux, and an emphasis on domesticity as well as certain masculine behaviours appropriate to corporate conformity replaced the wartime emphasis on the super-masculine military man. For women, do-it-yourself security relied on informed consumption and gender-normative domestic duties. According to civil defence literature, preparedness resided in a well-stocked larder and 'emergency housekeeping', responsibilities essential to women's role as homemaker. Even though this emphasis took place at a time when women were returning to the workplace at greater rates than at any other

Image 22 Office of Civil and Defense Mobilization Poster. Record Group 304, Still Pictures Branch, National Archives, College Park, Maryland.

time since the Second World War, they remained housekeepers and childcare providers first. Such expectations were carried into the construction of the home fallout shelter and helped perpetuate gendered stereotypes into the post-nuclear world—literally building them into a concrete form.[2]

In a world increasingly perceived as uncertain, the do-it-yourself home fallout shelter signified the solidity of domestic 'American values' and safety. Just as the government advocated political containment to minimize the destructive power of the Soviet Union and the atomic threat, historian Elaine Tyler May has suggested that 'domestic containment' was 'now the key to survival in the nuclear age'. The do-it-yourself shelter placed the suburban home and family on the front lines of national defence. It promoted the idea of security, while revealing larger cold war insecurities of daily life. The do-it-yourself fallout shelter was

the indispensable space that people hoped never to use.[3]

[...]

'IF YOU'RE NOT ALL THUMBS': BUILDING THE HOME SHELTER

To facilitate the construction of do-it-yourself shelters, government literature, popular magazines, and educational films provided detailed plans and step-by-step instructions. *Walt Builds a Family Fallout Shelter: A How-To-Do-It Project* (1961), for example, a film co-sponsored by the National Concrete Masonry Association (NCMA) and the OCDM [Office of Civil and Defense Mobilization], followed Walt, an amiable, bespectacled older man, through the process of building his home shelter.[4]

Using the popular civil defence booklet *The Family Fallout Shelter* as his guide, Walt builds the 'Basement Concrete Block Shelter'. The affordable model, estimated to cost approximately $150, required materials readily available in any hardware store and included: 535 solid concrete blocks, five bags of ready mix mortar, six wooden posts, 95 feet of board sheathing, and six pounds of nails. To build the shelter, Walt first draws a chalk guideline on the basement floor. He then lays a row of concrete blocks in wet mortar, affixes the wooden beams to the basement walls and, after waiting at least one day until the mortar in the block wall dries, installs a double layer of concrete blocks across the ceiling. Finally, he mortars the last row of blocks into position. As he explains, the shelter takes him only a few evenings and weekends to complete. 'Anybody', he notes, 'who isn't all thumbs can do it'. Walt's reassuring message and his avuncular demeanour encouraged the average do-it-your-selfer to roll up his sleeves and start building.

For those not inclined to watch a movie or write away for booklets, mass-circulation magazines also provided do-it-yourself information. In September 1961, *Life* ran the lead story 'Fallout Shelters: A New Urgency, Big Things to Do—and What You Must Learn'. The article optimistically promised that 97 per cent of the population could survive a nuclear attack if only they knew what to do when the bomb hit. *Life* endorsed the national call for shelters and superimposed an image of an exploding mushroom cloud over a letter written by President Kennedy. Kennedy encouraged readers to participate in a voluntary shelter programme for the good of themselves and America, by calling on civilian patriotism and self-reliance: 'Nuclear weapons and the possibility of nuclear war are facts of life … [but] there is much that you can do to protect yourself—and in doing so strengthen your nation … . The ability to survive coupled with the will to do so therefore are essential to our country'.[5]

Life laid out a series of do-it-yourself plans ranging from the simple to the complex, complete with renderings of constructed shelters, detailed blueprints, and supply lists. It featured: the 'Simple Room in Basement Built with Concrete Blocks', the 'Big Pipe in the Backyard Under Three Feet of Earth', 'A Double-walled Bunker for Safety Above Ground', Which 'could be built by any enterprising do-it-yourself family', and 'A $700 Prefabricated Job to Put up in Four Hours'.[6] In keeping with the money saving message of do-it-yourself, the magazine estimated the shelters would cost one-third of those supplied and constructed by professional contractors.

Three months later *Popular Mechanics* published 'You Can Build a Low-Cost Shelter Quickly', which outlined plans for four shelters. Like *Life*, the article contained illustrations and detailed shelter plans. The most basic and least expensive shelter consisted of little more than a 4 × 6 foot wooden frame covered with sandbags. The 'Under-the-Patio', the 'Store-Away', and the 'Basic Sit-Down' shelters provided more space, and conceivably more protection, but necessitated more advanced do-it-yourself skills such as working with concrete.[7]

SECURITY IN A BOX: THE HOME FALLOUT SHELTER KIT

Owing to the often complex and daunting shelter construction process, some companies eased the burden on the builder by manufacturing shelter kits. Just as the cake mix provided post-war housewives an error-free confection—all dry ingredients were pre-measured—so too did the shelter kit relieve men of the responsibility of carpentry expertise, not to mention endless trips to the hardware store for forgotten items.[8]

The idea of do-it-yourself assembly using ready-made components was well known since the Berlinwork canvasses of the mid-nineteenth century. Kits of the post war period offered an array of choices and encompassed everything from audio sets to paint by numbers. Hobby kits had grown into an economic force, expanding from a $44 million industry in 1945 to a $300 million one by 1953. In 1961, *Life* featured the assembly of the low cost Kelsey-Hayes shelter (the company was a major supplier to the automobile industry) as an additional civil defence option. Assembled from a kit of four modular steel panels, the 2 × 66 × 8 foot shelter, available at Sears that autumn, could reportedly be erected by two men in four hours with only a screwdriver and a wrench. *Life's* picture series of Art Carlson and his adolescent son Claude effortlessly snapping the shelter together clearly expressed that building a shelter was not only easy but also fostered father and son relationships.[9]

BONDING AND THE BOMB: FATHERS AND SONS BUILD SHELTERS

The image of a father and son building a do-it-yourself shelter domesticated nuclear war. It endorsed the notion that all was well by making shelter construction part of everyday life, and helped normalize war preparations by representing a father and son engaged in everyday tasks such as cleaning the car or mending the garden fence. It was an appropriately gendered activity and provided boys with 'wholesome outlets' for their creative and youthful energies. Fathers engaging in do-it-yourself were deemed to set 'a fine example' for boys, especially at a time when society considered teenagers at high risk of juvenile delinquency and homosexuality.[10] Fathers were expected to provide positive role models for their sons, and failing to do so could have dire consequences. Images of fathers and sons working together abound in shelter literature, reinforcing these ideals.[11]

Building a shelter together could also provide quality time where the father could impart to his son ideas of patriarchal and family duty and responsibility. The family followed defined gender roles to ensure that life in the shelter was 'Snug, Equipped, and Well Organized'.[12] *Life* depicted the finished Kelsey-Hayes shelter filled with supplies and occupied by the entire Carlson family. Mrs Carlson tended the larder and water supply, while daughter Charlene minded the linens and daughter Judy worked as the 'shelter librarian'.

Mr Carlson, on the other hand, managed the emergency equipment and tools, while his son looked after the flashlights, transistor radio, and battery supply. Grim-faced but resilient, and holding a shovel rather than a pitchfork, Mr Carlson and his family present an atomic update to Grant Wood's *American Gothic* (1930).

FAMILY FALLOUT: FEMININITY, MASCULINITY, AND THE GENDERED NATURE OF DO-IT-YOURSELF PREPAREDNESS

Like many other gender stereotypes depicted in mass culture, images of home repair in magazines and advertisements in the 1950s often reduced gender to stereotypical roles: men work with tools and build things while women open boxes and decorate.[13] As the Carlson family demonstrates, the same can be said for home fallout shelters. Although both men and women participated in do-it-yourself projects, the responsibility of constructing the home shelter, at least according to the promoters, fell squarely on the man of the house. Depictions of male shelter builders dominated civil defence brochures and popular magazines. Men are almost invariably shown building the shelter or, once inside, actively operating equipment such as the air ventilator. Women, on the other hand, are depicted engaged in domestic tasks such as tending children, stocking the pantry, or decorating. An image of Ben Smith and his children, published in the 1961 *Time* article 'Civil Defense: The Sheltered Life', depicts the typical division of labour promoted by shelter literature: Mr Smith and his son cement the shelter wall while his daughter decorates it by painting a 'picture window'.[14]

The highly domesticated vision of mid-century women, however, occurred during a time when the number of women in the workplace matched wartime highs, and by 1960 women were one-third of the nation's workforce. Despite greater numbers of middle- and working-class women active in the labour force, and marking a significant shift in 'women's work', many women still found themselves confronted by societal pressure that urged 'traditional' domestic roles and circumscribed career opportunities. Women were expected to be the primary—if not the sole—homemakers, housekeepers, and childcare providers. Not surprisingly, these gendered roles were repeated in fallout shelter literature. The extreme nature of the emergency, however, validated these roles and acknowledged the crucial significance of this type of unpaid domestic labour.[15]

Women provided safety and security though informed consumption and domestic tasks. From furniture to foodstuffs, shelter life demanded specialized goods. Castro Convertibles produced a space-saving 'Jet Bed', a foldaway metal bunk designed specifically for shelter use, and General Foods appealed to 'families believing in preparedness' with a protein-rich product called 'Multi-Purpose Food'.[16] This was consumption in the name of civil defence; cooking equipment, medical supplies, a battery-powered radio, flashlight, a can opener, sanitary napkins (which could also double as bandages), toothache pills, deodorant, books, games for the kids, and tranquillizers were just some of the items recommended for shelter life. Women were responsible for making sure these and other items were purchased and ready.

The well-stocked larder became a central metaphor for shelter preparedness. In his *Fallout Shelter Handbook* (1962), Chuck West provided tips for a successful shelter that included careful checking of items on a grocery list. No campaign exemplified women's role in shelter preparedness more than 'Grandma's Pantry'. Headed by the Federal Civil Defense Administration's Director of Women's Activities, Jean Wood Fuller, with the help of the National Grocers' Association and the National Dietetic Association, the campaign linked American 'heritage' to cold war policy and sought to appeal to women's role as nurturer by evoking nostalgic images of the past. Its promotional material included a drawing of a 'traditional' American kitchen with curtained windows, a cast iron stove, a circular hook rug, a large box of firewood, and

shelves stocked with foodstuff. A caption read, 'Grandma's Pantry Was Ready—Is Your "Pantry" Ready in Event of Emergency?'.[17]

Civil defence increasingly 'militarized' the family home, and historian Laura McEnaney has argued that women assumed the role of 'atomic housewife'. In keeping with more 'traditional' gender roles, much shelter literature conflated cleaning up after nuclear attack with gender-normative 'feminine' duties such as everyday housework. Good housekeeping after the blast was also purportedly one of the best protections against fire (loose items could ignite from the heat), as well as fallout. In *How to Survive an Atomic Bomb* (1950), Richard Gerstell, using the language of domesticity, argued that unopened food was safe to eat after an attack, but could become 'dirty' if it came into contact with radioactive 'dust'. Careful homemakers only need 'wash the outside' of packages for safety. The warning signs were clear: good housekeeping inside the shelter could mean the difference between life and death.[18]

While women protected the family home through domestic duties, men did so through construction, and the gendered nature of shelter building demanded that they fit into mid-twentieth century ideas of acceptable 'masculine' behaviour. According to historian Steven M. Geller, 'by the 1950s being handy had, like sobriety and fidelity, become an expected quality in the good husband'.[19]

Do-it-yourself furnished men with a paraphernalia of masculinity that forged their domestic identities. Working with tools demonstrated masculine ideals of power and competence, ideals reinforced by a 1957 *Better Homes and Gardens* article featuring male film stars. The article pictured Rory Calhoun, Glenn Ford and George Montgomery, among others, mixing cement and working with table saws. According to the author, these men, whose success in 'Western' movies lent them an added aura of strength and competent masculinity, reputedly found 'complete relaxation and enjoyment working with … tools'.[20] Skill in the workshop signified maleness; 'The hammer, saw, and quarter-inch electric drill', Gelber argues, 'became the emblems of the new masculinity, and men who refused to master them did so at some risk to their standing in the eyes of spouse and community'.[21]

For many men, do-it-yourself also helped them grapple with the post-war 'crisis of masculinity' in which they wrestled with shifting gender roles, expectations, and the very meaning of maleness itself. In *The Organization Man* (1956), William H. Whyte lamented the loss of male identity and individualism in the wake of corporate conformity.[22] Indeed, Jack Arnold's novel and subsequent film, *The Incredible Shrinking Man* (1956), summed up the anxieties of many mid-century men who saw their masculinity disappearing before their very eyes.[23] The older ideal of the 'Heroic Artisan', virile, independent, and in control of his own labour, was vanishing. 'If we want to have *men* again', Arthur Schlesinger Jr wrote, '… we must first have a society which encourages each of its members to have a distinct identity'.[24] As men sought out other means to express their masculine identity, do-it-yourself, including fallout shelters, became an arena in which they could demonstrate their manhood. Through shelter construction, men reaffirmed their masculine identity by building protection not only for themselves, but also for the 'weaker sex'[25] and for children.

[…]

Building the family shelter drew on the gendered stereotypes associated with the ideal of post-war family life. 'Traditional' gender roles offered stability and change, in an era shadowed by the threat of nuclear attack. The ideals of do-it-yourself supplied both men and women with appropriate male and female tasks that strengthened domestic identity and gave them a sense of contained purpose and control in an increasingly uncertain world. The home fallout shelter, though intended to reassure, however, was a site of anxiety. Shelters, even if built, could only provide symbolic security. The home fallout shelter was a paradoxical space that domesticated war by militarizing the family home. As such, it was doomed to fail in reality, even if it was to survive as an icon in post-war America.[26]

NOTES

Extracted from S. Lichtman, 'Do-It-Yourself Security: Safety, Gender, and the Home Fallout Shelter in Cold War America', *Journal of Design History* 19/1 (2006), pp. 39–40 and pp. 46–54. Reproduced with the permission of Oxford University Press via Copyright Clearance Center.

I would like to thank Paul Atkinson, Marilyn Cohen, Juliet Kinchin, Pat Kirkham, Rachel Kueny, Amy Ogata and Kate Papacosma for their insight and encouragement.

1. Pat Kirkham and Janet Thumim, 'You Tarzan,' in *You Tarzan: Masculinity, Movies and Men*, Pat Kirkham and Janet Thumim (eds.) Lawrence and Wishart, London, 1993, pp. 11–26.

2. 'The New American Domestic Male,' *Life*, 4 January 1954, pp. 42–5; James Gilbert, 'A Feeling of Crisis: The 1950s,' in *Men in the Middle: Searching* for *Masculinity in the 1950s* (University of Chicago Press, Chicago and London, 2005), pp. 62–80; US Department of Defense, Office of Civil Defense, *Fallout Protection: What to Know and Do About Nuclear Attack* (GPO, Washington D.C. 1961), p. 29; William H. Chafe and Harvard Sitkoff (eds.) *A History of Our Time: Readings* on *Postwar America*, 4th edn. (Oxford University Press, New York and Oxford, 1995), p. 224; Stephanie Coontz, The *Way We Never Were: American Families and the Nostalgia Trap* (Basic Books, New York, 1992), p. 161.

3. Elaine Tyler May, *Homeward Bound: American Families in the Cold War Era* (Basic Books, New York, 1988), p. 14 and p. 103. Several noteworthy civil defence studies devote chapters to the fallout shelter. See Margot A. Henriksen, *Dr. Strangelove's America: Society and Culture in the Atomic Age* (The University of California Press, Berkeley and Los Angeles, 1997); Laura

McEnaney, *Civil Defense Begins at Home: Militarization Meets Everyday Life in the Fifties* (Princeton University Press, Princeton and Oxford, 2000); Guy Oakes, *The Imaginary War: Civil Defense and American Cold War Culture* (Oxford University Press, New York and Oxford, 1994); Kenneth D. Rose, *One Nation Underground: The Fallout Shelter in American Culture* (New York University Press, New York and London, 2001); Tom Vanderbilt, *Survival City: Adventures Among the Ruins of Atomic America* (Princeton Architectural Press, New York, 2002), and Allan M. Winkler, *Life Under a Cloud: American Anxiety About the Atom* (Oxford University Press, New York and Oxford, 1993). For investigations into the early years of civil defence, see Paul Boyer, *By the Bomb's Early Light: American Thought and Culture at the Dawn of the Atomic Age* (Pantheon Books, New York, 1985).

4. NCMA, *Walt Builds a Family Fallout Shelter: A Do-It-Yourself Project,* RG 311, Video. 096, National Archives, also mentioned in Stoke, p. 49.

5. John F. Kennedy, 'A Message to You From the President,' *Life,* 15 September 1961, p. 95.

6. Ibid., pp. 92–3, and pp. 100–104. Also discussed in Henriksen, *Dr. Strangelove's America,* pp. 207–8.

7. 'You Can Build a Low-Cost Shelter Quickly,' *Popular Mechanics,* December 1961, pp. 85–9. In addition to shelter construction, *Popular Mechanics* also provided instructions for other do-it-yourself shelter projects. See, 'Outdoor Antenna for Fallout Shelter,' *Popular Mechanics,* February 1962, p. 204. Handling concrete numbered among the most important tasks for building a home fallout shelter. As author Chuck West advised in the *Fallout Shelter Handbook,* 'No matter what type of shelter you build, working with concrete will be a major part of the construction.' West, *Fallout Shelter Handbook,* pp. 50–51. Laying concrete was a topic often covered in hobby magazines. See 'How to Lay Concrete Blocks,' *Popular Mechanics,* August 1958, pp. 164–7, W. B. Eagan, 'Eight Types of Mortar Joints and How to Make Them,' *Popular Mechanics,* July 1958, pp. 176–9, 'Cement Jobs Are Easy,' *New York Times,* 10 June 1956.

8. For more information on cake mixes and their significance in the 1950s, see Karal Ann Marling, 'Betty Crocker's Picture Cook Book,' in *As Seen on TV: The Visual Culture of Everyday Life in the 1950s* (Harvard University Press, Cambridge and London, 1994), pp. 202–40.

9. Gelber, *Hobbies,* pp. 166–7. Berlinwork is a form of cross-stitch embroidery done on canvas with a pre-traced image and colour guide. It was popular in the early to mid-nineteenth century and was predominantly used for accessories, furnishings, firescreens and decorative pictures; Gelber, *Hobbies,* p. 265. For an investigation into post-war hobbies, see Marling, 'Hyphenated Culture: Painting by Numbers in the New Age of Leisure,' in *As Seen On TV,* pp. 50–85. For the popularity of hobby kits, see Gelber, 'Kits: Assembly and Craft,' in *Hobbies,* pp. 255–67. For a survey of ready made shelters, see 'It's Time to Take Another Look at Fallout Shelters,' *House and Home,* July 1961, pp. 215–7.

10. Penny and David Hellyer, 'Keep Those Home Fires Burning … With Hobbies,' *The American Home,* December 1948, p. 52. For an examination of American fatherhood, see Robert L. Griswold, *Fatherhood in America: A History* (Basic Books, New York, 1993), Ralph I.aRossa, *The Modernization of Fatherhood: A Social and Political History* (University of Chicago Press, Chicago, 1997), May, *Homeward Bound,* pp. 146–50, and Gelber, *Hobbies,* pp. 290–1. After 1948, official juvenile court case records and FBI arrests reflect a sharp increase in apprehensions and trials of young people for crimes ranging from burglary to murder. See James Burkhart Gilbert, *Another Chance: Postwar America, 1945–1968* (Temple University Press, Philadelphia, 1981), p. 68.

11. US Department of Defense, Office of Civil Defense, *Fallout Protection,* p. 20. In the *Fallout Shelter Handbook,* Chuck West, for example, depicts a father and son inspecting tools in a completed shelter. West, *Fallout Shelter Handbook,* p. 81. The tragic ending of *Rebel Without a Cause* presented a popular parable for the disastrous effects of poor parenting. In the film, James Dean plays Jim Stark, a troubled teen whose father is cowed by his overbearing wife. Jim's father is weak and feminized; he wears women's aprons around the house. Jim recognizes his father's inadequacy both as a father and as a husband and he yearns for him to act like a 'real' man. 'If he had guts to knock mom cold once,' Jim laments, 'then maybe she'd be happy.' *Rebel Without a Cause,* Director, Nicholas Ray, 1955. For the role of the 1950s father in television and film, see Nina C. Leibman, *Living Room Lectures: The Fifties Family in Film and Television* (University of Texas Press, Austin, 1995).

12. 'Family in the Shelter, Snug, Equipped and Well Organized,' *Life,* 15 September 1961, p. 105, also discussed in Henriksen, *Dr. Strangelove's America,* p. 208.

13. For an investigation into the gendered nature of do-it-yourself, see "Handyman, Handywomen," in Goldstein, *Do-It-Yourself,* pp. 67–82. Penny Sparke notes that feminine domesticity, and the gendered division of labour during the 1950s were still predicated on "Darwinian ideas" of differences between men and women. Sparke, *As Long as It's Pink,* p. 169.

14. Goldstein, *Do-It-Yourself,* p. 74; U.S. Department of Defense, Office of Civil Defense, *Family Shelter Designs,* p. 19; 'Civil Defense: The Sheltered Life,' p. 23.

15. Chafe and Sitkoff (eds.) *A History of Our Time,* p. 224; Stephanie Coontz, *The Way We Never Were,* p. 161. For domestic duties as a sign of feminine resistance in the home, see "The Happy Housewife": Domesticity Renewed' in Sparke, *As Long as it's Pink,* pp. 165–186.

16. West, *Fallout Shelter Handbook,* p. 9 and p. 1. For an investigation into the intersection of consumption and national defence, see Stocke, 'Suicide on the Installment Plan.'

17. West, *Fallout Shelter Handbook,* p. 93; Federal Civil Defense Administration, *Grandma's Pantry Was Ready—Is Your Pantry Ready in Event of Emergency?* (GPO, Washington D.C., 1955); for 'Grandma's Pantry,' see May, *Homeward Bound,* pp. 104–6; Rose, *One Nation Underground,* p. 142, and Winkler, *Life Under a Cloud,* p. 122. For women's role in civil defence, see Rose, 'The Gendered Holocaust,' in *One Nation Underground,* pp. 141–149; Oakes, 'The Nuclear Family,' in *The Imaginary War,* pp. 105–144, and McEnaney, 'The Nuclear Family: Militarizing Domesticity, Domesticating War,' in *Civil Defense Begins at Home,* pp. 68–87.

18. McEnaney, 'Atomic Housewifery,' in *Civil Defense Begins at Home,* pp. 108–113; Richard Gerstell, *How to Survive an Atomic Attack* (Combat Forces Press, Washington D.C., 1950), p. 76. Poor housekeeping could also adversely affect shelter morale. Chuck West relates the experience of the Perkins family, who spent seven days in a test shelter. Mrs Perkins realized that when 'dirty clothes began to pile up,' she and her family became discouraged. West, *Fallout Shelter Handbook,* p. 97.

19. Men's work in this particular type of home was also unpaid. For investigations into the nature of masculinity, see James Gilbert, *Men in the Middle;* Michael S. Kimmel, *The History of Men: Essays in the History of American and British Masculinities* (State University Press, New York, 2005); Michael Kimmel, *Manhood in America: A Cultural History* (The Free Press, New York and London, 1996); Pat Kirkham and Janet Thumim (eds.) *You Tarzan: Masculinity, Movies and Men* (Lawrence and Wishart, London, 1993); and Pat Kirkham and Janet Thumim (eds.) *Me Jane: Masculinity, Movies and Women* (Lawrence and Wishart, London, 1995); Gelber, 'Do-It-Yourself,' p. 99.

20. Richard Nunn, 'Hollywood Handymen,' *Better Homes and Gardens,* November 1957, p. 78, also mentioned in Marling, p. 7.

21. Gelber, *Hobbies,* p. 294. For masculinity and do-it yourself, see Gelber, 'Do-It-Yourself.' In the post-war period the increased use of power tools ironically lessened the physical burden and skill level previously required to complete projects. 'Machines,' *Harper's* writer Eric Larrabee contended, 'are not destroying skills; they are putting them in the hands of every unskilled householder.' Companies such as Skill Corp and Shopmaster flooded the market with home tools. Black and Decker, one of the most successful tool companies, alone featured 150 different models, and driven by the popularity of their portable drill, earned an annual revenue of over $35,000,000. 'Power tools: The Newest Home Appliance', *Industrial Design,* February 1954, p. 31; 'Do-it-Yourself is Big Business,' *The New York Times,* 10 June 1966; *Time,* 2 August, 1953, p. 66; Gelber, 'Power Tools,' in *Hobbies,* pp. 278–82.

22. William Hollingsworth Whyte, *The Organization Man* (Simon and Schuster, New York), 1956.

23. For an investigation into the re-definition of man's place in post-war society as seen through science fiction, see Paul Wells, 'The Invisible Man: Shrinking Masculinity in the 1950 Science Fiction B-Movie,' in *You Tarzan* (eds.) Kirkham and Thumim.

24. Arthur Schlesinger, Jr., 'The Crisis of American Masculinity;' *Esquire,* November 1958, p. 66.

25. Michael Kimmel, ' "Temporary About Myself": White-Collar Conformists and Suburban Playboys, 1945–1960,' in *Manhood in America,* 223–258. On the 'feminization' of manhood see Michael S. Kimmel, 'Consuming Manhood: The Feminization of American Culture and the Recreation of the Male Body, 1832–1920,' in *The History of Men,* pp. 37–59.

26. William Bird, 'How One Old Shelter Got a Face-Lift-and a Permanent Home: The Bomb Shelter Installation at the National Museum of American History,' *Smithsonian,* April 1994, p. 52. For discussion of the bomb shelter on television during the Cold War, see Margot A. Henriksen, 'The Berlin Crisis, the Bomb Shelter Craze and Bizarre Television: Expressions of an Atomic Age Counterculture,' in *The Writing on a Cloud,* pp. 151–173. For a recent film about a family who spent thirty-seven years living in a fallout shelter, only to realize the nuclear war they were hiding from never happened, see Hugh Wilson, Director, *Blast from the Past,* 1999. For a recent television programme highlighting a bomb shelter, see, *The Simpsons,* 'Bart's Comet,' 5 February 1995, which features Homer and the people of Springfield commandeering Ned Flanders' fallout shelter.

48

CRITIQUE OF COMMODITY AESTHETICS

Appearance, Sexuality and Advertising in Capitalist Society

W. F. Haug

In the course of a partial socialization of commodity production and distribution, the dynamics of valorization are released to force the constituent moments of the sales act further and further apart, and with their differentiation they become fixed separately and developed in the most profitable arrangement. Presentation and *mise en scene* of the commodities, design of sales location, its architecture, lighting,[1] colours, background noise, and odours; the sales staff, their external appearance and behaviour; the whole business of the sale; each moment in the commodity's metamorphosis, and the environment in which it takes place and which influences it, are all held in the grip of the basic valorization calculation and are functionally adapted towards that end.

All these developments benefit specialized capital, whose profit interest furthers the development. The aesthetics of shops and window displays is the object and means of competition amongst shop-fitters as well as retailers. In this way aesthetic innovation becomes economically indispensible in the field of sales technique which no capitalist trader can afford to ignore. The mechanism does have a tendency increasingly to limit the period of the shops' aesthetic innovation. Thus 'shops are considered outmoded after five to seven years, rather than 20 to 30 years in the old days, and therefore must be completely refurbished.'[2]

The market for shop interior design and sales areas goes on display at a special fair, the 'Euroshop'. 'Many firms who wish to make shops even more modern and attractive', reads the pious report in the trade section of a bourgeois paper (to which one might add 'and those who profit from the competition in the retail sector through their aesthetic of selling'), 'discuss the aspects of shopping experience we need to stimulate in order to increase turnover … Ever more sophisticated techniques, and more tasteful designs for the salesroom, are conceived by the shop-fitters.'[3] It is the old story of 'you scratch my back, I'll scratch yours' within capitalism. The shop-fitting capital helps retail capital with a valuable aesthetic weapon for the competitive struggle, the use of which, as it increases in sophistication, becomes compulsory. The shop-fitting capital's advertising conceals a threat: 'If you want to sell, you've got to provide *entertainment*.'[4]

This 'shopping entertainment' offers an additional attraction for buyers, and is thus an armament in the competition between retail capital, which they can no longer do without. 'It was a revelation' the *Frankfurter Allgemeine Zeitung* commented subsequently on the brand new 1967 commodity presentation at Globus, the Zurich department store. The then director, appropriately named Kaufmann [which means salesman or trader], was applying in the new store 'a philosophy of commerce which he later presented again in his fascinating book, *The Key to the Consumer.*'[5]

The commodities are no longer to be displayed in their traditional categories 'but should be arranged thematically to fulfill the needs and dreams of the buyers'. One must not confront the buyer brusquely with a commodity but 'guide them into the "entertainment".' So it can be seen that even the miracle of the transubstantiation of value from the commodity's use-form into the value-form of money, under the pressure of capital's anxieties, can be turned into a mysterious cult, an initiation ceremony for the buyer lured into acting as the saviour of exchange-value.

'He must not stand aloof,' according to Kaufmann's principles of sales philosophy. 'He must become a participant.' The exhibition of commodities, their inspection, the act of purchase, and all the associated moments, are integrated into the concept of one theatrical total work of art which plays upon the public's willingness to buy. Thus the salesroom is designed as a stage, purpose-built to convey entertainment to its audience that will stimulate a heightened desire to spend. 'On this stage the sale is initiated. This stage is the most important element in sales promotion.'

This aesthetic innovation of the salesroom into a 'stage for entertainment' on which a variety of commodities are arranged to reflect the audience's dreams, to overcome their reservations, and provoke a purchase, was a pioneering exercise at a time marked by a general change in the selling trend. 'Fashion in the meantime, had developed into a totality which affected the individual's whole appearance. A new dress required new stockings and shoes in a matching colour-scheme, a suitable handbag and new make-up. Fashion even spread beyond clothing, affecting other areas such as house interiors.' Boutiques led the way in conquering this market, 'mushrooming ever since', probably because their profits were well above the average in the retail trade.

In this situation,[6] it was the department stores in particular which had to keep up with what was euphemistically and naively termed 'a rising standard of living'. Kaufmann's innovation was immediately demonstrated to be a pioneering breakthrough. 'The entertainment-stage at the Globus department store became a mecca to which retailers from all over the world made an annual pilgrimage.' There they hoped to gain access to their Holy of Holies, to receive newly disclosed their driving force and determining aim.

The outcome was that, to turn a proverb on its head, the early bird lost his worm. Kaufmann was obliged to resign because 'the entertainment programme at Globus did not fulfill expectations.' The turnover per employee in 1970 was only 29,000 Swiss Francs, while department stores in the Federal Republic had figures of between DM70,000 and DM84,000 per worker. Kaufmann's successor, Calveti, pragmatically reduced the task. 'Entertainment shopping' in his revised formula, 'has to be initiated by the commodity and not from the stage.'

However, the 'Seven Worlds of Globus' are already undergoing a resurrection in the new Wertheim store in West Berlin's Kurfürstendamm.

In a row of elegantly furnished shops and boutiques, groups of commodities which fulfill the most sophisticated of needs are arranged. Among other things, customers can find a 'Trend Shop, Fifth Avenue', a Western shop, 'Chisolm Trail, Santa Fe', and a beauty salon, 'Madame'. Fashionable footwear is for sale at 'Boots Inn', and the latest records at 'Blues Inn.'[7]

The language of capital draws greatly on Wall Street even when the valorization standpoint is persuasively denied. Those who are to be fooled must pay for their entertainment. The management calculates that the new store will be one 'which, despite offering the full range of everyday products, is consciously aimed at the more sophisticated market (fashionable brand-name goods). Moreover, Wertheim, like the other stores, prefers a younger clientele in the high income bracket.'[8]

In contrast to the strategy of 'entertainment shopping', it appears that the 'purchasing strategy' is hardly perceived as such. From the standpoint of exchange-value and on a higher level, from the standpoint of valorization, it would be ideal if the monied class could be made to buy without reflecting on the necessity of an acquisition',[9] as suggested by the soul of capital in a bourgeois newspaper's financial section. In pursuit of this ideal, in so far as it is achieveable, capital and its applied science of consumer research have invented the term 'impulse buying.' In order to induce it, styling, display and pricing of the commodity are assigned specific tasks. It is intended for a surprise encounter with the distracted customer. The commodity put on view is not displayed as the main article one is looking for, but appears as a seemingly incidental commodity. For example, the shoe firm Wosana achieved 'the highest growth rate (in 1971 around 100 per cent) … by distributing through food stores and supermarkets as well as drugstores and perfumeries (around 20 per cent growth).'[10]

The prices are consciously calculated to attract 'impulse buying' by ensuring that they retail at under DM20. The styling displays the commodity as if it had already been bought. 'Accordingly, some Wosana products are offered in clear plastic with a handle.' Viewing the merchandise through the wrapping replaces any physical contact or testing of the commodity which acts as a synthetic reminder that the actual test for use-value has been made to seem superfluous. The handle is already familiar from the carrier bags in which one carries away one's commodities. Everything is arranged so as not to inconvenience, since every pause in the act of buying can provide a break-off point, allowing time for reflection on the necessity of what one is actually acquiring. The purchase, being hardly recognized as such, and therefore unconsidered also depends like "entertainment shopping" on an element of distraction. If the unconsidered purchase happens, literally by chance on the sidelines, the development of 'entertainment shopping' itself places the incidental at the centre of its aesthetic efforts at representing commodity capital, thus operating as an entertaining distraction for the public.

In the 1970 Euroshop fair in Dusseldorf this new style of selling appeared on the horizon to establish a general standard. 'One can expect,' reported the biggest shopfitters in the Federal Republic, 'that the activation of the sales process will culminate in an increasingly strong attempt to combine supply with entertainment.'[11] With entertainment, or amusement, an additional vehicle for aesthetic commodity attraction arrives on the salesroom's 'entertainment' stage.[12] This involves new functions for the sales agents. At the fair it was said that 'the retailer of the future must be both shopkeeper and impresario rolled into one.'[13] As an experiment, some department stores changed the emphasis of their advertising. 'Relax with us,' proposed a West Berlin concern in the autumn of 1971, 'in the fascinating world of a large department store. Where you can buy a lot of fun for very little money. And without cash! Simply use your Gold Card. We wish you an enjoyable time shopping at *XYZ*.'[14]

These performances, an extra means of seduction evolved from the commodity, still have to be paid for by the buyers. The thinking behind the 'amusement store' remains the same as in the 'entertainment stage', i.e. takings per employee and profit on turnover. Here the borderline between the commodity and the sales process begins to blur, as already happened long before between use-value, and commodity aesthetics. Now, when a commodity is sold, the customer not only pays for its styling and the name made famous through advertising, but also for the styling of the selling process. As far as the commodity is concerned, conscious efforts are made to shift the emphasis from the specific commodity to the experience of consumption.

Ultimately the aestheticization of commodities means that they tend to dissolve into enjoyable experiences, or into the appearance of those experiences, detached from the commodity itself. The tendency to sell these processes as material/immaterial types of commodities leaves no time to consider their use value. By selling the commodity in the form of absolute consumption, the market remains unsatiated.

To establish this trend, it is not enough to mould and remould the army of sellers; one must condition the instincts and behaviour of the 'public at large.' And since young people are easiest to manipulate, they become the instrument and expression of a general trend towards moulding. Their fetishization is both expression and instrument in one.

NOTES

Extracted from W. F. Haug, *Critique of Commodity Aesthetics: Appearance, Sexuality and Advertising in Capitalist Society* (Minneapolis: University of Minnesota Press, 1986), pp. 67–72. Reprinted by permission of Sukrkamp Verlag.

1. Kracauer mentions in his study of employees at the end of the twenties, years in which lighting techniques in the sales area had been greatly developed, the 'beneficial influence'—beneficial as far as capital is concerned—'that lighting has on both the desire to buy and on sales assistants … the light dazzles rather than illuminates … and thus the illusion is preserved' (*Schriften*, p. 284).
2. *Frankfurter Rundschau*, 26 February 1970. According to this same source the sales area in retail shops in the Federal Republic increased from 23 million to 32 million square metres between 1960 and 1970. Thus according to these figures, the investment in salesrooms costs around DM4 thousand million a year (1970). According to more recent figures on the other hand, 1970 saw a DM3.6 thousand million (5 per cent) drop in investment in comparison with retail trade in the previous year. But according to an Ifo survey, 1971 will enter a period of investment of at least 10 per cent increase. 'This growth in investment should chiefly be borne by the larger retail outlets, which register a yearly turnover of over DM10 million' (*FAZ*, 13 August 1971).
3. *Der Tagesspiegel*, 24 February 1970.
4. Quoted in *Der Tagesspiegel*, 24 February 1970.
5. 'Das Warenhaus als Erlebnisbühne. Nachbemerkungen zum Fall Globus' by J. Jürgen Jeske, *FAZ*, 4 August 1971. Other quotations and information on 'Globus' are also from this source.
6. The extensive aesthetic innovation in department stores which followed the success of boutiques occurred in the same year (1967) in which even men's fashion came under pressure from economic crisis and declining turnover. It gave itself a boost of aesthetic innovation, following a sideways glance at the growing number of boutiques which sell imported commodities. 'The second effect of monopolization—aesthetic innovation' in the present work.
7. *FAZ*, 2 September 1971, p. 15. This also mentions the story of the legendary pioneer in the world of commodities—the Wertheim store which was completed in 1927 in Leipzig Square.

    Its ground floor was more than double the size of the Reichstag's ground floor. The building, erected by Professor Messel, was richly decorated with sculptures and bronze reliefs by famous sculptors. Its interior was covered in marble inlay-work, and silver-plated terracotta pieces were on display. The carpet department was panelled in Italian walnut and in the numerous inner courtyards, fountains worked in Istrian limestone were playing.
8. Ibid.
9. *FAZ*, 20 August 1971, p. 15.
10. Ibid.
11. *Der Tagesspiegel*, 24 February 1970.
12. A new name has already been coined for the new stage-management of the sales-area and the whole sales-experience: 'Amusement Store' (*Der Tagesspiegel*, 24 February 1970). Coining new names is a standard component in the process of carrying out innovations and thus devaluing a portion of the retail invested capital.
13. *Der Tagesspiegel*, 24 February 1970.
14. Ka-De-We advertisement in *Der Tagesspiegel*, 17 October 1971.

49

FASHIONING UNIQUENESS

Mass Customization and the Commodization
of Identity

Heike Jenß

Welcome to PUMA Mongolian Shoe BBQ … Taking our inspiration from the preparation of Mongolian cuisine, Puma lets you taste the art of shoemaking and pick from a generous assortment of pre-cut materials to design your own custom-made shoes. … Unlike the bland and impersonal of mass production, this is your art and your invention—dream and spice it up as you please. (http://www.mongolianshoebbq. puma.com. Accessed April 1, 2008)

With this recipe for creating personal uniqueness, sports-brand Puma invites customers to "cook up" their individual pair of sneakers as a visual and material assurance and display of taste and distinction. Unlike the concepts of Puma's competing brands, Nike*ID* and *mi*adidas, which already indicate in their name the marriage of the global corporation with the individual identity of the consumer, Puma offers the creation of difference by adding the exotic flavor of otherness and orientalism, christening the concept "Mongolian Shoe BBQ." To provide a different or unique shopping experience, the company merges fashion consumption, as the constitutive bodily practice of representing oneself, with the idea of food consumption, as the essential bodily practice of sustaining oneself. Both practices link body and identity with the social and economic sphere, relying on the availability of a necessary range of commodities and their selection, purchase, arrangement and processing or preparation

according to sociocultural custom and individual taste. Thus the concept capitalizes in a quite direct way on the pleasure of the sensual experience, material feeling, and sampling associated with consumption and taste in the physical or sensory, as well as in a classificatory sense as the display of social positioning and distinction (see Bourdieu 1984). Starting with some field notes on the experience offered by PUMA's Mongolian Shoe BBQ, this essay explores the implications of mass customization within the dynamics of uniformity in fashion consumption, the fabrication of identity, and the idealization of uniqueness.

CUSTOMIZATION EXPERIENCE

Mass customization, as a production and marketing tool that allows the personal finishing or processing of mass products, adapts to the desire for individualization achieved through commodities and consumer practices. It is also defined as a "customer co-design process of products and services which meet the needs of each individual customer with regard to certain product features" (http://www.mass-customization.de/glossary. htm#mc). The idea is not to custom-make products but to combine the efficiency of high-volume or mass-production with customization at a price level "that does not imply a switch in an upper market segment" (http://www.mass-customization. de/glossary.htm#mc). The principle has been discussed in the marketing and business publications of Stan Davis (1987), Joseph Pine (1993) and Frank Piller (1998) and has become an important strategy among bigger corporations as well as among companies that target niche markets and use the Internet as the central form of interaction with the customer.

The concept offered by PUMA is available both online and in selected stores. In the PUMA store in New York's SoHo district, customers can approach a small counter station not unlike in a self-service restaurant. They pick up a plastic tray printed with the order and outline of the diverse pieces that have to be selected and assembled to create a real pair of sneakers. The customization process then begins by first selecting one of the two shoe silhouettes on offer: In spring 2008 customers could choose either the running shoe "RS-11," which was first introduced in the late 1980s, or "Basket," according to PUMA one of the "iconic hoops styles from the 70s." After selecting the preferred pair, either in its male or female variant, as well as its size, the customer starts sampling and selecting the material raw ingredients for the shoe. In line with the reference to the Mongolian BBQ, represented here in the form of the industrial kitchen counter, the shoe ingredients are kept in a series of professional catering bowls. These stainless steel containers, which one usually only encounters filled with food in a canteen or menu bar, are here filled with the eighteen precut components of a sports shoe, multiplied by their variations in color and texture, that circulate, instead of food aromas, the smell of rubber. From loose soles, to laces, tongues, and finally the brand symbol, the PUMA form-stripe, in colors and textures ranging from purple suede to green reptile pattern, the customer can pick and mix the bits and pieces from the bowls and rearrange their combination on the tray until the combination turns out just the way he or she likes them to be. Ideally the plastic tray now is covered with all the loose eighteen pieces that form the matrix of the final dish. A computer is assisting in this process and displays the composition of the new shoe in

a virtual image that can be turned around 360° to give a three-dimensional impression of the finished result.

After this process, the customer's personal selection from the shoe menu is processed through the PUMA Web site. The customer pays for the order by credit card (either $100 for the 1980s-style Basket or $130 for the RS-100) or continues to shop or create an additional design, filling his or her virtual shopping cart (or "doggy bag," as PUMA refers to it) for later checkout. In contrast, however, to the customer's personal hand-selection of precut ingredients, the shoe will be finished in a standardized industrial production process, which, together with shipping to the customer, can take between five and seven weeks.

The Puma store itself sells otherwise rather conventional mass-produced sports and leisure-wear products, as well as more expensive limited-edition articles. However, within the range of the standardized and branded products, Mongolian Shoe BBQ provides the customer with a very sensual and creative shopping experience. The customer can hand-select each of the ingredients of his future sneaker—touching, sampling, choosing, evaluating, replacing colors, fabrics, textures—and thereby rise from consumer to the rank of designer or "shoe artist." The concept partly resembles do-it-yourself strategies, as a response to the uniformity perceived with the continuing rise of mass fashion. It could even be seen as an educational tool that allows the development of manual competencies and specialist knowledge, as the consumer gets some rudimentary insights into the "art of shoemaking," or respectively, into the material side of creation and fabrication, usually invisible to the consumer of mass fashion. However, in contrast to an autonomous do-it-yourself activity pursued by an individual, here the production or creation process is clearly defined by the relationship between the consumer and the corporation, who provides the customer with the final product and thereby lets him or her not only take part in the creation but also be a part of the brand.

FASHION—UNIFORM—UNIQUENESS

As the introductory slogan implies, this customization experience or assortment of the variants of the branded shoe is "generously" offered as an alternative to mass fashion and particularly to counter the "blandness or impersonal" effect of uniformity that is associated with it. Apparently the uniformity of mass-produced fashion, as the dominant raw material for dressing the body in the industrialized world, does not fit the diversity and individuality of consumers. Rather, the uniformity of mass-produced fashion stands in stark contrast to the societal process of individualization, the fragmentation of modern lifestyles, the emergence of hybrid consumers, as well as to the cultural idealization of uniqueness that goes along with this. *Uniqueness,* already a term emotionally charged, is the highly sought-after ideal that Undine Eberlein even declares as a substitute for religion (2000: 283). However, the uniqueness or individuality of a person is not a given, but it has to be constructed as social categories or values. Individuality, not necessarily autonomy, but meaning to be or appear individual is a commandment or a social expectation (Schulze 2001). Individuality is regarded a constitutive value of modern democratic society, despite the consequences individualization as a social process may provide in the post-industrial world, and its realization or achievement involves hard identity work.

In this context the uniformity and seriality associated with mass production is seen as a burden and an anxiety causing threat (see Jenß 2007: 253; Mentges 2005). Of course as a historically grown dress culture, the development of fashion is immediately linked with the process of individuation in modernity, as the self-determined visual and material fashioning of oneself demands social autonomy (Mentges 2005: 21). Uniforms and uniformity obviously are therefore the negative "other" of fashion, as they are "indifferent to

individual differences" (Calefato 2000: 195–204, 196), limiting and regulating appearances and the freedom of choice. Dressed in a uniform, the individual ideally becomes incorporated into the greater body and order of an institution, where the creation of individual appearance is subordinate to detailed regulations from above: "everything is codified, nothing is left up to personal initiative" (Craik 2003: 127–48, 128). But while institutional uniforms are one extreme form of limiting individual appearances, we can find principles of uniformity also in fashion: The individual follows fashion in order to pursue and prove its own uniqueness and by doing so aligns itself with a common tendency (Esposito 2004: 13, Simmel 2004). Beyond this societal dynamic of imitation and differentiation, visually and symbolically negotiated through appearances that "fit in" or "stick out," uniformity is also materially inherent in fashion, as the mass production of civil clothing evolved from the fabrication of standardized military uniforms, based on the measurements of a high number of soldier's bodies and their categorization into the order of a rational, standardized sizing system (Krause 1965, Mentges 1993). While this basis for the serial production of clothing in standardized sizes, which came with the professionalization of the standing army, was once a great milestone in the development of ready-made clothing, it is now perceived as mass fashion's great burden.

One of the most dominant reasons why today a garment is not purchased is because it does not fit the body (Rissiek and Piller 2001: 38). Reasons for this include obsolete sizing systems that no longer match the ongoing development of the human body, whose height and shape alters with improved nutrition and different modes of physical exercise and labor. The simplification of sizes over the last decades further complicates this, as well as the lack of an international sizing system, despite the global spread of international fashion chains (such as Swedish company Hennes & Mauritz or Spanish company Zara, with differences in clothing size and fit). The dissatisfaction of consumers with the fit of standardized garments certainly provides a huge market potential, and more and more fashion suppliers started in the 1990s to cater this market with mass-customization strategies in which standardized clothing is adapted to the individual bodily measurements of the consumer (Rissiek and Piller 2001: 39–40).

However, the reality of bodily fit is only one side of the dissatisfaction with standardized fashion; the other, maybe more emotional, side refers to the notion of personal taste and the perception that mass fashion cannot satisfactorily provide the wearer with the sense of individuality and uniqueness he or she wishes or is expected to project through clothing choice. Consumption as a complex cultural practice means not simply the purchase of things but involves the whole process of observation, searching, selecting, imagining, the consumption of images and things, the shopping experience, looking at things, comparing, trying on, taking home, and the use, composition, and integration of things into one's own wardrobe (see Miller 1995). Consumption is the practice through which mass-produced fashion becomes singular and personally invested with meanings, including charging it with the value of the personal and unique. Therefore, it is a key practice in identity work and in localizing oneself in society, and, respectively, commodities or the things people use to perform identity are of key significance as well.

In order to serve the desire for individual things and experiences, and of course also to benefit from its economic potential, the concept of mass customization as exemplified with PUMA's Mongolian Shoe BBQ addresses the consumer in his or her active role of creator, inventor, or artist, turning him or her into a "prosumer," who is consumer and producer at the same time. Therefore, the act of singularization, usually achieved independently through the personal appropriation and usage of things and the meanings subjectively invested in them over time, now happens almost instantly and in direct dialogue with the company. Hence, the customer does not need to work autonomously on the construction of his or her uniqueness; rather, this freedom or

service is provided by the brand that "lets you taste the art of shoemaking and pick from a generous assortment of pre-cut materials to design your own custom-made shoes" (http://www.mongolianshoebbq.puma.com).

In this process the customer also becomes more personally and emotionally involved in the concept or world of the brand. The great advantage for the company in turn is to establish a direct relationship to the consumer, and with that also a profitable infrastructure to gather with the consumer's desires an invaluable amount of so-called "individualization information" (Piller 1998: 277). This includes not only the name and address of the customer, and physical or bodily characteristics like size and gender, but also more social information such as age, spending habits, and, most importantly, personal taste and preferences, which in turn can be directly addressed via personalized or customized product marketing. Eventually, however, all the diverse tastes, desires, dreams, characteristics, interests, and bodily features of the various individual consumers coagulate into a profitable and efficiently processable amount of data that can be transformed and materialized into new standardized commodities (see Jenß 2005: 199–219). It is an attempt not only to involve the consumer in the design process, but also to establish a closer or more direct relationship between the brand and the volatile consumer, who has—despite the assumed uniformity of mass fashion—the potential liberty to choose between uncountable suppliers who can provide him with potential material for his or her individual identity construction.

UNIQUE TASTE—COLLECTIVE DISTINCTION

According to John Thackara, mass customization is only "the latest twist in a hundred-year-old struggle between standardization and customization" (1998: 148–52, 151), and he refers to the automotive industry: "When you consider that Ford's Model T began production in 1911, and that by 1924 a new model was launched every year, you could say that 'pure' mass production (or Fordism) lasted precisely thirteen years" (1998: 151). The industry has probably never really believed in a homogenous group of people sharing "collectivized consumption" and "uniformed taste" as envisioned in Werner Sombart's early twentieth-century idea of the "big uniform masses of … consumers whose entire history is signified by a uniformization of thought and will" (1986: 80–105, 83).

As Sarah Berry remarks with respect to fashion, the development of mass consumption does not evolve from the principle of mass production but relied on an early form of mass customization. The invention of the sewing machine, for example, did not cause a simplification or uniformization of fashion but instead enabled a higher complexity and increased change of fashionable forms (2000: 49–60, 54). Based on a system of subcontractors and using sweated labor, retailers "were able to place orders at the last minute in tiny production runs, making new fashions affordable for the masses" (Fine and Leopold 1993: 107, quoted by Berry 2000: 54). Variation and change fuel the desire for consumption, and the participation in it provides a temporary satisfaction in the individual's hunt for uniqueness.

Of course, at the same time, the attempts of consumers to create individuality outside of industrial production processes fuel change and variation in the market. A good example is the early American hot-rod culture that developed among teenagers and former GIs shortly after World War II. In opposition to the term *customizing,* the term *kustomizing* or *kustomized kars* (that replaces the c with a k) connotes an independently pursued destandardization of cars that is not offered by the industry. As vividly described by Tom Wolfe, the car was a significant part of the emerging teenage culture in America, and an embodiment of "freedom, style, sex, power, motion, color" (Wolfe 1965: 79). The tuning of cars was a subversive act that was, however, quickly incorporated by the car industry catering to youth culture with special customizing events (see Wolfe 1965).

In a similar way, we can understand the mass-customization of sneakers. We can clearly link the phenomenon with the subculture of sneakerheads (see Bartholomew Jr. 2005) who define themselves as similar to vintage enthusiasts, through the focus on the consumption of the rare and authentic, usually purchased through the search and discovery of old-stock or secondhand markets (Jenß 2004, 2007). The scene of the (still predominantly male) sneakerheads, which evolved from hip-hop culture into a global scene of sneaker connoisseurs, is now directly targeted by the brands themselves, which cater to this market with new, expensive, limited editions and customized shoes like PUMA. Their consumption focus is linked with a striving for authenticity and realness as quasi-ideological means of differentiation, as well as sometimes with a certain degree of nostalgia (for the sneaker that reminds one of old days in the school gym, or the shoes one always wanted but never could afford). Consumers who are labeled sneakerheads possess, in some cases, several hundred pairs of sneakers and often tend to get a couple of pairs of the same type; one pair is worn while a spare one is stored neatly in the original box and kept in a special sneaker closet (see Bartholomew Jr. 2005).

This may be a rather extreme form of consumption; however, it shows how commodities become trophies in the hunt for authenticity and can be invested with the aura of uniqueness, even if they were at some point mass-produced. It also shows how it is the act of consuming and the experience involved in it that ascribes personal meanings into commodity. This form of sneaker consumption clearly involves the practices, specialist knowledge, and emotions that are usually involved in the process of collecting. "An excessive, sometimes even rapacious need to *have* is transformed into rule-governed, meaningful desire" (Clifford 1993: 53). And as James Clifford further reminds us, collecting, or the assemblage of a "material world," is a "strategy for the deployment of a possessive self … it involves the notion that this gathering involves the accumulation of possessions, the idea that identity is a kind of wealth (of objects, knowledge, memories, experiences)" (1993: 52). With the collectible being fashion, or in this case specifically shoes, sneakerheads focus the accumulation of possessions on the commodity that is closest to the body and representation of self.

Clothing is constituted to make an appearance and to make the body culturally and socially visible. It is the material that enables the immediate embodiment of identity and the objectification of wealth in knowledge and competencies, or, in Bourdieu's sense, the display of taste, and with that, cultural or subcultural capital (Thornton 2005). And shoes, as the objects that physically connect the human body to the world or environment, have long been used as special markers of distinction and as a means for classification and categorization. And it is, of course, not only the high-quality handmade shoe that helps to project taste and distinction, but, looking at the development of youth cultures, from pointed winkle pickers to Doc Martens and Chucks, shoes have always been a key in the negotiation of difference. This is even more the case with respect to sneakers, which have diversified so much and are an integral component of youth cultural activities, from skateboarding and breaking to the basketball courts. They serve sportive activities and, beyond that, signify casualness, youthfulness, modernity, mobility, and urban lifestyle.

Further, sneakers are a particular item of dress that is instantly associated with a brand. Unlike other forms of body wear, which often can only be signified or branded through the application or print of a label, sneakers represent the brand in their entire design. The high-top canvas Chuck from Converse can be immediately identified as such, as can a pair of Nike Dunks or Adidas Superstars, not only by the iconic brand logo, and the form stripes, which are an integral aesthetic component of the shoe, but usually by the entity of the shoe design. Sneakerheads who pay high prices to own a pair of Nikes that are only produced in a very limited quantity, so that they are almost unique, or at least not shared with anybody but a selected few,

as well as prosumers who codesign their Pumas or Adidas, possess the symbol of the quasi-individual, which is at the same time, however, collective, because it is a branded commodity.

"If modern personhood is defined in large part through the disposition to possess ... then the specificities of both individual and collective life narratives increasingly depend upon the ownership of branded goods, both licit and illicit, for their expression and recognition. For what brands confer is precisely not the generic and ordinary, but the specific and particular" (Moor 2007: 113). And this is what makes them attractive in the contemporary fashioning of uniqueness, since the desire is not to be unique in the sense of total self-reliance or even social disconnection, but to achieve social status, acceptance, and a sense of belonging through the projection of individuality, and the display of taste and distinction that only makes sense if it is recognized by, and thus part of, the community.

With the breakdown of stable social structures, people are incited and required to develop their own senses of selfhood and to be responsible to fashion their own identities and social networks. The necessary efforts and identity work related with this is constructively supported and promoted through the economy, which not only responds to but, with concepts like mass customization also fosters, the desire and commandment of uniqueness. Individuality has become a "mass-desire" (Schulze 2001) that apparently can be fulfilled through more and more specialized forms of consumption and commodities, ranging from an increasing product variety to built-in personalization options (engraving the iPod) and mass customization. Disconnected from the sense of individuality as the autonomy of the individual—as if the freedom of the individual means primarily its freedom to consume—it designs or creates individuality as a commodity or a commodity feature and thereby turns it again into a component of a "collective semantic" (Schulze 2001: 564) through which uniqueness and individuality become standardized.

ANNOTATED GUIDE TO FURTHER READING

There has been considerable scholarly interest in consumption and identity and their relationships in recent years, and while many publications do not identify design specifically, design is very much a part of that conversation. This is particularly so in the consumption of virtual identity, in which books such as Richard Bartle's comprehensive *Designing Virtual Worlds* (2004) serves as more than a do-it-yourself manual, but encourages readers also to think about the issues of virtual world design. Similarly, N. Katherine Hayles, *How We Became Posthuman: Virtual Bodies in Cybernetics, Literature, and Informatics* (1999), brings a critical and historical framework to issues of embodiment in the information age. Hayles echoes the concerns of Donna Haraway, whose conception of "nature" in *Primate Visions: Gender, Race, and Nature in the World of Modern Science* (1989) was formative for feminist theory. From a different perspective, the essays contained in Roger Horowitz and Arwen Mohun, *His and Hers: Gender Consumption and Technology* (1998), provide a helpful analysis of gender, technology, and consumption as both a material and a cultural process.

The study of fashion and dress continues to produce valuable insights into gender and identity. While it is invidious to choose specific examples, Diana Crane's *Fashion and Its Social Agendas: Class, Gender and Identity in Clothing* (2001) provides an accessible introduction to this issue, as does John Harvey's focus on the role of color in dress in *Men in Black* (1995). Amy de la Haye and Elizabeth Wilson's edited volume, *Defining Dress: Dress as Object, Meaning and Identity* (1999), concentrates on objects, identity, and consumer culture and follows a similar trajectory to Pat Kirkham's *The Gendered Object* (1996). Kirkham's work on feminism and design is significant, including her appraisal of the work of two designing partners, *Charles and Ray Eames: Designers of the Twentieth Century* (1995), as well as *A View From the Interior: Feminism, Women and Design* (1989), co-edited with Judy Attfield, and Kirkham's edited *Women Designers in the USA 1990–2000: Diversity and Difference* (2000). In comparison, in *As Long As It's Pink,* Penny Sparke (1995) considers the sexual politics of taste. Along side these historically based texts, we can place publications such as Frank Mort's *Cultures of Consumption: Masculinities and Social Space in Late Twentieth Century Britain* (1996) as an exploration of gender, commerce, and geography.

There are many important studies of consumption that have an impact on our reaction to identity and design, from Thorstein Veblen's classic study of conspicuous consumption in *The Theory of the Leisure Class* (1899), to Brewer and Porter's *Consumption and the World of Goods* (1993), which concentrates on seventeenth- and eighteenth-century Europe, through economist Ben Fine's comprehensive and recently revised *The World of Consumption* (2002), Grant McCracken's *Culture and Consumption II*

(2005), and Robert Bocock's key ideas in *Consumption* (1993), to Daniel Miller's substantial body of work on consumption and material culture (1987; 1998a; 1998b; 2001). The numerous readers on consumption also provide introductions to the field of studies, such as *The Consumer Society Reader* (Schor and Holt 2000), or *The Consumption Reader* (Clarke et. al. 2003). Brands are another important area of study of the issues of identity and consumption and include *Brand.new,* the book of the exhibition at London's Victoria and Albert Museum (Pavitt 2000), as well as investigations such as *The Rise of Brands* (Moor 2007), or *Brands: Meaning and Value in Media Culture* (Arvidsson 2006), which may helpfully be read in conjunction with Jonathan Schroeder's *Visual Consumption* (2002). Broader cultural interpretations of identity and consumption include Garon and Maclachlan, *The Ambivalent Consumer, Questioning Consumption in East Asia and the West* (2006).

SECTION 5

LABOR, INDUSTRIALIZATION, AND NEW TECHNOLOGY

SECTION INTRODUCTION

Many historians argue that industrialization ushered out the production of craft and prompted our current conception of design. Thus, this section explores industrialization and mass production in the late eighteenth and early nineteenth centuries. To thoroughly assess the role of industrialization in the design process, these three subsections focus on production, consumption, and new technology. The first subsection examines different ideas about labor, and how work, both physical and intellectual, creates design. The second subsection posits the importance of industrialization in relation to design and concludes with a discussion about our current postindustrial condition. Finally, the subsection on technology investigates how technology changes our perceptions of politics and individual power within civic culture, fashion, and the workplace.

As Marxism has taught us, in our capitalist system we often disassociate labor from design. We see things in the marketplace but are not aware of the work, or human energy, that goes into the production of goods. The readings in the first subsection on labor pick up on Marx's contention and either support his theory, or describe the problems with his approach. We can assess the Marxist perspective by examining the economic forces that define the production of design, thus interrogating the myth of production and pointing out the gendered and socioeconomic division of labor that allows many of our goods to be made inexpensively. Others contend that our understanding of capitalism should not be as focused on labor, as Marx demands, but instead we need to assess how capitalism signifies, or represents, things in the marketplace. It is the power of signification, not the brawn of physical labor, that does the real work in our current economic system.

Labor is, of course, what allowed industrialization to take place. The second subsection contains readings that reveal how industrialization shifted the practice of design into the realm of mass production. In the early twentieth century, many argued that industrialization was an opportunity to make bodies work harmoniously with manufacturing to foster more productivity. Scholars have critiqued the advent of this use of bodies, revealing how corporations mistreated workers with the rise of new factories. Today we live in a world where the notion of nonphysical, postindustrial production (think of software) exists. Hence, the immaterial—that which is not tangible—is much more important than goods produced during the industrial process. This is a vision of the present and future that privileges the intangible (for instance, JPEGS and MP3 downloads) over the physical (for instance, computer hardware).

This description of the immaterial is rooted in our growing reliance on new technology. Many contemporary critics see over-dependence on this new technology, which has not, they decry, led to better-designed computer systems that can make our lives easier. Still, there are examples of a rising tide of democratized political cultures that have utilized technology. It appears that technology can bring people together to help create a unified voice. There, is, however, a dark side to technology that can foster desires that lead to brutality and abuse. The interpretations of technology in this section suggest other ways of thinking about our computers, our cell phones, our iPods, our cars, and our obsession with these contrivances.

These articles on labor, industrialization, and technology are closely related to the ethical and political concerns covered in the Theorizing Design and Visuality section of this book (Section 3). In the world of work, our ideas about labor are always changing. However, the fact that labor creates design, manufactures design, and markets design to the public remains constant. Although our contemporary notion of labor may be more closely aligned with a conception of a postindustrial society, we need to think about the role that different types of work continue to play in design.

SECTION 5: LABOR, INDUSTRIALIZATION, AND NEW TECHNOLOGY

5.1: Labor and the Production of Design

INTRODUCTION

The methods of mass manufacture, based on the division of labor, established in Britain in the eighteenth century, laid the ground for labor and design practices that still continue, as documented by British eighteenth-century historian John Styles. The profit-driven increase in the manufacture and consumption of design was dependent on the successful transmission of visual information. Technical innovation enabled a greater use of printed and hand-drawn two-dimensional designs: as sources of visual ideas, as instructions for the execution of work, for recording information about products, and for visualizing products for customers. In this process, visualization became subject to a hierarchical division of labor, with designers emerging as a separate and specialized occupation, distinguished from pattern drawers. Yet, despite the emergence of proto-professional roles, the commonplace written and spoken word remained an important means for transmitting design information, as indeed remains the case in our own times (see also the reading from David Brett in Section 5.2).

In the intervening two centuries, mass production has been characterized in particular by Fordism, the system originated by Henry Ford for the production of automobiles. The question for the twentieth-century manufacturer was similar to that of his eighteenth-century counterpart—how to produce standardized items that would be affordable to the given consumer market, and would bring a profit to the manufacturer. By dividing the work force, breaking down complicated tasks into simpler ones, and using unskilled workers and standardized components on a moving assembly line, profit margin is increased, but the potential for worker satisfaction is diminished.

Sociologist Paul du Gay and his colleagues at the U.K. Open University analyze the production at Sony as part of the "circuit of culture," a very useful articulation of the five major cultural processes identified as essential to the study of any "cultural text or artefact": representation, identity, production, consumption, and regulation. Their classification is one we endorse and have addressed in the earlier sections of this *Reader,* as providing a comprehensive framework for the analysis and understanding of designed objects or things (see also Section 7). According to this premise, du Gay argues that production must be "articulated" with consumption. Before producing or designing the Sony Walkman, however, its "imagined" consumer had to be addressed. The designers function in the space of Marx's "intermediary movement" between production and consumption. They do not serve as quasi-artists, as in the eighteenth century, but as "cultural intermediaries" charged with instilling the things being manufactured with symbolic meanings.

Sony is exemplary for a large global corporation in giving their designers a central and respected part of the organizational structure, which functions between production and consumption and has the potential "to stitch the two spheres together." The product is the effective outcome of this connection, in which the consumer is kept at the forefront in the design decision-making process. However, the text also draws attention to the often neglected "hub" of labor and production in the form of an anonymous female global workforce. The assembly line enabled labor and production costs to be kept low, keeping the retail price of the product at a level where it could be appealing to the target market of younger consumers with limited spending power, through the Fordist model and the sexual division of labor. Women workers in Asian manufacturing countries have a central role, yet they are as under-valued as the alienated labor force to which Marx referred in the nineteenth century. (This point is also reinforced in the extract by Barbara Ehrenreich and Annette Fuentes extracted in Section 4.2, Gender and Design).

But the relationships between design, production, and consumption have many variations, depending on the larger intention. New initiatives are emerging outside of the profit-driven global conglomerates. Stuart Walker reassesses scales of production by considering manufacture, repair, and reuse at the local or regional level. Walker provides examples of specific products: the Lumière Floor Lamp and the Remora Box, which have been fabricated from standardized and interchangeable parts. Such products take into consideration environmental and social considerations, which reveals how the notion of sustainability can be integrated into product design. Using regionally produced parts and materials in combination with mass-produced parts, the resulting products can be disassembled then reassembled and reused in new combinations. This shifts the relationship of designer, producer, and consumer (discussed in Section 4) and enable the latter to take on the role of the former and potentially to achieve a greater understanding of and empathy with the things they own and use (a concept that is explored further in Section 7 of the *Reader*). Such developments challenge the way we conceptualize labor and production and provide alternatives that do not focus on factories or on retail stores, but return to the local level (see also Manzini in Section 6.2) and the domestic sphere.

Each of these extracts explores different periods of time and different cultural contexts, yet they arrive at similar conclusions about the importance of recognizing and valuing all aspects of human labor in the design and production of the material world.

50

MANUFACTURING, CONSUMPTION AND DESIGN IN EIGHTEENTH-CENTURY ENGLAND

John Styles

THE DICTATES OF THE MARKET AND THE IMPLEMENTATION OF DESIGN

Eighteenth-century manufacturers of batch-produced consumer goods faced markets that were often keenly attuned to the visual appearance of their products. Novelty and fashion could be important, although not necessarily dominant, at every level in the market. In some markets, goods that missed the latest fashion trend could not be easily sold. On receipt of a consignment of hats from Stockport, Cheshire that had to be returned for reworking because they were damaged, a London hatmaker commented in 1784, 'they will be good for little; they certainly will look like old hats; let them be done as soon as possible'.[1] The imperatives of constantly changing fashion were particularly pressing on those like the Spitalfields manufacturers of fine patterned silks who supplied dress materials to the extremely wealthy and fashionable, but they also extended to the makers of more modest buttons, buckles, hats, handkerchiefs and other patterned cloths.

As we have seen, the manufacturers of products such as these were often geographically distant from the final consumer. Moreover, they were, more often than not, the manufacturers of products such as these were often geographically distant from the final consumer. Two questions arise regarding the design of their products. First, how did such manufacturers determine the way their products should look in order to enjoy success in a variety of markets? Second, how did they ensure that their workers, often using hand techniques in their own homes, produced goods that accorded with the desired and often very precise visual specifications?

Most existing work on these subjects has focused either on the activities of those producing high design goods for the elite market, or on the distinctive ways design was exploited by Josiah Wedgwood and Matthew Boulton. Particular emphasis has been placed on the latter's initiation of new designs (both in the sense of new products and new forms of decoration) in accordance with or in advance of changes in fashionable taste, in order to secure a privileged place in the market. By making products to original designs, Boulton and Wedgwood were simply doing what had long been established practice in the London luxury trades. Not all metropolitan producers of luxury goods developed new designs, but it could be an important element in the success of such a business. In his discussion of cabinetmaking in *The London Tradesman* of 1747, Campbell emphasized that

A youth who designs to make a Figure in this Branch must learn to Draw; for upon this depends the Invention of new Fashions, and on that the Success of his Business: He who first hits upon any new Whim is sure to make by the Invention before it becomes common in the Trade; but he that must always wait for a new Fashion till it comes from *Paris,* or is hit upon by his Neighbour, is never likely to grow rich or eminent in his Way.[2]

The fruits of innovation were similar in many of the other luxury trades. The Spitalfields silkmakers, for example, systematically commissioned novel designs in order to pre-empt changes in fashion.[3]

Producers of more modest consumer goods did not generally exercise the same degree of initiative in staying ahead of fashion. They simply adapted the broad trend of prevailing London high fashion to the prejudices and pockets of their intended customers. As in many aspects of eighteenth-century industrial innovation, a process of copying combined with small incremental adjustments was the norm. Stanley Chapman has pointed out the importance of systematic piracy of expensive London designs by Lancashire cotton printers producing for the lower end of the market in the 1780s.[4] During the same decade, the Leeds merchant house of Horner and Turner often arranged for their manufacturing suppliers to imitate woollen and worsted cloths sold by their competitors in continental Europe.[5] Manufacturers were often secretive, but successful copying and adaptation required information about what other producers, and particularly fashion leaders, were doing, as well as information about what different markets were anxious or prepared to accept.[6] Hence the constant monitoring by manufacturers of what producers of similar goods were up to, hence the desperate efforts to secure information on changes in London taste, hence the voluminous advice from agents and wholesale customers on market trends.

If design depended for most producers on copying and adaptation, precisely how was visual information on what was to be copied communicated? One way was simply to acquire an example of the product to be pirated. This was common. In textiles, for example, it was fairly easy to secure a small piece of a competitor's fabric. A 1787 parliamentary committee was informed that a print of a new design from a Surrey printworks had been sent by a London warehouseman to the Peel printworks in Lancashire to be copied. Within a fortnight it was on sale in London at two-thirds of the price of the original.[7]

Another means of communicating visual information was to use two-dimensional depictions of an object or its ornament. One of the most striking new features of late seventeenth- and eighteenth-century manufacturing in England was a dramatic increase in the use of two-dimensional paper plans for subsequent three-dimensional execution. Designs on paper had been employed long before the mid-seventeenth century, by architects and goldsmiths for example, but over the next century and a half there was a massive expansion, at first concentrated in London, but later more extensive; of activities reliant on sophisticated design and ornament, such as cabinetmaking, coachmaking, cotton printing, silkweaving and the manufacture of decorative metalware. At the same time, there were important technical innovations in two-dimensional and low relief ornament: for example, copper plate printing on fabrics, stamping on the softer metals, the use of transfers on ceramics. The consequence was a vastly increased use of both printed and hand-drawn two-dimensional designs in the manufacturing of consumer goods, for a variety of purposes. They were used as sources of visual ideas, as instructions for the execution of the work, for recording information about products and as a means of visualizing products for customers.

As two-dimensional design became more important, designer and pattern drawer emerged as distinct occupational designations. The term designer was first used early in the eighteenth century to describe those who performed the highly specialized task of providing new designs for fine patterned textiles, often on a freelance basis, but by mid-century it was being used more extensively.[8] The demand for drawing and associated skills like engraving grew apace. By the middle years of the eighteenth century there was much complaint about skill shortages in this area. Some of the deficiency had to be made up from overseas and considerable efforts were mounted to provide training. In 1759 it was claimed 'that there are two or three drawing schools established at Birmingham, for the instruction of youth in the arts of designing and drawing, and 30 or 40 Frenchmen and Germans are constantly employed in drawing and designing'.[9]

From the later seventeenth century, the London book and print trade catered to the expanding industrial market for two-dimensional designs with prints and subsequently illustrated source books. As early as the 1660s, the London bookseller and print dealer Robert Walton stocked prints which he advertised as 'extraordinarily useful for goldsmiths, jewellers, chafers, gravers, painters, carvers, drawers, needlewomen and all handicrafts'.[10] In the eighteenth century, design source books were often targeted at particular trades, like Smith and Linnell's *A New Book of Ornaments Useful for Silver-Smith's Etc.* of 1755 or Chippendale's *The Gentleman and Cabinet Maker's Director* of 1754, although designs for one material could be transferred to another, given the ubiquity of certain types of classical and rococo ornament within elite material culture.[11] From mid-century, if not before, printed designs also circulated in the illustrated trade catalogues issued by some manufacturers of ceramics, light consumer metalwares and even tools.[12] These were unabashed marketing devices, for use in showrooms, by travelling salesmen and by wholesale customers, similar in purpose to the pattern cards and books which were widely employed by textile manufacturers and merchants to circulate samples of fabric.

Clearly the increasing availability of drawing and design skills and the growing circulation in various guises of design illustrations facilitated the acquisition of design information by manufacturers and its adaptation for use in their products (legitimately or otherwise).[13] "It is therefore surprising to realize the extent to which manufacturers in many eighteenth-century industries producing batches of relatively modest products on a large scale secured design information by means of the written or spoken word. This was partly because in these industries the crucial design changes were often quite simple—a new range of colours here, a different width of stripe there. In textiles, for example, weaving simple patterned cloths did

not necessarily require the painstakingly prepared patterns on point paper used in weaving elaborate designs on unwieldy draw looms in the Spitalfields silk industry. One should not, however, underestimate the richness of the information that could be communicated by means of the written word. The degree of complexity is indicated in a letter that Matthew Boulton wrote to his London buckle agent in 1793 on the need to settle on a terminology for describing changes in fashion: 'As you and I shall often have occasion to speak of forms and proportions of buckles, it is necessary we should settle a distinct language that our definitions may be precise.'[14] In most trades, however, an appropriate language of visual description already existed. Indeed, it was a fundamental aspect of that elusive but much prized knowledge of the trade which was essential to participation in it.[15] But it was also possible for non-specialists to use a verbal language of visual description in the same way. For example, information about new fashions in clothes sufficiently precise to instruct a local mantua maker was sent to a Lancashire gentlewoman from a London relative mainly through the medium of words, not drawings or illustrations.[16]

The importance of a verbal language of visual description was not confined to the process whereby manufacturers secured information about design innovation. It was also central to their ability to adapt that information to their own advantage; to get their workers successfully to produce goods which incorporated those innovations. In other words, it was crucial to communication within the firm. For example, the late eighteenth-century London hat-maker Thomas Davies was accustomed to communicate the design of new hats to the manager of his manufacturing operation in Stockport, Cheshire by letter along the following lines: 'a short napp, almost like a French hat but not so bare, pleasant stiffen'd, rather smart, by no means raggy and not a heavy hat; they are to be from 7¼ to 7½, 3¼ to 3¾ high, not quite upright, a little taper.'[17] Here we observe the use of a specialist vocabulary in combination with a system of standard sizes to communicate precise specifications for a batch of goods.

This kind of verbal communication to specify the intended look of a product was common in other industries. Sometimes words were used in conjunction with three-dimensional devices for communicating visual information, like moulds or sample objects. In the 1770s and 1780s, the London agent for the Royal Northumberland Bottle Works sent his orders to the works manager by letter in the following manner:

> Be so good to send me by first opportunity 6 doz. bottles to the pattern sent, which holds near 2 gallons, must be imitated both in strength and shape as near as possible. 7 doz. parting glasses to 3 patterns sent. 4 doz. 4 gallon bottles, exact to the size of the pattern sent, the neck straight up, the mouth 2½ inch diameter and no less. 100 3 gallon bottles to pattern, no larger in size with good stopper mouths.[18]

The patterns mentioned here were sample bottles.

Even when two-dimensional information was transmitted, words were often an essential accompaniment, because manufacturers did not simply want their workers to copy, but to adapt, adjust and elaborate in ways appropriate to their markets, their materials and their skills. The partners in one Lancashire cotton printing firm at the beginning of the nineteenth century sent samples of other firms' prints to their pattern drawer with accompanying verbal instructions, usually to vary the ground or the motifs, or to change the direction, the emphasis or the size of the pattern. For example, 'Enclosed you have a pattern of one of the Busy House's plate furnitures. Joseph Peel desires you will draw up and engrave two or three patterns similar, they must be showey and full of work.'[19]

Success in the consumer industries depended not only on the products being of a marketable and therefore often a fashionable design, but also on each individual item conforming strictly

to a precise visual specification embodying that marketability. Distant wholesale customers who bought on the basis of samples and illustrated trade catalogues expected the goods delivered to them to conform to the look of the sample or the illustration. Uniformity was crucial, but was often extremely difficult to achieve, especially when making adaptations of more expensive products in large batches using inferior materials and cheaper, less skilled and more pressured labour.[20] Consequently manufacturers, agents, wholesalers and retailers were constantly monitoring the appearance of batch-produced goods and chiding their workers and suppliers about visual deficiencies. This kind of visual policing was conducted mainly in words.

In 1781 the London agent for the Royal Northumberland Bottle Works complained to the works manager,

> I have returned you by Dawson some of the [bottles] which are of a very bad quality … half the cargoe is such, some of the bottles have necks ¾ of an inch too long, flat shoulders and blown in different moulds. I beg you will take care not to send me any more of those blown in that narrow mould, but let it be destroyed as I cannot sell them on any account.[21]

Davies the London hatmaker commented to his Stockport manager in 1783:

> We have received a little order from Vain as under which beg your attention to; he complains that our hats are not so good as those from other houses, which occasions our having so few of his orders and that we never send them exact to the sizes he orders them at.[22]

The same problem obliged a Cumbrian glovemaker to offer the following tortuous excuse to a London wholesale customer in 1733: 'The leather is as good as … our country affords, not but that there may [be] some of them not so good as other some, for 'tis impossible to have all equally alike.'[23]

Implementing design in large-batch manufacturing of consumer goods in the eighteenth century depended on the dexterity and adaptability of the individual worker, and on the employer's capacity to direct and instruct a workforce. The initiative in specifying design flowed predominantly from master manufacturer to worker, but the ability of workers autonomously to interpret and adapt the manufacturer's instructions was also essential. Much turned on the capacity of employees, frequently working in their own homes within an intense division of labour, to use what were often general purpose tools to produce the required specification uniformly across hundreds or thousands of objects. Much also turned on the ability of the employer to communicate his requirements to such employees with sufficient precision. All sorts of devices for specifying, transmitting and reproducing visual information could play a part here, including moulds, models, dies, transfers, scale patterns and paper designs. In the course of the eighteenth century the use of two-dimensional designs probably increased, but their importance should not be overestimated. In many of these industries a specialized and sophisticated verbal language of visual description remained crucial.[24]

NOTES

Extracted from J. Styles, 'Manufacturing, Consumption and Design', in John Brewer and Roy Porter, eds, *Consumption and the World of Goods* (London: Routledge, 1994), pp. 543–7. Reprinted by permission of Taylor and Francis Books, U.K.

1. Public Record Office, C107/104: Davies letter book, undated letter (summer 1784?).
2. R. Campbell, *The London Tradesman* (London, 1747), 171.
3. N. Rothstein, 'The silk industry in London, 1702–1766' (University of London, M.A. thesis, 1961).
4. S. D. Chapman and S. Chassagne, *European Textile Printers of the Eighteenth Century* (London, 1981) 78–81.
5. For example, Public Record Office, C108/101: letter books of Horner and Turner, merchants, Leeds; letter to Mr George Darby, merchant in Naples, 30 December 1789.
6. For secrecy see M. Berg, *The Age of Manufactures, 1700–1820* (London 1985) 296. For similar practices in the nineteenth century Toshio Kusamitsu, '"Novelty, give us novelty", London agents and northern manufacturers', M. Berg (ed.), *Markets and Manufacture in Early Industrial Europe* (London, 1991).
7. Referred to in Chapman and Chassagne, *European Textile Printers*, 81, from *Journal of the House of Commons*, xlii (1787), 584–5; see Public Record Office, C108/101: letter books of Horner and Turner, merchants, of Leeds for similar activities.
8. Information from Charles Saumarez Smith. See his 'Design and economy in mid-eighteen century England', paper presented at Oxford University, 1987, and 'Eighteenth-century man' *Designer* (March 1987), 19–21. For designers in the Spitalfields silk industry, see Rothstein, 'The silk industry in London', *passim*.
9. *Journal of the House of Commons*, xxviii (1757–61), 496–7. For a discussion of the whole issue of skill shortages and training, see Saumarez Smith, 'Eighteenth-century man'.
10. Quoted in Leona Rostenberg, *English Publishers in the Graphic Arts* (New York, 1963), 45.
11. S. Lambert (ed.), *Pattern and Design: Design for the Decorative Arts, 1480–1980* (London, 1983), sect. 2.
12. See D. Towner, *Creamware* (London, 1978), Appendix 2; M. B. Rowlands, *Masters and Men* (Manchester, 1975), 152–3; N. Goodison, 'The Victoria and Albert Museum's collection of metal-work pattern books', *Furniture History*, xi (1975), 1–30; T.S. Ashton, *An Eighteenth-Century Industrialist: Peter Stubbs of Warrington 1756–1806* (Manchester 1939), 60.

13. The law on design copyright was extremely weak at this period.

14. Quoted in E. Robinson, 'Eighteenth-century commerce and fashion: Matthew Boulton's marketing techniques', *Economic History Review*, xvi (1963–4), 49.

15. See D. Defoe, *The Complete English Tradesman*, vol. 1 (London, 1745), 19–23.

16. Elizabeth Shackleton of Alkincoats, Colne, … I would like to thank Amanda Vickery for this information.

17. Public Record Office, C107/104: Davies letter book, letter dated 3 February 1785.

18. Northumberland Record Office, Delaval Mss., 2/DE.11.11/72; correspondence with Broughton and Harrison, London, bottle traders, 1769–1807: Harrison to Brotherick, 1 September 1781.

19. Letter of 1807, quoted in Chapman and Chassagne, *European Textile Printers*, 84. Also see H. Clark, 'The anonymous designer', in Design Council, *Design and Industry*, 33–8 and idem, 'The design and designing of Lancashire printed calicoes during the first half of the 19th century', *Textile History*, xv (1984), 109–10.

20. A witness before a 1787 parliamentary committee claimed that the Lancashire cotton printers who copied southern firms' designs executed 'them in a much inferior style, and consequently are not at the same expense in cutting their blocks', as well as using cheap colours that ran; *Journal of the House of Commons*, xlii (1787), 584.

21. Northumberland Record Office, Delaval Mss., 2/DE.11.11/76; Correspondence with Broughton and Harrison, London, bottle traders, 1769–1807; Harrison to Brotherick, 9 October 1781.

22. Public Record Office, C107/104: Davies letter book, letter dated 26 July 1783.

23. Public Record Office, C105/15: letters received by James Hudson, linen draper, London, 1731–4; Anthony Wilson, Broughton, Cumberland to James Hudson at his warehouse in Three King Court, Lambert Street, London, 24 March 1733.

24. This calls into question the extent of the contrast identified by Craig Clunas between the 'visual' design practice of Europe and the 'verbal' design practice of China during the seventeenth and eighteenth centuries; C. Clunas, 'Design and cultural frontiers: English shapes and furniture workshops, 1700–90', *Apollo*, cxxvi (October 1987), 259.

51

THE SONY WALKMAN

Paul du Gay, S. Hall, L. Janes, H. Mackay, and K. Negus

MAKING THE WALKMAN TO SELL: CONNECTING PRODUCTION AND CONSUMPTION

At this point in our cultural circuit we turn to some of the ways in which 'consumption' is an integral part of the relations of 'production'. Although often separated for the purpose of study and analysis, we wish to emphasize the way in which production and consumption are interrelated and overlap. This is an important theoretical issue that has a long history: it is a theme that concerned Karl Marx in his analysis of the relations of capitalist production during the middle of the nineteenth century:

> Production is ... at the same time consumption, and consumption is at the same time production. Each is directly its own counterpart. But at the same time an intermediary movement goes on between the two. Production furthers consumption by creating material for the latter which otherwise would lack its object. But consumption in its turn furthers production, by providing for the products the individual for whom they are products. The product receives its last finishing touches in consumption. A railroad on which no one rides, which is consequently not used up, not consumed, is only a potential railroad ... Without production, no consumption; but, on the other hand, without consumption, no production; since production would then be without a purpose.
>
> (Marx, 1980/1857–8, p. 24)

Following Marx, we could say that a portable stereo that nobody listens to is only a *potential* portable stereo. For it to be fully realized, for it to have any social meaning, production has to be connected to consumption. This is what Stuart Hall, drawing on this particular part of Marx's work, has referred to as 'articulation'—a process of connecting together—in which the dynamic of the 'circuits of production' can be understood as involving an 'articulation of the moments of production, with the moments of consumption, with the moments of realization, with the moments of reproduction' (Hall with Cruz and Lewis, 1994, p. 255).

You should bear in mind that whilst we can divide production from consumption for the purpose of study, our analysis should make an attempt to understand how production and consumption are made to 'articulate'. We should attempt to trace the specific dynamics of articulation involved. We will do this here in the following ways. First, by considering how the Walkman was aimed at an imagined consumer who was young. Secondly, by pointing out how the name of the machine was guided by assumptions about consumers' responses to it. Thirdly, we shall consider aspects of marketing and, finally, we shall highlight how Sony attempted to monitor and gain feedback about consumer activity. These will give some indications of what Marx called the 'intermediary movement' that occurs between production and consumption. This will lead into a longer section in which we consider how design is centrally located at this point where production is articulated to consumption.

ASSEMBLING FOR THE YOUNG CONSUMER: THE MOTHERS OF THE INVENTION

We can start to pursue this issue by considering how the personal stereo-cassette player was initially produced with a specific target audience in mind. A number of accounts of the production of the Walkman indicate that the device was directed at young consumers. It was aimed at those people who already listened to music whilst moving around the home, driving in a car or walking on the street. Observing that young people seemed to need to have music constantly with them, whether in New York or Tokyo, Morita [Akio Morita, Sony founder] and colleagues felt that the Walkman would enable people to take their music with them and bring the added advantage that it would not disturb other people.

It was with these considerations in mind that the first Walkmans were produced. A particular *imagined* consumer (based on observation and knowledge of existing patterns of music listening) guided the process of production and also the manufacturing schedule. With a young consumer in mind, the aim was to get the new device into the shops just prior to the school, college and University holidays (Kuroki, 1987). These considerations in turn meant that the small tape-machine had to be marketed at a price that made it affordable for young people.

This consideration about the identity of the envisaged potential consumers of the device thus had a further impact on production: it was important that the price be kept down. The first way in which production was organized to keep costs down was by making all the most important parts (such as motors, stereo-heads and headphones) on site within the company. This eliminated negotiations with suppliers over price and delivery time and enabled the company's management to monitor,

oversee and control the processes of production directly (Sony, 1989). Further technical ways were found to reduce costs by using very small integrated circuits instead of individual transistors and resistors. This reduced the number of component parts required and in turn cut both the length of time and the cost of assembling them.

Once the Walkman was in production and selling, there were continual attempts to reduce the cost of production. This culminated in the production of a Walkman Mark 2, launched in February 1981, which was a lighter, smaller model with 50 per cent fewer parts (Borrus, 1987). Technical modifications meant that the time required to assemble the machine was again reduced.

In referring to the process of assembling Walkmans from a number of component parts, we come to a significant contribution to the Walkman's success that is even further removed from the idea of inspired heroes and happy accidents: the routine, rigidly organized and monotonous task carried out by a predominantly female labour force in electronic assembly-plants.

As a number of feminist scholars have argued, the practice of assembling components should not be thought of as simply a secondary activity—as something that just takes place after 'innovation' (Glucksmann, 1990). Instead, assembly-line tasks can be thought of as constituting the 'productive hub' of the manufacturing process. Miriam Glucksmann (1990), for example, points out that ever since the 1920s women assembly-workers have become an increasingly important part of the industrial workforce of the world. Yet the importance and significance of the female assemblers have been undermined by a distinct sexual division of labour in which 'women assemble and men do everything else'. As you will probably have noticed, so far all the 'voices' of the participants in the Sony Walkman story have been male executives. You might recall that some of these men have been referred to as the 'father' of this 'invention'. Here, we might suggest that such fathers are dependent upon the 'mothers' of invention who are found on the assembly-lines.

The production of the Walkman is thus based on a distinctive sexual division of labour. The work of the assembly-line was crucial to the Walkman's initial success. Keeping the costs down depended on controlling the assembly-line and making components that could be assembled rapidly. In this way we can see that the women occupying the assembly-lines have 'a centre-stage significance as workers at the very heart of the production process' (Glucksmann, 1990, p. 4). Without the women assemblers in their rows in Japan, Malaysia and Taiwan, working away putting components together, the Walkman would not have appeared and would not continue to be manufactured in such large numbers.

[...]

DESIGNERS AS CULTURAL INTERMEDIARIES

So far we have outlined some of the accounts which can be found of the origins of the Walkman and we have explained how its origins—quite typically for a successful technology—are bound up in numerous, often contradictory, narratives. In discussing the design of the Walkman, our interest is not with *who* designed it, but with what its design embodies or represents—in other words, with how its very design 'makes meaning'.

Our first task is to clarify what a designer is. One of the most common assumptions is that the designer is some sort of artist. Nearly all the literature on design is concerned with aesthetics; it uses much the same language as is used in discussing art. But designers are different from artists because their main purpose is to make artefacts attractive so that they sell. To make artefacts sell, as we shall see in the case of the Walkman, designers have to *embody* culture in the things they design. Designed artefacts are certainly there to *do* something, they are often functional (for playing tapes, for instance); but, more than this, they are inscribed with *meanings* as well as uses. So, in addition to creating artefacts

with a specific function, designers are also in the game of making those artefacts meaningful. In other words, design produces meaning through encoding artefacts with symbolic significance; it gives functional artefacts a symbolic form. Designers are key cultural intermediaries, to use the terminology of the cultural theorist Pierre Bourdieu (1984).

By the term 'cultural intermediaries' Bourdieu is referring to that increasingly important group of workers who play an active role in promoting consumption through attaching to products and services particular meanings and 'lifestyles' with which consumers will identify. Put simply, they can be defined as people involved in the provision of *symbolic* goods and services. They are most frequently found in the media, fashion, advertising and design industries. In their symbolic work of making products 'meaningful', designers are a key link in our cultural circuit; for, amongst many other things, they articulate production and the world of engineers with the market and consumers. Indeed, the perpetual attempt to achieve that magic 'fit' between production and consumption is often represented as the 'holy grail' of the designer (Gardner and Sheppard, 1989, p. 74).

THE ORGANIZATION OF DESIGN AT SONY

Sony is an organization which is both represented and represents itself as the paradigm of a 'design-led' corporation (Morita et al., 1987; Sparke, 1987; Aldersey-Williams, 1992). Design at Sony, it is often claimed, is *organized* in a way which enables the company to make products which both create and respond to consumer 'needs' in a highly flexible manner. There are three elements of the organization of design at Sony which have been represented as providing the key to its success in achieving this 'fit' between production and consumption.

First, the functional and occupational status of design and designers at Sony is held to be greater—particularly vis-à-vis that of engineering and engineers—than at other comparable

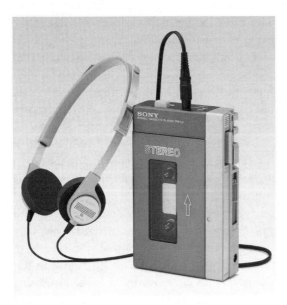

Image 23 Sony Walkman, TPS-L2, 1979. Courtesy of Sony Corporation.

organizations. Until comparatively recently the status of design within the occupational hierarchy of many manufacturing corporations was considerably lower than that of engineers, the influence of the former being confined to styling and a little ergonomics. Secondly, designers at Sony have enjoyed relatively easy access to senior management and, indeed, have become the most senior of managers—again, most unusual in a manufacturing organization. Thirdly, design at Sony has been organized in such a way that designers are kept closely in touch with contemporary cultural trends and with the cultural practices of target consumer groupings.

We can begin to gauge the importance of these first two elements by focusing upon the design 'hub' at Sony: the Design or PP—Product Planning, Product Proposal and Product Presentation—Centre. The multiple meanings contained within the acronym 'PP' suggest the extended role that design plays within the Sony corporation. Product design at Sony involves production and marketing within its remit—in other words, it is involved in developing entire product concepts—as well as the usual styling function, thus guaranteeing it a more

strategic role than that usually attributed to design within manufacturing organizations. It is possible to understand the centrality of design at Sony when we turn our attention to the role that the Design Centre played in the creation of the most popular of the Sony Walkman range, the 'classic' Walkman II (WM-2).

When the term Sony Walkman is mentioned, it is rarely the original Walkman that people recall—the TPS-L2; rather it is the WM-2. Its design, which deviated quite distinctly from that typical of cassette-players, is deemed by Sony, amongst others, to have firmly 'established the new product concept of the Walkman' (Sony, 1989).

The design, which features switches located at the front of the machine rather than at the side, was developed by the Sony Design Centre as an entry for a commercial design competition. This model also had another original feature: the tape-head was installed on the back of the cassette housing cover. This mechanism, which assured that the tape made even contact with the head when inserted, achieved considerable space-savings over the conventional mechanism in the TPS-L2 which moved the head when the playback button was pushed down. Although the model had originally been envisaged as a cassette tape-recorder, the company decided to use the design for the next generation of Sony Walkmans.

Conventionally, as we have already indicated, product development begins with the general locational requirements of basic mechanisms and switches specified by engineers, and then the designers incorporate them into their design development. At Sony, because of the centrality of the Design Centre within the overall organizational structure, the design development of the WM-2 was turned upside down, with the engineers required to work within the parameters specified in advance by the Design Centre—including body size and layout of switches.

As a result, the body of the WM-2 weighed only 280 grams (9.9 oz). This made it 110 grams (3.9 oz) lighter than the original TPS-L2 model and very close to the conceptual image of the size of two 'AA' batteries and an audiocassette that is represented in so much of Sony's advertising and publicity material for the Walkman where the Walkman is represented as 'a cassette player so small you could hide it behind a cassette box'. Brought onto the market in 1982, the WM-2 has since achieved sales of over 2.5 million units and remains the best-selling Walkman model of all time.

The role of the Design Centre in creating the WM-2 indicates the important position that design occupies within Sony. Rather than simply developing the ideas and specifications of engineers and others, the Design Centre was the initiator of the entire product concept. According to the former head of design at Sony, Yasuo Kuroki, the Design Centre was not limited to look and shape. The whole concept—how a product is sold, how a product is marketed, how a product is advertised—really developed there. In this way, design at Sony does not just 'add value' to existing technology, but has been a fundamental element of product innovation, linking the complex worlds of production and consumption.

Not only has the design function occupied a central position within the overall organizational structure of Sony, individual designers have also played crucial roles in the management of the organization. Yasuo Kuroki, for example, head of the Design Centre during the early days of the Walkman's development and production, was the only departmental head at Sony who reported directly to Akio Morita's deputy, Norio Ohga. And Ohga, himself a former head of design at Sony, later became President of the corporation.

As we indicated earlier, design at Sony is also organized to stay close to the cultural practices and preferences of target consumer groupings, focusing designers on reading the 'signs on the street' as well as concentrating on the function and form of product concepts. As Kuroki's comments above indicate, design at Sony is not simply concerned with creating functionally apposite and intelligible products but with specifying design that symbolizes subjects and meanings beyond the ones that are obvious. As one commentator has argued, seen in this way the designer is a 'radar—scanning art, architecture, technology, fashion, pop, everything

and ... translating it into design' (Powell quoted in Gardner and Sheppard, 1989, p. 74).

At Sony there are a number of ways in which this scanning takes place. We have already mentioned the importance of market research in the targeting of the Walkman. Another way, and one in which designers are heavily implicated, is through the Sony Showroom concept. Located in some of the world's 'global cities'—Tokyo, New York and Paris, for example—Sony's showrooms are part shop, part playground and part R&D laboratory. In a highly 'designed' environment—furnished with 'lifestyle settings' such as bedrooms, offices, lounges—consumers are encouraged to walk in and play with Sony products, to be assisted in using them if they so desire and, at the same time, their behaviour and preferences are monitored by Sony staff.

In the Chicago showroom, for example, staff meet daily to discuss consumer reactions to different products. The information is then passed on to Sony headquarters where it can be used to refine the design of products yet to go to market or to develop new marketing and merchandising strategies for existing products (Miller, 1992, p. 2). Through encouraging consumers to interact with products in a space that does not have the threatening appearance of a shop—in other words, where people will not feel an overt pressure to purchase—Sony hopes to see consumers using technology as they would in their everyday lives. This is important to Sony because the more 'realistic' the reaction in this environment— whether good or bad—the more likely it is that this reaction might be enhanced or modified with suitable adjustments in design, or in marketing and so on. In this sense, the showroom is very much a laboratory designed to further articulate production with consumption.

LIFESTYLING THE WALKMAN

As we saw in our discussion of advertising, and of marketing, these forms of symbolic expertise attempt to sell products through addressing consumers as certain sorts of subjects. The language of advertising and marketing attempts to create *identification* between consumer and product. It inscribes or encodes the product with meanings with which it is hoped consumers will identify. Design operates in a similar way. The visual 'look' and tactile 'feel' of a product are crucial means of communicating with consumers, not simply about function or basic 'use' but simultaneously about identity and meaning. Design in a very fundamental way speaks on behalf of the product to the consumer. It addresses the consumer as a certain sort of person.

We can better understand how design works to encode a product with a particular meaning or identity by focusing upon the massive expansion in the range of Sony Walkmans available for consumption since the launch of the original model in 1979. In particular, we will focus upon the role of design in 'lifestyling' a range of Sony products—including two versions of the Walkman—targeted at young children, what the company terms their 'My First Sony' range.

As we indicated, the Walkman was originally designed for and marketed to a particular target consumer grouping: mobile, young music-listeners. However, the company soon became aware that a much more diverse range of people than had originally been envisaged were actually purchasing and using the Walkman. As Sony began to realize that there was more than one market for the Walkman, its advertising strategy, for example, underwent a subtle change of emphasis—appealing to lovers of outdoor pursuits in the country and not simply to urban youth. Sony recognized, in effect, that the Walkman had an appeal for an identity beyond that of the initial imagined consumer.

Gradually, as Walkman sales increased worldwide it was not simply *representations* of the Walkman that began to change but the *very 'look' and 'feel' of the product itself*. In other words, Sony shifted from registering the increasing diversity of consumer use through changes in its advertising and marketing materials alone to inscribing those changes onto the 'body' of the Walkman itself, through changes in its *design*. Instead of a single Walkman model sold worldwide, Sony began to customize the product, targeting different sorts of Walkman at different consumer markets. Or to put it another way, Sony began to lifestyle the Walkman.

So what does the term 'lifestyle' mean in this context? Well, basically, the term refers to the combination of responsive design and visual communication with techniques of market segmentation. In contrast with selling the same basic model to a mass market, lifestyling involves tailoring or customizing a product to the lifestyle of a particular niche or target market segment. Lifestyling is also made possible by the development of new methods of production linked to novel forms of flexible, electronics-based automation technologies, often referred to as 'flexible specialization' (Piore and Sabel, 1984). In contrast to mass production techniques, where particular products were manufactured in large batches on assembly-lines that required great investment in inflexible plant, flexible specialization techniques make small batch production possible. So whereas in the past motor companies, for example, would produce one model of a particular car, nowadays using computer-based technologies and a functionally flexible labour force, it is common for a particular model to be available in a large number of different versions, each designed for and marketed at a distinct consumer grouping.

We can see this combination of new production technologies, responsive design and market segmentation operating at Sony where the Walkman is now available in over seven hundred versions. There are Walkmans for all tastes and prices: they can be solar-powered, waterproof, and attachable to a sweatband (for racquet sports); they come designed specifically for skiing, jogging or camping; they can come with a clock and/or a radio; they are even available in gold!

One of the most publicized of Sony's 'lifestyling' initiatives was its decision in 1987 to create a range of products aimed specifically at young children—the 'My First Sony' range. Taking a closer look at this initiative can help us to understand better how designers encode products with particular meanings and more generally how the practice of 'lifestyling' works.

A senior executive at Sony describes how the company set about developing a line of products aimed specifically at children. One of their primary objectives in targeting this group appears to have been the desire to build 'brand loyalty' from a young age. By getting children—through their parents—to identify with Sony products from their earliest years, the company hoped to keep those consumers on board for the rest of their lives. The very title of the range—'My First Sony'—connotes a potential life-long relationship between company and consumer. From cradle to grave, it seems to be suggesting, Sony will have a product for you at every stage of your life.

Although the products were designed for use by young children, the company defined its target audience as being 'adults, generally working couples who are reasonably affluent'. As young children generally have their consumption mediated by their parents, Sony aimed their marketing and advertising materials mainly at parents—and middle-class parents specifically—advertising on television at times when both parents would be assumed to be viewing, rather than children alone, and deliberately placing cute 'embraceable' kids in the frame who were thought likely to elicit a favourable emotional response, especially from women.

The company was also keen to stress that the 'My First Sony' range did not represent a move by Sony into the toy business. Rather, they stressed that the range was a 'niche' within their wider market of 'quality' consumer electronics. This stress on 'quality' can be found in the advertising materials used to promote the range. One campaign in Australia appealed directly to parents in the name of quality, establishing a chain of meaning between the quality of Sony's products, high-quality parenting and a child's quality of life. Your children, the copy boldly pronounced, are 'Never too young to experience the best'.

From the focus groups which marketeers ran to assess parents' views about the desirability and market potential of the range, through to the advertising strategy aimed at appealing to middle-class parents as typical purchasers of the products, symbolic expertise played a crucial role in creating the market for 'My First Sony'. For our purposes, it is the role of design in this 'lifestyling' process that is of most interest.

As we can see, design operated on the very cusp of production and consumption, attempting to stitch the two spheres together. On the one hand, designers were charged with translating adult models of basic Sony products—such as the Walkman—into products suitable for children. This involved considerable work not simply of a 'technical' kind, utilizing more durable materials and making 'sharp' edges more rounded and hence less likely to cause injury, but also of a cultural kind—constructing a 'look' for the products—in this case using bright primary colours—that would appeal to children of both sexes. On the other hand, the design team did not just work within the sphere of production—creating products in their offices—they also spent time in retail toy-stores observing, for example, the behaviour of parents and children at first hand. This first-hand observation not only contributed to their decisions concerning the look of the actual products, but also to their choice of packaging and visual presentation.

Overall, through their deployment of a range of competencies—technical and cultural and operating in the domains of both production and consumption—designers played a crucial role in translating a number of fairly disparate adult electronic products into a niche range of children's goods, with their own distinct 'brand identity'. Or, to put it another way, through the deployment of their particular 'symbolic' expertise, designers made a series of products achieve a new register of meaning.

NOTE

Extracted from P. du Gay, S. Hall, L. Janes, H. Mackay, and K. Negus, *Doing Cultural Studies: The Story of the Sony Walkman* (London: Sage Publications, 1997), pp. 52–55 and 62–69. Reprinted by permission of Sage Publications Ltd via Copyright Clearance Center.

52

INTEGRATION OF SCALES—MASS-PRODUCED PLUS LOCALLY MADE PARTS

Stuart Walker

An important but little explored aspect of sustainable product design is a reassessment of our scales of production so that products can be made, repaired and reused within an industrial ecology of cyclic resource use at the local or regional level. Where appropriate, products and parts could be made using locally available resources, but there would remain many components that would be more appropriately manufactured in high quantities. For example, light sockets, bulbs and electronic parts would be difficult to manufacture at the local level and it would be inappropriate to do so. It is important to retain standardization of these types of components for safety reasons and to ensure compatibility. Sustainable product design must, therefore, combine and integrate scales—using locally and regionally produced parts from regional materials in combination with mass-produced parts. If the mass-produced parts are designed so that they are not specific to a particular product, they can be recovered and more easily reused in other applications. A standard, mass-produced lamp socket can be used in a variety of lighting designs; similarly, a length of threaded rod, electrical cable or a keypad has many possible design applications. On the other hand, a specialized moulding produced for one particular product application might be difficult to reuse.

The Lumière Floor Lamp is a simple design that illustrates this integration of scales. It utilizes a number of off-the-shelf, mass-produced components, including a lamp socket, a mini fluorescent lamp, cable, a floor switch, threaded rod and fasteners, together with locally produced and found components—reused hardwood components for the cross-arms and base, a sheet of locally made paper as the shade and a large pebble for the base weight. Packaging and shipping of components is reduced to a minimum. Fabrication of several parts and product assembly is done locally and the basic design can be modified and adapted to suit local requirements. In addition, the design is such that its construction is explicit and easily comprehended—this facilitates repair and disassembly for replacement or recovery of parts. Reuse is encouraged by the fact that all mass-produced components are standard, off-the-shelf parts. Another design that combines a mass-produced part with a locally made base is shown—the G-Clamp Nutcracker.

ELEGANCE AND EMPATHY THROUGH DESIGN

When developing products within the limitations imposed by locale, processes, techniques and human skills must be used imaginatively to convert often uninspiring or non-ideal materials into elegant forms that contribute in a positive way to our material culture.

The Remora Box is a legged, leaning chest constructed from recovered planks with screw fastenings and threaded-rod legs. Here an attempt was made to bring an element of finesse to an otherwise prosaic item constructed in

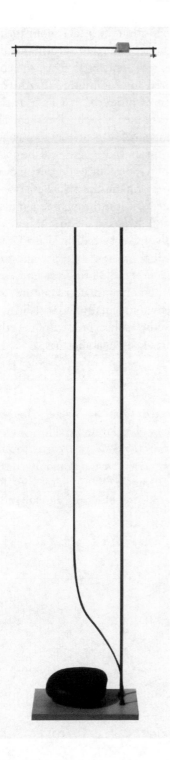

Image 25 G-Clamp Nutcracker: G-clamp, concrete.

an expeditious and rudimentary fashion from commonplace materials. An additional feature of this approach is that the simplicity and evidently basic means of construction allow a certain empathy with the object that is based on an understanding of what the object is made from and how it is constructed. The materials and finishes bring a character to the piece, which can contribute to its sustainable value. Many contemporary products lack this sense of connection because they are made using processes, materials and fastenings that are unfamiliar to the user or owner. This lack of understanding of one's material environment not only hinders product repair and maintenance, it also distances us from the objects we use. Without a greater sense of rapport with our material surroundings, we tend to value products only for their functional convenience but not as material things. Consequently, when products fail to perform their intended task they are discarded

Image 24 Lumière Floor Lamp: Threaded rod, recovered ash wood, handmade paper, steel rod, pebble, standard electrical parts.

and replaced rather than maintained, repaired or upgraded.

These examples represent an approach whereby environmental and social considerations inherent to the notion of sustainability can be made relevant to the discipline of product design. These initial explorations were conducted through direct engagement in the creative activity of designing itself, rather than through investigation of technical issues, which can inform, but are not central to, the design process. It suggests that a reassessment of our approaches to product manufacturing is both necessary and feasible. A greater emphasis on the local could start to transform our infrastructures, our economy and our attitudes, and begin to align them with the principles of sustainability. Large manufacturing plants located in industrial zones and producing a limited number of models of new products in large quantities would be replaced by the local production and re-production of a variety of products in smaller quantities for local consumption.

This could be accompanied by the evolution of a more service-oriented economy where products could be maintained, repaired and upgraded, and parts could be reused and recycled. Consumers and users of local products would have the assurance that their products could be maintained within the local region. Smaller-scale, less-intrusive, production facilities could be located closer to residential areas, thereby reducing the need for commuting. Furthermore, the production of products that have aesthetic and cultural attributes, which raise them above the merely functional, can help reduce emphasis on consumerism and 'the new' and begin to foster attitudes of responsibility and care. However, it is the designer who must put the flesh on the bones of this potential. It is through design that we can envision and demonstrate how 'things' could be, how products can be redefined for local and regional conditions, how a diverse and thoughtful variety of routes could bring a richness and depth to the creation of our material culture so that it is not only environmentally and socially responsible but also aesthetically expressive of the ethical core at the heart of sustainability.

NOTE

Extracted from S. Walker, 'Integration of Scales—Mass-Produced Plus Locally Made Parts', *Sustainable by Design Explorations in Theory and Practice* (London and Sterling, Va.: Earthscan, 2006), pp. 93–97. Reprinted by permission of Earthscan Publications Ltd.

SECTION 5: LABOR, INDUSTRIALIZATION, AND NEW TECHNOLOGY

5.2: Industrialization and Post-Industrialization

INTRODUCTION

Industrialization has shaped the production of design. Many historians claim that design did not begin until the Industrial Revolution, when the relationship between arts and the commercial sphere radically shifted, thus creating design, where objects could be invented, mass-produced, and sold to a larger audience of consumers. With the rise of industrialization, the days of the unique object began to wane, as a world of multiples came to the fore. How design shaped and responded to industrialization continues to be an area of great interest that tells us about the design process and the objects and artificial environments that come out of that process.

David Brett, in his article, "Drawing and the Ideology of Industrialization," reveals how the shift to mass production led to a new reliance on drawing. According to Brett, the "industrial revolution required new graphic conventions to communicate its need for precision, and, therefore, many books and pamphlets on drawing were written in the first decades of the nineteenth century." Thus, in places like Great Britain, where many claim the Industrial Revolution first took hold, the language of drawing changed from one based on metaphor to a vocabulary centered on "instrumental thought." Instead of creating a drawing of symbolic possibilities, drawing had to impart a new "flow of information" in which the "visual language of experts" could be understood by "operatives." Drawing is John Styles points to in the previous subsection (5.1), became the great communicator of design ideas, and a new prescriptive literature arose in England that demonstrated how the technology of drawing could help devise good design.

Industrialization not only altered the representation of design, it also changed how workers lived. Margaret Crawford explains how "The 'New' Company Town" arose out of the growing need for worker housing in the United States. However, this housing belied the realities of factory life, and, rather than use design motifs that would signify industry, this new housing type "symbolically counteracted in the domestic sphere the realities of the workers' daily activity" in factories. Moreover, these workers' "landscapes acted as a form of social engineering, synthesizing architecture, landscape, and planning into coherent images that embodied illusions of social unity and coherence during a period of dramatic social and economic change." Utilizing suburban planning ideas found in locations such as Forest Hills Gardens, New York, these American company towns might have looked similar to expensive suburban communities on paper; yet, when constructed, they lacked "parks, playgrounds, and other recreational amenities" that were part of the designer's original intent. The company built an attractive façade without including community-based services, thus creating "a visible gap between the designer's vision and what the sponsor was willing to pay for." As Karl Marx explains in the excerpt of his work in the Politics subsection (3.3), the pragmatics of design in the new industrial economy ignored the actual needs of workers.

Frederick Winslow Taylor, the American famous for promoting the idea of scientific management, claimed to understand the connection between workers and the new economy. In fact, Crawford mentions Taylor as part of the cultural milieu that produced the company towns. Writing in 1911, Taylor, in his book *The Principles of Scientific Management,* observes that we focus so much attention on being careful with monetary concerns, yet we refuse to look at laborers as an integral resource that could radically improve our quality of life. Using a series of examples, he reveals how owners can work in conjunction with workers to set goals, based on timed performance, which will lead to higher profits. These profits, in turn, can be shared with workers, whose newfound success with productivity will ultimately lead to a better economy. By applying the principles of scientific management to every industry, Taylor contends, the workplace will become more efficient and prosperity will soar. He gives the example of a foreman directing workers to handle pig-iron in a different way than what was, at the time, considered best practice. The foreman told the workers to shovel at specific intervals, and, because of this change in pace, production rose dramatically. Although Taylor's language toward these workers is condescending to the twenty-first-century reader, he claims that this use of a scientific approach to work led to an almost quadrupling in the output of work, and, even more convincing, "the men were receiving 60 per cent more wages than other workmen around them" because of this increase in productivity.

Unlike the other three readings in this subsection, which focus on themes related to industrialization, Abraham Moles discusses our move to the realm of immateriality in his essay, "Design and Immateriality: What of It in a Post Industrial Society?" Moles explains how our contemporary condition is one based on images and "communicational opulence," in which designers manipulate information rather than objects. He eloquently describes the new designers' workspaces, where "drafting tables, sculptor's tools or carpenter's chisels" are absent. In place of these objects, one finds "drawing and image-creating machines." The importance of drawing during the Industrial Revolution, described by David Brett, has given way, according to Moles, to a "conceptual immateriality." Yet, regardless of this virtual reality of imagery and bits, the material object still exists as an ironic but critical artifact from a previous era. We still have to plug in our computers, we still have to handle CDs, and we still have to tune radio reception. However, our dependence on these objects only comes to the fore when we witness their defects, such "as the smudge on a poorly cleaned vinyl disk." Moles argues that with our world's growing complexities, our designed existence is more precarious than ever and "subject to mishaps." Thus, there continues to be a dire need for technicians and others who can fix our ever-growing "demon of disorder" with "maintenance." We live in a postindustrial era, but this does not negate our continued grappling with the products of industrialization that support our current epoch.

Moles's discussion raises the question of what tomorrow will bring. Will we continue to move into a world where virtuality, as discussed in Section 4.1 of the *Reader,* becomes more pervasive, or will there be a cultural backlash that demands the preeminence of the object and the "real"? Regardless of the answer to this query, it is design that will mediate our response. It is design that will either become more integral to the realm of what many term *invisible design*, or it is design that will go back to the drafting table and utilize the historic authority of drawing to conceptualize a return to the import of physical reality. Within this probable negotiation, it is workers who will be managed, policed, and supervised—as explained by Crawford and Taylor—to insure that production and consumption continues to endure and transform in the face of future challenges.

53

DRAWING AND THE IDEOLOGY OF INDUSTRIALIZATION

David Brett

Drawing is an activity fundamental to human action. It belongs with counting and speaking as being a primary form of cognition. A people that did not draw would be as unimaginable as one that did not count or speak, and, if not too pedantic about how drawing is defined, we may assert that the activity of making lines is a mode of thought. A line, as it extends, takes in the world, and because drawing may be both descriptive and prescriptive, lines can model possible worlds. The form used to represent the worlds (the objects) we seek to make is, preeminently, drawing.

The first industrial revolution required new graphic conventions to communicate its need for precision, and, therefore, many books and pamphlets on drawing were written in the first decades of the nineteenth century. Some of these were fundamental textbooks in isometric projection; others were useful manuals for tradesmen and apprentices. Still others were for the general education of young people and amateur artists or for the developing profession of "designer." (In British usage, this term meant those who drew designs for applied ornament and was distinguished from mechanical drawing.) The majority of these books attempted to treat drawing in a systematic manner, and a smaller number treated it as a science, presenting sets of axioms to use to analyze a drawing problem. The latter now encroach on the territory occupied by teaching machines and computer-driven drafting tables.[1] Most taught a dry, linear style of drawing.

Literature is part of the process of mass education that any newly industrialized society demands; it was the earliest example of the process still under way in Third World countries. The process entails a profound epistemological upheaval, a shift from metaphorical to instrumental thought, and the teaching of drawing at such a juncture is obviously part of an ideological struggle to transform human understandings.

Descriptive drawings of machines, mines, and buildings are, of course, very ancient types of drawing; but industrial production at that time demanded a prescriptive clarity that could convey unambiguous instructions in a universally comprehensible code. This was equally true in both decorative and mechanical design.

In the preface to his description of the building of the Eddystone lighthouse (1786), John Smeaton found it necessary to write about his plates as such: "They are little more than geometric lines, drawn to explain geometric and mechanical subjects. If any of them put on the appearance of anything further, it is to render it more explanatory and descriptive. They are, in reality, not meant as pictures ... "[2] The plates, splendid large engravings, are a mix of mechanical drawing and picturesque detail—some distance from modern engineering drawing. For that style to be achieved, a uniform industrial practice was essential so that a uniform graphic convention could both mirror and create it.

This codification took place in naval dockyards and the workshops of engine designers and railway builders,[3] creating a new professional group with its own self-conscious values and powers. In 1836, George Stephenson complained, "They have no sooner come into an office, and become acquainted in every detail with our plans, than they leave and carry away what has cost us a great deal of money and more thought."[4]

The prescriptive nature of such drawing indicates a change in the nature and flow of information; it is the visual language of experts instructing operatives. This operational necessity is also the creation of a social function. "An engineer is a mediator between the philosopher and the working mechanic, and like an interpreter between two foreigners, must understand the language of both. ... Hence the absolute necessity of his possessing both practical and theoretical knowledge."[5] Engineering drawing is the language of such mediation, as have been the innumerable other forms of diagram, chart, map, and instructional sheet developed since the 1820s. The tacit understanding of the craft-based ship or millwright is being replaced by the explicit science of the industrial manager and technologist. A recent writer observed, "If we divest ourselves of any notion of instrumental rationality as a Geist-like disembodied wraith, and see it instead as a part of the occupational culture of experts and technicians who constitute a specific status group, with status interests they wish to protect and advance, and for which they require political allies, and which, in turn, require an ideology acceptable to these allies, then it becomes clear: technicians and experts are forced to go beyond instrumental rationality, and to generate a larger morality."[6]

In the domain of decorative design, a similar process of codification took place, and two determinants can be identified. The first was the technical constraints of designing motifs and patterns capable of production by mechanical means; the second involves intellectual and esthetic factors, being a theory of what was appropriately beautiful for the new age.[7]

Technical constraints hampered the design of patterns for the newly mechanized textile trades, notably printed cottons. The use of engraved or punched copper rollers, printing on an evenly stretched continuous belt of cloth, demanded a certain simplification of drawing and the abandonment of shading. A writer suggested, "The combination of the cylindrical, never-ending surface, with the small mill and die, tended to produce overall patterns, minute florals, geometric and optical effects. The pervasiveness of the small repeat, in texture and motif, is so widespread that textile students today, when asked to produce a dress print, often instinctively produce designs of this sort."[8]

However, this tendency to linear simplicity, flatness, and close repeat remained a stylistic desideratum even when no longer technically necessary. These qualities were approved by Augustus Pugin, the writers in the *Journal of Design and Manufactures*, and Richard Redgrave, Owen Jones, and Christopher Dresser,[9] but to describe the patterns merely as contemporary taste avoids interpretation. D. Greysmith observed, "Despite the many factors at work bringing design into being, the new machine-produced patterns can be seen, anthropologically, as the sign language of a people changing from a predominantly rural to an increasingly urban culture."[10]

This linearity and flatness did not simply appear; it had to be taught in the design schools. Redgrave later described the instruction as "a method wholly new." When viewing nature, the trainee designer had to perform an "ornamental analysis ... displaying each part separately according to its normal law of growth, not as viewed perspectively, but diagrammatically flat to the eye ... this flat display was specially suitable to the requirements of the manufacturer, to reproduction by painting, weaving, stamping, etc., to which naturalistic renderings do not readily lend themselves."[11] Dresser developed the same idea still further, arguing that "for ornamental purposes we deem literal copies altogether insufficient; representations of a more rigid character and analytic nature being necessary ...," and asserted that plant drawing for decorative purposes must "generally ... coincide with the architect's plans of the building … a series of drawings which shall convey a perfect knowledge of every part."[12] The expected manner of drawing was always hard, clear, unshaded pencil work.

This approach to drawing, which by mid-century became known as "conventional art," was given its first full expression in *The Drawing Book of the Government Schools of Design*, produced by William Dyce in 1842–43.[13] This book followed a progression, familiar to all who have studied these drawing manuals, from simple linear elements to increasingly complex ornamental forms abstracted from botanical study. It was intended to teach young people to be designers. "Beauty," wrote Dyce, "is a quality separable from nature's objects. … [The designer] makes the separation in order to impress the cosmetic of nature on the productions of human industry. Works of industry thus molded into shape are not imitations of nature because they are covered with pictures or sculptured resemblances of natural objects, but because they are adorned on the same principles as the works of nature themselves." The purpose of drawing was to study nature and its "operating and governing laws" to form "abstractions … beauties of form and color [which] … by the very fact that they are abstractions, assume, in relation to the whole progress of art, the character of principles or facts, that tend by accumulation to bring it to perfection."[14] By these means, ornamental design was to become "a kind of practical science, which, like other kinds, investigates the phenomena of nature for the purposes of applying natural principles and results to some new end."[15]

To understand this highly cognitive and positivist concept of drawing, the pedagogical and philosophical assumptions that preceded it need review. These assumptions were broadly shared by Dyce, Redgrave, Dresser, David Hay, Jones, Cole, Pugin, and, indeed, all the major British decorative designers and theorists of the early and mid-century, with the exception of Ruskin and his followers. The drawing manuals published in Britain during the first 30 years of the century were based on the assumption that all drawing is founded upon a set of primary or elementary lines. The ability to form these lines must be imparted before any attempt is made to produce images, because the linear elements have priority. They are, indeed, the *a priori* conditions of any kind of drawing. A characteristic formulation can be found in the pages of William Robson's *Grammigraphia* (1799): "Lines are four; perpendicular, horizontal, oblique, and curve. All the variety of appearance in nature are presented by a combination of these four lines placed agreeably to proportion and position." The production of a line should be considered as "properly the continuation of a point. A point can proceed in four ways only … and from these we derive a mathematical account of all the common figures: angle, square, circle, ellipsis, oval, pyramid, serpentine, weaving, and spiral." The student was expected to use a line "as distinct and determinate as possible."[16]

Robson's scheme of four lines is similar in kind to that of George Field, for whom "from the direct, reflect, and inflect motions of a point are generated the three primary figures: the right line, the angle, the curve."

From these, "all possible figures constituted of lines, surfaces, and solids [are produced] by the variation and composition of the three primary figures. It follows that all graphic art, and that of drawing in particular, consists elementarily in the ability to form the three primary lines—straight, angular, and curve—in all their variations of position, gradation, and composition."[17]

From such beginnings—though not all manuals were so axiomatically organized—students were expected to progress to the drawing of regular solids, simple perspective, and, finally, effects of light and shade. Some authors encouraged students to draw from wood or plaster "models" of cubes, cylinders, and tetrahedrons, and some manuals were published with sets of such wooden blocks provided.[18] Dyce's *Drawing Book* (which was, significantly, usually called the "Outlines") may be regarded as the summary of this pedagogy, which had both this native British element and one much indebted to German ideas.

In Germany, this approach had been incorporated by Pestalozzi and his followers, notably J. C. Buss, into part of all elementary education. It was known there as *pedagogische Zeichnen* and was held to be quite distinct from expressive or *Kunstzeichnen*. Inasmuch as in the philosophy of Kant space and form are *a priori*, the activity of drawing should begin with exercises that enlarged and developed a child's existing understanding of space and form. Drawing based on empirical observation came a decided second.[19]

Buss, in an account of Pestalozzi's methods published in 1828, wrote that "Angles, parallels, and arcs comprise the whole art of drawing. Everything that can possibly be drawn is only a definite application of these three primary forms. We can imagine a perfectly simple series arising out of these primary forms, within which an absolute standard is to be found for all drawing; and the esthetic beauty of all forms can be evolved from the nature of these primary forms." He went on to elaborate an "ABC of Form," which built exercises from the simple to the complex and linked them with the development of measuring and mathematical skills. He remarked, significantly, "This is a new art that should precede the usual, old-fashioned, well-known ideas of art-culture."[20]

Pestalozzian ideas were first favorably reported in England in 1814, and the first school using these principles was founded in London in 1836, where Hermann Krusi taught the ABC of Form as an algorithmic method for the production of decorative motifs through the combination and permutation of simple elements. The evidence presented to the Parliamentary Committee in Arts and Manufactures (1835–36) reflected this German teaching, as well as the native British element.[21]

Similar ideas were in circulation in the United States, where there was a considerable publishing effort by artist-writers and educationalists such as J.G. Chapman, W.B. Fowle, and Rembrandt Peale. Peale's "Graphics" (2nd ed. 1838) quotes extensively from Pestalozzi. These ideas were tried out by A.B. Alcott in his experimental schools in Boston between 1834 and 1839; but the appeal of the drawing manual was very strong in a country in which the education system was still in an early stage. W.B. Fowle's self-teaching handbooks were written to supply the want of teachers.[22] However, the main force of the Anglo-German pedagogical tradition reached the United States through the work of Horace Mann, the secretary of the Massachusetts State Board of Education; Mann was responsible, on one hand, for bringing over Walter Smith of the Leeds School of Design to teach the South Kensington system in the Massachusetts Normal Art School (in 1873) and, on the other, for introducing Peter Schmid's system of Naturzeichnen through the pages of the *Common School Journal*.[23] Smith wrote of the Normal Art School that "it is intended as a training school for the purpose of qualifying teachers and masters of industrial drawing. In the future it may be necessary to provide for high skill in technical drawing and art-culture, but the immediate pressing demand is for teachers who know the elementary subjects thoroughly." He had written earlier, "To do this, [the teacher] must first learn the alphabet of the subject and know by name and at sight any feature of form from the dot to the most subtle compound curve, and from the simplest geometric form to the last problem in perspective."[24]

Ideas similar to Pestalozzi's were also developed by Friedrich Froebel, who envisaged an *a priori* perceptual grid, or network, in which "The vertical and horizontal directions mediate our apprehension of all forms … in our imagination we constantly draw these lines across our field of vision, we see and think according to these, and thus there grows in our consciousness a network of lines keeping pace in clearness and distinction, without consideration of the form of things." His drawing exercises, as described in *The Education of Man* (1828), consisted of linear adventures within this network. From this network developed his notion of "gifts"—sets of blocks and other materials in which the child can explore simple spatial and volumetric experience.[25]

Other systems of pedagogical drawing came into existence in both Britain and Germany, but discussing the fine distinctions that contemporaries perceived among them is not necessary. Worthy of note, however, is dictation drawing, devised by Platz in 1818. Every child was provided with a matrix of dots, each one numerable. A relatively complex design could be converted into a code and then dictated at regular speed to the class, which drew it in unison. "It is clear that in this way the full attention of the little draughtsman is demanded. The slightest inattention to the word of the teacher leads unavoidably to mistakes."[26] Such is one first step toward the computer-driven drafting table.

Neither in Britain nor in Germany was conventional art or pedagogical drawing regarded as an attempt at art education. Influential writers regarded such drawing as a useful mechanical skill, attainable by all. A typical apologia was provided by the *Encyclopaedia Mancuniensis* (Manchester, 1813), which under "Drawing" stated, "It should be learned by every person as answering the same purposes with writing … we are convinced that it is of the utmost importance to society that this should always form part of common school education, in the same manner as writing."[27] In the 1840s, Dyce was fond of pointing out to recalcitrant staff of the British Schools of Design that the regulations stated that "no person making Art his profession should be eligible as a student." Many similar examples might be given.

These schemes were justified in both idealistic and narrowly utilitarian terms. For Froebel, "Form … reveals in various ways inner spiritual energy. To recognize this inner energy is part of man's destiny. … It is therefore an essential part of human education to teach the human being, not only how to apprehend but also how to represent form; and inasmuch as the perpendicular relations (of the vertical and horizontal) aid the development of form consciousness, the external representation of these relations as a means for study and representation of form is based on the very nature of man, and of the subject of instruction."

However, "The use of this instruction would supply one of the greatest wants of our schools in town and country; … it teaches the eye a knowledge of form and symmetry and trains the hand in representing them; and these find much to do in all relations and activities of practical life."[28] Logan noted, "Widespread approval of this kind of drawing was based on its value in the manual training of a population (employed) in industry and the skilled crafts."[29]

That these arguments should be both idealistic and utilitarian is a consequence of the intellectual tradition that brought them into being, as well as the ideological process of which they were a part. The first argument is clearly a combination of lore and assumptions embedded in the academic tradition, both of which were reinforced by eighteenth-century natural philosophy, with its assumptions about the regularity and inexorable precision of the functioning Universe.

In the pages of Rosicrucian writers such as John Dee or Robert Fludd, the expansion of the point to line, plane, and solid was given a mystical significance as being emblematic of the unfolding of the manifold creation. The capacity to "frame" lines and geometrical diagrams was part of the natural magic that accompanied this occult philosophy, a body of ideas that many writers have shown to be germinal of the academic tradition. The magical framing was not perfectly distinguishable from the utilitarian drawing of masons, architects, and carpenters. An important feature of Dee's *Praeface to Euclid* (1577) is the separation it attempts between practical workman and learned architect, through the instrumental skill of drawing. "The hand of the carpenter is the architect's instrument … the whole feate of architecture in building consisteth of lineaments and in framing. And the whole power and skill of lineaments tendeth to this; that a right and absolute way may be had of coapting and joining lines, by which the face of the building, or frame, may be comprehended and concluded. … the form and figure of the building may rest in the very lineaments, etc. And we may prescribe in mind and imagination the whole forms, all material stuff being secluded."—the immateriality of perfect architecture.[30] The frame for these writers meant both the elevation of the building and its abstract and mathematical scheme as depicted in "lineaments." Thus, when they spoke of the frame of the Universe, they meant its geometrical configuration expressed in number and line.

NOTES

Extracted from D. Brett, "Drawing and the Ideology of Industrialization," Design Issues 3, no. 2 (1986): 59–67. Reprinted by permission of the author and the University of Illinois at Chicago, School of Art and Design.

1. Typical titles in these categories include *Geometrical and Graphical Essays*, by George Adams (1791), *The Practice of Isometrical Perspective*, by Joshua Jopling (1833), *Treatise on Isometrical Drawing*, by Peter Sopwith (1834), *The Carpenter's Guide: a Complete Book of Lines for Carpenters* (8th ed. 1828), *Rudiments of Drawing Cabinet and Upholstery Furniture*, by R. Brown (1822), *An Essay in Ornamental Design*, by D. R. Hay (1844), *A Manual for Teaching Model Drawing from Solid Models*, by B. Williams (1843), *The Science of Drawing Simplified, or the Elements of Form Demonstrated by Models*, by B. W. Hawkins (1843), *The Oxford Drawing Book*, etc., by N. H. Whittock (1825 several eds.), *Elements of Perspective Drawing*, by A. O. Deacon (1841), *Drawing for Young Children*, by H. Grant (1833), *First Exercises for Children in Light, Shade and Colour*, by H. Cole (1840), *The Lessons in Art*, by J. D. Harding (1835, etc. many eds.). I am indebted in some points to an unpublished thesis by David Jeremiah entitled "Drawing and Design: Theory and Practice, 1830–1870," University of Reading, 1971. Accompanying these texts are many manuals on drawing instruments and their use and a spate of inventions to assist the draftsman,

culminating in the camera. Machines were devised for drawing ellipses and parabolas, for enlarging or contracting drawings, and so forth. Beam and telescopic compasses came into regular use, as did "geometrical pens," complex dividers, proportional compasses, and innumerable forms of rulers. The modern T-square and protractor were first illustrated in 1830. The primary instrument of all, the humble pencil, was also coded for the first time, and by 1830, HH for engineers, H for architects, F for sketching, and B for shading were recorded. The combination of drawing instrument and hard pencil was devised to provide exactly that determinate line that the drawing manuals demanded and mechanical drawing required. See: P. J. Booker, *A History of Engineering Drawing*, (1963), K. Baynes, *The Art of the Engineer* (1983) and *Drawing Instruments R.I.B.A. catalog.* (1982).

2. J. Smeaton, *A narrative ... of the building of the Eddystone light ... etc.* 2nd ed. (1813).

3. The role of military and naval requirements in the long war years has clearly some part to play in this, especially in France, where the organization of the polytechnics created the first real engineering education. The preponderance of books in English indicates the lack of regular schooling; Nicholson's *The Carpenter's Guide* (see note 1) has to begin with a short course on Euclid to do the work of a school class. It was not until the 1830s and 1840s that the mechanics institutes became numerous enough to supply the want of instruction.

4. See K. Baynes, "Drawing as Design Method," in *Design and Industry: the Effects of Industrialization and Technical Change on Design*, ed. N. Hamilton. (London: The Design Council, 1980), 46–47.

5. H. R. Palmer of the newly formed Institute of Civil Engineers (1818) as quoted in W.H.G. Armytage, *A Social History of Engineering* (London: Faber and Faber, 1961), 22.

6. A. W. Goulden, *The Dialectic of Ideology and Technology* (London: Macmillan, 1976), 269.

7. To treat the technical constraints first does not imply their logical priority. Monocausal explanations of culturally complex realities should be rejected as a naive idealism. In studying design, we need to be careful not to confuse different orders of explanation. Technical constraints seems to belong to one such order and nexus of causality, and esthetic and intellectual assumptions, to another. Design occurs at the meeting place of several such trains of implication. I have found useful an article by P. G. Dickens, entitled "Social Science and Design Theory," *Environment and Planning B* Vol. 7 (1980), 353–360, which discusses the interaction between production and ideology.

8. D. Greysmith, contribution to *Design and Industry,* ed. Hamilton (see note 4), 62–65.

9. For a very interesting discussion of "flatness" see J. Maschek, "The Carpet Paradigm: Critical Prolegomena to a Theory of Flatness," *Arts Magazine* (September 1976): 82–106.

10. D. Greysmith, *Design and Industry.*

11. S. and R. Redgrave, *A Century of Painters* (London: Smith, Elder, 1866), 5645. See also Macdonald, *The History and Philosophy of Art Education* (London: University of London Press, 1970), Ch. 12.

12. C. Dresser, "Botany as adapted to the arts and Art Manufacture," *Art Journal* (December 1, 1858): 362.

13. William Dyce's intellectual biography included a scientific education and lengthy experience of German artistic life and design training. He had some association with D. R. Hay and the circles in Edinburgh in which the relationship between science and art was discussed (see note 14 below).

14. William Dyce, *The Drawing Book of the Government Schools of Design* (London: Chapman and Hall, 1842), Introduction. A full unpacking of the concepts carried in this passage would be most revealing. See also Dickens's lampoon of it in *Hard Times* (1854), Ch. II.

15. In *The Journal of Design and Manufacture,* Vol. 1 (March–August 1849).

16. William Robson, *Grammigraphia; or the Grammar of Drawing* (London: Wilson, 1799). An interesting little book that contains evidence for most of the themes discussed here. It was recently mentioned by Stafford (1979)(see below).

17. The interesting figure of George Field touches on these topics at several points. The leading color chemist of his day, he was the author of a standard work on color, *Chromatography* (1835: several eds.), and a number of highly theoretical writings in which he developed an analogical philosophy whereby primary forms and colors were construed as part of a logical system of universal analogy that linked written and spoken language, and even machine parts, with the fundamental constituents of the universe. See D. Brett, "The Aesthetical Science: George Field and the 'Science of Beauty'," *Art History* Vol. 9, No. 3 (September, 1986): 336–350.

18. Clive Ashwin has written, "The progressive adoption of geometric models at all levels of art teaching, including the art schools and academies, is a subject . . . worthy of further research." In what follows I am particularly indebted to C. Ashwin, *Drawing and Education in German-speaking Europe, 1800–1900* (Ann Arbor, MI: UMI, 1981), and for other writings by Ashwin.

19. See C. Ashwin, "Pestalozzi and the Origins of Pedagogical Drawing," *The British Journal of Educational Studies* Vol. XXIX No. 2 (June 1981): 138–151. Also G. Sutton, *Artisan or Artist: a History of the Teaching of Arts and Crafts in English Schools* (London: Pergamon, 1967).

20. Quoted by Sutton, *Artisan or Artist,* 30.

21. See *Parliamentary Papers: Select Committee* (1836) Pt. 1., p. vii. "Such elementary instruction should be based on an extension of the knowledge of form, by the adoption of a bold style of geometrical and outline drawing, such as is practiced in the national schools of Bavaria." See also D. R. Hay, *The Laws of Harmonious Colouring* (4th ed. 1836)

for a discussion of the evidence. In the *Parliamentary Report on Foreign Schools of Design for Manufacture* (1840), Dyce describes himself as "looking for something constituted out of both."

22. I am here indebted to Diane Korzenik, whose collection of early drawing books is very useful. Her *Drawn to Art: A Nineteenth-Century American Dream* (Hanover, N.H.: University Press of New England, 1986) contains much interesting material. For A. B. Alcott, see F. M. Logan, *The Growth of Art in American Schools* (New York: Harper, 1955), 16–19.

23. For a detailed description and discussion of Schmid's work, see C. Ashwin, "Peter Schmid and Das Naturzeichnen: An Experiment in the Teaching of Drawing," *Art History* Vol. 5, No. 2 (June 1982): 154–165. Schmid produced a huge book supported by a kit of wooden models (1828–32). Ashwin observed that "What Schmid had devised was a primitive teaching machine, complete with self- checking mechanism in the form of the plates which represented what the learner should be producing, and, like all well-designed teaching machines, it had the great advantage that the learner could progress at his own pace even when working in a class context." A number of simplified versions of Schmid's system appeared in Germany in the 1830s; in Britain, A. O. Deacon's *Elements of Perspective Drawing, or the Science of Delineating Real Objects* (1841) came accompanied by a box containing 57 wooden elements. Also see Logan, *The Growth of Art in American Schools,* 19.

24. See Logan, *The Growth of Art in American Schools,* 66 et. seq. Smith's *Teacher's Manual of Freehand Drawing and Designing* (Boston: L. Prang, 1873) set out to do for American pupils what Dyce's *Outlines* were intended to do for British, 30 years earlier: to take the student from simple squared lines and polygons to curves, complex curves, scrolls, ornaments, symmetries, and botanical analyses to snow crystals and beyond. All drawing was to be done in a clear style with hard pencils. Smith's book was preceded by R. Demcker's *A Course of Systematic and Progressive Drawing* (Cincinnati: Ehrgott, Forbriger, 1868); it was a Schmid-based manual.

25. Writers on Frank Lloyd Wright have noticed the importance he attached to the Froebel education he received. We should probably think of Wright and Sullivan before him as the direct inheritors of this tradition of decorative design. The role of Frank Furness is probably seminal in this transmission of precepts. Furness had access to both Jones's and Dresser's ideas directly and to those of Jones's French associates, Cesar Daly and Labrouste. Furness's decorative interiors seem to be what Owen Jones and Dresser were wanting to achieve.

26. See Ashwin, *Drawing and Education in German-speaking Europe, 1800–1900,* 124.

27. The argument that writing and drawing are somehow congruent with one another is very common in this literature; its most complete statement is in the pages of Field's *Analogy of Logic* (1850). Robson, *Grammigraphia; or the Grammar of Drawing,* also thought that drawing could be taught "with nearly as much truth and certainty as a sum in arithmetic" and that "Musick is a science founded on the same principle of quantity as drawing." Horace Mann was another who thought that "Drawing is a form of writing and should be taught with it." (See Logan, *The Growth of Art in American Schools,* 21.)

28. See F. Froebel, *The Education of Man* (1828) trans. W. N. Hailman (New York: Appleton-Century Co., 1887), 278–299. See also Sutton, *Artisan or Artist,* 35–44.

29. Logan, *The Growth of Art in American Schools,* 19.

30. John Dee, *The Mathematical Praeface to Euclid* (1577) (New York: reprinted by Science History Publications, 1977). I have simplified his erratic spelling. Dee is an early example of the combination of mystical idealism and utilitarian intentions.

54

THE "NEW" COMPANY TOWN

Margaret Crawford

The "new" company town constitutes a distinct chapter in the history of American industrial settlement. Designers of new company towns created fictional environments and established an important episode in a continuing American design tradition of "themed living." Until 1900, most American company towns were industrial landscapes, direct translations of the technical and social necessities of a particular method of production into a settlement form. Based on expediency, structured by habit, and laid out by pragmatic owners or company engineers, their patterns mirrored the demands of industrial processes. After 1900, professional designers—architects, planners, and landscape architects—took over the task of designing company towns. Unlike vernacular expression, professional design explicitly effaced the visual connection between the living environment and its industrial origins. Overlays of physical and social planning rendered the towns' industrial purpose almost unrecognizable as designers replaced the rigid geometry and hierarchical order of earlier company towns with picturesque imagery and garden city planning, all aimed at promoting social harmony and industrial peace. These new company towns constitute an important chapter in a continuing American design tradition of fantasy environments. Carefully constructed landscapes acted as a form of social engineering, synthesizing architecture, landscape, and planning into coherent images that embodied illusions of social unity and coherence during periods of dramatic social and economic change.

Designs for new company towns resemble those of elite planned suburbs such as Forest Hills Gardens, New York, or Mariemont, Ohio, and rival them in the skill and sophistication of their design. However, in spite of the formal planning similarities, the two settlement types are significantly different in their intent and meaning. If barely legible in the plans, these differences become immediately evident when examining the physical and social contexts in which the towns were built.

In contrast to the convenient access of the elite suburb, located within easy commuting distance of city centers, the new company towns were, like the older company towns, still linked to the factory. The primary requirement was physical proximity to the workplace, usually measured in pedestrian distances. Unlike earlier company towns, however, visual separation from the factory was a key element in their design. These locational determinants often came into conflict, dictating remote and inconvenient sites. Cost considerations also influenced siting decisions; large tracts of inexpensive land, necessary for the layout of the new towns, were often hilly, inaccessible, or otherwise undesirable. Scale issues also became design determinants for the new company town. In contrast to ample suburban lots, winding streets, and substantial houses characteristic of the elite planned suburbs, company towns were miniaturized. Small houses, lots, and settlements cost less, met workers' limited expectations, and could be easily navigated by foot. The gap between the plan and the towns as they were finally built is even more revealing. Architects and planners designed the settlements as both social and physical entities, focusing their plans around town centers with social and community facilities and providing numerous parks, playgrounds, and other recreational amenities. However, invariably, companies neglected to build these amenities, providing housing and commercial services but little else. Thus, these towns were left incomplete—a visible gap between the designer's vision and what the sponsor was willing to pay for.

RETHINKING THE COMPANY TOWN

Vernacular company towns, spawned by regional industries all over the country, followed no single pattern. In contrast, new company towns embodied a consistent ideology, adapted from the Industrial Betterment movement, and a coherent formal vocabulary, derived from the English garden city.[1] These settlements constituted one aspect of a broader effort to create a more systematic industrial order. During the late nineteenth century, manufacturers began to replace time-honored methods of shop organization and labor relations with newly coordinated managerial systems. Introduced by trained mechanical engineers, this approach culminated in the scientific management system popularly known as Taylorism, named after its founder, Frederick Winslow Taylor.[2] Similarly, an allied field, the industrial betterment or welfare capitalism movement, transformed the informal and highly personal paternalism that prevailed in company towns into an institutionalized and professionalized operation. Under the direction of "expert" welfare workers, firms introduced systematic social programs designed to improve workers' living and working environments.

The political and social motivations behind these new methods of "social engineering" were complex; one clear impetus was the growing tension between labor and capital. After 1870,

increasing numbers of strikes and the development of new labor organizations such as the Knights of Labor demonstrated the growing power of bigger and more militant working classes. The 1873 panic brought a wave of strikes, and the subsequent depression led to the "Great Upheaval" of 1877, the first mass strike in America. After 1880, new waves of immigrant workers from eastern and southern Europe strained the gulf between employers and employees even further. The panic of 1893 brought widespread layoffs, triggering a dramatic march of the unemployed on Washington known as "Coxey's Army." Strikes occurred at an unprecedented rate and broad scale. The 1894 Pullman strike paralyzed rail traffic across the country and cost more than five million dollars in lost wages and earnings. After 1905, a new series of strikes broke out, bringing with them radical labor organizations like the Industrial Workers of the World (IWW). By 1911, labor struggles were so intense that a group of social workers, philanthropists, and college professors, interviewed by *The Survey,* a social work journal, concluded that "actual class warfare exists in the United States and the conditions leading to such warfare have to be changed.[3]

Progressive reformers appointed themselves as the agents of change. Their position, articulated by intellectuals such as Richard Ely and Jane Addams, occupied a middle ground in the increasingly hostile standoff between capital and labor. If the reformers feared the unfettered power of huge corporations, they also rejected the growing strength of militant labor organizations. As labor upheavals multiplied, reformers sought to act as mediators. Seeing their goal as an orderly and stable society, the progressives replaced class conflict with a vision of social harmony under the leadership of the "competent," that is, the educated middle class. These concerns overlapped with the growing size and power of the urban middle class, then demanding a strong voice in setting the nation's social and political priorities. Concerned with improving social and environmental conditions, progressive reformers proposed a scientific reorganization of the social environment, a task that demanded full-time, organized and skilled efforts. This inevitably expanded the realm of middle-class professionalism. In turn, architects, landscape architects, and planners, seeking to strengthen their own professional position, allied themselves with these reform movements.

OBJECT LESSON ABOUT OUTDATED AND EXCESSIVE PATERNALISM

Searching for scientific solutions to the urgent problems presented by the slum and the factory, reform agendas and professional aspirations converged on a single solution, namely, the planned industrial community. Far from the bad influences of the city, planners believed, a socially-engineered environment could offer a *tabula rasa* on which capital and labor could renegotiate their differences. Financed by employers and designed by professionals, the planned industrial community appeared to provide a comprehensive answer to urban and industrial problems. Employers, acknowledging their social responsibilities, would upgrade working and housing conditions for their workers. Designers would create new types of exurban communities. The resulting decentralization of industry and housing would reduce urban congestion, thus improving living conditions in cities.

The confluence of interests between social reformers and design professionals provided the basis for the new company town, but realizing it in physical form took the support of industrial employers. Their willingness to sponsor costly housing, town planning, and welfare programs was closely related to the crisis in industrial relations. Concerned with attracting skilled workers and avoiding unionization, employers hoped that appealing and well-designed communities would build loyalty and stability and thus head off more strikes. Designers claimed to offer new and more effective ways of addressing these persistent problems while avoiding paternalism. The 1894 railroad strike, ignited by George Pullman's refusal to lower rents in his company housing after lowering wages in his plant, dramatically demonstrated the dangers of excessive personal control. The town of Pullman, Illinois, created as a model of urban beauty and industrial harmony, now served an object lesson about outdated and excessive paternalism, no longer appropriate in a large-scale corporate economy. To avoid such problems, employers turned over the task of building company towns to independent professionals, who, they hoped, would act as buffers between capital and labor.

The company town provided the design professions an ideal medium to demonstrate their growing expertise. For architects, the complete town was a laboratory situation where they could test the profession's new self-definition as "modern," that is, systematic, rational, and socially efficient. By adopting the role of mediator, architects could claim at least rhetorical independence from their traditional client base of wealthy individuals. For planners, private commissions such as company towns offered opportunities to develop comprehensive plans without obstacles such as individual ownership, real estate speculation, and conflicting political demands, all of which plagued large-scale planning projects. Landscape architects brought an existing ideology of social and moral improvement and an aesthetic vocabulary, dual legacies of Andrew Jackson Downing and Frederick Law Olmsted.

Whatever their professional intentions, designers faced contradictory demands from their clients and the users—the employers and the workers. Large corporations, under increasing public scrutiny, incorporated designers and their work into the company's publicity, focusing national attention on their efforts to improve living conditions. At the same time, concerned about protecting their investments, employers refused to take excessive risks. Attempting to attract a stable force of skilled workers, they began to finance homes for sale. To convince their employees to buy, employers had to address them as consumers as well as workers. Increasingly beset with strikes and labor problems, employers were anxious to demonstrate their lack of paternalism. Looking beyond merely improving the workers' living conditions, they became interested in satisfying their housing preferences. In response, employees began insisting that they be given the type of houses they preferred, with prices and styles that would appeal to them. This in turn forced architects to begin investigating workers' tastes and concerns. Employers sponsored informal surveys and meetings, but workers made their housing preferences known directly through their purchases. Thus, with the company's investments at stake, the workers became the final arbiters of a town's design and success.

THE SEARCH FOR A STYLE

Although the design professions enthusiastically assumed responsibility for these new settlements, initially there was no consensus about their form or style. The sponsors of the new company town were generally large-scale corporate enterprises, operating on a national scale. With limited local interests, they usually selected nationally-known practitioners with offices in large cities, rather than local designers. These architects, with well-established approaches to housing and town planning, reinforced professional aspirations to establish nationally-accepted norms of good design. Thus, like most managerial and reform ideologies of the progressive era, company towns and their architects offered generalized and standardized solutions. Designed by outsiders unfamiliar with industrial processes or the local situation, new company towns rarely reflected these concerns. Instead, architects sought to distinguish themselves from aggressive commercial competitors. Manufacturers of prefabricated housing such as the Aladdin Company and Sears, Roebuck, boasted that they could erect a complete community in only twenty-six days. Sears marketed simple, inexpensive houses for under 400 dollars, far undercutting even the cheapest architect-designed house. To compete, architects focused on their most secure professional skill: aesthetics. They designed inexpensive houses in distinctive styles, searching for imagery that counteracted the influence of the factory. Landscape architects and planners similarly looked for new ways of combining planning, landscape, and architecture to create a new coherence.

In Fairfield, Alabama, an ambitious town sponsored by U.S. Steel in 1910, planner George Miller and architect William Leslie Walton designed a range of bungalows in a park-like setting. The craftsman style, with its natural building materials and complex detailing, symbolically counteracted in the domestic sphere the realities of the workers' daily activity in the steel mill. But the style's beneficial associations had limits. Fundamentally domestic, the craftsman style was difficult to adapt to urban and public uses; it couldn't be used at the scale of a comprehensive plan or provide the town with a unified identity. Instead, Fairfield had two separate images—an attractive, informal residential area and a commercial block indistinguishable from that of any other small town. The same year (1910), in the company town of Torrance, California, planner Frederick Law Olmsted, Jr. and architect Irving Gill tried to overcome the same challenges of architectural expression and urban design, and met opposition. Engineers hired by the developer, objecting to the high costs and wasted land in building the gently curving streets, plazas, and public areas that Olmsted planned, eliminated them. Similarly, the town's working-class home-buyers emphatically rejected the modern housing models Gill designed. They found their pure cubic forms, concrete floors, and stripped down planes too much like the town's factory buildings, also designed by Gill. They believed that Gill's designs were more suggestive of poverty and austerity than the emancipatory values intended by the architect. Instead they opted for heavily detailed California bungalows, identifying them with a sense of home, comfort, and flattering associations with upper middle class individuality.

Ultimately, it was the English garden city movement, particularly the work of Barry Parker and Raymond Unwin, that provided design solutions for the new company town. Although Ebenezer Howard's original conception of the garden city contained more radical features, such as cooperative ownership, economic self-sufficiency, and innovative living arrangements, the movement also had strong ties with picturesque English company towns built in the 1890s, such as Bournville and Port Sunlight. Designed as theatrical evocations of pre-industrial villages, these towns offered self-consciously rural and English alternatives to urban and industrial life. Parker and Unwin's 1904 design for Letchworth, the first garden city, expanded on this, creating a new planning style with an extensive repertoire of techniques. Letchworth's trademarks, a formal center spreading out into a loose network of roads lined with houses, low density and extensive landscaping, along with a range of devices such as "street pictures," subtle changes in street patterns, cul-de-sacs, and group housing, provided new towns with a strong and unified physical identity.

Letchworth had an immediate impact in the United States; architects, planners and urban reformers quickly adapted it as a new ideal. In 1909, the first, and probably the most sophisticated, adaptation of the style appeared at Forest Hills Gardens, just outside Manhattan in the borough of Queens. Sponsored by the Russell Sage Foundation, the garden suburb was a demonstration project to educate the public about the benefits of decentralization, comprehensive planning, and good housing. Planner Frederick Law Olmsted, Jr., and architect Grosvenor Atterbury utilized a number of techniques from Unwin's book, *Town Planning in Practice,* which had been published earlier that year and included many of the ideas of the Austrian architect Camillo Sitte. Olmsted and Atterbury orchestrated a sequence of scenographic spaces that moved from the enclosed space of Station Square through streets defined by continuous row houses, culminating in the open fields of Forest Park. Atterbury's picturesque architecture worked perfectly with Olmsted's landscaping and carefully calculated site planning to create a highly compelling suburban environment. Like the English picturesque company towns, Forest Hills was a newly created old place. Its vague medieval associations—one writer compared it to "a college or cathedral city,"[4]—offered suburban commuters an escape from modern life, only minutes from Manhattan.[5]

Atterbury took this lesson from Queens, now acting as both architect and planner, and transformed the company town. The industrial suburb of Indian Hill in Worcester, Massachusetts (1913) was the first full-fledged example of the new company town. Synthesizing picturesque imagery, colonial revival architecture, and garden city planning, Atterbury created the image of a charming new England village with cozy colonial cottages, tree-lined streets, and a town square. Communicating stability, domesticity, and traditional American values, Indian Hill's design was intended to encourage social harmony and industrial peace. A complete, if fictional, environment, it offered the Norton Company, beginning to experience labor problems, an alternative to the troubled industrial landscape. Other architects and planners quickly followed Atterbury's example. Bertram Goodhue adapted garden city techniques to a southwestern setting in Tyrone, New Mexico. The planner John Nolen standardized company town design, producing more than 25 company town plans, ranging from New England textile villages to Arizona copper camps. The new company town reached its peak during World War I. Responding to desperate housing shortages, high labor turnover rates, and the threat of strikes, government agencies began to build housing for war workers. Thoroughly familiar with the issues of designing workers' housing and complete living environments, architects and planners took full advantage of government support to produce even more comprehensive (and better funded) projects such as Union Park Gardens in Wilmington, Delaware, and Yorkship Village in Camden, New Jersey.

NOTES

Extracted from M. Crawford, "The 'New' Company Town," *Perspecta* 30 (1999): 49–55. Reprinted by permission of Yale School of Architecture.

1. For discussions of the Industrial Betterment or the Welfare Capitalism movement, see Stuart Brandes, *American Welfare Capitalism* (Chicago: University of Chicago Press, 1976); Daniel Nelson, *Managers and Workers* (Madison: University of Wisconsin Press, 1975); Gerald Zahavi, *Workers, Managers, and Welfare Capitalism: The Shoe-Workers and Tanners of Endicott Johnson* (Chicago: University of Illinois Press, 1988); Sanford Jacoby, *Modern Manors* (Berkeley: University of California Press, 1998). Standard works on the Garden City movement include Walter Crese, *The Search for Environment* (New Haven, CT: Yale University Press, 1966) and Raymond Unwin, *Town Planning in Practice* (London: Unwin, 1909).

2. On Taylorism, see Samuel Haber, *Efficiency and Uplift* (Chicago: University of Chicago Press, 1964) and Harry Braverman, *Labor and Monopoly Capital* (New York: Monthly Review Press, 1974).

3. *The Survey* (30 December 1911), pp. 1430–31.

4. Samuel Howe, "Forest Hills Gardens," *Architectural Record* 87 (January 1930), p. 14.

5. Initially intended to house those of modest means, the high cost of land so near Manhattan immediately altered the town's social composition. Since the Sage Foundation had to earn a 3% return on its investment, it passed these costs onto buyers, driving up housing prices, thus ensuring that Forest Hills Gardens would become an upper middle class enclave.

55

THE PRINCIPLES OF SCIENTIFIC MANAGEMENT

Frederick Winslow Taylor

One of the first pieces of work undertaken by us, when the writer started to introduce scientific management into the Bethlehem Steel Company, was to handle pig iron on task work. The opening of the Spanish War found some 80,000 tons of pig iron placed in small piles in an open field adjoining the works. Prices for pig iron had been so low that it could not be sold at a profit, and it therefore had been stored. With the opening of the Spanish War the price of pig iron rose, and this large accumulation of iron was sold. This gave us a good opportunity to show the workmen, as well as the owners and managers of the works, on a fairly large scale the advantages of task work over the old-fashioned day work and piece work, in doing a very elementary class of work.

The Bethlehem Steel Company had five blast furnaces, the product of which had been handled by a pig-iron gang for many years. This gang, at this time, consisted of about 75 men. They were good, average pig-iron handlers, were under an excellent foreman who himself had been a pig-iron handler, and the work was done, on the whole, about as fast and as cheaply as it was anywhere else at that time.

A railroad switch was run out into the field, right along the edge of the piles of pig iron. An inclined plank was placed against the side of a car, and each man picked up from his pile a pig of iron weighing about 92 pounds, walked up the inclined plank and dropped it on the end of the car.

We found that this gang were loading on the average about 12 1/2 long tons per man per day.

We were surprised to find, after studying the matter, that a first-class pig-iron handler ought to handle between 47 and 48 long tons per day, instead of 12 1/2 tons. This task seemed to us so very large that we were obliged to go over our work several times before we were absolutely sure that we were right. Once we were sure, however, that 47 tons was a proper day's work for a first-class pig-iron handler, the task which faced us as managers under the modern scientific plan was clearly before us. It was our duty to see that the 80,000 tons of pig iron was loaded on to the cars at the rate of 47 tons per man per day, in place of 12 1/2 tons, at which rate, the work was then being done. And it was further our duty to see that this work was done without bringing on a strike among the men, without any quarrel with the men, and to see that the men were happier and better contented when loading at the new rate of 47 tons than they were when loading at the old rate of 12 1/2 tons.

Our first step was the scientific selection of the workman. In dealing with workmen under this type of management, it is an inflexible rule to talk to and deal with only one man at a time, since each workman has his own special abilities and limitations, and since we are not dealing with men in masses, but are trying to develop each individual man to his highest state of efficiency and prosperity. Our first step was to find the proper workman to begin with. We therefore carefully watched and studied these 75 men for three or four days, at the end of which time we had picked out four men who appeared to be physically able to handle pig iron at the rate of 47 tons per day. A careful study was then made of each of these men. We looked up their history as far back as practicable and thorough inquiries were made as to the character, habits, and the ambition of each of them. Finally we selected one from among the four as the most likely man to start with. He was a little Pennsylvania Dutchman who had been observed to trot back home for a mile or so after his work in the evening; about as fresh as he was when he came trotting down to work in the morning. We found that upon wages of $1.15 a day he had succeeded in buying a small plot of ground, and that he was engaged in putting up the walls of a little house for himself in the morning before starting to work and at night after leaving. He also had the reputation of being exceedingly "close," that is, of placing a very high value on a dollar. As one man whom we talked to about him said, "A penny looks about the size of a cart-wheel to him." This man we will call Schmidt.

The task before us, then, narrowed. itself down to getting Schmidt to handle 47 tons of pig iron per day and making him glad to do it. This was done as follows. Schmidt was called out from among the gang of pig-iron handlers and talked to somewhat in this way:

"Schmidt, are you a high-priced man?"

"Vell, I don't know vat you mean."

"Oh yes, you do. What I want to know is whether you are a high-priced man or not."

"Vell, I don't know vat you mean."

"Oh, come now, you answer my questions. What I want to find out is whether you are a high-priced man or one of these cheap fellows here. What I want to find out is whether you want to earn $1.85 a day or whether you are satisfied with $1.15, just the same as all those cheap fellows are getting."

"Did I vant $1.85 a day? Vas dot a high-priced man? Vell, yes, I vas a high-priced man."

"Oh, you're aggravating me. Of course you want $1.85 a day—every one wants it! You know perfectly well that that has very little to do with

your being a high-priced man. For goodness' sake answer my questions, and don't waste any more of my time. Now come over here. You see that pile of pig iron?"

"Yes."

"You see that car?"

"Yes."

"Well, if you are a high-priced man, you will load that pig iron on that car to-morrow for $1.85. Now do wake up and answer my question. Tell me whether you are a high-priced man or not."

"Vell—did I got $1.85 for loading dot pig iron on dot car to-morrow?"

"Yes, of course you do, and you get $1.85 for loading a pile like that every day right through the year. That is what a high-priced man does, and you know it just as well as I do."

"Vell, dot's all right. I could load dot pig iron on the car morrow for $1.85, and I get it every day, don't I?"

"Certain you do—certainly you do."

"Vell, den, I vas a high-priced man."

"Now, hold on, hold on. You know just as well as I do that a high-priced man has to do exactly as he's told from morning till night. You have seen this man here before, haven't you?"

"No, I never saw him."

"Well, if you are a high-priced man, you will do exactly as this man tells you to-morrow, from morning till night. When he tells you to pick up a pig and walk, you pick it up and you walk, and when he tells you to sit down and rest, you sit down. You do that right straight through the day. And what's more, no back talk. Now a high-priced man does just what he's told to do, and no back talk. Do you understand that? When this man tells you to walk, you walk; when he tells you to sit down, you sit down, and you don't talk back at him. Now you come on to work here to-morrow morning and I'll know before night whether you are really a high-priced man or not."

This seems to be rather rough talk. And indeed it would be if applied to an educated mechanic, or even an intelligent laborer. With a man of the mentally sluggish type of Schmidt it is appropriate and not unkind, since it is effective in fixing his attention on the high wages which he wants and away from what, if it were called to his attention, he probably would consider impossibly hard work.

What would Schmidt's answer be if he were talked to in a manner which is usual under the management of "initiative and incentive"? say, as follows:

"Now, Schmidt, you are a first-class pig-iron handler and know your business well. You have been handling at the rate of 12 1/2 tons per day. I have given considerable study to handling pig iron, and feel sure that you could do a much larger day's work than you have been doing. Now don't you think that if you really tried you could handle 47 tons of pig iron per day, instead of 12 1/2 tons?"

What do you think Schmidt's answer would be to this?

Schmidt started to work, and all day long, and at regular intervals, was told by the man who stood over him with a watch, "Now pick up a pig and walk. Now sit down and rest. Now walk—now rest," etc. He worked when he was told to work, and rested when he was told to rest, and at half-past five in the afternoon had his 47 tons loaded on the car. And he practically never failed to work at this pace and do the task that was set him during the three years that the writer was at Bethlehem. And throughout this time he averaged a little more than $1.85 per day, whereas before he had never received over $1.15 per day, which was the ruling rate of wages at that time in Bethlehem. That is, he received 60 per cent. higher wages than were paid to other men who were not working on task work. One man after another was picked out and trained to handle pig iron at the rate of 47 1/2 tons per day until all of the pig iron was handled at this rate, and all the men were receiving 60 per cent. more wages than other workmen around them.

The writer has given above a brief description of three of the four elements which constitute the essence of scientific management: first, the careful selection of the workman, and, second and third, the method, of first inducing and then training and helping the workman to work according to the scientific method. Nothing has as yet been said about the science of handling pig iron. The writer trusts, however, that before leaving this illustration the reader will be thoroughly convinced that there is a science of handling pig iron, and further that this science amounts to so much that the man who is suited to handle pig iron cannot possibly understand it, nor even work in accordance with the laws of this science, without the help of those who are over him.

NOTE

Extracted from F. Taylor, *The Principles of Scientific Management* (New York: Harper, 1911), pp. 41–48.

56

DESIGN AND IMMATERIALITY

Abraham Moles

An immaterial culture is emerging. It exists only because a heavily material base supports it and makes it possible. It is from the very outset a phenomenon—indeed, an epiphenomenon—resulting from technology. The future of design, then, for an artificial reality depends on the design of the hardware and specialized techniques, that are the fundamental constituents of an artificial reality and that contribute to the creation of what one could call imago—generalized images, not necessarily confined to a visual mode. Thus, a post industrial society (Bell) is a superindustrialized society, or one which has pushed to extremes the consequences of its industrialization.

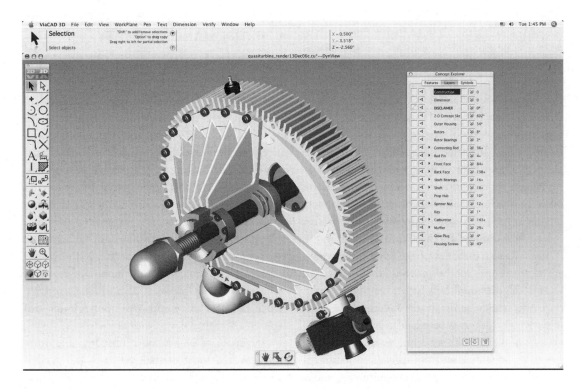

Image 26   ViaCAD screen shot. Courtesy of Punch! Software LCC.

It is true that we are surrounded by so-called electric phantoms, to use a phrase of Villiers de l'Isle Adam, which more and more are invading both our work and recreational environments. One of the problems posed to the human spirit is its capacity to exercise control over reality, while adjusting to the blurring of barriers between reality and images, or between real objects and their appearances. As we enter the age of *telepresence* we seek to establish an equivalence between "actual presence" and "vicarial presence." This vicarial presence is destroying the organizing principle upon which our society has, until now, been constructed. We have called this principle the *law of proximity*: what is close is more important, true, or concrete than what is far away, smaller, and more difficult to access (all other factors being equal).

We are aspiring, henceforth, to a way of life in which the distance between us and objects is becoming irrelevant to our realm of consciousness. In this respect, telepresence also signifies a feeling of equidistance of everyone from everyone else, and from each of us to any world event. At the same time, we live in an age of *communicational opulence*. We now have at our disposal more sources of communication and interaction than we will ever be able to make use of in our relatively short lifetime. This is the age of a social system of networks, decorated with the futuristic name of the "Information Society." Henceforth, the bulk of our effort will be spent more for manipulating information than for manipulating objects, which are now no more than products of far-out robots, controlled by abtruse programs, inaccessible models, and a ubiquitous creator.

Nevertheless, these new living conditions, which are also cultural conditions, and thus what one used to call the conditions for art, can subsist only on a spectacular hardware or material base. This underlying structure is spectacular, most evidently, because of the astonishing omnipresence and sheer size of the machines and the specialized manufacturing plants making cars, video equipment, audio components, and so on. While generally unaware of the highly specialized, technical origin of such objects, the layman has to live with this material accumulation. But sheer size is not the most significant aspect of this material base. Rather, it is especially spectacular because of its complexity which stands as today's paradigm for technological advancement. A 3cm² microprocessor comprises more "things" than an automobile—more components, more functions, more connections, more relays, and, conceivably, more raw intelligence.

Yet, the structural complexity of today's hardware, which can be quantitatively measured, finds itself subject to one of the general laws of the universe, the law of entropy, or, simply put, the tendency of all conjunctions of things toward disorder. This irrepressible agitation of the physical world counteracts and eventually destroys the order imposed by the hardware creator. The consequences are overloads, short circuits, and equipment failure.

A MAINTENANCE SOCIETY REPLACES A PERFORMANCE SOCIETY

While transmitting and receiving messages and imagoes constituting an artificial reality, man encounters more frequently, like the *diabolus in machina* ("devil in the machine") of the religious era, the bug, the hitch, and the malfunction, largely random in nature, which erode the fundamental virtue that any mechanical aid or appliance must possess: reliability. All other factors being equal, the more our world is complex, in reality or appearance, the more it is fragile, and the more it is subject to mishaps. As a result, the hardware builder must adopt particular strategies or plans of action designed to control the demon of disorder. Such action gives rise to a *maintenance mentality*, which perfuses the world of support groups and technicians, for making "immaterials."

The creators of the new immaterial culture have devoted most of their effort to the permanent reproduction of what, for them, was once practically inconceivable—the transmission of sounds and speech over distance and the storage of data in memory banks. All this, which a century ago was hailed as "the miracle of communication," has become commonplace in our lives. From a social perspective, the inventors and the builders seem to have won the battle waged on the continual insurrection of nature against the complex pattern of circuits and transistors. They have learned how to incorporate a reasonable degree of reliability into an uncertain miracle, and have mastered the multiple and diverse causes of disorder through deduction and quantitative reasoning. The digital compact disc or the satellite numerical repeater are two noteworthy examples. *The immaterial civilization must be reliable;* otherwise, it could have no social impact and would be the subject of little or no debate today.

But the minimal reliability established by the industrial complex still does not inspire in the individual sufficient confidence to participate in an immaterial culture. He or she is reluctant to depend completely on telerepresentations being confronted by a heterogenous array of equipment that originated from various sources, was assembled at random, and offers uncertain compatibility. The situation of the individual, then, is different from that of the society at large, and consequently the meaning of the term "reliability" becomes more strict according to the scope of the human or material circumstances to which the word is applied. To live and experience a culture is to interact with innumerable, disparate forms of that culture, as well as to find oneself presented with a myriad of possibilities for successful—and unsuccessful—operation. The demands that the individual presents to society, therefore, are more important than the demands of society on its subjects, which is the situation we are faced with today.

The task of the designer is, precisely, to ensure reliability by mastering the factors that jeopardize it. Therefore, the first field of investigation of design for an immaterial culture is to furnish largely material assurance of the *universal reliability* of the systems that make it possible.

DESIGN BY A MODEL OR IMMATERIALISM OF DESIGN?

A second direction of inquiry into the relationship between design and the immaterial culture is to investigate the impact of the stratagem on the designer's *task* in a computerized society. We used to say that the designer, an environmental engineer, was responsible for each of the systems he installs, as well as for their integration into the particular life-style of each person. Each of these systems required a material task of design, done in a workshop that until now, was hardly susceptible to automation. All this is changing, however, with the advent of computer processing and computer-aided manufacturing, which are modifying the phenomenological *nature of the design process* (Tuchny, Larroche).

It is useless to ask if design is an artistic activity or a scientific one; the etymology of the word "technology," or *techne* (art), provides a sufficient response. With respect to doing, the confusing etymology of the word "engineer" (the genius who drives the engine or machine) applies also.

The designer creates the environment of others. Until now the designer's vocation has been both conceptual and concrete. The workshop has been a place to perceive and build models destined to be copied for mass production. The question now, however, is how this vocation has been modified, for better or for worse, by the inexorable development of the immaterial culture. The design activity itself is changing because the designer's tools are becoming immaterial, as are the lives of those to whom the products are marketed. Design by holographic models may still be far in the future, but the concrete activity of design even now partakes substantially of immaterial techniques, or usage of artificial representations, images, and diagrams composed by image-generating machines.

Affecting more than workshop activity alone, the trend toward immaterialism includes all projectional conception in a concrete model, a process which used to depend on a situation of permanent interaction between conception and construction. The dialectic game between the abstract (the idea, the mental vision) and the concrete (the struggle with the material and disparate tools and appliances) is giving way to work done essentially with computer-integrated manufacturing at a computer desk. The designer's task now consists of construction based on three precepts: (a) the work order, (b) the rules of an exploratory program, (c) articulated in a field of liberty defined by certain parameters—often of ergonomic origin and eventually of creative fantasy. This suggests to the designer, regarded as the master of the work, an ensemble of more or less pertinent variations on which he will have to exercise his critical abilities, themselves controlled by functional optimization principles in the broadest sense. The designer, who assumes a more and more important social role in a society where power is evanescent, must confront the new fundamental idea of "Initial Form plus Variations," in order to realize an often monotonous variation of possible forms with respect to given parameters. This is what we have called "variational creativity."

We are passing from a time of hands-on creation of a model to one of an initial form plus a field of variations, which stem from any already existing object, whether traditional or modern. Thus, from this established model a whole series of new models is determined, with the intention of forever satisfying the avidity of the consumer market. This process is done using the most refined and the most abstract creative techniques, in order to express them in programs, through creative methods (Alexander).

Not only the designer, but also the manufacturer of forms and models faces this situation, but with a different perspective. The manufacturer confronts a kind of creation in immateriality, which encompasses the definition of the field of possibilities and its methodical exploration, which, in turn, generates auxiliary criteria for judgment. These criteria are then reapplied in order to furnish yet another new field of possibilities. Henceforth, one expects no longer to find drafting tables, sculptor's tools or carpenter's chisels in the design room. They are being phased out by drawing and image-creating machines that yield computer graphics, so that the material objects themselves, as products of these images or of audio and visual simulations, are, at a distance, mere products of the imagination, and seem more *credible* than *real*.

From 1850 to 1950, industrialization was characterized by the predominance of a system of drafted plans and diagrams, which were essential to the materialization of ideas, and which caused a proliferation of design patents. DeForge, in a noteworthy book, illustrated well this "kingdom of drawings" or technical diagrams, which were the rule in nineteenth century workshops.

For several decades the complexity and precision of drawings have rendered them amenable to both the computer's memory and the drafting table. Now, however, the draftsman and the modelist are disappearing from the finishing laboratory or the graphic workshop itself; the computer is supplanting them with its ability to generate, on demand, any view, profile, or cross section of any part or whole of the factory or machine in question. Furthermore, the implicit and intuitive relationship itself of a small part to the whole, or of a particular machine to the whole factory, is vanishing. In many complex systems the global design breaks loose, becomes accessory, indeed superfluous, because the whole changes with each moment of its construction. Certain parts are replaced by others and modifications are made during construction, even during the useful life of the product itself, because the conditions determining the integration of smaller parts into the whole are automatically taken into account by the computer. In short, the scale model is losing its significance; it serves only as a rough estimate or guide to the builder. It is only a palpable illustration of the concept involved and, most important, is no longer necessary. One could say that neither the designer, the engineer, nor the architect knows the system in all its exact detail, though any one of these persons could simply ask the computer for any piece of information concerning the function of the object under construction. Thus, we are arriving at a kind of conceptual immateriality of complex systems in the wake of those who create them in fragments.

THE DESIGNER AT THE CENTER OF COMBINATIONS OF ESTHETIC EFFECTS

Finally, it seems appropriate to consider the relationship of design with a fundamentally artificial reality, which is another systematic exploration of the field of possibilities and which will be one new sensorial combination, generated from a "new art," defined by the sensory parameters that it manipulates and the new esthetic arrangement it proposes. If, in the foreseeable future, art remains (for those unperfused to or allergic to the idea of chance) a programmed sensualization of the environment, the designer, as an environmental engineer, finds himself endowed with considerable ability to manipulate the new artistic matter, a step which transforms the designer himself into a neo-artist. Or, could the designer be called a meta-artist, the potential maker of new "art"? In this respect, our senses of the close range of those affecting us by contact (touch, smell, sensitivity to temperature, vibration, and balance) remain a relatively unexplored area of human sensoriality. We lack the means to evaluate objectively certain aspects of the real, which we could call *transduction* (to transform messages from one medium to another) or *interfacing* (to set up a partition of illusions for the projection of tele-images for example, a screen, a tactile sensor, a sonorous background, a simulated landscape, or a virtual actor). The immense technological structure proposed by the post industrial society seems precisely to have to fill quickly this gap.

It is becoming the function of design to examine this new field of "programmed sensualizations" (what one used to call a "work of art" and what one could call from now on a "scene of esthetic action"). What would become, for example, of an electronic tactile detector combined with a Minitel or Compuserve system? In a purely philosophical sense, would the result be a by-product of the immaterial culture, or would it be a new event in the sphere of esthetic valorization?

THE POSITIONS OF DESIGN DURING THE AGE OF THE INVASION OF IMMATERIALITY

Any immaterial civilization will be heavily materialized because its immaterial products are necessarily linked to the mechanical infrastructure that generates, stabilizes, and governs them. By misinterpretation, a recent exposition celebrated, not an "immaterial world," but a form of the binomial object-images, forms, and support. This is another attitude of man vis-a-vis an artificial world—a world created by him as the only source of his reactions. Does such an attitude imply a danger of technological narcissism, at the moment when nature becomes inaccessible or restricted to parks with limited access?

Thus, every symphony has its compact disc; every audio experience its loudspeaker; every visual image its camera and video disc. Behind every outward image or symbol lies mechanical support, and if the immateriality of these images and symbols gives rise to a new approach to the relationship between human being and object, the analysis will be one of the individual's connection with the material support underlying the new culture of immateriality.

The real problem, though, resides in the kind of relationship man will establish with the new material foundation that he will consider simply as part of the decor of the environment, consequently that he rejects from his own field of consciousness, and thus forgets entirely for the benefit of the immaterial imago (which is slightly material in itself), which directs him and the *credibility* of which is becoming more important than its *verity*.

But since this same individual is constantly reminded of this material base by screens and terminals, the question is this: under what conditions of reliability will the material foundation be truly forgotten and replaced by the dubious, hazy, generalized images as only points of reference for a subsequent conscious activity?

These material supports reveal themselves only by their imperfections—by the necessity to plug in a computer, for example, and to turn it on in order to make it work. The infrastructure subsists in the fact that the elimination of the most insignificant contact—indeed, a telecontact—can extract all that the most advanced technology has put into a computer. The material supports remind us of our dependence on them, especially by such defects as the smudge on a poorly cleaned vinyl disc, the highrise apartment building that interferes with radio reception, or the interfering lines that intrude in our private telephone conversations.

As an individual, here and now, I could forget all the hardware, if only it were to reach perfection, something rarely attained in practice. Striving for that perfection and that absolute reliability is precisely the fundamental role of the one who *designs* the machinery of imagery, simulation, and communication; the standing of quality, without which no post industrial world could subsist, is always questioned, as is the fleeting "perfect moment" of my relationship with the world.

The role of the designer, then, is not so much to create "new" objects to serve as structural supports of an immaterial culture, as to insist on an environment of implacable stability. Before introducing something new, the designer must protect the status quo, which permits individuals to participate spontaneously and with little effort in the seductive immateriality of today's world.

NOTE

A. Moles, "Design and Immateriality: What of it in a Post Industrial Society?" trans. David Jacobus, *Design Issues* 4, nos. 1/2 (1988): 25–32. Reprinted by permission of the University of Illinois at Chicago, School of Art and Design.

SECTION 5: LABOR, INDUSTRIALIZATION, AND NEW TECHNOLOGY

5.3: New Design and New Technologies

INTRODUCTION

As technology continues to transform our world through the power of globalization, many are upset with the changes that attend our ongoing technological revolution, and others embrace these developments. The four articles in this subsection address these points of view. Bradley Quinn looks at a fashion designer who questions the boundaries between clothing and machines. Donald Norman claims that technology can be harnessed to make our lives easier, but, in its current form, the computer industry only hinders our pleasure and denies us an easier way of completing necessary tasks. Vicente Rafael, on the other hand, explores the political potential of technology and a specific example of the public's enthusiastic adaptation of a type of information appliance, the cell phone. Theodore Adorno frightens us with a short excerpt about how technology can empower us in ways that are cruel.

Bradley Quinn uses Donna Haraway's ideas about the cyborg, found in the virtual identity subsection (4.1) of the *Reader,* in his essay on Turkish designer Hussein Chalayan. Quinn explores the technological wonders of Chalayan's Remote Control Dress. In this garment, "computer devices and remote-control communication" change the dress to function in different ways depending on the wearer's environment. The design potentialities for a dress that allows "the body ... [to] be linked to other machines, and linked to other bodies also linked to machines" are endless. Chalayan's dress is the manifestation of a cyborg fantasy, but like so many instances of design that engage technology, it offers a vision of the future in which technology can transform how bodies function.

Donald Norman wants the makers of both computer hardware and software design to heed the call for a sane approach to technology that focuses on human use rather than technological possibility. Norman, in his book, *The Invisible Computer,* claims that the device "tries to be all things to all people," and, perhaps most daunting, it is such a complex machine that users are unable to make the computer do what it is that we want it to do. Even though the computer has a remarkable range of functions—from Computer Aided Design (CAD) for architects to word processing for writers—it does too much for an audience that is too varied. It is, as Norman explains, like a Swiss Army knife that contains an inordinate number of blades, but each of the individual blades works terribly. Norman wants computers to "disappear from sight" (this is what, in fact, Moles claims has happened with so much technology in his essay from the Industrialization and Post-Industrialization subsection [5.2]), so that "we can once again concentrate upon our activities and goals in life." We need, in short, "information appliances" that communicate with each other and give us pleasure and usability in a manner that fits our own specific user agendas.

What Norman does not tackle in his argument are the larger political ramifications and embrace of technology that Vicente Rafael contends with in his essay, "The Cell Phone and the Crowd: Messianic Politics in the Contemporary Philippines." It is through new design that technology often enables forms of political engagement. This connection, as embodied in the design of the cell phone, is what Rafael discusses in his article. Rafael explains the cultural significance of the cell phone as a widely owned communication device in the Philippines that can foster political subversion through its anonymity

Image 27 Carbon chair. Designed by Bertjan Pot and Marcel Wanders.

and portability. He notes that people become attached to this design object in a type of fetishistic mania, in which the "cell phone gives its owner a sense of being someone even if he or she is only a street vendor or a high school student—someone who can reach and be reached and is thus always in touch." Hence, the phone is an information appliance that functions in an almost mythical manner. It tethers the user to a vast network of technologically induced possibilities that can be utilized in the contested public sphere of politics.

In the Philippines, it was through the cell phone that protestors were able to muster forces against what they viewed as the abuses of President Joseph Estrada's administration in 2001. Using power texting to "disrupt protocols of recognition and accountability," groups were able to assemble protestors whose upset stemmed from the unexpected interruption of the Estrada impeachment hearings, in which his administration's corrupt history was being aired. In a circular route that traveled readily and with ease, Filipinos learned about public protests against Estrada. They paid close attention to the electronic missives' calls for action and created mass protests in Manila.

Like the texters in the Philippines, we continue to sustain our faith in technology. We believe it will improve the world and foster radical changes that will lead to betterment. In our horizon of artificiality, it is impossible to disenfranchise ourselves from technology, and we are more dependent than ever on our "mania" for cell phones, personal computers, and other devices that make our network of interconnectivity a navigable terrain of virtual interfaces. Regardless of this love affair with technology, it is, as Theodor Adorno notes in the short passage that concludes this subsection, a dangerous relationship, with "brutal" ramifications. He asks what machines do to our civility. Indeed, Adorno queries, "which driver is not tempted, merely by the power of his engine, to wipe out the vermin of the street, pedestrians, children and cyclists?"

Adorno implores the reader to grapple with what technology does to our sense of self and society. He, like other critics, understands our ongoing conundrum about our growing need for these devices in the face of an increasingly complex world. Adorno's brief excerpt asks us to think about the possibilities and limitations inherent in our designed world, where technology drives our desires and alters our impulses. His assessment gets us to reexamine the ideas about technology offered in the other readings in this subsection.

57

HUSSEIN CHALAYAN, FASHION AND TECHNOLOGY

Bradley Quinn

Chalayan had been exploring the interaction between the body and technology for some time, expressing it on the catwalk in his *Panoramic* collection and several seasons later in his *Echoform* collection (Fall/Winter 2000). The Altitude project was based on exploring the relationship of the body's inherent mobility on the creation of forms that give it speed. "With Altitude I wanted to recreate environmental systems that mirror how the body moves. Thinking of speed led me to focus on car interiors which generated the idea of ergonomically amplifying the body's own speed and movement. I saw speed as something created by technological means to enhance the body's natural capacity to move quickly," Chalayan explained.

As Chalayan's work engages further with technological systems, he is pioneering garments that place wireless technology, electrical circuitry and automated commands directly onto the body's surface. His Remote Control dress (Spring/Summer 2000) was a hi-tech triumph that married fashion to technology and technology to the body, establishing a dialogue between the body and the environment. "The dress expressed the body's relationship to a lot of invisible and intangible things—gravity, weather, flight, radio waves, speed, etc.," Chalayan said. "Part of it is to make the invisible tangible, showing that the invisible can transform something and say something about the relationship of the object—the dress in this case—between the person wearing it and the environment around it."

The dress, like those in the Aeroplane series, was designed by means of the composite technology used by aircraft engineers, mirroring the systems that enable remote-control aeroplanes to fly. It is made from a combination of glass

Image 28 *Mechanical Dress 40's–60's*, from the One Hundred and Eleven Collection (Spring/Summer 2007). Photography by Chris Moore, courtesy of Hussein Chalayan.

fiber and resin, molded into two smooth, glossy, pink-colored front and back panels that fasten together by metal clips. Each panel is encased within grooves two millimeters in width that run throughout the length of the dress. These seams create the only textural differences in the dress, revealing interior panels made in translucent white plastic, accentuated by lighting concealed within the solar plexus panel and the left side elevating panel. The dress is designed to remain on the ground, where the principles behind it also mirror the "intelligent" systems controlling and regulating the functions of modern buildings. This establishes a new affinity between the human and the environment, mediated by clothing designed to be intimately involved with their wearer's activities.

Starlab, the now-defunct research laboratory pioneering technologized clothing, developed prototype garments that could be programmed to anticipate and respond to the wearer's needs by communicating wirelessly with remote systems. Charmed Technology, a research organization exploring the potentials of wireless clothing, conducted similar studies with wireless technology to adapt it for fashion. Although their prototypes featured state-of-the-art technology that provided the wearer with a broad range of functions, they never evolved into a finished model before the projects were terminated in 2001. Chalayan's Remote Control Dress, though less sophisticated, was the first wireless device to be presented as a fully functioning fashion garment. The Remote Control Dress is a ground-breaking achievement on many levels, not least because it showed that the technological principles behind it could be achieved in fashion as well as science.

Chalayan described the dress' cyborgian attributes as "something of a side effect." The Remote Control Dress was not designed specifically to explore the relationship of technology to the body, but to examine how the form of the garment could evolve around the body in a spatial relationship to its environment. "If you alter the way the body comes across in the space around it, then the body alters everything in the space

that affects it," Chalayan said. "The dress can also be transformed invisibly by the environment. The idea was a technological force between the environment and the person." Extending the function of a dress beyond clothing is central to Chalayan's work, and the Remote Control dress demonstrates that garments are capable of interaction with other humans and computerized systems distant in time and space.

The Remote Control Dress lines the body with computer devices and remote-control communication that aligns it to other systems. This reveals how technological enhancement means that the wearer must allow technology to come uncomfortably close to the body, all the while knowing that the systems themselves are ambivalent, capable of many contradictory uses. As the wearer puts on the Remote Control Dress, it literally becomes a cog in the machine. Through the technology in the dress, the body could then be linked to other machines, and linked to other bodies also linked to machines. This would connect the wearer to larger bodies of people, businesses, and governments through the agency of wireless communication technologies. This gives the axis of fashion and technology another dimension, signaling the integration of the constructor and the constructed.

The concept of the human cyborg resulted from Manfred Clynes and Nathan Kline's theories of how humans could survive in extraterrestrial environments by being equipped with medical implants and prostheses. (Clynes and Kline 1960: 26–7, 75–6) More recently, Donna Haraway has expanded this definition to suggest that cyborgs represent more than the classical distinction between nature and artifice, as "a hybrid of machine and organism, a creature of social reality as well as a creature of fiction." (Haraway 1999: 50–9) In Haraway's thinking, those surfing the net, designing virtual bodies or operating equipment can be considered cyborgs, since their own nervous systems operate in direct connection with the artificial intelligence of the machine.

The cyborg body is a paradox of technological power and control, mirroring how the fashioned body is also determined by the ideals and values of a wider society. As scientists define the categories of cyborg bodies, the attributes of the fashioned body can also be identified in their studies. According to the research of Chris Hables Gray, Steven Mentor and Heidi Figueroa-Sarriera, technologies of the body can enhance it in four categories: they can be *restorative,* replacing lost functions, lost limbs, and failed organs; *normalizing,* creating a generic aesthetic while imposing technologized bodies as social or esthetical norms; *reconfiguring,* like the performance artist Stelarc, who equips the body with additional limbs or communication systems; or merely *enhancing* by increasing vision, optimizing mobility, hearing, etc. (Hables Gray *et al.*). In fashion terms, the cyborg body is for the most part *reconfiguring* and *enhancing* through products like sunglasses, spectacles, mobile phones, palm pilots, and even athletic shoes.

In addition to containing the principles of the *reconfiguring* and *enhancing* categories, the Remote Control dress suggests *normalizing* properties as it charts the techno-sexualization of the body. In its ability to reveal/conceal erogenous zones and shape the body into a uniform feminine silhouette, the dress forecasts the future means of equipping and manipulating the body to conform to body ideals and dynamics of sex appeal. The structural architecture of the Remote Control Dress echoes the attributes of a fashioned body rather than an organic body. The structure of the dress forms an exoskeleton around the body, incorporating elements of body consciousness; its contours mimic the curves of the fashioned female body, arcing dramatically inward at the waist and outward in the hip region, echoing the silhouette of the corset and the crinoline. This gives the dress a defined hourglass shape that incorporates principles of corsetry in its design, emphasizing a conventionally feminine shape, while creating a solid structure that simultaneously masks undesirable body proportions.

As the dress's panels and components are activated to open and close, it evokes the allure of exposed skin and flesh, while concealing the body underneath its lining. "I made a tulle dress to be worn under the remote control dress, so that's what you see when it opens. I don't show erogenous zones in an obvious, cliched way," he said. "Sexiness doesn't come from what you wear, or from your physical appearance—it's all to do with feeling good about yourself." The sensuality associated with revealing and concealing the body is central to Chalayan's work, which challenges the way fashion defines erogenous zones, and avoids creating clothes that scream sex appeal. Chalayan views these pleasure centers as highly individual; zones to be explored and identified on individual bodies rather than dictated by fashion. In 1997 he sent models onto the catwalk wearing black chadors of varying lengths and nothing else, alluding to fashion's continual shift of erogenous zones around the female body arises in response to changing ideals.

The dress confronts one of the most profound issues raised by new technologies: the possibility that human identities would take on the properties of machines or be at their mercy. Though the wearer can access external symptoms via the remote, inherent in the dress is a sinister reversal—the potential for those systems to control the wearer. The interface of flesh and technology is both thrilling and terrifying, if technology holds the potential to override the body's commands and take control of it before the wearer is able to escape.

As a technologized object the dress is loaded with symbolic value: it is a tool of communication, a man-machine hybrid, and a hallmark of scientific progress. For fashion, it achieves innovations never thought possible, and amplifies the potential fashion has always had to interact and communicate. As the dress interacts with its immediate environment, or performs maneuvers originating from a command center, it enables the body to extend its range of movements and control beyond arm's reach. The dress makes it clear that the fashioned mechanization of the body and the integration of both into a larger technological system produces a whole new range of practices, possibilities, and aesthetics that transgresses the body/machine boundary.

This marks a radical departure from a world where distinctions between body and machine, body and dress, present and distant, natural and artificial once seemed clear. This illustrates how, as Michel Foucault described, social and cultural discourses construct our bodies in a way that makes us as analogous to a machine as possible. The design of the dress is imbued with technologies that make interaction efficient, productive, and empowered, akin to the machine-like principles of controlled automation. The presence of hi-tech systems in fashion fuses its body conscious ideals with a belief in automation, speed and accuracy as the means to achieve it.

While, historically, fashion has defined the human body according to social values, technological progress is radically changing the way it is perceived. As Chalayan's work reflects these changes, his Remote Control Dress showed what science could not yet represent: the icon of the technological age. The Remote Control Dress reminds us that we are always embodied, while showing that the future choices of embodiment, like choices of clothing, may not always be simple. As Chalayan continues to expand his thinking behind these representations, his clothing requires a body with confidence to carry off clothing still heavy with the thought process that created it.

Chalayan is among the most ambitious innovators working with fashion today, those whose work avoids commercially minded values and fashion trends. In ignoring these restrictions, they have set up a critical discourse of the principles of clothing. His work imbues garments with architectural, environmental, and technological principles. As he explores fashion's relationship to the built environment, he reveals the extent to which fashion, interiors and architecture can be truly integrated in design. "This way of thinking about fashion is still quite new to the fashion world, but it's what is moving things forward. The fashion audience doesn't really know about technology or architecture," Chalayan explained, "but they soon will."

NOTE

Extracted from B. Quinn, "A Note: Hussein Chalayan, Fashion and Technology," *Fashion Theory* 6, no. 4 (2002): 364–68. Reprinted by permission of Berg Publishers.

58

WHAT'S WRONG WITH THE PC?

Donald Norman

If there is any device that characterizes modern technology, it is the personal computer (PC). It gives all of us computational power that earlier scientists and business people could only dream of in their wildest fantasies. The world has been transformed once again, this time through the power of technologies available to the individual: communications, computation, access to information of all sorts in multifarious shapes and forms, all available through our personal computers, the instrument of power. But despite this, the PC is hardly a technological blessing; it is as much a curse as a wonder, and it is attacked as much as it is praised.

What's wrong with the PC? Everything. Start with the name. The personal computer is not personal nor is it used to do much computing. Mostly, it is used for writing, reading, and sending things to one another. Sometimes it is used for games, entertainment, or music. But most of the time it is using us. When I prowl the halls of my workplace, I often see people on their hands and knees beside their computer. No, not praying, but installing new things, rebooting, checking the cable connections, or just muttering under their breath. The *personal* computer isn't very personal. It's big and clumsy, sitting there on the desk, occupying space, requiring more and more time to maintain, requiring lots of help from one's family, friends, and neighbors. Rather than being personal, friendly, and supportive, it is massive, impersonal, abrupt, and rude.

Rebooting. Even the word is strange technical jargon. The word *booting* is derived from *bootstrap,* a small loop at the side or rear of a boot to help the owner pull it on. To bootstrap is to pull yourself up by those straps, not that many people have them on their boots anymore. A computer, when first turned on, starts up with no knowledge. No matter that you have long been using it, when first turned on it is completely ignorant of the past. In order to get started, it must find its operating system, that massive program that is the infrastructure for all else. But the computer doesn't even know how to find the operating system; it has to start off with a tiny program that has been permanently implanted in its memory and use that to load a larger program that in turn lets it load even larger programs that let it load the operating system. And, of course, the whole purpose of the operating system is to give you, the user, some way of calling up the stuff you want to work on. This process of bringing in a program whose sole purpose is to load yet a larger program is called *bootstrapping.* But why am I telling you this? Why do you need to know? You shouldn't have to know or care.

Boot, RAM, DRAM, ROM, floppy disk, hard disk, megahertz, gigabyte: Why should we want to know any of these terms? Answer: We don't. We are told we need to know because we are driven by technology and technologists.

The personal computer tries to be all things to all people. It casts all the activities of a person onto the same bland, homogeneous structure of the computer: a display screen, a keyboard, and some sort of pointing device. This is a certain guarantee of trouble. Any single set of tools is a compromise when faced with a wide range of tasks. It's like trying to do all your cooking with a knife, a fork, a spoon, and one saucepan over an open fire. It can be done. Campers do it. In olden times, people managed with less. But the myriad cooking utensils, stoves, cooktops, ovens, and so forth are in the kitchen for a reason; they make life easier, they do a better job.

A second problem is that of complexity. Try to make one device do many things and complexity increases. Try to make one device suffice for everyone in the whole world and complexity increases even more. The single, general purpose computer is a great compromise, sacrificing simplicity, ease of use, and stability for the technical goals of having one device do all.

We humans are social beings. We work best with other people. The real promise of the new technologies comes with the merger of the communication and computing industries, keeping people in touch with one another, communicating, socializing, working together, playing together. Sure, there are times when we do things alone. Creative work requires solo, silent, concentrated periods. Reading is a solitary activity. But much of our time is spent in talking to others, whether by mail, on the phone, or in person. The exciting new services are social and interactive, yet here we are, trying to build them on a device whose first name is "personal."

How many hours a week do you spend keeping your computer working, updating hardware or software, reading instruction manuals, help files, or the monthly PC magazine? Too many. How many hours a day do you spend keeping your TV set or telephone or refrigerator working? Updating it? Reading instruction manuals and help files? Not very many. There is a lesson to be learned from that contrast.

Today's PC has, gotten too big, too expensive, too complex, demanding more and more attention. It is a general purpose machine, which means it can do anything. This is not a virtue.

Take another look at the Swiss Army knife, one of those knives with umpteen blades. Sure, it is fun to look at, sure it is handy if you are off in the wilderness and it is the only tool you have, but of all the umpteen things it does, none of them are done particularly well. Yes, my Swiss Army knife has a screwdriver and scissors and corkscrew—it even has a knife blade—but when I am home, I much prefer to use a real screwdriver, a real scissors, a real corkscrew, and even a real knife. Not only are the simpler devices superior, but they are easier to use; with the Swiss Army knife, I invariably pry up the wrong blade until I find the one I am seeking.

Now take another look at the PC: It does everything, serves all masters, works all around the world. The end result is that it comes with large instruction manuals, multiple layers of menus and screen icons and toolbars. Each item presents me with options that I neither understand nor care about. Today, the PC has become more complex than the old main-frame computer it was intended to replace. Why is this? In part because of the business model of the personal computer business, in part because we have let ourselves be trapped.

But finally, and much more important, I don't normally need to compute anything, so why do I want a computer? Sure, I need to write, yes, I am a habitual user of email, and yes, I use my personal computer for all sorts of activities; but the machine itself is an imposing technology, and I don't want to be controlled by a technology. I just want to get on with my life, enjoy my activities and friends. I don't want a computer, certainly not one like today's PC, whether or not it is personal. I want the benefits, yes, but without the PC's dominating presence. So down with PCs; down with computers. All they do is complicate our lives.

Don't get me wrong: There have indeed been many important virtues of our new technologies. After all, it is things that make us smart, things that allow us to represent our ideas in a permanent manner, things that allow ideas to be transmitted from one generation to another, that allow people to collaborate over time and space.

We shouldn't give up the virtues. Moreover, I'm technically savvy, well versed in the technology. In my home, where I write these words, I have four desktop computers, two laptops, two laser printers, and an ethernet network. The problem is that the clumsiness and flaws of the technology tend to overwhelm the virtues, at least for most people. So, what we need is to keep the virtues of the machines without the overhead, without the clumsiness. We need to move to the third generation of the PC, the generation where the machines disappear from sight, where we can once again concentrate upon our activities and goals in life. We are ready for the generation of information appliances.

THE FIRST TWO GENERATIONS OF THE PC

We are now in the second generation of the personal computer. The first generation was the era of the Apple II and the IBM PC. Before that, computers were large and expensive. They were sold to companies, governments, and universities. Then, suddenly, for the first time, computers were available as small, relatively inexpensive machines that could be bought and used by average individuals. These were awkward machines, quite puny by today's standards, but they were able to perform some useful functions, primarily word processing, creating spreadsheets, and playing games. These machines were limited in capability, difficult to learn, and difficult to use. But these early machines made a difference, primarily because they empowered their users. For the first time people could do their own accounts and budget projections without waiting for information technologists in their company to get around to them. The first word processors enhanced the ease of writing and revising. Computer games started to evolve. And thousands of individuals developed educational tools for schools. For the first time people were in control of their computing tools.

The second generation of the PC was that of the Graphical User Interface—the GUI (pronounced "gooey"). This is where we are today. The first successful machine of this generation was the Apple Macintosh, which followed upon the unsuccessful Xerox Star and Apple Lisa. Soon, other companies followed, IBM with OS/2 and Microsoft with Windows. In the GUI generation, the primary philosophy is "ease of use," making the complex machinery of the personal computer relatively simple to operate. And therein lies the rub: The machine is indeed complex, and the GUI goal is to sugarcoat this complexity so that it won't be noticed. Alas, complex things are truly complex, and an attractive image on the screen doesn't overcome the fundamental problems. Rather than trying to make a complex machine easy, the better way would be to make a simple machine in the first place.

WHAT'S WRONG WITH THE GRAPHICAL USER INTERFACE

The Graphical User Interface was right for its time, but wrong for today. Why? First, it has outgrown its usefulness. The basic interface design was developed back in the days when personal computers were small by today's standards. The essential design principle was to make everything visible, so that instead of memorization of archaic commands, one could see the entire array of possible commands, file names, and directory names. Second, the basic operation was by selection, dragging, and direct manipulation. These principles worked well as long as the machines themselves were small.

The graphical user interface really worked. Buy a new computer program, take it home, stick the floppy in the computer, and use it right away. Don't bother to open the manual; why would you need to do that? Just pull down each menu and look at it, and you have seen all the commands. Don't understand some? Just try them out—you couldn't do any harm, and everything is reversible anyway.

But those were the "good old days." The computer had a really small memory (128K, or 128 thousand bytes), and a small floppy diskette (that could only hold 400K, 400,000 bytes), and no network or hard drive. The programs were small and simple. And you couldn't store anything permanently in the computer. So making everything visible worked, for there wasn't that much to be visible. And learning by trying out everything worked, because there wasn't that much to try out.

Today, machines have expanded in power thousands of times. Today, all machines have internal disk storage, and many are connected to networks that enable them to receive millions of documents from locations all over the world. My home computer has almost ten thousand files in it, most of which are meaningless to me. My company network has hundreds of locations all over the world, each with thousands or even millions of documents. The design philosophy of making everything visible fails miserably in this context.

What's the matter with the graphical interface today? The solution doesn't scale. Making everything visible is great when you have only twenty things. When you have twenty thousand, it only adds to the confusion. Show everything at once, and the result is chaos. Don't show everything, and then stuff gets lost.

But although the computer has changed dramatically since the 1980s, the basic way we use it hasn't. The Internet and the World Wide Web give much more power, much more information, along with more things to lose track of, more places to get lost in. More ways to confuse and confound. It is time to start over.

Reality check: The early Apple Macintosh computer was small and convenient, but the screen was small, too—small and inconvenient. Tiny is more like it. No color, just black and white. And it was slow. S-L-O-W. And no hard disk, just floppies, so you had to store your stuff on piles of floppies. If you didn't label those floppies and then keep the labels up to date (and who could ever do that?) it was awfully hard to find the stuff again. And if you think they don't hold much today, well, they held a lot less then. No large capacity storage devices, no CDROMs, no

DVD, no hard disk, no networking. But easy to use? Yup. Nice and easy. You truly did not need to read the manuals. Those were the good old days, which, like most good old days, are happier in memory than in reality.

WHY YOU REALLY DON'T WANT TO USE A COMPUTER (EVEN THOUGH YOU THINK YOU DO)

Do you really want to use a computer? Do you want to use a word processor? Of course not. The fact that you think you do is the triumph of marketing and advertising over common sense. Now, maybe if you are a confirmed technology addict, or a computer programmer, sure you love using computers, but not the rest of us. We want to get on with our lives.

I don't want to use a computer. I don't want to do word processing. I want to write a letter, or find out what the weather will be, or pay a bill, or play a game. I don't want to use a computer, I want to accomplish something. I want to do something meaningful to me. Not "applications," not some bizarre complex computer program that does more than I ever want to know about and yet doesn't really do exactly what I need. I want computing that fits my activities. I want the technology hidden away, out of sight. Like electric motors. Like the computers that control my car.

Once upon a time, cars were difficult to use. They had all those controls and meters and gauges. Spark adjustment, fuel priming, choke, and throttle. And there was little standardization, so every car worked differently. Some were steered with wheels, some with tillers, some with levers. The speed of the engine was adjusted by foot, by hand, by pedals, levers, or knobs. In the real early days you had to take your mechanic along with you when you went for a drive. To start it you had to prime the fuel line, adjust the spark setting, set the choke, open the throttle, and then stand outside the car beside the engine and crank it over by hand, being careful that it didn't start at the wrong time and break your arm. There were gauges for all sorts of things.

Today, now that the cars are extremely reliable, all you really need is a speedometer to tell you how fast you are moving, a fuel gauge to tell you when you are running low, and that's about it. Anything else can be done with warning lights or messages that only come on when they are needed, ideally to warn you a bit before serious problems arise, when there is still enough time to take corrective action or get help.

Even the fuel gauge isn't what you want. You don't really want to know how much fuel you have left (no, honest, you don't); what you really want to know is how far you can drive. Some cars provide this information. The normal fuel gauge can't do this because it is a simple float that rides up and down on the surface of the fuel, allowing its level to be translated into how much fuel is left in the gas tank. To translate fuel level into how many more miles of driving is possible requires some computation. The fuel level has to be converted to the amount of fuel, either liters or gallons. Then, an estimate of the efficiency has to be made: How much gasoline have you been using per mile or kilometer recently? Multiply the efficiency by the amount of fuel and you have the predicted range. Do the same computation in kilometers and liters as well as in miles and gallons so you can accommodate inhabitants of both the more advanced countries that use metric measurements and lesser advanced countries that don't. These computations require a computer; hence the moral of this story.

Computers ought to be like the embedded ones that tell you how far you can drive with the amount of fuel remaining in the fuel tank: invisible, automatic, and useful. It's invisible, so you don't have to do anything to it. It provides valuable information. Drive more efficiently, and the remaining distance goes up; drive less efficiently and the distance goes down. It wouldn't be difficult to add a time estimate: "Twenty minutes to empty."

This is the way the fuel tank meter ought to be: Get rid of the current gauge that tells what fraction of the fuel tank still has fuel in it and replace it with one that says how far or how long we can go. Notice, too, that this computer-controlled gauge is very limited in its functionality; it tells the range of driving with the remaining fuel. Nothing more, nothing less.

This is the way computers ought to be, not just in the car, but in the home, at schools, and in the office. Useful for doing things, for getting answers, for having fun, presenting us with the information we need to know, information we can use directly without further thought. According to this model they will be far easier to use. They will be designed specifically to fit the task, to fit the needs of their users. This also means that they will be specialized, so we are apt to need many of them. No problem, because they will be like all our other appliances: We buy just the ones we want, just the versions that fit our lives. Their simplicity and utility make up for their specialization.

WHY THE PERSONAL COMPUTER IS SO COMPLEX

The major problem with today's PC is its complexity. The complexity of the PC is pretty fundamental; it is built into its foundation. There are three major reasons for the complexity: the attempt to make a single device do too many things; the need to have a single machine suffice for every person in the world; and the business model of the computer industry.

Make a single device do everything, and each task will be done in a manner that is adequate, but not superior. As I have explained before, a multiple purpose device cannot be optimized for any single task; it has to be a compromise. Its physical shape, the nature of its controls and displays, are all compromises. Imagine a musical instrument that combines the violin, guitar, flute, and piano keyboard. Can it be done? Oh yes, your handy-dandy music synthesizer program will produce the sounds of all these instruments from a typewriter keyboard. But will it be inspired music? Will a real musician use it? Of course not.

The second cause of the computer's inherent complexity is that computer companies make products intended to be used by hundreds of millions of people all around the world. "Know your user" is the mantra of good design, but how can you possibly know your user when it could be millions of people, of every age, every educational level, and every social and cultural group, while hoping to satisfy every conceivable need and style of work? Because each country, each culture, and for that matter, each individual, has different interests and needs, this means that the product has to have a large set of features and operations in order to satisfy everyone who might use it. No matter that any individual is apt to use only a very small number of features or commands; to satisfy the world market, the product must have everything. Making one device try to fit everyone in the world is a sure path toward an unsatisfactory product; it will inevitably provide unnecessary complexity for everyone.

Finally, there is the business model, the strategy that the computer industry follows in order to ensure that it can make a profit year after year There is nothing wrong with this: A company that fails to make money soon goes out of business, and then it cannot be of use to anyone, even if its products were loved and respected. But the strategy adopted by the computer industry is also one that dooms it to an ever-increasing level of complexity in its products. Let us look at this issue in greater detail.

HOW THE BUSINESS MODEL OF THE PC GUARANTEES COMPLEXITY

All companies need to make a profit in order to survive. It doesn't do anyone any good to make great products if the company fails for a lack of funds. Now, how do you make a profit in the computer business? By selling computers and software, right? Yes, but the problem is that the vast majority of people, if they need a computer

at all, only need one. And each user of a machine only needs one word processor, one spreadsheet, one email program.

Think about it. Suppose you could buy a computer and software that would make you completely happy. From your point of view, that's good. But, oops, from the point of view of the computer manufacturers, that's a problem. How would they make money if their customers were so happy that they wouldn't need to buy anything else? Horrors. There is only one solution to their dilemma: They need to make you unhappy with what you have and make you want something else. Isn't this wonderful: An industry whose business model is based upon the need to make their customers unhappy.

Every year, the computer companies have to convince you that this year's version of software has features in it that you simply can't live without, even though you have lived without them all your life up to now. Moreover, because you think you are already happy with your software, the new software has to do everything that the old software did, while adding those exciting new features that you can't live without. Each year the hardware manufacturers make their systems more powerful, with more memory capacity, and faster, better graphical display capability, all absolutely necessary, of course, if you are to be able to use that new software with all those new features you suddenly can't live without. Year after year after year there will be new releases of that original, perfectly adequate software, with new feature after new feature added. Year after year you will need faster, bigger, more capable hardware. The result: guaranteed complexity.

All industries have a problem of ensuring a continuing revenue stream from their customers. They need a business model: a plan for ensuring a continual stream of revenue. The business model for some industries is trivial. If you sell consumable goods such as food, people eat it, and therefore need to buy more. Similarly, in the newspaper business, fresh news continually arrives, so customers naturally seek your services to find out about the latest events. In other businesses the life of the product is made artificially short, by making it into a fashion. Once things become fashion, a whole new industry of trendsetters emerges to produce the social pressures that cause people to buy new items so that they will never appear to be old-fashioned, never appear to be out of fashion. This, of course, is the mainstay of the clothing industry, so much so that it is called the fashion industry.

Most industries use a combination of methods. Automobiles are both consumable and fashionable. Cars fall apart after a while, which makes them consumable. And through clever advertising, autos can also fall out of fashion. Government regulation also helps by mandating new emission controls, fuel efficiency, and safety features, thereby enhancing the value of newer autos and diminishing that of older ones.

In the computer industry, the answer is to convince users that whatever hardware and software they are now perfectly happy with is, in actuality, unsatisfactory. This is done through the introduction of new features. The strange thing is that this strategy appears to work. Every six months the hardware side of the computer industry comes out with new models, each better and faster, with more capacity and lower cost than the previous model. These are called *speed bumps,* where the same basic computer as before is being offered, only speeded up a bit. In similar fashion, the software is "improved" every year. And every year the software industry comes out with new products and new versions of existing products, each with brilliant new features that are essential for the health, safety, and well-being of the planet.

Creeping featurism, is what I called this problem in 1988,[1] the symptom of the dreaded disease of *featuritis.* By 1992 the word processing program Microsoft Word had 311 commands. Three Hundred and Eleven. That's a daunting amount, more than I dreamed was possible when I wrote my 1988 book. Who could learn over three hundred commands for a single program? Who would want to? Who would ever need them? Answer: nobody. They are there for lots of reasons. In part, they are there because

this one program must cover the whole world, so, in principle, for every command, there is at least one user somewhere who finds it essential. In part, though, they are there because the programmers dreamed them up; if it was possible to do, it was done. But the most important reason is for marketing. My program is bigger than yours. Better. It can do more. Anything you have, I have too, and more besides.

Creeping featurism may be the wrong term: perhaps it should be called *rampant featurism.* Do you think 311 commands is a lot for a word processing program? Five years later, in 1997, that same word processing program, Microsoft Word, had 1,033 commands. One Thousand Thirty Three. That made the program easier to use?

The problem is made even more complex by the way the computer marketplace has developed. Computer magazines review the new products, and the major things they think of looking for are comparisons of speed, lists of features, and artificial performance measurements. The stores that sell PCs also have certain requirements they look for when they decide to order machines from a manufacturer: *Hygienic* features is what the industry calls them. How fast is the machine in megahertz, how many megabytes of RAM, how many megabytes of hard disk space? Once again, it doesn't matter that speed measured in megahertz is not only a meaningless number to the consumer, but that it doesn't really measure computer speed either. It doesn't matter that the old speeds were perfectly satisfactory. It doesn't matter that consumers have no idea what a hard drive is compared to RAM. What matters is the numbers game: Bigger is better, and if your numbers don't compete, neither will your products. To sell its products, a computer company has to sell to the stores that stock them and deal with stores' purchasing agents, the "channels." And these channels have their own opinion of what sells. In particular, they like features, the more the merrier, so they have a standard set of hygienic features that the company's products must have in order to be purchased, properly displayed, and sold by the store. If it fails in the hygienic tests, the company will fail in the sales channels. The fact that the hygienic features have little to do with usage is irrelevant.

Actually, it isn't true that the current speeds and memory capacities are sufficient. They aren't, because it isn't in the industry's best interest to let them be. Nathan Myhrvold, one of the senior executives and gurus of Microsoft, once proposed, only partially in jest, "Nathan's First law": "Software is a gas, it expands to fill its container." Moreover, he added, "It's a good thing for the computer industry that computer power expands so rapidly. This way we can build bigger and fancier software that require you to get a bigger and faster computer, so we can use up all that space too."[2]

Think about it. When you go into a store to buy a stove or refrigerator, television set or telephone, you are bombarded with rows of almost identical-looking items, each barely distinguishable by price, perhaps by appearance, and by a comparison list of features. Whether or not you can use the device, whether it really does the job for you is usually not a major decision point, even if it should be. You have been taken over by the channel.

Whatever happened to the consumer? Whatever happened to the notion that one should solve the consumer's needs, which are really expressed in such terms as having fun, doing homework, writing letters, and the like, and not in megahertz and megabytes? What happened?

The computer industry works under a peculiar view of the world. The goal is to manufacture a machine that can do everything, that fits all people with the same basic hardware and software, that provides applications that have little to do with real work, and that grow ever more complex over time. It's a great business to be in, but a horrible way to affect people's lives. There are better ways to serve the customer, better ways to make money.

ACTIVITY-BASED COMPUTING

With today's PC, we buy the hardware, the computer, in order to support computer programs, also known as *applications.* Applications: what a terrible term. What a terrible concept. Applications have little to do with the tasks that people are attempting to accomplish. Look. We don't do word processing; we write letters, or memos, or reports, or notes to ourselves. Some of us write books. I do not want to go to my computer to do word processing. I don't want to go to my computer at all. What I do want is to be able to write, with a tool that *fits* my needs. When I write, I need some way of getting my ideas onto paper or screen, some way of reviewing them, of outlining and restructuring. I need to be able to incorporate notes I have made and sometimes drawings or photographs.

When I write business memos, I need a different writing tool. I may want to insert some budget tables and calendar schedules. When I write a letter I may want the letters I am responding to, and perhaps a calendar, and maybe my address book. Each task has its own special requirements, each of which encompasses several different applications. Today's applications have far too much power for the use I make of them, yet lack all the necessary components for any given task.

On top of all of this, life is filled with interruptions. It is a rare event when I can finish a task at one sitting. At almost any task I am interrupted by other people, by the telephone, by the next scheduled event, or because I need other material and can't proceed without it. Sometimes more urgent matters intrude, and sometimes I simply need to stop and do other things, such as eat, or sleep, or socialize.

People do activities, and the software ought to support this. At Apple Computer, we called this approach "Activity Based Computing" (ABC), and together with a hardy band of souls[3] we tried to interest the company in the notion that software based upon ABC would fit the lives of our customers better than the traditional application model that we and our competitors were selling. (What happened? It's a long story, so see the endnote.[4])

The basic idea is simple: Make it possible to have all the material needed for an activity ready at hand, available with little or no mental overhead.

Tools, documents, and information are gathered together into packages maximally designed for the particular activities in which they participate, without interfering with other activities. Of course, it must be possible to make changes in the choices and to switch rapidly and easily among the activities. Finally, items not needed for the current activity are hidden so they do not distract and do not take up valuable work space.

An *activity* is a goal-directed set of tasks. Activities, tasks, and actions provide a hierarchy; an activity is composed of tasks, which in turn are composed of actions. Examples include "doing one's mail," "doing the weekly home banking activity of paying bills and balancing the checkbook," "writing a technical report." Tasks are lower-level activities, aimed at fulfilling particular subgoals of an activity. The activity of doing the mail will have in it the tasks of "read the new mail," "write a new message," and "forward the mail from Sonia to Fred." Similarly, the activity of "banking" might have subactivities, such as "balance the checkbook," or "send payment to a merchant." Actions are a lower level of interest and refer to such things as selecting a particular menu command, or typing a particular name or phrase, or naming a file. In the scientific research field of activity theory,[5] of which this set of specifications is a special case, there are further distinctions. Thus, an *operation* would be the physical movement of the hand in order to move the mouse so as to highlight a menu, with yet another operation being to move the appropriate finger so as to depress the mouse button and select the item of interest. Operations make up actions. Actions make up tasks, and tasks make up activities.

Work within any single activity can take a long time. It may involve numerous people. As a result, it is necessary to allow different people to share the activity spaces, and to figure out how to coordinate the work so that one person's actions do not interfere with another's.

Because activities take place over extended periods, it is necessary to make it possible to return to the tasks without disruption. If you are interrupted while doing an activity, you should be able to resume at a later time, whether it be an hour or a month, and find the activity space exactly as it was left, with all the items and tools in the same place and same state. If the cursor was in the middle of a highlighted word, it is still in the same place, with the same highlighting still present. All this would aid memory, would aid the resumption of the task, and would be built to reflect the way people really work. In everyday life there are multiple interruptions and it is important to be able to resume work at some later time exactly where one left off. This requires restoration of the exact context of the activity.

Activity spaces could be shared with other people or copied from one machine to another. A company might wish to provide standardized activity spaces for its procedures, such as for filling out expense reports or purchase orders. Small software companies might provide specialized activity spaces, much as stationery stores provide a wide variety of forms and notebooks. Users could then further customize these spaces to meet their particular requirements.

This would be a very different way of doing software than the homogeneous, super-duper general purpose software packages we now must use. Instead of long menu commands, one would have a chest of tools from which to select, much like working on a project in the home, where you select only those tools needed for the task and have only those at the worksite; activity spaces would allow just the needed selection. But, just as in the home where it is possible to go back and get another tool, it is possible in an activity space to add or subtract tools as needed.

Activity spaces are not a magical cure to all that ails the PC. The "C" in ABC still stands for "computing." Many of the negative characteristics I have described for the PC would be unchanged. All activities would still be mapped onto the very same set of interface tools: a screen, a keyboard, and a pointing device. And the same machine would still be doing everything, with the extra requirement that it manage the variety of activity spaces and tools that each user would need. Activity spaces are probably difficult to implement in today's world of the personal computer, although there have been numerous attempts.[6]

A far better approach is to implement ABC without the "C"—without the computer. The goal is to make it so that the tools match the activities. There is an alternative way of getting to this state: Build special purpose devices, information appliances, where each device is tuned especially for an activity. With separate devices, some of the properties come automatically. If you are interrupted, just put the device away. When you wish to resume, pick it up and get to work. There would be no interference from other activities, no problem of keeping the original state. If we made special devices for activities, we could tailor them appropriately. The banking activity could have a special check printer and dedicated connection to the bank and to your stock broker. The letter writer could have a built-in address book and print letters and envelopes.

The main barrier to the introduction of technology that is aligned with people's real needs and desires, with people's real activities, is the mindset of the computer industry. This industry has grown up being dominated by technology. The result has been the development of powerful tools that have become essential to modern life. The computer industry feels vindicated: It has been highly successful. It has prevailed in the face of skepticism. And it did it all through the power of modern information processing technology. Why should it change?

The problem is that the resulting device is technology-centric. To make it usable by the vast majority of people who lack the detailed technical skills, the industry has been forced to add all sort of add-ons: wizards, help systems, telephone support lines, books, training courses, Internet sites that feature the answers to "Frequently Asked Questions," whose numbers have grown so large that we now need help systems to navigate through all those answers. All these add-ons contribute to the complexity; now, in addition to the ever-increasing complexity of the computer applications, we must cope with the ever-increasing complexity of the help systems and support services. The computer industry is stuck in a rut from which it can't escape. Its very success has driven it further and further down a path of no return. Its business strategy is caught in the endless loop of added features, continual upgrades, and, as a result, ever-increasing complexity and ever-increasing help systems to let us cope. The only way out is to start all over.

There are many hurdles in the way of information appliances, but the goal is worth it: devices that fit the person, that fit the task. Devices that are easy to use, not only because they will be inherently simpler, but because they fit the task so well that to learn the task is to learn the appliance.

Now let us take a look at the fundamental issues, the better to understand how to do better. In the next chapter I look at problems with the PC and the attempts to overcome them. I conclude that these are all doomed to fail. The problems are too fundamental; there is no simple magical cure. In chapter 6 I point out that the infrastructure is wrong. In chapter 7 I examine the mismatch between the needs and abilities of people and the requirements of machines. People are analog and biological; information technology is digital and mechanical. Being digital may be good for machines, but it is bad for people. This sets the framework for chapter 8's examination of why things have become so difficult to use.

In the final chapters of this book I propose an alternative approach: a human-centered development process coupled with a set of disruptive technologies, the better to yield a family of information appliances designed to fit human tasks, tailored for human needs and abilities.

NOTES

Extracted from D. Norman, *The Invisible Computer* (Cambridge, Mass.: MIT Press, 1998), pp. 69–87. © 1998 Massachusetts Institute of Technology, by permission of The MIT Press.

1. Creeping featurism is what I called this problem in 1988. D. A. Norman, *The Psychology*

of Everyday Things (New York: Basic Books, 1988), p. 172. (Also published in paperback as D. A. Norman, *The Design of Everyday Things* [New York: Doubleday, 1990]).

The numerical values for the number of commands in the 1992 and 1997 versions of Microsoft Word come from W. Gibbs, "Taking Computers to Task," *Scientific American* 277, no. 1 (July 1997): 88.

2. **Nathan's First law: "Software is a gas. … "** Statements made in 1997 at the ACM's 50th Anniversary party, at their annual convention in San Jose, California. These are actually paraphrases, not actual quotations, for although I was in attendance, I was not taking notes. But these are precisely the sentiments that Nathan expressed: for corroboration, see Wayt Gibbs's provocative article, "Taking Computers to Task," 82–89 (see note 1).

3. **Together with** a **hardy band of souls.** The ABC group consisted of Thomas Erickson, Charlie Hill, Austin Henderson, Dan Russell, Harry Saddler, and Mitch Stein, all of whom have left Apple.

4. **What happened? See the endnote.** Activity-based computing never did make it to product. The idea failed for many reasons. It was a disruptive technology offered to an industry that wasn't interested. It suffered from all the common ailments of disruptive technologies (discussed in chapter 11). In part, the idea failed because it connected itself to a superior, new technology (object-oriented component parts) that itself never reached any market acceptance. In part, it was too difficult to convince the critical senior executive staff that the approach would make a difference in the marketplace. Apple was already suffering from its use of a nonstandard operating system, the nonsubstitutable, infrastructure problem, and it wasn't clear why offering a nonstandard set of applications would help in this battle, even if the new approach was a superior way of doing things.

Apple had developed a component-based software architecture that it called "OpenDoc" (as in Open standards for Documents), which provided the perfect vehicle upon which to implement activity-based computing. It was easy to convince the members of Apple's OpenDoc team and together we made the rounds of the other companies that were part of the OpenDoc consortium. But OpenDoc had its own political problems, both within Apple and outside, so this effort never got off the ground. OpenDoc itself failed to receive widespread usage, and it was finally abandoned. Established companies, even innovative ones (which Apple prided itself on being), have great difficulty in moving outside the established paradigm.

5. **In the scientific research field of activity theory.** See B. Nardi, ed., *Context and Consciousness: Activity Theory and Human-Computer Interaction* (Cambridge, MA: MIT Press, 1996). My interest first started in the early 1980s: see Y. Miyata and D. A. Norman, "Psychological Issues in Support of Multiple Activities," in *User Centered System Design,* ed. D. A. Norman and S. W. Draper (Hillsdale, NJ: Lawrence Erlbaum Associates, 1986).

6. **There have been numerous attempts.** Austin Henderson and Stuart Card of the Xerox Palo Alto Research Center developed an early version of Activity Spaces, "Rooms," which a division of Xerox released as a product. D. A. Henderson, Jr., and S. K. Card, "Rooms: The Use of Multiple Virtual Workspaces to Reduce Space Contention in a Window-Based Graphical User Interface," *TOGS 5,* no. 3 (1986): 211–243. "Lotus Notes," a business communication and organizing tool by the Lotus Corporation includes related notions, although within a restricted (confining) framework. To be completely successful requires a somewhat different model of software than the current application-based framework. It requires component-based software as well as the appropriate task-centered design philosophy (hence our use of Open Doc: see note 4).

59

THE CELL PHONE AND THE CROWD

Vicente Rafael

Telephones were introduced in the Philippines as early as 1885, during the last decade and a half of Spanish colonial rule.[1] Like telegraphy before it, telephony provoked fantasies of direct communication among the colonial bourgeoisie. They imagined that these new technologies would afford them access to colonial leaders, enabling them to hear and be heard directly by the state. We can see this telecommunicative ideal, for example, in a satirical piece written by Filipino national hero Jose Rizal in 1889. Entitled *Por Telefono,* it situates the narrator as an eavesdropper. He listens intently to the sounds and voices that travel between the Spanish friars in Manila— regarded as the real power in the colony—and their superiors in Madrid.[2] The nationalist writer wiretaps his way, as it were, into the walls of the clerical residences, exposing their hypocrisy and excesses. In this sense, the telephone shares the capacity of that other telecommunicative technology, print, to reveal what was once hidden, to repeat what was meant to be secret, and to pass on messages intended for a particular circle.[3] It is this history of tapping into and forwarding messages—often in the form of ironic commentaries, jokes, and rumors—that figured recently in the civilian-led coup known as "People Power H." From 16 to 20 January 2001, more than one million people assembled at one of Metro Manila's major highways, Epifanio de los Santos Avenue (commonly called Edsa), site of the original People Power revolt in 1986. A large cross section of Philippine society gathered there to demand the resignation of President Joseph "Erap" Estrada, after his impeachment trial was suddenly aborted by the eleven senators widely believed to be under his influence. The senators had refused to include key evidence that purportedly showed Estrada had amassed a fortune from illegal numbers games while in office. The impeachment proceedings were avidly followed on national TV and the radio. Most viewers and listeners were keenly aware of the evidence of corruption on the part of Estrada and his family; once the pro-Estrada senators put an abrupt end to the hearing, hundreds of thousands of viewers and listeners were moved to protest in the streets.[4] Television and radio had kept them in their homes and offices to follow the court proceedings, but at a critical moment, these media also drew them away from their seats. Relinquishing their position as spectators, they now became part of a crowd that had formed around a common wish: the resignation of the president.

Aside from TV and radio, another communications medium was given credit for spurring the coup: the cell phone. Nearly all the accounts of People Power II available to us come from middle-class writers or by way of a middle-class-controlled media with strong nationalist sentiments. And nearly all point to the crucial importance of the cell phone in the rapid mobilization of demonstrators. "The phone is our weapon now," we hear from an unemployed construction worker quoted in a newspaper article. A college student in Manila testified that "the power of our cell phones and computers were among the things which lit the fuse which set off the second uprising, or People Power Revolution II." And a newspaper columnist advised "would-be foot-soldiers in any future revolution" that "as long as you[r cell phone] is not low on battery, you are in the groove, in a fighting mood."[5] A technological thing was thus idealized as an agent of change, invested with the power to bring forth new forms of sociality.

Introduced in the latter half of the 1990s, cell phones in the Philippines had become remarkably popular by 1999.[6] There are a number of reasons for their ubiquity. First, there is the perennial difficulty and expense of acquiring land line phones in the Philippines, and the service provided by the Philippine Long Distance Company (PLDT) and the more recent, smaller Bayan Tel is erratic. Cell phones offered the promise of satisfying this need for connectivity. In addition, cell phones cost far less than personal computers, which are owned by less than 1 percent of the population (though a larger proportion has access through Internet cafes). By contrast, there are over 10 million cell phone users in a population of about 77 million. The vast majority of users buy prepaid phone cards that, combined with the relatively low cost of phones (as little as $50 in the open market and half this amount in secondary markets), make wireless communication more accessible and affordable than regular telephones or computers.

More importantly, cell phones allow users to reach beyond traffic-clogged streets and serve as an alternative to slow, unreliable, and expensive postal service. Like many Third World countries recently opened to more liberal trade policies, the Philippines shares the paradox of being awash with the latest communication technologies, like the cell phone, while being mired in deteriorating infrastructures: roads, postal services, railroads, power generators, and land lines. With the cell phone, one seems able to pass beyond these obstacles. And inasmuch as these broken, state-run infrastructures represent government ineptitude, passing beyond them gives one the sense of overcoming a state long beset by corruption.[7] It is not surprising, then, that cell phones could prove literally handy in spreading rumors, jokes, and information that steadily eroded whatever legitimacy President Estrada and his congressional supporters still had during the impeachment hearings. Bypassing the broadcasting media, cell phone users themselves became broadcasters, receiving and transmitting both news and gossip, and often confounding the two. Indeed, one could imagine each user becoming his or her own broadcasting station: a node in a wider network of communication that the state could not possibly monitor, much less control.[8] Hence, once the call was made for people to mass at Edsa, cell phone users readily forwarded messages they received as they followed the messages' instructions.

Cell phones, then, were not only invested with the power to overcome the crowded conditions and congested surroundings brought about by the state's inability to order everyday life, they were also seen to bring about a new kind of crowd that was thoroughly conscious of itself as a movement headed toward a common goal. While telecommunication allows one to escape the crowd, it also opens up the possibility of finding oneself moving in concert with it, filled with its desire and consumed by its energy. In the first case, cell phone users define themselves against a mass of anonymous others. In the second, they become those others, accepting anonymity as a condition of possibility for sociality. To understand how the first is transformed into the second, it is worth noting how, specifically, the vast majority of cell phone messages are transmitted in the Philippines: as text messages.

TEXTING

Text messages are e-mails sent over mobile phones that can also be transferred to the Internet. Recently, the verb *texting* has emerged to designate the act of sending such messages, indicating its popularity in such places as England, Japan, and Finland (where text messaging was first available). In the Philippines, texting has been the preferred mode of cell phone use since 1999, when the two major networks, Globe and Smart, introduced free and, later on, low-cost text messaging as part of their regular service. Unlike voice messages, text messages take up less bandwidth and require far less time to convert into digitized packets available for transmission. It thus makes economic sense for service providers to encourage the use of text messaging in order to reserve greater bandwidth space for more expensive—and profitable—voice messages. Calling cards and virtually free texting, as opposed to expensive long-term contracts, give cell phone service providers a way to attract a broad spectrum of users from different income levels. Thus, from an economic standpoint, texting offers a rare point of convergence between the interests of users and providers.[9] But it is obviously more than low costs that makes cell phones popular in the Philippines. In an essay sent over the Internet by "An Anonymous Filipino," the use of cell phones in Manila is described as a form of "mania." Using Taglish (the urban lingua franca that combines Tagalog, English, and Spanish), this writer, a Filipino *balikbayan* (one who resides or works abroad and periodically visits the motherland), remarks:

> HI! WNA B MY TXT PAL? They're everywhere! In the malls, the office, school, the MRT [Manila Railroad Transit], what-have-you, the cellphone mania's on the loose! Why, even Manang Fishball [Mrs. Fishball, a reference to older working-class women who sell fishballs by the side of the road] is texting! I even asked my sisters how important they think they are that they should have cells? Even my nephew in highschool has a cell phone. My mom in fact told me that even in his sleep, my brother's got his cell, and even when they have a PLDT [land line] phone in the house, they still use the cell phone.[10]

According to the *Oxford English Dictionary, mania* is a kind of madness characterized "by great excitement, extravagant delusions and hallucinations, and, in its acute stage, by great violence." The insistence on having cell phones nearby, the fact that they always seem to be on hand, indicates an attachment to them that surpasses the rational and the utilitarian, as the remarks above indicate. The cell phone gives its owner a sense of being someone even if he or she is only a street vendor or a high school student—someone who can reach and be reached and is thus always in touch. The "manic" relationship to the cell phone is just this ready willingness to identify with it, or more precisely with what the machine is thought capable of doing. One not only has access to it; by virtue of its omnipresence and proximity, one becomes like it. That is to say, one becomes an apparatus for sending and receiving messages at all times. An American journalist writing in the *New York Times* observes as much in an article on Manila society:

> "Texting?" Yes, texting—as in exchanging short typed messages over a cell phone. All over the Philippines, a verb has been born, and Filipinos use it whether they are speaking English or Tagalog. The difference [between sending e-mail by computers and texting] is that while chat-room denizens sit in contemplative isolation, glued to computer screens, in the Philippines, "texters" are right out in the throng. Malls are infested with shoppers who appear to be navigating by cellular compass. Groups of diners sit ignoring one another, staring down at their phones as if fumbling with rosaries. Commuters, jaywalkers, even mourners—everyone in the Philippines seems to be texting over the phone. … Faye Siytangco, a 23-year-old airline sales representative, was not surprised when at the wake for a friend's father she saw people bowing their heads and gazing toward folded hands. But when their hands started beeping and their thumbs began to move, she realized to her astonishment that they were not in fact praying. "People were actually sitting there and texting," Siytangco said. "Filipinos don't see it as rude anymore."[11]

Unlike computer users, cell phone owners are mobile, immersed in the crowd, yet able to communicate beyond it. Texting provides them with a way out of their surroundings. Thanks to the cell phone, they need not be present to others around them. Even when they are part of a socially defined group—say, commuters or mourners—cell phone users are always somewhere else, receiving and transmitting messages from beyond their physical location. It is in this sense that they become other than their socially delineated identity: not only cell phone users but cell phone "maniacs." Because it rarely leaves their side, the phone becomes part of the hand, the digits an extension of the fingers. In certain cases, the hand takes the place of the mouth, the fingers that of the tongue. One Filipino-American contributor to Plaridel, an on-line discussion group dealing with Philippine politics, referred to a Filipino relative's cell phone as "almost a new limb."[12] It is not surprising then that the consciousness of users assumes the mobility and receptivity of their gadgets. We can see how this assumption of the qualities of the cell phone comes across in the practice of sending and receiving messages:

The craze for sending text messages by phone started [in 1999] when Globe introduced prepaid cards that enabled students, soldiers [and others] too poor for a long-term subscription to start using cellular phones. ... People quickly figured out how to express themselves on the phone's alphanumeric keypad. ... "Generation Txt," as the media dubbed it, was born. Sending text messages does not require making a call. People merely type in a message and the recipient's phone number, hit the phone's send key and off it goes to the operator's message center, which forwards it to the recipient, ... Sending text messages by phone is an irritating skill to master, largely because 26 letters plus punctuation have to be created with only 10 buttons. Typing the letter C, for example, requires pressing the No. 2 button three times; an E is the

No. 3 button pressed twice; and so on. After the message is composed it can be sent immediately to the phone number of the recipient, who can respond immediately by the same process. People using phones for text messages have developed a shorthand. "Where are you?" becomes "WRU." And "See you tonight" becomes "CU 2NYT." People have different styles of keying in their messages. Some use their index fingers, some one thumb, others both. ... [Others] tap away with one hand without even looking at [their] phone.[13]

As with e-mail, conventions of grammar, spelling, and punctuation are frequently evaded and rearticulated in texting. The constraints of an alphanumeric keypad require users to type numbers to get letters. As a result, counting and writing become closely associated. Digital communication requires the use of digits, both one's own and those on the phone keypad, as one taps away. But this tapping unfolds not to the rhythm of one's speech or in tempo with one's thoughts, but in coordination with the numbers by which one reaches letters: three taps on *2* to get a C, for example, or two taps on *3* to get an *E*. Texting seems to reduce all speech to writing and all writing to a kind of mechanical percussion, a drumming that responds to external constraints rather than an internal source. In addition, there are no prescribed styles for texting: one or two fingers or a thumb will do, and skilled typists can text without looking at the screen. Nor are standardized body postures required while texting: one can sit, walk, or drive while sending messages. If handwriting in the conventional sense requires classroom instruction in penmanship and posture under the supervision of teachers, texting frees the body, or so it seems, from these old constraints.

Mimicking the mobility of their phones, texters move about, bound to nothing but the technological forms and limits of the medium. The messages they send and receive condense whatever language—English or Tagalog and, more frequently, Taglish—they are using, and so are proper to none. This hybrid language follows the demands of the medium itself rather than the idiosyncrasies of its users. The phone companies' recent introduction of limits on free text messaging, and their assessment of a fee per character of text, has led to the further shortening of words and messages. Instant messaging, along with the mechanical storage and recall of prior messages, requires only highly abbreviated narrative constructions with little semantic deferral or delay. Using the cell phone, one begins to incorporate its logic and techniques to the point of identifying with an apparently novel social category: *Generation Txt.*

An obvious pun on *Generation X*, Generation Txt was first used as an advertising gimmick by cell phone providers to attract young users to their products. Defined by its attachment to and ease with the cell phone, Generation Txt has troubled older generations uneasy about the rise of texting. An anthropologist from the University of the Philippines addresses the dangers of texting in terms that are familiar from other countries where the practice has become popular, especially among youth. He cites the cell phone's propensity to stifle literacy by "[wreaking] havoc" on spelling and grammar, and its erosion, "in tandem with mindless computer games and Internet chat rooms, [of] young people's ability to communicate in the real world in real time."[14] Rather than promote communication, texting obstructs it; indeed, cell phones cultivate a kind of stupidity. For the anthropologist, this is evident in young people's gullibility for the marketing ploys of cell phone providers: they end up spending more money sending messages of little or no consequence. He further charges cell phones with leading to "anti-social" behavior: children "retreat to their own cocoons," while the parents who give them the cell phones evade responsibility for "interacting" with them in any meaningful way.[15] Other writers report students' use of texting to cheat on exams, or the role of cell phones in spreading slanderous rumors and gossip that may ruin someone's reputation.[16] As one Filipino on-line writer put it, cell phones are like "loaded weapons," and their use must be tempered with caution. Another contributor writes: "If the text [I received] felt like a rumor masquerading as news, I didn't forward it." An office worker from Manila adds: "Sometimes whenever you receive serious msgs, sometimes you have to think twice if it is true or if perhaps someone is fooling you since there is so much joking [that goes on] in txt."[17]

Part of the anxiety surrounding texting arises from its perceived tendency to disrupt protocols of recognition and accountability. Parents are disconnected from their children, who in turn defy parental authority. Cheating is symptomatic of the inability of teachers to monitor students' cell phone use. And the spread of rumors and gossip, along with irreverent jokes, means that the senders of messages readily give in to the compulsion to forward messages without, as the writers above advise, weighing their consequences or veracity. Indeed, it is the power to forward messages almost instantaneously that transforms the cell phone into a "weapon." The urge to retransmit messages is difficult to resist and, under certain conditions, irrepressible, as we learn from the events leading up to People Power II. Actor and writer Bart Guingona, who organized a demonstration at Edsa on 18 January, describes his initial doubts about the effectiveness of cell phones in a posting to the Plaridel listserv: "I was certain [texting] would not be taken seriously unless it was backed up by some kind of authority figure to give it some sort of legitimacy. A priest who was with us suggested that [the church-owned broadcasting station] Radio Veritas should get involved in disseminating the particulars. ... We [then] formulated a test message ... and sent it out that night and I turned off my phone. ... By the time I turned it on in the morning, the message had come back to me three times. ... I am now a firm believer in the power of the text!"[18]

The writer was initially hesitant to use texting, reasoning that messages sent this way would be perceived as groundless rumors. Anonymously circulated from phone to phone, the text seemed unanchored to any particular author who could be held accountable for its content. Only when the church-owned radio station offered to broadcast the same information did he agree to send a text message. Upon waking up the next day, he saw the effect of this transmission. Not only did his message reach distant others; it returned to him threefold. He is converted from a doubter to a believer in the "power of the text." Such power has to do with the capacity to elicit numerous replies.

There are two things worth noting, however, in this notion of the power of texting: first, that it requires, at least in the eyes of this writer and those he sends messages to, another power to legitimate the text's meaning; and second, that such a power is felt precisely in the multiple transmissions of the same text. The power of texting has less to do with the capacity to elicit interpretation and stir public debate than it does with compelling others to keep messages in circulation. Receiving a message, one responds by repeating it. The message is forwarded to others who are expected to do the same. In this way, the message returns, mechanically augmented but semantically unaltered. They crowd one's phone mailbox just as those who believed in the truth of the call they received crowded the streets of Metro Manila. On this account, the formation of crowds answers the repeated call of texts deemed to have legitimacy by virtue of being grounded in an authority outside the text messages themselves: the electronic voice of the Catholic Church. The voice of the church in effect domesticates the dangers associated with texting. Users forward texts and likewise feel forwarded by the expectations these texts give rise to. Finding themselves called by the message and its constant repetition, they become "believers," part of Generation Txt.

Generation Txt thus does not so much designate a new social identity as a desire for seeing in messages a meaning guaranteed by an unimpeachable source residing outside the text. In this sense, there is nothing very new or different about the technological fantasy. Most of those who gathered at Edsa and marched toward Mendiola—the road leading to the presidential palace—were united by anger at the corrupt regime of President Estrada and by their wish to replace him with a more honest leader. This said, the protesters challenged neither the nature of the state nor its class divisions. Indeed, everything I have read by supporters of People Power II emphasizes the constitutional legality of these protests and their institutional legitimacy vis-à-vis the Supreme Court and the Catholic Church (as opposed to the army or left-wing groups). In the end, Estrada's replacement came from within his own circle of power: Gloria Macapagal-Arroyo was his vice-president and the daughter of a previous Philippine president. It would appear then that Generation Txt comes out of what its "believers" claim to be a "technological revolution" that sets the question of social revolution aside.

Texting is thus "revolutionary" in a reformist sense. Its "politics" seeks to consolidate and render authority transparent, whether this is the authority of the state or of text messages. In an exemplary manifesto titled "Voice of Generation Txt" [Ting ng Generation Txt], which appeared in what was, until recently, one of Manila's more widely read tabloids, the *Pinoy Times,* Ederic Penallor Eder, a twenty-something University of the Philippines graduate, credits the "power" *(lakas)* of "our cellphones and computers" for contributing to the "explosion" of People Power II. Texting, he declares, became the medium through which "we" responded quickly to the "betrayal" *(kataksilan)* of the pro-Estrada senators who had sought to block the impeachment hearings. Elaborating on the "we" designating Generation Txt, Eder writes in Taglish:

> We are Generation Txt. Free, fun-loving, restless, insistent, hard-working, strong and patriotic.
>
> We warmly receive and embrace with enthusiasm the revolution in new technology. Isn't it said that the Philippines rules Cyberspace and that the Philippines is the text messaging capital of the world? Our response was rapid to

the betrayal of the eleven running dogs *(tuta)* of Jose Velarde (a.k.a. Joseph Estrada). The information and calls that reached us by way of text and e-mail were what brought together the organized as well as unorganized protests. From our homes, schools, dormitories, factories, churches, we poured into the streets there to continue the trial—the impeachment trial that had lost its meaning. …

Our wish is for an honest government, and a step towards this is the resignation of Estrada. We are patriotic and strong and with principles, since our coming together is not merely because we want to hang out with our friends, but rather to attain a truly free and clean society brought by our love for the Philippine nation. …

There were those from our generation that have long since before the second uprising chosen to struggle and fight in the hills and take up arms, trekking on the harsh road towards real change. Most of us, before and after the second uprising, can be found in schools, offices, or factories, going about our everyday lives. Dreaming, working hard for a future. Texting, internetting, entertaining ourselves in the present.

But when the times call, we are ready to respond. Again and again, we will use our youth and our gadgets *(gadyet)* to insure the freedom of our Motherland. … After the second uprising, we promise to militantly watch over the administration of Gloria Macapagal Arroyo while we happily push Asiong Salonga (a.k.a. Joseph Estrada) into the doors of prison.

We are Generation Txt.[19]

This statement of identity curiously enough does not specify the "we" except as those who "warmly accept and embrace" the "revolution" in new technology. The "we" is established through an identification with technological novelty and the status of the Philippines as the "text messaging" capital of the world. This is perhaps why the message reads as if it were meant to be received, then forwarded: it begins and ends with exactly the same lines: *Kami ang Generation Txt* (We are

Generation Txt). Instead of ideals or a critique of social relations, Generation Txt is characterized here by attitudes and affects: it is *malaya* (free), *masayahin* (fun-loving), *malikot* (restless), *makulit* (insistent), *masipag* (hardworking), and so forth. Its members pride themselves on having principles and courage, and, unlike the rudderless and Westernized Generation X, they have direction. They stand for "transparent" government and a "free" and "clean" society. In this sense, they do not see themselves as different from their elders: they are patriots *(makabayan)* dedicated to using their "gadgets" for the sake of the motherland *(Inang Bayan)*. Such commitment comes in the form of a "militant" readiness to watch over the workings of the new government in order to ensure "justice" *(katarungan)*. Unlike those who have chosen to take up arms and go to the mountains, Generation Txt can be found in schools, offices, and factories, ready to respond to the call of the times. They watch, they wait, and they are always ready to receive and forward messages.

Generation Txt is concerned not with challenging the structures of authority but with making sure they function to serve the country's needs. This reformist impetus is spelled out in terms of their demand for accountability and their intention of holding leaders under scrutiny. Through their gadgets, they keep watch over their leaders, rather than taking their place or putting forth other notions of leadership. Thus does Generation Txt conceptualize its historical agency: as speedy *(mabilis)* transmitters of calls *(panawagan)* that come from elsewhere and have the effect of calling out to those in their "homes, schools, dormitories, factories, churches" to flood the streets in protest. Rather than originate such calls, they are able to trace them to their destination, which, in this case, is the nation of middle-class citizens that seeks to renew and supervise its government. Like the first generation of bourgeois nationalists in the nineteenth century mentioned earlier, Generation Txt discovers yet again the fetish of technology as the capacity to seek access to, and recognition from, authority.[20]

NOTES

1. See the bundle entitled "Telefonos, 1885–1891" at the Philippine National Archives, Manila, for sketches of a plan to install a telephone system in the city as early as November 1885. By December 1885 an office of Telephone Communication had been established, and the first telephone station at Santa Lucia, Manila, was operational.

2. Jose Rizal, "Por Telefono" (Barcelona, 1889); reprinted in *Miscellaneous Writings* (Manila: R. Martinez and Sons, 1959) and in various other anthologies of Rizal's writings. For a more extended discussion of telegraphy and the formation of a wish for a lingua franca among the first generation of nationalists, see Vicente L. Rafael, "Translation and Revenge: Castilian and the Origins of Nationalism in the Philippines," in *The Places of History: Regionalism Revisited in Latin America,* ed. Doris Sommer (Durham, N.C.: Duke University Press, 1999).

3. For an elaboration of other modalities of these telecommunicative fantasies and their role in shaping nationalist consciousness, see Vicente L. Rafael, *White Love and Other Events in Philippines History* (Durham, N.C.: Duke University Press, 2000), especially chapters 4 and 8 on rumor and gossip as populist modes of communication in Philippine history.

4. For a useful collection of documents and newspaper articles relating to the corruption case against Estrada, see Sheila Coronel, ed., *Investigating Estrada: Millions, Mansions and Mistresses* (Metro Manila: Philippine Center for Investigative Journalism, 2000).

5. The quotations above come, respectively, from Uli Schmetzer, "Cell Phones Spurred Filipinos' Coup," *Chicago Tribune,* 22 January 2001; Ederic Penaflor Eder, "Tinig ng Generation Txt" [Voice of Generation Txt], *Pinoy Times,* 8 February 2001; and Malou Mangahas, "Text Messaging Comes of Age in the Philippines," *Reuters Technology News,* 28 January 2001.

6. Much of the information that follows was gathered from Wayne Arnold, "Manila's Talk of the Town Isn't Talk at All," *New York Times,* 5 July 2000, Cl; "Text Generation," special issue of *I: The Investigative Reporting Magazine* 8, no. 2 (April–June 2002), especially 14–21, 28–32; and Elvira Mata, *The Ultimate Text Book* (Quezon City: Philippine Center for Investigative Journalism, 2000), which is especially good for examples of the more common text messages that circulate among Filipino users.

7. For a succinct historical analysis of the Philippine state, see Benedict Anderson's "Cacique Democracy in the Philippines" in his book *The Spectre of Comparisons: Nationalism, Southeast Asia, and the World* (London: Verso, 1998). See also John Sidel, *Capital, Coercion, and Crime: Bossism in the Philippines* (Stanford, Calif.: Stanford University Press, 1999); and Paul D. Hutchcroft, *Booty Capitalism: The Politics of Banking in the Philippines* (Ithaca, N.Y.: Cornell University Press, 1998).

8. Technologies for monitoring cell phone use do exist, and there is some indication that the Philippine government is beginning to acquire them. It is doubtful, however, that cell phone surveillance technology was available to the Estrada administration. It is also not clear whether the current regime of Gloria Macapagal-Arroyo has begun or intends to monitor cell phone transmissions.

9. See Arnold, "Manila's Talk of the Town"; Mangahas, "Text Messaging Comes of Age"; and Schmetzer, "Cell Phones Spurred Filipinos' Coup." See also Leah Salterio, "Text Power in Edsa 2001," *Philippine Daily Inquirer* (hereafter indicated *PDI*), 22 January 2001, 25;

Conrado de Quiros, "Undiscovered Country," *PDI,* 7 February 2001, 8; and Michael L. Tan, "Taming the Cell Phone," *PDI,* 6 February 2001. However, the economic advantages of texting are limited. For example, any transmission across cell networks is expensive, so that calling or texting from a Globe phone to a Smart phone is rarely done. Indeed, the Department of Transportation and Communication (DOTC) had to intervene in late 1999 to get the two companies to improve interconnectivity and service as well as lower their costs.

10. This article was circulated on the listservs of various nongovernmental organizations in the Philippines and bore the title "Piny Lifestyle." I have no knowledge of the original source of this piece, so it exists in some ways like a forwarded text message. Thanks to Tina Cuyugan for forwarding this essay to me. All translations are mine unless otherwise indicated.

11. Arnold, "Manila's Talk of the Town."

12. Message posted by mrsarreal@aol.com, in Plaridel (plaridel_papers@egroups.com), 25 January 2001.

13. Arnold, "Manila's Talk of the Town"; see also Richard Lloyd Parr's untitled article on People Power II and cell phone use in the *Independent* (London), 23 January 2001.

14. Tan, "Taming the Cell Phone."

15. Tan, "Taming the Cell Phone"; De Quiros, "Undiscovered Country."

16. Arnold, "Manila's Talk of the Town."

17. These messages were forwarded by rnrsarreal@aol.com to the Plaridel discussion group (plaridel_papers@yahoogroups.com), 25 January 2001.

18. Bart Guingona, Plaridel (plaridel_papers@yahoogroups.com), 26 January 2001. Texting is widely credited with bringing about the rapid convergence of crowds at the Edsa Shrine within approximately seventy-five minutes of the abrupt halt of the Estrada impeachment trial on the evening of 16 January. Even prior to Cardinal Sin and former president Cory Aquino's appeal for people to converge at this hallowed site, it has been estimated that over 20,000 people had already arrived there, perhaps drawn by text messages they received. As Danny A. Gozo, an employee at Ayala Corporation, points out in his posting on Plaridel (plaridel_papers@yahoogroups.com), 23 January 2001, during the four days of People Power Globe Telecom reported an average of 42 million outgoing messages and roughly an equal number of incoming ones as well, while Smart Telecom reported over 70 million outgoing and incoming messages texted through their system per day. He observes enthusiastically that "the interconnectedness of people, both within the country and outside is a phenomenon unheard of before. It is changing the way that we live!"

19. Eder, "Tieing ng Generation Txt." The translation of this text is mine.

20. I owe this term to James T. Siegel, *Fetish, Recognition, Revolution* (Princeton, N.J.: Princeton University Press, 1997).

60

DO NOT KNOCK

Theodor Adorno

Technology is making gestures precise and brutal, and with them men. It expels from movements all hesitation, deliberation, civility. It subjects them to the implacable, as it were ahistorical demands of objects. Thus the ability is lost, for example, to close a door quietly and discreetly, yet firmly. Those of cars and refrigerators have to be slammed, others have the tendency to snap shut by themselves, imposing on those entering the bad manners of not looking behind them, not shielding the interior of the house which receives them. The new human type cannot be properly understood without awareness of what he is continuously exposed to from the world of things about him, even in his most secret innervations. What does it mean for the subject that there are no more casements windows to open, but only sliding frames to shove, not gentle latches but turnable handles, no forecourt, no doorstep before the street, no wall around the garden? And which driver is not tempted, merely by the power of his engine, to wipe out the vermin of the street, pedestrians, children and cyclists? The movements machines demand of their users already have the violent, hard-hitting, unresting jerkiness of Fascist maltreatment. Not least to blame for the withering of experience is the fact that things, under the law of pure functionality, assume a form that limits contact with them to mere operation, and tolerates no surplus, either in freedom of conduct or in autonomy of things, which would survive as the core of experience, because it is not consumed by the moment of action.

NOTE

Extracted from T. Adorno, *Minima Moralia,* trans. E.F.N. Jephcott (London: Verso, 1984), p. 40. Reprinted by permission of Verso Books.

ANNOTATED GUIDE TO FURTHER READING

In order to get a better sense of the connections between labor, design, and the affects of industrialization, there are several key texts that should be read. One of the first historians to deal with this complicated issue was E. P. Thompson, who, in *The Making of the English Working Class* (1963), set out to prove that social history could be better understood through a broader cultural analysis that assessed the history of laborers. Like Eric Hobsbawm's *Labouring Men: Studies in the History of Labour* (1964), Thompson's Marxist perspective contends that economic shifts, fostered by industrialization, formed new social classes in late eighteenth- and nineteenth-century England.

Other important sources that will help ground a better understanding of the Industrial Revolution include Thomas Ashton's *The Industrial Revolution: 1760–1830* (1968), which looks at this period as a time of social and economic progress in Great Britain, and M. J. Daunton's *Progress and Poverty: An Economic and Social History of Britain, 1700–1850* (1995), which assesses how England changed as a nation during this tumultuous era.

Historically, there have been a number of authors who consider labor and industrialization through the lens of empire. These writers contend that the Western European desire for empire building led to overseas trading and production, which were some of the world's first forays into global markets. The importance of imperialism to the industrial project cannot be ignored, and two classic texts that make these connections are J. A. Hobson's *Imperialism* (1902) and Vladimir Lenin's *Imperialism, the Highest Stage of Capitalism* (1916). Additionally, Hobsbawm's *Industry and Empire: From 1750 to the Present Day* (1968) provides a comprehensive examination of this enormous topic.

Industrialization changed design aesthetics, and there is a growing body of literature that focuses on industrial design. John Heskett's *Industrial Design* (1980) is a helpful reference source. Jeffrey Meikle's *Twentieth-Century Limited: Industrial Design in America* (1979), provides a survey of major designers in the United States and reveals why and how certain aesthetics thrived. Other design historians, such as Christina Cogdell in *Eugenic Design: Streamlining America in the 1930s* (2004), are now revising the standard take on industrialization and asking how race, gender, and sexuality played into cultural fantasies about the industrial aesthetics that emerged in the twentieth century. Additionally, Carma Gorman's *The Industrial Design Reader* (2003) provides primary sources on this topic. Finally, Daniel Bell's *The Coming of Post-Industrial Society: A Venture in Social Forecasting* (1973) is one of the first texts that predicted how our future would be less focused on material goods and more indebted to information and information systems.

There are countless books about new technology and its impact on design. Lewis Mumford's grand, and historically sweeping, *Technics and Civilization* (1934) assesses the power of the machine and its impact on society, especially in terms of the history of technology. Alan Trachtenberg's study, *Brooklyn Bridge: Fact and Symbol* (1965), is also a good example of a historical and cultural approach to the power of new technology. For a look at contemporary design and society in terms of new potentialities that can interrupt traditional stereotypes about gender and the body, The Cutting Edge Women's Research Group's *Desire by Design: Body, Territories and New Technologies* (1999) is a useful resource. Groups like The Cutting Edge, at the University of Westminster, envisage an exciting future in which design will offer possibilities never before imagined.

SECTION 6

DESIGN AND GLOBAL ISSUES

SECTION INTRODUCTION

Design transpires in an international arena. Since the world's resources are not divided equally, the globalization of design has led to concerns related to social justice and economic parity. Furthermore, the use and overuse of resources by those privileged few who have access to the world's financial prosperity has created a debate about sustainability, or the way in which design impacts the environment. Design, as the excerpts in this section contend, can either alleviate the problems associated with our global condition or ignore these predicaments, thus deepening our current economic and environmental crises.

Design has become a truly global concept. In a world where we can fly across the planet in less than twenty hours and communicate internationally via mobile phones and the Internet, design, as discussed in the first subsection in this section, has become more accessible. The old barriers are gone, and in their place are faster transactions that have altered our conceptions of culture and economics. If we think of globalization as the process whereby world markets become linked and interdependent, the ramifications of this world system, and its reliance on design, become apparent. In fact, the global marketplace has encouraged a type of group imagination where new forms of media, such as the type discussed in the virtual identity subsection (Section 4.1), have caused our global interconnectivity. This subsection specifically takes the idea of globalization into the realm of design and reveals that cities and nations are now working to brand themselves in relation to the global marketplace. Ironically, it is only by marking geography as unusual and different, in the face of an increasingly homogeneous world, that cities and nations can brand themselves to create identities that further economic success.

Globalization has led to enormous disparities, especially, as the subsection on Equality and Social Justice (6.2) details, in terms of economics. As the proliferation of design magazines and television shows makes evident, customized design is a privileged realm only available to the few. In fact, only two percent of the population works closely with architects to build new homes. Several of the authors here ask that culture get past the idea of only looking at design as the purview of the rich. Good design can create better living situations that are more affordable and more accessible to the masses. The readings here should be read in conjunction with the Ethics subsection (3.1), as these readings make it evident that our decisions around design issues affect others.

As the sections on Ethics and Politics make clear (Sections 3.1 and 3.3), design has implications that can create change beyond the designer's imagined conception of his or her product's impact, and the subsection on Sustainability (6.3) takes this important conversation further. Since design creates waste—think, for instance, of plastic water bottles—and the possibility for controlling waste—think, for instance, about designing recyclable uses for those water bottles—we need to assess how to better monitor and alter design's global footprint. There are ways to control design's over-reliance on producing waste. In fact, design has begun to embrace its inherent tension between constantly producing waste (all goods, after all, do create the future potential for more artificially constructed waste) and formulating new ways to enhance the environment's resilience. Our obsession with disposability and consumerism (see Section 4) has instituted a "throwaway" culture that can be changed with vigilance and a new approach toward ecology.

The things we make, the products we sell, and the processes in which design takes place all impact the future of the Earth. Tossing a plastic water bottle into a nonrecyclable bin in New York City can take up more landfill, create gasses that cause global warming, and end the life cycle of nonbiodegradable material that could be used by individuals in other parts of the world. The ethical and global implications of our throwaway culture may seem irrelevant on a local scale, but, as this section reveals, the global influence of our everyday decisions are becoming increasingly significant.

SECTION 6: DESIGN AND GLOBAL ISSUES

6.1: Globalization

INTRODUCTION

The process of globalization, identified as such in the 1980s, but begun with global explorations and colonization in the sixteenth century, continues to shape the world: politically, economically, technologically, socially, and culturally. Debate continues as to whether globalization homogenizes or leads to greater local autonomy, whether it internationalizes or Americanizes, whether it is a force of good or one of evil. There are no clear answers to these questions, but however we look at it, design is central to many aspects of globalization, in production, markets, economies, and symbolic roles. In this subsection three writers provide perspectives on design and the global context.

Arjun Appadurai begins with a strategy for addressing the disjunctures between global economy, culture, and politics. His concept of scapes provides contemporary frameworks for examining the relationship between global cultural flows, beyond the limitations of national or cultural stereotypes, which he calls ethnoscapes, mediascapes, technoscapes, financescapes, and ideoscapes, all of which to some extent depend on and impact design. These frameworks structure a global economy in which Marx's commodity fetishism has been replaced by production fetishism and fetishism of the consumer. Fetishism with production obscures the increasingly transnational forces that drive that process. They compound Marx's concept of alienation (see Section 3.3), which is now "increasingly global" and involves also the consumer, who has lost real agency to the global processes of production. Appadurai emphasizes that the globalization of culture is not the same as its homogenization but involves many of the same instruments. In this process design is complicit, as both a facilitator and as an outcome.

But can and should we then speak of "global design"? This question is discussed by Hugh Aldersey-Williams in the second reading. At the time he was writing, in the early 1990s, Williams notes how global design had no clear definition in terms of function or of style. It should not, for example, be confused with the principles of universal design mentioned in Section 6.2 by John Hockenberry. According to Aldersey-Williams, global design "is nothing more than good old-fashioned functionalism decked out in softer shapes and brighter colors." It is more often a misnomer for global *branding*, and specifically for brands from America or other economically, technologically, and politically dominant nation states (see also Jenß's essay in Section 4.3). Yet the fear that as a result of such corporate ventures national cultures would converge, aired in the 1970s, has not come to pass. In fact design has become more reflective of national and cultural identities, proving Erskine Childers's assertion of the designer's pivotal role in the affirmation of cultural identities.

Evidence of this is referred to in the third reading as the "Barcelona paradigm." Guy Julier considers the positive role of design interventions in the urban regeneration of Barcelona and in the region of Catalonia prior to the 1992 Olympics as an example of how the development of European regionalism had allowed for the retrieval of a local identity. Barcelona became recognized globally through a "branding of place," where design culture was developed successfully through the collaboration of designers and other interested parties in a shared mission. The local was designed and presented for recognition and consumption at a global level. But opinions vary as to the propriety of such initiatives. Scholars have argued that such exercises in branding can only reinforce generalized and banal values, as opposed to the nuances that constitute the culture of any city, region, or nation. We can compare the success, or otherwise, of Wolff Olins's positioning of new Britain as "Cool Britannia." Is the nation, city, or region any longer the appropriate vehicle through which to address the cultural diversity that it would typically comprise in a globalized world?

Julier returns us to Appadurai's scapes as an alternative way of addressing global cultural flows. It can be argued that it is the role of designers to reflect the complexities of what actually exists, while recognizing also that they can have the authority to design or brand a place or a product with the purpose of projecting a defined concept within a larger global imaginary.

61

MODERNITY AT LARGE

Arjun Appadurai

The new global cultural economy has to be seen as a complex, overlapping, disjunctive order that cannot any longer be understood in terms of existing center–periphery models (even those that might account for multiple centers and peripheries). Nor is it susceptible to simple models of push and pull (in terms of migration theory), or of surpluses and deficits (as in traditional models of balance of trade), or of consumers and producers (as in most neo-Marxist theories of development). Even the most complex and flexible theories of global development that have come out of the Marxist tradition (Amin 1980; Mandel 1978; Wallerstein 1974; Wolf 1982) are inadequately quirky and have failed to come to terms with what Scott Lash and John Urry have called disorganized capitalism (1987). The complexity of the current global economy has to do with certain fundamental disjunctures between economy, culture, and politics that we have only begun to theorize.[1]

I propose that an elementary framework for exploring such disjunctures is to look at the relationship among five dimensions of global cultural flows that can be termed (a) *ethnoscapes,* (b) *mediascapes,* (c) *technoscapes,* (d) *financescapes,* and (e) *ideoscapes.*[2] The suffix *-scape* allows us to point to the fluid, irregular shapes of these landscapes, shapes that characterize international capital as deeply as they do international clothing styles. These terms with the common suffix *-scape* also indicate that these are not objectively given relations that look the same from every angle of vision but, rather, that they are deeply perspectival constructs, inflected by the historical, linguistic, and political situatedness of different sorts of actors: nation-states, multinationals, diasporic communities, as well as subnational groupings and movements (whether religious, political, or economic), and even intimate face-to-face groups, such as villages, neighborhoods, and families. Indeed, the individual actor is the last locus of this perspectival set of landscapes, for these landscapes are eventually navigated by agents who both experience and constitute larger formations, in part from their own sense of what these landscapes offer.

These landscapes thus are the building blocks of what (extending Benedict Anderson) I would like to call *imagined worlds,* that is, the multiple worlds that are constituted by the historically situated imaginations of persons and groups spread around the globe. An important fact of the world we live in today is that many persons on the globe live in such imagined worlds (and not just in imagined communities) and thus are able to contest and sometimes even subvert the imagined worlds of the official mind and of the entrepreneurial mentality that surround them.

By *ethnoscape,* I mean the landscape of persons who constitute the shifting world in which we live: tourists, immigrants, refugees, exiles, guest workers, and other moving groups and individuals constitute an essential feature of the world and appear to affect the politics of (and between) nations to a hitherto unprecedented degree.

This is not to say that there are no relatively stable communities and networks of kinship, friendship, work, and leisure, as well as of birth, residence, and other filial forms. But it is to say that the warp of these stabilities is everywhere shot through with the woof of human motion, as more persons and groups deal with the realities of having to move or the fantasies of wanting to move. What is more, both these realities and fantasies now function on larger scales, as men and women from villages in India think not just of moving to Poona or Madras but of moving to Dubai and Houston, and refugees from Sri Lanka find themselves in South India as well as in Switzerland, just as the Hmong are driven to London as well as to Philadelphia. And as international capital shifts its needs, as production and technology generate different needs, as nation-states shift their policies on refugee populations, these moving groups can never afford to let their imaginations rest too long, even if they wish to.

By *technoscape,* I mean the global configuration, also ever fluid, of technology and the fact that technology, both high and low, both mechanical and informational, now moves at high speeds across various kinds of previously impervious boundaries. Many countries now are the roots of multinational enterprise: a huge steel complex in Libya may involve interests from India, China, Russia, and Japan, providing different components of new technological configurations. The odd distribution of technologies, and thus the peculiarities of these technoscapes, are increasingly driven not by any obvious economies of scale, of political control, or of market rationality but by increasingly complex relationships among money flows, political possibilities, and the availability of both un- and highly skilled labor. So, while India exports waiters and chauffeurs to Dubai and Sharjah, it also exports software engineers to the United States—indentured briefly to Tata-Burroughs or the World Bank, then laundered through the State Department to become wealthy resident aliens, who are in turn objects

of seductive messages to invest their money and know-how in federal and state projects in India.

The global economy can still be described in terms of traditional indicators (as the World Bank continues to do) and studied in terms of traditional comparisons (as in Project Link at the University of Pennsylvania), but the complicated technoscapes (and the shifting ethnoscapes) that underlie these indicators and comparisons are further out of the reach of the queen of social sciences than ever before. How is one to make a meaningful comparison of wages in Japan and the United States or of real-estate costs in New York and Tokyo, without taking sophisticated account of the very complex fiscal and investment flows that link the two economies through a global grid of currency speculation and capital transfer?

Thus it is useful to speak as well of *finance-scapes,* as the disposition of global capital is now a more mysterious, rapid, and difficult landscape to follow than ever before, as currency markets, national stock exchanges, and commodity speculations move megamonies through national turnstiles at blinding speed, with vast, absolute implications for small differences in percentage points and time units. But the critical point is that the global relationship among ethnoscapes, technoscapes, and financescapes is deeply disjunctive and profoundly unpredictable because each of these landscapes is subject to its own constraints and incentives (some political, some informational, and some technoenvironmental), at the same time as each acts as a constraint and a parameter for movements in the others. Thus, even an elementary model of global political economy must take into account the deeply disjunctive relationships among human movement, technological flow, and financial transfers.

Further refracting these disjunctures (which hardly form a simple, mechanical global infrastructure in any case) are what I call *mediascapes* and *ideoscapes,* which are closely related landscapes of images. *Mediascapes* refer both to the distribution of the electronic capabilities to produce and disseminate information (newspapers, magazines, television stations, and film-production studios), which are now available to a growing number of private and public interests throughout the world, and to the images of the world created by these media. These images involve many complicated inflections, depending on their mode (documentary or entertainment), their hardware (electronic or preelectronic), their audiences (local, national, or transnational), and the interests of those who own and control them. What is most important about these mediascapes is that they provide (especially in their television, film, and cassette forms) large and complex repertoires of images, narratives, and ethnoscapes to viewers throughout the world, in which the world of commodities and the world of news and politics are profoundly mixed. What this means is that many audiences around the world experience the media themselves as a complicated and interconnected repertoire of print, celluloid, electronic screens, and billboards. The lines between the realistic and the fictional landscapes they see are blurred, so that the farther away these audiences are from the direct experiences of metropolitan life, the more likely they are to construct imagined worlds that are chimerical, aesthetic, even fantastic objects, particularly if assessed by the criteria of some other perspective, some other imagined world.

Mediascapes, whether produced by private or state interests, tend to be image-centered, narrative-based accounts of strips of reality, and what they offer to those who experience and transform them is a series of elements (such as characters, plots, and textual forms) out of which scripts can be formed of imagined lives, their own as well as those of others living in other places. These scripts can and do get disaggregated into complex sets of metaphors by which people live (Lakoff and Johnson 1980) as they help to constitute narratives of the other and protonarratives of possible lives, fantasies that could become prolegomena to the desire for acquisition and movement.

Ideoscapes are also concatenations of images, but they are often directly political and frequently have to do with the ideologies of states and the counterideologies of movements explicitly oriented to capturing state power or a piece of it. These ideoscapes are composed of elements of the Enlightenment worldview, which consists of a chain of ideas, terms, and images, including *freedom, welfare, rights, sovereignty, representation,* and the master term *democracy.* The master narrative of the Enlightenment (and its many variants in Britain, France, and the United States) was constructed with a certain internal logic and presupposed a certain relationship between reading, representation, and the public sphere. (For the dynamics of this process in the early history of the United States, see Warner 1990.) But the diaspora of these terms and images across the world, especially since the nineteenth century, has loosened the internal coherence that held them together in a Euro-American master narrative and provided instead a loosely structured synopticon of politics, in which different nation-states, as part of their evolution, have organized their political cultures around different keywords (e.g., Williams 1976).

As a result of the differential diaspora of these keywords, the political narratives that govern communication between elites and followers in different parts of the world involve problems of both a semantic and pragmatic nature: semantic to the extent that words (and their lexical equivalents) require careful translation from context to context in their global movements, and pragmatic to the extent that the use of these words by political actors and their audiences may be subject to very different sets of contextual conventions that mediate their translation into public politics. Such conventions are not only matters of the nature of political rhetoric: for example, what does the aging Chinese leadership mean when it refers to the dangers of hooliganism? What does the South Korean leadership mean when it speaks of discipline as the key to democratic industrial growth?

These conventions also involve the far more subtle question of what sets of communicative genres are valued in what way (newspapers versus cinema, for example) and what sorts of pragmatic genre conventions govern the collective readings of different kinds of text. So, while an Indian audience may be attentive to the resonances of a political speech in terms of some keywords and phrases reminiscent of Hindi cinema, a Korean audience may respond to the subtle codings of Buddhist or neo-Confucian rhetoric encoded in a political document. The very relationship of reading to hearing and seeing may vary in important ways that determine the morphology of these different ideoscapes as they shape themselves in different national and transnational contexts. This globally variable synaesthesia has hardly even been noted, but it demands urgent analysis. Thus *democracy* has clearly become a master term, with powerful echoes from Haiti and Poland to the former Soviet Union and China, but it sits at the center of a variety of ideoscapes, composed of distinctive pragmatic configurations of rough translations of other central terms from the vocabulary of the Enlightenment. This creates ever new terminological kaleidoscopes, as states (and the groups that seek to capture them) seek to pacify populations whose own ethnoscapes are in motion and whose mediascapes may create severe problems for the ideoscapes with which they are presented. The fluidity of ideoscapes is complicated in particular by the growing diasporas (both voluntary and involuntary) of intellectuals who continuously inject new meaning-streams into the discourse of democracy in different parts of the world.

[…]

But the relationship between the cultural and economic levels of this new set of global disjunctures is not a simple one-way street in which the terms of global cultural politics are set wholly by, or confined wholly within, the vicissitudes of international flows of technology, labor, and finance, demanding only a modest modification of existing neo-Marxist models of uneven development and state formation. There is a deeper change, itself driven by the disjunctures

among all the landscapes I have discussed and constituted by their continuously fluid and uncertain interplay, that concerns the relationship between production and consumption in today's global economy. Here, I begin with Marx's famous (and often mined) view of the fetishism of the commodity and suggest that this fetishism has been replaced in the world at large (now seeing the world as one large, interactive system, composed of many complex subsystems) by two mutually supportive descendants, the first of which I call production fetishism and the second, the fetishism of the consumer.

By *production fetishism* I mean an illusion created by contemporary transnational production loci that masks translocal capital, transnational earning flows, global management, and often faraway workers (engaged in various kinds of high-tech putting-out operations) in the idiom and spectacle of local (sometimes even worker) control, national productivity, and territorial sovereignty. To the extent that various kinds of free-trade zones have become the models for production at large, especially of high-tech commodities, production has itself become a fetish, obscuring not social relations as such but the relations of production, which are increasingly transnational. The locality (both in the sense of the local factory or site of production and in the extended sense of the nation-state) becomes a fetish that disguises the globally dispersed forces that actually drive the production process. This generates alienation (in Marx's sense) twice intensified, for its social sense is now compounded by a complicated spatial dynamic that is increasingly global.

As for the *fetishism of the consumer,* I mean to indicate here that the consumer has been transformed through commodity flows (and the mediascapes, especially of advertising, that accompany them) into a sign, both in Baudrillard's sense of a simulacrum that only asymptotically approaches the form of a real social agent, and in the sense of a mask for the real seat of agency, which is not the consumer but the producer and the many forces that constitute production. Global advertising is the key technology for the worldwide dissemination of a plethora of creative and culturally well-chosen ideas of consumer agency. These images of agency are increasingly distortions of a world of merchandising so subtle that the consumer is consistently helped to believe that he or she is an actor, where in fact he or she is at best a chooser.

The globalization of culture is not the same as its homogenization, but globalization involves the use of a variety of instruments of homogenization (armaments, advertising techniques, language hegemonies, and clothing styles) that are absorbed into local political and cultural economies, only to be repatriated as heterogeneous dialogues of national sovereignty, free enterprise, and fundamentalism in which the state plays an increasingly delicate role: too much openness to global flows, and the nation-state is threatened by revolt, as in the China syndrome; too little, and the state exits the international stage, as Burma, Albania, and North Korea in various ways have done. In general, the state has become the arbitrageur of this repatriation of *difference* (in the form of goods, signs, slogans, and styles). But this repatriation or export of the designs and commodities of difference continuously exacerbates the internal politics of majoritarianism and homogenization, which is most frequently played out in debates over heritage.

Thus the central feature of global culture today is the politics of the mutual effort of sameness and difference to cannibalize one another and thereby proclaim their successful hijacking of the twin Enlightenment ideas of the triumphantly universal and the resiliently particular. This mutual cannibalization shows its ugly face in riots, refugee flows, state-sponsored torture, and ethnocide (with or without state support). Its brighter side is in the expansion of many individual horizons of hope and fantasy, in the global spread of oral rehydration therapy and other low-tech instruments of well-being, in the susceptibility even of South Africa to the force

of global opinion, in the inability of the Polish state to repress its own working classes, and in the growth of a wide range of progressive, transnational alliances. Examples of both sorts could be multiplied. The critical point is that both sides of the coin of global cultural process today are products of the infinitely varied mutual contest of sameness and difference on a stage characterized by radical disjunctures between different sorts of global flows and the uncertain landscapes created in and through these disjunctures.

NOTES

Extracted from A. Appadurai, *Modernity at Large: Cultural Dimensions of Globalization* (Minneapolis: University of Minnesota Press, 1996), pp. 32–37 and 41–43. Copyright, 1990, Duke University Press. All rights reserved. Used by permission of the publisher.

1. One major exception is Fredric Jameson, whose work on the relationship between postmodernism and late capitalism has in many ways inspired this essay. The debate between Jameson and Aijaz Ahmad in *Social Text,* however, shows that the creation of a globalizing Marxist narrative in cultural matters is difficult territory indeed (Jameson 1986; Ahmad 1987). My own effort in this context is to begin a restructuring of Marxist narrative (by stressing lags and disjunctures) that many Marxists might find abhorrent. Such a restructuring has to avoid the dangers of obliterating difference in the Third World, eliding the social referent (as some French postmodernists seem inclined to do), and retaining the narrative authority of the Marxist tradition, in favor of greater attention to global fragmentation, uncertainty, and difference.

2. The idea of *ethnoscape* is more fully engaged in chap. 3.

62

GLOBALISM, NATIONALISM, AND DESIGN

Hugh Aldersley-Williams

Ask designers what they think "global design" is, and the impulsive answer often comes back in a torrent of familiar brand names, with the likes of McDonald's and Coca-Cola high on the list. These brands are indeed global in their reach: Coca-Cola topped the 1990 "ImagePower" survey conducted by the San Francisco-based corporate identity consultants, Landor Associates. McDonald's ranked eighth and Pepsi tenth in this measurement of the recognition of international brands.[1]

Yet their products are not "designed." Despite the fact that they are prepared in many localities, their appearance and the appearance of the companies that make them are effective in suggesting their American origins. The products of The Walt Disney Company, which ranked fifth in the Landor league table, not only reflect their American origins but are also generally made in America. This, then, is not global design but global distribution of a national product.

[…]

Most global products reflect nothing more profound than the power of their manufacturers. Global food and drink is American food and drink. Global movies are Hollywood movies, despite the fact that the environment and behavior they portray is patently alien to much of their audience. Global electronics goods are Japanese electronics goods. The world's luxury items are French luxury items, and so on.

[…]

It is small wonder that globalism and globalization have become an obsession in business and culture alike. Since the Second World War, our lives have been transformed in many ways that appear to diminish the importance of national borders. Trade between nations has multiplied by a factor of thirteen since 1950.[2] The effect of technologies—not least the technology of war—has served to bring communities closer together. Nuclear annihilation threatens us all. The media have an ever-greater reach. People are more mobile. Capital is held internationally and, as a consequence, economic and political events in one country affect those in another more than ever before. The French essayist Paul Ricoeur coined the term "mondialization" to reflect this growing interdependence, observing that "the foreign policy of every country has become the domestic policy of humanity."[3]

There is a moral argument in favor of globalization, although this aspect of the matter does not appear to have detained the globalists of the business world. Throughout modern history there have been utopian thinkers who have wished for the dissolution of national boundaries. For their part, designers are often people of a liberal cast of mind who are inclined to believe that national borders are invidious things. Their dilemma is that they do not wish to abet the emergence of narrow political nationalism through design that celebrates national cultures, but neither have they seen much to inspire them in the only apparent alternative of global design. Ricoeur states the paradox succinctly in his essay "Universal Civilization and National Cultures": "The phenomenon of universalization, while being an advancement of mankind, at the same time constitutes a sort of subtle destruction, not only of traditional cultures, which might not be an irreparable wrong, but also of ... the creative nucleus of great cultures."[4]

The designers' dilemma becomes more pressing as it becomes more apparent that global design will not sweep all before it. The supposition made in the 1970s by Theodore Levitt and other business theorists that national tastes and cultures would converge, does not appear to be coming true. People's habits of eating, drinking, washing, working, and playing remain distinct. Thus, the products that help them do these things will and should continue to reflect the different ways they do them from country to country, even if many manufacturers would rather they did not.

[...]

Although "global design" has its adherents and its detractors, little thought appears to have been given to a working definition of the phrase. It is not clear what it means in terms of either function or style. The protagonists of global design cited here produce work that is solidly rooted in the tradition of the Bauhaus and Ulm schools. Platonic geometry dominates the form. The function is generally transparent. Decoration is kept to a minimum, although colors are bright. The use of simple shapes rounded off with large radii is well suited to the process by which molded plastic parts are produced in large numbers. It would seem that in stylistic terms global design is nothing more than good old-fashioned functionalism decked out in softer shapes and brighter colors.

Ostensibly, globalists are more sensitive than centralized multinationals to local requirements. According to Ohmae: "A global corporation today is fundamentally different from the colonial-style multinationals of the 1960s and 1970s. It serves its customers in all key markets with equal dedication."[5] This statement is disingenuous, and many people in those markets would disagree with it. Just because the

dedication is "equal" does not mean it is absolute or sufficient for all customers in all markets or even for most customers in any market.

Ohmae describes five stages through which a corporation evolves to become "genuinely global." Stages one and two involve the export of its products, first through local distributors and then through its own agencies. In stage three, the company also begins to locate some manufacturing, marketing, and sales activity in the countries to which it exports. By stage four, the company has become an insider, undertaking local research and development, design, and engineering, which allows it "to replicate in a new environment the hardware, systems and operational approaches that have worked so well at home."[6] In stage five, companies must devolve all operations, relying on a network of local managers sharing the same corporate culture. Says Ohmae: "Moving to stage five is another matter entirely. What is called for is what Akio Morita of Sony has termed global localization, a new orientation that looks in both directions. At base the problem is psychological, a question of values.

"Before national identity, before local affiliation, before German ego or Italian ego or Japanese ego, comes the commitment to a single, unified global mission."[7]

[...]

There is no doubt that design that pays closer heed to national cultural identity is growing in importance as designers begin to voice their concern that global design is not all to the good. The Internationales Forum für Gestaltung Ulm—a foundation that seeks to revive the spirit of the city's famous design school—held a conference and workshop on the subject in September 1989. The unspoken aim was to reconcile the conflicting views on the importance of, and prospects for, the expression of cultural identity in design of the peripatetic capitalists of the international design community on the one hand and the sandaled saviors of the culturally oppressed on the other. It came as no great surprise that little common ground had been established by the end of the seminar.

For the latter camp, Erskine Childers, a director of the United Nations Development Program, set the tone in a keynote address that set out the aims of the UNESCO Decade for Cultural Development (1988–97), one of which is the "affirmation of cultural identities." Worryingly, Childers appeared to advocate a kind of protectionism for vulnerable cultures, but he also recognized that cultural renewal can and must happen in the context of the overlapping and cross-pollinating network of cultures that has arisen from growth in media and personal mobility. With regard to this second, and more significant, process of cultural affirmation, Childers issued a call to arms: "The designer emerges as having a far more pivotal role than has generally been realized. If we look along the entire sequence of effort involved in modern living, it is in fact the design profession that provides the essential links in the chain."[8]

The power of the designer to affirm cultural identity is an unknown quantity. Many designers are confused both about the nature of cultural identity and about whether and how to express it in their work. Some clearly believe there is no such thing. Interviewed on the occasion of the "Triad Design Project" exhibition of the Design Management Institute, for example, Arnold Wasserman, vice president of industrial design at Unisys, listed some design stereotypes: "If you want rigor, you go to German designers. If you want flair, you go to Italians. If you want Zen intuitions about people's needs and desires, it's the Japanese. For tail fins, go to American designers." But he added, "These stereotypes are absolutely wrong."[9]

Although these stereotypes may be of little interest to Unisys, the one thing they are not is absolutely wrong. The design globalists, including Wasserman and the Design Management Institute, may wish that stereotypes did not exist because they disrupt their commercial world order, but by definition they are never absolutely wrong.

[...]

Nevertheless, it is the nation—and in the context of design and other commercial activities, this means the nation-state—that remains the principal designator of cultural character. Although the existence of a national border is not a sufficient proof of the presence of a nation (how did that border come to be drawn?), the facts of political, economic, and commercial life often give that border a disproportionate weight. Regions are effectively transformed into nations (Lombardy, the economic powerhouse around Milan, represents Italy as a whole, for example) and nations into regions (the Benelux countries; Canada as a province of the United States). When a nation's design industry is located almost entirely within a region, as is the case in Catalonia and Lombardy, it is already hard to say whether its output is a fairer reflection of national character or of that region's character, which becomes the national character by default.

The nation-state seems likely to persist despite the ever-greater integration and interdependence of national economies. Indeed, its importance may be growing as pan-national political ideologies such as communism go into decline. As *The Economist* points out, "Unless the nation-state fails to satisfy its other purposes as well—defence, social identification, rule-making—the global economy will not be in a position to pronounce its obituary."[10] And if the nation-state survives because it can offer these securites, national identity will doubtless continue to be more important than the identity either of larger regions invented for economic convenience or of small subnational communities. In addition, design has been more closely linked with the nation-state than other creative pursuits. Design is promoted by national organizations, and in exhibitions and published works it is frequently pigeonholed by nation.

Although it is the nation-state upon which cultural identity in design centers, all nation-states are not equal. Some small or strongly focused nations (the Netherlands, France, Japan, for example) display a relatively cohesive national identity through their design. Others, too large, too diffuse, or too divided (the United States, India, the Soviet Union, Yugoslavia) cannot. The problem of defining and exploiting a national design character varies greatly among the more homogeneous nations (Japan,

Korea, Denmark), the melting pots (the United States, the Netherlands, Great Britain), the multicultural societies (Canada, India), and the city-states (Singapore, Hong Kong) (see Table 62.1.)

A further obstacle to the promotion of national design is its unavoidable association with political nationalism. The link or potential link between cultural identity (virtually unquestioned as

Table 62.1 Estimated evolution of national competitive development since 1945 (from Porter). The table has been adapted to suggest the character of the design that emerges from each manufacturing regime. The entries above the horizontal rule are from Porter. Entries for other countries are added.

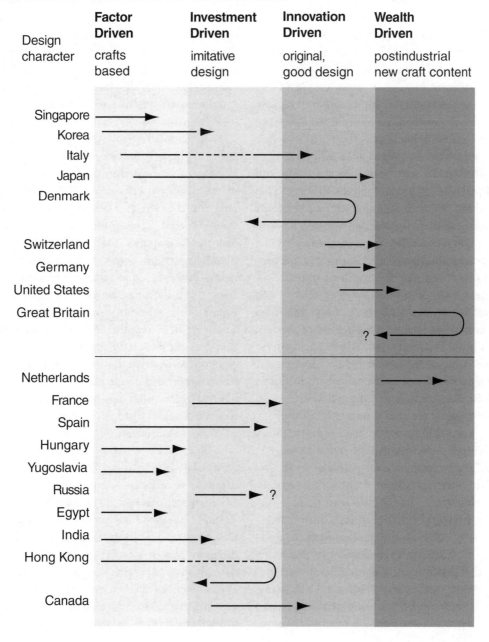

"a good thing") in design and the resurgence of nationalism in many corners of the world ("a bad thing") cannot be denied. In this regard, it might be said that designers believe in nations but not in the borders that separate them.

Nationalism per se need not be a bad thing, however. In the first half of the nineteenth century, nationalism had a positive connotation at a time of free-trade mercantilism. It was only in the twentieth century that trade suffered in proportion to the rise of more dangerous forms of nationalism accompanied by protectionism and a resistance to progress and modernity.

It is conceivable that the expression of national cultural identities by design could prove instrumental to the emergence of benign new nationalisms. This is not to say that a national style (or styles) would be applicable to all products or even to most products, but it could renew and enrich national cultures if applied to some types of product. Such nationalisms would have to be compatible with technological progress and with free-trade practices. They could encourage product diversity, stimulate market demand, and perhaps even do a little to improve mutual understanding among the peoples of different nations and cultures. They would not be incompatible with the "mondialization" in other realms of modern life. In his book, *Nations and Nationalism*, Ernest Gellner writes, "The nationalist principle can be asserted in an ethical, 'universalistic' spirit. There could be, and on occasion there have been, nationalists-in-the-abstract, unbiased in favor of any special nationality of their own, and generously preaching the doctrine for all nations alike: let all nations have their own political roofs, and let all of them also refrain from including non-nationals under it. There is no formal contradiction in asserting such non-egoistic nationalism. As a doctrine it can be supported by some good arguments, such as the desirability of preserving cultural diversity, of a pluralistic international political system, and of the diminution of internal strains within states. ... Late industrial society (if mankind is spared long enough to enjoy it) can be expected to be one in which nationalism persists, but in a muted, less virulent form."[11]

[Eric] Hobsbawm believes that nationalism, for all its prominence, is of less historical importance now than it has been in the past: "It is no longer, as it were, a global political programme, as it may be said to have been in the nineteenth and earlier twentieth centuries. It is at most a complicating factor, or a catalyst for other developments." He illustrates his argument with reference to the Catalans, whose "culture flourishes, but on the tacit assumption that it is Catalans who will communicate with the rest of the world through Spanish and English, since few non-residents in Catalonia will be able to communicate in the local language."[12]

Such nationalism may no longer serve much political purpose, but it could contribute materially to company performance. Against the tide of multinational commerce and global business talk, the concern of a few designers to protect their national styles could seem romantic and forlorn. Reassurance that such thinking is not merely nostalgic comes from Michael Porter in his book *The Competitive Advantage of Nations:* "The globalization of industries and the internationalization of companies leaves us with a paradox. It is tempting to conclude that the nation has lost its role in the international success of its firms. Companies, at first glance, seem to have transcended countries. Yet ... differences in national economic structures, values, cultures, institutions, and histories contribute profoundly to competitive success."[13]

[...]

What is true of the role of the nation in the dry matters of business must surely be truer still where the cultural ingredient is stronger. There are or have been at various times strong regional and national identities in music and architecture, for example. Design is where culture and commerce meet. If these other arts and those businesses that Porter describes can continue to show national and regional characteristics—and, in the global village, to trade upon them—then surely design can too.

It might be said that this is nationalism as sideshow. Stripped of its political purpose, can this nationalism serve any purpose other than to provide trading companies with a spurious means of differentiating themselves from their competitors? At worst, the expression of national character could become no more profound than the nation-themed village sets at Disneyworld. But it has a more worthy potential. If pursued with sufficient skill and vigor, national design could begin to restore to artifacts some of the meaning they have lost as societies have become more secular, more industrialized, and more intertwined.

It is in the context of these developments, for example, that Loek van der Sande of Global Design in the Netherlands, a former president of the International Council of Societies for Industrial Design, is able to remark that "culture is the world commodity of the twenty-first century."[14] In the seventeenth and eighteenth centuries, he argues, wealth was determined by access to natural resources, and in the nineteenth and twentieth centuries it came through the ability to manufacture goods and control the money and credit supply. In the future, he believes, national character will become a tradeable resource. Although his comment sounds cynical at first, it quickly becomes apparent that there is no other course. Cultures do not grow in a vacuum. For the expression of cultural identity to survive in any valid sense, it must acknowledge, and indeed swim with, the powerful tides that engulf it. As Porter notes: "National differences in character and culture, far from being threatened by global competition, prove integral to success in it."[15]

The view of culture as a commodity gains credibility upon closer consideration of what a designer is called upon to do. Different sets of factors bear on work done in different creative fields. The composer of music has a fairly free hand in determining the character of his or her work. An architect, on the other hand, has less creative autonomy and is bound by factors of teamwork, raw materials, and a building's context. In design, the character of the individual is important at one level, as it is in all creative acts. National character

may be important, too. But for a designer, other factors are often present, such as the collective character or house style of the company where he or she works and the character or "corporate culture" of clients. It would be foolish to say that a given design was 20 percent individual, 50 percent corporate, and 30 percent national, but clearly an immigrant designer working as part of a multinational team in close cooperation with a foreign client's engineering department to create, say, a piece of medical equipment is subject to a very different mix of cultural ingredients from a single designer collaborating with a local craftsperson on a glass vase.

Central to this issue is the question of how much of each design may be the product of an individual's creative psyche and how much is the result of education, working and living environment, peers, magazines, and all the other unavoidable clutter of national and international influences. One possible clue as to the balance between the personal and the contextual is provided by an examination of the few works published on design exclusively by women. It is difficult to discern any consistent quality of these designs that distinguishes them from designs by men. All other things being equal, one would surely expect more difference between women's and men's design than between the design of country X and country Y. If no difference is discernible in this case, one might conclude that circumstantial and traditional factors in design creativity are powerful in relation to individual temperament.

Matters are further complicated because national, corporate, studio, and individual identities are not mutually exclusive. They overlap and distort one another. A good studio will influence a designer's individual technique; a powerful client will, to some extent, determine the character of the work of the studio it employs. Nationality bears on the character of client, studio, and individual alike.

The traditional pattern, which predates the establishment of the design profession, is that of a local artisan creating a product for local use. Many designers today still frequently work for local clients who will sell their products primarily on the domestic market. However, the patchwork nature of cultural identities in the modern world is making more complex patterns commonplace. Increasingly, more than one nationality is involved in the design process.

[...]

But to what degree should designers act as chameleons, adopting regional or national style characteristics other than their own simply for the gratification of themselves or their clients? The apparent deceptiveness of some examples of national design need not detract from their validity. Composers have proved adept at writing music in the style of countries other than their own. The execution of contextual and new vernacular architecture is not restricted to local architects. In design, one need look no further than to the Frenchman Raymond Loewy, who created some of America's most distinctive icons, or to David Lewis, the Englishman who has helped make Bang and Olufsen a paragon of Danish design. As Hobsbawm points out, "more often than not the discovery of popular tradition and its transformation into the 'national tradition' of some peasant people forgotten by history was the work of enthusiasts from the (foreign) ruling class or elite, such as the Baltic Germans or the Finnish Swedes."[16]

[...]

The consciousness and perception of cultural identity vary greatly from country to country, as does the perceived need to reinforce or reinvent that identity.

NOTES

Extracted from H. Aldersey-Williams, "Globalism, Nationalism, and Design," in *World Design Nationalism and Globalism in Design* (New York: Rizzoli, 1992), pp. 8–17. Used with permission from Rizzoli International Publications, Inc.

1. "Europe Resists Global Brands," *Design Week* (September 21, 1990): 6.
2. "The State of the Nation-State," *The Economist* (December 22, 1990): 73.
3. Paul Ricoeur, "From Nation to Humanity: Task of Christians" in *Political and Social Essays by Paul Ricoeur,* David Stewart and Joseph Bien, eds. (Ohio University Press, 1974).
4. ———, *History and Truth,* trans. Charles A. Kelbley (Northwestern University Press, 1965).
5. Kenichi Ohmae, *The Borderless World* (Harper Business, 1990).
6. Ibid.
7. Ohmae, *The Borderless World.*
8. "Design and Cultural Identity," Internationales Forum für Gestaltung, Hochschule für Gestaltung, Ulm, Germany, September 1989.
9. Jane Holtz Kay, "Analyzing Success Stories of Products," *The New York Times* (October 26, 1989).
10. "The State of the Nation-State," *The Economist* (December 22, 1990): 73.
11. Ernest Gellner, *Nations and Nationalism* (Blackwell, 1983).
12. Eric Hobsbawm, *Nations and Nationalism Since 1780* (Cambridge University Press, 1990).
13. Michael E. Porter, *The Competitive Advantage of Nations* (Free Press, 1990).
14. "Design and Cultural Identity." Internationalès Forum für Gestaltung, Hochschule für Gestaltung, Ulm, Germany, September 1989.
15. Porter, *The Competitive Advantage.*
16. Hobsbawm, *Nations and Nationalism.*

63

RESPONSES TO GLOBALIZATION
The Branding of City-Regions and Nations

Guy Julier

More benignly, this reorientation of political and cultural discourse towards regions musters some interesting results. As in the case of Catalonia, European regionalism allows for the retrieval of local identities. But technological and economic change may indeed create new regional identities. Such was the case of Øresund where the building of a bridge linking Copenhagen, Denmark and Malmö, Sweden across the Øresund sound would open up opportunities for the concentration of specific shared or complementary partnerships in a transnational region. The new region brings together Zealand on the Danish side and Scania in Sweden. Steps to their integration originated partly in an historical study of their shared past and cultures (Weibull et al. 1993). Making up a population of 3 million the new region shares expertises in bio-industry, environmental technology, life sciences and food, tourism, trade and distribution as well as information technology, media and communications. The region is therefore constituted less in formal structures of governance—since these reside within their respective nation-states—but in their shared physical environments and human resource bases.

The Øresund Konsortiet, a consortium of organizations involved in the promotion of the region, engaged the London-based design consultancy Wolff Olins to develop a brand identity for it. The ensuing study consolidated an appreciation of the shared features of history, environment and economy. It also identified attitudinal factors to the region's personality—being openness,

inclusivity, responsibility and innovation—which flavour the brand. Eventually all these facets are distilled into the Øresund marque. Here two organic shapes and the palette of earth and sky colours represent the coming together of the two areas, but also the shared 'attitude and visual language of the region' (Øresund Committee 1999) in its natural environment and the human values of its population.

The use of 'attitudinal' factors to identify a city, region or nation is evidence of an emergent tendency by politicians and their design consultants to consider them as brands. Hans Arnold working at Wolff Olins developed a structure for identifying different levels of branding within a region which integrates place factors and human resources. The regional brand was equated with its overall 'attitude'. This is subsequently made up of: 'local brands', which incorporate its various environmental features such as its towns and cities; category brands which describe its competences as evidenced in its economy and educational infrastructure; and, finally, its product or service brands, such as specific leisure attractions which are sold and consumed as part and parcel of the place (Øresund Committee 1999; Vinogradoff 1999). These categories are then distilled into a central idea which provides a short-hand, by way of a slogan or a simple image to communicate its essence.

Co-founder of Wolff Olins, Wally Olins reinforces the notion that governments can control the brand image, and thus the attitudinal markers, of an entire nation. In a report written for a British government think-tank, The Foreign Policy Centre, he stated that,

> Governments can create the mood and lead and co-ordinate the image. … All countries communicate all the time. … Collectively, all these millions of messages represent an idea of what the nation as a whole is up to, what it feels, what it wants, what it believes in. It should be the task of government—with a very light touch—to set the tone of these messages.
>
> (Olins 1999: 25–6)

Wolff Olins was highly influential in promoting the idea of rebranding places during the late 1990s. In November 1996 it approached BBC2's *Money Programme* with an idea for a programme in which it would develop a brand for Britain. Their research had shown that Britain's image and reputation was damaging the country's ability to compete in world markets. Furthermore, British people had a uniquely poor self-image of their country. They determined 16 key signals and values which 'encapsulate the essence and personality of a new brand for modern Britain' (Wolff Olins 1999a), these being: Original; Invest in; Made in; Educating; Creative; Leading; Team; Skilled; Discovering; Welcoming; Diverse; Innovative; Strategic; Exporting; Popular; Serving. Their recommendations were that the word 'Great' be taken out of Great Britain, arguing that, 'New Britain will demonstrate greatness without having to say so'. The visual scheme they proposed to substitute the use of the Union Jack—which had become associated with football hooliganism, imperialism and right-wing politics—would not make particular emphasis on red over blue or vice versa. The brand, they claimed, was 'post-political'.

The resulting television programme, 'Made in UK' was followed by a report produced by the think-tank Demos entitled *Britain™ Renewing our Identity* (1997) and a pamphlet produced by the British Tourist Authority *Branding Britain* (1997).

They coincided with the emergence of the 'Cool Britannia' slogan, used liberally by politicians to describe this new Britain. The term 'Cool Britannia' originates in the title of a song by the Bonzo Dog Dooda Band released in 1967, and was re-used both in a headline in *The Sunday Times* and in an ice-cream brand in 1996. In 1997, the British Council commissioned design consultancy Johnson Banks to develop a campaign to promote the 'new Britain' brand abroad. In each of these cases, the drive was to manoeuvre the national image away from historical associations of empire and cultural conservatism towards one of modernity and pluralism.

This 'softening' of national image through brand strategies clearly reflects the shifting status of nations in the new world order. Wolff Olins undertook a similar study to their 'Made in UK' programme for the German television station, ZDF in 1998 in which they developed proposals and sketches for a rebranding of Germany. The recommendations included redesigning the national colours by introducing the European blue in place of black and using a typographic signature of 'DE' to stand for 'Deutschland Europa' (Wolff Olins 1999b). The applications of this in the resultant television programme and an exhibition which opened in Berlin in January 1999 played up such values as tolerance, diversity, non-conformism, creativity and peace, values which are easily generalizable to other European nations. Pluralism, as we have seen, is readily appropriated as a core value in (post)modern fortress Europe.

PROBLEMATIZING THE BRANDING OF PLACE

Unsurprisingly, attempts to create a cohesive brand image for a locality under relatively loose headings such as 'creativity', 'modernity' or 'multiculturalism' are easily problematized. In the first instance, it locates identity less in the unique characteristics of a focused place (if they indeed exist) than in a constellation of transnational shared values. This might immediately result in contestation as to exactly what those shared values might really be. But equally where a localized 'flavour' is placed alongside such brand building, the contradictions between the two are immediately recognizable.

The Barcelona paradigm is powerful not just because of the strength of the sum of individual design interventions deployed in a single context. There was also a tight fit between different components of du Gay et al.'s 'circuit of culture' (1997). Local and global demand was met by design production. Local taste-makers, be they famous architects or TV channels, effectively regulated the nature and scale of design culture. Specific design products satiated notions of self-identity. Looking at the Barcelona paradigm in terms of 'systems of provision', it is clear that the city and its industrial and commercial infrastructure provided a tightly-woven and highly localized channel linking production, distribution and consumption, which was self-supporting, self-legitimating and self-authenticating.

This 'success', however, was not without its critics. Catalan journalist Arcadi Espada noted that the nation-building of the regional autonomous government so effectively reached all areas of everyday life (including its design) that one seemingly could never cease to be a Catalan (1997: 43). He questioned whether the very specific identity of Catalanism was truly inclusive of its population—a sizeable proportion of whom were not of Catalan family background—and whether its claim to inclusivity was met in practice. For Espada, Catalan identity was constantly represented and reproduced through what he called *cultureta* (literally meaning 'small culture'). This placed cultural 'normalization' at the level of the everyday (such as in the design of studio sets on the local TV station) whereby national values and myths of nationhood were more insidiously inculcated.

Espada's argument coincides with what Michael Billig (1995) saw as 'banal nationalism' in action on a wider scale. While in liberal democracies the state could only dictate national values through minimal legislative means, so these were reproduced more effectively at a more domestic level—through language, the attitudes expressed in television soap operas, the commentaries made in sporting events or identities carried by particular food products. Equally, the branding of cities, regions or nations seeks to implement values at a 'banal', nuanced and symbolic level: through the subtle application of a logo to a poster or a product, through the provision of public seating of a particular aesthetic pitch or through inflexions used in copywriting. It seems that attempts to communicate and promote cohesion are brought down to the everyday material and visual features of private and public life. Marxist geographer David Harvey (1989) argues that the kinds of initiatives to define, distinguish and broadcast the cultural capital of cities are merely a gloss. In appealing to bourgeois tastes and aspirations for urban living, it patches over class, racial or ethnic divisions.

This process, within which design culture plays a significant part, may even enhance these fissures. Gentrification may result in traditional communities being displaced—as indeed happened in a limited way around Barcelona's Plaça Real as part of its renovation prior to the 1992 Olympic Games. Sharon Zukin (1991: Ch. 7) presents an equally critical viewpoint. She contends that the new middle classes of global, disorganized capitalism exercise cosmopolitan tastes as a vehicle of their cultural capital. She discusses how this has resulted in a growth of demand for international cuisine since the 1970s. The 'vernacular' of diverse immigrant communities (to New York in her discussion) is thus appropriated and consumed by this class, displacing it from its traditional function in serving its own community. Identities are served up or even themed for this new audience. In doing so, their original vernacular is superseded by a conformity to and coherence with the values of the marketplace.

Coherence, as indeed purveyed by the machinations of design culture in the city, region or nation-state, others argue, can only be momentary, or may only address particular levels of social experience. Global cultural flow of ethnic groups, media, technology, finance and ideologies means that place and identity may be understood in several different dimensions. Their shifting nature and rapid movement continually disrupt the unity of economics, culture and politics. The disjunctures between these five elements are experienced and articulated in different ways, by different people and groupings in different localities (Appadurai 1990).

Movement can also lead to hybridization, as distinct global cultural sections are assembled to present new identities. With the weakening of the nation-state, globalization can result in a growth of various modes of ideological and cultural organization so that groups and individuals may be represented at transnational, international, macro-regional, national, micro-regional, municipal and local levels. This ladder of representation is crisscrossed by functional networks of corporations, international organizations, non-governmental organizations as well as professionals and even, simply, internet users (Nederveen Pieterse 1995).

Cultural coherence may therefore be destabilized by a range of organizations, conflicting flows and activities. And if designers and other cultural producers are mustered to protect that stability, they may as easily attack it. Commenting on the 'Cool Britannia' phenomenon and its incorporation into the British Tourist Authority marque, cultural critic Robert Hewison wrote that:

What the Cool Britannia phenomenon does tell us is how symbolic goods—music, movies, food, fashion, art, design, architecture—all of which convey values over and above their value in exchange, have become vital to the moral as well as the material economy. But in the end, symbolic goods have to symbolise something—and that is why the buzzword Britain has become so significant. When our evangelical Prime Minister Tony Blair uses the words Britain or British 53 times in his speech to the Labour Party conference he is not reinforcing our sense of identity, he is betraying a profound anxiety about it ... it is up to the creators of symbolic goods—the designers, artists and architect readers of *Blueprint*—to scribble all over [the marque], to break in from the margins of an ersatz, marketised identity and reveal just what our collective sense of ourselves could be.

(Hewison 1997: 31)

NOTE

Extracted from Guy Julier, 'Responses to Globalization (2): The Branding of City-Regions and Nations', in *The Culture of Design* (London: Sage Publications, 2000), pp. 135–42. Reprinted by permission of Sage Publications Ltd.

SECTION 6: DESIGN AND GLOBAL ISSUES

6.2: Equality and Social Justice

INTRODUCTION

The complex and diverse roles of design and its practices creates a janus-like identity. On the one hand, it is implicated in the development of capitalism, consumption, and greater profit margins, while on the other hand, design is being used to address the 80/20 conundrum—in which 20 percent of the global population controls 80 percent of the world's resources. Globalization has reinforced this inequality, which design has the potential to address through the creation of new possibilities and radical transformations that can revolutionize the lives of those in need. The writers included in this subsection of the Reader bring different perspectives to the creative possibilities and radical transformations that design can achieve toward developing greater equality and social justice between human beings.

The first extract is from a very valuable survey of 100 years of humanitarian design, written by Kate Stohr, a cofounder of Architecture for Humanity, a charitable association that promotes the role of architecture and design in resolving global social and humanitarian crises (http://www. ArchitectureForHumanity.org). Stohr raises the thorny issue of whether the role of the architect should be "limited to design," a question that suggests that design has become a restrictive practice, divorced from the act of making and from users. To play a more meaningful role in design, architects and other design practitioners must have a more active engagement. Stohr reflects on the development of the self-help housing movement to improve the quality of life, resolve global disasters, and build sustainable communities as an outcome of the failure of professional architects to become actively involved in more humanitarian projects. She advocates that the success of socially conscious design in the twenty-first century will depend on architects and designers venturing "beyond the design community" to work more humbly, at the grass roots level.

An example of the professional architect taking the self-help approach toward greater social equality is provided in the second extract, with reference to one man, the designer and architect Michael Graves. The article is written by journalist and paraplegic John Hockenberry, who brings intelligence and empathy to the concept of universal design, which is intended to be usable by everyone, not only for those with disabilities. While universal design recognizes the importance of appearance, it does not prioritize it. To understand its application we can cite, for example, the OXO Good Grips utensils as socially sensitive designs that have also proved to be commercially successful due to their effectiveness for as wide a range of users as possible, irrespective of their age, gender, or particular physical needs.

Acknowledging fundamental commonalities and differences in human existence is a key to design for equality and social justice. Ezio Manzini, a world-recognized expert on sustainable design, has acknowledged this in his work and his particular interest in the everyday and the local. Manzini directs our thoughts to social learning and project-based activities as another form of design "self-help," in which sustainable local development is redefined positively in the context of globalization. He references Appadurai's (Section 6.1) concept of global flows to inform his concept of "cosmopolitan localism"

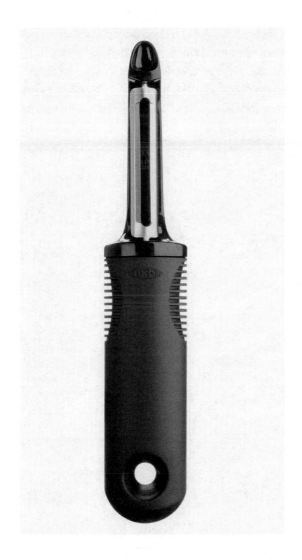

Image 29 OXO Peeler. Courtesy of OXO.

and networking. Here again, the question arises of the designer's role. Like Stohr, Manzini advocates designers "rolling up their sleeves" and working in communities, collectively with nonprofessionals.

Finally, Earl Tai provides a philosophical foundation and a method for distributive justice in design, seen as an ethical imperative rather than an optional nicety. He discusses the ethical and functional foundations of the topic and seeks to identify a framework for understanding distributive justice in general, and with particular reference to design. What role can and should design serve in the fair allocation and distribution of goods and services in any given society? Tai asks whether design is merely a "negotiable luxury" or an essential ingredient in this process. The answers are fundamental to the way that design is conceived and functions, to its professional, social, and historical development. Design can, and as Tai would argue should, be instrumental in the creation and operation of more equal and socially just systems, services, products, and environments. He references John Rawls's "veil of ignorance" scenario as the basis for societies where "everyone would be considering and looking out for everyone else," regardless of their professions or social status. While design has some way to go to achieve this, there is some evidence of the application of these theories within design consultancies, especially those focusing on human factors design, such as IDEO, the California-based global design consultancy. But for the majority of design professionals, equality and social justice are not, as of yet, issues fundamental to their practices.

64

SELF-HELP AND SITES-AND-SERVICES PROGRAMS

Kate Stohr

"Of all the participants in the business of home building, the architect is the only one qualified to guide the house and its environment toward a civilized form. Well-trained and possessed of practical experience, he should be intellectually constituted to prevent abuses, develop new methods and impart originality to the design. Yet he fails in each of these responsibilities," wrote Abrams in his landmark survey of the housing industry, *The Future of Housing*. Leadership in improving the design of low-cost homes was coming from the materials industry, he argued, not architects. Others felt that architects tripping over their own stylish egos in the pursuit of wealthy clients "had lost sight of the requirements for elementary shelter."[1]

A debate emerged in the profession: Should the work of the architect be limited to design? Or should architects roll up their sleeves and take on the job of the housing activist, working to influence not only implementation but also policy and planning decisions? Could architects play a meaningful role in providing shelter to those who needed it most? And if so, what should that role be?

The self-help housing movement grew out of this disillusionment. Homeowners had been successfully building their own homes for generations. Moreover, they had been doing it without the aid of government agencies, architects, or outside funding. What were slums but just another form of owner-built housing? Rather than pour money into government-built housing projects,

why not use government funding to support and empower families to upgrade and build their own homes? This was the idea at the crux of the self-help movement.[2]

[...]

Over time a variety of approaches to the basic self-help housing concept emerged. One variant was the roof-loan scheme. In this approach, first developed by Abrams and Otto Koenigsberger as part of a United Nations mission to Ghana in the 1950s, families who had built the foundation and walls of a structure themselves received loans from a revolving fund, repayable over a fixed period, to buy the roof, doors, and windows. Another variant was the "core-housing" scheme, in which agencies provided a number of identical "cores," typically consisting of one room that in some cases included basic services such as water and electricity. The families could then expand these cores as time and money allowed. Many houses erected in the later years of Puerto Rico's self-help program followed this "core" model.

Then in 1968 a young American couple named Millard and Linda Fuller took the basic tenets of self-help and mutual aid in yet a new direction. The idea for Habitat for Humanity was born at Koinonia Farm, a small, interracial Christian farming community founded in 1942 outside Americus, Georgia, by farmer and biblical scholar Clarence Jordan. Working with Jordan the Fullers helped set up a revolving loan fund and orchestrated a program to build 42 homes. Future owners and volunteers worked "in partnership" to construct the homes, which were sold to families in need at no profit with no interest. Jordan died before the first home was completed, but the Fullers carried on his work.

Although Habitat for Humanity is considered an American organization, the first housing project the Fullers undertook on their own was in Zaire (now the Democratic Republic of the Congo). Starting in 1973 they built 100 cement-block houses over three years. On returning to America they officially formed Habitat for Humanity International in 1976, with its headquarters in Georgia. The mission of the organization, which the Fullers described as a "Christian housing ministry," was to eradicate "poverty housing" by building "simple, decent homes" based on the "economics of Jesus." Within 30 years Habitat for Humanity would claim to be the fifteenth-largest homebuilder in the United States.

The Habitat for Humanity "partnership" model offered a number of advantages over typical self-help and mutual-aid programs. Whereas prior self-help initiatives relied primarily on the labor of families themselves, often forcing wage earners to give up paid work, Habitat for Humanity involved volunteers, speeding the construction process and lessening the burden on already struggling families. Moreover, whereas administrative and organizational costs absorbed as much as 25 percent of the funding for a typical self-help and mutual aid program, Habitat for Humanity relied on the built-in organizational skills of local churches to help set up and run its housing initiatives. This not only cut down on costs but also helped overcome local resistance and potential siting hurdles, while guaranteeing a steady supply of volunteers and funding.

Habitat for Humanity published a how-to guide entitled *Community Self-Help Housing Manual* in 1982.[3] It included everything from basic house plans (which have changed little since then) to family selection guidelines to instructions on setting up your own Habitat for Humanity affiliate. Perhaps more than anything else, however, it was Habitat for Humanity's ability to build a grassroots

network of zealous housing advocates, including former President Jimmy Carter, that secured its success.

The 1970s also saw a number of significant policy shifts. As the concept of self-help gained momentum, the poor were seen no longer as a burden but as a resource. The United Nations held a number of conferences focusing on urban settlements, at which Turner and others presented their work, and in 1972 the World Bank, drawing on the work of Abrams, Turner, and others, launched an urban lending program that paved the way for slum-improvement initiatives. Rather than investing in housing, the bank advocated investing in land, services, and utilities and, in some cases, granting secure land tenure to residents in existing squatter settlements.

One of the first of these "sites-and-services" projects the bank funded was in Lusaka, Zambia. Carried out between 1972 and 1975, it provided the construction of roads, installation of piped water to standpipes, security lighting, and garbage removal. The project also offered small loans to residents for housing improvements, including $375 to those forced to relocate to an overspill area to make way for the new services.[4]

Gradually slum redevelopment gave way to "upgrading."[5] The introduction of micro-credit lending helped spur the construction of pit latrines, water delivery, and self-help housing in former squatter settlements. Architects such as Reinhard Goethert and nonprofit groups such as the Cooperative Housing Foundation (CHF) in America and FUNDASAL in El Salvador began to play a significant role in advising governments on housing policy and implementing large-scale self-help and sites-and-services programs.[6]

Unlike previous government-managed programs, the sites and services and self-help models promoted self-reliance over institutional support. In terms of sheer numbers, at least, it was difficult to find fault with the approach. For example, between 1969 and 1984 the Kampung Improvement Program, funded by the World Bank, brought essential services to some 15 million people in Indonesia, and by 1996 Habitat for Humanity alone had dedicated some 50,000 homes.

However, in time housing experts recognized a number of shortcomings to the approaches.[7] Because people were unlikely to invest time and money in building or upgrading homes they didn't own, the self-help and sites-and-services models could not be adopted in areas where formal land-tenure was a political impossibility. Others pointed out that both models tended to relocate people who relied on work in the inner city to the city's periphery.

The need to meet financial targets placed an emphasis on quantity above quality. This resulted in homes so basic as to be almost bereft of design, lessening their value over time. Program mandates and policies did little to encourage green building or to mitigate the impact of human settlements on the environment. And whereas public housing—permanent and well serviced—had provided shelter at little to no cost to the tenant, self-help and sites-and-services occupants invariably paid more for less. In most areas, improvements still struggled to keep pace with population growth.

Although architects participated in and in many cases mobilized self-help housing programs, the very concept was a negation of the traditional role of the architect. Design was not perceived as adding value. Architects in the self-help housing model were mere trainers if not unnecessary inconveniences. As Turner, one of the movement's most prominent advocates, put it:

The certified professional makes a fool of himself, and often does a great deal of harm to other people, by assuming that he knows more than the uneducated by virtue of his schooling. All that second- and third-hand knowledge and intellectual exercising does for him, however, is to reduce his ability to listen and learn about situations significantly different from his own social and economic experience—with consequences that can be tragic when he has the power to impose his solutions on those who are not strong enough to resist.[8]

Once again the relevance of design and of the design professional was called into question. It would require a new generation of architects, policy makers, planners, humanitarian aid workers, and others to bridge the gap between design and policy. In doing so, they would not only reaffirm the essential role of design but demonstrate the importance of building sustainable communities.

[...]

A century after the San Francisco earthquake, the solution to housing the world's displaced and disenfranchised remains as stubbornly situation-specific and complex as ever. Even as we compiled this book, a series of tsunamis, hurricanes, and earthquakes reminded the world once again how vulnerable and unprepared we are against the awesome powers of nature—whether we live in the world's poorest country or its wealthiest. The Red Cross estimates that over the past two decades, on average more than 75,000 people have been killed annually by natural and man-made disasters, and another 211 million have been affected by disaster each year—more than 98 percent of them in the developing world. What's more, the agency reports that over the last decade the number of disasters—and the number of people affected by disasters—has climbed.[9]

Likewise, systemic substandard housing conditions continue to plague the world's cities. UN-HABITAT estimates that nearly one billion people, a third of the world's urban population, live in slums. The agency projects that number will double by 2030.[10]

Fortunately, we also live in a time when technology, particularly the ubiquitous Internet, has enabled the rapid exchange of ideas on an unprecedented scale. Groups such as Slum Dwellers International are using the Web to network and exchange models of development between slum dwellers in different countries. CAD software has made professional design services more affordable and enabled architects to volunteer their services in communities near and far. At the same time, computer modeling systems have led to technical advances promoting safer, more disaster-resistant building design.

A wider appreciation for the importance of design in disaster mitigation and community development has spurred greater collaboration between designers and communities. In addition to the many architects and groups engaged in community design and development profiled in this book, organizations such as the Aga Khan Development Network, Architects Without Frontiers, Architecture + Development, Architectes de l'Urgence, the Buckminster Fuller Institute, Builders Without Borders, Building and Social Housing Foundation, Association for Community Design, Architects/Designers/Planners for Social Responsibility, the Enterprise Foundation, Design Corps, Design Matters, Public Architecture, Shelter Associates, shelterproject, World Shelters, the Volunteer Architects' Network, and many others have emerged, promising a more innovative and inclusive approach to designing shelter.

Will the start of the twenty-first century be remembered as the golden era of socially conscious design? The answer will likely depend on the willingness of architects and designers to reach beyond the design community and its traditional audience—to humbly venture into the communities in which they live, listen to the needs of their neighbors, and offer their services. As Samuel Mockbee once said: Proceed and be bold.

NOTES

Extracted from K. Stohr, "100 Years of Humanitarian Design," in Architecture for Humanity, ed. *Design Like You Give a Damn: Architectural Responses to Humanitarian Crises* (New York: Metropolis Books, 2006), pp. 42, 44–45, 52–53. Reprinted by permission of Metropolis Books.

1. Charles Abrams, *The Future of Housing,* New York: Harper & Brothers, 1946, 129.
2. The first "self-help and mutual aid" project in America took place in the coal-mining areas of Pennsylvania during the Depression. In the wake of mass unemployment at the mines, the program sought to bring unemployed mine workers living in slum conditions "back to the farm" by paying them to build their own housing. Peter M. Ward, *Self-Help Housing: A Critique,* London: Mansell, 1982, 26.
3. Robert William Stevens and Habitat for Humanity eds., *Community Self-Help Housing Manual: Partnership in Action,* Croton-on-Hudson, NY: Intermediate Technology Development Group of North America, 1982.
4. It was intended that the squatter community help defray the costs of the new services by paying for water usage and other services and by repaying their loans. Ultimately, though, many residents were slow to pay their loan installments and resented being charged for services. If wealthy Lusakans did not have to pay for them, they argued, why should they, especially when they received much lower levels of service (for example, trash was often not collected at all in the project area). Nonetheless, the program was considered a success and offered an alternative approach for cities struggling with an explosion of squatter settlements. "Lusaka Sites and Services Project," Upgrading Urban Communities, The World Bank Group, 1999–2001, http://web.mit.edu/urbanupgrading/upgrading/case-examples/ce-ZA-lus.html
5. Nabeel Hamdi, *Housing Without Houses: Participation, Flexibility, Enablement,* London: Intermediate Technology Publications, 1995.
6. Ibid., 20.
7. Ward, *Self-Help Housing.*
8. John F. C. Turner and Robert Fichter, *Freedom to Build: Dweller Control for the Housing Process,* New York: MacMillan, 1972, 147.
9. Between 2000 and 2004 disasters affected one-third more people than between 1995 and 1999. International Federation of the Red Cross, World Disasters Report 2005, table 3, 196.
10. "Millennium Development Goals," 2003, UN-HABITAT, http://www.unhabitat.org/mdg/

65

THE RE-EDUCATION OF MICHAEL GRAVES

John Hockenberry

For most of my life I have had a love-hate relationship with architecture and architects. It has generally been my experience that the making of physical spaces to welcome people in wheelchairs has ranked on the low end of the scale of importance for most architects, down there with selecting the paint for a stairwell. Accessibility is fine for ugly strip malls in Texas but somehow eludes the stair-encrusted Four Seasons Hotel in Manhattan. Universal design seems like more of an architectural afterthought than a central tenet of building, even today. So upon visiting the personal domain of a world-renowned architect—especially one who reveres Le Corbusier's "expressive" spiral staircases and "five points" zealotry about roof gardens and suspended entrances—ease of access is not my expectation.

I had last seen Michael Graves in early 2003, when we shared a stage at Manhattan's Javits Center as part of a panel on innovation in retailing. Graves, David Rockwell, and I took turns speaking about "branding" or some such fashionably urgent bull-shit that has long ago faded from memory. Graves, I remember vividly, was athletically trim in hipster black and slightly wizened in a handsome, meticulously tailored way. He was soft-spoken but acid-tongued about the state of design. I clearly recall that I was the only one of the three of us who used a wheelchair.

Much has changed in Graves's life since that encounter. For one thing, we both use wheelchairs now. Shortly after our appearance at the Javits Center a virus destroyed nerves in his spinal cord, bringing on paralysis from his midchest down.

In a quirky coincidence he and I were paralyzed at virtually the same level—he from a disease three years ago and I from a car accident 30 years ago. So as I steer my Audi sedan into the gravel parking lot of Graves's impressive terra-cotta home in Princeton, New Jersey, I look for telltale signs of retrofitting, door widening, and makeshift ramps. There are none. These outward details of accessibility—items associated with the 16-year-old Americans with Disabilities Act, which critics have famously cited as a scourge of modern architecture—are invisible if they're present at all. Perhaps, I think, some architect had figured out a way to live with the ADA.

As I remove the disassembled titanium wheelchair from my car's passenger seat, where it was stowed for driving, and begin to snap the quick-release wheels back on, two people rush into the parking lot transfixed by what I'm doing. "Michael is going to want a videotape of this," Karen Nichols says, introducing herself. A principal of Michael Graves & Associates (MGA), she absorbs every detail of my transfer from car to chair and then carefully watches me roll in my chair to the house. "We've been trying to gather data about how disabled people solve physical problems. We've learned that the only way is to just pay attention to see precisely how people use their tools for getting around." This is a degree of interest in my physical details that I had rarely seen from doctors, let alone designers.

I observe that Graves's house is, apparently, accessible. It was built at ground level with wide doors and no stairs. I ask Nichols how long Graves has lived here. "Michael's been here forever," she says. "The amazing thing is how little needed to be done to make the house work for him." Inside I roll effortlessly past furniture that exudes comfort and shelves packed with well-loved books and art pieces. Flat, straight, spacious corridors connect wide, sedate rooms appointed with ornate colorful tiles and intriguing arrangements of household objects, some sculptural, some more whimsical, such as a Bauhaus-looking chess set. A newly constructed elevator is similarly appointed. It opens onto a second floor flooded with natural light and framed by solid classical doorways. The numerous skylights and many levels of overhead space give the impression that there's no ceiling at all.

When I visit Graves again one steamy morning last summer, he is confined to his bed due to a prolonged bedsore, under strict medical orders to heal it by staying down and out of his wheelchair, so he insists that we speak in his room. A number of chairs are set up for his designers to join what will be a long meandering conversation about design, disability, and one of Graves's favorite subjects: America's obsession with originality for its own sake and transitory fashion over beauty. The man whose sparkling eyes greet me from the large hospital bed, I discover, is much younger than me. After all, in wheelchair years Graves is 27 my junior, and it shows.

Physically, however, he seems frailer than the last time I saw him. His voice wavers at first; but he's bursting with curiosity about me and my chair, brimming with invective about the lack of accessibility in the world and the dreadful state of design for people with disabilities—and full of plans to fix it all tomorrow. It's a feeling of mission and outrage I recall from my own early days as a paraplegic: Graves, the architect, is the wide-eyed idealist about what might be done to improve the world for the disabled, while the visiting journalist in the wheelchair is the curmudgeonly skeptic, jaded from the many times in the last three decades that architecture and design has said, "Sorry, no access here."

"People who become disabled have to radically redesign their outlook about the physical world," Graves says, remembering the first days after he was out of danger and learning to live with paralysis. "They redesign their sense of privacy and their sense of independence. Yet in the products they have to use, design has abandoned them."

Three years after the illness that changed him forever, Graves and his team are hard at work on a line of products that fuse one-dimensional medical utility with style, multifunctional elegance, and beauty. The product line (eventually to number in the hundreds) from the Michael Graves Design Group is called Michael Graves Solutions. Nearly a decade ago at Target, Graves leveraged brand identity into a loyal, lucrative customer base that sought out his products with the expectation of higher quality and smart design. Much the same trajectory is anticipated with Solutions. It begins as an exercise in branding, with an ambitious end point of reconfiguring medical devices that in many cases have remained static for decades.

The first products include heating pads and simple shower seats for the mobility impaired. They experiment with unifying colors and styling, and add some important improvements. Graves anticipates that Solutions eventually will have its design stamp on everything from walking canes to complicated wheelchairs. "I'm looking forward to doing a chair," Graves says with the gusto of someone designing a new sports car for Maserati. Though its roots are clearly in the designer's recent health setbacks, Solutions represents a fusion of ideas that Graves has lived throughout his career. When I clumsily suggest that in my experience most architects care as much about universal design for people with disabilities as they do about choosing doorknobs, Graves blurts out impatiently, "But I love doorknobs. I've done doorknobs in almost every one of my buildings. I always thought that was the job of architects to do like Le Corbusier and Saarinen— design rooms and the objects that went in them. I discovered it wasn't quite like that."

[…]

Graves's health problems have had little impact on his diverse businesses. One of his best years was 2004, the year after his illness, when he had $800 million worth of projects under contract.

There's a special enthusiasm for this medical line, to be manufactured by Drive Medical Design & Manufacturing, of Port Washington, New York. Graves and designer David Peschel demonstrate how simple additions to standard safety items transform and humanize them without increasing costs. "Here we can make a soft tub-rail cover with a pocket molded into its surface, and it becomes a place for a cell phone in case someone needs to call for help," Peschel says. "A few strategic grips and the cover becomes a much safer aid for transferring from chair to bath." All of these improvements were developed from careful observation of people using existing devices. "I can't wait to take notes on how you load your chair back into your car," he says to me. Watching people lose the lock button on telescoping walker legs inspired a simple redesign of the legs of a bath seat—making the telescoping aluminum tube elliptical rather than circular so they can't drift out of alignment. "See, you never lose the lock button; it's always right in line," Peschel says, snapping the tube in and out in a single efficient move.

Tremendous effort has been made in the few prototypes to standardize color and function. "This orange here says adjustability on all of our products," Peschel says, pointing to a locking pin on an adjustable tub rail. "The shades of blue indicate our brand and also show the user that some care was taken in making these." He demonstrates an ergonomically designed handheld shower with snap-on brushes in two shades of the Graves signature blue. Peschel believes the medical field has been so neglected by design that it is a wide-open opportunity for a brand like Michael Graves Solutions to project health, functionality, independence, and beauty. Still in development are prototypes for walkers and a Rollator, both of which contain design improvements gleaned from stroller advancements, Japanese rolling shopping carts, and state-of-the-art caster technology. All have Graves's human and playful rules-be-damned quality. Something about being a part of this community of users has freed him to be utterly unselfconscious about his identity as an iconoclast.

"We're changing the rules here, period. I want people to look at these objects and immediately get a message," Graves says, after pointing critically to a rubber grip end of a new folding walking cane to indicate that it still looks too institutional. "The message I want is, 'Made by us for us.'" He points to his own chest.

Graves is certainly one of "us," and I am grateful to have him on my team; however, any disabled person might ultimately prefer to have his former life restored. Graves has said that he would like to walk again, if only to play golf like he used to. But three years after the onset of his paralysis he is going to make the best of what he can do, and that includes using design, as he always has, to make things better. Graves's passion reminds me of my own frustrations over badly designed wheelchairs and other tools when I was first injured decades ago. I made plenty of prototypes and improvised improvements. Some worked; some didn't. Most disabled people have closets full of their own solutions to bad design as well as failed devices that were too much trouble to use and so were tossed aside. Graves is determined that his solutions not end up in any closet unless he designs them explicitly to go there.

He says it all comes back to the choice of whether to make something beautiful or to tolerate something ugly. Allowing something to be simply ugly leads to permitting something that's not functional, that doesn't work right, that can be unsafe. "It's all the same," he says. "It all begins with thinking about beauty. Look around you: people can tolerate a lot of bad design," he says with a twinkling smile to his staff, who have heard it all before. "I can't tolerate any of it, of course. And I won't."

NOTE

Extracted from J. Hockenberry, "The Re-Education of Michael Graves," *Metropolis* 26, no. 3 (October 2006), pp. 123–25 and 127. Posted October 11, 2006. Reprinted by permission of Metropolis Magazine.

66

A COSMOPOLITAN LOCALISM

Prospects for a Sustainable Local Development and the Possible Role of Design

Ezio Manzini

Contrary to what was thought in the past, the joint phenomena of globalisation and networking have given rise once again to the local dimension. By the expression 'local' something very removed is meant from what was understood in the past (i.e. the valley, the agricultural village, the small provincial town, all isolated and relatively closed within their own culture and economy). Indeed, it combines the specific features of places and their communities with the new phenomena generated and supported world-wide by globalisation and by cultural, socio-economic interconnection. Unfortunately, these phenomena are characterised today by extremely negative dominant tendencies, on the one hand, that swing between traditionalist stances, supporting local interests, and reactionary stances (all the different forms of fundamentalism hidden behind the protecting veil of traditions and identity); and, on the other hand, by inclinations towards turning what remains of traditions and landscapes into a show for tourist purposes (the tourist-related 'supermarket type' of localism, which is just another side of the standardising aspect of globalisation, from which there is the desire to break away).

Luckily, however, at a closer look, more interesting and promising cases can be observed. Local communities that invent unprecedented cultural activities, forms of organisation and economic models; initiatives which, as a whole, represent an interesting development scenario, which we can refer to as cosmopolitan localism (Sachs, 1998; Manzini, Vugliano, 2000; Manzini, Jegou, 2003). A scenario which emerges at the point of intersection of two complementary strategies: a balanced interaction between the local and the global dimension, on the one hand, and a sustainable enhancement of local resources, on the other hand (intended both as physical and as socio-cultural resources).

In the following presentation these two strategies are discussed, focusing on some of their implications, particularly, highlighting the role designers could play in their implementation.

COSMOPOLITAN LOCALISM AND NETWORKING

Cosmopolitan localism is the result of a particular condition characterised by the balance between being rooted (rooted in a place and in the community related to that place) and being open (open to global flows of ideas, information, people, things and money—Appadurai, 1990). This is quite a delicate balance as, at any time, one of the two sides can prevail over the other leading to an anti-historical closure or, on the opposite side, it can lead to a destructive openness of the local social fabric and of its peculiar features.

Based on this unstable balance, the cosmopolitan localism, which we are discussing here, generates a new sense of place and culture[1]: a place and local community which are no longer (almost) isolated entities, but junctions of a network, points of connection among short networks, which generate and regenerate the local social and production fabric; and long networks, which connect that place and that community with the rest of the world (De Rita, Bonomi, 1998).

Within the frame of this cosmopolitan localism, successful local handicraft products emerge, which are linked to the identity of the place of origin and to the cultural and social values that characterise handicraft. The most commonly known and quoted examples are quality wine and some niche food products, such as those promoted by Slow Food. Other examples, however, are the essential oils of the Provence region, the Murano glassware, the Casentino wool etc., all products that carry with them the spirit and history of a place and a community, to the end consumer.

However, for the success of this model, the place and the community, to which these products are related, need to be alive, thriving and of high quality. In other words, if there are products that carry with them the spirit of the place, the quality of this place (and of the community which characterises it) must also be guaranteed. Therefore, a double link needs to be established between the place, the community and the product: the quality of the place and of the community is a decisive element for a product's success; vice versa, the success of a product, to be long-term, needs to favour the qualitative regeneration of the place and the community of origin. In a few words, the products of controlled origin require places and communities of guaranteed quality.

This is not enough, though. Within cosmopolitan localism another remarkable aspect arises which, up to now, has not yet been emphasised. If, on the one hand, the balanced interaction between local and global can be seen as the realisation of a vertical link, on the other hand, there are other links within this connection which are equally important and can be synthetically defined as horizontal. These links connect activities that are different among themselves but which, if adequately devised, can produce symbiotic systems (able to co-operate, strengthening one another) and scope economies (where efficiency and effectiveness are pursued, through the symbiotic integration of different activities). The most effective example, thanks to its renown, of this original economic and organisational model is farm holidays, intended as symbiosis between non-industrial agriculture and non-standardised tourism[2] (Bimonte, Punzo, 2003; Simonicca, 2004). Given its success, this symbiosis tends to spread to other pairs of activities (e.g., the integration between tourism and fishing, tourism and handicraft, tourism and cultural heritage conservation etc.).

In conclusion, we have seen that all examples mentioned above are characterised by the connection between local and global relationships and between various specialised networks (related to specific activities, functions and interests). In practice, this complex networking system, which is the necessary condition for any example of cosmopolitan localism, can be the result of different actions, occurred at different times thanks to the combination of particular starting conditions and of equally particular personal abilities. However, if the purpose is to spread this approach, with the view of a sustainable local development, it is necessary to effectively and consciously design such networking system in terms of a cultural, economic and operational platform (which we will call local tier) able to promote the vertical and horizontal interactions mentioned above. Clearly, for this platform's design different social players can play and will play their role. Among them designers are also involved. I will go back to this subject later on.

DISCOVERY AND DEVELOPMENT OF LOCAL RESOURCES

Let's move on to consider the second strategic element of local development, i.e. the aspect linked to the issue of resources. In order to do that, we have to start from some remarks aimed at better understanding their nature.[3]

Each territorial resource (Magnaghi, 2000; Medesign, 2003) is a complex entity based on two fundamental components: endowment, corresponding to one or more territorial values (Dematteis, 1995); and capability of resident communities, that is, the ability to recognise potential resources, to transform them into actual resources, and to develop them with the prospect of their sustainability. The combination of endowment and capabilities allows for the rise of different types of resources: physical, historical, infrastructural resources (the availability of water or of fertile soils, the natural and built landscape, the communication infrastructure, etc …), production resources (agricultural, craft and industrial activities, …), and social resources (the existence of strong local communities, the presence of traditions, the spread of skills and know-how, the proposal of significant cultural events, etc …).

This way of presenting things leads us to highlight the human and project-based component involved in the concept of resource: a resource is not a gift of nature, nor is it a legacy from preceding generations. A resource is the result of a deliberate activity which operates on an existing system, interpreting it and transforming it in relation to a purpose.

Within this conceptual framework, it may be added that, in order to exist and to last through time, a resource needs to be discovered, enhanced and adequately developed. It is, indeed, necessary to focus on a pre-existing territorial value to see how, in a certain social, technological and economic context, this can take the shape of a potential resource; it is necessary to find the way and the means to transform such potential resource into an actual resource; finally, in order to avoid that this enhanced resource deteriorates or is exhausted, it is necessary to use it within the limits of its regeneration possibilities. In other words, a resource needs to be developed in the sense that it has to be managed so as to produce new value without exhausting the starting capital, that is, without deteriorating the territorial value on which it is based and from which it gets nourishment. It goes without saying, that sustainability of development is, exactly, the result of this: the ability to combine the enhancement of a resource to the need of safeguarding it from overexploitation.

LEARNING PROCESSES AND PROJECT-BASED APPROACH

Discovering, enhancing and developing resources are human activities which have accompanied the entire history of our species. Traditionally, it has consisted in social learning processes, which have taken place over time, without employing specific and conscious project-based interventions. In other words, human beings have gradually discovered resources (that is they have discovered the possible use of existing territorial values) and, by trial and error, they have learnt to use them without necessarily learning to develop them. In the past, in the slow unfolding of history, this has then been possible, as already mentioned, through progressive adjustment processes alternated by casual events (inventions, introduction of new solutions imported by other populations).

Over the last century, the pace of change (combined with the spread of networking and with the new challenges brought about by the issue of sustainability) has interrupted this traditional way of proceeding, requiring to move from a largely implicit social learning process to an explicit one.[4] The latter being a social learning process which is increasingly taking the form of a project-based activity. This is an articulated and complex process, involving different players, which aims at identifying a development objective together with the necessary steps to reach it.

Today, this process seems to give rise also to the need for design. That is the need for particular skills and competences that designers could provide. This statement needs to be grounded. Indeed, traditionally, designers have been recognised as project professionals who operate for and with the manufacturing industry, conceiving and developing standardised and non-localised products (whose characteristics are almost unrelated to the place in which they are produced and by which they are employed). This has been the case for a long time.

If things were still the same there would be no reason to talk about a possible and significant role of designers in local development. However, things have changed. Today, what manufacturers, or at least most advanced manufacturing companies, produce are systems of products, services and communication[5] (Norman, Ramirez, 1994; Mont,

2002; Manzini, Vezzoli, 2002; Manzini, Collina, Evans, 2004). In this new context designers are asked to conceive and develop these product-systems. This means, applying their skills and competencies to systems that, for their nature, are the result of the interaction of a multiplicity of partners (not just industrial partners), and which are developed and implemented through structured localisation strategies. It is, therefore, from these experiences that those skills and abilities also emerge which make of this new design a discipline potentially useful for the local development we are dealing with here.

LOCAL DEVELOPMENT
AND DESIGN

Design, therefore, enters the local development arena. In so doing, it introduces new and interesting opportunities. At the same time, though, it also introduces a big risk, that is, reinforcing a distorted and, today unfortunately, widespread view, according to which places and territories are considered as commodities; entities that are reduced to something that can be produced, sold and consumed exactly as a commodity. This view and the practical implications that this entails are the most serious risk that the issue of local development is challenged with. The objective of this paper is not to present an in-depth discussion of this topic.[6] It is clear, however, that the introduction of design in the arena of local development could also reinforce this dangerous trend. Indeed, the simplest and most immediate concept which tends to emerge can be summed up as follows: if designers, who traditionally deal with products, now deal with places and the territory, this means that places and the territory today need to be treated in the same way as products. In effect, this is, unfortunately, what is happening. And it is also what many designers contribute to make happen. But maybe things might also go in another direction. And maybe designers could also work together to reverse this negative trend.

Therefore, let's try and bet on the possibility that the involvement of design in the local development process introduces a set of skills and competencies that are potentially useful for its actual trend towards sustainability (Cipolla, 2004; Villari, 2004). As with any bet, there is no certainty of winning. However, in my opinion, it has good prospects for success. And this is mainly because design (in the sense of the extended community of designers) is founded on an independent culture which is able to play a critical and constructive role. If this cultural root is preserved and regenerated, an interesting and rewarding transfer might possibly take place between what designers have learnt from their experiences in the most advanced manufacturing companies, and what is required in the local development processes which have been discussed in this paper.[7]

In detail, what designers could do, in line with what has been said, is promoting convergence among players around a shared vision (landscape design); developing this shared vision in various practicable initiatives (strategic design) and designing the derived services interfacing (service design); promoting and developing an effective communication within the process (communication design). Last, but not least, designers should update the concept and meaning of being a designer today, accepting the fact of having to deal with different other players who, despite not being "professionals of design" are, nonetheless, designers in their own right. In sum, accepting that local development will undoubtedly be the result of a collective process in which, if capable, they may take on an active and proactive role.

NOTES

Extracted from E. Manzini, 'A Cosmopolitan Localism: Prospects for a Sustainable Local Development and the Possible Role of Design'. 2008. http://sustainable-everyday.net/manzini/?m=200401. Accessed March 18, 2008. Reprinted by permission of Ezio Manzini.

1. It should be added that cosmopolitan localism generates and is generated by a new idea of well-being. This well-being is based upon the awareness of the way and the extent to which some local qualities can contribute to the possibility of feeling good; moreover the awareness of how and the extent to which, for example, the sense of security resulting from a still active social fabric, the healthiness of the places, the beauty of the landscape etc. can contribute to well-being (Censis 2003). This awareness regarding the positive role of quality of context in the definition of well-being is what, first and foremost, distinguishes localism, on which we are focusing here, from the traditional local "village culture" (which, normally, did not attach any value to these characteristics of physical and social context). This awareness, combined with the delocalising potential of information and communication technologies, leads to the spread of new forms of local-global activities which strongly concur to the definition of cosmopolitan localism: why be a broker, a musician or a potter in an inhabitable place, when one can do the same in Tuscany without losing one's necessary international contacts?

2. Farm holidays demonstrate, indeed, the possibility of developing a symbiosis between local activities, which are weak in themselves but are characterised by high territorial qualities such as hill agriculture, and a non-standardised tourism, where the tourist is willing to establish a profound relationship with the places and the communities he/she visits and comes across.

3. Each territory has its heritage made up of territorial values ... resulting from its natural and social history (Magnaghi, 2000). These values are linked to the physical environment (eco-systems which have been changed in the course of history by man's intervention), to the built environment (historical legacy, infrastructures, production system and its products and services network) and to the anthropic environment (the social fabric and its forms of organisation, the shared beliefs, the production-related know-how, etc.)

At the same time, these territorial values are not yet resources. That is to say, they are not yet entities that are able to promote development strategies. In order for this to happen they need to be recognised as such. This means that resident communities need to develop an attitude according to which a certain territorial value is seen as a resource that can be used for a certain purpose.

Hence it appears that each territory is characterised by a specific heritage consisting in territorial values and by an equally specific capital of resources. The former (heritage) exists irrespective of its recognition as a whole set of resources and, therefore, irrespective of their use. Whilst the latter, which we will refer to as territorial capital (Medesign, 2003), represents, on the contrary, the result of the way in which and the extent to which, up to that moment, resident communities have recognised the potential resources present in the territorial heritage and have been able to transform them into actual resources.

4. Today the communities who reside on a territory often consciously face the need to redefine the territorial capital available to them, generate new resources or adjust some of the existing resources to the new context. And not only that. The increase in networking connections, on the one hand, and the rise of issues involving the sustainability of social and technical systems, on the other hand, give rise to the need for a profound change of the idea of development and, as a consequence, of which resources to use and how to use them.

5. Industrial production, at least in its highest performances, does no longer match the simplified view of companies producing tangible products for indefinite and non-localised consumers. Today, in fact, industrial production tends to be defined as the creation of complex and interactive systems which emerge from

the interrelation of a multiplicity of various and differently motivated players (Norman, Ramirez, 1995; Mont, 2002; Manzini, Vezzoli, 2002). In particular, in relation to the subject treated here, industrial production involves systems where globalisation processes go hand in hand with as many and as equally necessary localisation processes. This refers both to activities involving the final user and his contextualisation, and to those which are strictly project-based and production-related.

Design has followed this transformation, changing its profile and redefining the object and procedures of its activities. In so doing, it has initiated significant experiences concerning new ways of conceiving production and consumption activities and it has promoted the development of a series of tools that meet the new needs. These tools and especially these gathered experiences are what design, intended as industrial design of an advanced industrialisation (Manzini, Collina, Evans, 2004), can bring to local development today.

6. In any case, places and territory are not products. They are not products and services systems either. The places and the territory remain complex entities of which are part also the people that inhabit them. And even if at times their exchange value seems clear, they cannot be reduced to a commodity: every place and every territory, even the most backward ones, are also common goods. Something which cannot be produced by someone and sold to someone else. Considering places as goods to produce, communicate and sell, implies trivialising enormously the very concept of place and territory. This is a loss that transforms them, in the best case scenario, in theme parks and, in the worst case scenario, in disposable consumer goods (in the sense that a possible interest aroused at first, immediately disappears immediately transforming them into waste—it is the case of abandoned industrial areas or of declining tourist resorts). If, on the other hand, places and the territory are not products, they are, nonetheless, entities which are increasingly influenced by them. Therefore, a project-based approach designing the relationship between product, service and communication systems together with other territorial variables is fundamental. It is exactly for this reason that, as pointed out above, also design comes into play.

7. These experiences and these tools do not obviously replace the ones other designing disciplines (architecture, urban planning and territorial planning) can offer. They can, however, complement them in order to better understand, promote and communicate the complex system of interactions that local development requires.

67

A CASE FOR DISTRIBUTIVE JUSTICE IN DESIGN

Earl Tai

When we look at the work of designers such as Samuel Mockbee and the Rural Studio, Cameron Sinclair and Architecture for Humanity, Ross Evans and Worldbike, and Robert Young and the Red Feather Development Group, we intuitively know that these efforts to bring design value to the concerns of populations in economic distress are noble and deserve our highest approbation. When asked to articulate a philosophical or moral argument as to why this is so, however, most of us find ourselves at a loss for a good explanation. *It just is.* We know it is important, but trying to express the reason why, or trying to describe the degree of its importance relative to our other aims as designers and citizens, is an altogether different matter. I would like to begin to address this issue by laying forth an introductory framework for a philosophy of distributive justice in design. I hope to show that our core ideas about what it means to come together as a contractual civil society compel us to take hold of design justice, not merely as an optional nicety, but as an ethical imperative.

Our contemporary conceptions of distributive justice, or the fair allocation and distribution of goods and services in a society, find their roots in discussions from the seventeenth and eighteenth centuries by such thinkers such as Hugo Grotius (*Commentary on the Law of Prize and Booty,* 1603, and *Commentary on the Law of War and Peace,* 1625), John Locke (*First and Second Treatise on Government,* 1689), and Jean-Jacques Rousseau (*The Social Contract,* 1762).

To sum up the legacy of these early thinkers we can identify the following. First, from Grotius comes the declaration of a concept of natural rights belonging to all people and transcending any single cultural or religious tradition. Second, due to the potential abrogation of these rights, a social contract, not based on power, is necessary for their preservation. Third, particularly for Locke, the appropriate distribution of property according to just principles is central to the expression and preservation of these rights. Such principles include the idea that natural resources are given commonly to all humans, that personal labor is a criterion for ownership, and that there is an ethical limit to how much property an individual can rightly amass. Fourth, whether in Locke's allocation of stewardship of property or in Rousseau's submission of individual will, there arises an affirmation of the importance of general will and societal good. Fifth, and perhaps most importantly, these thinkers affirm the equality of individuals under just social contracts. It is embedded in the soil of these assertions that contemporary discussions of distributive justice find their roots.

Following in the vein of the earlier thinkers, John Rawls articulates in *Theory of Justice* in 1971 a concept he calls "justice as fairness," which operates from a social contract. Like Grotius, Locke, and Rousseau, Rawls begins with the concept of natural rights belonging to all individuals. Rawls's unique contribution lies in his remedy to the natural tendency of individuals to create biased systems aligned with ones own gifts, abilities, and status. The definitions of justice that emerge from these biased systems simply represent a negotiation of power, wherein those with power are able to enact laws that favor their own positions and gifts, exactly the type of situation against which philosophers like Rousseau were trying to mitigate.

The solution comes in the use of what Rawls calls a "veil of ignorance," a proposition that basic principles about the ordering of society and about the distribution of resources be made according to a hypothetical, nonhistorical scenario in which people would not know what gifts they would eventually be granted at birth. Rawls writes:

> No one knows his place in society, his class position of social status, nor does any one know his fortune in the distribution of natural assets and abilities, his intelligence, strength, and the like. I shall even assume that the parties do not know their conception of the good or their special psychological propensities. … Since all are similarly situated and no one is able to design principles to favor his particular condition, the principles of justice are the result of a fair agreement or bargain. (Rawls: 12)

Agreements made under this "veil of ignorance" in this "original position" would be fair, because people would have incentive to consider matters from every position in the social hierarchy and to vote with concern for everyone in the society, for each person could very well end up being one of the ones dealt the less favorable set of attributes. Put another way, existing manifestations of the social contract can be likened to playing poker and setting card values after hands have already been dealt and seen by the players. The rules of the game would be influenced by the cards in players' hands and by the relative power of the players. In contrast, Rawls's theory says that fairness and justice would require us to set the rules before dealing the cards and knowing our individual strengths.

What the veil of ignorance scenario assures is that in setting up policy, everyone would be considering and looking out for everyone else in society. Rawls goes on to posit two principles that he believes people under a veil of ignorance would select. First, there would be "equality in the assignment of basic rights and duties" (p. 14). No one would be given special preferences or advantages. Second, participants would select a system under which "social and economic inequalities, for example inequalities of wealth and authority, are [seen as] just only if they result in compensating benefits for everyone, and in particular for the least advantaged of society," and these benefits would be attached to positions and opportunities accessible to all (pp. 14, 16). This contrasts the utilitarian view that advocates adoption of any policy that adds to greater aggregate good, regardless of whether the least advantaged benefit or not.

Since its emergence thirty-five years ago, Rawls's theory has received the scrutiny and criticism of a number of scholars, including the well-known response by Robert Nozick, who comes from a utilitarian and libertarian point of view (*Anarchy, State, and Utopia,* 1974). It has also been praised and expanded upon by scholars such as Peter Singer, who expands the argument to the global scale (*One World: The Ethics of Globalization,* 2002), and Thomas Pogge, who advocates a global resources dividend to remedy unjust inequalities (*World Poverty and Human Rights,* 2002). Regardless, Rawls's statement remains one of the most compelling statements on economic or political philosophy of our time. This, I believe, is due in large part to its ability to harness our own inclination toward self-interest and self-preservation into a contemplation of others and a contemplation of the ideal.

When it comes to design and the visual world, however, discussions of distributive justice have been largely absent. The main reason for the exclusion of design from discussions about distributive justice is almost certainly due to a prevailing idea in our culture that design and visual concerns are luxuries, not necessities. We feel that only after our basic physical needs are met can we have the luxury to enjoy the benefits of design and visual concerns, in a manner reminiscent of Abraham Maslow's pyramid. And we believe society only has obligation to address the lower-level needs of people. That is why, for example, in public education, design education is almost nonexistent, and when funding runs out, art curricula are some of the first to be cut.

The first argument against this position is that design is not an esoteric luxury. In a primitive society, design could perhaps have been peripheral to everyday social dynamics, but in the contemporary world, this is not the case. Visual and spatial sensibilities and literacies have become requirements for full and equal participation in contemporary society, due to the exponential increase in the quantity and impact of visual and spatial media within our everyday lives; to the central role of new technology related to visual and spatial culture within our society; to the phenomenon of globalism and the resultant rise of design as one of the primary currencies of cultural exchange; to the increasing awareness of and co-option of the sociopolitical power of our visual and material world for political agendas; and maybe most importantly, to the rise in popular awareness and economic power of design.

As we move increasingly away from being a text-based culture to being an image-based culture, the power of the visual continues to grow, and the visual landscape continues to be consciously designed and shaped. That is why billions of dollars are spent in advertising. And that is why political entities go to great lengths to control visual images. It surely was no coincidence in March of 2003, just days before the start of the U.S. war against Iraq, when the ban on photography of the dead coming into Dover Air Force Base in Delaware was expanded to all bases throughout the world, even as the ban had been broken only a month earlier on February 5, 2003 for more "heroic" events, such as the widely publicized transport into Dover of

astronauts' bodies recovered from the Columbia space shuttle crash.

Marshall McLuhan lends further support to the inextricability of visual and material media from other activities of society. Taking his lead from Bernard Lonergan's identification of an empirical plane of consciousness that exists beyond the more widely acknowledged rational or logical plane, McLuhan declares that media are preeminent and are fundamental to our comprehension of ontological presence. In *The Gutenberg Galaxy*, McLuhan posits that with the introduction of new technology, new "sense ratios," that is, relative balances in the degree of activity of our senses, are forced upon us. This changes our reality and our experience of the world.

> a new technology extends one or more of our senses outside us into the social world, then new ratios among all of our senses will occur in that particular culture. It is comparable to what happens when a new note is added to a melody. And when the sense ratios alter in any culture then what had appeared lucid before may suddenly become opaque, and what had been vague or opaque will become translucent. (McLuhan: 41)

In *Understanding Media: The Extensions of Man*, McLuhan takes this one step further, declaring that media are extensions of human senses and are integral to our being. With his famous declaration that "the medium is the message," McLuhan asserts that content does not unproblemmatically get carried by the medium, but that the medium itself shapes the nature of the content and limits the extent of potential epistemological engagement. And in *Laws of Media*, published by his son posthumously, he demonstrates how media have the ability to enhance, to promote obsolescence, to retrieve, and to be transformed.

If the medium is so inextricably linked to our grasp of knowledge, then we would be hard pressed to argue that the medium only operates at the level of luxury, for the very foundations of knowledge are shaped by the medium. Therefore we would have difficulty arguing that exposure to literacy about that medium is unconnected to fundamental issues of fairness and access to opportunity. The material media of culture is not separate from other core goods. In such a configured world in which design and visual culture figure so prominently, it follows that exposure to and literacy in these areas would affect an individual's ability to succeed. Just like the book, *Dress for Success,* from the 1970s, posited that awareness of sartorial cultural codes can be important to success quite apart from academic or professional skills, so too can we make a declaration about general visual and spatial literacy. In other words, design can be translated into economic value. Therefore, our society cannot presume to be giving all members a fair and equal opportunity for success without considering the distribution of design value.

A second argument against a Maslovian hierarchical view, in which design is seen as a good that sits at the upper reaches of the pyramid order, comes from a critique of a simplistic separation of social goods into the categories of needs and luxuries. While Maslow's 1954 five-tiered "hierarchy of human needs," going from physiological needs, to security and stability, to psychological or social needs, to self-esteem, and finally to self-actualization through morality, creativity, and problem solving, might seem compelling, there is a flaw with the basic premise of this view. For humans do not necessarily satisfy completely the needs of one tier before seeking the needs of another. Even as the so-called lower needs push to be satisfied, upper-level needs are also very real and present. The strict hierarchical diagram implies a rigid relationship from tier to tier that is not upheld in empirical observation, as evident in the pursuits of higher activities on the pyramid, such as morality and creativity, by people whose basic physical and security needs are far from being established.

Virginia Postrel, in *The Substance of Style,* supports such a critique, discrediting a view in which

design and aesthetic concerns are placed in strict sequential structure, to be addressed only after other supposedly more basic concerns are fulfilled. She writes: "Human beings don't wait for aesthetics until they have full stomachs and a roof that doesn't leak. They do not pursue aesthetic needs only when basic needs have been satisfied. … Aesthetics is not a luxury, but a universal human desire. … There is no pyramid of needs, where each layer depends on completely satisfying the need under it.' (Postrel 2003: 45). As Elie Wiesel, chronicler of the Holocaust, reminded us, when children were being marched to the gas chambers, what they needed was not food for their stomachs, but stories to touch their souls. The spiritual benefits that can be wrought by the arts are not always second to our physical needs.

Additionally, such an attitude is evident in the foundational discussions of natural rights, for the argument was never about the preservation of bodily viability alone. Whether it is in Locke, Grotius, or Rousseau, the emphasis is on natural rights encompassing life and the free pursuit of personal fulfillment. Early framers of the social contract never discussed natural law and the social contract only in terms of physiological survival. Their goal was to cultivate respect for and preservation of personal liberty, leading toward self-fulfillment, under which bodily survival is only a subcategory. It seems we have too easily in our own era dismissed this wider aim of social contract theory that lies at the foundations of our social structures.

This point is further expressed in John Rawls's definition of basic goods, what he calls "primary social goods," that should be considered in discussions of social justice. The primary social goods to be assured for all people "are rights and liberties, opportunities and power, income and wealth" that allow for "greater success in carrying out their intentions and advancing their ends, whatever these ends may be" (p. 92). Moreover, Rawls emphatically includes in this bundle of primary social goods self-respect, stating "I have also said that self-respect and a sure confidence in the sense of one's own worth is perhaps the most important primary good" (p. 396). He says that this is true of even a "thin theory of good," that is, one that considers only the most basic level of just distribution (p. 397).

Such an argument depends on an Aristotelian definition of the good, which holds that the highest good for an individual includes the opportunity to freely pursue and exercise capabilities, both natural and learned, in ever-increasing enjoyment and complexity. Ultimately, defining basic needs in this way enhances the whole of society. Rawls reminds us that such values as "personal affection and friendship, meaningful work and social cooperation, the pursuit of knowledge and the fashioning and contemplation of beautiful objects … are not only good for those who enjoy them but they are likely to enhance the good of others. … These facts of interdependency are further reasons for including the recognized values in long term plans" (p. 425). The opposite of such an inclusion of self-respect is shame, a condition we easily recognize existing for many people at the lower rungs of the economic ladder.

The final question, then, is whether our present distribution of design and aesthetic value allows for the cultivation of self-respect and self-actualization that lies at the foundation of our social contract. In a capitalistic system, our physical environment and our material appurtenances will naturally bear the greater imprint of those in power. After all, those with economic power have the means to directly control design value and shape its character. However, we cannot continue to support such inequalities and think our system is just. Either we say design is not all that important and so it does not need to be included in discussions of justice. Or we say that design is extremely important and so it should be subject to the scrutiny of fairness. And if we subject design to the criteria of the veil of ignorance, can we honestly say that design value would be distributed as it is today?

SECTION 6: DESIGN AND GLOBAL ISSUES

6.3: Sustainability

INTRODUCTION

Design schools are beginning to teach students what can be done to make the human experience on Earth sustainable in the face of global warming and other environmental concerns. However, these efforts are not enough. As Joel Towers discusses in an article titled "Learning Deficiency" (see annotated reading guide at the end of this subsection), design education does not spend enough time assessing our planet's most pressing ecological problem. Schools offer courses that touch on issues related to the environment, and some classes ask students to design solutions to our climate-based predicament, but design curricula often ignore the importance of sustainability. We tend to move forward promoting the status quo, rather than seeking viable options that could begin the process of solving our current crisis. Designers often refuse to acknowledge the inherent dilemma that attends all design practice: Creating solutions inevitably leads to the creation of future waste. And, as Buckminster Fuller explained in the Design Philosophies and Theories subsection of the *Reader* (2.1), there are numerous options available, but we have been slow to take advantage of these opportunities.

The evidence about global warming is now overwhelming. The average temperature on the planet's surface has been rising each year. In fact, many scientists contend that the average temperature on Earth is approaching the highest level in a million years. These increases, caused by our use of fossil fuels that emit greenhouse gases, have warmed our oceans and raised the average air temperature. This has set off a chain of reactions, including the increased melting of the polar icecap and the intensity of tropical storms. As water levels rise and become warmer, the realities of flooding and catastrophes, such as hurricanes, become more frightening. Design offers possible solutions to these dilemmas. Indeed, design can help us solve these problems by creating products and infrastructure that remedy global warming. By implementing a new form of design education that teaches solutions, rather than business as usual, new possibilities about a sustainable future can be discussed and put into action.

William McDonough and Michael Braungart argue that issues related to sustainability and the environment are ideologically based concerns. In their seminal book, *Cradle to Cradle: Remaking the Way We Make Things,* they trace our relationship with nature to the Industrial Revolution when, because of "the desire of the acquisition of capital," a way of life emerged that "wanted to make products as efficiently as possible and to get the greatest volume of goods to the largest number of people." This model of production designed and manufactured commodities that have a life cycle identified by the authors as "cradle to grave." Everything that we use, from cars to computers to the ever-increasing volume of plastic water bottles that fill our enormous refrigerators, are designed to be thrown away. These nonbiodegradable products end up in "a landfill or incinerator," where they degrade the environment by taking up valuable space and producing greenhouse-gas emissions. This problematic cycle of creating vast quantities of consumables that end up being tossed aside is, according to McDonough and Braungart, the main culprit behind our current environmental conundrum. They contend that design can save this "cradle to grave" cycle, and in its place we can create things that are environmentally sensitive by insuring that consumables are constantly circulating and in use. In short, we need products that are "cradle to cradle," so that they cycle through a use and reuse sequence. Instead of making goods for a "worse-case scenario," which are designed for the largest pool of consumers, the authors hope that designers can begin to work creatively on solutions that will enable us to rethink our notion of disposability.

Victor Papanek explains how designers can create a safer future through better choices. He begins by detailing six ways in which design produces pollution. Materials, factories, packaging, products, transportation of goods, and, of course, waste all add to what Papanek describes as a frightening "life cycle assessment." Papanek writes that "we routinely over-package things" and produce excess waste that leads products, and their packaging, to landfill locations where toxins are released that interfere with the health of the planet. Tires, the rubber packaging that allow cars to move on wheels, are one of the most widely dumped products in the world. Papanek examines a process that would enable us to transform the mass graveyard of tires found all over the planet into "twelve thousand million gallons of oil." Like Towers, Papanek claims that "all design education must be based on ecological methods and ideas." As Susan Szenasy notes in the Ethics subsection (3.2), designers have an ethical obligation to question the link between the environment and design practices. This changing discourse about sustainability in the profession is taking hold, but sometimes with dubious results. Corporations, for instance, are beginning to use ideas about "green" design to advertise to potential consumers by placing bold graphics on products that claim ecological sensitivity. These ploys, such as the famous department store, Barneys, in New York using green-colored shopping bags for the holidays that declare "Have a Green Holiday," might raise the profile of this important cause, yet place their message on design packaging, one of the most prolific causes of consumer waste.

In a short article from *Design Week,* Trish Lorenz furthers what the other authors in this subsection assert about design's role in relation to ecology. She notes Tim Cooper's assessment that "80 percent of a product's environmental impact is fixed at the point of design." Cooper, who runs the Center for Sustainable Consumption at Sheffield Hallam University, contends that designers need to talk to clients about other possibilities that create different scenarios besides "our throw-away culture." Lorenz quotes another design thinker, Guy Robinson, as explaining, "We find that clients generally don't include sustainability issues as part of the brief, but we feel it's our responsibility to write that in."

As popular media sources, such as *Design Week,* focus on the importance of sustainability, some designers will continue to seek best practices that find sustainable solutions. Although still a nascent field, the imperative to create a viable future in the face of global warming is critical. As McDonough made clear in *The Hannover Principles* (1992), which assessed the importance of utilizing green design in the city of Hannover, Germany, for the world exposition of 2000, it is time to "inspire an approach to design which will meet the needs and aspirations of the present without compromising the ability of the planet to sustain an equally supportive future." Since the crux of good design is about seeking potential, it is exciting to think about a future when new practices will lead to workable alternatives.

68

A QUESTION OF DESIGN

William McDonough and Michael Braungart

In the spring of 1912, one of the largest moving objects ever created by human beings left Southampton, England, and began gliding toward New York. It appeared to be the epitome of its industrial age—a potent representation of technology, prosperity, luxury, and progress. It weighed 66,000 tons. Its steel hull stretched the length of four city blocks. Each of its steam engines was the size of a town house. And it was headed for a disastrous encounter with the natural world.

This vessel, of course, was the *Titanic,* a brute of a ship, seemingly impervious to the forces of the natural world. In the minds of the captain, the crew, and many of the passengers, nothing could sink it.

One might say that the *Titanic* was not only a product of the Industrial Revolution but remains an apt metaphor for the industrial infrastructure that revolution created. Like that famous ship, this infrastructure is powered by brutish and artificial sources

Image 30   Prius car. Courtesy of Toyota.

of energy that are environmentally depleting. It pours waste into the water and smoke into the sky. It attempts to work by its own rules, which are contrary to those of nature. And although it may seem invincible, the fundamental flaws in its design presage tragedy and disaster.

A BRIEF HISTORY OF THE INDUSTRIAL REVOLUTION

Imagine that you have been given the assignment of designing the Industrial Revolution—retrospectively. With respect to its negative consequences, the assignment would have to read something like this:

Design a system of production that

- puts billions of pounds of toxic material into the air, water, and soil every year
- produces some materials so dangerous they will require constant vigilance by future generations
- results in gigantic amounts of waste
- puts valuable materials in holes all over the planet, where they can never be retrieved
- requires thousands of complex regulations—not to keep people and natural systems safe, but rather to keep them from being poisoned too quickly
- measures productivity by how few people are working
- creates prosperity by digging up or cutting down natural resources and then burying or burning them
- erodes the diversity of species and cultural practices.

Of course, the industrialists, engineers, inventors, and other minds behind the Industrial Revolution never intended such consequences. In fact, the Industrial Revolution as a whole was not really designed. It took shape gradually, as industrialists, engineers, and designers tried to solve problems and to take immediate advantage of what they considered to be opportunities in

an unprecedented period of massive and rapid change.

It began with textiles in England, where agriculture had been the main occupation for centuries. Peasants farmed, the manor and town guilds provided food and goods, and industry consisted of craftspeople working individually as a side venture to farming. Within a few decades, this cottage industry, dependent on the craft of individual laborers for the production of small quantities of woolen cloth, was transformed into a mechanized factory system that churned out fabric—much of it now cotton instead of wool—by the mile.

This change was spurred by a quick succession of new technologies. In the mid-1700s cottage workers spun thread on spinning wheels in their homes, working the pedals with their hands and feet to make one thread at a time. The spinning jenny, patented in 1770, increased the number of threads from one to eight, then sixteen, then more. Later models would spin as many as eighty threads simultaneously. Other mechanized equipment, such as the water frame and the spinning mule, increased production levels at such a pace, it must have seemed something like Moore's Law (named for Gordon Moore, a founder of Intel), in which the processing speed of computer chips roughly doubles every eighteen months.

In preindustrial times, exported fabrics would travel by canal or sailing ships, which were slow and unreliable in poor weather, weighted with high duties and strict laws, and vulnerable to piracy. In fact, it was a wonder the cargo got to its destination at all. The railroad and the steamship allowed products to be moved more quickly and farther. By 1840 factories that had once made a thousand articles a week had the means and motivation to produce a thousand articles a day. Fabric workers grew too busy to farm and moved into towns to be closer to factories, where they and their families might work twelve or more hours a day. Urban areas spread, goods proliferated, and city populations increased. More, more, more—jobs, people, products, factories, businesses, markets—seemed to be the rule of the day.

Like all paradigm shifts, this one encountered resistance. Cottage workers afraid of losing work and Luddites (followers of Ned Ludd)—experienced cloth makers angry about the new machines and the unapprenticed workers who operated them—smashed labor-saving equipment and made life difficult for inventors, some of whom died outcast and penniless before they could profit from their new machines. Resistance touched not simply on technology but on spiritual and imaginative life. The Romantic poets articulated the growing difference between the rural, natural landscape and that of the city—often in despairing terms: "Citys … are nothing less than over grown prisons that shut out the world and all its beauties,"[1] wrote the poet John Clare. Artists and aesthetes like John Ruskin and William Morris feared for a civilization whose aesthetic sensibility and physical structures were being reshaped by materialistic designs.

There were other, more lasting problems. Victorian London was notorious for having been "the great and dirty city," Charles Dickens called it, and its unhealthy environment and suffering underclasses became hallmarks of the burgeoning industrial city. London air was so grimy from airborne pollutants, especially emissions from burning coal, that people would change their cuffs and collars at the end of the day (behavior that would be repeated in Chattanooga during the 1960s, and even today in Beijing or Manila). In early factories and other industrial operations, such as mining, materials were considered expensive, but people were often considered cheap. Children as well as adults worked for long hours in deplorable conditions.

But the general spirit of early industrialists—and of many others at the time—was one of great optimism and faith in the progress of humankind. As industrialization boomed, other institutions emerged that assisted its rise: commercial banks, stock exchanges, and the commercial press all opened further employment opportunities for the new middle class and tightened the social network around economic growth. Cheaper products, public transportation, water distribution and sanitation, waste collection, laundries, safe housing, and other conveniences gave people, both rich and poor, what appeared to be a more equitable standard of living. No longer did the leisure classes alone have access to all the comforts.

The Industrial Revolution was not planned, but it was not without a motive. At bottom it was an economic revolution, driven by the desire for the acquisition of capital. Industrialists wanted to make products as efficiently as possible and to get the greatest volume of goods to the largest number of people. In most industries, this meant shifting from a system of manual labor to one of efficient mechanization.

Consider cars.[2] In the early 1890s the automobile (of European origin) was made to meet a customer's specifications by craftspeople who were usually independent contractors. For example, a machine-tool company in Paris, which happened to be the leading manufacturer of cars at the time, produced only several hundred a year. They were luxury items, built slowly and carefully by hand. There was no standard system of measuring and gauging parts, and no way to cut hard steel, so parts were created by different contractors, hardened under heat (which often altered dimensions), and individually filed down to fit the hundreds of other parts in the car. No two were alike, nor could they be.

Henry Ford worked as an engineer, a machinist, and a builder of race cars (which he himself raced) before founding the Ford Motor Company in 1903. After producing a number of early vehicles, Ford realized that to make cars for the modern American worker—not just for the wealthy—he would need to manufacture vehicles cheaply and in great quantities. In 1908 his company began producing the legendary Model T, the "car for the great multitude"[3] that Ford had dreamed of, "constructed of the best materials, by the best men to be hired, after the simplest designs that modem engineering can devise … so low in price that no man making a good salary will be unable to own one."

In the following years, several aspects of manufacturing meshed to achieve this goal, revolutionizing car production and rapidly increasing levels of efficiency. First, centralization: in 1909 Ford announced that the company would produce only Model T's and in 1910 moved to a much larger factory that would use electricity for its power and gather a number of production processes under one roof. The most famous of Ford's innovations is the moving assembly line. In early production, the engines, frames, and bodies of the cars were assembled separately, then brought together for final assembly by a group of workmen. Ford's innovation was to bring "the materials to the man," instead of "the man to the materials." He and his engineers developed a moving assembly line based on the ones used in the Chicago beef industry: it carried materials to workers and, at its most efficient, enabled each of them to repeat a single operation as the vehicle moved down the line, reducing overall labor time dramatically.

This and other advances made possible the mass production of the universal car, the Model T, from a centralized location, where many vehicles were assembled at once. Increasing efficiency pushed costs of the Model T down (from $850 in 1908 to $290 in 1925), and sales skyrocketed. By 1911, before the introduction of the assembly line, sales of the Model T had totaled 39,640. By 1927, total sales reached fifteen million.

The advantages of standardized, centralized production were manifold. Obviously, it could bring greater, quicker affluence to industrialists. On another front, manufacturing was viewed as what Winston Churchill referred to as "the arsenal of democracy," because the productive capacity was so huge, it could (as in the two world wars) produce an undeniably potent response to war conditions. Mass production had another democratizing aspect: as the Model T demonstrated, when prices of a previously unattainable item or service plummeted, more people had access to it. New work opportunities in factories improved standards of living, as did wage increases. Ford himself assisted in this shift. In 1914, when the prevailing salary for factory workers was $2.34 a day, he hiked it to $5, pointing out that cars cannot buy cars. (He also reduced the hours of the workday from nine to eight.) In one fell swoop,

he actually created his own market, and raised the bar for the entire world of industry.

Viewed from a design perspective, the Model T epitomized the general goal of the first industrialists: to make a product that was desirable, affordable, and operable by anyone, just about anywhere; that lasted a certain amount of time (until it was time to buy a new one); and that could be produced cheaply and quickly. Along these lines, technical developments centered on increasing "power, accuracy, economy, system, continuity, speed,"[4] to use the Ford manufacturing checklist for mass production.

For obvious reasons, the design goals of early industrialists were quite specific, limited to the practical, profitable, efficient, and linear. Many industrialists, designers, and engineers did not see their designs as part of a larger system, outside of an economic one. But they did share some general assumptions about the world.

"THOSE ESSENCES UNCHANGED BY MAN"

Early industries relied on a seemingly endless supply of natural "capital." Ore, timber, water, grain, cattle, coal, land—these were the raw materials for the production systems that made goods for the masses, and they still are today. Ford's River Rouge plant epitomized the flow of production on a massive scale: huge quantities of iron, coal, sand, and other raw materials entered one side of the facility and, once inside, were transformed into new cars. Industries fattened as they transformed resources into products. The prairies were overtaken for agriculture, and the great forests were cut down for wood and fuel. Factories situated themselves near natural resources for easy access (today a prominent window company is located in a place that was originally surrounded by giant pines, used for the window frames) and beside bodies of water, which they used both for manufacturing processes and to dispose of wastes.

In the nineteenth century, when these practices began, the subtle qualities of the environment were not a widespread concern. Resources seemed immeasurably vast. Nature itself was perceived as a "mother earth" who, perpetually regenerative, would absorb all things and continue to grow. Even Ralph Waldo Emerson, a prescient philosopher and poet with a careful eye for nature, reflected a common belief when, in the early 1830s, he described nature as "essences unchanged by man; space, the air, the river, the leaf."[5] Many people believed there would always be an expanse that remained unspoiled and innocent. The popular fiction of Rudyard Kipling and others evoked wild parts of the world that still existed and, it seemed, always would.

At the same time, the Western view saw nature as a dangerous, brutish force to be civilized and subdued. Humans perceived natural forces as hostile, so they attacked back to exert control. In the United States, taming the frontier took on the power of a defining myth, and "conquering" wild, natural places was recognized as a cultural—even spiritual—imperative.

Today our understanding of nature has dramatically changed. New studies indicate that the oceans, the air, the mountains, and the plants and animals that inhabit them are more vulnerable than early innovators ever imagined. But modern industries still operate according to paradigms that developed when humans had a very different sense of the world. Neither the health of natural systems, nor an awareness of their delicacy, complexity, and interconnectedness, have been part of the industrial design agenda. At its deepest foundation, the industrial infrastructure we have today is linear: it is focused on making a product and getting it to a customer quickly and cheaply without considering much else.

To be sure, the Industrial Revolution brought a number of positive social changes. With higher standards of living, life expectancy greatly increased. Medical care and education greatly improved and became more widely available. Electricity, telecommunications, and other advances raised comfort and convenience to a new level. Technological advances brought the so-called developing nations enormous benefits, including increased productivity of agricultural land and vastly increased harvests and food storage for growing populations.

But there were fundamental flaws in the Industrial Revolution's design. They resulted in some crucial omissions, and devastating consequences have been handed down to us, along with the dominant assumptions of the era in which the transformation took shape.

FROM CRADLE TO GRAVE

Imagine what you would come upon today at a typical landfill: old furniture, upholstery, carpets, televisions, clothing, shoes, telephones, computers, complex products, and plastic packaging, as well as organic materials like diapers, paper, wood, and food wastes. Most of these products were made from valuable materials that required effort and expense to extract and make, billions of dollars' worth of material assets. The biodegradable materials such as food matter and paper actually have value too—they could decompose and return biological nutrients to the soil. Unfortunately, all of these things are heaped in a landfill, where their value is wasted. They are the ultimate products of an industrial system that is designed on a linear, one-way *cradle-to-grave* model. Resources are extracted, shaped into products, sold, and eventually disposed of in a "grave" of some kind, usually a landfill or incinerator. You are probably familiar with the end of this process because you, the customer, are responsible for dealing with its detritus. Think about it: you may be referred to as a consumer, but there is very little that you actually consume—some food, some liquids. Everything else is designed for you to throw away when you are finished with it. But where is "away"? Of course, "away" does not really exist. "Away" has gone away.

Cradle-to-grave designs dominate modern manufacturing. According to some accounts more than 90 percent of materials extracted to make durable goods in the United States become waste almost immediately.[6] Sometimes the product itself scarcely lasts longer. It is often cheaper to buy a new version of even the most expensive appliance than to track down someone to repair the original item. In fact, many products are designed with "built-in obsolescence," to last only for a certain period of time, to allow—to encourage—the customer to get rid of the thing and buy a new model. Also, what most people see in their garbage cans is just the tip of a material iceberg; the product itself contains on average only 5 percent of the raw materials involved in the process of making and delivering it.

ONE SIZE FITS ALL

Because the cradle-to-grave model underlying the design assumptions of the Industrial Revolution was not called into question, even movements that were formed ostensibly in opposition to that era manifested its flaws. One example has been the push to achieve universal design solutions, which emerged as a leading design strategy in the last century. In the field of architecture, this strategy took the form of the International Style movement, advanced during the early decades of the twentieth century by figures such as Ludwig Mies van der Rohe, Walter Gropius, and Le Corbusier, who were reacting against Victorian-era styles. (Gothic cathedrals were still being proposed and built.) Their goals were social as well as aesthetic. They wanted to globally replace unsanitary and inequitable housing—fancy, ornate places for the rich; ugly, unhealthy places for the poor—with clean, minimalist, affordable buildings unencumbered by distinctions of wealth or class. Large sheets of glass, steel, and concrete, and cheap transportation powered by fossil fuels, gave engineers and architects the tools for realizing this style anywhere in the world.

Today the International Style has evolved into something less ambitious: a bland, uniform structure isolated from the particulars of place—from local culture, nature, energy, and material flows. Such buildings reflect little if any of a region's distinctness or style. They often stand out like sore thumbs from the surrounding landscape, if they leave any of it intact around their "office parks" of asphalt and concrete. The interiors are equally uninspiring. With their sealed windows, constantly humming air conditioners, heating systems, lack of daylight and fresh air,

and uniform fluorescent lighting, they might as well have been designed to house machines, not humans.

The originators of the International Style intended to convey hope in the "brotherhood" of humankind. Those who use the style today do so because it is easy and cheap and makes architecture uniform in many settings. Buildings can look and work the same anywhere, in Reykjavik or Rangoon.

In product design, a classic example of the universal design solution is mass-produced detergent. Major soap manufacturers design one detergent for all parts of the United States or Europe, even though water qualities and community needs differ. For example, customers in places with soft water, like the Northwest, need only small amounts of detergent. Those where the water is hard, like the Southwest, need more. But detergents are designed so they will lather up, remove dirt, and kill germs efficiently the same way anywhere in the world—in hard, soft, urban, or spring water, in water that flows into fish-filled streams and water channeled to sewage treatment plants. Manufacturers just add more chemical force to wipe out the conditions of circumstance. Imagine the strength a detergent must have to strip day-old grease from a greasy pan. Now imagine what happens when that detergent comes into contact with the slippery skin of a fish or the waxy coating of a plant. Treated and untreated effluents as well as runoff are released into lakes, rivers, and oceans. Combinations of chemicals, from household detergents, cleansers, and medicines along with industrial wastes, end up in sewage effluents, where they have been shown to harm aquatic life, in some cases causing mutations and infertility.[7]

To achieve their universal design solutions, manufacturers design for a *worst-case scenario;* they design a product for the worst possible circumstance, so that it will always operate with the same efficacy. This aim guarantees the largest possible market for a product. It also reveals human industry's peculiar relationship to the natural world, since designing for the worst case at all times reflects the assumption that nature is the enemy.

[...]

A STRATEGY OF TRAGEDY, OR A STRATEGY OF CHANGE?

Today's industrial infrastructure is designed to chase economic growth. It does so at the expense of other vital concerns, particularly human and ecological health, cultural and natural richness, and even enjoyment and delight. Except for a few generally known positive side effects, most industrial methods and materials are unintentionally depletive.

Yet just as industrialists, engineers, designers, and developers of the past did not intend to bring about such devastating effects, those who perpetuate these paradigms today surely do not intend to damage the world. The waste, pollution, crude products, and other negative effects that we have described are not the result of corporations doing something morally wrong. They are the consequence of outdated and unintelligent design.

Nevertheless, the damage is certain and severe. Modern industries are chipping away at some of the basic achievements that industrialization brought about. Food stocks, for example, have increased so that more children are fed, but more children go to bed hungry as well. But even if well-fed children are regularly exposed to substances that can lead to genetic mutations, cancer, asthma, allergies, and other complications from industrial contamination and waste, then what has been achieved? Poor design on such a scale reaches far beyond our own life span. It perpetuates what we call *intergenerational remote* tyranny—our tyranny over future generations through the effects of our actions today.

At some point a manufacturer or designer decides, "We can't keep doing this. We can't keep supporting and maintaining this system." At some point they will decide that they would prefer to leave behind a positive design legacy. But when is that point?

We say that point is today, and negligence starts tomorrow. Once you understand the destruction taking place, unless you do something to change it, even if you never intended to cause such destruction, you become involved in a strategy of tragedy. You can continue to be engaged in that strategy of tragedy, or you can design and implement a *strategy of change*.

NOTES

Extracted from W. McDonough and M. Braungart, *Cradle to Cradle: Remaking the Way We Make Things* (New York: North Point Press, 2002), pp. 17–30 and 42–44. Reprinted by permission.

1. "Citys ... are nothing": John Clare (1793–1864), "Letter to Messrs Taylor and Hessey, II," in *The Oxford Authors: John Clare,* edited by Eric Robinson and David Powell (Oxford and New York: Oxford University Press, 1984), 457.
2. Consider cars: James P. Womack, Daniel Jones, and Daniel Roos, *The Machine That Changed the World* (New York: Macmillan, 1990), 21–25.
3. Henry Ford: Quoted in Ray Batchelor, *Henry Ford: Mass Production, Modernism, and Design* (Manchester and New York: Manchester University Press, 1994), 20.
4. "Power, accuracy, economy": Ibid., 41.
5. "Essences unchanged": Ralph Waldo Emerson, "Nature," in *Selections from Ralph Waldo Emerson,* edited by Stephen E. Whicher (Boston: Houghton Mifflin, 1957), 22.
6. More than 90 percent: Robert Ayres and A. V. Neese, "Externalities: Economics and Thermodynamics," in *Economy and Ecology: Towards Sustainable Development*, edited by F. Archibugi and P. Nijkamp (Netherlands: Kluwer Academic, 1989), 93.
7. Mutations and infertility: Marla Cone, "River Pollution Study Finds Hormonal Defects in Fish Science: Discovery in Britain Suggests Sewage Plants Worldwide May Cause Similar Reproductive-Tract Damage," *Los Angeles Times,* September 22, 1998.

69

DESIGNING FOR A SAFE FUTURE

Victor Papanek

Ecology and the environmental equilibrium are the basic underpinnings of all human life on earth; there can be neither life nor human culture without it. Design is concerned with the development of products, tools, machines, artefacts and other devices, and this activity has a profound and direct influence on ecology. The design response must be positive and *unifying*. Design must be the bridge between human needs, culture and ecology.

This can be clearly demonstrated. The creation and manufacture of *any* product—both during its period of active use and its existence afterwards—fall into at least six separate cycles, each of which has the potential for ecological harm.

When we speak of pollution as related to products, we usually think of end results: the exhaust fumes from automobiles, the smoke from factory chimneys, chemical fertilizers or truck tyres in a dump poisoning the ground-water. But pollution falls into several phases.

PRODUCTION AND POLLUTION

The Choice of Materials

The materials chosen by designer and manufacturer are crucial. Mining metal for cars creates atmospheric pollution, and uses oil and petrol, thus wasting natural resources that cannot be replaced. The designer's decision to use foam plastics to make cheap, throw-away food containers damages the ozone layer. This is not a prescription for doing nothing at all, but an attempt to make designers aware that every choice and dilemma in

their work can have far-reaching and long-term ecological consequences.

The Manufacturing Processes

The questions facing the designer are: Is there anything in the manufacturing process itself that might endanger the workplace or the workers, such as toxic fumes or radioactive materials? Are there air-pollutants from factory smokestacks, such as the gases that cause acid rain? Are liquid wastes from the factory leaking into the ground and destroying agricultural land or—worse still—entering the water supply?

Packaging the Product

Further ecological choices face the designer when developing the package in which the product is transported, marketed and distributed. Foam plastics, which pose acute dangers to the ecological balance, are used by designers as a protection for fragile products. It is now known that propellants (such as CFCs) for lacquer sprays and other products are directly implicated in the depletion of the ozone layer. Considerations of materials and methods are therefore crucial in the packaging phase of ecologically aware design.

The Finished Product

There are too many different versions of the same item available in many cases. Since the manufacture of most industrial or consumer products uses up irreplaceable raw materials, the profusion of objects in the market-place constitutes a profound ecological threat. To give a typical example: in western Europe, Canada, Japan and the USA there are now more than 250 different video cameras available to consumers; the differences between them are minimal—in some cases they are identical but for the name-plate. The choice of consumer products in the West is highly artificial.

Other products threaten the ecological balance even more directly. Snowmobiles, which are largely sold as winter-sports and recreation equipment, are so noisy that when they go into roadless terrain they destroy breeding grounds and habitats. Yet, at the same time, they have assumed an important role in hunting and herding cycles and are now important tools for survival among the Inuit of Canada and Alaska. 'Off-road' vehicles and 'mountain bikes' affect the precious layer of topsoil and humus that can grow crops. 'Dune buggies' harm the sand-dune layers at the critical edge between ocean and land.

Transporting the Product

The transporting of materials and products further contributes to pollution by the burning of fossil fuels, and by the necessity for a whole complex of roads, rails, airports and depots. There is transportation from the mill to the factory, the factory to the distribution centre, from there to the shops and, eventually, to the end-user.

Waste

Many products can have negative consequences *after the useful product life is over.* One only has to see the huge automobile graveyards in many countries to understand that these vast amounts of rusting metals, decaying paints and shellacs, deteriorating plastic upholstery, leaking oils and petrol are leaching directly into the ground, poisoning the soil, the water-supply and the wildlife, besides visually destroying the landscape. It has been estimated that the average family in the technologically developed countries throws away some 16 to 20 tons of garbage and waste a year. This is not only an environmental hazard, but is also an enormous waste of materials that could be recycled responsibly. This is one area in which the so-called Third World countries are leading the way—because of material scarcities, recycling is an accepted way of life there and has been for generations.

PRODUCT ASSESSMENT

The relationship between design and ecology is a very close one,[1] and makes for some unexpected complexities. The designed product goes, as shown, through at least *six* potentially ecologically dangerous phases. Product Life Cycle Assessment is the evaluation incorporating all of them, from the original acquisition of raw materials, through the manufacturing process and assembly, the purchase of the complete product (which also includes shipping, packaging, advertising and the printing of instruction manuals), the use, the collection of the product after use, and finally the re-use or recycling and final disposal. It can best be understood through the hexagonal diagram, the six-sided 'Function Matrix'. At the moment Life Cycle Assessment is very new, and can be profoundly complicated, demanding a great deal of study, testing and experimentation.

Environmental Issues in Life Cycle Assessment

- The exhaustion of scarce or finite resources
- The production of greenhouse gases
- The production of chlorofluorocarbons leading to ozone depletion
- The production of acid rain
- Habitat destruction and species extinction
- Materials or processes that harm plants, animals and humans
- Air, soil and water pollution

- Noise pollution with its deleterious effect on the human psyche
- Visual pollution

PACKAGING AND SHROUDING

Most goods need to be packaged. The package protects the contents in transit and in store from spoilage, vermin, moisture and damage. It can serve as a powerful marketing tool through design, colour and texture. Furthermore […], it will frequently signify not only the contents, but also lend identity to the product-line. In terms of goods that are nearly identical—washing-up powders, breakfast cereals or cigarettes—it can be said that *the package is the product.*

It is clear that we routinely over-package things. In some cases this is to lend a visual charisma to luxury goods such as perfumes that sell at enormously inflated prices. But the less luxurious package can be equally destructive of the environment. Fast-food suppliers have for decades used small coffins made of a plastic known as styrofoam in North America in which to serve their cheeseburgers and Big Macs. Some years ago, McDonald outlets in the American Midwest proudly proclaimed on an automatically changing neon sign: '*Seventy billion* sold so far' (italics supplied). More recently the McDonald corporation has been convinced of the ecological soundness of switching to paper containers.

Foam plastic is a very useful packing material, yet profoundly damaging to the environment. After it has been discarded, it is doubtful whether it is possible to re-use it, and it continues to be an environmental and toxic hazard in spite of the optimistic assurances of the manufacturers relayed to the public by their public relations people. The advantages of foam plastic are that it makes an extremely lightweight protection for precision parts, is easily formed around delicate optical instruments or electronic assemblies, and is quite inexpensive. But there are alternative and organic ways of packaging.

It is a valuable concept that there is really nothing new in the world that needs to be packed and shipped. The immediate objection will be that this is sheer nonsense. After all, there were no computers, CD players or camcorders in the distant past. Yet Van Leuwenhoek had to ship his microscopes from the Netherlands to Padua in the 16th century, Galileo needed to send telescopes to the Danish astronomer Tycho Brahe on the island of Hven off southern Sweden, and forward 'philosophical instruments' and optics to various other parts of Europe. More recently, during the Civil War in the United States, delicate surgical instruments had to be shipped from northern factories to the front. The materials used to pack such early precision instruments were Spanish moss, other dried mosses, sand, sawdust, crushed and dried leaves or dried grasses, thin cotton bags filled with down or feathers, wood chips, and much else. The one thing that these materials have in common is that they can be recycled; they are all organic and will return to the natural environment.

My earliest introduction to this way of packing was my first job as a young boy in New York. I worked in the basement of the Museum of Modern Art packing small sculptures or ceramics to send to members of the museum who were renting art objects for a few months at a time. I remember that, in addition to shipping-boxes (which were made of wood or cardboard), we had two gigantic popcorn machines, and made popcorn—unsalted and without cheese, I may add—in which to pack the sculpture pieces; polystyrene 'worms' did not then exist. It was an intelligent and decent way of packing which in 1992, to my delight, began to be revived by some mail-order firms as an ecologically responsible way of dealing with fragile objects.

In 1989 I was hired by a Japanese corporation, specializing in computers, cameras, and other high-tech products, and spent three years conducting research and feasibility studies in the use of organic packaging materials. Research eventually concentrated on plants that, when maturing, surround their seeds with an enormous protective cradle of fluffy material. The specific seed we researched expands its bulk to more than forty times the original volume.

The package was for a professional precision 35mm camera and its lenses. Normally, expensive small cameras are cradled in a shaped foam-plastic cushion that has been covered with an equally plastic fake-velveteen fabric. This in turn is topped by another velvet-like foam-plastic lid on top, and both are bedded in a sarcophagus-like box, made of high-impact polystyrene. The box is held, or suspended, by two foam-plastic spacers within an outer (again plastic) case. Lenses are normally placed in plastic tubes that are upholstered with foam on the inside, and covered with a leather-like vinyl, called 'leatherette' (the very word makes one's flesh crawl), or a plastic called 'naughahide' on the exterior. A hideous example of over-packaging and transparent make-believe.

Eventually we created a small quilt, about 15 inches (37cm) square. The 'shell' of the quilt is made of rice-paper, filled with fluffy plant fibres and then sewn into quilt squares with a hemp-derived thread. The quilt is wrapped around the camera body and inserted into a cardboard sleeve. Quilted pouches, made of 'green' cotton and filled with eiderdown, protect the lenses. In Japan this method of softly cradling precision parts is already in experimental use, and will probably soon be used for export models. The great advantages of this package are obvious. Reliance on oil-based plastics and the hazards of their manufacture are entirely eliminated. The new package is wholly organic, and will return to the soil. To exaggerate somewhat, theoretically it may be possible in a year or two for someone to buy a camera or CD player and literally dump the wrapping in the back garden where the recyclable, organic components of the package—augmented by trace amounts of nitrate boosters—will actually help the garden grow.

At the moment, packaging generally involves the use of plastics [...], metal, wood, cardboard and paper. The use of paper has two major effects on the ecology. One of these is the cutting-down of trees

and forests, the other the pollution that occurs in the paper production itself. Nine-tenths of paper products come from forests in northern temperate zones—Canada, the United States, and northern Europe. It is now widely known how to manage such forests commercially so that they can continue to function as renewable resources, but the timber industry generally refuses to engage in selective harvesting from multi-species mature forests, and continues to plant monocultural forests and to employ the clear-cutting of established woodlands.

Chlorines used in paper production as a bleach for wood fibres also pose an ecological hazard. Chlorine creates dioxins that are mutagenic, that is to say, they create genetic changes by bonding to the DNA structure of living cells. Furthermore the runoff of water tainted with dioxin and chlorine has endangered aquatic life (such as salmon in the Pacific north west of North America), as well as poisoning ground-water.

There are packaging items that are inherently impossible to recycle. Manufacturers can easily avoid using high-gloss papers, highly coated or plastic-coated papers, glues that are not water-soluble and plastic windows on envelopes. Instead designers could specify non-bleached papers or those whitened with new, bleach-free methods. More than three-quarters of all paper types can be recycled, but usually a percentage of new fibres are added. Recycling waste paper can be 50% more energy efficient than the use of virgin pulp. It is good practice to use paper with the highest percentage of re-cycled material. The Simpson Paper Company of San Francisco has emerged as one of the leaders in this field.

[...]

Packages come in various guises. With complex mechanisms and electronic parts forming a machine or device, the package in industrial design frequently turns into a 'shroud', that is, an external cover or shell that keeps dust from the working parts, protects them, and cuts down the visual confusion of a complicated working arrangement that can no longer be understood by the end-user.

[...]

PROFIT AND POLITICS

Industrialists, primarily in Germany, Japan and Sweden, have recognized the current environmental and ecological hazards for what they really are: vast new challenges for humankind that must be solved, and *vast possibilities for future earnings, since few governments or industrial powers yet take these threats seriously.*

The beneficial connection between economics and ecology has been systematically misrepresented by industrial and governmental apologists. When the Pacific Electric Company distributes thousands of low-wattage and therefore energy-saving fluorescent light bulbs (that retail at $16.95 each), at no cost to its domestic customers, and insulates private houses for free, this may be done out of altruistic concern for a benign environment, but it also saves 185 million dollars otherwise needed to build a new power-generating station.[2]

The slogan 'Re-use, recycle and dispose responsibly' is a familiar one. 'Use less', however, should be our over-riding maxim. Manufacturers and their designers are frightened by the idea of using less. It implies that less will be bought and that profits will shrink. Yet if we disengage ourselves from this linear way of thinking, we see that quite the reverse may happen. In a world in which less is used and less is bought, products that are designed to last longer and are more carefully crafted and assembled will obviously need to cost more.

Most designers today don't seem to feel comfortable with a term like 'social responsibility' in reference to the built or designed environment. The Post-Modern condition can be characterized as a vacuum of conscience in which such socially responsible notions as fair housing, a clean environment, health care or access to services are considered somewhat of an embarrassment. Product culture has been allowed to run wild, and has substituted trendy objects for community values, many of them provided by industry and their captive industrial designers, designers and architects.

NOTES

Extracted from V. Papanek, *The Green Imperative: Natural Design for the Real World* (London: Thames and Hudson, 1995), pp. 29–37 and 39 and 46–47. Used by permission from Thames & Hudson Ltd.

1. V. Papanek, 'Seeing the World Whole: Interaction Between Ecology and Design', Fifth Inaugural Lecture, University of Kansas, 1982.
2. R. Ingersoll, 'The Ecological Question', *Journal of Architectural Education*, Feb. 1992.

70

BRITISH DESIGNERS ACCUSED OF CREATING THROW-AWAY CULTURE

Trish Lorenz

Designers are complicit in the fuelling of Britain's growing 'throw- away culture', contributing to associated environmental issues, and must begin to 'balance creativity with their environmental responsibilities', a leading sustainability expert said today.

According to Tim Cooper, head of Sheffield Hallam University's Centre for Sustainable Consumption—which is holding a conference on the issue of product durability next week—80 per cent of a product's environmental impact is fixed at the point of design.

'The Earth can't cope with the ever-increasing demands of our throw- away culture and designers clearly have a massive part to play in making products that are longer lasting,' he says. 'Designers need to raise the issue with clients and say, "We can do this in different ways."'

Sustainability is clearly moving higher up corporate, consumer and Government agendas. According to the sustainability report released by electronics company Philips last week, its 160 Green Flagship Products—which include items such as energy-efficient light bulbs—doubled in sales last year to #1.3bn.

But there has been debate in the past as to whether designers are victims or culprits in the battle to stem the nation's appetite for short-lived disposable items. Eco-friendly consultancy Sprout Design director Guy Robinson believes designers need to take more responsibility for these issues.

'We find that clients generally don't include sustainability issues as part of the brief, but we feel it's our responsibility to write that in. Sustainable and inclusive factors are an [integral] part of good design,' Robinson says.

Cooper believes products, particularly consumer goods, are becoming less durable and says designers are in danger of losing credibility as a profession. 'If you boil [design] down so that all a designer does is tweak a product in order to fulfil a marketing need, then the profession becomes worthless,' he argues.

He calls for designers to take creativity further than stylistic changes that simply respond to passing fashion and consider both the emotional aspects involved in creating long-lasting appeal and the physical aspects of durability.

'Sustainable design involves more creativity and can be far more interesting,' he says. 'Designers need to think about how they build in both reparability and emotional attachment—designing products that people want to keep for years and years.'

Robinson believes environmental responsibility and sustainability can be a source of innovation. 'Our ideas come from that style of thinking; it actually helps us be more creative,' he says.

The Centre for Sustainable Consumption was established in 1996 and conducts research that focuses on consumer behaviour and the environmental impact of household goods. Its one-day conference, Design for Durability, takes place at the Design Council in London on 11 April. Topics will encompass the tools and techniques for long-lasting design and emotionally durable design—making products with which consumers bond.

Keynote speakers include sustainable design researcher Nicole van Nes, Jonathan Chapman, author of Emotionally Durable Design, and vice-president of SlowLab, Alistair Fuad-Luke.

WASTE NOT, WANT NOT

- The UK produces more than 434 million tons of waste every year. This rate of rubbish generation would fill the Albert Hall in less than two hours
- In 2001, UK households produced the equivalent weight of 245 jumbo jets per week in packaging waste
- Recycling two glass bottles saves enough energy to boil water for five cups of tea
- One litre of oil can pollute a million litres of drinking water
- The UK uses 20 times more plastic today than 50 years ago. Source: www.wasteonline.org.uk

NOTE

Extracted from T. Lorenz, 'British Designers Accused of Creating Throw-Away Culture', *Design Week* (April 6, 2006): 7. Used with permission from *Design Week* (www.designweek.co.uk).

ANNOTATED GUIDE TO FURTHER READING

There are a number of books that provide a helpful overview of globalization. For several points of view about this contested topic, Frank Lechner and John Boli's edited volume *The Globalization Reader* (2003) provides a comprehensive perspective and is very useful. Other academic approaches to globalization can be found in Martin Wolf's very optimistic *Why Globalization Works* (2004), which is a good counter to some of the antiglobalization arguments found in Lechner and Boli. Additionally, Michael Hardt and Antonio Negri's *Empire* (2000) takes a theoretical approach to globalization, in which social, political, and economic forces are increasingly interdependent and not hindered by geographic boundaries.

The rise of globalization has helped solidify and extend the bifurcated world of poverty and wealth. Two books that describe this issue and provide possible solutions are Stephen Smith's *Ending Global Poverty: A Guide to What Works* (2005), and Paul Collier's *The Bottom Billion: Why the Poorest Countries are Failing and What Can Be Done About It* (2007). Two unusual books that look at possible solutions to social inequities through design are John Clarkson, et. al.'s *Inclusive Design: Design for the Whole Population* (2003), and Selwyn Goldsmith's *Universal Design* (2000). A book that assesses design's potential—in the face of humanitarian crises, such as extreme poverty—is Cameron Sinclair and Kate Stohr's *Design Like you Give a Damn* (2006) (Section 6.2).

Our global economy has made the issue of sustainability a critical concern. One of the earliest writers to discuss the perils of industrialization with regard to our environment is Rachel Carson. She lays the foundation for the contemporary environmental movement in her 1962 book, *Silent Spring*. E. F. Schumacher's *Small Is Beautiful: Economics as if People Mattered* (1973) is another early book that questions the corporate mantra of expansion with no regard to ecological impact. Several contemporary writers, including Paul Hawken in *The Ecology of Commerce* (1993) and Janine Benyus in *Biomimicry: Innovation Inspired by Nature* (1997), assert that we can attain progress by looking to nature for guidance. And, in terms of design, one of the original thinkers to understand the connections between sustainability and the creative process of making products for a better world is William McDonough. His *The Hannover Principles: Design for Sustainability* (1992) is an outstanding example of a designer's attempts to apply ideas about environmental sensitivity to a real-world project. Joel Towers, who worked with McDonough, has written a succinct essay on sustainability and design education's lack of concern for this topic in an article titled "Learning Deficiency" (2005). Finally, although most of the sustainability literature continues to focus on architecture, other areas of design are starting to extol the virtues of ecologically friendly practices. In fashion, for instance, Cambridge University's Institute for Manufacturing put out a very informative report titled *Well Dressed?* (2006), which considers fashion design in relation to materials and production costs that adhere to, or sadly ignore, sustainable guidelines.

SECTION 7

DESIGN THINGS

SECTION INTRODUCTION

What are "Design Things"? We have chosen this term to refer to the tangible, visible, and material objects that are designed, produced, and used by people. In our own time these products of human labor are likely to have been made by mechanical or industrial processes and to be commodities, and therefore defined, in part, by their economic value and their appearance. The examples included in this section serve as a culmination of the themes addressed in the *Reader;* they are the material substance of design studies.

We invited a range of scholars in the study of design and material culture to analyze one example each, to exemplify the particular "design thing," but also to demonstrate the level of detail and complexity that is required to understand the artificial or designed world. Each of the examples began by being developed to suit a human purpose or need. Some can be identified with a professional designer, as in the case of the "Eames chair," or with another named originator, such as Henry Beck and the "Tube Map," or London Underground Diagram. Others have particular brand identities: the Swatch watch, and the Nike sneaker. Others still are ubiquitous and long-lived and have hardly changed form over time: the bicycle and Helvetica type. Each one has been widely acclaimed as somehow significant, yet the way that design has contributed to their reputation is varied. This is due in part to the multiple roles that design takes, which have been the subject of the *Reader.* It is also because the meanings and importance that things acquire are not only instilled by professional designers, but are developed in the process of consumption and use, relative to social, economic, historical, cultural, geographical, and other myriad factors.

Design is a practice of modernity, associated with mass production and mass consumption, capitalism, and globalization. In the commodity sphere, design has become most closely associated with the visual and aesthetic aspects of products, with fashion and advertising, with personal signification and status, with culturally formed meanings. Every one of the things discussed in this section has functional and symbolic roles; they do something to improve life while also taking on an appearance that is deemed acceptable to their use. Design enabled the cell phone to shrink in size and include new capabilities that suited a broad range of users. The Petronas Towers in Kuala Lumpur, for a time the world's largest building, "were designed with a particular place in mind." They both join the Shinkansen "bullet" train, in being a product of technological development, whereas the Michael Graves kettle for Target, in contrast, was conceived to bring a high-end product design to the mass market.

Designed things also have enormous social dimensions; objects, images, spaces, environments, and messages are the material, and increasingly also the immaterial, manifestations of human beings. By design they can be forces for good, but also for evil. Not only do people produce design, either professionally or as users, but those design things are also reflective of who we are—our wants, needs, desires, responsibilities, or the lack of them.

71

THE EAMES LOUNGE

The Difference between a Design Icon and Mere Furniture

Wava Carpenter

Labeled an icon, a classic, and a masterpiece, the Eames Lounge Chair and Ottoman set is possibly the most written about piece of furniture in existence. Launched in 1956, the Lounge has sustained its reputation among design academics and enthusiasts throughout more than fifty years of continuous production, surviving the criticisms of postmodernism and decades worth of competition from increasingly novel chairs. It is the only discrete work of American Modernist design given its own museum exhibition—*The Eames Lounge Chair: An Icon of Modern Design* (organized and circulated by the Grand Rapids Art Museum, shown also at the Museum of Arts and Design in New York City and the Henry Ford Museum in Dearborn, Michigan, between May 2006 and April 2007). The designers behind it, Charles and Ray Eames, maintain a heroic stature in design history, holding a special distinction for the unusually numerous celebrated designs for which they are responsible. The exalted status of this chair begs the questions: What, exactly, is a design icon and why is the Eames Lounge, by consensus, iconic?

At the time of the Eames Lounge Chair's debut, the definition of a design icon would have been agreed upon with a greater degree of consensus than is possible today. Design, as a category of material production, encompassed industrially produced consumer goods (especially furniture and housewares) and commercial graphics, as opposed to fine art (painting and sculpture), architecture (buildings), decorative arts (preindustrial interior

décor), and crafts (handmade objects associated with "primitive" peoples). Design, as a subject of criticism, was relatively new, especially in the United States, and the pool of design critics was considerably smaller, concentrated around a handful of museums, notably the Museum of Modern Art (MoMA), and a limited number of trade and lifestyle magazines and newspaper columns. There were some dissenting voices from more conservative, populist circles (for example, Elizabeth Gordon, editor of *House Beautiful* from 1939 to 1965) that tended to discuss furniture within the arena of "decoration" rather than "design" per se.

However, mid-century design authorities, arbiters of "cultured" or "highbrow" taste, such as Nikolaus Pevsner, Siegfried Gideon, Edgar Kaufmann Jr., and Eliot Noyes, established the most influential standards, which equated design to Modernist principles. Influenced by Arts and Crafts theorists who believed that beautiful objects should permeate everyone's everyday life, and by Bauhaus practitioners who exalted the role of architect-designers in the creation of innovative, standardized goods, these mid-century authorities believed the criteria for "legitimate" design objects to be universal and unchanging. For this group, a design icon, by extension, must be a Modernist or proto-Modernist object that has stood the test of time, reinforcing their teleological narrative of design evolution since the beginnings of the Industrial Revolution.

Charles Eames himself consistently articulated his approach to furniture design as an architectural

Image 31   Eames® Lounge Chair and Ottoman. © EAMES OFFICE LLC (eamesoffice.com).

exercise in structure, simplification, and the constraints of mass production. Toward the end of his life, Eames stated, "I think of myself as an architect. I can't help but look at the problems around us as problems of structure. ..." (quoted in Diehl 1972). He added, "The idea was to do a piece of furniture that would be simple and yet comfortable. It would be a chair on which mass production would not have anything but a positive influence; it would have in its appearance the essence of the method that produced it" (Diehl 1972). Although he probably had in mind his earlier molded-plywood experiments and his legendary LCW Chair from 1946, the Lounge Chair was similarly designed with these principles more or less as the starting point.

Charles Eames's strong commitment to a principled design practice secured his position among mid-century design authorities, and the Lounge was deemed successful even though it did not fully embody Modernist ideals. The tilting body of the Lounge comprises three segments of curved plywood, the material for which Eames first gained acclaim from Modernist authorities (winning first prize in MoMA's 1940 Organic Design Competition, Noyes 1941). While the Eames Office pioneered the use of molded plywood in furniture in the 1940s, the Lounge did not represent an innovative approach to plywood but rather employed the same technology developed in the previous decade. Moving even further away from the Modernist program, the Lounge features deep cushioning, tufted glove-leather upholstery, and richly striated rosewood veneer. While the base consists of a standardized-looking star-shaped cast aluminum pedestal more in keeping with Eames's earlier, more strictly Modernist designs, the luxurious aspects of the Lounge's body strained against Modernism's ostensible populist criteria. Although the Lounge in general upheld the Modernist aesthetic of sculptural, floating, structural form, it was bulkier than any other example of Eames's work. Technically, the design is mass-produced, but its assembly process requires a good many hands-on steps, which, coupled with the expensive materials, make the chair affordable only to the affluent. Such contradiction did not hinder the Lounge's triumph; from 1956 through much of the 1970s, the Eames Lounge seemed to be included in the permanent collections of every design-collecting institution, as well as in nearly every home owned by a successful architect, physician, auteur, or jazz musician in the United States—from Eliot Noyes to Miles Davis.

Beginning in the 1960s and continuing through the 1980s, however, the discourse around design expanded, both in terms of participants and perspectives. In the early 1960s, Reyner Banham critiqued Modernist theorists for their underlying inclination to judge good design chiefly by form, and he suggested that content, instead, is the superior criterion (Michael 2002). Over the following decades, the consensus equation of Modernist design with good design evaporated, resulting in increasing debate within academic and creative circles over the universality of Modernist criteria, with focused criticism directed toward the authorities from the previous generation. One voice in particular, Joseph Mashek, represented one of the earliest outright disparaging perspectives on MoMA's criteria for good design, suggesting that the institution's claim to apolitical universality was a farce and instead represented only the *outré* tastes of the *haute bourgeoisie* (Mashek 1975). Mashek's 1975 *Art Forum* article, "Embalmed Objects: Design at the Modern," supports this argument specifically by way of a comparison between the Modernist-approved Eames Lounge Chair and the mass-market, anonymously designed Barcalounger, epitomized by traditionalist upholstery options and massive, overstuffed

shell-bodies that conceal (rather than expose) the reclining mechanisms.

Mashek's article draws attention to the officially unacknowledged similarities between the Eames Lounge and the Barcalounger, while emphasizing the persistent class associations dividing them. Both chairs emerged and found success during the postwar era, the "Populuxe" era, as coined by Thomas Hine, when consumer incomes were on the rise and manufacturers responded with an explosion of consumer goods, especially for the home (Hine 1986; 2006). Both chairs were intended for use during activities such as reading the newspaper or watching television, affording grand comfort during prolonged sitting, through deep upholstered cushioning, pitched back supports, and the opportunity to elevate one's feet (the Lounge in conjunction with the separate Ottoman, the Barcalounger through the retractable foot-rest mechanism). As Mashek suggests, both chairs are associated with male users; in situ, both chairs have likely been called "daddy's chair" by countless consumers. Assuming that both chairs provide comfort during moments of supine pleasure, we can say that they both successfully achieve the Modernist criterion of fitness to purpose and functionality, yet they each appealed to different market demographics, primarily because the Lounge *looked* Modernist and expensive (indeed it was and is expensive), and the Barcalounger did not.

The implication is that mid-century design authorities selectively loosened their Modernist criteria while disparaging the "uninitiated" masses that chose their furniture according to what seems to be the true functionalist criteria of utility and cost. A decade later, Hine also juxtaposes the Eames Lounge and the Barcalounger as two well-known symbols of the postwar era, separated in appeal by class-based tastes (Hine 1986: 76–77). While he recognizes the Lounge as an emblem of Modernism, he gives greater weight to the Barcalounger. He celebrates its ubiquity amid average American homes and its customizability over the static, exclusive Eames Lounge,

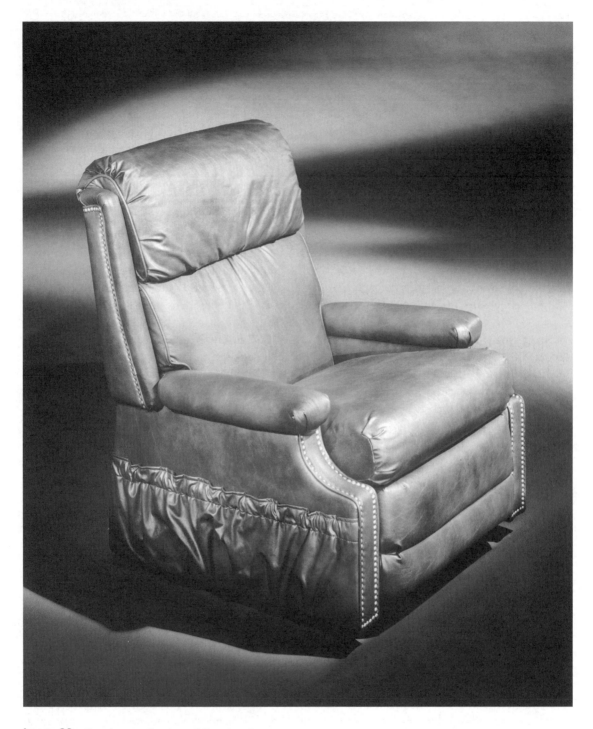

Image 32 Barcalounger. Courtesy of Barcalounger.

which did not come in a variety of shapes and only offered a small selection of approved upholstery options.

Why then is the Eames Lounge a design icon and the Barcalounger a mere piece of furniture? A partial answer to this question, and the original questions posed in the introduction to this essay, can be inferred from the 2002 book *What is Architecture?*, edited by Andrew Ballantyne, professor of architecture at the University of Newcastle upon Tyne, in the United Kingdom (Ballantyne 2002). The first essay, written by Ballantyne and called "The Nest and the Pillar of Fire," identifies within existing architectural discourse a dichotomy between what is deemed architecture proper versus run-of-the-mill buildings, arguing that "some buildings matter to us and others don't" (Ballantyne 2002: 48). As evidenced by the many textbooks that tend to focus on a relatively exclusive list of monumental structures, buildings that by consensus fall within the category of architecture tend to be innovative and surprising, embodying a compelling program or ideology as formulated by a visionary architect or coherent collective entity. Ballantyne labels these buildings "pillars of fire." In contrast, Ballantyne ascribes the term *nest* to buildings outside the mainstream architectural discourse—modest, undemanding, familiar-looking structures that comprise the vast majority of our built environment, and that, in truth, "most of us want most of the time" (Ballantyne 2002: 47–48).

Ballantyne argues that the essential difference between the two categories is culturally constructed and lies outside of the buildings in and of themselves: "the actual fabric of buildings is not sufficient to make architecture," but rather, "the buildings turn into architecture when we feel that we should notice them and treat them with respect, and this can happen to any building" (Ballantyne 2002: 11). This feeling is best evoked when a building is seen to carry within it an aspect of primacy, innovation, reification, or otherwise momentous narrative. If these associations last over time, the building is reexamined

again and again. Eventually the original associations become intermixed with new stories about its influence and hegemony, and the "pillar of fire" label becomes reinforced and leads to further study. Ballantyne advocates for increased examination of the "nests," but as yet such buildings to do not command that same attention as the "pillars of fire."

If we apply Ballantyne's dichotomy to the evaluation of design, then we can think of the Eames Lounge as a definite "pillar of fire," and the furniture that is left out of the discourse, such as the Barcalounger, as "nests." If these two categories are indeed shifting and mutable according to cultural consensus, then we can assume that the Lounge has maintained its iconic status because the content projected onto it has only become richer over time, while the Barcalounger, in contrast, has only been able to hold a limited quantity of meaning.

The Eames Lounge currently has a number of narratives attached to it. It can be appreciated both as a successful embodiment of the Modernist agenda, which is still considered a fertile field of study, and simultaneously, as a poor embodiment of the Modernist emphasis on innovation and "good design for everyone." Paradoxically, it has also been described as a cultural nexus, representative of the very "softening" of Modernism that eventually led to Postmodernism, or, as Pat Kirkham has written, the "humanizing" of Modernism (Kirkham 1995; 1998). Feminist critiques within design studies have also led to examinations of Ray Eames's role in what was formerly considered exclusively the work of her husband (Kirkham 1995). Precisely because the Lounge's form has remained frozen in deference to its designer(s), over time it has come to serve as a referent to another era, the postwar era, and the Lounge is now studied from a variety of perspectives that relate it to cultural developments such as the Cold War, the commodity boom, and feminist issues. Within the marketplace, the taste for objects from this era has emerged as a retro style, perhaps because the postwar era is now nostalgically remembered for its optimism and naïveté. Of course, the Eameses are still respected for the strong ideological convictions that underlie their work; this respect (heroizing) facilitates the projection of ideas onto the Lounge, because we know it was the product of a well-considered program. Clearly it remains important that furniture be attributable to an identifiable maker, so the design can be seen as deliberate and therefore encapsulating an intentional narrative.

In contrast to this type of semiotic layering, the Barcalounger's meanings have not significantly changed since the mid-century, even while its form has, paradoxically, continued to evolve. Even if our attitudes toward popular culture have changed, we still see the Barcalounger as a symbol of unsophisticated taste and the domain of working-class men who watch a lot of television. And without a known designer to attribute its creation, we assume that there is no philosophical foundation for the Barcalounger beyond purely commercial aspirations. While the commercial success cannot be denied, the constant re-creation of new models for changing markets leaves us without a single form to recognize, and we assume that the form does not matter. Even though the brand is familiar, the primary identifying characteristic of the Barcalounger is the retractable footrest mechanism, which it shares with chairs produced by other brands such as La-Z-Boy, Stratolounger, and the like. The perception remains that the Barcalounger plays too passive a role within the larger material culture (much like the stereotype of the consumers who buy it) to warrant the continuous reexamination that design icons elicit.

After fifty years of existence, the Eames Lounge continues to be collected by museums; it still sells successfully through Herman Miller (and Vitra in Europe); it is continuously added to revised lists of important design published in books, magazines, and Web sites; and it was given its own solo museum exhibition. This attention on the Lounge simultaneously results from and reinforces its iconic status within the realm of design studies, as well as within our culture in general. Even though the Modernist program has been critiqued over and over, the critical feedback loop set off by the mid-century authorities perpetuated their icons into the discourse that followed, and the Eames Lounge, more than any other single chair, has deftly embodied the changing values of design researchers and consumers.

72

THE TUBE MAP

Dipti Bhagat

During an everyday Tube (Londoners' familiar moniker for the London Underground) journey headed east on the (pink) Hammersmith and City Line, I observed an (everyday) moment of tourist confusion at the point where the Hammersmith Line heads toward Aldgate East and east London. Frantically, the tourist checked his pocket map and the one above the seats; the train was venturing beyond prescribed tourist London, outside of the (yellow) Circle Line. He needed to be on the Circle Line, to Tower Hill, of course: Tower Hill (and its proximity to the Tower of London) is the only reason for camera-clad, sneaker-wearing tourists to be on the Tube in that part of the city. Rectifying his way would be a little troublesome: London's colourful Tube Map, with its famous geometric order, elegantly angled lines, and spacious plan, which implies a swift and uncomplicated journey, belies the reality of London's complex underground network. Like many Londoners, however, I am rather fond of the Tube Map and take pride in being an expert of sorts in my use of it: as a daily user of the Tube, I know it and the best (and worst) interchanges well (despite its uniform depiction of easy interchange), understand the gap between its diagrammatic plan of the city's underground transport network and the real geography of London, and quickly recognize when tourists might be wandering beyond their usual path.

Lost tourists notwithstanding, the core diagrammatic design of the Tube Map, in use since 1933, is extraordinary for its endurance. It has been and is prolific, as card folders and poster maps in Tube stations and Tube trains and printed on the back of the London A–Z street maps, as a ubiquitous way-finding or navigational technology for Londoners and London's visitors. Beyond this site of (regular) production, the place of the diagrammatic design in the world of its everyday audience and users is one of iconic value: Metonymic of the transport network and of the city of London, it has become an iconic image of London itself. Inevitably, the enduring iconicity of the map of London's underground network has meant that it has "unfolded" many meanings as its audience of scholarly/academic experts have circulated the map through a "cycle of interpretation … in an effort to comprehend and understand" (Wood and Fels 1986: 88) its mythic quality. Such interpretations are variously "appraisive, evaluative, persuasive or rhetorical" (Scholes, 1982: 142) in their discourse, re-presenting the diagrammatic design, its history, and use in terms of functional modernity (Hadlaw, 2003), excellence in the history of graphic (Aynsley, 2001; Forty 1986; Garland 1994; Meggs 1992), information and schematic cartographic design (Avelar and Hurni 2004; Hong, Merrick, and do Nascimento 2004; Roberts 2005), as exemplary of semiotic richness (Hadlaw 2003), as revealing map use (Brown and Laurier 2003) and even as instructive of the use of the visual in science (Vertesi 2008). This essay will traverse these contexts and meanings of the diagrammatic design of the Tube Map, from the sites of its production and use, to the discourses that variously enframe it.

It is difficult to refer to "the Tube Map" as a singular object, for indeed, as artifacts there are millions of maps printed every year; equally, it is not quite correct to refer to a single London Underground diagram, as again, there have been many, visibly different diagrams issued during the history of the transport system (Roberts 2005). In terms of nomenclature, the "Tube Map," the term that is typical with Londoners, is also more formally called the "London Underground Map." Transport for London (TFL, the city's transport authority) uses the term "Journey Planner" in official documentation, as a correct description of what is technically a *diagram* of the London Underground Transport Network—it is not a literal representation of distance and geography and thus not actually a map. (Vertesi 2008) However, card folder versions produced for individual use

by passengers have been issued titled variously as: "Map of London's Underground Railways" (first issue of Beck's design, 1933), "Underground Diagram of Lines," "Underground Pocket Map," "Journey Planner," and recently "Tube Map" (Garland 1994: 19; Roberts 2005: 6).

Nevertheless, it is widely recognized that the "Tube Map" as we know it today (literally) is based on a core diagrammatic design devised by Henry ("Harry") C. Beck in 1931 and launched in 1933 by the London Passenger Transport Board (LPTB), which had been established that year as a unified corporate identity for what had been a collection of independent, competing railway companies built up piecemeal since the first trains in the 1860s (Forty 1986: 222–38; Hadlaw 2003: 28–31; Whitfield 2006: 185). That the diagrammatic design of today's map is visually consistent

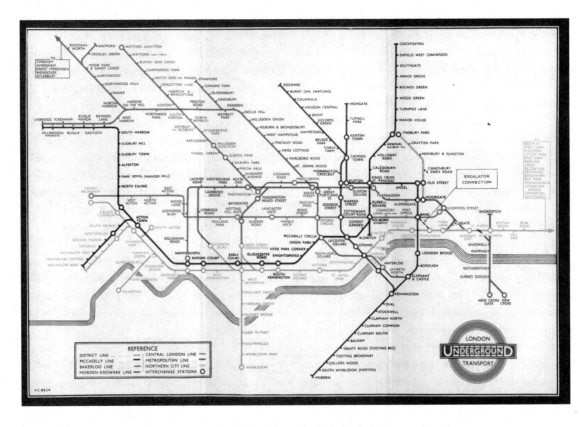

Image 33   Pocket Underground Map, no. 2, 1936, designed by H. C. Beck. © Transport for London.

with that of 1933 reveals that maps since this first issue cohere through employing key design conventions that echo Beck's first iteration. Maxwell Roberts (2005: 6) has distilled these design conventions as line, color, symbol, scale, space, and topology (vs. topography).

Beck's diagrammatic design is restricted to utilizing only horizontal, vertical, and 45-degree lines; each line is distinctive by color; stations are symbolized by ticks, and interchanges by a circle (variances from these are very few, see Garland 1994; Roberts 2005). The distance between each station is determined by the graphic scale of the page: the layout of station names, lines, and interchanges for clarity's sake insists that the center (city) of the diagram is scaled up, enlarged, and inflated in contrast to the periphery (suburbs), which is compressed, drawn in.[1] Indeed, this utilizes a purely graphic scale, and, in Beck's design, it replaces geographic scale; geographically scaled maps adhere to uniform scale to represent accurately the reality of specific places and spaces between them. Beck's design eliminates street details and attempts at geographic verity that had cluttered and confused maps of the Underground transport network prior to 1933 (Roberts 2005: 8–11). Thus, the space of the city above—chaotic, unorganized, echoing its medieval heart—is replaced by the graphic space of the design—ordered, geometric, artificial, compositional spaces of the page. The diagrammatic design abandoned topography—of the city above ground—to render the topology of the network—interchanges below the city— eminently understandable; only the Thames River is included, but as a highly stylized topological feature.

Ken Garland (1994: 7–21) details the early biography of Beck's diagrammatic design. When Beck (at the time an unemployed engineering draughtsman) first presented his diagram to the Underground Publicity Department, it was rejected. It was, however, accepted at his second attempt, and 750,000 copies were issued for trial in January 1933 as a card folder, with an invitation to the traveling public to comment on the new map. That the LPTB needed to reprint the card folder (100,000 copies) within a month of issue suggests its remarkable popularity. Thereafter, it was Beck himself that often reordered his diagrammatic design between 1933 and 1960, incorporating station closures, line extensions, and official directives for graphic variables. This period of design and redesign also incorporated Beck's shift, in 1947, from the LPTB to teaching at the London College of Printing and Kindred Trades, where he taught "theory and practice of typographic design, colour theory, the history of type design, lettering and general drawing" (Garland 1994: 42). Parallel to this, tutors at the Central School of Arts and Crafts exemplified their teaching of information design through Beck's diagrammatic design for the London Underground transport network.

Beck's core diagrammatic design is strictly copyrighted by the (now) Transport for London and alternative representations of the Underground transport network are heavily proscribed (Vertesi 2008: 10).[2] Its iconicity, as a "cultural enterprise … derives from [the designer's] ability to transcribe arrangements in space and mark them out in conventional symbols—in other words, to *map* them" (Wood and Fels 1986: 75). Under the authority of TFL, the official, *mapped*, diagrammatic design is prolific in myriad forms: from way-finding devices to decorating tourist objects as varied as T-shirts, socks, ties, neck scarves, underwear, tea towels, beach towels, bags, mugs, innumerable stationery items, umbrellas, postcards, and wrapping paper/posters. This abundant production for novelty's sake is matched by a TFL reissue of maps on a regular basis to account for shifts in the diagrammatic design that indicate changes in the Underground network, such as line or station closures. Ads for the Underground network, at the time of writing, utilize cameos extracted from the diagrammatic design to advertise maintenance/repair works; for example, workmen are pictured on the ground of the map, manually moving the interchange symbol of Bank Station; a bit in a large pneumatic drill is colored to match the Tube line affected by works; screws are lined up on the edge of the poster page, colored to match every Tube line, to advertise ongoing maintenance work. Such intertextual, graphic complexity is perhaps to be expected of a corporation aware of its image-savvy users of the twenty-first century.

The diagrammatic design is also boldly used at the entrance to the main galleries at the London Transport Museum: it is writ large—in scale and conception—as its lines, ticks (which symbolize stations), and interchange circles are extended beyond London to morph into the lines, ticks, and circles of the subway/transit/metro networks of New York, Tokyo, Paris, Shanghai, and Kolkuta (Calcutta). This global diagrammatic design is punctuated by screens relaying everyday, moving images of scenes of and from each city's transit system; it reverberates with the sounds of each city, its trains and its people. The display has the effect of expanding and concentrating the mind; it presents urban transit networks as civic culture; this giant, pulsating map suggests that the "subway [sic] is a modern [global] agora" (Berman 2001). Thus, the seemingly endlessly reproducible map comes not only to advertise London's transport network, but London itself; it even becomes other networks, and other cities.

It could be argued that this is the way of a mythic image, working through repetitive imaging of the diagrammatic design: or is it merely a diagram? Among its audience, scholars have regularly sought to unravel Beck's diagrammatic design as a form of discourse itself, one bound by rules that cover its visual system as well as its social production and exchange (Scholes 1982: 144). Histories of graphic and information design have focused on Henry Beck's authorship (Garland 1994) and the historical context of the diagrammatic designs (Hadlaw 2003), and on subsequent designers' authorship, paying close—train-spotter-like—attention to the intricate changes in each map, evaluating the impact on the essence of Beck's original design, described as "clear, useable, attractive, compact and trustworthy" (Roberts 2005).

It is these qualities of utility, function, form, and visual appeal that mythologize Beck's design as "the prototype of the modern map" (Meggs, in Hadlaw 2003: 35). Beck's original diagrammatic design has been hailed as a "classic British design"; it was one of many to which a BBC television program was devoted in a series called *Design Classics* (BBC4 2008). Recent exhibitions at London's Victoria and Albert Museum (Modernism: Designing a New World, 1914–1939, 2006) and Design Museum (Designing Modern Britain, 2006) have also fixed the 1933 Underground map not only in their chronologies of design icons, but also of *British* design. Indeed much is made of the diagrammatic design in comparison to New York's subway map and Paris's metro map, both geographically driven in design (Avelar and Hurni 2004; Garland 1994; Hong, Merrick, and do Nascimento 2004; Roberts 2005; Vertesi 2008); for while London lacks the organizing principles of New York's grid, or Paris's concentric arrondissements, the British capital's Underground network is "orderly, lucid, regular, efficient, and entirely functional" (Hadlaw 2003: 35). For Hadlaw, marshalling Roland Barthes's *Mythologies* and Henri Lefebvre's *The Production of Space*, Beck's original design is a "magical object," a "modern representation complicit with modern ideals ... [that] acted to overlay everyday life with modernism's [capitalist] concept of space and time."

While histories of design have been largely concerned with the sites and context of the production of Beck's design, and analysis of its visual form, it is scholars of cartography, science, computer science, and social sciences that have examined user interactions with and meanings made of the Underground map. For Brown and Laurier's users, way-finding with an Underground map is "irretrievably immersed in the organization of specific social settings ... [and is a] publicly available, transparent, accountable action" in situ in London (Brown and Laurier 2003: 30). London's Underground map—unique in its design differential from the city itself, stable in its copyright, and iconic in its ubiquity—has served Vertesi's study of the map as a "graphical interface" between the user and London; indeed, her interviewees revealed the extent to which the map image represented the Underground transport network *and* London. Vertesi's detailed study recommends a careful consideration of the power of the visual in science, for "*the study of representations in interaction is critical to the study of technological systems in action*" (Vertesi 2008: 26, emphasis original). Finally, Vertesi's interviewees return us to Beck's topographical design principles, for the expert users of this picture of London, who learn and navigate the city above and below with this map, "topology and topography become intertwined, enmeshed" in everyday practices of traveling and being in the city (Vertesi 2008: 12).

Henry Beck's diagrammatic design and London's subsequent Underground/Tube maps are presented here as exemplars of modern design and way-finding technologies, as discourse *and* the subject of discourse. From its sites of production to its mass use in London, the core diagrammatic design of the map endures as an instrument of communication and persuasion, as an icon, not only of a highly complex underground transport network, but also of London itself.

NOTES

1. Forty has interpreted this differential in the scaling of the city and suburbs on Beck's diagrammatic design as making London look smaller with suburbs appearing 'deceptively close to the centre', an effect he suggests 'induced people to undertake journeys they might otherwise have hesitated to make' (Forty 1986: 237). However, Beck's design was unsolicited by the Underground Publicity Department, and he has stated in an interview that 'clarity of connections' were the design principles at stake in his design (Garland 1994: 17). This refutes any suggestion that Beck's diagrammatic design of space was a tactic to advertise suburban rail use. Elsewhere, Frank Pick, the director of the LPTB responsible for unifying London's transport network, stated that the merging of rural and urban space (in practice) had more to do with the popularity of the automobile than the railways (see Hadlaw 2003: 34).

2. Roberts (2005: 81–91) discusses alternative representations that appear mostly in London travel guides that avoid copyright reproduction of official diagram. All make strong references to Beck's diagrammatic design; as a Londoner, I find that these alternative maps renew my fidelity to the Tube Map, not only for familiarity and thus ease of use, but as the only "correct" picture of the city.

73

SWATCH

Susan Yelavich

Remarkably inexpensive, produced in multiples of upwards of eighty different colorful designs each year, the Swatch watch is a case study in both modernist populism (affordable and good design for the masses) and postmodernist ephemerality. And as might be expected of a product of the early 1980s, the latter has proved far more dominant. Above all, the economical Swatch celebrates the idea of self-transformation. The weakening of fixed identities associated with global peregrinations is intrinsic to its form language, with its interchangeable watch faces and wrist bands, and proclaimed in its advertising language: "Be yourself, Swatch yourself" (Swatch 1991).

But for all its physical modularity and it semiotic mobility, a decidedly localized history is embedded in the Swatch. Indeed, the name Swatch, a concatenation of S(econd) + watch, is often, and justifiably, mistaken to be a merger of S(wiss) + watch. The confusion works to the advantage of the company, since, in fact, the Swatch Group is an umbrella for eighteen other watch brands, all but four of which are Swiss. More significantly, the success of the Swatch watch in the 1980s legendarily saved a complacent Swiss watch industry from bankruptcy—albeit at a pace that in the twentieth century nearly proved fatal.

Since 1931, the Swiss watch-making industry had been controlled by the Allgemeine Schweizer Uhrenindustrie AG (ASUAG), a federal holding company formed to create exclusive market value for the product, by constraining Swiss manufacturers to work only with Swiss suppliers (Glasmeier 2000: 151). But the same bureaucracies that kept a Swiss watch Swiss, hence, a valuable and limited commodity, were all but paralyzed by the rise of nonmechanical watches.

In the late 1960s, Swiss preeminence in the industry was seriously challenged by the introduction of quartz crystal technology, which relied on piezoelectric material that vibrated at a particular frequency when captured within an electric field. At this point, Swiss competency was completely bound up in the production of mechanical watches. Lacking a military-industrial complex, they did not have the same access to microelectronic developments available to the United States and Japan (Glasmeier 2000: 203). By the 1970s, the entire Swiss watch industry was in a perilous decline; its very existence was threatened by Japanese quartz brands such as Seiko, and, to a lesser extent, the emergence of the jewel-free American Timex.

Ralph Gautier, of the Siber Hegner World Watch Marketing group, is credited with restructuring and reorganizing one of the largest watch conglomerates, the Société Suisse pour l'Industrie Horlogerie (SSIH)—which included Tissot and Omega (Glasmeier 2000: 244). Under his direction, the percentage of quartz watches was increased from 8 percent to 60 percent between 1977 and 1980 (Glasmeier 2000: 244). When he brought the Swiss into the electronic market, Gautier had the foresight to reject the digital watch face (its popularity was short-lived) for the more culturally familiar analog face. But despite

Image 34 *Wrist Swatched* (2008). Michael Casy, artist, and with permission of Swatch.

the fact that Gautier predicted that wristwatches would soon be as disposable as plastic cigarette lighters, he chose not to compete in that arena (Glasmeier 2000: 245).

It took a major competitor to drive the process forward. In 1978, Seiko came out with a watch that was a mere 2.5 millimeters thick (Edwards 1998: 8). A subsidiary of ASUAG/SSIH, named ETA SA Fabriques d'Ebauches, took on the task of beating that figure. The project became known as the Delerium: ETA technicians thought it was madness. But within the next year they produced a movement that required no separate back plate. The plastic prototype—officially, the Delerium Vulgare—measured in at 1.98 millimeters (Avery 2004: 285). Assembly was fully automated, and

parts for the quartz watch were reduced from ninety-one to fifty-one components.

However, the name was bound to be a liability, something the Swiss could ill-afford. So, in the summer of 1981, a New York advertising agency was hired, and one Franz Xavier Sprecher rechristened the Delerium Vulgare as Swatch (Edwards 1998: 8). But since ETA only sold the watch components, the name would have been secondary to other company brand names, if, indeed, it appeared at all. Not surprisingly, its prelaunch in San Antonio, Texas, in 1982 was a failure.

Were it not for the intervention of Nicholas G. Hayek, the Swatch might well have been shelved. A Lebanese-born entrepreneur and the CEO of Hayek Engineering, Hayek was a consultant in the Swiss watch industry turn-around and had helped engineer the system that enabled a private individual such as himself, with relatively little history in the industry, to own a Swiss company. Hayek's first move was to establish an in-house marketing team and to consolidate distribution (Edwards 1998: 12). Within a year, the Swatch was relaunched in Switzerland, Germany, and Great Britain as a twelve-model collection, priced from SF39.90 to SF49.90 (roughly US$25–$35) (Edwards 1998:12). This time the venture was a success, one that reverberated throughout the entire Swiss industry. However, Glasmeier cautions against placing too much emphasis on the role of Swatch and credits the recovery of the Swiss to the structural reorganizations that gave birth to the company in the first place (2000: 247).

Instead of a traditional code number, each watch was given a name, to express its "personality." Furthermore, the marketing stress had shifted the emphasis away from the generic, that is, "features that make it suitable for everyday wear" to the particular, that is, "a new wave of Swiss watches for the young, and a symbol of a new lifestyle." Virtues like "the high standards of Swiss manufacture" were replaced by "a quality normally associated with more expensive watches—an accuracy of +/- one sec/day … at a price never before seen in Switzerland" (Edwards 1998: 11–12).

The usual order had been inverted. The customer came first, and the customer was youthful and fashion-savvy. Swiss values, present in the flag next to the company name, were also reinforced in the "S" of Swatch, even though the firm claimed it stood for "second." The name Swatch worked both ways for the young company. It signaled a hip, knowing confidence that the national reputation for precision was not lost, only an unflattering, conservative national stereotype. Banished were clichés of the stodgy Swiss watchmaker. Stability now rested only in two places: the constant use of the brand name, and the commitment to using round cases for the watch face, at least until 2000, when the first square Swatches were introduced.

The round case may have been unchanged for eighteen years, but all the other elements—the Swatch's dial, hands, and straps—were treated as blank canvases, not incidentally reinforcing public perception of design as styling. However, given the miniaturization of its workings, the argument can be made that the Swatch was a successful experiment in product semantics. The theory and practice of product semantics, in fact, emerged coincidentally in the 1980s with the introduction of micro-technologies. Its adherents argued that the form and meaning of electronic products now depended on imagery, since they were no longer determined by (or recognized by) the bulk of their old mechanical parts.

While the Swatch was not developed under the aegis of product semantics, per se, tremendous value was placed on the signs it carried. Once again, Switzerland's geographical location, and its multilingual culture (a mix of Italian, German, French, and indigenous Swiss), were used to advantage. In 1987, Carlo Giordanetti, who was already employed by Swatch, founded Swatch Labs in Milan, and the Milan-based designer Alessandro Mendini was hired as art director. Mendini, associated with both the Memphis design group and Studio Alchymia, was an ideal choice given his life-long interest in the emotional properties of artifacts. Since emotions are fleeting, the surface look of the Swatch was freed to mutate at the speed of fashion, once considered anathemic to product design. Furthermore, the imprimatur of design authority, implicit in Mendini's association and Milan's reputation as a design center, mitigated any stigma associated with fashion or bargains.

Mendini designed several Swatches himself, including Lots of Dots, Cosmesis, and Metroscape, and he created the template for Swatch's store designs in Europe. Mendini's key idea was to keep the stores open to the street, the ostensible source of the watch's populist credibility. (In America, Pentagram partners Daniel Weil and James Biber received the commission for the company's midtown Manhattan flagship, the Swatch Timeship, which opened in 1997. Shigeru Ban designed the Tokyo flagship, the Nicolas G. Hayek Center in the Ginza in 2007.)

Under the influence of Hayek and Giordanetti (creative director of Swatch until 2007), the Swatch was quickly positioned as an endlessly multiplying work of art. The early in-house watches—the Raspberry, Ice Mint, and Banana models in the Granita di Frutta series, and the transparent Jelly Fish— were soon joined by Swatch Art Specials. Kiki Picasso produced the first—AKIKI—in 1985. A partial list of those who have followed includes Jean Michel Folon (Perspective #2, 1987), Vivienne Westwood (Putti, 1992), Pedro Almovadar (Despiste, 1995), Yoko Ono (Film No. 4, 1996), David LaChapelle (Time Tranny, 2000), and the Blue Man Group (Paint in Blue, 2006). These Swatches became highly sought after, and, as early as 1989, a limited-edition Mimmo Paladino watch sold for $24,000 at auction (Avery, 2004: 270). However, it was the anonymous, in-house 1983 Jelly Fish that was selected by New York's Museum of Modern Art for its collection, no doubt for its catalytic role in the company's history as well as for its modernist purity.

The early decision to invite celebrity art-world figures, whether painters, designers, performers, or filmmakers, insured that Swatch could operate on two platforms: The affordable, everyday "second" watch would provide an economic base subject to market forces, while the more expensive, limited-edition art watch would sustain a consistently high public profile. The everyday watch witnessed technical innovations, yielding the scuba, solar, chrono, musical alarm, and electronic access wristwatches, even a steel-case line called Irony, with watchbands inspired by costume jewelry. Nonetheless, by the 1990s, Swatch no longer enjoyed the cult status that it had in the 1980s, when it was not uncommon to wear several at once, on the wrist, in the hair, and on clothing. The Swatch Art Specials and other lines, tied to sports figures and events like Earth Day, represented a modest form of insurance against new cycles of novelty. Swatch watches are designed to live in the consumer's imagination as a perpetually rejuvenated souvenir. As anthropologist Arjun Appadurai has observed, nostalgia operates paradoxically today: The present is saturated with images of pasts that consumers have never experienced themselves (Appadurai, 1996: 77).

Thus, with the demand for the Swatch diminishing under the pressure of fakes and competitors who used cheaper labor (Glasmeier 2000: 257), a calculated form of nostalgia has been used to attract a new generation of buyers. That nostalgia is especially apparent in the design language of its current lines, but it also thrives in the active collectors' market that exists outside of Swatch, though not without its manipulation. Because of their limited and uneven distribution, contemporary collectors seeking to assemble a coherent collection have to search out the inventory of all the Swatch outlets or order directly from Switzerland. The Swatches released in one season are not, and never have been, universally available in their stores. Consequently, this system of dispersion forges an oxymoron of accessibility (in price) and rarity (in accessibility), all within the same low-priced product line.

Another internal contradiction embodied in the Swatch brand lies in the inherently unsustainable nature of its eminently disposable watches and the company's corporate mission to further sustainability, articulated quite publicly by Nicholas Hayek. As early as 1992, Hayek addressed the General Assembly of the United Nations on the subject of environmental responsibility. But rather than focus on the most recognized product of his business enterprise—the Swatch watch—he directed his energies toward sustainable automobility. In 1994, Hayek formed a partnership between Swatch and Daimler-Benz that led to the introduction of the Smart car. In keeping with its approach to watch design, Swatch contributed the cosmetic component, with a system of interchangeable body parts in various colors (Avery 2004: 270). Daimler-Benz was supposed to produce a hybrid engine; however, when they failed to do so, Hayek broke off the relationship.

A report from 2007 by British journalist Matthew Sparkes notes that Hayek is now investing in the development of a fuel-cell driven car (2007). And his successor and son, Nick Hayek, the current CEO of the Swatch Group, has been using the expertise of the Omega division to further the production of solar aircraft. However, there is little evidence of the same attentiveness to sustainable design in the Swatch watch. No instructions for returning parts or recycling accompany its packaging. That said, the energy required to turn on a light bulb for a second can power a Swatch watch for a year (Tomassini 1998: 70).

74

ARCHITECTURE AND CULTURAL IDENTITY

The Case of the Petronas Towers in Kuala Lumpur

Catherine Walsh

Soaring dizzily above the more mundane hotels and office buildings that surround them, two buildings, joined at foot and waist into one evocative and gleaming silhouette, punctuate the skyline of Kuala Lumpur, Malaysia's capital city, with a population of 1.3 million (Peng 2005: 202). The Petronas Towers, so named after the country's national petroleum corporation, their chief tenant, have marked the City Centre of Kuala Lumpur since 1997, and for about seven years they claimed the title of the world's tallest buildings, rocketing this Asian city into the international limelight. Each eighty-eight-story tower stretches to a height of 452 meters above street level, narrowing to a thin pinnacle after five setbacks that emphasize the verticality and elegant proportions of the buildings. Two forty-four-story bustles flank the towers on their street-side north face, and a bilevel skybridge at the forty-first and forty-second floors spans the 58.4-meter distance between the identical towers (Petronas 2005). The symmetricality of the buildings' design profile is heightened by the skybridge and its support system, a three-hinged arch composed of legs bolted to the bridge and the sides of each tower, thus framing a geometrically divided space between the towers that takes on an active role in the architecture's composition. The towers are enlivened by a horizontally textured exterior comprising stainless steel cladding and glass windows, which flashes in the bright tropical sunlight, reflecting back purple, orange, and red hues from dramatic sunsets and cascading light shows that mark the towers'

nighttime exterior. Permanence, stability, and symmetricality combine with ever-changing light effects and fluctuating traffic through the bustling streets and parks that surround the buildings.

The Petronas Towers were designed with a particular place in mind. Not only do they accommodate the physical site located within the heart of the Golden Triangle financial district in Kuala Lumpur City Centre; in addition, both client and architect from the beginning conceived of the buildings as integrally related to a cultural space, their specifically Malaysian context. As a designed object, the Petronas Towers have come to embody a national and communal identity for Malaysia, whether imagined or actual, that hinges upon a combination of advanced technology and metaphorical interpretations assigned to the buildings' design.

During the early 1990s, the Malaysian economy experienced an upsurge in economic potential, which manifested itself in Kuala Lumpur as a booming real estate market that took advantage of demographic shifts and increasing population in the city center. Looking toward a prosperous future, Prime Minister Mahathir Mohammad instituted a nationwide plan to turn Malaysia into a "fully developed nation by 2020," with construction projects totaling $73 billion in planning stages. Part of this project of cultural and economic rejuvenation—or "building binge," according to environmentalist Gurmit Singh (Mydans 1996)—called for the sweeping away of the country's colonial heritage. The Malaysian government decided to move the Selangor Turf Club, a colonial

Image 35   Petronas Towers. Courtesy of Pelli Clarke Pelli Architects.

racetrack situated on 104 acres in the city's Golden Triangle. Thus, they instituted an international competition in 1990 to plan Kuala Lumpur City Centre (KLCC) as a mixed-use development that included office buildings, shopping, and a fifty-acre public park. The complex is integrated by a multi-story shopping and entertainment galleria connecting the Petronas Towers at their base.

Another competition, opened to twenty international architectural firms in 1991, resulted in the commissioning of the American company, Cesar Pelli & Associates, for Pelli's compelling Petronas Towers design, approved by a technical committee and Prime Minister Mohathir (Pelli 2001: 7–8). Project planning began in January of 1992, by March of 1993 foundation work was underway, and on August 31, 1999, the Towers were officially opened at a celebration presided over by the prime minister, as well as Petronas's CEO Tan Sri Azizan (Petronas Twin Towers 2005). The two towers were built by different sets of general contractors, creating a sense of competition and providing for technical experimentation (Pearson 1999: 94). The Petronas Towers can therefore be considered an "object" designed literally from the ground up, from its revolutionary interior structure to outside cladding, by a series of makers: the prime minister and Petronas representatives, the U.S. firm that won the competition to design KLCC, Pelli and the architects associated with his firm, the New York and Malaysian engineers that worked to design the structure, the contractors who made decisions based on feasibility and on-site affect (for instance, choosing steel over aluminum for the cladding), and the ultimate viewers and users, who make meaning for themselves. Design decisions were made as a negotiation among these makers, as they debated symbolism, finances, and feasibility, and in the process, the Petronas Towers went through various stages of objecthood, ranging from textual conception to penciled and computer-generated drawings and structural diagrams, over 2000 study models (including a full-size mockup of the exterior wall), and the massive buildings themselves, both in construction and as finished.

Throughout this process, makers continually placed a great deal of emphasis on one issue above all others: the building's relationship to *place* and the necessity of communicating a Malaysian identity, rather than adhering to an international style found in skyscrapers elsewhere. Yet how was this identity to be defined, considering the vast distance between paradigms of very tall buildings and traditional Malaysian architecture?

The design specifications offered during the competition requested that the finished building include advanced technology and local and national aspirations; Pelli was asked to make a "Malaysian building" ("Tower Power" 2005: 74). Much has been made of characteristics inherent to the design that draw on elements of Malaysian culture, especially Pelli's conception, adapted after discussion with Prime Minister Mohathir, of two intersecting squares, tilted at forty-five-degree angles, that created an eight-pointed star linked by eight semicircles. This geometricized footprint for each tower draws, in a kind of cultural pastiche, on "traditional Islamic patterns" found throughout the predominantly Islamic society of Malaysia (Campi, 2000: 182; Pearson 1999: 95; Pelli 2001: 6–10). The official Petronas Twin Towers Web site argues, "Architecturally, these forms reflect the paramount Islamic principles of 'unity within unity, harmony, stability and rationality'" (Petronas Twin Towers 2005).

Yet, unless the building's inhabitant is familiar with official rhetoric or the architect's schematic designs, this aspect is not ultimately visible. Due to structural requirements, individual floor plans do not conform to the geometric design, and from the exterior the geometric relationships created by the building's intersecting angles are largely obscured by steel and glass cladding. Surveys of public opinion show that most people do not recognize the intended Islamic character of the design, and one outspoken critic accuses this "arbitrary pattern of squares and circles" of degenerating into a "cocktail of superficialities" (Davey 1997). The debate rages as to whether the design taps into something inherent to its locale, or whether it is only superficially Malaysian, a kind of Orientalizing nod on the part of a Western architect to the demands of the "other" place for which he designs.

There is no decisive answer to settle this debate. Regardless, authors, businessmen, and workers in the buildings continually point to Petronas Towers with pride as a symbol of Malaysia. Perhaps this evolves out of the many ways designers attempted to tie the constructed and experiential building to Malaysia's unique culture and environment: the use of traditional Malaysian crafts, woods, tiles, and patterns to decorate the lobby of the buildings; the partnership between teams of American and Malaysian contractors; and the deep overhanging window shades that cut solar gain and cool the building in response to Malaysia's tropical climate (Binder 2001: 152; "Cesar Pelli" 1995: 63; Pearson 1999: 94; Petronas Twin Towers 2005; Sullivan 1996: 160).

However, it might also be beneficial to move beyond the construction so often set up by Western authors that seek the "Malaysian" in its traditional arts, religion, and materials. In his introduction to Pelli's book describing the design process and meaning inherent in the Towers, Michael J. Crosbie asserts that the Towers do their work by "stitching two cultures together, and stand as a world wonder that joins East and West" (Pelli 2005: 6). For Crosbie and Pelli, Eastern elements include the eight-pointed plan and the space between the towers, cast as a gigantic gateway or portal to the infinite, as stressed by Taoist philosopher Lao Tse's assertion that architecture's power lies in the space created by it. In contrast, inhabitants of Kuala Lumpur, while sometimes embracing these assertions, also point to the Towers' roles in the municipal and national future. For many, they signify ambition, technological advancement, dynamism, economic prosperity, and an international announcement of the desire to compete in a corporate and architectural sphere so long dominated by Western notions.

Although Pelli claims repeatedly that at no time did the Malaysian government require a design to overtake the Sears Tower as the world's tallest building, this nevertheless became a defining characteristic of the Towers, described by one author as "the great Asian steeple chase" (Myerson 1995). Very tall buildings have, since their first appearance on the international scene, been associated with a variety of ideas. They allow for an economical use of limited urban space in high-density population centers. They advance in leaps and bounds with the development of new technologies, ranging from the iron skeleton to the hydraulic lift to the twenty-three-square-meter high-strength concrete core and "soft tube" structure that enabled the Petronas Towers to reach record-breaking heights (for infinitely more detail on the buildings' structure, see Pearson 1999: 99, and especially Sullivan 1996). Furthermore, skyscrapers evoke poetical descriptions from viewers awed by their grandiosity. In 1896, Louis Sullivan described the tall office building: "It must be tall, every inch of it tall. The force and power of altitude must be in it, the glory and pride of exaltation must be in it. It must be every inch a proud and soaring thing, rising in sheer exultation that from bottom to top it is a unit without a single dissenting line" (quoted in Betsky 1995: 10).

The affective power of the Petronas Towers has not escaped those who inhabit and visit Kuala Lumpur. In his poem, originally published in the Bahasa language, Datuk A. Samad Said writes of the buildings' "Silver scales shining merrily,/glass slabs glittering brightly." He goes on to discuss the significance of the Towers for the Malaysian people:

It becomes a flag billowing mightily
in our grateful hearts.
It becomes a voice yearning for respect
in our sincere hopes.
It is the epitome of our pure dreams,
winking from afar, glittering from a near.
it states the determined achievement of the
nation which braved the world's turmoil
on its own efforts.

(Petronas Twin Towers 2005)

This "yearning for respect" and assertion of the nation's achievement took the form of a very tall building for a specific reason, that is, the long-time competitive drive for greater and greater height. In *Tall Buildings of Asia and Australia,* A. Eugen Kohn and Dennis Lau Wing-kwong argue that in the late 1990s, Asian clients sought tall buildings as "a symbol, as a vehicle for expressing their power" that resulted in intense competition between countries and cities— a competition that Kuala Lumpur eventually lost with the completion of Taipei 101 in 2004 (Kohn and Wing-kwong 2001: 6–7). This competition could be fierce. Indeed, after the Petronas Towers were constructed, the Council on Tall Buildings and Urban Habitat had to step in to still debates as to whether buildings should be measured based on spire, inhabitable floor, or antenna height—a debate that, if resolved differently, could have resulted in the Sears Tower's continued dominance as the tallest building in the world (Binder, 2001: 11; Sullivan 1996). Affective power ascribed to the Towers, due to their height and technological advancement, thus contributes as much to meaning, as well as civic and national identity, as those elements conceived as specifically Malaysian.

Any consideration of the objecthood of the Petronas Towers must move beyond the architects' sketches and rhapsodic rhetoric used by architect, prime minister, and the CEO of Petronas alike to describe the purpose and meaning of the building. These skyscrapers, visible from various parts of the city, dominate the skyline of Kuala Lumpur. Their distinctive silhouette, composed of the two towers connected by the skybridge and its V-shaped supportive struts, becomes a recognizable and iconic profile, a condensation of the buildings' design into an object concretized in the popular imagination, as well as in drawings, photographs, popular films, souvenirs, and newspaper diagrams that place the Towers in a series of the world's tallest buildings. Through their omnipresence of view in and around the environs of Kuala Lumpur, the Towers encroach

upon the everyday lives of its inhabitants as a visual image, seen from a multitude of perspectives in combination with many foregrounds. This visual object fits Charles Jencks's definition of the iconic building, which "must provide a new and condensed image, be high in figural shape or gestalt, and stand out from the city" (Jencks 2005: 23). At the same time, this profile, through its omnipresence and recognizability, becomes a unique silhouette that stands as a symbol for the city ("Cesar Pelli" 1996: 63). However, despite their exceptional nature as iconic buildings, the Petronas Towers also represent an enlivened space, experienced on a daily basis by office workers and shoppers, who find their recursive movements and social practices transformed by the physicality of the buildings' design. Thus, one must not neglect the ways in which the buildings construct the professional and commercial identities of individuals who engage with them.

As a designed structure, the Petronas Towers occupy a world of things and are surrounded by a constellation of other things, among them the human bodies that interact with them on a daily basis. Bill Brown has argued that this universe of things, although often ignored, sometimes springs into stark relief as something happens— an event, a moment of realization—to disclose a physicality of things, moving them from a "thing" to an "object" through which we examine society. Similarly, Sidney Nagel has argued that we as viewers can become optically conscious of an everydayness that otherwise exists on the perimeter of critical awareness (quoted in Brown 2004: 4–6). Paying critical attention to the objecthood of the Petronas Towers in Kuala Lumpur yields insight into the ways in which design can interact with place, identity, technology, and human perception in order to create meaning. The Petronas Towers become "things with attitude" that work "to express individual or group identity, to denote status or demonstrate technological prowess, to exercise social control or to flaunt political power" (Attfield 2000: 12).

75

HELVETICA

Love It or Leave It

R. Roger Remington

The year 2007 was a good one for the typeface Helvetica. It concurrently celebrated its fiftieth birthday with the release of a feature-length documentary film by Gary Hustwit, who brought together a talented array of graphic designers to speak about Helvetica, its ubiquity, its visual culture, and its popularity. This is a proper and appropriate celebration for one of the most widely used typefaces ever.

Helvetica arrived on the world graphics scene in the mid-1950s, based on the classic Akzidenz Grotesk font from 1898. A classic contemporary sans-serif typeface, Helvetica is known for its high degree of legibility and its clear-cut characters. Since its release, Helvetica has gained the reputation as the essence of modernity. Developed in the Haas'sche Schriftgiesserei Foundry (Haas Type Foundry) in Münchenstein, Switzerland, its designers were Max Miedinger, who made the drawings, and Edouard Hoffmann, who assisted Miedinger. Originally named Haas Grotesk, in 1957 the name was changed to Helvetica when it was marketed by D. Stempel AG.

Hoffmann was shocked when he learned that Stempel had changed the name. Its name stems from Confereratio Helvetia, which was the ancient Roman name for Switzerland. The typeface could not be marketed internationally with the name of a country; thus the change to Helvetica. Through the 1960s to the 1980s a number of new weights were added, including Helvetica Light and Helvetica Extra Bold. Likewise, Linotype and Monotype added new weights, and in 1983 a new version was designed by Linotype,

called Neue Helvetica (New Helvetica). IBM later created a font similar to Helvetica, which they called Arial, although some designers, such as Mark Simonson, have said that "Arial is a knockoff riding on Helvetica's coattails" (Roane 2007: 71). To its credit, Helvetica comes as standard on virtually every PC in the world. The Web site for Linotype now includes an overview of the original Helvetica font weights and all of the Neue Helvetica font as well. Helvetica has inspired new fonts such as Meta, designed by Erik Spiekermann in Berlin. Meta was used exclusively by the German State Post Office after 1984. Helvetica, therefore, has been part of the important progression of influences that have shaped many modern fonts, each one evaluating and building upon its predecessor.

There are a number of reasons why Helvetica is popular and noteworthy, which are discussed in the sections that follow.

IT IS CONTROVERSIAL AND MEMORABLE

The release of the Helvetica film has fanned the flames of disagreement that have surrounded this typeface. Because of its broad popularity, Helvetica has been and continues to stimulate differing points of view and therefore is regularly in the news. In the Lars Müller book, *Helvetica: Homage to a Typeface,* Wolfgang Weingart, a leader of the "Swiss Punk" style, called Helvetica "the epitome of ugliness" (Roane 2007: 71). This reflects the philosophical and geographic

Image 36 Helvetica showing on cover of the Swiss specimen book, *Handbücher guten Druckschriften,* vol. E (Zurich: Visualis AG, 1975).

distance in Switzerland between Basel (more artistic in point of view) and Zurich (more design-oriented.) The sans-serif font Univers, designed by Adrian Frutiger in 1957, has been, for many designers, a competitor of Helvetica. Charles Bigelow, designer of the typeface Lucida, remembers,

At a typographic conference in Mainz in the 1980s, I was with a group of French typographers, talking about signage and legibility. A youngster among sage elders, I voiced the opinion that Helvetica, while not especially good for bookwork, was adequately legible for signage. At this, the effervescent Ladislas Mandel, a fine designer who a quarter century earlier had been Adrian Frutiger's assistant in the development of the typeface Univers at Deberny & Peignot, retorted with Gallic panache: "But no! Univers, that is a LEGIBLE typeface! Helvetica? It is merely decipherable."[1]

Christian Larsen from the Museum of Modern Art says, "Helvetica is really a standout. It helped define the typographic look of the 20th century, and I think, is here to stay" (Roane 2007: 71). New York's Museum of Modern Art (MoMA), in fact, mounted, in the summer of 2007, a small exhibit of Helvetica print applications to coincide with the film. Hustwit, the Helvetica film's creator, is responsible for fueling the controversy. He said, "For over 50 years, Helvetica has picked up the baggage. Because it is used by big business and government, when we look at a word set in Helvetica, we pick up the subtle feelings of authority, efficiency and permanence" (Roane 2007: 71).

ITS TIMING WAS AUSPICIOUS

The timing of its availability had a great deal to do with this. It came on the market early in the formative days of the Swiss International Style and was adopted as the "house typeface" of this important movement in Modernist design. The introduction of the Apple Macintosh computer in 1985 gave users Helvetica as one of its fine standard fonts. Nowadays both Helvetica and Arial are recommended for use on the Web for screen design.

IT HAS A UNIQUE STYLE

Designers of an earlier generation in Zurich, Basel, and Milan, such as Richard P. Lohse, Hans Neuberg, Armin Hofmann, Max Bill, Carlo Vivarelli, Max Huber, Emil Ruder, and Karl Gerstner were all using Helvetica in their posters and other graphic works. For example, the Swiss design magazine, *Neue Graphik* (New Graphic Design), was, at the time, an international review of design and used Helvetica exclusively. The font was also extensively used in the series of posters done by Josef Müller-Brockmann in the 1950s and 1960s. Of particular note was the "der film" exhibition poster from 1960. This poster shows Müller-Brockmann's masterful use of Helvetica

and his ability at demonstrating universal design harmony by mathematical space division. These same visual values were applied in the series of music posters, done by Müller-Brockmann, for the Zurich Concert Hall over a two-decade span.

Typography, in the context of this "International Style," was seen as one important component in an approach to graphic design that stressed objective, structural, systematic, and rational values. In the 1960s it quickly became popular in the United States, largely through the work of Will Burtin, Rudolph de Harak, Chermayeff and Geismar, Fred Troller, and especially Massimo Vignelli. Remington and Fripp, in their new book, *Design and Science—The Life and Work of Will Burtin,* credit Burtin with an early use and appreciation for Helvetica. During a summer trip to Zurich in 1958, Burtin saw Helvetica in the works of Max Bill, Ernst Keller, and others. Being an advocate for functional information flow in graphic design, he was determined to bring this "clarity of Swiss style" to the world (Remington and Fripp, 2007: 84). Massimo Vignelli at Unimark International had been strongly influenced by Max Huber in Milan. At that time Vignelli used Helvetica for everything he designed.

Still today we see his Helvetica in the logos of JC Penney, Heller, Knoll International, and American Airlines. When designing the New York Subway signage in 1966 with colleague Bob Noorda, Vignelli originally used Akzidenz Grotesk, only because Helvetica was not available to him at that time. Subsequently the typeface has been systematically replaced by Helvetica with few noticing the difference. Two years later, Helvetica was used in the graphics and signage for the Washington, D.C. Metro. Many identity designs by other designers have joined the global branding parade, such as Crate & Barrel, Comme des Garçons, Nestlé, Target, 3M, Microsoft, Sears, Wal-Mart, Energizer batteries, Greyhound Lines, Jeep, Lufthansa, Marks & Spencer, Toyota, Karlsberger, National Car Rental, and Panasonic. to name a few. Apple, Inc.'s OS X integrates Helvetica as its default font for many applications. In a *Business Week* article,

Tobias Frere-Jones, director of typography at Hoefler & Frere-Jones in New York, stated, "Every typeface is made to solve some type of problem. They're design tools. Helvetica wasn't designed with anything specific in mind. It was designed to be a jack-of-all-trades. … Helvetica is so widely available. It has so many associations, namely to large corporate entities like American Airlines. These companies stay with it because of the brand equity they have invested in the typeface. Plus, the font's forms suggest stability" (quoted in Reena, 2007: 14).

IT IS VERY LEGIBLE

Helvetica has been popular as a font because of the inherent functionality in its basic design. The characters in the typeface are clear-cut. Its lower-case letters have an increased-height "x" height, which means that the lower-case or small letters are larger proportionately to the capital letters than in most sans-serif fonts. This is one reason why Helvetica is so commonly used for interior and exterior sign systems, especially in airports, such as Heathrow in London. In 1970, the book, *A Sign Systems Manual,* was published in London by Studio Vista. This reference book by Theo Crosby, Alan Fletcher, and Colin Forbes used Helvetica to establish sign standardization systems for the graphic designer. It quickly became a useful desktop volume for designers challenged with creating sign and way-finding systems.

Because the various heights and weights of Helvetica were designed by different individuals over the years, it has been criticized for lacking the systematic cohesiveness of Univers. With the development of the Neue Helvetica in 1983, however, many of these design inconsistencies were remedied, as the typeface became available in a fully systematic range of weights and postures.

GRAPHICALLY IT IS NEUTRAL

When compared to Bodoni or many other fonts, Helvetica has been successful because it is plain in appearance. It leaves the viewer with nothing but the message to see. Wim Crouwel, the Dutch designer, who appears in the Helvetica film, says "We were impressed with Helvetica's lack of manual details and because it was more neutral. It shouldn't have a meaning in itself; the meaning is in the content of the text and not in the typeface."[2] It is one of the contradictions of Helvetica that while it is touted as being neutral, it also has been a common typeface used in identities in which one would suppose that distinction was a priority. Over the years, typographic traditionalists have compared Helvetica to Akzidenz Grotesk, with the criticism that the newer font is blunt, colorless, and lacks the color of its parent typeface. The same is then said of its contemporaries and successors.

IT IS TIMELESS

Helvetica is an enduring exemplar in the history of graphic design and graphic arts. Michael Bierut of Pentagram, a New York design firm, says,

> Helvetica is a beautifully machined, rationally resolved, entirely modern typeface that seems absolutely suited to its times. Helvetica was introduced at a moment where postwar optimism was at its highest, at a time when—pre-Vietnam, pre-Watergate—people had real confidence in Modernism and modern institutions to solve the world's problems. Like most typefaces, Helvetica works its magic on an entirely subconscious level. Its ubiquity and inherent authority are inescapable. If it is important to people's lives, it's largely without their knowledge or consent. (Roane 2007: 71)

Even designer Paula Scher, when speaking about Helvetica, admits that a classic typeface (such as Helvetica) never goes out of style.

One graphic application that uses Helvetica exclusively is the large Stendig wall calendar. Designed by Vignelli in 1966, the calendar, which is 36 × 48 inches in size, has been represented in

The Design Collection of the Museum of Modern Art. Vignelli recalls that the calendar became so popular upon its introduction that it went directly from the printer to MoMA. It features huge Helvetica numerals with each month alternating in either positive or negative form for variety. Beyond the functionalism of the calendar, at this scale, the numerals individually and in concert become a tour-de-force of beautiful positive and negative shapes. It is as much a functional calendar as it is a piece of art that depends exclusively on the forms of the Helvetica typeface.

Whether we like it or not, we have all probably seen Helvetica a thousand times today. Designers will continue to use it for all the right reasons. Because of the plethora of available typefaces, its detractors can easily seek out another sans-serif font. However, they need to consider the words of Massimo Vignelli, in a lecture to graphic design students at the School of Design, Rochester Institute of Technology, on October 21, 2002: "In the new computer age the proliferation of typefaces and type manipulations represents a new level of visual pollution threatening our culture. Out of thousands of typefaces, all we need are a few basic ones, and trash the rest." But in the end, we can all agree with Matt Zoller Seitz as he wrote in his film review, "Helvetica is an emblem of the machine age, a harbinger of globalization and an ally of modern art's impulse toward innovation, simplicity and abstraction" (Seitz 2007: 6). Either way, we had better get used to it because it is going to be with us for a long time and, as Vignelli says, "Every society gets the design it deserves."[3]

NOTES

1. Interview with Charles Bigelow, Rochester Institute of Technology, Rochester, New York, January 17, 2008.
2. *Helvetica.* Dir. Gary Hustwit. Perf. Wim Crouwel. Veer, 2007.
3. "Medalists: Massimo and Lella Vignelli," http://www.aiga.org/content/cfm/medalist-massimoandlellavignelli

76

THE ARCHITECT AND THE TEAKETTLE

Shirley Teresa Wajda

The teakettle designs of American architect Michael Graves for the American discount department store Target provide a case study of the late twentieth-century democratization of design. The phenomenal success of the 1985 "whistling bird" kettle for the Italian firm Alessi reintroduced to the American public the idea that an architect could design more than buildings. Facilitated by the prosperity created in the New Economy of the 1980s and 1990s and the corresponding desire by consumers and retailers for domestic goods and authentic design, Michael Graves, as well as other architects and product designers, achieved celebrity status as they altered both the consumer and domestic landscapes.

Kettles are to be seen *and* heard. Filled with water and set upon heat, a metal kettle's lid shakes and rattles, bullied by escaping steam at boiling point. Through the kettle's spout a white plume of urgent steam ensures that the heated metal container does not burst. The smaller the circumference of the spout, the more insistent the hum of the escaping steam. Attach a spout cover with a small hole, and that hum becomes a whistle; dependent on the shape and size of the hole, that whistle may be shrill or harmonious, insistent or inviting. Many a morning's silence has been interrupted by the ritual call of the kettle, summoning a household to breakfast. Many an afternoon's bustle has been calmed by the call to tea.

Indeed, the English craze for right-tasting "China drink" in the seventeenth and eighteenth centuries, and the rise of associated tea-taking rituals, reinvested the lowly, often blackened iron kettle with a more singular purpose. *Teakettle,* according to the *Oxford English Dictionary,* was coined in 1705, signaling the introduction of the lowly cooking vessel into the genteel rituals of tea drinking. Fashioned in silver, copper, or japanned tin, modeled with a flat bottom, and placed on a tripod stand from which heating sources such as spirit lamps were suspended, the teakettle, "a covered metal vessel with a spout, used to boil water for domestic purposes," adorned tasteful tables. The kettle's purpose at tea was more than making available hot water to dilute strong tea infusions poured from the ceramic teapot. The kettle's stylish makeover fit it to sets of teawares as well as the room decors in which it was displayed.

Since the early nineteenth century, however, the kettle has been more often found in the kitchen. The enclosure of fire in stoves created a ready resting place for the multipurpose kettle. Boiling water was a daily necessity in households, not only for the preparation of food but also for cleaning and laundering. The introduction of gas, kerosene, and electric stoves did not alter the form of the kettle, although new materials— enameled sheet iron, spun and cast aluminum, stainless steel, and later tempered glass, Bakelite, and other plastics and resins for handle and spout cover—introduced in the late nineteenth and twentieth centuries, were adapted to kettle design and manufacture.

Over the course of the twentieth century, the domestic dwelling was reconfigured to facilitate more informal sociability in living rooms and kitchens rather than parlors. By the 1920s and

Image 37 Alessi Whistling Bird teakettle. Photo credit: Joseph Andris.

continuing today, American decorating manuals and periodicals have consistently dedicated pages to efficient and delightful kitchens—all the more delightful because of the constant introduction of conveniences, from gas ranges to microwave ovens. Nevertheless, the kettle rests squarely on the stovetop, its presence a testament to efficiency, sociability and—especially since the mid 1980s—decor. "Putting the kettle on" presages the informal hospitality that takes place in the kitchen.

Whatever the style, these utensils sport the same attributes of lid, spout, and handle. These three elements protect the user from the scalding contents as they facilitate use. The lid shields the steam from the hand. The handle, fashioned of wood or some other insulating material, eases lifting and pouring. The slowing of the water stream through the employment of the spout averts accidental splashing. Whether called *kettle* in England and on the Continent, or *teakettle*, as coffee-drinking Americans prefer, this kitchen tool serves historically and consistently as an icon of hearth, home, and hospitality. These are the considerations the historicist architect-designer Michael Graves took into account in his first two teakettle designs for the discount retail department store chain, Target Corp., of Minneapolis, Minnesota.

FROM HIGH (HEAT) STYLE TO READY-TO-BOIL: MICHAEL GRAVES'S KETTLES FOR ALESSI AND TARGET

Michael Graves's success in Minneapolis began in Italy. In 1980, Alberto Alessi sought to enhance his Italian, family-run firm's reputation and expand its market within the United States. Alessi, founded in 1921 as a metalware manufacturer, had already expanded its luxury line of kitchen tools and tablewares. German industrial designer Richard Sapper's popular Melodic Whistle Kettle, sporting a pitch pipe spout and designed for Alessi, proved that evocative design was both marketable and profitable. Buoyed by this success, Alessi undertook the Tea and Coffee Piazza program, inviting eleven architects to create services in which the teapot, coffeepot, creamer, and sugar bowl (with spoon) were "buildings" standing on the tray, which served as the "piazza."

One of those eleven architects was Michael Graves, who designed a classical "domestic landscape" of square, sterling silver pieces with fluted walls and columns. Limited to editions of ninety-nine, these costly piazzas were displayed at American museums (including the Whitney Museum of American Art) when they were finished in 1983. More aesthetic concept and advertising experiment than viable marketing strategy, orders were few, though the Graves service (U.S.\$25,000) outpaced the other architects' designs by a ratio of two to one (Patton 2004: 31). As Max Protetch, whose New York City gallery exhibited the collection and took orders, recalled, "It was silver-coated architectural theory that you could use for pouring coffee" (Pearlman 2003, F8). Alessi, however, had achieved his goal of introducing his firm's wares to the American market while learning that market's shifting character. With many piazzas left unsold, Alessi learned how "to turn mass production into something like mass customization" (Pearlman 2003).

What would become its best-selling kettle was the product of Alessi's effort to remedy design flaws in Sapper's version and tap the growing American taste for designer goods. As Michael Graves recounted in 2005, Alberto Alessi wanted Graves "to update the Sapper tea kettle with functionality—it had to whistle but had to come with a removable option. It had to blow [sic] water faster than anything else in the market, and we designed that by having as broad a base you can have that fits into a stove top." Alessi also "came loaded with plans on minute technical requirements on how the joints would come together in the kettle" (Gogoi 2005). Sapper's design failed in two other respects: The handle retained too much heat and was attached so low on the vessel that it risked melting from direct exposure to the heating source. Utility, as well as facilitating consumer preference (to whistle or not to whistle), were the problems to be solved.

Graves brought to the project more than twenty years of architectural, interior, and product design. He adapted what he terms "figurative architecture" to the task of designing housewares, embracing "humanistic concerns" and exploring "a language of forms that express the myths and rituals of our culture." Counter to Modernism's aesthetic of abstraction, Graves argues that, in figurative design, "forms that are familiar and accessible can convey meaning because we associate with them" (Patton 2004: 28). His postmodern buildings—notably the Portland Building (1982, Oregon) and the corporate headquarters of Humana in Louisville, Kentucky (1985)—incorporate surface color as a key symbolic element. "For me, color—along with form—is representational," Graves observed in 2004.

To counter the hot handle of Sapper's design, Graves insulated the handle of his version in a "cool blue-gray" (now known as Graves Blue) polyamide grooved to be gripped by fingers and finished by thin black discs and red balls on either end. The curved lid's round polyamide knob, echoing the circular handle, is a neutral black. To indicate heat, Graves had intended the series of dots (imitating the heads of hobnails, referencing historic forms of manufacture) circling the broad base of the conically shaped kettle to be red, "because of their proximity to the flame of the stove, but that was technically not feasible" (Patton 2004: 71).

Red, however, is the color used to signal, by sight and by sound, the hot steam escaping from the vessel's spout. Graves chose a removable bird that could "perch" on the spout, wings spread as if flying or merely animated. "I grew up in Indiana," Graves explained, "where we really did get up to the sound of the rooster in the morning. I initially thought of the teakettle as the red rooster and wanted to name it *gallo rosso,* which is Italian for red rooster" (Patton 2004: 35). This whimsical addition of the "whistling" bird, and a "real" one based in nature and in personal experience rather than an abstraction, gave the polished stainless steel kettle, according to Graves, a "personality." "Architecture and product designs have a narrative capacity—you can start to tell a story about them and imagine a lot of things" (Gogoi 2005). Initially priced at U.S.$125 (although Graves suggested that it should sell at "about what a Revereware kettle costs"—between U.S.$30 and U.S.$40), the popularly called Whistling Bird kettle became Alessi's best seller: some two million by 2007. Its success led to the additions of teapots, creamers, sugar bowls, and serving platters.

Graves's successful avian whimsy brought him to the attention of Target Corp. executives, who, in 1997, were seeking a designer "with wit" (Patton 2004: 72) to create a scaffolding for the Washington Monument during a two-year restoration. This commission led to collaboration between the architect-designer and the expanding "big box" store. Target Corp., once the upscale Dayton-Hudson department stores, drew upon a long practice of retailing what it once called "trend forward" merchandise and now calls "design for all." Humorously called in pseudo-French "Tarzhay," the company had begun to concentrate on consumers with an average annual household income of U.S.$47,000, calling them "guests" and offering a boutique experience in a mass-market retail store. According to Graves, Ron Johnson, Target's vice-president of general merchandise, asked him, "We've been knocking you off for years. Why don't we come to the source?"—a ready admission of the allure of originality and market exclusivity and the new problem of brand marketing when imitation has always served as a strategy (Lipman 1999). A visit to a Target store followed, during which the architect affixed yellow Post-It Notes on the items he thought he could improve—though Johnson worried that he wouldn't have enough Post-It Notes.

Of the 350 items in the Michael Graves Design Collection, 150 debuted in January 1999 at the Whitney Museum of American Art, and in each of the 851 Target stores then in the United States. Included in the Whitney display was a wall full of narrow, almost bullet-shaped, stub-spouted teakettles, each featuring a reverse-mounted, screwed-on handle swathed in Graves Blue Santoprene and a red whistle, described, in terms firmly within American popular culture, either as a "Cracker Jack prize" (Patton 1999) or a "red coach's whistle" (Lipman 1999). Graves employed a yellow, egg-shaped Santoprene knob set at an angle on the lid opposite the handle so as to facilitate handling. The egg form was, according to the promotional literature, "familiar … an object both basic to cooking and easy to hold" (Thau 1999). This egg form, along with the use of colors such as Graves Blue and an earthy red, united the housewares line as a "product family"—Graves's term suggesting family relations (Patton 2004: 62). This strategy appealed to a new type of consumption based on connoisseurship and collecting, all the while imitating the traditional practice of harmonized, seasonal couture collections. It also celebrated the practices of architects to rethink their designs, in that the strategy provided the possibility of a "genealogy" of design, in creating successive product "generations" sporting "family resemblances."

Ron Johnson's easy admission of copying Graves's designs stands in stark contrast to Alberto Alessi's protestation of Target's new product family. Soon after the line's launch, Alessi targeted (!) as "inferior" the U.S.$34.99 teakettle, calling it a "knockoff" of the 1985 whistling bird version. His objections, he stated, arose not from the possibility of competition (he saw none), but about poor quality, which he attributed to Graves's staff, thereby invoking traditional definitions of genius,

Image 38 Target Spinner Whistle teakettle. Photo credit: Joseph Andris.

originality, and authenticity. "I'm sure this is easily recognizable if you compare the objects designed by Target to those originally designed by Michael for Alessi." In reply, Graves observed that the "general understanding Alberto and I have is that I would endeavor to avoid confusion in the marketplace resulting from designing similar products in the same price range." Alberto Alessi would not be appeased on this point. "Even with the price difference, how can such an unequivocally ugly object be desired by the American public? In my opinion, this only reinforces the classic design of our kettle as one of the design icons of the 1980s." Graves's final word? "I'm sorry to hear that he does not like the kettle we designed for Target. I think it has great spirit, and it appears to be a hit with the American public" (Zisko 1999).

Yet, only three years later Graves birthed the Spinner Whistle Teakettle (U.S.$34.99) into his Target product family. The problems of the previous model had been noted earlier by design journalist Phil Patton: "the kettle's egglike handle is awkward, steam can lift the lid, and the removable whistle is almost too hot to handle" (1999). In addition, the requirements of mass-market retail dictated different criteria for this teakettle: Design aside, these included the placement and number of the product in stores, as well as the necessity of changing over time while retaining identity for repeat customers (Patton 2004: 79). The new dome-shaped, stainless steel version, like its predecessor, features an attached, reverse-mounted insulated handle, in Graves Blue, with a yellow egg-shaped finial on the lid. Strikingly, however, this teakettle's shape approximates more closely the Alessi kettle, even to the employment on the tubular spout of a red spiraling spinner whistle activated by steam, which offers another whimsical interpretation of nature (unlike the "coach's whistle").

Whatever the true purpose of Alberto Alessi's lament or Michael Graves's motivation in this version, what constitutes good design in the mass market still requires that authenticity, and not necessarily originality, ultimately be linked to the hand of the designer. Rather than a selected coterie of star architects, each expressing simultaneously their interpretations of the things we use—Alessi's strategy to achieve both prestige and market through "mass customization"—Target Corp. and other mass-market retailers are underwriting long-term, evolving "mass-tige" collections that may, like many a Parisian couture house, outlive their founders.

Alessi is right, however, when he states that Graves's whistling bird kettle is a cultural icon. It has become Graves's signature piece, used in his firm's promotional materials, able to bear replication as well as evolution. Nevertheless, Graves's iconic kettle for Alessi and its "estranged" cousins created for Target ensure the former's position as "timeless" design as well as chronicle a sense of time passing. Both the whistling bird and Spinner Whistle kettles have been added to the Brooklyn Museum's permanent collection. In 2008 Alessi offered a miniature version of the architect's famed postmodern kettle, a souvenir eliciting in its sculptured smallness a nostalgic sense of what the firm calls "the recurrent desire to surround oneself with beautiful things that represent the physical expression of distinctive taste" (Alessi.com). The designer himself, now wheelchair-bound, has dedicated his energies to Universal Design, meshing his new projects for his Target collection with the socially conscious retailer's motto of "design for all." In a photograph of Michael Graves appearing on the retail giant's Web site, the Spinner Whistle teakettle sits on the table, more than an arm's reach from the seated architect, while two of his new, smaller, ergonomic, wide-mouth, enamel-clad whistling teakettles, in black and in white, sit on a display shelf behind him. The quotation, "Good design should be accessible to all," superimposed on the image, links the architect and the teakettle—and the consumer—in a new relationship, one based less on whim and more on necessity (http://www.target.com).

77

BULLETS AND BEYOND (THE *SHINKANSEN*)

Greg Votolato

With the inauguration of pure jet passenger aircraft in the 1950s, the world's railroads faced increasingly tough competition with airlines for passengers and express goods delivery, such that their survival would demand a fundamental reappraisal of their services and a quantum leap in the idea of what a modern railroad should be. Although airlines soon captured the great majority of long-haul travelers with planes, such as the Boeing 707, a new generation of high-speed intercity trains could offer competitive door-to-door travel times over distances of four to five hundred miles. However, trains moving at more than 120 miles per hour would need their own dedicated infrastructure and a state-of-the-art management system. Such a railroad was developed first in Japan, where the revolutionary *shinkansen* (new main network) "bullet" trains covered the 320 miles between Tokyo and Osaka in just three hours. Drivers were guided for the first time by an innovative electronic telecommunication and information system displayed in the cab, while passengers were accommodated in pressurized, airline-style carriage interiors, dramatizing the competitive aspirations of the *shinkansen*.

Proposals for a high-speed rail line were first mooted in the 1930s, when the Japanese Empire was spreading its domain into Asia; but planning, land acquisition, and construction of a new electrified railway system were halted during the later part of World War II and were not revived until the 1950s. Then, its major impetus was the country's dramatic postwar reconstruction, spurred by

the Japanese role in supplying goods to American and allied forces during the Korean conflict between 1950 and 1953. While Japan's railways, and indeed its total transport infrastructure, were overstretched and underdeveloped in relation to the country's burgeoning economy, it was also dangerous. Existing narrow gauge railways followed the difficult topography of the country's four main islands, which were linked by train-ferry services that became notorious for accidents at sea with high mortality rates.

Nationalization of the railways and the formation of Japan National Railways (JNR) in 1949 facilitated the creation of a modern rail network in the following decade, while postwar reconstruction and the ensuing economic expansion placed intense pressure on the rail operators to devise radical solutions to the problems of rail transport in Japan. The two main authors of the high-speed intercity rail lines were the engineer, Shima Hideo (1901–1998, "the father of *shinkansen*"), whose own father had initiated plans for a *shinkansen* during World War II, and Sogo Shinji, President of JNR and the political genius behind the scheme (Kirkup 1998). New routes were planned to cut through the landscape, following the straightest path possible, to increase speed and reduce travel times between major city centers. In 1957 JNR announced the plan to construct the first of its 210 km/hr (130 mph) *shinkansen* covering the 322 kilometers (515 miles) between Tokyo and Osaka in less than four hours, halving the previous best travel time. Construction

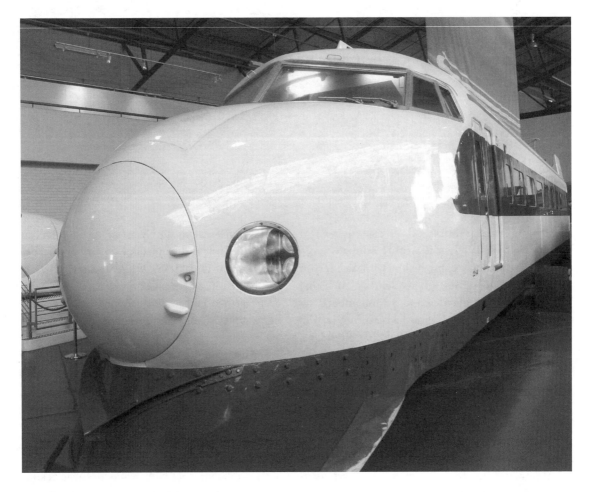

Image 39 Bullet Train. Photo by Greg Votolato.

started in 1959, and the Tokaido Shinkansen began passenger service on October 1 1964, just in time to dazzle visitors to the Tokyo Olympics, which opened on October 10. The word *shinkansen* means "new main network" but was quickly applied to the trains as well as the infrastructure. In addition to the striking appearance of the new trains, their three main attractions were high speeds, city center departure and arrival, and the frequency and punctuality of the service.

Japan is a disjointed, island landmass stretching more than three thousand miles, with extremes of climate, and mountainous terrain prone to earthquakes, all of which contributed significantly to the character of the *shinkansen* design and to its spectacular constituent elements: bridges, viaducts, stations, depots, train sets, and extravagant record-breaking structures such as the Seikan tunnel, the world's longest under-sea tunnel. This ensemble of elements enabled the new lines to connect Japan's major cities according to relatively straight routes, passing through, rather than around, mountains and eliminating the need for ferries by bridging over or crossing under the many bodies of water they encountered. Just as important and innovative as the physical infrastructure, the new Automatic Train Control (ATC) system provided a speed and braking safety net to support the work of the drivers, whose cabin instruments replaced line-side signaling. Together, these features provided the key electronic elements enabling *shinkansen* trains to achieve consistently high speeds with no accident fatalities in all their years of operation (Semmens 1997: 14–17).

Trains designed for the *shinkansen* service were powered by overhead electrical cables and driven by motors running under the carriages the full length of the train, rather than being housed in a locomotive. The resulting lowered center of gravity made the ultra-lightweight carriages particularly stable in an earthquake-prone environment. This, coupled with a new Urgent Earthquake Detection and Alarm System, which can quickly bring the train to a stop in the event of a serious tremor, have protected the *shinkansen* effectively throughout its history. Yet, earthquakes are not the only forces of nature to threaten the railways in Japan. Heavy rainfall causes landslides, against which the *shinkansen* was shielded by concrete reinforced cuttings. Snow is a seasonal threat, which was counteracted by a variety of measures, including heated signaling points on the line, heaters to prevent snow from building up under the train, and the extensive network of tunnels through which trains run. In the summer months, typhoons play havoc with all transport systems, and in this event the *shinkansen* has been nearly as vulnerable to delay as aircraft or road traffic.

The streamlined profiles of the original 0-series train of 1964, and particularly the aerodynamic nose of its control car, gave that vehicle a distinctive appearance and earned it the popular nickname "bullet train." The 0-series's iconic status as the preeminent symbol of modern Japan is at least partly due to its striking appearance. Among the design team that created the 0-series bullet train, Tadaneo Miki had established his reputation as the designer of the Ginga, a World War II Navy dive-bomber, whose sleek shape influenced the sweeping lines of the 0-series. The nose and windscreen of the train also closely resemble another, better-known global product, the Douglas DC3 airliner, which dominated air transport around the world from 1935 to around 1950. The train's overall

aesthetic, however, can be attributed to the broad notion of functionalism, which spread internationally between the late nineteenth century and the 1950s, entering Japanese design through the Mingei (Folkcraft) Movement guided by Yanagi Soetsu, who promoted the aesthetics of everyday useful objects. Although later Shinkansen trains achieved ever more aerodynamically efficient shapes, partly by abandoning the bullet nose, they have all retained their cutting-edge image of sleek modernity (Semmens 1997: 44–56).

Aboard the bullet train, ninety percent of passengers traveled in the Ordinary Class, sitting three abreast, while the small percentage of First Class passengers sat two abreast and enjoyed more leg and elbow room. However, class distinctions were minimal, and the *shinkansen* has been appreciated as a highly democratic form of transport, although its fares were typically higher than those of its competitor airlines. Whereas first-generation trains offered the civility of a dining car, these were eventually replaced with stand-up buffets; and crew members also served bento boxes to passengers at their seats, airline-style. As these trains were high-volume mass transporters and passengers were on board for only a few hours, their commuter-style interiors were robust and rather plain. However, recent carriages have featured more innovative interiors, such as those of the 800-series train designed by Eiji Mitooka for the Hitachi Kasodo Works and used by the Japan Railway (JR) Kyushu line since 2004. These interiors reflect traditional Japanese aesthetics through their use of timber-framed chairs upholstered in nishijin-ori brocade fabric, cherry-wood window blinds, and rope curtains covering the lavatory entrances. The use of such natural materials in a sleek contemporary style suggests a synthesis of Mingei craftsmanship and twenty-first century ecological consciousness.

The visual image of the *shinkansen* became of particular importance with the partial privatization of JNR in 1987 and the creation of several regional JR companies, whose services by then linked most of the major cities in Japan. Thus, branding of the high-speed railway, including all its infrastructure and rolling stock, became a tool of corporate enterprise. It also became important in the development and dissemination of a new postwar national identity for reconstructed Japan. The bullet train became an Asian equivalent of transport icons from other times and nations, such as the American Model T Ford, the London bus, and the French ocean liner *Normandie.* Widespread reproduction of photos showing the bullet train passing Mt. Fuji has created one of the central images of late twentieth-century Japan—the timeless and the timely, speed and stasis, nature and technology—an image that captures the great contradictions of the modern world and, particularly, of modern Japan.

Global recognition of the bullet train in the 1960s and 1970s also coincided with the emergence of other modern Japanese products and technologies that became world-famous in a variety of fields; the miniature audio-visual products of Sony, the precision cameras of Japan's optics manufacturers, such as Canon and Nikon, the radically efficient Toyota system of automobile production, the technologically inventive treatment of materials in the fashion garments of Issey Miyake, and the influential Metabolist architecture of Kisho Kurokawa.

Despite its symbolic importance, Japan's rail system in general and the *shinkansen* in particular have been the objects of both political and popular controversy, due largely to the compulsory purchase of land, which has made its construction possible, the "compensation game" played by some individuals and companies to benefit excessively from compulsory purchase, and its consequent cost to the taxpayer (Hood 2006: 85–90). Shinkansen Citizen Movements have sprung up locally to demonstrate the objections of neighbors and businesses affected by particular *shinkansen* construction projects and aspects of environmental pollution caused by the trains.

Whereas the *shinkansen* is considerably more efficient than cars, buses, and its principal rival, jet aircraft, in terms of carbon dioxide emissions and energy consumption, it faces additional environmental challenges, including noise and vibration. Although the trains do not operate between midnight and early morning, the proximity of tracks to areas of housing makes it imperative that the impact of the train's movement be kept to acceptable levels. This was accomplished initially by the carefully calculated streamlining of the 0-series body, improved gradually in the design of each successive generation of trains. Skirtings, which cover the underside of the carriages, have been added to reduce noise emitted by the wheels, and quieter pantographs (which transfer the electrical supply from overhead lines to the train's motors) have been developed. Over seven hundred kilometers of tunnel, approximately thirty-seven percent of the combined six *shinkansen* lines, keep the trains out of sight and earshot in many sensitive locations. In above-ground sections of the lines, sound walls at the sides of the track limit noise but also restrict vision, blocking some of the most potentially impressive views from the train. Compression waves, producing a "boom" effect when the train enters or leaves a tunnel, have also been muted through improved streamlining of the control car and the addition of noise-muffling hoods to tunnel mouths. Vibration has proved to be a far stickier problem, and although research is ongoing, a satisfactory counter-measure is yet to be found.

Some critics also list the appearance of the overhead pantographs and the heavy concrete infrastructure of the elevated sections of track as visual pollution, scarring the landscape. Such critiques may also point to the poor design of some *shinkansen* stations (Hood 2006: 177–78). With privatization, JNR was broken up to form six regional passenger railways, with a national company responsible for the carriage of freight, an arrangement that has allowed and encouraged a more entrepreneurial approach to development, particularly through the construction of office buildings and hotels on former JNR land adjacent to *shinkansen* terminals. While the aesthetic quality of some JR developments may be questionable, companies have made efforts to include community amenities and a sense of style in their new stations and other commercial buildings. Among recent projects, JR Kyushu's Shin Minamata station, designed by architect Makoto Sei Watanabe, stands out for its high-tech construction and its aesthetic of dynamism and transience, visual qualities sympathetic to its purpose and location.

Among the Japan Railway companies, JR East is by far the largest; in fact it is the world's largest railway, carrying around twice the passengers of the British, German, French, and Swiss railways combined, a comparison that confirms Japan as the preeminent railway nation (Semmens 1997: 62). Thus, it is not surprising that Japan's major railroad achievement, the *shinkansen*, has had significant influence abroad, particularly in Europe, where the French TGV, the Spanish AVE, and the German ICE trains emulated the *shinkansen* system and, in the case of the TGV, became its chief competitor for speed. While at present the TGV holds the world's railway speed record, the *shinkansen* retains the record as the fastest passenger service, calculated as the average speed between two stations on a route (Hood 2006: 122–23). This rivalry echoes the hectic interwar Blue Riband competition for the fastest crossing of the North Atlantic by a passenger ship.

Although speed may have been its raison d'être, the bullet train also offers its passengers the comfort of its pressurized carriages, with roomy reclining seats. Its punctuality is legendary, with the great majority of trains running within a minute of the schedule. They are also staffed by personnel trained to the highest standards of efficiency and politeness. The culture of intercity rail travel in Japan is relaxed, with many passengers using their trips to nap in their seats. Yet there is also a convivial atmosphere aboard many services, with passengers chatting, drinking beer, and smoking. The trains' relatively large windows would also suggest that gazing out may be a significant pastime. Yet on a fast train, things are not that simple. Noise walls and tunnels obscure all external views for significant parts of many routes. And according to Mitchell Schwarzer, when there is a view,

images of buildings multiply, simplify and compress into montage-like sequences. In Japan, the bullet train between Osaka and Tokyo routinely exceeds 180 miles per hour. Leaving Osaka is hardly distinguishable from entering nearby Kyoto, so fast does the train amalgamate each city's furthest suburbs. As the train passes through Nagoya … the view consists of distant megastructures surrounded by a bleary cityscape. … The Japan of the bullet-train view contains little more than factory complexes, high-rise buildings, and expansive, netted golf driving ranges. (Schwarzer, 2004: 55)

In the near future, *shinkansen* passengers could become accustomed to viewing the passing landscape at speeds around 220 mph (350 kph) (Thorne, 2001: 54). At such speeds, panoramic views from the train's windows will be limited to distant objects of considerable mass. Anything near the line will be reduced to a blur. And as safety considerations associated with increased speeds will ensure that secure seating becomes a greater priority, any opportunities to walk around the train freely will be reduced to a minimum as they are in current airliners. "Please keep your seatbelts fastened throughout the flight."

78

SNEAKERS

Alison Gill

A sullied, worn, very-much-alive object to be left on the front step or coveted dead-stock to be kept in a climate controlled vault? This contrasting view of the sneaker divides the collecting community down the middle, as there are those that wear their shoes and those that do not. As a ubiquitous object of avid consumer spending, the physical, emotional and sociocultural impact of the sneaker clearly exceeds its presence as a collectable. As athletic footwear is a global industry estimated at U.S.$26 billion dollars, the sneaker commodity is probably most remarkable for its assertive and multiplying market presence as both a specialist sports shoe and a leisure shoe over a forty-year period, and its segmentation during this period as an iconic example of niche-marketing and as a transforming agent of the casual shoe market.[1] The sneaker form has rapidly multiplied across many sport and leisure categories, as the leading brands release products in various shoe categories every sixty days, and smaller brands respond with a handful of variations. In order to maintain this pace, the industry practices both planned obsolescence with the release of new, improved models and the reissue of classic models (sometimes with new colors and features).

In terms of terminology, the sneaker is an American term for a rubber-soled canvas shoe produced beginning in 1870, using vulcanizing technology developed in the U.S. and British rubber and tire industry, and the term *sneaker* was derived from *sneak,* describing the soft sound of the rubber soles. Vulcanization strengthens rubber and allows the sole to be bonded with a canvas upper, a process still used in traditional sneaker models such as Keds (1916), Converse (1917), P. F. Flyers (1930s) and Vans (1966), many of which have been produced throughout the twentieth century as a staple of American youth footwear. Colloquially in the United States, sneakers are often called Chucks, based on the Converse "Chuck Taylor" made from 1923 on, or skips, for a nonbranded version. While the flat-soled look of the sneaker seems far removed from the feature-laden performance shoe of the 1980s, the term *sneaker* still applies in the United States to various specialist sports and casual shoes. In Great Britain, the *sand-shoe* was the preferred term for a canvas and rubber-soled shoe produced by the New Liverpool Rubber Company (later Dunlop) from the 1870s on, and used for gym and lawn sports. *Trainer* (from training shoe) is used by the British and some Europeans to refer to either specialist or cross-training applications of performance technology, for instance in aerobics, athletics, and basketball. In summary, while the generic industry term is athletic shoes, it encompasses a range of shoe subcategories—running, basketball, tennis, skate, walking, fitness, outdoor, classics, and so on—that have also been inflected in use with national, regional, and subcultural (shits, kicks, plates, or footcovers) differences of terminology.

Frequently cited as an iconic commodity of the twentieth century in cultural studies, journalism, and specialist studies of the athletic shoe, the sports shoe functions as a key indicator of cultural, social and economic change (Busch 1998; Cardona 2005; "Post-National Economy" 1996; Lury 2007; Quinn 2002; Tickle 2002; Vanderbilt 1998). In these studies, the manufacture and marketing of the athletic shoe, and exponential consumer responses to it, stand out as a preeminent examples of post-industrial manufacturing and global economic organization, the growth of brand culture, and lifestyle niche marketing. The "modern era" of the athletic shoe industry is defined by two rapid growth periods, which cemented the shoe's iconic status; the first was in the late 1970s and early 1980s in the United States, and the second, a decade later as the Western European market was established.[2] While the industry has experienced intermittent periods of nongrowth, it has resiliently mixed innovation in performance design, marketing, trend/fashion analysis, and cheap subcontracted labor to forge

vast new market segments and sustain consumer desire for athletic shoes.

Thus, there are many layers to the sneaker's iconic commodity status. It is an indicator of global economic change and post-industrial manufacturing and organization. By the mid-1970s the sneaker manufacturing industry was reorganizing internationally due to the challenge that a new foreign breed of company was yielding on domestic industries that had produced relatively unchanged sneaker models for decades. A series of increasingly marketing-driven firms such as Adidas, Puma, Onitsuka Tiger (later ASICS), Reebok, and Nike began promoting specialized performance shoes for individual sports and updating models annually, which introduced new materials and design innovations, and they relied on offshore manufacture and assembly. The *Far Eastern Economic Review* in 1996 put forward the sneaker as a new product model for economics

Image 40 Hype DC shoe store in central Sydney, Australia. Store design by DesigningSpace 2007.

education: "the once lowly sports shoe—the end product of an increasingly complicated design, production, and delivery process coordinating dozens of multinational companies under ever shorter deadlines—illustrates the realities of trade and globalisation more clearly than the widget of classic economic texts ever did" (cited in Vanderbilt 1998: 3–4).

Vanderbilt writes that the term "sneakerisation of the economy" has been used to describe the continuing trend of multiplying products and niche-market segmentation that extends endlessly under an ascending brand image (1998: 4). Offshore production of shoe components and their assembly in factories in Japan, South Korea, Taiwan, and more recently, China, Vietnam, and Indonesia fostered this trend, as Asian subcontractors out-competed domestic labor and production costs. A global network of shoe parts and human relations is constituted in the design, manufacture, and distribution of the sneaker. There is debate about the application of the term *post-industrial* to apply to the industry's organization, and differences within each company are to be observed. For example, Michael T. Donaghu and Richard Barff argue that Nike is neo-Fordist: "Nike's system of production has clearly moved beyond Fordist mass production with the complex subcontracting network and the production partnerships. Yet the company still relies on large volume production by semi- and unskilled labour" (Cited in Vanderbilt 1998: 85). Nike and Adidas-Salomon are the industry leaders based on net profits, with the January 2006 acquisition by Adidas of rival Reebok.

Beginning in 1990, media stories in the West began to tell of the poor labor conditions in South Korean and Indonesian factories, and the illegal practice of paying a "training" wage to long-standing workers. Groups such as Nike Watch and other antisweatshop lobbyists continue to exert pressure on the industry leaders to regulate the labor practices of their contractors.[3] Products such as Worn Again sneakers (made from recycled materials and 100% recyclable

in the United Kingdom) and the fair-trade No Sweat Mojo Sneaker have become an ethical alternative for consumers and an exertion of consumer pressure on companies that are perceived as nonethical, nonsustainable, and all-powerful. Perhaps in response to the negative publicity of antisweatshop campaigning and culture-jamming of groups like Adbusters, Nike publicly redefined its core business, stating in 2001 "we're a design and marketing company," not a shoe manufacturer, and other companies have followed suit in hiding their involvement in production (Gill 2006: 379; Tickle 2002).

The sneaker's iconic status is also an indicator of progressive design and performance technology. Companies continue to invest heavily in research and development of high-performance technology—cushioning and anti-shock systems, traction, lightweight, sustainable, and synthetic materials—in order to gather a design edge against their rivals in profits and consumer awareness. Combining the expertise of aeronautical engineers, biomechanics, sports physiologists, and textile scientists to combine shock-absorbent materials with compression-molded forms that interact with spring technologies, there is a view that sports equipment and athletic shoe design is a hotbed of innovation that flows into other product fields such as casual shoe design, apparel/sportswear, and accessories; as one trend analyst puts it, "Technological innovations start with sport but reshape fashion fast" (Kathy Deane, cited in Hennock 2003).[4] While industry leaders have market categories such as "performance shoes," "fashion shoes," and "classics/heritage," it is frequently difficult to ascertain the features that distinguish performance from fashion, and it is equally difficult for consumers to separate these in their motivations and decision making. The twenty-first-century frontiers of innovation are to deliver lightness in both material and form—that is, reducing midsole depth, as well as over-padding—to allow the subtle movements of the foot to occur and thus to turn away from the corrective technology of the earlier trainer.

An additional layer of the sneaker's iconic status is that it is an indicator of social distinction and movements; the sneaker has been a staple of youth cultural expression, as part of the youth kit for school, sport, and recreation, throughout the twentieth century. It has often functioned as a medium of individual or group expression through color or model choice, or through customization via shoelaces, drawing, or painting.

The example of hip-hop can illustrate an adoption of specialized shoes as part of a social movement or subculture that draws together interests in sports, fashion, music, and dance and expresses racial pride and lifestyle. Neal Heard has called hip-hop, along with Californian skate culture and the Football Casuals in the United Kingdom, an example of a "trainer tribe" due to the centrality of the athletic shoe to this social formation (2005: 12–20). Hip-hop, with its roots in 1970s basketball, break-dancing, and music, documented in films such as *Wild Style,* witnessed the proud adoption of athletic and basketball shoes as part of the uniform of black urban youth, with notable brand allegiances such as that expressed in song by Run DMC's "My Adidas" in the mid-1980s to the (unlaced, spotless) Adidas Superstar model (or Shell-toe classic, now in its thirty-seventh year). An American magazine such as *Sole Collector* documents the dandyesque attention afforded to choosing and collecting models and color-ways of athletic shoes in the hip-hop scene. In addition to taking the viewer inside the shoe vaults of key collectors and their addiction, the film *Just for Kicks* argues that the popularity of hip-hop worldwide has been the dominant force in the growth of a global sneaker culture. The sneaker culture has also grown from over-hyped shoe releases, marketing politics, and sponsorship deals, as well as the networking of enthusiasts and collectors, producing market demand for specialist magazines, retail outlets, and Web sites for news and trade. The sneaker-wearing preferences of "tribes" (subcultural groups of young people who follow a particular style) continues to be a lucrative source of design research, as it can provide essential technical and trend analysis to both the product and marketing fields of the industry, and rich cultural knowledge to sociologists and design theorists.

Additionally, the unstoppable flow of brand culture is a factor; sports shoes, along with computers, youth fashion, and fast food are a primary example of the marketing practice of building a brand image and a set of lifestyle qualities for an expanding product range. To illustrate the consumer hyper-awareness of shoe brands, one can point to the naming of shoes by their brand names and/or models rather than a generic product term like *athletic shoe*—for example, Chucks, Nikes, Air Jordans, Superstars, and so on. According to a 2006 Research and Markets report, "The active sportswear and footwear product group is one of the most heavily branded areas of apparel" (quoted in Lury 2007). A brand is an interaction between consumer, company, and product, an exchange of meaning, emotion, experience, and lifestyle qualities, in an open-ended production that is not finished as is the product it promotes; a brand can always express itself in a new form or set of consumer options (Lury 2007: 308–24). For example, the Nike brand was built around a core image of a runner's authentic experience (determination, self-competitiveness, etc.), and the brand image has been successfully designed to respond to trends in consumer lifestyle, fashion, and sport, thus expanding the core image into alternative athletic pursuits and carving out niche markets (Gill 2000: 93–128). All the while, as new products are released they inherit and finesse qualities and associations already established by the brand. A sneaker brand—with its logo functioning to magnify and consolidate associations—has become a powerful device for the management of flows of products in highly dynamic global markets.

Finally, because of the many dimensions to the iconicity of this commodity, the contemporary sneaker promises a very appealing and rich shoe culture—embodying progressive design, fashion, global belonging, status, and consumer responsiveness. It is for this reason that the athletic shoe and the other rubber-soled casual and business shoe variants it has spawned continue to be seen by consumers as the ultimate shoe liberation.

NOTES

1. The value of U.S.$26 billion is cited by the directors of a 2005 documentary film, *Just For Kicks*. The U.S. Sporting Goods Manufacturers Association reports the annual value of U.S. wholesale to be U.S.$11.9 billion in 2005, $12.3 billion in 2006, and $12.9 billion in 2007. The 2002 UK market was valued at 1.15 billion pounds in a 2003 Key Note publication.

2. Following the second period, a 1994 market report found that on average Europeans would buy a new pair of athletic shoes every twenty months, by which time the average U.S. consumer had purchased more than 2.5 pairs (Sporting Goods Manufacturing Association 1994).

3. See Jeff Ballinger's Nike/Anti-Sweatshop Chronology at the Web site of the Centre for Communication and Civic Engagement, University of Washington, http://depts.washington.edu/ccce/polcommcampaigns/Nike.htm

4. Bradley Quinn would agree that it is an influential sector of innovation, writing, "The level of innovation and the pace of change in sports shoes remain higher than in any other field of fashion design" (2002: 197).

79

THE BICYCLE

Considering Design in Use

Bess Williamson

Everyone knows what a bicycle is. So ubiquitous, this human-powered machine, consumer product, and mode of transport is recognizable in nearly every corner of the world. It is so familiar one need not be an artist to draw one—two wheels, triangles for the frame, a seat and handlebars will do. Yet, beyond these standard features there are endless small variations. Design differences among bicycles are rarely radical but instead involve subtle changes for distinct uses: small wheels on a low frame that folds for easy storage; a large, soft seat for long rides; reverse handlebars to pull the rider lower and diminish air resistance. These variations distinguish one bicycle from another, but standing on the street, locked to a public rack, they have little meaning. A bicycle is not simply an assemblage of angles, lines, and curves in metal and rubber; it is a way of moving. In order to understand the design of the bicycle and its history, we must understand bicycle riders and where they are going.

The study of design is a study of objects and the people who make them, but it is also a study of users. The features of a given category of object—bicycle, telephone, automobile, and so on—become accepted through a social process involving not only the plans of designers and engineers, but also the experience of users. When a technology first emerges, different social groups receive it differently, embracing some elements and rejecting others. When there are competing versions of the same product, each representing a different interpretation of the best design, the

technology remains "open" and its form unstable. When the "safety" bicycle we are familiar with today, with two wheels of equal size, a diamond frame, air-filled tires, and a chain drive, appeared in the mid-1880s, it was neither the only option nor the most popular one (Pinch & Bijker 1987). The "Ordinary," or "Penny-Farthing" bicycle, with a tall wheel directly under the rider and a smaller wheel for back support, was among the preferred models at the time. Although the Penny-Farthing was, like the safety, a two-wheeler and thus a "bi-cycle," it operated on different mechanical principles. In current-day terms, it resembled a unicycle, whose pedals directly turn the axis of the dominant wheel, in contrast to the safety bicycle's chain-driven rear wheel, which provides greater power for each turn of the pedals.

The sociologists Wiebe Bijker and Trevor Pinch have described this early phase of the bicycle's development as one in which the technological design remained "open"; it would take more than a decade for the safety bicycle to become the "closed," or standard design. The form and meaning of "a bicycle" has continued to change over time and space, often in response to the input of new users and new kinds of use. Looking at the bicycle in history and across cultures, we can see how, in different places and times, the function of the bicycle has been defined and redefined, open and closed. In the following examples, gender, politics, and the individual rider's body contribute to the ongoing social construction of the bicycle.

Image 41 Bicycles awaiting riders. Photograph by Bess Williamson.

As Pinch and Bijker explain, the safety bicycle triumphed over others for reasons of use, not mechanics. In the early years when the Penny-Farthing and other axle-pedaled models dominated, the bicycle was considered primarily a sporting instrument, used by men of the middle and upper classes in racing clubs. As one account of 1877 described the activity, bicycling was "a healthy and manly pursuit," to be recommended as much for its contribution to character as for transportation (quoted in Pinch & Bijker 1987: 35). The shift away from the Penny-Farthing to the safety bicycle came about for a variety of reasons, including changing ideas of who would be riding and why. As women slowly began to try out cycling, their long skirts made it

difficult to reach their legs around the large front wheel to pedal. Further, when bicycling became more of an urban activity, including for working-men, the bumpy surfaces of cobblestone streets were a concern, as the distribution of weight over the large front tire made for less stability in the tiny back wheel. These new users and new kinds of use tipped the balance toward the lower-riding, more stable safety bicycle.

The safety bicycle, with its diamond frame and chain-driven back wheel, has remained the standard form since the late nineteenth century. But if the technological definition of the bicycle became closed in this era, subtler variations in design remained open. The safety bicycle better accommodated skirts, but deeper concerns persisted. As a new and publicly visible invention, the bicycle became the subject of Victorian American and European anxieties about mobility and modernity, especially when it came to women cyclists. The idea of women setting out in public alone, energizing their delicate bodies, and, most shockingly, discovering sexual pleasure through a bicycle seat was most unsettling (Garvey 1995). To confront these ideas, women riders and their supporters had to reconstruct the cultural associations of speed, mechanics, and bodily agitation to better align with Victorian ideas of femininity. Seeking to improve their market, bicycle makers helped this process along. Advertisements showed composed, upright-sitting riders, their dresses safely covering their ankles even in motion. Manufacturers rolled out ladies' bicycles with graceful curves and decorative metalwork, presenting the activity as delicate and fashionable; a higher handlebar and broader seat countered the idea of a woman improperly thrust forward over the seat. As the historian Wendy Gruber Garvey has written, these commercial messages offered a new image of the woman bicyclist as "both decorative and decorous" (1995: 70).

Beyond these defensive measures against moral concerns, social construction of bicycling as an acceptable women's activity involved changing the very idea of mobility in relation to gender. In a late nineteenth-century society still becoming familiar with the speed of railroads and steamships, rapid telegraph communication, and the short cycles of fashion, mobility was both thrilling and destabilizing. The reassuring images of women in refined motion may have helped ease acceptance of the bicycle, but women themselves also embraced some of the riskier connotations. The feminist suffragette Frances Willard referred to her bicycle as an "implement of power," and even a rather tame ladies' bicycle manual reflected that "[r]iding the wheel, our powers are revealed to us. ... You have conquered the world, and exultingly you take possession of it" (quoted in Garvey 1995: 72). Social reconstruction was thus a product of changing images, not only of the bicycle, but also of the woman riding it.

The concept of modernity, embedded in the gendered discourse around bicycles in the 1890s, is even more charged in a non-Western context. Bicycles, as they emerged in an era of European colonialism, were introduced into many non-Western countries almost concurrently to Europe and America. In China, the first bicycles appeared in the early twentieth century in port cities, ridden by missionaries, diplomats, and the children of wealthy families with Western connections (Esfehani 2003). Their presence, like that of other Western goods, represented both the appeals and the threats of outside commercial influence. Over time, however, China developed its own bicycle industry and cultural usage, such that, by the mid-twentieth century, bicycles were as much symbols of Chinese modernity as they had ever been for the West.

If the controversial issue of women riding bicycles was settled by redefining its gender associations, the Chinese bicycle was subject to moments of closure based on political priorities. For the new Communist regime established in 1949, bicycles were well suited to economic and political goals. Bicycles were one of the few light, consumer-oriented industries to gain government support, though demand still overwhelmed supply into the 1980s (Xunhai 1992). The three dominant brands, Phoenix, Forever, and Flying Pigeon, were relatively affordable, sturdy models that provided personal mobility without the corrupt luxury of Western commercial products. Bicycles also required little change to the existing infrastructure of such cities as Shanghai, where tiny alleyways would not accommodate a public transport system. Government planners supported bicycle use by providing subsidies for commuting workers to buy bicycles and by designating bicycle lanes on roads (Esfehani 2003).

After 1979 in particular, when new market reforms helped to boost production, the bicycle became a symbol of a modern, mobile Chinese society that—ideally at least—favored equal consumption for all rather than capitalist materialism. In recent years, however, the status of bicycles has changed again in China. Economic planning has made a turn to the dramatically modern, encouraging private industry and global competitiveness. Entire swaths of cities have been renovated to make way for wide expressways, and new financial districts, crowded with automobiles, do not allow bicyclists in the street. Through a shift in emphasis in urban and economic policy, the function of the bicycle is once again redefined, this time as an artifact of the old rather than a harbinger of the new. "Bicycles are for old people and children," one young businesswoman told the *New York Times* in 2002. "My generation does not ride to work" (Kahn 2002).

While the function of the bicycle depends on the age, profession, and nationality of the rider, it also depends on the individual body. As Maria Ward wrote in her 1896 advice book, *Bicycles for Ladies*, "to understand the adjustment of the human machine to environment requires cultivated perception and special knowledge" (Ward 1896: 6). Indeed, the subtleties of how a rider physically uses her bicycle are hard to perceive from afar: The way one tenses going over a bump, relaxes in coasting, and feels the slight inclines and drops in terrain are all part of the experience of the ride that go beyond physical design. The rider in turn will evaluate these sensations as easy or hard, invigorating or stressful, according to his or her own cultural perception of "normal" levels of exertion and effort in bicycling. Traveling between the United States and Europe, for example, one can easily identify a different social construction of the bicycle based on effort. Many American bikers approach the bicycle as athletes, donning spandex, cycling shoes, and helmets even for short trips. In Europe, especially in the Netherlands, elegantly clad women in heels and men in suits are a common sight, using the bicycle with minimal exertion to go to work or out to dinner. These expressions of bodily composure on the bicycle indicate subtle differences in attitude about personal mobility: How hard should one work to transport oneself? What are the cultural

associations of sweat, muscle, and speed from country to country, or across categories of age, gender, and class?

Once we describe the bicycle in terms of the body that rides it, we can think of it among other forms of transportation. The body's movement on a bicycle contrasts with the automobile, a newer invention and one that represents a dramatically different technological and sensory experience. Why, given the choice, might we select cars over bicycles, and vice-versa? The first responses that come to mind are personal: we have too far to travel, or too much to carry. But these choices also reflect the social and political status of riding as opposed to driving. A new generation of professionals in China and other non-Western nations reject the seemingly antiquated bicycle in favor of cars, a symbol of economic accomplishment. On the other hand, environmentally aware Westerners claim the bicycle as an alternative form of transportation that helps lower individual energy consumption. In contemporary society, these different ways of transporting oneself often represent choices of one technology over another, indicating the embedded social meanings of each.

Across history and around the world, bicycles have changed form and meaning because of shifting processes of social construction. We will remember that the Penny-Farthing, the first widely used bicycle, fell to near extinction not because of mechanical failure or poor design, but because new groups of people wanted to use bicycles for new purposes. These new groups and new purposes represent the story of design beyond the particular object, in the realm of use. In use, mass-produced, seemingly mundane things become personal, embodying social concerns, political debates, and subjective experiences far beyond manufacturers' predictions. The full definition of a bicycle must include not only two wheels, a frame, and a chain, but also the rider who makes this arrangement of mechanical parts his or her own.

80

CELL PHONE

Gerard Goggin

The cell phone is a perfect example of an object embraced by twenty-first century society. In 2007 the number of cell phone subscribers worldwide surpassed the three billion mark, which does not include the actual number of cell phones that still figure in everyday life—whether disused, discarded, or back-up devices. From its prosaic origins in predecessor technologies, including wireless telegraphy, the telephone, radio, and the pager, the cell phone has become a much-desired, lovingly crafted thing—an artifact in which we may observe many entwined, sinuous facets of contemporary design.

The moveable phone is often referred to in the Americas as the "cell phone," or just "cell." Elsewhere it is often called a "mobile" or, in languages other than English, given a word associated with its portability, especially to convey its status as a handheld device. Various kinds of portable mobile telephony were used in the post–World War II era, especially from the 1960s onward. However, the commercial deployment of mobile networks, based on sharing of spectrum through cell-based technology, waited until the late 1970s (Agar 2003). In the early days, then, of the public offerings of cell phones, the design revolved around reconceiving a formerly fixed telephone instrument for the portable technology of the vehicle. Mobile phones were bulky, heavy, and expensive. And their design remained firmly anchored in the industrial, engineering, and scientific realms of telecommunications.

Early ideas about the design of the cell phone were strongly influenced by the archetype of the telephone. Telephones had moved from requiring communication with the operator for connection to automatic dial, in which the subscriber herself could dial a number, switching would be initiated, and, if answered, connection with the "B" party established. How people thought about the phone as an object in domestic settings had also changed, as this mid-twentieth-century discussion reveals:

> At one time a common practice was to conceal or disguise telephones because their appearance detracted from the pleasing effects that were sought from the furnishings and decorations by which they were surrounded. This practice emphasised the importance of shape, which really received first acknowledgment when plastic-cased telephones with some pretensions to good shape were introduced (Jones 1956).

The relationship between the user and the user's hands, voice, and body, on the one hand, and the telephone instrument or device, on the other, had become reasonably well-established—as we can see in the iconic black Bakelite telephone, common from the 1930s to the 1950s. From the late 1950s on, telephones were conceived and made in plastic. In the 1960s and 1970s, one can marvel at groovy telephone designs, including the airplane phone, the doughnut phone, the ball phone, and the first one-piece phone, the Ericofon (made by North Electric, in a fabulous orange). The rotary dial telephone was succeeded by the push-button

Image 42 CE Mobira Talkman, Nokia 8810, and Mobira Cityman. Courtesy of Nokia and copyright Nokia.

phone, initially using pulse dialing, and later tone dialing.

When the cell phone was introduced, it was of necessity quite bulky. Mobile phones had already been used since the 1960s, especially in cars. Once it became technically possible for cell phones to be lighter and more easily transported, indeed carried by a person, design opened up. This can be observed in the staged photos of the ritual of making the "first" cell phone call. In 1973, such a media event saw Dr. Martin Cooper of Motorola making a call while walking the streets of New York City, using the prototype of the Motorola DynaTAC—which a decade later was the first handheld mobile available to the U.S. market.

Such phones were typical of those used in the first-generation analog phone. With the advent of second-generation digital networks and handsets in the early 1990s, the size of phones became

dramatically smaller. Interesting to contemplate here is a 1992 patent from a Nokia engineer for a "stand-alone portable telephone unit," which is described as belonging to a species of "battery-power, small-sized portable telephone devices which work like mobile (car) phones and use a mobile phone system," but comprising "all parts including the antenna required for a mobile station" (Tattari, 1992). Indeed, Nokia launched its first digital GSM (Global Standard for Mobiles) phone, the 1011, in 1992.

DESIGN AND CELL PHONE CULTURE

This decisive shift to a stand-alone portable telephone provided the material basis for a set of new affordances and design features that now are regarded as standard for a cell phone. If Motorola had played an important role in the first generation of cell phones, and their recognized design outlines, then it was Nokia (though among many other firms, of course) that became synonymous with the definition and entrenchment of cell phone culture—and also with the entrance of the cell phone into the annals of design.

The shrinking of the cell phone paradoxically was accompanied with the inclusion of new features, capabilities, and new communicative architectures and cultural expectations and routines into this now genuinely pocket-sized, yet overstuffed, thing. The address book was incorporated into the phone. Like computers, cell phones were installed with games (starting with the famous Nokia snake game). The cell phone jostled with the wristwatch for displaying the time, and with the alarm clock and other alert technologies for offering reminders.

An important design breakthrough in the 1990s was the invention of changeable faces for mobile phones. Users could buy relatively inexpensive faces for their phones, to change the color or look. The phone also became a device that was adorned with personal objects and decorations. The cell phone had not only become part of people's everyday lives but was now an integral part of how they dressed themselves, decorated their surroundings, and signaled their identities and meaning making. Not only did users customize it for their self-fashioning, the object itself entered the reckonings and representations of the fashion industry (Fortunati, Katz, and Riccini 2003). The cell phone became recognized as a notable object of design, with Nokia's Frank Nuovo enjoying the limelight as the first celebrity cell phone designer. Over the coming years the cell phone took center stage at fashion and design events.

In 2002 Nokia set up a subsidiary called Vertu (http://www.vertu.com), headed by Nuovo. Initially the avowed focus was upon the premium, luxury market, with price tags of £15,000 for the top-of-the-line platinum handset. Here the cell phone has played a role in the commodification of previously luxury goods, and their marketing to the wealthier elites, not least in the emerging economic giants, such as China and India—as affordable luxury. Thus, the cell phone is also tied into the important new dynamics of brands in contemporary society.

SMARTENING UP THE PHONE

While the cell phone was becoming part of the fashion worlds, it was also developing in other directions. Once the capability was possible, one recurrent idea had it that the cell phone would combine a number of work and business functions, competing, for instance, with the alternate technology of the "portable digital assistant." So the smart phone was born (the first appears to be have offered by IBM in 1992)—offering advanced functions, and combining versions of now standard computer programs.

With the Internet taking off around the world from the early 1990s on especially, designers addressed the idea of how to offer online services on a cell phone. One early way to do this was the Wireless Access Protocol (WAP), introduced in the late 1990s, offering browsing on a cell phone. This was not initially popular, but in its later incarnations it was being more widely used from 2007 onward. What did become avidly used, especially by certain groups of users (for instance, lawyers, managers, and professionals) were mobile e-mail devices. Ironically, the stalwart cell phone companies, despite many attempts, were not so successful here. The iconic mobile e-mail device—featuring heavily in television programs with characters with wealthy, busy, glamorous lives—was the Blackberry. Introduced in 1997 by the Canadian company Research in Motion (RIM), the Blackberry was customized for business e-mail, with a handy track wheel on the side.

The 1990s was a time preoccupied with the convergence and digitization of media. Again, the cell phone as a ubiquitous personal technology was viewed as a promising site for seizing the initiative on digital technologies and cultures. Nokia was most systematic here in covering the various options. Its N-series offered mobiles customized for different user preferences: a cell phone with high-quality lens and storage for the keen photographer; a phone dedicated for music; a phone for mobile blogging, with Nokia's own "lifeblog" software; and the celebrated N-gage device, aimed at the mobile gaming market. Other cell phone manufacturers targeted particular facets of the mobile entertainment or "content" market, especially music—notably Sony Ericsson (Sony having, of course, pioneered the classic Walkman). Critically, here the design challenge was to position the cell phone as a real alternative to other digital music players such as the MP3 player or Apple iPod.

The rise of online video—an auspicious sign of which was the acquisition of video-sharing site YouTube by Google in late 2006—also had implications for the cell phone. With the advent of the camera phone, mobile phone users could easily produce their own videos. However, the widespread, rapid, viral distribution of video did not come, as perhaps expected, from circulation on mobile phone networks; rather it came from the crossover of the cell phone with the Internet. Short videos produced on cell phones were uploaded to the Internet, and the peer-to-peer dynamics and architecture of photo and video-sharing sites, Web sites, blogs, and social networking technologies, saw an explosion of content. The Bluetooth protocol was a decisive innovation here, allowing the transferring of files between users for free.

In 2002–2003, the much-heralded arrival of mobile television was hoped to extend this enormously influential twentieth-century medium to the mobile and handheld device. Though there was a great deal of experimentation and some production of programs specifically for cell phone, for the first years most of the content comprised well-known programs offered on conventional free-to-air, public broadcasting, and subscription television, modified for the cell phone platform—at first using the third-generation network platforms, and later through direct broadcasting to cell phones. Designers had to confront the challenges of keeping cell phones small and portable, while increasing screen size, resolution, and quality. Again, particular phones were devised for dedicated mobile television viewing, while with other handset models, compromises were made.

These new media and cultural dynamics of the cell phone were on display in the rapturous reception given the launch of Apple's iPhone in mid-2007. Here we saw the meeting of the much-vaunted Apple design culture, and its cool thing, the iPod, with the cell phone. For many, the iPhone underlined the proposition that the cell phone could seriously be also a portable music device—and so offer the preferred way to access the digital, online world of contemporary music. For the geeks, there was relief that finally the relatively closed world of cell phones and networks could be opened up to the computing and Internet culture. There had been intimations of this, previously, with the placement of WiFi (wireless Internet) chips in mobile phones, which made it possible for users to connect to either the cellular network or wireless Internet hot-spots. However, these had been slow to be taken up, hence the hope that the Apple gambit would stand a good chance of opening up, and transforming, the political economy of the cell phone companies and vendors.

CODESIGNING WITH USERS

An unexpected and highly significant development in the cell phone was the popularity of text messaging. This was a facility included in the second-generation digital mobile (GSM) standard, but not thought to be particularly important. The role of users was critical in discovering the possibilities for text messaging, and making it a central part of cell phone culture. Text messaging was a deceptively simple function that users very much valued. This rudimentary communicative affordance eclipsed for at least a decade the apparently richer technologies of 3G, smart phones, and various media and entertainment reframings of the cell phones. Text messaging is especially instructive because it underlines an important trend in cell phone design—the role of the user.

Thus, the cell phone is an exemplary case in how it actualizes, and has shaped, discussions of the importance of users in contemporary design and innovation. From overlapping perspectives, theorists and practitioners have urged the importance of including the user in the design of technology, and indeed in recognizing that often the humble user plays a collaborative role in design (Oudshoorn and Pinch 2003). We are familiar with this from the motifs of Internet culture and innovation—user-generated content, consumer-producers, prosumers, and so on. The cell phone also has been shaped by this design philosophy (Fortunati 2006).

As well as users being influential in design through their avid adoption, or shunning of, particular technologies and applications, there is also the theme of customization that runs through the formative period of cell phone culture, as we have seen. There is a related issue now deepening the focus on, and tensions obtaining, to the role of the user. This springs from the fact that the decisive, indeed massive, markets for cell phones now and into the future, lie in the "new markets"—in Asia-Pacific countries, in Eastern Europe, and in Latin America, and notably also in developing countries, where the cell phone is used even by quite poor users.

With the cell phone having arrived as a global technology come new forces shaping design that we are only now beginning to grasp. Countries such as China are manufacturing and designing cell phones for their own markets and also for export. Pioneers such as Japan and Korea are playing an even more important role. European and North American countries are systematically changing their design and product processes, to build in design capacity and user input from target countries. Multidisciplinary research is playing an important part in this endeavor, for instance, with ethnography being incorporated into design cycles. A crucial aspect is the recognition of the cross-cultural dimensions of the cell phone. While many features of the cell phone may be captured with universal notions of design, society and culture are a strong force in shaping technology, and design must deal and reckon with the cultural, linguistic, gender, class, and other specificities of how the cell phone is conceived—the rich ambiguities and possibilities of constructing an eminently global thing.

ANNOTATED GUIDE TO FURTHER READING

There is a substantial body of literature on the subject of "things," which has proved of interest to a range of scholars from philosophy, phenomenology, anthropology, material culture studies, and psychology. This writing brings greater understanding to the relationships between people and the made, or designed, world. Consumption is a central focus of this interest, because many designed things are commodities (as discussed in Section 4.3). In his insightful *Material Culture and Mass Consumption* (1987) (see also Section 3.4), anthropologist Daniel Miller employs an innovative concept of objectification, which addresses the implications of the particular physical nature of artifacts in the study of their meanings.

Ethnographic scholarship has been important in the study of objects, as shown in the important book *The Social Life of Things: Commodities in Cultural Perspective* (1986), edited by anthropologist Arjun Appadurai, which addresses the circulation and use of things in the construction of their meanings. Ground for such work was also laid by French sociologist and anthropologist Marcel Mauss in his acclaimed *The Gift: The Form and Reason for Exchange in Archaic Societies* (translated from the French 1954; 1990). Neil Cummings and Marysia Lewandowska demonstrate how the collection and the exchange of objects play a vital role in the definition of their cultural value by contrasting the histories and development of the British Museum and Selfridges department store in London in *The Value of Things* (2000). A further approach to commodities is offered in Jean Baudrillard's Marxist-influenced *The System of Objects: For a Critique of the Political Economy of the Sign* (1996 [1968]). Victoria de Grazia and Ellen Furlough focus on historical and gendered understanding in their co-edited anthology, *The Sex of Things: Gender and Consumption in Historical Perspective* (1996).

The way that meanings are constructed for objects by their consumers and users has been the subject of a number of important texts, including M. Csikszentmihalyi and E. Rochberg-Halton's *The Meaning of Things: Domestic Symbols and the Self* (1981), and Judy Attfield's *Wild Things: The Material Culture of Everyday Life* (2000), both of which have an interest in the domestic interior. In their series of essays, *Reading Things,* N. Cummings and M. Lewandowska similarly investigate the making of meanings at the level of the vernacular and the local. As psychoanalyst Christopher Bollas demonstrates in his essay, "The Evocative Object," published in his *Being a Character: Psychoanalysis and Self Experience* (1993), each person unconsciously invests ordinary objects with particular and private meanings, which in turn evokes their own individuality. This view is clearly demonstrated by Siu King Chung in his visually fascinating *Designs You Don't Know What to Do With: A Book about (the Meanings of) Design and Its Alternatives* (2002).

Media critic and philosopher Vilem Flusser, in *The Shape of Things: A Philosophy of Design* (1999), proposes that the future depends on design. In the similarly titled *Shaping Things* (2005), cultural critic and science fiction writer Bruce Sterling offers a view of the future rich with new kinds of designed things. He coined the neologism "spime" to define a new breed of highly sophisticated technological objects. Designer and teacher Jonathan Chapman also looks to the future in *Emotionally Durable Design, Objects, Experiences and Empathy* (2005), a call for professionals and students alike to prioritize the relationships between design and its users, as a way of developing more sustainable attitudes to, and in, design things.

BIBLIOGRAPHY

Abercrombie, N., S. Hill, and B. Turner. 1986. *Sovereign Individuals of Capitalism.* London and Boston: Allen and Unwin.

Abrams, C. 1946. *The Future of Housing.* New York: Harper and Brothers.

Adam, P. 1987. *Eileen Gray.* London: Thames and Hudson.

Adams, G. 1791. *Geometrical and Graphical Essays.* London: R. Hindmarsh.

Adamson, G. 2003. *Industrial Design Strength: How Brooks Stevens Shaped Our World.* Cambridge, Mass.: MIT Press and Milwaukee Art Museum.

Adorno, T. 1974. *Minema Moralia.* London: Verso.

Agar, J. 2003. *Constant Touch: A Global History of the Mobile Phone.* Cambridge: Icon Books.

Ahmad, A. 1987. "Jameson's Rhetoric of Otherness and the 'National Allegory,'" *Social Text* 17: 3–25.

Ainley, R., ed. 1998. *New Frontiers of Space, Bodies, and Gender.* London: Routledge.

Albrecht, D., R. Schonfeld, and L. S. Shapiro. 2001. *Russel Wright: Living with Good Design.* New York: Cooper Hewitt, National Design Museum and Harry N Abrams.

Aldersey-Williams, H. 1992. *World Design Nationalism and Globalism in Design.* New York: Rizzoli.

Alessi.com. 2008. "Alessi Spring/Summer New Products, 2008: Miniatures of Alessi Classics." Available at: http://www.alessi.com/stampa/communicati/display.jsp?id=86

Alexander, C. 1963. "The Determination of Components for an Indian Village." In *Proceedings of the Conference on Design Methods*, ed. C. Jones and D. G. Thornley. New York: MacMillan Co.

Alexander, C. 1964. *Notes on the Synthesis of Form.* Boston: Harvard University Press.

Alexander, S. 1994. *Becoming a Woman and Other Essays in Nineteenth- and Twentieth-Century Feminist History.* London: Virago.

Allen, F. H. 1938. *Classification Scheme: Records of the Committee on Public Information, 1917–1919.* Washington, D.C.: Division of Classification, The National Archives.

Amin, S. 1980. *Class and Nation: Historically and in the Current Crisis.* New York and London: Monthly Review Press.

Anderson, B. 1983. *Imagined Communities: Relflections on the Origin and Spread of Nationalism.* London: Verso.

Anderson, B. 1998. *The Spectre of Comparisons: Nationalism, Southeast Asia, and the World.* London: Verso.

Anscombe, I. 1984. *A Woman's Touch: Women in Design from 1860 to the Present Day.* New York: Viking.

"Anti-Sweatshop Activists Score in Campaign Targeting Athletic Retailers." 1999. *Boston Globe* (April 18).

Appadurai, A., ed. 1986. *The Social Life of Things: Commodities in Cultural Perspective.* Cambridge: Cambridge University Press.

Appadurai, A. 1990. "Disgiunzione e differenza nell' economia culturale globale." In *Cultura globale,* ed. M. Featherstone. Rome: Seam.

Appadurai, A. 1996. *Modernity at Large: Cultural Dimensions of Globalization.* Public Worlds, vol. 1. Minneapolis: University of Minnesota Press.

Archer, B. 1965. *Systematic Method for Designers.* London: Council of Industrial Design.

Armytage, W.H.G. 1961. *A Social History of Engineering.* London: Faber and Faber.

Arnheim, R. 1969. *Visual Thinking.* Berkeley and Los Angeles: University of California Press.

Arnold, W. 2000. "Manila's Talk of the Town Isn't Talk at All." *New York Times* (July 5): 14–21, 28–32.

Arnold, W. 2002. "Text Generation." Special issue of *I: The Investigative Reporting Magazine* 8, no. 2 (April–June), especially 14–21, 28–32.

Arnold, W. 2003. "Vertically Challenged in Malaysia: Petronas Is Long on Views, Short on Tenants." *New York Times* (March 8).

Arvidsson, A. 2006. *Brands: Meaning and Value in Media Culture.* London and New York: Routledge.

Ash, J., and E. Wilson. 1992. *Chic Thrills: A Fashion Reader.* London: Pandora.

Ashton, R. 1939. *An Eighteenth-Century Industrialist: Peter Stubbs of Warrington, 1756–1806.* Manchester, UK: Manchester University Press.

Ashton, T. 1964. *The Industrial Revolution: 1760–1830.* Oxford: Oxford University Press.

Ashwin, C. 1978. "Art and Design History: The Parting of the Ways?" In *Design History: Fad or Function?*, ed. Design Countil, 98–102. London: Design Council.

Ashwin, C. 1981. *Drawing and Education in German-speaking Europe, 1800–1900.* Ann Arbor, Mich.: UMI.

Ashwin, C. 1981. "Pestalozzi and the Origins of Pedagogical Drawing." *The British Journal of Educational Studies* 29, no. 2 (June): 138–51.

Ashwin, C. 1982. "Peter Schmid and Das Naturzeichnen: An Experiment in the Teaching of Drawing." *Art History* 5, no. 2: 154–65.

Asimow, M. 1962. *Introduction to Design.* New York: Prentice Hall.

Athanasiou, T. 1987. "High-Tech Politics: The Case for Artificial Intelligence." *Socialist Review* 92: 7–35.

Atkinson, P., ed. 2006. "Special Issue: Do it Yourself: Democracy and Design." *Journal of Design History* 19, no. 1: 1–10.

Attfield, J. 1987. "Invisible Touch." *Times Higher Educational Supplement* (June 19): 26.

Attfield, J. 1989. "FORM/female FOLLOWS FUNCTION/male: Feminist Critiques of Design." In *Design History and the History of Design,* ed. J. Walker, 199–225. London: Pluto Press.

Attfield, J., ed. 1999. *Utility Reassessed: The Role of Ethics in the Practice of Design.* Manchester, UK, and New York: Manchester University Press.

Attfield, J. 2000. *Wild Things: The Material Culture of Everyday Life.* Oxford and New York: Berg.

Attfield, J. 2007. *Bringing Modernity Home: Writings on Popular Design and Material Culture.* Manchester, UK: Manchester University Press.

Attfield, J., and P. Kirkham. 1989. *A View from the Interior: Women and Design* [Also titled *A View from the Interior: Feminism, Women, and Design.*]. London: Women's Press.

Avelar, S., and L. Hurni. 2004. "On the Design of Schematic Transport Maps." *Cartographica* 41, no. 3: 217–28.

Avery, G. 2004. *Understanding Leadership: Paradigms and Cases.* Thousand Oaks, Calif.: Sage Publications.

Aynsley, J. 2001. *A Century of Graphic Design: Graphic Design Pioneers of the 20th Century.* London: Mitchell Beazely.

Aynsley, J., and F. Berry, eds. 2005. "Publishing the Modern Home: Magazines and the Domestic Interior 1870–1965." *Journal of Design History* 18, no. 1: 1–5.

Aynsley, J., and Forde, K. 2007. *Design and the Modern Magazine.* Manchester, UK: Manchester University Press.

Aynsley, J., and C. Grant, eds. 2006. *Imagined Interiors: Representing the Domestic Interior since the Renaissance.* London: Victoria and Albert Press.

Ayres, R., and A. V. Neese. 1989. "Externalities: Economics and Thermodynamics." In *Economy and Ecology: Towards Sustainable Development,* ed. F. Archibugi and P. Nijkamp, 89–118. Deventer, Netherlands: Kluwer Academic.

Badiou, A. 2001. *Ethics: An Essay on Understanding Evil.* London: Verso.

Badiou, A. 2005. *Meta-Politics.* London: Verso.

Bain, A. D. 1964. *The Growth of Television Ownership in the United Kingdom since the War: A Log-Normal Model.* Cambridge: Cambridge University Press.

Ballantyne, A. 2002. *What Is Architecture?* London and New York: Routledge.

Banham, R. *A Critic Writes.* Berkeley: University of California Press, 1996.

Barmé, G. R. 1999. In *The Red: On Contemporary Chinese Culture.* New York: Columbia University Press.

Barthes, R. 1970–1971. "Remarks." *Architecture d'aujourd'hui* 153: 11–13.

Barthes, R. 1972. *Mythologies.* London: Paladin.

Bartholomew, S. J. Jr. 2005. *Just for Kicks.* [Film] Image Entertainment.

Bartle, R. 2004. *Designing Virtual Worlds.* Boston, Indianapolis, London, Munich, New York, San Francisco: New Riders.

Batchelor, Ray. *Henry Ford: Mass Production, Modernism, and Design.* Manchester, UK, and New York: Manchester University Press, 1994.

Baudrillard, J. 1981. *For a Critique of the Political Economy of the Sign.* St Louis, Mo.: Telos Press.

Baudrillard, J. 1983. *Simulations,* trans. P. Foss, P. Patton, and P. Beitchman. New York: Semiotexte.

Baudrillard, J. 1996 [1968]. *The System of Objects: For a Critique of the Political Economy of the Sign,* trans. J. Benedict. London and New York: Verso.

Bauman, Z. 2004. *Wasted Lives: Modernity and Its Outcasts.* New York: Blackwell.

Bauman, Z. 2006. *Liquid Fear.* Cambridge, UK: Polity Press.

Bayly, C. A. 1986. "The Origins of Swadeshi: Cloth and Indian Society 1700–1930." In *The Social Life of Things: Commodities in Cultural Perspective,* ed. A. Appadurai, 285–321. Cambridge: Cambridge University Press.

Baynes, K. 1980. "Drawing as Design Method." In *Design and Industry: The Effects of Industrialization and Technical Change on Design,* ed. N. Hamilton, 46–47. London: The Design Council.

Baynes, K. 1982. *Drawing Instruments.* London: Royal Association of British Architects.

Baynes, K. 1983. *The Art of the Engineer.* Woodstock, N.Y.: Overlook Press.

BBC4. 2008. "London Underground Map." *Design Classics* (August 2).

Beattie, W. 1950. "The Merchant Seaman." Masters thesis, Department of Sociology, University of Chicago.

Beebe, J. 1995. "Basic Concepts and Techniques of Rapid Appraisal." *Human Organization* 54, no. 1: 42–51.

Bell, D. 1973. *The Coming of Post Industrial Society: A Venture in Social Forecasting.* New York: Basic Books.

Bellah, R. M., R. Madsen, W. M. Sullivan, A. Swidler, and S. M. Tipton. 1985. *Habits of the Heart: Individualism and Commitment in American Life.* Berkeley: University of California Press.

Bennett, F. J. 1995. "Qualitative and Quantitative Methods: In-Depth or Rapid Assessment?" *Social Science and Medicine* 40, no. 12: 1589–90.

Benson, S. P. 1988. *Counter Cultures: Saleswomen, Managers, and Customers in American Department Stores, 1890–1940.* Urbana: University of Illinois Press.

Bentham, J. 1843. *Works,* published under the Superintendence of his Executor, John Bowring. Edinburgh: William Tait.

Benton, C. 1985. "Charlotte Perriand: Un Art de Vivre." *Design History Society Newsletter* 25: 12–15.

Benton, T., and C. Benton, eds. 1975. *Form and Function.* London: Crosby, Lockwood and Staples.

Benveniste, E. 1966. *Problèmes de linguistique générale.* Vol. 1. Paris: Gallimard.

Benveniste, E. 1974. *Problèmes de linguistique générale.* Vol. 2. Paris: Gallimard.

Benyus, J. 1997. *Biomimicry: Innovation Inspired by Nature.* New York: Morrow.

Berg, M. 1985. *The Age of Manufactures: Industry, Innovation and Work in Britain, 1700–1820.* London: Fontana; Totowa, N.J.: Barnes and Noble Books.

Berg, M., ed. 1991. *Markets and Manufacture in Early Industrial Europe.* London and New York: Routledge.

Berman, M. 1985. *All That Is Solid Melts into Air.* London: Verso.

Berman, M. 2001. "Notes from Underground: Plato's Cave, Piranesi's Prison, and the Subway." *Harvard Design Magazine* 15 (Fall).

Berney, A. 2001. "Streamlining Breasts: The Exaltation of Form and Disguise of Function in 1930's Ideals." *Journal of Design History* 14, no. 4: 327–42.

Berry, S. 2000. "Be Our Brand: Fashion and Personalization on the Web." In *Fashion Cultures: Theories, Explorations and Analysis,* ed. S. Bruzzi and P. C. Gibson, 49–60. London and New York: Routledge.

Betsky, A. 1995. "Lost Horizons: The Birth and Death of the Skyscraper." *Architectural Design* 75, nos. 7–8: 8–15.

Betts, P. 2004. *The Authority of Everyday Objects: A Cultural History of West German Industrial Design.* Berkeley: University of California Press.

Bicknell, J., and L. McQuiston, eds. 1977. *Design for Need.* Oxford: Pergamon Press.

"Big Brand Firms Know the Name Is Everything." 1998. *Irish Times* (February 27).

Billig, M. 1995. *Banal Nationalism.* London: Sage.

Bimonte, S., and L. F. Punzo. 2003. "Turismo, sviluppo economico e sostenibilità: Teoria e pratica." *Collana Economia dell Ambiente e del Turismo Sostenibile. Pubblicazione del Corso di Laurea.* Siena, Italy: Università degli Studi di Siena, Pratagon Editori Toscani.

Binder, G., ed. 2001. *Tall Buildings of Asia and Australia.* Mulgrave, Victoria, Australia: The Images Publishing Group.

Bird, W. 1994. "How One Old Shelter Got a Face-Lift and a Permanent Home: The Bomb Shelter Installation at the National Museum of American History." *Smithsonian* (April): 52.

Birmingham, J. 1975. "Traditional Potters of the Katmandu Valley." *Man* 12: 370–86.

Bishop, T., ed. 1977. *Leisure in the Twentieth Century: History of Design. Fourteen Papers Given at the Second Conference on Twentieth Century Design History 1976.* London: Design Council Publications.

Bishop, T., ed. 1978. *Design History: Fad or Function?* London: Design Council Publications.

Blake, J. 1978. "The Context for Design History." In *Design History: Fad or Function?* ed. T. Bishop, 56–59. London: Design Council Publications.

Blau, P. 1955. *The Dynamics of Bureaucracy.* Chicago: University of Chicago Press.

Bleier, R. 1984. *Science and Gender: A Critique of Biology and Its Themes on Women.* New York: Pergamon.

Boas, F. 1955. *Primitive Art.* New York: Dover.

Bocock, R. 1993. *Consumption.* London and New York: Routledge.

Bogel M., ed. 2002. *Designing Australia: Readings in the History of Design.* Annandale, New South Wales: Pluto Press.

Bollas, C. 1992. *Being a Character: Psychoanalysis and Self Experience.* New York: Hill and Wang.

Bonsiepe, G. 1978. *Teoría y Práctica del Diseño Industrial.* Barcelona: Gustavo Gili.

Bonsiepe, G. 1997. "Some Virtues of Design." In *Design beyond Design,* ed. J. van Toorn, 105–10. Maastricht, Netherlands: Jan van Eyck Akademie.

Bonsiepe, G. 2006. "Design and Democracy." *Design Issues* 22, no. 2 (Spring): 27–34.

Booker, P. J. 1963. *A History of Engineering Drawing.* London: Northgate Publishing Co.

Booker, P. J., ed. 1964. *Conference on the Teaching of Engineering Design.* London: Institution of Engineering Designers.

Borrus, A. 1987. "How Sony Keeps the Copycats Scampering." *Business Week* (June 1): 43.

Bourdieu, P. "L'invention de la vie d'artiste." *Actes* 2 (1975): 67–93.

Bourdieu, P. 1984. *Distinction: A Social Critique of the Judgment of Taste,* trans. R. Nice. Cambridge, Mass.: Harvard University Press.

Bourdieu, P. 1993. *The Field of Cultural Production: Essays on Art and Literature,* ed. R. Johnson. Cambridge, UK: Polity Press.

Boyer, P. 1985. *By the Bomb's Early Light: American Thought and Culture at the Dawn of the Atomic Age.* New York: Pantheon Books.

Braidotti, R. 1994. *Nomadic Subjects: Embodiment and Sexual Difference in Contemporary Feminist Theory.* New York: Columbia University Press.

Brandes, S. 1976. *American Welfare Capitalism.* Chicago: University of Chicago Press.

Braverman, H. 1974. *Labor and Monopoly Capital.* New York: Monthly Review Press.

Brecht, B. 1964 [1949]. "A Short Organum for the Theatre." In his *Brecht on Theatre: The Development of an Aesthetic,* ed. and trans. John Willett. London: Methuen.

Brett, D. 1986. "The Aesthetical Science: George Field and the 'Science of Beauty.'" *Art History* 9, no. 3: 336–50.

Brett, D. 1986. "Drawing and the Ideology of Industrialization." *Design Issues* 3, no. 2: 59–72.

Breward, C. 2003. *Fashion.* Oxford: Oxford University Press.

Breward, C. 2004. *Fashioning London.* London: Berg.

Brewer, J. 2004. "The Error of Our Ways: Historians and the Birth of Consumer Society." *Culture of Consumption, Working Paper Series* (June). Available at: http://www.consume.bbk.ac.uk/publications.html#workingpapers

Brewer, J., and T. Porter, eds. 1993. *Consumption and the World of Goods.* London and New York: Routledge.

Brown, B. 2004. "Thing Theory." In *Things,* ed. B. Brown, 1–16. Chicago: University of Chicago Press.

Brown, B., and E. Laurier. 2003. "Maps and Journeys: An Ethno-Methodological Investigation." *Cartographica* 40, no. 3: 17–33.

Brown, R. 1835 [1822]. *Rudiments of Drawing Cabinet and Upholstery Furniture.* London: Printed for M. Taylor.

Bruckmann, H., and J. Meier-Graefe, eds. 1897. *Dekorative Kunst.* Munich, Germany.

Bucciarelli, L. 1994. *Designing Engineers.* Cambridge, Mass.: MIT Press.

Buchanan, R. 1990. "Metaphors, Narratives, and Fables in New Design Thinking." *Design Issues* 7, no. 1: 78–84.

Buchanan, R. 1991. "Wicked Problems: Managing the Entrapment Trap." *Innovation* 10 (Summer): 3.

Buchanan, R. 1992. "Wicked Problems in Design Thinking." *Design Issues* 8, no. 2: 5–21.

Buchanan, R. 1998. "Books: Twentieth-Century Design: Jonathan Woodham." *Journal of Design History* 11, no. 3: 259–63.

Buckley, C. 1986. "Made in Patriarchy: Towards a Feminist Analysis of Women and Design." *Design Issues* 3, no. 2: 1–31.

Buckley, C. 1989. "Made in Patriarchy: Towards a Feminist Analysis of Women and Design." In *Design Discourse: History Theory Criticism,* ed. V. Margolin, 251–62. Chicago: University of Chicago Press.

Buckley, C. 1989. "The Noblesse of the Banks: Craft Hierarchies, Gender Divisions, and the Roles of Women Paintresses and Designers in the British Pottery Industry, 1890–1939." *Journal of Design History* 2, no. 4: 257–74.

Buckley, C. 1990. *Potters and Paintresses: Women Designers in the Pottery Industry, 1870–1955.* London: Women's Press.

Buckley, C. 1994. "Design, Femininity, and Modernism: Interpreting the Work of Susie Cooper." *Journal of Design History* 7, no. 4: 277–94.

Buckley, C. "Made in Patriarchy: Theories of Women and Design—A Reworking." In *Design and Feminism: Re-Visioning Spaces, Places, and Everyday Things,* ed. Joan Rothschild, 109–18. New Brunswick, N.J., and London: Rutgers University Press, 1999.

Burkhauser, J. 1990. *Glasgow Girls: Women in Art and Design, 1880–1920.* Edinburgh: Canongate Press.

Busch, A., ed. 1998. *Design for Sport.* London: Thames and Hudson.

Buss, C. 1996. "Talking with Karen Finley." *Provincetown Arts* 12. Available at: http://www.capecodaccess.com/Gallery/Arts/talkingKaren.html

Calefato, P. 2000. "Signs of Order, Signs of Disorder: The Other Uniforms." In *Uniform: Order and Disorder,* ed. F. Bonami, 195–204. Milan, Italy: Edizioni Charta.

Calvera, A. 2002. "The Influence of English Design Reform in Catalonia: An Attempt at a Comparative History." *Journal of Design History* 15, no. 2: 83–100.

Calvera, A. 2005. "Local, Regional, National, Global and Feedback: Several Issues to Be Faced with Constructing Regional Narratives. *Journal of Design History* 18, no. 4: 371–83.

Calvera, A., and M. Mallol, ed. 2001. *Historiades de la periferia: Historia e historias del diseño. Actas de la 1ºReunión Científica Internacional de Historiadores y Estudios del Diseño, Barcelona 1999* [Design History Seen from Abroad: History and Histories of Design. Proceedings of the 1st International Conference of Design History and Design Studies, Barcelona 1999]. Barcelona: University of Barcelona Publications.

Campbell, R. 1969 [1747]. *The London Tradesman.* Newton Abbot, UK: David and Charles; New York: A. M. Kelley.

Campi, M. 2000. *Skyscrapers: An Architectural Type of Modern Urbanism.* Basel, Switzerland: Birkhäuser.

Cardona, M. 2005. *The Sneaker Book: 50 Years of Sport Shoe Design.* Atglen, Pa.: Schiffer Publishing.

Cardozo, B. 1921. *The Nature of the Judicial Process.* New Haven, Conn.: Yale University Press.

Carey, S. 1985. *Conceptual Change in Childhood.* Cambridge, Mass.: MIT Press.

Carson, R. 1962. *Silent Spring.* Boston: Houghton Mifflin.

Casey, E., and L. Martens. 2007. *Gender and Consumption: Domestic Cultures and the Commercialisation of Everyday Life.* Aldershot, UK: Ashgate Publishing.

Castoriadis, C. 1984. *Crossroads in the Labyrinth.* Brighton, UK: Harvester Press.

Cazeaux, C., ed. 2000. *The Continental Aesthetics Reader.* London: Routledge.

"Cement Jobs Are Easy." 1956. *New York Times* (June 10).

Censis. 2003. *XXXVII Rapporto sulla situazione sociale del paese.* Rome: Censis.

Certeau, M. de. 1984. *The Practice of Everyday Life,* trans. S. Randall. Berkeley: University of California Press.

Certeau, M. de. 1988. *The Writing of History,* trans. T. Conley. New York: Columbia University Press.

"Cesar Pelli: The Petronas Towers, Kuala Lumpur, Malaysia." 1995. *Architectural Design* 75, nos. 7–8: 62–65.

Chafe, W. H., and H. Sitkoff, eds. 1995. *A History of Our Time: Readings on Postwar America,* 4th ed. Oxford: Oxford University Press.

Chamberlin, E. R. 1976. *The Awakening Giant: Britain in the Industrial Revolution.* London: Batsford.

Chambers, R. 1983. "Rapid Appraisal for Improving Existing Canal Irrigation Systems." Discussion Paper Series No. 8. New Delhi, India: Ford Foundation.

Chapman, J. 2005. *Emotionally Durable Design, Objects, Experiences and Empathy.* London: Earthscan.

Chapman, S. D., and S. Chassagne. 1981. *European Textile Printers in the Eighteenth Century: A Study of Peel and Oberkampf.* London: Heinemann Educational, Pasold Fund.

Cherlin, A. J. 1999. "I'm OK, You're Selfish." *The New York Times Magazine* (October 17). Available at: http://lwww.nytimes.comfiibrary/millenniunt/m5/poll-cherlin.html

Childers, Erskine. 1989. "Design and Cultural Identity." Keynote address for Internationales Forum für Gestaltung, Hochschule für Gestaltung, Ulm, Germany, September.

Choay, F. 1973. "Figures d'un discours inconnu." *Critique* (April): 293–317.

Churchman, C. 1967. "Wicked Problems." *Management Science* 4, no. 14: 141–42.

Cipolla, C. 2004. "Tourist or Guest—Designing Tourism Experiences or Hospitality Relations?" In *Design Philosophy Papers: Collection Two,* ed. Anne-Marie Willis. Ravensbourne, Australia: Team D/E/S Publications.

Clare, J. 1984. "Letter to Messrs Taylor and Hessey, II." In *The Oxford Authors: John Clare,* ed. E. Robinson and D. Powell, 457. Oxford and New York: Oxford University Press.

Clark, H. 1980. "The Anonymous Designer." In *Design and Industry: The Effects of Industrialisation and Technical Change on Design,* ed. N. Hamilton, 33–38. London: Design Council.

Clark, H. 1984. "The Design and Designing of Lancashire Printed Calicoes during the First Half of the 19th Century." *Textile History* 15, no. 1: 101–18.

Clark, H. 2005. "The Difference of Female Design." In *Dish: International Design for the Home,* ed. Julie Stahl, 158–61. New York: Princeton University Press.

Clark, J. 2005. "Get a Life." *I.D.* 52: 4.

Clarke, A. J. 1999. *Tupperware: The Promise of Plastic in 1950s America,* Washington, D.C.: Smithsonian Institution Press.

Clarke, D. B., M. A. Doel, and K.M.L. Housiaux, eds. 2003. *The Consumption Reader.* New York: Routledge.

Clarkson, J., R. Coleman, S. Keates, and C. Lebbon, eds. 2003. *Inclusive Design: Design for the Whole Population.* New York: Springer.

Clifford, J. 1993. "On Collecting Art and Culture." In *The Cultural Studies Reader,* ed. S. During, 57–76. London and New York: Routledge.

Clunas, C. 1987. "Design and Cultural Frontiers: English Shapes and Furniture Workshops, 1700–90." *Apollo* 126 (October): 259.

Clynes, M. E., and N. S. Kline. 1960. "Cyborgs and Space." *Astronautics* 26–27: 75–76.

Cockburn, C. 1983. *Brothers: Male Dominance and Technological Change.* London: Pluto.

Cockburn, C. 1985. *Machinery of Dominance.* London: Pluto.

Cogell, C. 2004. *Eugenic Design: Streamlining America in the 1930s.* Philadelphia: University of Pennsylvania Press.

Cohen, R., and M. Wartofsky. 1965. *Boston Studies in the Philosophy of Science.* Vol. 2. New York: Humanities Press.

Cohn, C. 1987a. "Nuclear Language and How We Learned to Pat the Bomb." *Bulletin of Atomic Scientists:* 17–24.

Cohn, C. 1987b. "Sex and Death in the Rational World of Defense Intellectuals." *Signs* 12, no. 4: 687–718.

Cole, H. 1840. *First Exercises for Children in Light, Shade and Colour.* London.

Coleridge, N. 1988. *The Fashion Conspiracy.* London: William Heinemann.

Collier, P. 2007. *The Bottom Billion: Why the Poorest Countries Are Falling Apart and What Can Be Done about It.* Oxford: Oxford University Press.

Collinson, M. 1981. "A Low Cost Approach to Understanding Small Farmers." *Agricultural Administration* 8: 463–71.

Colomina, B., ed. 1992. *Sexuality and Space.* Princeton, N.J.: Princeton Architectural Press.

Colville, Q. 2004. "The Role of the Interior in Constructing Notions of Class and Status: A Case Study of Britannia Royal Naval College, Dartmouth, 1905–39." In *Interior Design and Identity,* ed. S. McKellar and P. Sparke, 114–32. Manchester, UK: Manchester University Press.

Complete Report of the Chairman of the Committee on Public Information, 1917:1918:1919/Washington, DC. 1917–1919. Washington, D.C.: U.S. Government Printing Office.

Cone, M. 1998. "River Pollution Study Finds Hormonal Defects in Fish Science: Discovery in Britain Suggests Sewage Plants Worldwide May Cause Similar Reproductive-Tract Damage." *Los Angeles Times* (September 22).

Conekin, B. 2003. *The Autobiography of a Nation: The 1951 Festival of Britain.* Manchester, UK: Manchester University Press.

Conekin, B., F. Mort, and C. Walters, eds., 1999. *Moments of Modernity: Reconstructing Britain 1945–64*. London and New York: Rivers Oram Press.

Connellan, K. 2007. "White Skins, White Surfaces: The Politics of Domesticity in South African Domestic Interiors 1920–1950." In *Taking up the Challenge: Critical Race and Whiteness Studies in a Postcolonising Nation,* ed. D. Riggs, 248–59. Adelaide, Australia: Crawford House.

Conway, H. 1987. *Design History: A Students' Handbook*. London: Allen and Unwin.

Coontz, S. 1992. *The Way We Never Were: American Families and the Nostalgia Trap*. New York: Basic Books.

Coronel, S., ed. 2000. *Investigating Estrada: Millions, Mansions and Mistresses*. Manila: Philippine Center for Investigative Journalism.

Cowin, R. 1983. *More Work for Mother: The Ironies of Household Technology from the Open Hearth to the Microwave*. New York: Basic.

Craik, J. 2003. "The Cultural Politics of the Uniform." *Fashion Theory* 7, no. 2: 127–48.

Cramer, J. S. 1958. "Ownership Elasticities of Consumer Durables." *Review of Economic Studies* 25: 87–96.

Crane, D. 2001. *Fashion and Its Social Agendas: Class, Gender and Identity in Clothing*. Chicago: University of Chicago Press.

Crawford, M. 1999. "The 'New' Company Town." *Perspecta* 30 (1999): 48–57.

Creel, F. 1956. *The National Cyclopedia of American Biography*. New York: James T. White and Company.

Creel, G. 1920. *How We Advertised America*. New York and London: Harper and Brothers Publishers.

Creel, G. 1947. *Rebel at Large: Recollections of Fifty Crowded Years*. New York: G. P. Putnam's Sons.

Crese, W. 1966. *The Search for Environment*. New Haven, Conn.: Yale University Press.

Crespin, Adolphe. 1897. *Art et Decoration: Revue Mensuelle d'Art Moderne*. Paris: Librairie Centrale des Beaux-Arts.

Critchley, S. 1997. *Very Little … Almost Nothing: Death, Philosophy, Literature*. London: Routledge.

Crosby, T., A. Fletcher, and C. Forbes. 1970. *A Sign Systems Manual*. London: Studio Vista.

Cross, N. 1984. *Developments in Design Methodology*. New York: Wiley.

Crowley, D. 2006. *Magazine Covers*. London: Mitchell Beazley.

Csikszentmihalyi, M., and E. Rochberg-Halton. 1981. *The Meaning of Things: Domestic Symbols and the Self*. Cambridge: Cambridge University Press.

Cumming, E. 1993. *Phoebe Anna Traquair*. Edinburgh: National Galleries of Scotland.

Cummings, N., and M. Lewandowska. 2000. *The Value of Things*. Basel, Switzerland: Birkhäuser.

The Cutting Edge Women's Research Group. 1999. *Desire by Design: Body, Territories and New Technologies*. London: I. B. Tauris.

Danto, A. C. 1981. *The Transfiguration of the Commonplace*. Cambridge, Mass.: Harvard University Press.

Daunton, M. J. 1995. *Progress and Poverty: An Economic and Social History of Britain, 1700–1850*. Oxford: Oxford University Press.

Davey, P. 1997. "Outrage: Malaise in Malaysia." *Architectural Review* 201, no. 1201: 27.

Davis, S. 1987. *Future Perfect*. New York: Addison Wesley.

Deforge, Y. 1995. "Avatars of Design: Design before Design." In *The Idea of Design: A Design Issues Reader,* ed. V. Margolin and R. Buchanan, 21–28. Cambridge, Mass.: MIT Press.

Deacon, A. O. 1841. *Elements of Perspective Drawing, or the Science of Delineating Real Objects*. London: Taylor and Walton.

Dee, J. 1977 [1577]. *The Mathematical Praeface to Euclid*. New York: Science History Publications.

De Grazia, V., and E. Furlough, eds. 1996. *The Sex of Things: Gender and Consumption in Historical Perspective*. Berkeley and Los Angeles: University of California Press.

De la Haye, A., and E. Wilson. 1999. *Defining Dress: Dress as Object, Meaning and Identity*. Manchester, UK: Manchester University Press.

Dematteis, G. 1995. *Progetto implicito*. Milan, Italy: Angeli.

Demcker, R. 1868. *A Course of Systematic and Progressive Drawing*. Cincinnati, Ohio: Ehrgott, Forbriger.

De Rita, G., and A. Bonomi. 1998. *Manifesto per lo sviluppo locale*. Torino, Italy: Bollati Boringhieri.

De Waal, F. 1982. *Chimpanzee Politics: Power and Sex among the Apes*. New York: Harper and Row.

Dewey, J. 1938. *Logic: The Theory of Inquiry*. New York: Holt, Rinehart and Winston.

Dickens, P. G. 1980. "Social Science and Design Theory." *Environment and Planning B* 7, no. 3: 353–60.

Dieha, D. 1972. "Q&A Charles Eames." *Los Angeles Times* (October 8): N140. ProQuest Historic Newspapers.

Dilnot, C. 1984a. "The State of Design History: Part One, Mapping the Field." *Design Issues* 1, no. 1: 4–23.

Dilnot, C. 1984b. "The State of Design History, Part Two: Mapping the Field." *Design Issues* 1, no. 2: 3–20.

Dilnot, C. 1989. "The State of Design History, Part I and Part II." In *Design Discourse: History Theory Criticism*, ed. V. Margolin, 213–50. Chicago: University of Chicago Press.

Dilnot, C. 1995. "The Gift." In *The Idea of Design*, ed. V. Margolin and R. Buchanan, 144–55. Cambridge, Mass.: MIT Press.

Dilnot, C. 2003. "Which Way Will the Dragon Turn? Three Scenarios for Design in China over the Next Half-Century." *Design Issues* 19, no. 3: 5–20.

Dilnot, C. 2005. "Ethics? Design?" In *Archeworks Papers* 1, no. 2, ed. Stanley Tigerman: 1–149.

"Do-It-Yourself Is Big Business." 1966. *The New York Times* (June 10).

Doordan, D. 1995. "On History." *Design Issues* 11, no. 1: 76–81.

Douglas, A. 1977. *The Feminization of American Culture.* New York: Knopf.

Douglas, M. 1963. *The Lele of the Kasai.* Oxford: Oxford University Press.

Douglas, M. 1967. "Primitive Rationing." In *Themes in Economic Anthropology*, ed. R. Firth, 119–147. London: Tavistock.

Douglas, M., and B. Isherwood. 1979. *The World of Goods.* New York: Basic Books.

Downey, F. 1936. *Portrait of an Era as Drawn by C. D. Gibson.* New York: Charles Scribner's Sons.

Dresser, C. 1858. "Botany as Adapted to the Arts and Art Manufacture." *Art Journal:* 362.

Dresser, C. 1873. *Principles of Decorative Design.* London and New York: Cassell, Peter and Galpin.

Du Gay, P., S. Hall, L. Janes, H. Mackay, and K. Negus. 1997. *Doing Cultural Studies: The Story of the Sony Walkman.* London: Sage, The Open University.

Dumont, L. 1977. *From Mandeville to Marx.* Chicago: University of Chicago Press.

Dyce, W. 1842. *The Drawing Book of the Government Schools of Design.* London: Chapman and Hall.

Eagan, W. B. 1958. "Eight Types of Mortar Joints and How to Make Them." *Popular Mechanics* (July): 176–79.

Eagleton, T. 1983. *Literary Theory: An Introduction.* Oxford: Blackwell.

Eastman, C., W. McCracken, and W. Newsletter, eds. 2001. *Design Knowing and Learning: Cognition in Design Education.* Amsterdam: Elsevier Science.

Eberlein, U. 2000. *Einzigartigkeit: Das romantische Individualitätskonzept der Moderne.* Frankfurt am Main and New York: Campus.

Eder, E. P. 2001. "Tinig ng Generation Txt" [Voice of Generation Txt]. *Pinoy Times* (February 8).

Edwards, C. 1994. *Twentieth-Century Furniture: Materials, Manufacture and Markets.* Manchester, UK: Manchester University Press.

Edwards, C. 2001. "Aluminum Furniture 1886–1986: The Changing Applications and Reception of a Modern Material." *Journal of Design History* 14, no. 3: 207–25.

Edwards, F. 1998. *Swatch: A Guide for Connoisseurs and Collectors.* Richmond Hill, Ontario: Firefly Books.

Edwards, P. 1985. "Border Wars: The Science and Politics of Artificial Intelligence." *Radical America* 19, no. 6: 39–52.

Eeden, J. van. 2004. "The Colonial Gaze: Imperialism, Myths, and South African Popular Culture." *Design Issues* 20, no. 2: 18–33.

Ehrenreich, B., and A. Fuentes. "Life on the Global Assembly Line." *MS Magazine* (Spring 2002). Available at: http://www.msmagazine.com/spring2002/ehrenreichandfuentes.asp

Ellis, E. R. 1975. *Echoes of Distant Thunder: Life in the United States 1914–1918.* New York: Coward, McCann and Geoghegan.

Ellmann, R. 1972. *Ulysses on the Liffey.* London: Faber and Faber.

Emerson, R. W. 1957. "Nature." In *Selections from Ralph Waldo Emerson*, ed. S. Whicher, 22. Boston: Houghton Mifflin.

Epstein, B. 1991. *Political Protest and Cultural Revolution: Non-Violent and Direct Action in the 1970s and 1980s.* Berkeley: University of California Press.

Esfehani, A. M. 2003. "The Bicycle's Long Way to China: The Appropriation of Cycling as a Foreign Cultural Technique, 1860–1941." *Cycle History* 7: 94–102.

Eskilson, S. 2007. *Graphic Design: A New History.* New Haven, Conn.: Yale University Press.

Espada, A. 1997. *Contra Catalunya: Una Crónica.* Barcelona: Flor del Viento.

Espin, Ivan. *Diseño y subdesarrollo.* Havana, Cuba.

Esposito, E. 2004. *Die Verbindlichkeit des Vorübergehenden: Paradoxien der Mode.* Frankfurt am Main: Suhrkamp.

"Europe Resists Global Brands." 1990. *Design Week* (September 21): 6.

Evans, C., and M. Thornton. 1989. *Women and Fashion.* London: Quartet.

Exhibition of Modern Design in Japan. 1969. Kyoto: National Museum of Modern Art.

"Extreme Spreadsheet Dude." 1998. *Baffler* no. 9: 79, and *Wall Street Journal* (April 16).

Falk, P. H., ed. 1999. *Who Was Who in American Art 1564–1975: 400 Years of Artists in America.* Madison, Conn.: Sound View Press.

Faludi, S. 1991. *Backlash.* New York: Crown; London: Chatto and Windus.

"Family in the Shelter, Snug, Equipped and Well Organized." 1961. *Life* (September 15): 105.

Farr, M. 1966. *Design Management.* London: Hutchison.

Farrell, M. J. 1952. "Irreversible Demand Function." *Econometrica* 20: 171–86.

Faurschou. G. 1988. "Fashion and the Cultural Logic of Postmodernity." In *Body Invaders: Sexuality and the Postmodern Condition,* ed. A. Kroker and M. Kroker, 79. London: New World Perspectives.

Fausto-Sterling, A. 1985. *Myths of Gender: Biological Theories about Women and Men.* New York: Basic Books.

Federal Civil Defense Administration. 1955. *Grandma's Pantry Was Ready—Is Your Pantry Ready in Event of Emergency?* Washington, D.C.: Government Printing Office.

Fernández, A. 1992. *Prologo al proyes to del trembus.* Havana.

Field, G. 1835. *Chromatography.* London: Tilt.

Field, G. 1850. *Analogy of Logic.* London: David Bogue.

Fielden, G.B.R. 1963. *Engineering Design.* London: Her Majesty's Stationery Office.

Fine, B. 2002. *The World of Consumption: The Material and Cultural Revisited.* New York: Taylor and Francis Group.

Fine, B., and E. Leopold. 1993. *The World of Consumption.* London: Routledge.

Flax, J. 1990. *Thinking Fragments: Psychoanalysis, Feminism, and Postmodernism in the Contemporary West.* Berkeley and Los Angeles: University of California Press.

Flinchum, R. 1997. *Henry Dreyfuss: Industrial Designer: The Man in the Brown Suit.* New York: Copper-Hewitt, National Design Museum, Smithsonian Institution, and Rizzoli.

Flusser, V. 1999. *The Shape of Things: A Philosophy of Design.* London: Reaktion.

Forde, D. 1934. *Habitat, Economy and Society.* London: Methuen.

Fortunati, L. 2006. "User Design and the Democratization of the Mobile Phone." *First Monday* special issue 7. Available at: http://firstmonday.org

Fortunati, L., J. E. Katz, and R. Riccini, eds. 2003. *Mediating the Human Body: Technology, Communication, and Fashion.* Mahwah, N.J.: Lawrence Erlbaum Associates.

Forty, A. 1985. "Lucky Strikes and Other Myths." *Designer:* 16–17.

Forty, A. 1986. *Objects of Desire: Design and Society 1750–1980.* London: Thames and Hudson; New York: Pantheon.

Forty, A. 1995. "Debate: A Reply to Victor Margolin." *Design Issues* 11, no. 1: 16–18.

Foster, H. 1985. *Postmodern Culture.* London: Pluto.

Foucault, M. 1975 [1963]. *The Birth of the Clinic: An Archeology of Medical Perception,* trans. A. M. Smith. New York: Vintage.

Foucault, M. 1978 [1976]. *The History of Sexuality.* Vol. 1. *An Introduction,* trans. Robert Hurley. New York: Pantheon.

Foucault, M. 1977 [1975]. *Discipline and Punish: The Birth of the Prison,* trans. Alan Sheridan. New York: Vintage Books.

Foucault, M. 1977. "L'Oeil du pouvoir." In *Le Panoptique,* J. Bentham, 16. Paris: Belfond.

Fox, R. W., and J. Lears, eds. 1983. *The Culture of Consumption: Critical Essays in American History, 1880–1980.* New York: Pantheon.

Franklin, L. C., and R. Alice. 2003 "Kettles." In *The Oxford Encyclopedia of Food and Drink in America,* ed. Gordon Campbell. Oxford: Oxford University Press.

Frascara, J. 2004. *Communication Design: Principles, Methods, and Practice.* New York: Allworth.

Fraser, K. 1984. *Something (even Human Voices): in the Foreground, a Lake.* Berkeley, Calif.: Kelsey St. Press.

Friedman, M., ed. 1989. *Graphic Design in America: A Visual Language History.* New York: Harry N. Abrams; Minneapolis, Minn.: Walker Art Center.

Froebel, F. 1887 [1828]. *The Education of Man,* trans. W. N. Hailman. New York: Appleton-Century Co.

Frow, J. 2005. "Australian Cultural Studies: Theory, Story, History." *Australian Humanities Review* 37. Available at: http://www.lib.latrobe.edu.au/AHR/archive/Issue-December-2005

Fry, T. 1988. *Design History Australia.* Sydney: Hale and Iremonger.

Fry, T. 1989. "A Geography of Power: Design History and Marginality." *Design Issues* 6, no. 1: 15–30.

Fry, T. 2008. *Design Futuring.* Oxford: Berg.

Fuller, B. 1981. *Critical Path.* New York: St. Martin's Press.

Galbraith, J. K. 2004. *The Economics of Innocent Fraud.* Boston: Houghton Mifflin Company.

Gaines, J., and C. Herzog. 1990. *Fabrications: Costume and the Female Body.* London and New York: Routledge.

Galileo Galilei. 1638. *Discorsi e dimastrazioni mateingtiche, intorno a due nuoue scienze.* Leiden, Netherlands: Appresso gli Elsevivii.

Galt, D. 1985. "How Rapid Rural Appraisal and Other Socio-Economic Diagnostic Techniques Fit into the Cyclic FSR/E Process." Paper presented at the International Conference on Rapid Rural Appraisal, Khon Kaen, Thailand.

Gardner, C., and J. Sheppard. 1989. *Consuming Passion: The Rise of Retail Culture.* London: Unwin Hyman.

Garland, K. 1994. *Mr Beck's Underground Map, A History.* London: Capital Transport.

Garner, T., and A. Stratton. 1911. *Domestic Architecture during the Tudor Period.* London: BT Batsford.

Garon, S. M. and P. L. Maclachlan, eds. 2006. *The Ambivalent Consumer, Questioning Consumption in East Asia and the West.* Ithaca, N.Y.: Cornell University.

Garvey, E. G. 1995. "Reframing the Bicycle: Advertising-Supported Magazines and Scorching Women." *American Quarterly* 47: 66–101.

Gassiot-Talabot, G., P. Gaudibert, G. Lascault, M. Le Bot, J.-F. Lyotard, and C. Lyotard. 1973. *Figurations 1960–1973.* Paris: Union Generale des Editions.

Gatz, Felix M. 1935. "Die Theorie de l'art pour l'art und Theophile Gautier." *Zeitschrift für Aesthetik und allgemeine Kunstwissenschaft* 29: 116–40.

Gay, P. 1976. *Art and Act: On Causes in History—Manet, Gropius, Mondrian.* New York: Harper and Row.

Geertz, C. 1983. *Local Knowledge: Further Essays in Interpretive Anthropology.* New York: Basic Books.

Gellner, E. 1983. *Nations and Nationalism.* London: Blackwell.

Gerchuk, I. 2000. "Festival Decoration of the City: The Materialization of the Communist Myth in the 1930s." *Journal of Design History* 13, no. 2: 123–36.

Gerstell, R. 1950. *How to Survive an Atomic Attack.* Washington D.C.: Combat Forces Press.

Gibbs, W. 1997. "Taking Computers to Task." *Scientific American* 277, no. 1 (July): 64–71.

Giedion, S. 1948. *Mechanisation Takes Command: A Contribution to Anonymous History.* Oxford: Oxford University Press.

Gilardi, J. 1995. "Adidas Share Offer Set to Win Gold Medal." *Reuters* (October 26).

Gilbert, J. 2005. *Men in the Middle: Searching for Masculinity in the 1950s.* Chicago and London: University of Chicago Press.

Gilbert, J. B. 1981. *Another Chance: Postwar America, 1945–1968.* Philadelphia: Temple University Press.

Gill, A. 2000. "Belonging with the Swoosh." *Form/Work* 4: 93–128.

Gill, A. 2006. "Limousines for the Feet: The Rhetoric of Sneakers." In *Shoes: A History from Sandals to Sneakers,* ed. G. Riello and P. McNeill, 372–85. Oxford: Berg.

Glanville, P., and J. F. Goldsborough. 1990. *Women Silversmiths, 1685–1845.* Washington, D.C.: National Museum of Women in the Arts.

Glasmeier, A. K. 2000. *Manufacturing Time: Global Competition in the Watch Industry, 1795–2000.* New York, London: Guilford Press.

Glassie, H. 1975. *Folk Housing in Middle Virginia: A Structural Analysis of Historic Artifacts.* Knoxville: University of Tennessee Press.

Glassie, H. 1977. "Meaningful Things and Appropriate Myths: The Artifact's Place in American Studies." In *Prospects: An Annual of American Cultural Studies,* ed. Jack Salzman, vol. 3, 1–49. New York: Burt Franklin.

Glucksmann, A. 1977. "Le Totalitarisme en effet." *Traverses,* no. 9: 34–40.

Glucksmann, M. 1990. *Women Assemble.* London: Routledge.

Godelier, M. 1972. *Rationality and Irrationality in Economics.* London: Monthly Review Press.

Goffman, E. 1953. "Communication Conduct in an Island Community." Ph.D. dissertation, University of Chicago.

Goffman, E. 1996. *The Presentation of Self in Everyday Life*. Garden City, N.Y.: Doubleday.

Goggin, G. 2006. *Cell Phone Culture: Mobile Technology in Everyday Life*. London: Routledge.

Gogoi, P. 2005. "Michael Graves: Beyond Teakettles." *BusinessWeek* (August 18).

Goldman, I. 1975. *The Mouth of Heaven*. New York: Wiley.

Goldsmith, S. 2000. *Universal Design*. London: Architectural Press.

Golec, M. 2004. "Books: *Graphic Design History*, Heller, S. and Balance, G. (eds.), and *Tests on Type: Critical Writings on Typography*, Heller, S. and Meggs, P. B. (eds.)." *Design Issues* 20, no. 4: 91–94.

Gombrich, E. H. 1966. *Norm and Form: Studies in the Art of the Renaissance*. London and New York: Phaidon Press.

Gombrich, E. 1979. *The Sense of Order*. London: Phaidon.

Gonse, L. "L'art japonais et son influence sur le goût européen." *Revue des arts decoratifs* 18, 1898.

Goodison, N. 1975. "The Victoria and Albert Museum's Collection of Metal-Work Pattern Books." *Furniture History* 11: 1–30.

Goodman, N. 1978. *Ways of Worldmaking*. Indianapolis, Ind.: Hackett.

Gorman, C. 2001. "Reshaping and Rethinking: Recent Feminist Scholarship on Design and Designers." *Design Issues* 17, no. 4: 72–88.

Gorman, C., ed. 2003. *The Industrial Design Reader*. New York: Allworth Press.

Gorman, W. M. 1959. "Separable Utility and Aggregation." *Econometrica* 27: 469–81.

Gould, S. 1981. *Mismeasure of Man*. New York: Norton.

Goulden, A. W. 1976. *The Dialectic of Ideology and Technology*. London: Macmillan.

Grant, H. 1833. *Drawing for Young Children*. London: C. Knight and Co.

Gregory, S. 1966. *The Design Method*. London: Butterworths.

Greysmith, D. 1980. "The Impact of Technology on Printed Textiles in the Early 19th Century." In *Design and Industry: The Effects of Industrialization and Technical Change on Design*, ed. N. Hamilton, 62–65. London: The Design Council.

Griswold, R. L. 1993. *Fatherhood in America: A History*. New York: Basic Books.

Gronberg, T., and J. Attfield, eds. 1986. *A Resource Book on Women Working in Design*. London: London Institute/Central School of Art.

Grosz, E., and E. Probyn, eds. 1995. *Sexy Bodies: The Strange Carnalities of Feminism*. London: Routledge.

Grotius, H. 1984 [1625]. *De jure belli ac pacis, libri tres* [Commentary on the Law of War and Peace], trans. F. Kelsey, with Arthur E. R. Boak, Henry A. Sanders, Jesse S. Reeves, and Herbert F. Wright. Oxford: Clarendon Press.

Grotius, H. 1950 [1603]. *De Jure Praedae Commentarius* [Commentary on the Law of Prize and Booty], trans. G.L. Williams et al. for the Classics of International Law series, Oxford: Oxford University Press.

Gulliver, P. H. 1955. *The Family Herds, a Study of Two Pastoral Tribes in East Africa: The Jie and the Turkana*. London: Routledge and Kegan Paul.

Gurwitsch, A. 1965. "Comments on Marcuse." In *Boston Studies in the Philosophy of Science*, ed. R. Cohen and M. Wartofsky, vol. 2, 293. New York: Humanities Press.

Haber, S. 1964. *Efficiency and Uplift*. Chicago: University of Chicago Press.

Habermas, J. 1970. *Towards a Rational Society*. Boston: Beacon Press.

Hables, G., S. Mentor, and H. Figueroa-Sarriera, eds. 1995. *The Cyborg Handbook*. London: Routledge.

Habraken, J. 1985. *The Appearance of the Form*. Cambridge, Mass.: Atwater Press.

Hacking, I. 1983. *Representing and Intervening*. Cambridge: Cambridge University Press.

Hadlaw, J. 2003. "The London Underground Map: Imagining Modern Time and Space." *Design Issues* 19, no. 1: 25–35.

Hage, R. 2008. "The Great Design Art debate"; "House and Home." *The Financial Times* (Saturday, April 12/ Sunday, April 13): 1.

Hall, S. 1977. "Culture, Media and the 'Ideological Effect.'" In *Mass Communication and Society*, ed. J. Curran, M. Gurevitch, and J. Woollacott, 315–48. London: Edward Arnold.

Hall, S., with J. Criz and J. Lewis, eds. 1994. "Reflections of the Encoding/Decoding Model: An Interview with Stuart Hall." In *Viewing, Reading, Listening: Audiences and Cultural Reception*, ed. J. Cruz and J. Lewis, 253–74. Boulder, Colo.: Westview.

Hall, S., and T. Jefferson. 1993 [1976]. *Resistance through Rituals*. New York: Harper and Collins.

Hamdi, N. 1995. *Housing without Houses: Participation, Flexibility, Enablement*. London: Intermediate Technology Publications.

Hannah, F., and T. Putnam. 1980. "Taking Stock in Design History." *BLOCK* (London: Middlesex Polytechnic) 3. Reprinted 1980 in *The BLOCK Reader in Visual Culture,* ed. J. Bird, 134–47. London: Routledge.

Harary, F., R. Norman, and D. Cartwright. 1965. *Structural Models: An Introduction to the Theory of Directed Graphs.* New York: Wiley.

Haraway, D. 1989. *Primate Visions: Gender, Race, and Nature in the World of Modern Science.* New York: Routledge.

Haraway, D. 1991. *Simians Cyborgs, and Women: The Reinvention of Nature.* London: Routledge.

Haraway, D. 1999. "A Manifesto for Cyborgs." In *The Gendered Cyborg,* ed. G. Kirkup. New York: Routledge.

Harding, J. D. 1835. *The Lessons on Art.* London: W. Kent and Co.

Harding, S. 1978. "What Causes Gender Privilege and Class Privilege?" Paper presented at the meeting of the American Philosophical Association, Philadelphia.

Hardt, M., and A. Negri. 2000. *Empire.* Cambridge, Mass.: Harvard University Press.

Harris, D. 2001. *Cute, Quaint Hungry and Romantic: The Aesthetics of Consumerism.* New York: Basic Books/Perseus Books Group.

Harvey, D. 1989. *The Condition of Postmodernity: An Enquiry into the Origins of Cultural Change.* Oxford: Basil Blackwell.

Harvey, J. 1995. *Men in Black.* Chicago: University of Chicago Press.

Haug, W. F. 1986. *Critique of Commodity Aesthetics: Appearance, Sexuality and Advertising in Capitalist Society.* Minneapolis: University of Minnesota Press.

Hauser, Arnold. 1972. "Sociology in Art." In *Marxism and Art: Writings in Aesthetics and Criticism,* ed. B. Lang and F. William, New York: David McKay Co.

Hawken, P. 1993. *The Ecology of Commerce: A Declaration of Sustainability.* New York: Harper Business.

Hawkins, B. W. 1843. *The Science of Drawing Simplified, or the Elements of Form Demonstrated by Models.* London: Smith, Elder.

Hay, D. R. 1836. *The Laws of Harmonious Colouring,* 4th ed. London: W. Blackwood and Sons.

Hay, D. R. 1844. *An Essay in Ornamental Design.* London: D. Bogue.

Hayles, N. K. 1999. *How We Became Posthuman: Virtual Bodies in Cybernetics, Literature, and Informatics.* Chicago: University of Chicago Press.

Hazlewood, Sara. "Martha Stewart Kicks Ass." *Salon.com.* Available at: http://www.salon.com/business/feature/2000/11/07/marthalindez.html

Heard, N. 2005. *Trainers.* London: Carlton Books.

Hebdige, D. 1988. "Object As Image: The Italian Scooter Cycle." In his *Hiding in the Light: On Images and Things,* 77–115, 249–50. London and New York: Routledge.

Hebdige, D. 1987. *Subculture: The Meaning of Style.* London: Routledge.

Heller, S., ed. 2002. *Graphic Design Reader.* New York: Allworth.

Heller, S., and G. Balance. 2001. *Graphic Design History.* New York: Allworth Press.

Hellyer, P., and D. Hellyer. 1948. "Keep Those Home Fires Burning … with Hobbies." *The American Home* (December): 52.

Henderson, D. A. Jr., and S. K. Card. 1986. "Rooms: The Use of Multiple Virtual Workspaces to Reduce Space Contention in a Windows-Based Graphical User Interface." *TOGS* 5, no. 3: 211–43.

Hennock, M. 2003. "Sports Brands Score vs Style Thieves." BBC News Online. Available at: http://news.bbc.co.uk/1/hi/business/3260407.stm

Henriksen, M. A. 1997. "The Berlin Crisis, the Bomb Shelter Craze and Bizarre Television: Expressions of an Atomic Age Counterculture." In *The Writing on the Cloud: American Culture Confronts the Atomic Bomb,* ed. A. M. Scott and C. D. Geist, 151–73. Lanham, Md.: University Press of America.

Henriksen, M. A. 1997. *Dr. Strangelove's America: Society and Culture in the Atomic Age.* Berkeley and Los Angeles: University of California Press.

Henriques, D. B. 1999. "Martha Stewart, the Company, Is Poised to Go Public. But Is It a Good Thing?" *New York Times* (October 12): C1.

Heskett, J. 1980. *Industrial Design.* New York and Toronto: Oxford University Press.

Hewison, R. 1997. "Fool Britannia." *Blueprint* 144: 30–31.

Hewitt, J. 1995. "East Coast Joys: Tom Purvis and the LNER." *Journal of Design History* 8, no. 8: 291.

Higginbothom, N. 1994. "Capacity Building for Health in a Social Science: The International Clinical Epidemiology Network, Social Science Program and International Forum for Social Science in Health." *Acta Tropica* 57, nos. 2/3: 231–37.

Hildebrand, P. 1982. "Summary of the Sondeo Methodology Used by ICTA." In *Farming Systems Research and Development: Guidelines for Developing Countries,* ed. W. W. Shaner, P. F. Philipp, and W. R. Schmehl, 89–291. Boulder, Colo.: Westview.

Hillier, W., and A. Leaman. "How Is Design Possible? A Sketch for a Theory." *DMG IDRS Journal* 8, no. 1: 4–11.

Hindless, B., and P. Hirst. 1975. *Pre-Capitalist Modes of Production.* London: Routledge.

Hine, T. 1986. *Populuxe.* New York: Knopf.

Hine, T. 2006. "Half a Century of Lounging: Sightings and Reflections." In *The Eames Lounge Chair: An Icon of Modern Design,* ed. M. Eidelberg, T. Hine, P. Kirkham, D. Hanks, and C. F. Peatross, 30–39. London and New York: Merrell.

Hobsbawm, E. 1964. *Labouring Men: Studies in the History of Labour.* London: Weidenfeld and Nicolson.

Hobsbawm, E. 1968. *Industry and Empire: An Economic History of Britain since 1750.* London: Weidenfeld and Nicholson.

Hobsbawm, E. 1990. *Nations and Nationalism since 1780.* Cambridge: Cambridge University Press.

Hobson, J. A. 1902. *Imperialism: A Study.* New York: J. Pott and Company.

Hockenberry, J. 2006. "The Re-Education of Michael Graves." *Metropolis* 26, no. 3 (October): 123–25 and 127.

Honadle, G. 1979. "Rapid Reconnaissance Approaches to Organizational Analysis for Development Administration." Paper presented at Rapid Reconnaissance Approaches Conference, at the Institute of Development Studies, University of Sussex, Brighton, UK.

Hong, S.-H., D. Merrick, and H.A.D. do Nascimento. 2004. "Metro Map Layout Problem." In *Graph Drawing,* ed. J. Pach, 482–91. Heidleberg and Berlin: Springer-Verlag, London Transport Museum.

Hood, C. P. 2006. *Shinkansen, from Bullet Train to Symbol of Modern Japan.* London: Routledge.

hooks, b. 1991. *Yearning: Race, Gender and Cultural Politics.* London: Turnaround.

Horowitz, R., and A. Mohun, eds. 1998. *His and Hers: Gender Consumption and Technology.* Charlottesville: University of Virginia Press.

Houthakker, H. S. 1960. "The Influence of Prices and Incomes on Household Expenditures." *Bulletin of International Institute of Statistics* 37: 9–22.

Howe, S. 1930. "Forest Hills Gardens." *Architectural Record* 87 (January): 14.

"How to Lay Concrete Blocks." 1958. *Popular Mechanics* (August): 164–67.

Hubbard, R., M. Henifin, and B. Fried, eds. 1982. *Biological Woman, the Convenient Myth.* Cambridge, UK: Schenkman.

Huppatz, D. J. 2005. "Globalizing Corporate Identity in Hong Kong." *Journal of Design History* 18, no. 4: 357–69.

Hutchcroft, P. D. 1998. *Booty Capitalism: The Politics of Banking in the Philippines.* Ithaca, N.Y.: Cornell University Press.

Ingersoll, R. 1992. "The Ecological Question." *Journal of Architectural Education* 45, no. 2: 125–27.

Ironmonger, D. S. 1972. *New Commodities and Consumer Behaviour.* Cambridge: Cambridge University Press.

"It's Time to Take Another Look at Fallout Shelters." 1961. *House and Home* (July): 215–17.

Jackson, S. 2002. "The 'Stump-jumpers:' National Identity and the Mythology of Australian Industrial Design in the Period 1930–1975." *Design Issues* 18, no. 4: 14–23.

Jacobs, J. 1961. *The Death and Life of Great American Cities.* New York: Random House.

Jacoby, S. 1998. *Modern Manors.* Berkeley: University of California Press.

Jakobson, R. 1970. *Essais de linguistique générale.* Paris: Seuil Points.

Jameson, F. 1984. "Post-Modernism, or the Cultural Logic of Late Capitalism." *New Left Review* 146: 53–92.

Jameson, F. 1986. "Third World Literature in the Era of Multi-National Capitalism." *Social Text* 15: 65–68.

Jameson, F. 1991. *Postmodernism, or, the Cultural Logic of Late Capitalism.* Durham, N.C.: Duke University Press.

Jencks, C. 2005. *The Iconic Building.* New York: Rizzoli.

Jenß, H. 2004. "Dressed in History: Retro-Styles and the Construction of Authenticity in Youth Culture." *Fashion Theory* 8, no. 4: 387–404.

Jenß, H. 2005. "Customize Me! Anmerkungen zur Massenindividualisierung in der Mode." In *Schönheit der Uniformität: Körper, Kleidung, Medien,* ed. G. Mentges and B. Richard, 199–220. Frankfurt am Main and New York: Campus.

Jenß, H. 2007. *Sixties Dress Only: Mode und Konsum in der Retro-Szene der Mods.* Frankfurt am Main and New York: Campus.

Jeremiah, D. 1971. "Drawing and Design: Theory and Practice, 1830–1870." Unpublished thesis, University of Reading.

Jervis, S. 1984. *Penguin Dictionary of Design and Designers.* London: Penguin.

Jeske, J. 1971. "Das Warenhaus als Erlebnisbühne: Nachbemerkungen zum Fall Globus." *Frankfurter Allgemeine Zeitung* (August 4).

Jhally, S. 1987. *The Codes of Advertising.* London: Pinter.

Jobling, P., and C. Crowley. 1996. *Graphic Design: Reproduction and Representation since 1800.* Manchester, UK: Manchester University Press.

Jones, A. F. 1956. *The G.E.C. 1000 Telephone.* Coventry: The General Electric Company Limited of England, Telephone, Radio and Television Works.

Jones, B. J. 1957. "C.F.A. Voysey." *Architectural Association Journal* 72: 238–62.

Jones, C. J., and D. Thornley, eds. 1963. *Conference on Design Methods.* London: Pergamon Press.

Jones, J. C. 1966. "Design Methods Reviewed." In *The Design Method,* ed. S. Gregory, 295–309. London: Butterworths.

Jones, J. C. 1981. *Design Methods: Seeds of Human Futures.* New York: John Wiley and Sons.

Jones, O. 1867. *Examples of Chinese Ornament.* London: Day and Son Ltd.

Jopling, J. 1833. *The Practice of Isometrical Perspective.* London: Published for the author, sold by S. Salmon.

Julier, G. 2000. *The Culture of Design.* London: Sage Publications.

Julier, G. 2006. "From Visual Culture to Design Culture." *Design Issues* 22, no. 1: 64–76.

Julier, G., and V. Narotzky. 1998. "The Redundancy of Design History." Presented at Practically Speaking Conference, Wolverhampton University, West Midlands, UK.

Kahn, J. 2002. "Shanghai Journal: Today's China, in a Rush, Has No Time for Bikes." *New York Times* (September 6).

Kahn, J., and J. Llobera. 1981. *The Anthropology of Pre-Capitalist Societies.* London: MacMillan.

Karf, A. 1988. "On a Road to Nowhere." *Guardian* (March 8).

Kasson, J. 1990. *Rudeness and Civility: Manners in Nineteenth-Century Urban America.* New York: Hill and Wang.

Kates, R. 1989. "The Great Questions of Science and Society Do Not Fit Neatly into Single Disciplines." *Chronicle of Higher Education* (May 17): 81.

Katz, D. 1994. *Just Do It.* Holbrook, Mass.: Adams Media.

Kay, J. H. 1989. "Analyzing Success Stories of Products." *New York Times* (October 26).

Keller, E. F. 1985. *Reflections on Gender and Science.* New Haven, Conn.: Yale University Press.

Kelley, T. 2005. *The Ten Faces of Innovation: IDEO's Strategies for Beating the Devil's Advocate and Driving Creativity Throughout Your Organization.* New York: Doubleday.

Kennedy, J. F. 1961. "A Message to You from the President." *Life* (September 15): 95.

Kernaghan, C. 1998. *Behind the Label: 'Made in China.'* New York: Prepared for the National Labor Committee.

Kimmel, M. S. 2005. *The History of Men: Essays in the History of American and British Masculinities.* New York: State University of New York Press.

King, A. G. 1997. "Right Time for Martha to Control Her Empire." *Daily News* [New York] (February 5): 26.

King, F. H. H. 1991. *History of the Hongkong and Shanghai Banking Corporation.* Vol. 4. *The Hongkong Bank in the Period of Development and Nationalism, 1941–1984: From Regional Bank to Multinational Group.* Cambridge: Cambridge University Press.

Kinross, R. 1998. "Herbert Reed and Design." In *Herbert Reed Reassessed,* ed. D. Goodway. Liverpool: Liverpool Univ. Press, 145–62.

Kirkham, P. 1995. *Charles and Ray Eames: Designers of the Twentieth Century.* Cambridge, Mass.: MIT Press.

Kirkham, P. 1998. "Humanizing Modernism: The Crafts, Functioning Decoration and the Eamseses." *Journal of Design History* 11, no. 1: 15–29.

Kirkham, P., and J. Thumim, eds. 1993. *You Tarzan: Masculinity, Movies and Men.* London: Lawrence and Wishart.

Kirkham, P., ed. and J. Thumim, eds. 1995. *Me Jane: Masculinity, Movies and Women.* London: Lawrence and Wishart.

Kirkham, P. 1996. *The Gendered Object.* Manchester, UK: Manchester University Press.

Kirkham, P., ed. 2000. *Women Designers in the USA 1990–2000: Diversity and Difference.* New Haven, Conn.: Yale University Press.

Kirkup, J. 1998. "Obituary: Hideo Shima." *The Independent* [London] (March 24).

Klein, N. 2002. *No Logo.* New York: St. Martin's Press.

Knorr-Cetina, K. 1981. *The Manufacture of Knowledge.* Oxford: Pergamon.

Knorr-Cetina, K., and M. Muklay, eds. 1983. *Science Observed: Perspectives on the Social Study of Science.* Beverly Hills, Calif.: Sage.

Kohn, A. E., and D. L. Wing-kwong. 2001. "Preface." In *Tall Buildings of Asia and Australia,* ed. G. Binder, 5–8. Mulgrave, Victoria, Australia: Images Publishing Group.

Korzenik, D. 1986. *A Nineteenth-Century American Dream.* Hanover, N.H.: University Press of New England.

Krause, G. 1965. *Altpreussische Uniformfertigung als Vorstufe der Bekleidungsindustrie.* Hamburg: Helmut G. Schulz Verlag.

Kroker, A., and M. Kroker. 1988. *Body Invaders: Sexuality and the Postmodern Condition.* London: New World Perspectives.

Kuhn, T. 1962. *The Structure of Scientific Revolutions.* Chicago: University of Chicago Press.

Kuhn, T. 1977. *The Essential Tension.* Chicago: University of Chicago Press.

Kundera, M. 1998. *The Art of the Novel.* New York: Harper and Row.

Kuntz, T. 1999. "Culture Clash; Martha vs. the W.W.F.—The Final Confit." *New York Times* (October 24): 4, 7.

Kuroki, Y. 1987. *Walkman Style Planning Technique.*

Kyrk, H. 1933. *Economic Problems of the Family.* New York: Harper.

LaFramboise, D. 1998. " 'Tell Them Martha Sent You': Lifestyle-Guru Stewart in Marketing Pact with Zellers." *The Gazette* [Montreal] (May 30): F3.

Lakoff, G., and M. Johnson. 1980. *Metaphors We Live By.* Chicago and London: University of Chicago Press.

Lambert, S., ed. 1983. *Pattern and Design: Design for the Decorative Arts, 1480–1980.* London: Victoria and Albert Museum.

Lancaster, C. 1952. "Oriental Contribution to Art Nouveau." *Art Bulletin* 34, no. 4: 297–310.

Lancaster, K. J. 1966. "A New Approach to Consumer Theory." *Journal of Political Economy* 174: 132–57.

Lancaster, K. J. 1971. *Consumer Demand: A New Approach.* New York: Columbia University Press.

LaRossa, R. 1997. *The Modernization of Fatherhood: A Social and Political History.* Chicago: University of Chicago Press.

Lasch, C. 1979. *The Culture of Narcissism.* London: W. W. Norton.

Lash, S., and J. Urry. 1987. *The End of Organized Capitalism.* Madison: University of Wisconsin Press.

Latour, B., and S. Woolgar. 1979. *Laboratory Life: The Social Construction of Science Facts.* Cambridge, Mass.: Harvard University Press.

Lau, J. L., ed. 1986. *Models of Development: A Comparative Study of Economic Growth in South Korea and Taiwan.* San Francisco: ICS Press.

Lavedan, H. 1942. *Les Représentations des vales dans l'art du Mayen Age.* Paris: Van Oest.

Lavin, M. 2001. *Clean New World: Culture, Politics, and Graphic Design.* Cambridge, Mass.: MIT Press.

Lawson, B. 1980. *How Designers Think.* London: Architectural Press.

Leach, E. R. 1967. "Magical Hair." In *Myth and Cosmos: Readings in Mythology and Symbolism,* ed. J. Middleton, 77–108. New York: Natural History Press.

Leach, W. 1993. *Land of Desire: Merchants, Power, and the Rise of a New American Culture.* New York: Vintage Books.

Lechner, F., and J. Boli, eds. 2003. *The Globalization Reader.* Malden, Mass.: Blackwell.

Lees-Maffei, G. 2001. "From Service to Self-Service: Advice Literature as Design Discourse." *Journal of Design History* 14, no. 3: 187–206.

Lees-Maffei, G. 2008. "Mediation: From Design History to Cultural History?" Unpublished conference paper delivered at The State of Design History session at the CAA Design Studies Forum Conference, Dallas, Texas.

Lefebvre, H. 1971. *Everyday Life in the Modern World.* Philadelphia: Allen Lane.

Leibman, N. C. 1995. *Living Room Lectures: The Fifties Family in Film and Television.* Austin: University of Texas Press.

Lenin, V. 1916. *Imperialism: The Highest Stage of Capitalism.* Moscow: Foreign Languages Publishing House.

Leonhardt, D. 1998. "Sara Lee: Playing with the Recipe." *Business Week* (April 27): 114.

Lethaby, W. R. 1924. *Ernest Gimson, His Life and Work.* London: Shakespeare Head Press.

"Levi Strauss and Co. to Close 11 of Its North American Plants." 1999. *Business Wire* (February 22): Bl.

Levy-Bruhl, L. 1966. *The Soul of the Primitive.* London: George Allen and Unwin.

Lewontin, R. C., S. Rose, and L. Kamin. 1984. *Not in Our Genes: Biology, Ideology, and Human Nature.* New York: Pantheon.

Lichtman, S. 2006. "Do-It-Yourself Security." *Journal of Design History* 19, no. 1: 39–55.

Lindinger, H. 1990. *Ulm Design: The Morality of Objects.* Cambridge, Mass.: MIT Press.

Lipman, Mary Jo G. 1999. "Bullseye! Michael Graves Does Target. A Teapot, and a Buying Tempest." *CNN.com.* Available at: www.cnn.com/style/9902/11/target. Accessed January 12, 2008.

Locke, John. 2003 [1689]. *Two Treatises of Government* [First and Second Treatise on Government], reprint with introduction by Ian Shapiro. New Haven, Conn.: Yale University Press.

Loewy, R. 1951. *Never Leave Well Enough Alone.* New York: Simon and Schuster.

Loewy, R. 1979. *Industrial Design.* New York: Overlook Press.

Logan, F. M. 1955. *The Growth of Art in American Schools.* New York: Harper.

Loisel, G. 1912. *Histoire des Ménageries.* Paris: O. Doin et fils.

Lorenz, T. 2006. "British Designers Accused of Creating Throw-Away Culture." *Design Week* (April 6): 7.

Lupton, E. 1993. *Mechanical Brides: Women and Machines from Home to Office.* New York: Cooper-Hewitt National Museum of Design, Smithsonian Institution, and Princeton Architectural Press.

Lury, C. 1996. *Consumer Culture.* New Brunswick, N.J.: Rutgers University Press.

Lury, C. 2007. "Just Do It: The Brand as New Media Object." In *New Media Worlds: Challenges for Convergence,* ed. V. Nightingale and T. Dwyer. South Melbourne, Victoria: Oxford University Press.

"Lusaka Sites and Services Project." *Upgrading Urban Communities, The World Bank Group, 1999–2001.* Available at: http://web.mit.edu/urbanupgrading/upgrading/case-examples/ce-ZA-lus.html

Lynch, M., and S. Woolgar, eds. 1990. *Representation in Scientific Practice.* Cambridge, Mass.: MIT Press.

Macdonald, S. 1970. *The History and Philosophy of Art Education.* London: University of London Press.

Madsen, S. T. 1975. *The Sources of Art Nouveau.* New York: Da Capo Press.

Maffei, N. 2000. "John Cotton Dana and the Politics of Exhibiting Industrial Art in the US, 1909–1929." *Journal of Design History* 13, no. 4: 301–18.

Magnaghi, A. 2000. *Il progetto locale.* Torino, Italy: Bollati Boringhieri.

Mailer, N. 1974. "The Faith of Graffiti." *Esquire* 81 (May): 77–99, 88, 154, 157, 158.

Majtenyi, C. 1996. "Were Disney Dogs Treated Better Than Workers?" *Catholic Register* (December 23–30): 9.

Maldonado, T. 1991. *Design Industriale: Un Riesame,* rev. and enl. ed. Milan, Italy: Feltrinelli.

Mandel, E. 1978. *Late Capitalism.* London: Verso.

Manderson, L., and B. Aaby. 1992. "An Epidemic in the Field? Rapid Assessment Procedures and Health Research." *Social Science and Medicine* 35, no. 7: 839–50.

Manderson, L., A. Almedom, J. Gittelsohn, D. Helitzer-Allen, and P. Pelto. 1996. "Transferring Anthropological Techniques in Applied Research." *Practicing Anthropology* 18: 33–35.

Mangahas, M. 2001. "Text Messaging Comes of Age in the Philippines." *Reuters Technology News* (January 28).

Manner, G. 1997. "Martha Has a New Home on the Web." *Daily News* [New York] (September 5): 83.

Mansell, R., and R. Silverstone, eds. 1998. *Communication by Design.* Oxford: Oxford University Press.

Manzini, E. 2008. "A Cosmopolitan Localism: Prospects for a Sustainable Local Development and the Possible Role of Design." Available at: http://sustainable-everyday.net/manzini/?m=200401

Manzini, E., I. Collina, and E. Evans, eds. 2004. *Solution Oriented Partnership: How to Design Industrialised.* Bedfordshire, UK: Cranfield University.

Manzini, E. and F. Jegou. 2003. *Sustainable Everyday.* Milan, Italy: Edizioni Ambiente.

Manzini E., and C. Vezzoli. 2002. *Product-Service Systems and Sustainability: Opportunities for Sustainable Solutions.* Paris: UNEP Publisher.

Manzini, E., and C. Vezzoli. 2008. *Design for Environmental Sustainability.* New York: Springer.

Manzini, E., and S. Vugliano. 2000. "Il locale del globale: La localizzazione evoluta come scenario progettuale." *Pluriverso*: N1.

Margolies, J. 2004. "Getting Tough About Kids' Stuff: Four Designing Mothers Sound Off on Baby Products." *I.D.* (March/April): 42–49.

Marcuse, H. 1964. *One-Dimensional Man: Studies in the Ideology of Advanced Industrial Society.* Boston: Beacon.

Margolin, V. 1987. *Design History Bibliography.* London: ICOGRADA.

Margolin, V., ed. 1989. *Design Discourse: History Theory Criticism.* Chicago: University of Chicago Press.

Margolin, V. 1995. "Design History or Design Studies: Subject Matter and Methods." *Design Issues* 11, no. 1: 4–15.

Margolin, V. 2002. *The Politics of the Artificial: Essays on Design and Design Studies.* Chicago: University of Chicago Press.

Margolin, V. 2005. "A World History of Design and the History of the World." *Journal of Design History* 18, no. 3: 235–43.

Margolin, V., and R. Buchanan, eds. 1995. *The Idea of Design: A Design Issues Reader.* Cambridge, Mass.: MIT Press.

Marin, L. *Utopiques: Jeux d'espaces.* Paris: Minuit, 1973.

"The Markets: Market Place; Big Board Fumbles Martha Stewart Deal." 1999. *New York Times* (October 21): C1.

Marling, K. A. 1994. *As Seen on TV: The Visual Culture of Everyday Life in the 1950s.* Cambridge, Mass. and London: Harvard University Press.

"Martha Stewart Living Omnimedia Acquires Martha Stewart Living from Time Inc." 1997. *PR Newswire* (February 4).

"Martha Stewart Tidies Up Wall St." 1999. *New York Times* (October 19).

Marx, K. 1906. *Capital: A Critique of Political Economy.* New York: The Modern Library.

Mascheck, J. 1975. "Embalmed Objects: Design at the Modern." *Art Forum* (February): 49–55.

Maschek, J. 1976. "The Carpet Paradigm: Critical Prolegomena to a Theory of Flatness." *Arts Magazine* (September): 82–106.

Maslow, A. H. 1954. *Motivation and Personality.* New York: Harper.

Massey, D. 1994. *Space, Place, and Gender.* London: Polity.

Mata, E. 2000. *The Ultimate Text Book.* Quezon City: Philippine Center for Investigative Journalism.

Matchett, E. 1968. "Control on Work in Creative Thought." *The Chartered Mechanical Engineer* 14, no. 4.

Matrix. 1984. *Making Space: Women and the Man-Made Environment.* London: Pluto Press.

Mauss, M. 1979. *Sociology and Psychology.* London: Routledge.

Mauss, M. 1990 [1950]. *The Gift: The Form and Reason for Exchange in Archaic Societies.* London: Routledge.

Maxim, H. 1915. *Defenseless America.* New York: Hearst's International Library Co.

May, E. T. 1988. *Homeward Bound: American Families in the Cold War Era.* New York: Basic Books.

Maynard, M. 2000. "Grassroots Style: Re-Evaluating Australian Fashion and Aboriginal Art in the 1970s and 1980s." *Journal of Design History* 13, no. 2: 137–50.

Mazur Thomson, E. 1997. *The Origins of Graphic Design in America 1870–1920.* New Haven, Conn.: Yale University Press.

McCloskey, D. N. 1990. *If You're So Smart: The Narrative of Economic Expertise.* Chicago: University of Chicago Press.

McCracken, G. 2005. *Culture and Consumption II: Markets, Meaning and Brand Management.* Bloomington: Indiana University Press.

McDonough, W. 1997. *The Hannover Principles: Design for Sustainability.* Charlottesville, Va.: Island Press.

McDonough, W., and M. Braungart. 2002. *Cradle to Cradle: Remaking the Way We Make Things.* New York: North Point Press.

McEnaney, L. 2000. *Civil Defense Begins at Home: Militarization Meets Everyday Life in the Fifties.* Princeton, N.J.: Princeton University Press.

McKellar, S., and P. Sparke, eds. 2004. *Interior Design and Identity.* Manchester, UK: Manchester University Press.

McLuhan, M. 1962. *The Gutenberg Galaxy: The Making of Typographic Man.* Toronto: University of Toronto Press.

McLuhan, M. 1964. *Understanding Media: The Extensions of Man.* London: Routledge.

McLuhan, M., with E. McLuhan. 1988. *Laws of Media: The New Science.* Toronto: University of Toronto Press.

Médam, A. 1976. "New York City." *Les Temps Modernes* (August–September): 15–33.

Médam, A. 1977. *New York Terminal.* Paris: Galilée.

Me.Design. 2003. "Strategies, Tools and the Practicality of Industrial Design in Order to Enhance and Develop the Resources of the Mediterranean Area between the Local and Global." Research program financed by MURST (Ministry of University Research in Science and Technology). Internal document.

"The Media Business: Martha Stewart to Buy Her Company." 1997. *New York Times* (February 5): D5.

Meggs, P. B. 1992. *A History of Graphic Design.* New York: Van Nostrand Reinhold. 3rd ed. New York: John Wiely and Sons, 1998.

Meglin, N. 1975. "Charles Dana Gibson and the Age of Exclusivity." *American Artist* 39 (March): 62.

Meikle, J. 1979. *Twentieth Century Limited: Industrial Design in America, 1925–39.* Philadelphia: Temple University Press.

Meikle, J. 1998. "Material Virtues: On the Ideal and the Real in Design History." *Journal of Design History* 11, no. 3: 191–99.

Mentges, G. 1993. "Der vermessene Körper." In *Der neuen Welt ein neuer Rock: Studien zu Kleidung, Körper und Mode an Beispielen aus Württemberg,* ed. C. Köhle-Hezinger and G. Mentges, vol. 9. Stuttgart: Forschungen und Berichte zur Volkskunde.

Mentges, G. 2005. "Die Angst vor der Uniformität." In *Schönheit der Uniformität: Körper, Kleidung, Medien,* ed. G. Mentges and B. Richard. Frankfurt am Main: Campus.

Merchant, C. 1980. *The Death of Nature: Women, Ecology and the Scientific Revolution.* New York: Harper and Row.

Merleau-Ponty, M. 1976. *Phénoménologie de la perception.* Paris: Gallimard Tel.

Meyer, N. 1999. "Martha Stewart Garden Furniture Rolls Out." *Brandmarketing* 6, no. 4 (April): 6.

Michael, V. 2002. "Reyner Banham: Signs and Designs in the Time without Style." *Design Issues* 18, no. 2: 65–77.

"Millennium Development Goals," 2003. UN-HABITAT. Available at: http://www.unhabitatorg/mdg/

Miller, C. 1992. "Sony's Product 'Playground' Yields Insight on Consumer Behaviour." *Marketing News* (February): 2, 13.

Miller, D. 1985. *Artifacts as Categories: A Study of Ceramic Variability in Central India.* Cambridge: Cambridge University Press.

Miller, D. 1986. "Alienation and Exchange in the Jajmani System." *Journal of Anthropological Research* 42, no. 2: 535–56.

Miller, D. 1987. *Material Culture and Mass Consumption.* Oxford: Basil Blackwell.

Miller, D., ed. 1995. *Acknowledging Consumption: A Review of New Studies.* London and New York: Routledge.

Miller, D. 1998a. *A Theory of Shopping.* Ithaca, N.Y.: Cornell University Press.

Miller, D., ed. 1998b. *Material Cultures: Why Some Things Matter.* Chicago: University of Chicago Press.

Miller, D., ed. 2001. *Consumption: Critical Concepts in the Social Sciences.* New York: Taylor and Francis Group.

Miller, D., and S. Küchler, eds. 2005. *Clothing as Material Culture.* Oxford: Berg.

Miller, G. 1978. "Practical and Lexical Knowledge." In *Cognition and Categorisation,* ed. E. Rosch and B. Lloyd, 305–20. Mahwah, N.J.: Lawrence Erlbaum Associates.

Miller, G., and P. Johnson-Laird. 1976. *Language and Perception.* Cambridge: Cambridge University Press.

Mitchell, J., and A. Oakely. 1987. *What Is Feminism?* Oxford: Blackwell.

Miyata, Y., and D. A. Norman. 1986. "Psychological Issues in Support of Multiple Activities." In *User Centered System Design,* ed. D. A. Norman and S. W. Draper, 265–84. Mahwah, N.J.: Lawrence Erlbaum Associates.

Mock, J. R., and C. Larson. 1939. *Words That Won the War: The Story of the Committee on Public Information 1917–1919.* Princeton, N.J.: Princeton University Press.

Moeran, B. 1984. *Lost Innocence.* Berkeley: University of California Press.

Moles, A. 1988. "Design and Immateriality: What of It in a Post Industrial Society?," trans. David Jacobus. *Design Issues* 4, nos. 1/2: 25–32.

Mollerup, P. 1997. *Marks of Excellence: The Function and Variety of Trademarks.* London: Phaidon Press.

Molloy, J. T. 1975. *Dress for Success.* New York: P. H. Wyden.

Mont, O. 2002. *Functional Thinking: The Role of Functional Sales and Product Service Systems for a Functional Based Society.* Research report for the Swedish EPA, IIIEE. Lund, Sweden: Lund University.

Moor, L. 2007. *The Rise of Brands.* Oxford and New York: Berg.

Moore, S. 1988. "Getting a Bit of the Other: The Pimps of Postmodernism." In *Male Order: Unwrapping Masculinity,* ed. R. Chapman and J. Rutherford, 165–92. London: Lawrence and Wishart.

Moran, T. 1999. "Kmart Corp.'s Billion-Dollar 'Brand-Aid' Is Martha Stewart." *HFN: The Weekly Newspaper for the Home Furnishing Network* (May 24): 1.

Morgan, M., ed. 1992. *Classics of Political and Moral Theory.* Indianapolis, Ind.: Hackett Publishing.

Morita. A., E. Reingold, and M. Shimomure. 1987. *Made in Japan: Akio Morita and Sony.* London: Collins.

Morris, M. 1988. *The Pirate's Fiancée: Feminism, Reading, Postmodernism.* London: Verso.

Mort, F. 1996. *Cultures of Consumption: Masculinities and Social Space in Late Twentieth Century Britain.* New York: Routledge.

Mumford, L. 1934. *Technics and Civilization.* New York: Harcourt, Brace and Co.

Mumford, L. 1961. *The City in History: Its Origins, Its Transformations, and Its Prospects.* New York: Lindner.

Munk, N. 1999. "How Levi's Trashed a Great American Brand." *Fortune* (April 12): 83.

Munn, N. 1977. "Spatiotemporal Transformations of Gawa Canoes." *Journal de la Société des Océanistes* 33: 39–52.

Muth, R. F. 1966. "Household Production and Consumer Demand Functions." *Econometrica* 24, no. 3: 699–708.

Muthesius, H. 1904–1905. *Das englische Haus.* 3 vols. Berlin: E. Wasmuth.

Mydans, S. 1996. "Malaysia Looks Down on World from 1,483 Feet." *New York Times* (May 2).

Myerson, A. R. 1995. "The Great Asian Steeple Chase." *New York Times* (June 25).

Nardi, B., ed. 1996. *Context and Consciousness: Activity Theory and Human-Computer Interaction.* Cambridge, Mass.: MIT Press.

National Association for the Advancement of Art and its Application to Industry. 1890. *Transactions, Edinburgh Meeting, 1889.* NAAA London.

Naylor, G. 2000. "Design History: A Personal Perspective." *Design History Society Newsletter* 86, no. 3.

Nederveen Pieterse, J. 1995. "Globalization as Hybridization." In *Global Modernities,* ed. M. Featherstone, S. Lash, and R. Robertson, 45–68. London: Sage.

Nelson, D. 1975. *Managers and Workers.* Madison: University of Wisconsin Press.

Nelson, J. S., A. Megill, and D. N. McCloskey, eds. 1987. *The Rhetoric of the Human Sciences: Language and Argument in Public Affairs.* Madison: University of Wisconsin Press.

Neumann, J. V., and O. Morgenstern. 1947. *The Theory of Games and Economic Behaviour,* 2nd ed. Princeton, N.J.: Princeton University Press.

"The New American Domestic Male." 1954. *Life* (January 4): 42–45.

Nicholson, P. 1867. *The New Carpenter's Guide.* Philadelphia: J. B. Lippincott.

Nodelman, S. 1970. "Structural Analysis in Art and Anthropology." In *Structuralism,* ed. J. Ehrmann, 79–93. Garden City, N.Y.: Anchor Books/Doubleday.

Norman, D. A. 1988. *The Psychology of Everyday Things.* New York: Basic Books.

Norman, D. 1998. *The Invisible Computer.* Cambridge, Mass.: MIT Press.

Norman, R., and R. Ramirez. 1994. *Designing Interactive Strategies, From Value Chains to Value Constellations.* Chichester, UK: John Wiley and Sons.

Noyes, E. 1941. *Organic Design in Home Furnishings.* New York: Museum of Modern Art.

Nozick, R. 1974. *Anarchy, State, and Utopia.* New York: Basic Books.

Nunn, R. 1957. "Hollywood Handymen." *Better Homes and Gardens* (November): 78.

Oakes, G. 1994. *The Imaginary War: Civil Defense and American Cold War Culture.* Oxford: Oxford University Press.

Ohmae, K. 1990. *The Borderless World.* New York: Harper Business.

Olins, W. 1989. *Corporate Identity: Making Business Strategy Visible through Design.* London: Thames and Hudson.

Olins, W. 1999. *Trading Identities: Why Countries and Companies are Taking on Each Others' Roles.* London: The Foreign Policy Centre.

O'Malley, G. O. 2006. "Virtual Worlds: The Latest Fashion." *Advertising Age* (July 10): 3.

O'Neill, M. 1999. "But What Would Martha Say?" *New York Times Magazine* (May 16). Available at: http://lwww.nytimes.com/libraryfinagazine/millennium/m2lrecipes.html

Open University. 1975. *History of Architecture and Design 1890–1939.* Milton Keynes, UK: The Open University Press.

Opitz, G. B., ed. 1987. *Memorial Fielding's Dictionary of American Painters, Sculptors and Engravers,* 2nd newly revised, enlarged, and updated edition. Poughkeepsie, N.Y.: Apollo Books.

Øresund Committee. 1999. *Hello* (pamphlet). Copenhagen: Øresund Committee.

Ortega, B. 1999. *In Sam We Trust.* New York: Times Books.

Oswald, A. 1935. *Country Houses of Dorset.* London: Country Life.

Oudshoorn, N., and T. Pinch, eds. 2003. *How Users Matter: The Co-Construction of Users and Technologies.* Cambridge, Mass.: MIT Press.

"Outdoor Antenna for Fallout Shelter." 1962. *Popular Mechanics* (February): 204.

Packard, V. 1957. *The Hidden Persuaders.* New York: David McKay and Company.

Page, J. K. 1966. *Contribution to Building for People.* London: Ministry of Public Buildings and Works.

Palmer, J., and M. Dodson, eds. 1996. *Design and Aesthetics: A Reader.* New York: Routledge.

Pansera, A., ed. 1988. *Tradizione e Modernismo, 1918/1940: Atti del Convegno* [Tradition and Modernism: Design between the Wars, 1918–1940: Congress Minutes]. Milan, Italy: L'Arca Edizioni.

Papanek, V. 1972. *Design for the Real World: Human Ecology and Social Change.* London: Thames and Hudson. Reprinted London: Paladin, 1974.

Papanek, V. 1982. "Seeing the World Whole: Interaction Between Ecology and Design." Fifth Inaugural Lecture, University of Kansas, Lawrence.

Papanek, V. 1995. *The Green Imperative: Natural Design for the Real World.* London: Thames and Hudson.

Papert, S. 1980. *Mindstorms: Children, Computers and Powerful Ideas.* New York: Basic Books.

Parker, R. 1984. *The Subversive Stitch.* London: Women's Press.

Paroush, J. 1965. "The Order of Acquisition of Consumer Durables." *Econometrica* 33: 225–35.

Parr, R. L. 2001. Untitled article on People Power II and cell phone use in the *Independent* [London] (January 23).

Parret, H. 1975. *La Pragmatique des modalités.* Urbino, Italy: Centro di Semiotica.

Parry, J. 1986. "The Gift, the Indian and the 'Indian Gift.'" *Man* 21: 453–73.

Patton, P. 1999. "For the Mall Rats, A New Piper." *The New York Times* (January 14).

Patton, Phil. 2004. *Michael Graves Designs: The Art of the Everyday Object.* New York: DK Meichior Media.

Pavitt, J. 2000. *Brand.new.* London: V & A Publications.

Pearlman, C. 2003. "From Alessi, a Second Chance to Buy a $50,000 Teapot." *New York Times* (March 27): F8.

Pearson, C. A. 1999. "Other Than Their Status as the World's Tallest Buildings, What Else Do Cesar Pelli's Petronas Towers Have Going for Them?" *Architectural Record* 187, no. 1: 92–101.

Peirce, C. S. 1931. *Collected Papers,* 8 vols. Cambridge, Mass.: Harvard University Press.

Pelli, C., and M. J. Crosbie. 2001. *Petronas Towers: The Architecture of High Construction.* New York: Wiley.

Pendleton, M. 1988. "Discouraging Local Innovation and Design Expertise in Hong Kong's Colonial Intellectual Property Law." Presented at the conference, Design and Development in South and Southeast Asia, Hong Kong University, December.

Peng, T. N. 2005. "Trends and Patterns of Urbanization in Malaysia, 1970–2000." In *Asian Urbanization in the New Millennium,* ed. G. Ness and G. P. Talwar, 178–221. Singapore: Marshall Cavendish International.

Pennell, E. R., and J. Pennell. 1908. *The Life of James McNeill Whistler.* London: J. P. Lippincott and Heinenmann.

Pennell, J. 1918. *Joseph Pennell's Liberty Loan Poster: A Text Book for Artists and Amateurs, Governments and Teachers and Printers, with Notes, an Introduction and Essay on the Poster by the Artist.* London: J. P. Lippincott.

Perloff, M. 1984. "Dirty Language and Scramble Systems." *Sulfur* 11: 178–83.

Peters, T. 1999. *The Circle of Innovation.* New York: Vintage Books.

Petronas. 2005. *The Petronas Twin Towers Official Website.* Available at: http://www.petronas.com

Petroski, H. 2006. *Success through Failure: The Paradox of Design.* Princeton, N.J.: Princeton University Press.

Pevsner, N. 1936. *Pioneers of the Modern Movement from William Morris to Walter Gropius.* London: Faber and Faber.

Pevsner, N. 1940. "Charles F. Annesley Voysey." *Elsevier's Maandschrift:* 343–55.

Pevsner, N. 1991 [1949, 1960]. *Pioneers of Modern Design: From William Morris to Walter Gropius.* London: Penguin.

Piller, F. 1998. *Kundenindividuelle Massenproduktion: Die Wettbewerbsstrategie der Zukunft.* Munich: Hanser Fachbuch.

Pinch, T. J., and W. E. Bijker. 1987. "The Social Construction of Facts and Artifacts: Or How the Sociology of Science and the Sociology of Technology Might Benefit Each Other." In *The Social Construction of Technological Systems: New Directions in the Sociology and History of Technology,* ed. W. E. Bijker, T. P. Hughes, and T. J. Pinch, 17–50. Cambridge, Mass.: MIT Press.

Pine, J. 1993. *Mass Customization: The New Frontier in Business Competition.* Cambridge, Mass.: Harvard Business School Press.

Piore, M. J., and C. Sabel. 1984. *The Second Industrial Divide: Prospects for Prosperity.* New York: Basic Books.

Pirsig, R. 1974. *Zen and the Art of Motorcycle Maintenance.* New York: William Morrow.

Pogge, Thomas. 2002. *World Poverty and Human Rights.* Cambridge, UK: Polity Press.

Ponsonby, Sir F. 1952. *Recollections of Three Reigns.* New York: Dutton.

Porter, G. 1998. "Cultural Forces and Commercial Constraints: Designing Packaging in the Twentieth-

Century United States." *Journal of Design History* 12, no. 1: 25–44.

Porter, M. E. 1990. *The Competitive Advantage of Nations.* New York: Free Press.

"The Post-National Economy: Goodbye Widget, Hello, Nike." 1996. *Far Eastern Economic Review* 159 (August 29): 5.

Postrel, V. 2003. *The Substance of Style.* New York: HarperCollins.

"Power Tools: The Newest Home Appliance." 1954. *Industrial Design* (February): 31.

Powner, J. 2000. "International Corporate Identity Insert." *Design Week* [UK] 15, no. 33 (August): 24–25.

Poynor, R. 2002. *Typographica.* New York: Princeton Architectural Press.

Prest, A. R. 1949. "Some Experiments in Demand Analysis." *Review of Economics and Statistics* 13: 33–49.

Prown, J. 1980. "Mind in Matter: An Introduction to Material Culture Theory and Method." *Winterthur Portfolio* 17, no. 1: 1–19.

Prown, J. D. 1980. "Style as Evidence." *Winterthur Portfolio* 15, no. 3: 197–210.

Pulos, A. 1983. *American Dream Ethic: A History of Industrial Design in American to 1940.* Cambridge, Mass.: MIT Press.

Putnam, T., and C. Newton, eds. 1990. *Household Choices.* London: Futures.

Pyatt, F. G. 1966. *Priority Patterns and the Demand for Household Durable Goods.* Cambridge: Cambridge University Press.

Quinn, B. 2002. "A Note: Hussein Chalayan, Fashion and Technology." *Fashion Theory* 6, no. 4: 359–68.

Quinn, B. 2002. *Techno Fashion.* Oxford: Berg.

Quiros, C. de. 2001. "Undiscovered Country." *PDI* (February 7).

Radway, J. 1991. *Reading the Romance: Women, Patriarchy, and Popular Literature.* Chapel Hill: University of North Carolina Press.

Radway, J. 1994. "On the Gender of the Middlebrow Consumer and the Threat of the Culturally Fraudulent Female." *South Atlantic Quarterly* 93, no. 4: 871–93.

Radway, J. A. 1996. "Reading Is Not Eating: Mass-Produced Literature and the Theoretical, Methodological, and Political Consequences of a Metaphor." *Book Research Quarterly* 2: 7–29.

Rafael, V. L. 1999. "Translation and Revenge: Castilian and the Origins of Nationalism in the Philippines."

In *The Places of History: Regionalism Revisited in Latin America,* ed. D. Sommer, 214–35. Durham, N.C.: Duke University Press.

Rafael, V. L. 2000. *White Love and Other Events in Philippines History.* Durham, N.C.: Duke University Press.

Rafael, V. 2003. "The Cell Phone and the Crowd: Messianic Politics in the Contemporary Philippines." *Public Culture* 15, no. 3: 399–425.

Raizman, D. 2003. *History of Modern Design: Graphics and Products since the Industrial Revolution,* London: Laurence King Publishing.

Raizman D., and C. Gorman, eds. 2007. *Objects, Audiences, and Literatures: Alternative Narratives in the History of Design.* Newcastle, UK: Cambridge Scholars Publishing.

Ramey, J. 1998. "Levi's Will Resume Production in China after 5-Year Absence." *Women's Wear Daily* (April 9).

Rawls, John. 1971. *A Theory of Justice.* Cambridge, Mass.: Harvard University Press.

Redgrave, S., and R. Redgrave. 1866. *A Century of Painters.* London: Smith, Elder.

Reed, S. 1997. "Destalinization and Taste, 1953–1963." *Journal of Design History* 10, no. 2: 177–203.

Reed, W. 2001. *The Illustrator in America 1860–2000.* New York: The Society of Illustrators.

Remington, R. 1989. *Nine Pioneers in American Graphic Design.* Cambridge, Mass.: MIT Press.

Remington, R. R., and R. Fripp. 2007. *Design and Science—The Life and Work of Will Burtin.* Hampshire, UK: Lund Humphries.

A Report Concerning Papers, Films, Records, Public Property, and Liabilities, etc. of the Committee on Public Information. Made by the Director of the United States Council of National Defense in Response to Senate Resolution 323 of the 65th Congress, Second Session, adopted March 5, 1920. Washington, D.C.: National Archives.

Reswick, J. B. 1965. *Prospectus for Engineering Design Centre.* Cleveland, Ohio: Case Institute of Technology.

Rewald, J. 1946. *The History of Impressionism.* New York: Museum of Modern Art.

Rhoades, R. E. 1982. *The Art of the Informal Agricultural Survey.* Training Document 1982–2, Lima, Peru: Social Sciences Department, International Potato Center.

Riccini, R. 2005. "Design e teorie degli oggetti." *It Verri* 27 (February): 48–57.

Ricoeur, P. 1965. *History and Truth,* trans. C. Kelbley. Evanston, Ill.: Northwestern University Press.

Ricoeur, P. 1974. "From Nation to Humanity: Task of Christians." In *Political and Social Essays by Paul Ricoeur*, ed. D. Stewart and J. Bien. Athens: Ohio University Press.

Rissiek, A., and F. Piller. 2001. "Mass Customization in der Bekleidungsindustrie: Der Wandel als Chance." In *Zukunft Maßkonfektion: Technik, Markt und Management*, ed. A. Seidl, 1–68. Frankfurt am Main: Deutscher Fachverlag.

Rittel, H.W.J. 1972. "Son of Rittelthink." Design Methods Group 5th Anniversary Report, January, pp. 5–10.

Rittel, H.W.J. 1984. "On the Planning Crisis: Systems Analysis of the First and Second Generations." *Bedriftsokonomen* no. 8: 390–96.

Rittel, H.W.J., and M. M. Webber. 1972. "Dilemmas in a General Theory of Planning." Working paper presented at the Institute of Urban and Regional Development, University of California, Berkeley, November.

Rizal, J. 1889. "Por Telefono." Barcelona; reprinted in *Miscellaneous Writings*. Manila: Martinez, R. and Sons, 1959.

Roane, K. R. 2007. "A Typeface for All Time." *U.S. News and World Report* (August 13–20). Available at: http://www.usnews.com/usnews/news/articles/070805/13helvetica.htm

Roberts, M. 2005. *Underground Maps after Beck*. London: Capital Transport.

Robinson, E. 1963–1964. "Eighteenth-Century Commerce and Fashion: Matthew Boulton's Marketing Techniques." *Economic History Review* 16: 49.

Robson, W. 1799. *Grammigraphia; or the Grammar of Drawing*. London: Wilson.

Rohrlich, M. 1999. "Personal Shopper: Perches for the Armchair Gardener." *New York Times* (March 25): F10.

Romanenko, N. 1999. "Material Girl: Martha Stewart Unfolds Fabric Collection." *Asbury Park Press* [Neptune, N.J.] (August 19): D1.

Rosch, E. 1978. "Principles of Categorization." In *Cognition and Categorization*, ed. E. Rosch and B. Lloyd, 133–59. Hillsdale, N.J.: Lawrence Erlbaum.

Rose, G. 1996. *Mourning Becomes the Law*. Cambridge: Cambridge University Press.

Rose, K. D. 2001. *One Nation Underground: The Fallout Shelter in American Culture*. New York: New York University Press.

Rosenbluth, A., N. Wiener, and J. Bigelow. 1943. "Behavior, Purpose, and Teleology." *Philosophy of Science* 10: 18–24.

Rostenberg, L. 1963. *English Publishers in the Graphic Arts*. New York: B. Franklin.

Rothschild, J., ed. 1983. *Machina ex Dea: Feminist Perspectives on Technology*. New York: Pergamon.

Rothstein, N. 1961 "The Silk Industry in London, 1702–1766." Masters thesis, University of London.

Rousseau, Jean-Jacques. 1968 [1762]. *The Social Contract*, trans. M. Cranston. London: Penguin Books.

Rowlands, M. B. 1975. *Masters and Men in the West Midlands Metalware Trades before the Industrial Revolution*. Manchester, UK: Manchester University Press.

Rubin, E. 2006. "The Form of Socialism without Ornament: Consumption, Ideology and the Fall and Rise of Modernist Design in the German Democratic Republic." *Journal of Design History* 19, no. 2: 155–68.

Russell, E., P. Garner, and J. Read. 1980. *A Century of Chair Design*. Chicago: Academy Editions.

Sachs, W. 1998. a cura di, (ed.). *Dizionario dello sviluppo*. Torino, Italy: Gruppo Abele.

Sahlins, M. 1976a. *Culture and Practical Reason*. Chicago: University of Chicago Press.

Sahlins, M. 1976b. *The Use and Abuse of Biology*. London: Tavistock.

Said, E. 1978. *Orientalism*. New York: Pantheon.

Said, E. W. 2003. *Humanism and Democratic Criticism*. New York: Columbia University Press.

Salen, K., and E. Zimmerman. 2003. *Rules of Play: Game Design Fundamentals*. Cambridge, Mass.: MIT Press.

Salterio, L. 2001. "Text Power in Edsa 2001." *Philippine Daily Inquirer* (January 22).

Sartre, J.-P. 1956. *Being and Nothingness*, trans. H. Barnes. New York: Philosophical Library. Reprinted London: Methuen, 1969.

Sassure, F. de. 1986. *Course in General Linguistics*, trans. R. Harris. Chicago: Open Court Press.

Scarry, E. 1985. *The Body in Pain*. Oxford: Oxford University Press.

Schaeffer, H. 1970. *The Roots of Modern Design: Functional Tradition in the Nineteenth Century*. London: Studio Vista.

Schapiro, J. J. 1970. "One Dimensionality: The Universal Semiotic of Technological Experience." In *Critical Interruptions*, ed. P. Breines, 136–86. New York: Herder and Herder.

Schlesinger, A. Jr. 1958. "The Crisis of American Masculinity." *Esquire* (November): 66.

Schmetzer, U. 2001. "Cell Phones Spurred Filipinos' Coup." *Chicago Tribune* (January 22).

Scholes, R. 1982. *Semiotics and Interpretation.* New Haven, Conn.: Yale University Press.

Schön, D. 1988. "Designing: Rules, Types, and World." *Design Studies* 9, no. 3: 181–90.

Schor, J., and D. B. Holt, eds. 2000. *The Consumer Society Reader.* New York: New Press.

Schreber, D. P. 1975. *Mémoires d'un névropathe.* Paris: Seuil.

Schroeder, J. 2002. *Visual Consumption.* London: Routledge.

Schulze, G. 2001. "Inszenierte Individualität: Ein modernes Theater." In *Die Entdeckung des Ich: Die Geschichte der Individualisierung vom Mittelalter bis zur Gegenwart,* ed. R. V. Dülmen, 557–82. Cologne, Germany: Böhlau.

Schumacher, E. F. 1973. *Small Is Beautiful: A Study of Economics as if People Mattered.* London: Blond and Briggs.

Schwarzer, M. 2004. *Zoomscape: Architecture in Motion and Media.* New York: Princeton Architectural Press.

Schweitzer, P. Undated. "People Buy Products Not Brands," J. Walter Thompson White Papers series.

Scotford, M. 1994. "Messy History vs. Neat History: Toward an Expanded View of Women in Graphic Design." *Visible Language* 28, no. 4: 367–87.

Searle, J. 1965. "What Is a Speech Act?" In *Philosophy in America,* ed. Max Black, 221–39. London: Allen and Unwin; Ithaca, N.Y.: Cornell University Press.

Seddon, J., and S. Worden. 1994. *Women Designing: Redefining Design in Britain between the Wars.* Brighton, UK: University of Brighton.

Segal, L. 1990. *Slow Motion: Changing Masculinities, Changing Men.* London: Virago.

Seitz, M. Z. 2007. "The Life and Times of a Typeface." *New York Times* (September 12).

Semmens, P. 1997. *High Speed in Japan, Shinkansen—The World's Busiest High-Speed Railway.* Sheffield, UK: Platform 5.

Shalom, F. 1999. "Curtain Fell So Fast: Bonavista Fabrics Is Suing Zellers and Martha Stewart. ..." *The Gazette* [Montreal] (September 7): E1.

Shaner, W. W., P. F. Philipp, and W. R. Schmehl. 1982. *Farming Systems Research and Development: Guidelines for Developing Countries.* Boulder, Colo:: Westview.

Sidel, J. 1999. *Capital, Coercion, and Crime: Bossism in the Philippines.* Stanford, Calif.: Stanford University Press.

Siegel, J. T. 1997. *Fetish, Recognition, Revolution.* Princeton, N.J.: Princeton University Press.

Silk, J. 1980. "Adoption and Kinship in Oceania." *American Anthropologist* 82: 799–820.

Silverman, D. 1989. *Art Nouveau in Fin-de-Siecle France: Politics, Psychology and Style.* Berkeley: University of California Press.

Simmel, G. 1950. *The Sociology of Georg Simmel,* ed. K. H. Wulf. Glencoe, Ill.: The Free Press.

Simmel, G. 1978. *The Philosophy of Money.* London: Routledge.

Simmel, G. 2004. "Fashion." In *The Rise of Fashion: A Reader,* ed. D. Purdy. Minneapolis: University of Minnesota Press.

Simon, H. 1976. *Administrative Behavior.* New York: Macmillan.

Simon, H. 1977. *Models of Discovery.* Boston: D. Reidel.

Simon, H. 1996. *The Sciences of the Artificial.* Cambridge, Mass.: MIT Press.

Simonicca, A. 2004. *Economia sostenibile, comunità culturali e isole.* Economia dell'Ambiente e del Turismo Sostenibile, Working Papers Series, N3 (January).

Singer, P. 1993. *Practical Ethics.* Cambridge: Cambridge University Press.

Singer, P. 2002. *One World: The Ethics of Globalization.* New Haven, Conn.: Yale University Press.

Siu, K. C., P. Wong, and N. Ip, eds. 2002. *Designs You Don't Know What to Do With: A Book about the Meanings of Design and Its Alternatives.* Hong Kong: MCCM Creations.

Sloterdijk, P. 1989. *Thinker on Stage: Nietzsche's Materialism.* Minneapolis: University of Minnesota Press.

"Sluggish National Chains Continue to Lose Ground." 1999. *HFN, The Weekly Newspaper for the Home Furnishing Network* (August 9): 6.

Smeaton, J. 1813. *A Narrative ... of the Building of the Eddystone Light ... etc.* London.

Smith. C. S. 1987. "Design and Economy in Mid-Eighteenth Century England." Paper presented at Oxford University.

Smith, C. S. 1987. "Eighteenth-Century Man." *Designer* (March): 19–21.

Smith, S. 2005. *Ending Global Poverty: A Guide to What Works.* New York: Palgrave, Macmillan.

Smith, W. 1873. *Teacher's Manual of Freehand Drawing and Designing.* Boston: L. Prang.

Sofia, Z. 1984. "Extermination Fetuses: Abortion, Disarmament and the Sexo-Semiotics of Extra-Terrestrialism." *Diacritics* 14, no. 2: 47–59.

Sony. 1989. *The Case of the Walkman.* Sony's Innovations in Management Series, vol. 1. San Diego, Calif.: Corporate Communications, Sony Corporation.

Sopwith, P. 1834. *Treatise* on *Isometrical Drawing.* London: John Weale.

Soucy, C. 1971. *L'Image du centre dans quatre romans contemporains.* Paris: CSU.

Sparke, P. 1983. *Consultant Design: The History and Practice of the Designer in Industry.* London: Pembridge Press.

Sparke, P. 1986. *An Introduction to Design and Culture in the Twentieth Century,* 1st ed. London: Unwin Hyman.

Sparke, P. 1987. *Japanese Design.* London: Michael Joseph.

Sparke, P. 1995. *As Long As It's Pink: The Sexual Politics of Taste.* London: Pandora; Harper Collins.

Sparke, P. 2004. *An Introduction to Design and Culture: 1900 to the Present.* London: Routledge.

Sparke, P. 2005. *Elsie de Wolfe: The Birth of Modern Interior Decoration.* New York: Acanthus Press.

Sparkes, M. 2007. "Smart Inventor Dreams Up Fuel Cell Car." (August 27). Available at: http://www.treehugger.com/files/2007/08/smart_car_inven.php. Accessed March 19, 2008.

Spillers, W. 1974. *Basic Questions of Design Theory.* Amsterdam: North Holland Publishing Company.

Sporting Goods Manufacturers Association. 1994. "The US Athletic Footwear Market Today." Available at: http://www.sgma.com/reports/archives. Accessed March 29, 2008.

Squires, S. 1999. "Rapid Ethnographic Assessment, American Breakfast and the Mother-in-Law." Paper presented at the American Anthropology Association meetings, Chicago.

Squires, S. 2002. "Doing the Work: Customer Research in the Product Development and Design Industry." In *Creating Breakthrough Ideas: The Collaboration of Anthropologists and Designers in the Product Development Industry,* ed. Bryan Byrne, 103–24. Westport, Conn.: Bergin and Garvey.

"The State of the Nation-State." 1990. *The Economist* (December 22): 73.

Steadman, C. 1985. "Landscape for a Good Woman." In *Truth, Dare, or Promise: Girls Growing Up in the Fifties,* ed. L. Heron, 103–26. London: Virago.

Stephen, A., A. McNamara, and P. Goad. 2006. *Modernism and Australia: Documents on Art, Design and Architecture 1917–1967.* Melbourne: Melbourne University Press.

Stephen, A., A. McNamara, and P. Goad, P. 2008. *Modern Times.* Melbourne: Melbourne University Press.

Sterling, B. 2005. *Shaping Things,* Cambridge, Mass.: MIT Press.

Stevens, W., and Habitat for Humanity, eds. 1982. *Community Self Help Housing Manual: Partnership in Action.* Croton-on-Hudson, N.Y.: Intermediate Technology Development Group of North America.

Stocke, J. G. 1997. "'Suicide on the Installment Plan': Cold-War Era Civil Defense and Consumerism in the United States." In *The Writing on the Cloud: American Culture Confronts the Atomic Bomb,* ed. A. M. Scott and C. D. Geist, 44–60. Lanham, Md.: University Press of America.

Stones, J. 2005. "Incendiary Devices." *Design Week* 20, no. 17: 16–17.

Stohr, K. 2006. "100 Years of Humanitarian Design." In *Design Like You Give a Damn: Architectural Responses to Humanitarian Crises,* ed. Architecture for Humanity. New York: Metropolis Books, 32–55.

Strathern, N. 1985. "Kinship and Economy: Constitutional Orders of a Provisional Kind." *American Ethnologist* 12, no. 2: 191–208.

Strotz, R. H. 1957. "The Empirical Implication of a Utility Tree." *Econometrica* 25: 269–80.

Strotz, R. H. 1959. "The Utility Tree—A Correction and Further Appraisal." *Econometrica* 27: 482–88.

Sturgeon, N. 1986. "Feminism, Anarchism, and Non-Violent Direct Action Politics." Ph.D. dissertation, University of California at Santa Cruz.

Styles, J. 1994. "Manufacturing, Consumption and Design." In *Consumption and the World of Goods,* ed. John Brewer and Roy Porter, 527–54. London: Routledge.

Sullivan, A. C. 1996. "Asia's Tallest Towers." *Architecture* 85, no. 9: 159–65.

Sunderland, P. 1999. "Glancing Possibilities: Three Weeks to Understand the Nature of Family Life in the United States." Paper presented at the American Anthropology Association meetings, Chicago.

Sutton, G. 1967. *Artisan or Artist: A History of the Teaching of Arts and Crafts in English Schools.* London: Pergamon.

"Swatch Watches Collection Catalogue—Be Yourself, Swatch Yourself." 1991. Collection Fall/Winter 1991, title on front wrapper, S.I., Swatch AG. Antiquariaat Gemilang, 117. Available at: http://www.gemilang.nl/catalogues.php?catnr=386&pg=115

Szenasy, S. S. 2003. "Ethical Design Education: Confessions of a Sixties Idealist." In *Citizen Designer: Perspectives of Design Responsibility,* ed. S. Heller and V. Vienne, 20–24. New York: Allworth Press.

Tambiah, S. 1984. *The Buddhist Saints of the Forest and the Cult of the Amulets.* Cambridge: Cambridge University Press.

Tan, Michael L. 2001. "Taming the Cell Phone." *Philippine Daily Inquirer* (February 6).

Taragin, D. S. 2002. *The Alliance of Art and Industry: Toledo Design for a Modern America.* Toledo, Ohio, and New York: Toledo Museum of Art and Hudson Hills Press.

Tattari, J. 1992. *U.S. Patent 5,265,158—Construction of a Standalone Portable Telephone Unit.* Jouko Tattari (Nokia), filed May 11, 1992, issued November 23, 1993.

Taylor, F. 1911. *The Principles of Scientific Management.* New York: Harper.

Thackara, J. 1998. "One-to-One On-Line Fashion, the Internet and the Role of Design." In *The Style Engine: Spectacle, Identity, Design and Business: How the Fashion Industry Uses Style to Create Wealth,* ed. G. Malossi. New York: Monacelli Press.

Thau, B. 1999. "Target Rolls Out Calphalon, Michael Graves Designs." *HFN: The Weekly Newspaper for the Home Furnishing Network.* Available at: http://www.highbeam.com/doc/1G1-54053451.html

Thompson, E. P. 1963. *The Making of the English Working Class.* New York: Pantheon Books.

Thorne, M. 2001. *Modern Trains and Splendid Stations, Architecture Design and Rail Travel for the Twenty-First Century.* Chicago: Art Institute of Chicago.

Thornton, S. 2005. "The Social Logic of Subcultural Capital." In *The Subcultures Reader,* ed. K. Gelder. London: Routledge, 184–92.

Tickle, M., producer. 2002. "The Running Shoe—Symbol of Our Time." ABC Radio National's *The Sports Factor* (transcript, Australian) (December 27).

Todorov, T. 2002. *Devoirs et delices: Une Vie de Passeur.* Paris: Seuil.

Tomassini, M. C. 1998. "Birth and Development of a Total Project." *Domus* 805.

Torre, S. 1981. "Space as Matrix." *Heresies* 3, no. 11: 51–52.

"Tower Power: Petronas Towers, Kuala Lumpur, Malaysia." 2005. *Architectural Review* 217, no. 1295: 74–75.

Towers, J. 2005. "Learning Deficiency." *Print* (July/August): 110–11.

Towner, D. 1978. *Creamware.* London and Boston: Faber and Faber.

Trachtenberg, A. 1965. *Brooklyn Bridge: Fact and Symbol.* New York: Oxford University Press.

"Trade and Development Report, 1997." 1997. United Nations Conference on Trade and Economic Development.

Traweek, S. 1988. *Beamtimes and Lifetimes: The World of High Energy Physics.* Cambridge, Mass.: Harvard University Press.

Trentmann, F. 2004. "Beyond Consumerism: New Historical Perspectives on Consumption." *Journal of Contemporary History* 39, no. 3: 373–401.

Trotter, R. and J. Schensul. 1999. "Methods in Applied Anthropology." In *Handbook of Methods in Cultural Anthropology,* ed. H. R. Bernard, 691–735. Walnut Creek, Calif.: Alta Mira Press.

Troy, N. 1991. *Modernism and the Decorative Arts in France: Art Nouveau to Le Corbusier.* New Haven, Conn.: Yale University Press.

Tuchman, B. 1962. *The Guns of August.* New York: Macmillan Company.

Tuchny, L. 1985. *Objet Industriel en Question.* Paris: Ed du Regard.

Turner, J.F.C., and R. Fichter. 1972. *Freedom to Build: Dweller Control for the Housing Process.* New York: MacMillan.

Turner, M. 1988. "A History of Export Design in Hong Kong (1900–1960)." In *Made in Hong Kong: A History of Export Design 1900–1960,* ed. J.S.P. Ting, 7–15. Hong Kong: Hong Kong Museum of History with the Urban Council.

Turner, M. 1995. "Early Modern Design in Hong Kong." In *Design History, An Anthology: A Design Issues Reader,* ed. D. Doordan, 200–213. Cambridge, Mass.: MIT Press.

Tybout, A., and T. Calkins, eds. 2005. *Kellogg on Branding: The Marketing Faculty at the Kellogg School of Management.* Hoboken, N.J.: Wiley.

University of Cambridge Institute of Manufacturing. 2006. *Well Dressed?* Cambridge: Cambridge University Press.

Unwin, R. 1909. *Town Planning in Practice.* London: Unwin.

Upton, D. 1986. *Holy Things and Profane.* Cambridge, Mass.: MIT Press.

Uriarte, L. F. 2005. "Modernity and Postmodernity from Cuba." *Journal of Design History* 18, no. 3: 245–55.

U.S. Department of Defense, Office of Civil Defense. 1961. *Fallout Protection: What to Know and Do About*

Nuclear Attack. Washington, D.C.: Government Printing Office.

Vanac, M. 1999. "Hudson, Ohio-Based Fabrics Retailer Signs Up Martha Stewart." *Akron Beacon Journal* (July 28).

Vanderbilt, T. 1998. *The Sneaker Book: Anatomy of an Industry and an Icon.* New York: New Press.

Vanderbilt, T. 2002. *Survival City: Adventures Among the Ruins of Atomic America.* New York: Princeton Architectural Press.

Van Praag, B. S. 1968. *Individual Welfare and Consumer Behavior, A Theory of Rationality.* New York: Elsevier-North Holland Publishing Co.

van Toorn, J. 1994. "Rethinking the Visual: Essayistic Fragments on Communicative Action." In *And Justice for all ...,* ed. O. Bouman. Maastricht, Netherlands: Jan van Eyck Akadmie.

van Toorn, J. 1997. *Design beyond Design.* Maastricht, Netherlands: Jan van Eyck Akadamie.

Van Schaak, E. 2006. "The Division of Pictorial Publicity in World War I." *Design Issues* 22, no. 1: 32–45.

Vastokas, J. 1978. "Cognitive Aspects of North-West Coast Art." In *Art in Society,* ed. M. Greenhalgh and V. Megaw, 243–66. London: Duckworth.

Vattimo, G. 1988. *The End of Modernity.* Baltimore, Md.: Johns Hopkins University Press.

Vaughn, S. 1980. *Holding Fast the Inner Lines: Democracy, Nationalism, and the Committee on Public Information.* Chapel Hill: University of North Carolina Press.

Veblen, T. 1970. *The Theory of the Leisure Class.* London: George Allen and Unwin. Reprinted New York: Cosimo Inc.

Venturi, R. 1966. *Complexity and Contradiction in Architecture.* New York: Museum of Modern Art.

Vertesi, J. 2008. "Mind the Gap: The London Underground Map and User's Representations of Urban Space." *Social Studies of Science* 38, no. 7: 7–33.

Vickers, G. 1978. *Information Memorandum.* Cambridge, Mass.: Division for Study and Research in Education, MIT.

Villari, B. 2004. *Il design per la valorizzazione delle risorse territoriali.* Milan, Italy: Dottorato di Ricerca in Disegno industriale e comunicazione multimediale, INDACO; Politecnico di Milano: documenti interni.

Vinogradoff, P. 1999. Consultant, Wolff Olins, *Interview with the author,* 2/11/99.

Vitruvius, M. P. 1960. *The Ten Books on Architecture,* trans. M. H. Morgan. New York: Dover Publications.

Volosinov, V. N. 1973. *Marxism and the Philosophy of Language.* New York: Seminar Press.

Vyas, H. K. 2006. "Design History: An Alternative Approach." *Design Issues* 22, no. 4: 27–34.

Wajda, S. 2001. "Kmartha." *American Studies* 42, no. 2: 71–88.

Walens, S. 1981. *Feasting with Cannibals.* Princeton, N.J.: Princeton University Press.

Walker, J. 1989. *Design History and the History of Design.* London: Pluto Press.

Walker, J. B. 1915. *America Fallen! The Sequel to the European War.* New York: Dodd, Mead and Company.

Walker, L. 1997. *Drawing on Diversity: Women, Architecture, and Practice.* London: Royal Institute of British Architects.

Walker, S. 2006. *Sustainable by Design: Explorations in Theory and Practice.* London and Sterling, Va.: Earthscan.

Wallerstein, I. 1974. *The Modern World System.* 2 vols. New York and London: Academic Press.

Ward, M. E. 1896. *The Common Sense of Bicycling: Bicycling for Ladies.* New York: Brentano's.

Ward, P. M. 1982. *Self-Help Housing: A Critique.* London: Mansell.

Warner, M. 1990. *The Letters of the Republic: Republication and the Public Sphere in Eighteenth-Century America.* Cambridge, Mass.: Harvard University Press.

Wasserman, B., P. Sullivan, and G. Palermo. 2000. *Ethics and the Practice of Architecture.* New York: Wiley.

Waters, J. 1997. "After Euphoria, Can Sara Lee Be Like Nike?" *Crain's Chicago Business* (September 22).

Way, T. R., and G. R. Dennis 1903. *The Art of James McNeil Whistler.* London: George Bell and Sons.

Weber, M. 1956. *The Protestant Ethic and the Spirit of Capitalism,* trans. Talcott Parsons. New York: Charles Scribner's Sons; London: Allen and Unwin.

Weibull, J., C. W. Matthiessen, L. Nordstrom, P. Lauring, and L. Holmqvist. 1993. *Oresund: Past, Present and Future.* Svedab, Sweden: Corona/Norden.

Weiner, N. 1948. *Cybernetics or Control and Communication in the Animal and the Machine.* Paris: Hermann and Cie.

Weizenbaum, J. 1976. *Computer Power and Human Reason.* San Francisco: Freeman.

Wells, P. 1993. "The Invisible Man: Shrinking Masculinity in the 1950 Science Fiction B-Movie." In *You Tarzan: Masculinity, Movies and Men,* ed. P. Kirkham and J. Thumim, 181–99. London: Lawrence and Wishart.

West, C. 1962. *The Fallout Shelter Handbook.* Greenwich, Conn.: Fawcett Publications.

White, A. R. 1975. *Modal Thinking.* Ithaca, N.Y.: Cornell University Press.

White, L. 1959. *The Evolution of Culture.* New York: McGraw-Hill.

Whitehouse, D. 2002. "The Question of Relevance." In *Opening Pandora's Box: Curriculum Research into History and Theory of Design in Australia,* ed. K. Conellan. Adelaide: University of South Australia.

Whitehouse, D. 2005. "The Panoramic Narrative and the Production of Historical Consciousness: This is Australia." Presented at Futureground, Design Research Society International Conference Proceedings, Monash University, Melbourne.

Whittock, N. H. 1825. *The Oxford Drawing Book.* Oxford: Bartlett and Hinton.

Whyte, W. H. 1956. *The Organization Man.* New York: Simon and Schuster.

Wiener, A. 1985. "Inalienable Wealth." *American Ethnologist* 12, no. 2: 210–27.

Wiesel, E. 1966. *The Gates of the Forest.* New York: Schocken Books.

Wilk, C., ed. 2006. *Modernism: Designing a New World, 1914–1939.* London: Victoria and Albert Press.

Williams, B. 1843. A *Manual for Teaching Model Drawing from Solid Models.* London: J. W. Parker.

Williams, M. E. 1997. "Perfect World." *Salon* (March 14). Available at: http://www.salon.com/march 97/medialmedia970314.html

Williams, R. 1965. *The Long Revolution.* Middlesex, UK: Penguin.

Williams, R. 1976. *Keywords.* New York: Oxford University Press.

Williams, R. 1977. *Marxism and Literature.* Oxford: Oxford University Press.

Wilson, E. 1985. *Adorned in Dreams: Fashion and Modernity.* London: Virago.

Wimsatt, W. K. Jr. 1947. "The Structure of the 'Concrete Universal' in Literature." *Publications of the Modern Language Association of America* 62: 262–80.

Winkler, A. M. 1993. *Life under a Cloud: American Anxiety about the Atom.* New York and Oxford: Oxford University Press.

Winner, L. 1977. *Autonomous Technology: Technics out of Control as a Theme in Political Thought.* Cambridge, Mass.: MIT Press.

Winner, L. 1980. "Do Artifacts Have Politics?" *Daedulus* 109, no. 1: 121–36.

Winner, L. 1986. *The Whale and the Reactor.* Chicago: University of Chicago Press.

Winograd, T., and F. Flore. 1986. *Understanding Computers and Cognition: A New Foundation for Design.* Norwood, N.J.: Ablex.

Wittgenstein, L. 1953. *Philosophical Investigations.* Oxford: Blackwell.

Wittkower, R. 1962. *Architectural Principles in the Age of Humanism.* New York: Norton.

Wolf, E. 1982. *Europe and the People without History.* Berkeley: University of California Press.

Wolf, M. 2004. *Why Globalization Works.* New Haven, Conn.: Yale University Press.

Wolfe, T. 1965. *The Kandy Kolored Tangerine Flake Streamline Baby.* Toronto: Farrar, Straus, Giroux.

Wolff, J. 1981. *The Social Production of Art.* New York: MacMillan.

Wolff Olins. 1999a. *Britain, Bye Bye Bulldog* (pamphlet). London: Wolf Olins.

Wolff Olins. 1999b. *Deutschland Als Globale Marke/A Global Brand for Germany* (pamphlet). London: Wolf Olins.

Womack, J. P., D. Jones, and D. Roos. 1990. *The Machine That Changed the World.* New York: Macmillan.

Wong, W. S. 2001. "Detachment and Unification: A Chinese Graphic Design History in Greater China since 1979." *Design Issues* 17, no. 4: 51–71.

Wood, D., and L. Fels. 1986. "Designs on Signs/Myth and Meaning in Maps." *Cartographica* 23, no. 3: 54–103.

Woodham, J. 1995. "Resisting Colonization: Design History Has Its Own Identity." *Design Issues* 11, no. 1: 22–37.

Woodham, J. 1997. *Twentieth Century Design.* Oxford: Oxford University Press.

Woodham, J. 2001. "Recent Trends in Design Historical Research in Britain." In *Historiades de la periferia: Historia e historias del diseño. Actas de la 1ºReunión Cientifica Internacional de Historiadores y Estudios del Diseño, Barcelona 1999* [Design

History Seen from Abroad: History and Histories of Design. Proceedings of the 1st International Conference of Design History and Design Studies, Barcelona 1999], eds. Anna Calvera and Miguel Mallol, 85–97. Barcelona: University of Barcelona Publications.

Woodham, J. 2005. "Local National and Global: Redrawing the Design Historical Map." *Journal of Design History* 18, no. 3: 257–67.

Woodward, I. 2007. *Understanding Material Culture.* Los Angeles, Calif.: Sage.

Worden, S. 1978. "A Voice for Whose Choice?" In *Design History: Fad or Function?,* ed. Design History Society, 41–48. London: Design Council.

Worden, S., and J. Seddon. 1995. "Women Designers in Britain in the 1920s and 1930s: Defining the Professional and Redefining Design." *Journal of Design History* 8, no. 3: 177–94.

Worrell, S. 1997. "Million Dollar Apple Pie; Profile: Martha Stewart; She's Turned Herself into a Saint, Home-Making into an Industry." *The Independent* [London] (October 12): 3.

Xunhai, Z. 1992. "Enterprise Response to Market Reforms: The Case of the Chinese Bicycle Industry." *The Australian Journal of Chinese Affairs* 28: 111–39.

Yates, F. 1966. *The Art of Memory.* London: Routledge.

"You Can Build a Low-Cost Shelter Quickly." 1961. *Popular Mechanics* (December): 85–89.

Young, R. 1979. "Interpreting the Production of Science." *New Scientist* 29: 1026–28.

Young, R., and L. Levidow, eds. 1985 [1981]. *Science, Technology and the Labour Process.* 2 vols. London: CSE and Free Association Books.

Zahavi, G. 1988. *Workers, Managers, and Welfare Capitalism: The Shoe-Workers and Tanners of Endicott Johnson.* Chicago: University of Illinois Press.

Zimmerman, J. 1983. *The Technological Woman: Interfacing with Tomorrow.* New York: Praeger.

Zisko, A. 1999. "Tempest in a Teapot: Alessi Objects to Target's Graves Line." *HFN: The Weekly Newspaper for the Home Furnishing Network.* Available at: http://www.highbeam.com/doc/1G1-54251537.html

Zukin, S. 1991. *Landscapes of Power: From Detroit to Disney World.* Berkeley: University of California Press.

INDEX